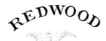

The Illustrated Encyclopedia of
PLANTS
AND ANIMALS

The Illustrated Encyclopedia of
PLANTS
AND ANIMALS

NEW YORK

Academic Advisor:
Doctor Wilma George,
Lecturer in Zoology,
University of Oxford.

Editors:
Michael Bisacre
Richard Carlisle
Deborah Robertson
John Ruck

Copyright © 1979 Marshall Cavendish Limited
First published in the United States of America
by Exeter Books

Printed in Great Britain

Distributed by Bookthrift Inc.
New York, New York 10018

Library of Congress Catalog Card Number: 79-51907
ISBN 0-89673-014-X

K9
// I79

Introduction

The plants and animals of the world are a constant source
of wonder and delight – and also a major area of scientific
study. *The Illustrated Encyclopedia of Plants and Animals* is
an invaluable source of information on the development of
the living world over literally millions of years. It is a
comprehensive work of reference on the many varieties
of botanical and zoological species, clearly divided into
the following parts: evolution, classification and anatomy,
plants and animals, and finally their habitats
and behavior.

The encyclopedia relates the history and development of life
on earth to more modern concerns such as horticulture and
conservation. The articles are detailed and
thought-provoking as well as providing a source of reliable
information. What do Darwin's once unconventional theories
tell us about ourselves and primitive forms of life? How has nature
produced such extremes as the giant Californian
redwood and the fragile beauty of the orchid? How do lions
rear their young? Plant life from viruses to vegetables,
animals, insects and fish are all carefully classified
and examined.

The entries are arranged into easily accessible sections to help
the reader find his way through this huge range of knowledge.
For example, plants are subdivided into categories such as
algae, herbaceous and flowering, while animals
are considered under headings such as vertebrates, invertebrates
and primates. There are also general chapters discussing the
origins of life and evolution, and plant and animal habitats,
showing how the two forms of life depend upon each other
for existence.

Numerous color illustrations, maps and diagrams reinforce
and expand in clear visual terms the vast source of
knowledge provided in this volume.

Contents

Part IV Plant and Animal Habitats

Part I

The Origin and Evolution of Species

Chapter 1 The Origin of Life

The Origin of Life

Four thousand million years ago the Earth was an inhospitable place, quite unlike the planet we know today. Most of the surface was covered by water and the land was rocky and forbidding, constantly being broken up by volcanic activity and eroded by wind, rain and extremes of heat and cold. The atmosphere was unbreathable, consisting mainly of hydrogen, methane, ammonia and, of course, water vapour. Oxygen was absent altogether. It was in this unpromising environment that the first simple chemical reactions occurred that were eventually to lead to life itself.

Early beliefs

The idea that life sprang from simple chemical compounds is a relatively recent one, and it succeeds a whole variety of beliefs that commanded authority in past centuries. The most popular theory, still adhered to by some, was the biblical teaching that living species were created by God and that each was constant and unchangeable.

For smaller forms of life such as insects and microscopic organisms 'spontaneous generation' was a popular theory. Its proponents believed that life was created directly from decaying organic matter and their view was apparently confirmed when maggots emerged from rotting meat or bacteria appeared in water left to stand. The possibility of there being flies' eggs in the meat or contamination of the water by airborne bacteria was ignored or dismissed without proper consideration. The great French scientist Louis Pasteur, by a long and painstaking series of experiments, finally disposed of the spontaneous generation theory in the 1860s and at about the same time in Britain Charles Darwin and Alfred Wallace published their theory of evolution of species by natural selection.

Darwin and Wallace suggested that every species (plant or animal) changes slowly as a result of the struggle for survival among its members. Because there is a natural variation among the members of a species (for example there are obvious differences in height, weight and physical strength among humans), some individuals will inevitably be slightly better equipped to survive than their fellows and it will tend to be these that sire the next generation.

Over a time scale of millions of years this slow selection process leads to the transformation of one species into another and over thousands of millions of years an animal as complex as man could develop through countless intermediate forms from a simple single-celled organism. Speculation about the origin of life is therefore concerned with how the simplest imaginable single-celled organism could have come into being.

The first steps

Before life could begin, the basic building blocks such as amino acids and sugars must have been formed somewhere on the Earth, in the atmosphere or the sea. In an attempt to find out how this might have

Above: Early ideas about the origins of life and the relationships between plants and animals seem very odd today. This illustration of lambs dropping as ripe fruit from a tree comes from a 16th century edition of 'The Voyages and Travels of Sir John Mandeville', a book first published in French in about 1360.

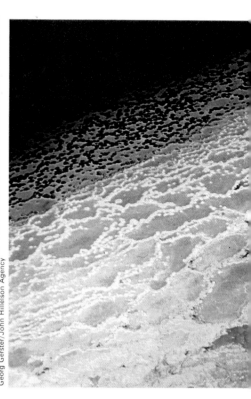

Right: The shore of a salt lake in Ethiopia seen from the air. The water evaporates away in the sun leaving behind a white deposit of salt crystals. Concentration by evaporation may well have been an important step in the formation of the first proteins, carbohydrates and nucleic acids from simpler compounds.

happened the American scientist Stanley Miller conducted a remarkable experiment in 1953. He took a closed flask containing a solution whose composition he thought corresponded closely to that of the primitive ocean and filled the space above the liquid with gases thought to have been once common in the atmosphere, notably methane, ammonia and hydrogen.

To simulate the effect of sunlight, volcanic activity and lightning, the flask was heated and sparked (two electrodes were fitted to the upper part of the flask for this purpose). After a week, the experiment was stopped and the composition of the liquid in the flask determined. The results were encouraging: three of the most common amino acids found in living systems had been formed—*glycine*,

alanine and *aspartic acid*.

Not surprisingly Miller's experiment stimulated further research and it was soon shown that a number of other amino acids and a variety of simple compounds such as *hydrogen cyanide*, *cyanoacetylene* and *formaldehyde* were also formed under similar conditions. These simple compounds, though not important in themselves, are vital building blocks for larger, more significant molecules. It has long been known, for example, that formaldehyde can easily be transformed into sugars. The most remarkable discovery of all was the isolation of *adenine* from the liquid of one of the experiments, for adenine is one of a group of only four 'bases' which carry the genetic code on nucleic acid molecules.

The results of Miller's experiment, and

Dr. J. A. L. Cooke/Oxford Scientific Films

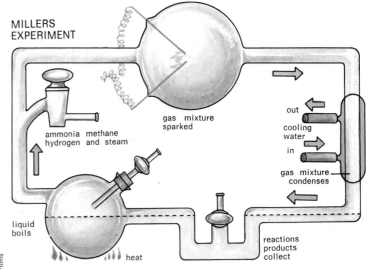

gas mixture sparked

ammonia methane hydrogen and steam

out

cooling water in

gas mixture condenses

liquid boils

heat

reactions products collect

Left: Although it lasts for only a fraction of a second, a flash of lightning can promote a variety of unusual chemical reactions. It was probably a key factor in the formation of the first building blocks of life. Other sources of energy included heat from volcanoes and radiation from the Sun.

Above: Apparatus of this sort was used by Stanley Miller in 1953 to reproduce the conditions prevailing on the primitive Earth. Miller was able to show that many of the basic compounds needed for life could be produced from simple gases like hydrogen, ammonia, methane and water vapour by heating and sparking.

Below: A photograph taken with an electron microscope of a modern blue-green alga, *Anabaena*. It resembles a bacterium in having no nucleus (the nucleic acid is distributed throughout the cell) but gets its energy by photosynthesis. The earliest living cells may have looked rather like this.

Left: Another method of concentrating solutions is by freezing, so important reactions may have taken place at the Earth's poles.

Below: The fossilized remains of an alga from the Silurian period some 430 million years ago. Though relatively simple, this fossil plant is already highly evolved. The earliest remains of cellular organisms come from Swaziland and are about 3,100 million years old.

Courtesy of the Institute of Geological Sciences

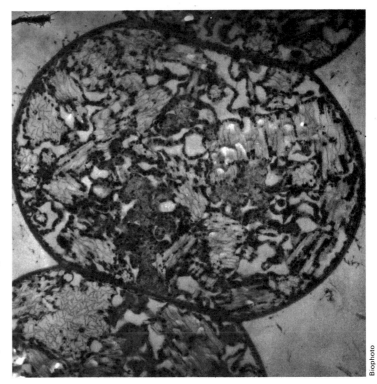

Biophoto

others like it, make it reasonable to suppose that many of the basic chemicals of life were formed by purely physical means in the primitive oceans of the Earth. These chemicals must then have reacted together to form the larger, more complex molecules such as *proteins*, *carbohydrates* and *nucleotides*. On the face of it these reactions are quite plausible because proteins are merely chains of amino acids joined together chemically, carbohydrates like cellulose are chains of sugar units, and nucleotides consist of a sugar unit linked both to a phosphate unit and to a base such as adenine. Just as proteins are made of chains of amino acids, *nucleic acids* are composed of chains of nucleotides linked together by chemical bonds between phosphate and sugar of adjacent units—

the bases stick out to one side of the main chain.

After many millions of years, chemical reactions of this sort eventually gave rise to a compound, probably a type of nucleic acid, which was able to reproduce itself. Whether this took place in many different parts of the world or whether it was confined to one particular site is not known, but it was undoubtedly the most important single event in the birth of life on Earth.

Nucleic acids

As has already been mentioned, a nucleic acid consists of a chain of nucleotide units. In effect the chain is composed of alternating sugar and phosphate units, with any one of four bases (*adenine*, *thymine*, *cytosine* or *guanine*) projecting

from each sugar unit. Since the chain may be many thousands of units long, the number of possible combinations of bases along the chain is enormous and because the sugar and phosphate units do not change, a nucleic acid chain can be defined simply by indicating the order of the bases along the chain: ATTCGATGC- TC . . . and so on. It is now known that it is the sequence of bases on the nucleic acid that carries genetic information, much as a series of dots and dashes carries a message by morse code.

In 1953, working in Cambridge, England, James Watson and Francis Crick worked out the structure of the best known nucleic acid, DNA (*deoxyribonucleic acid*). They found that it was composed of two nucleic acid strands running side by side in the shape of a

In 1923 J. B. S. Haldane in England and A. I. Oparin in the USSR suggested for the first time that the atmosphere of the primitive Earth was quite different from that which we know today. They believed, and this is now the accepted view, that its chief constituents were methane, hydrogen and ammonia (1). Oxygen was a notable absentee.

Over a period of millions of years these simple compounds reacted together to produce, in the sea, a 'soup' of more complex substances (2) such as amino acids, sugars and bases like adenine. The energy for these reactions would have been supplied by sunlight, lightning and volcanic activity.

After concentration by evaporation, freezing or adsorption on to the surface of a mineral such as clay, the new compounds reacted further to produce more complex molecules (3)— particularly long-chain compounds like proteins and polysaccharides (starch and cellulose). The chemical reactions by which amino acids were converted into proteins, sugars into polysaccharides and nucleotides into nucleic acids would almost certainly have required *catalysts*, even where the concentration of the starting materials was reasonably high. A catalyst is a substance which promotes a chemical reaction without itself being consumed in the reaction, much in the same way as oil makes a machine run smoothly. These early catalysts were either relatively simple chemical compounds or, more likely, adsorbent minerals present on the sea floor.

The most important single step in the creation of life on Earth was the production of the first self-replicating molecule—probably a double-stranded nucleic acid (4). This would have had a unique sequence of bases along its length and probably reproduced by 'unzipping' and then base pairing to create two identical daughter molecules.

Eventually the nucleic acid 'learnt' to use compounds such as proteins, and this at length led to the first primitive cell.

1 methane hydrogen

hydrogen
carbon
nitrogen
oxygen

ammonia water

2 formaldehyde

hydrogen cyanide

cyanoacetylene

adenine (base)

glucose

helix. As usual, each strand consisted of alternating sugar and phosphate units (the sugar being *deoxyribose*) and there were the usual bases projecting from the sugar units. Holding the two chains together, rather like the two halves of a zip fastener, were chemical bonds between the bases of the opposing chains.

Watson and Crick discovered that the adenine units on one chain were bonded to thymine units on the other, and cytosine was bonded to guanine. The linkages were totally specific: adenine was always bonded to thymine and never to cystosine or guanine, and cytosine was likewise always bonded to guanine, never to adenine or thymine. This curious arrangement means that if one knows the sequence on one strand, the sequence on the other strand can be worked out. In other words the two strands are 'mirror images' of each other.

Replication
If the structure of the earliest nucleic acid was anything like modern DNA, it becomes possible to understand how, in theory at least, replication might have occurred. Under the right conditions a double-stranded nucleic acid might 'unzip' to give two separate strands with their bases exposed. Such an unzipping reaction, actually the breaking of the base-to-base bonds between the chains, would almost certainly have required a catalyst, possibly a mineral or even a primitive enzyme (a catalyst made of protein).

Once the strands were separated and removed from the presence of the catalyst, the exposed bases on each strand might well have attracted nucleotides by base pairing. For example, thymine units on the nucleic acid strands would tend to react with molecules of the nucleotide *adenosine phosphate* (a sugar bonded to the base adenine and to a phosphate group) by forming bonds with the adenine residues. If this were to happen along the length of both strands, and the sugar-phosphate units of adjacent nucleotides became linked chemically, the end product would be a pair of double-stranded nucleic acid molecules identical to the original one both in structure and in sequence of bases. In this way, by unzipping and reforming, a single nucleic acid molecule might generate two identical daughter molecules.

Once the process of replication began,

12

3

polysaccharide
(sugar chain)

protein
(amino acid chain)

sugar
phosphate
adenine
thymine
guanine
cytosine

4

nucleic acid
double helix

nucleic acid unzips, two
new double helixes form

nucleotides

natural selection would have ensured that it gradually improved. As generation followed generation mistakes in the replication process would inevitably have occurred occasionally, leading to nucleic acids with slightly different base sequences from their parents. Most of these freak nucleic acids would have reproduced more slowly than normal or not at all, and so they would not survive. Very occasionally, however, one which replicated faster than its parents would appear, and such a molecule would soon become the dominant form.

Eventually nucleic acids developed the ability to manufacture and make use of proteins. At first these proteins were probably used simply to form a protective sheath around the nucleic acid, rather like a modern virus, but gradually they

developed the ability to catalyze a variety of reactions important to the replication of the nucleic acid—in other words they became enzymes. Such reactions would have included the unzipping and reforming reactions of the nucleic acid itself, as well as reactions involving the synthesis and breakdown of other proteins and carbohydrates which were found to be useful in speeding up the whole replication process.

As the system became increasingly complicated, more space would have been needed and so the protein envelope grew larger creating a bacterium-like cell. Finally, the nucleic acid became concentrated in a separate structure within the cell, the *nucleus*, and specialized structures developed within the *cytoplasm* (the region between the cell wall and the

nucleus) to undertake the routine reactions involved in energy production and other vital processes. One process which evolved at an early stage was *photosynthesis*, the energy-producing mechanism of green plants. Releasing oxygen as a by-product, it gradually changed the composition of the Earth's atmosphere to the one familiar today.

Because there is so little evidence available, theories about the origin of life are necessarily speculative. Just how particular reactions occurred, or even if they occurred at all, is at best very uncertain. Not until a living system is constructed in the laboratory from chemical building blocks will scientists be sure that they are on the right track, and confirmation of this sort seems a long way off.

Chapter 2
Evolution

Iguanas are descendants of one of the
groups of reptiles which were the
dominant form of life on earth for
about 150 million years. The iguanas
of the Galapagos, which Charles
Darwin visited in 1835, influenced his
ideas on evolution.

The History of Evolution

One of the foundations of modern biology is the theory of *evolution*, which proposes that all species of plants and animals are the result of modifications of other species—often now extinct—and are ultimately descended from simpler organisms or earlier still, from inanimate chemical compounds. The theory implies that man, like any other animal species, is a product of evolution, and it opens our eyes to the possibilities that the human species could also become extinct.

Research into evolution could not begin until somebody had suggested a *hypothesis*, a tentative explanation of how evolution might work, that could be tested by doing experiments or by further observations. By an extraordinary coincidence, two men working on opposite sides of the world in the middle of the nineteenth century reasoned simultaneously to the same explanation of how evolution happens.

In February 1858, Alfred Russel Wallace, working as a naturalist in the East Indies, suffered a severe attack of malaria. While recovering, he called to mind a book he had once read—the *Essay on Population* by Robert Malthus (1766-1834). Malthus put forward the idea that the human population tends to increase geometrically: if every couple have four children, then the number in succeeding generations

Below: An engraving of James Ussher (1580-1656), archbishop of Armagh, after a portrait by Sir Peter Lely. He is remembered now for his attempt to establish a biblical chronology— he put the Creation at 9 am on 23 October 4004 BC. Such a short time scale would rule out any possibility of species evolution.

Above: The Flood as depicted in an early Luther Bible. In an attempt to reconcile what they observed with traditional biblical teaching, 18th century geologists proposed that the Earth had undergone a number of catastrophic upheavals in the distant past, the most recent being the Flood.

Below: Baron Georges Cuvier (1769-1832) the great French naturalist. He was one of the first scientists to make a detailed study of fossil animals. He recognized the great diversity of creatures which had once populated the Earth, but believed that the extinction of a species was a sudden event, the result of some local catastrophe. He also worked on a classification of the animal kingdom, dividing its members into four main classes—radiates (such as starfish), articulates (such as insects), molluscs (such as snails) and vertebrates (such as mammals). He was a distinguished member of the Académie Francaise.

During 50 million years
of evolution the African
elephant's upper lip has
become a trunk, and its
tusks hugely extended
in the search for food.

Above: Jean Baptiste Lamarck (1744-1829) was the first person to distinguish clearly between invertebrate and vertebrate animals. In his theory of evolution, published at the beginning of the 19th century, he suggested that the vertebrates could have evolved from the simpler invertebrates.

Right: Dinosaur remains in the state of Utah, USA. Only when a realistic time scale for geological processes was worked out (by men like James Hutton and Charles Lyell) was it possible to estimate the age of such remains. Fossils were to provide strong evidence in favour of Darwin's theory of evolution.

Above: Before Darwin and Wallace's theory of evolution was published ideas about how, for example, the elephant got its trunk were as varied as some of them were bizarre.

Right: According to modern theories of evolution, the African and Indian elephants of today are descended from a pig-like animal, *Moeritherium*, which lived in northeast Africa during the Eocene epoch (54 to 38 million years ago). *Moeritherium* was only about 60 cm (2 ft) high, and it had small tusks and a longish skull. As its body size increased so its tusks and upper lip grew longer to help it forage on the ground.

will be two, four, eight, sixteen, thirty-two and so on. However, food supply is likely to increase much more slowly, so—concluded Malthus—it is inevitable that human population increase will be checked by famine or war. Malthus was not entirely right, because he ignored the fact that most human societies practise other, less drastic, methods of limiting population increase, such as infanticide, abortion and restrictions on marriage. Nevertheless, his theory, as applied to plant and animal populations which cannot expand their food supplies, forms the basis of the idea of *natural selection*.

All organisms produce enough offspring for a continual increase in population, if all the offspring survive. Wallace gave as an example a pair of birds laying four eggs a year and dying after four years. In

1 Moeritherium
2 Phiomia
3 Palaeomastodon
4 Mammut
5 Elephas
6 Gomphotherium
7 Stegodon
8 Loxodonta
9 Mammuthus

Left and above: By the time of the Great Exhibition, held at the Crystal Palace in London in 1851, the public had become familar with the discoveries of the early palaeontologists. This reconstruction of an iguanodon (left) was specially made for the exhibition by Sir Richard Owen, then conservator of the natural history department of the British Museum. Prehistoric creatures even featured in a cartoon (above) which lamented the lack of alcoholic refreshment at the exhibition. It was to be another eight years before Darwin's revolutionary book, *On the Origin of Species*, was published. It sold out on its day of publication.

15 years, the single pair would increase to more than 10 million birds. But natural populations of plants or animals rarely increase to such an extent, except when new species are introduced to an area; many of the offspring die through lack of food, while others are excluded from suitable habitats by competition from established individuals, and some are eaten by predators. The result is that over quite long periods of time, populations of most species remain roughly constant.

Now Wallace, like other biologists of his time who studied plants and animals in their natural habitats, was aware that even though the members of a species may look very much alike, there are always small differences between any one individual and the next. This *variation*, as it is called, affects structure, physiology and behaviour: it might mean slight differences in the coat markings of an animal, or in the shape of a plant leaf, affecting its rate of growth. During the 'struggle for existence' in which the majority of individuals of a species are doomed to die before they are old enough to reproduce, these slight differences could allow one individual to survive at the expense of another, where both are competing for the same food or space, or fleeing from the same predator.

This idea has been summed up as the 'survival of the fittest'—although in modern evolutionary theory it is more correct to say that fitness is defined as survival, and measured by the number of offspring produced. The point is that if some individual plants or animals, differing slightly from other members of the species, have a greater chance of survival and produce a larger number of offspring,

and if their offspring inherit these differences, the species will in each succeeding generation include a larger proportion of the variant type. Eventually, over a long period of time, the number of variant individuals could be great enough to count as a new species—although this would also require some sort of barrier to interbreeding between the original species and the new one.

This idea, of the origin of species by natural selection, so excited Wallace that within three days he had written a paper entitled *On the Tendency of Varieties to Depart Indefinitely from the Original Type* and posted it to another naturalist, in England, Charles Darwin. Its arrival posed a serious problem for Darwin. Twenty years earlier, he too had read Malthus' *Essay on Population;* before that, he had travelled round the world on HMS *Beagle*, and, like Wallace, he had his own observations of plants and animals in the tropics to provide evidence for a theory of natural selection.

But in 1858 Darwin had not completed his planned book on the subject, and he realized that, according to the rules of the scientific game, Wallace had won the race to be the first person to publish a theory of evolution by natural selection. Darwin's friends suggested a compromise, and in July 1858 Wallace's paper and part of Darwin's unfinished book were presented jointly to a meeting of the Linnean Society in London, and shortly afterwards published in the Society's journal.

As often happens with papers to learned societies, it attracted little notice at the time. On the other hand, when Darwin's own book, *On the Origin of Species*, appeared a year later, there was major

excitement: the first edition of 1,250 copies was sold out on publication day, and another edition came out six weeks later. Although the book contained only one reference to the likelihood that man, too, had evolved by natural selection, the message was clear. The book and its ideas were seen by many not as a contribution to rational and scientific understanding of nature, but as an affront to their belief in the literal truth of the description of the Creation found in the Bible.

In the eighteenth century the Biblical account of the age of the Earth was first challenged by a group of practical scientists, the geologists. In trying to understand the appearance of geological formations, early geologists had always been faced with direct evidence of massive upheavals in the Earth's crust. For these to have occured within 6,000 years (a Biblical chronology had suggested that the Creation occurred in about 4000 BC), they reasoned that the surface of the Earth must have undergone a series of catastrophes such as the Flood described in the Bible. These catastrophes would also have been responsible for the extinction of animals such as the dinosaurs, whose fossils the geologists were finding in particular strata.

A succession of Scottish geologists, notably James Hutton (1726-1797) and Sir Charles Lyell (1797-1875) developed alternative explanations for the geological formations which they saw around them in Scotland or knew about from the reports of scientists travelling in distant parts of the world. These new explanations were based on the principle of *uniformitarianism*, which states that geological changes in the past were the result of processes that continue to operate in the present. Since most observable geological processes, such as the deposition of ocean sediments or the weathering of rocks, are very slow, it follows that the geological history of the Earth must be measured in hundreds of millions of years. The idea of slow geological change was the basis of Lyell's book *Principles of Geology*, which was first published in 1830 and ran to 11 editions in his lifetime. Darwin carried a copy of the newly-published first volume on the *Beagle*.

The new geological timetable allowed realistic dating of fossils, and these in turn gave direct evidence of the evolution and extinction of species over hundreds of millions of years. Biologists were then free to develop theories of evolution as a correspondingly slow process.

At the beginning of the nineteenth

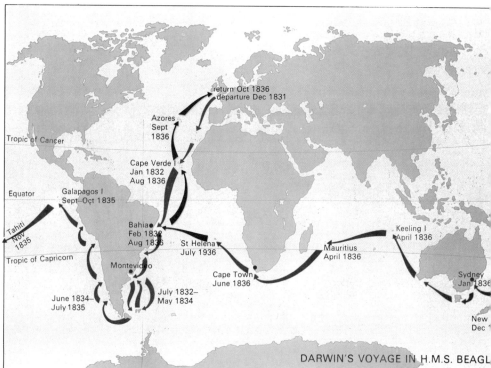

DARWIN'S VOYAGE IN H.M.S. BEAGL

Map labels:
Tropic of Cancer
Equator
Tropic of Capricorn

return Oct 1836
departure Dec 1831
Azores Sept 1836
Cape Verde I Jan 1832 Aug 1836
Galapagos I Sept–Oct 1835
Tahiti Nov 1835
Bahia Feb 1832 Aug 1836
Montevideo
St Helena July 1936
Cape Town June 1836
Mauritius April 1836
Keeling I April 1836
Sydney Jan 1836
New Dec
June 1834– July 1835
July 1832– May 1834

Above: Alfred Russel Wallace (1823–1913) came independently to the same conclusion as Darwin about the origin of species by natural selection. In 1858 he wrote about his ideas to Darwin, and the latter, previously reluctant to do so, felt compelled to publish his own theories about evolution.

Below and above right: In 1831, at the age of 22, Darwin sailed around the world as naturalist aboard the Admiralty survey ship HMS *Beagle.* He had no formal training in botany, zoology or geology. The voyage was to take five years and it provided Darwin with material for a lifetime of scientific thought and publication. Among the most significant places visited by Darwin were the Galápagos Islands. He was particularly interested in the way a species (notably finches and giant tortoises) varied from island to island. The illustration (below) of three species of palm was done by Darwin during the voyage.

century, the French naturalist Jean Baptiste Lamarck published his theory of evolution. It was based on systematic study of fossils, and on a new classification of the animal kingdom, in which Lamarck was the first person to make a fundamental distinction between vertebrates (animals with backbones) and invertebrates (those without), with the implication that the higher animals, the vertebrates, had evolved from the invertebrates. Also, for example, in his theory the long legs of flamingos result from a physical stretching continuing over generations. Its drawback is that physical deformities are not passed on in this way, to the offspring of a bird with stretched legs will have normal length legs. But the theory paved the way for that of Darwin and Wallace.

The careers of Darwin and Wallace were to a large extent the result of chance circumstances. Darwin, regarded as dull by his school teachers, at first intended to become a doctor and spent two years as a medical student in Edinburgh. Bored by lectures and horrified by the sight of surgery without anaesthetics, he cultivated an interest in natural history. After two years, when it was obvious that Darwin had little interest in medicine, his father proposed that he go to Cambridge, to prepare for a career as a clergyman. His commitment to the Church of England was no deeper, it appears, than his commitment to medicine, but Darwin was able to continue his informal studies in natural history, collecting beetles and learning some geology.

In these interests he was helped by the friendship of Professor J. S. Henslow, a botanist with wide interests in natural history and geology. After three years at Cambridge, Darwin obtained a degree but his intended career in the church remained in doubt. Then occurred the great opportunity: through Henslow, Darwin was offered the post of naturalist on board the Admiralty survey ship HMS *Beagle*, shortly to sail on an expedition round the world. Thus in 1831, at the age of 22, with no formal training in botany, zoology or geology, Darwin was able to spend five years studying these subjects in the field during a voyage of 40,000 miles.

Although he never achieved the reputation of Darwin, Wallace's career shows some intriguing parallels. Born 14 years after Darwin, he trained first as a surveyor, not from any special interest but from the need to earn a living, since, unlike Darwin, his family was not wealthy. In 1844, at the age of 21, there was no work for him as a surveyor, so he found a job as a teacher in Leicester. With a long-held interest in botany and geology, Wallace read in Leicester public library the books by Darwin and Humboldt describing their expeditions to the tropics. He also read Malthus' *Essay on Population* and probably Lyell's *Principles of Geology*, the two books that exercised the greatest influence on Darwin as he independently developed his ideas.

He travelled for four years in South America, and after a further two years in England, unable to find a scientific job— like Darwin, he never held any academic post—he returned to the tropics, spending a further eight years in the islands of the East Indies. It was during his second expedition that Wallace arrived at his theory of natural selection.

This theory, as we have seen, created an outcry when it was first brought to public notice by Darwin's book. It was badly reviewed—George Eliot described *On the Origin of Species* as 'not impressive from want of luminous and orderly presentation'—and criticized by prominent members of the scientific and religious establishments. Nonetheless, the theory of evolution by natural selection, despite its shortcomings, such as those caused by the lack of any corresponding theory of genetics, became within a few years the most generally accepted explanation of the origin of species. In a sense, this is surprising, because even today there is little direct evidence of the operation of natural selection in the ways proposed by Wallace and Darwin, and 100 years ago there was even less.

But Darwin and Wallace, as practical scientists with the experience of years of field work in the tropics behind them, were able to support their theory with such a mass of indirect evidence that most of the criticisms made at the time could be answered by good scientifically reasoned examples, many based on personal observation. As a result, many of their contempories were persuaded of the truth of the theory, thinking with John Stuart Mill, 'Nothing can be at first sight more implausible than his theory, and yet after beginning by thinking it impossible one arrives at something like an actual belief in it'.

Right: On 25 April 1977 a Japanese trawler reportedly caught a strange sea monster off the coast of New Zealand. This photograph was taken by a crew member before the creature was thrown back into the sea. Ever since man has become aware that huge creatures once populated the Earth, he has been fascinated by the possibility of finding a few individuals still surviving. If such creatures do exist, and the Pacific Ocean is one of the few places where they might still live undetected, they will have evolved as much as any other animal living today. There can be no such thing as a 'living fossil'.

Left: A cartoon of Charles Darwin published in the periodical *Vanity Fair* **in September 1871. Darwin's view that man and apes share a common ancestor, though widely accepted today, was much ridiculed by his contemporaries. The Church found it a particularly hard idea to accept.**

Below: Work on the theory of evolution continues today. Here a group of dinosaur's eggs are examined.

Popperfoto

Camera Press

The Evolution of Species

When Wallace and Darwin gave the world their theory of evolution by natural selection in the middle of the nineteenth century, they also gave biologists three great problems to solve. Modern understanding of evolution, which is far from complete, stems from the research inspired by these problems, which can be summed up in three questions: How are the characters that differ among members of a species inherited? How can these differences lead to one individual leaving more offspring than another? And how does a new species become separated from the species within which it evolves?

The separation of species

A cat is a member of one species, while a dog is a member of another one, admittedly a very variable one. The two types of animal differ in shape, size and colour, as well as in behaviour. Also, cats and dogs do not interbreed, whereas even the most different breeds of dog, so long as they are not too dissimilar in size, can mate and produce healthy offspring. Common sense maintains that members of a species breed together, and different species do not. This *reproductive isolation* is more important than differences in appearance, which can be misleading. For example, the females of many different species of ducks are more

Left and below: The hamadryas baboon, *Papio hamadryas*, and the olive baboon, *Papio anubis*, are separated both by patterns of behaviour and by geography so they do not interbreed. The hamadryas baboon lives in northeast Africa whereas the olive baboon is found further south, closer to the equator. Other species of baboon are found elsewhere in Africa. Such separation shows how an original species can become divided into two, each of which evolves in its own way. Where the original species is distributed over a wide area, or over different habitats, it may split into a number of reproductively isolated populations.

Above: When natural isolation mechanisms are disrupted by man, crosses between species are possible. This herd is composed of domestic horses, *Equus caballus*, and zebroids—crosses between horses and zebras, *Equus zebra*. Similarly, crosses between lions and tigers are possible. All such hybrids are sterile.

Bruce Coleman Ltd

Jen & Des Bartlett/ Bruce Coleman Ltd

A. J. Deane/Bruce Coleman Ltd

Feeding Habits of Darwin's Finches

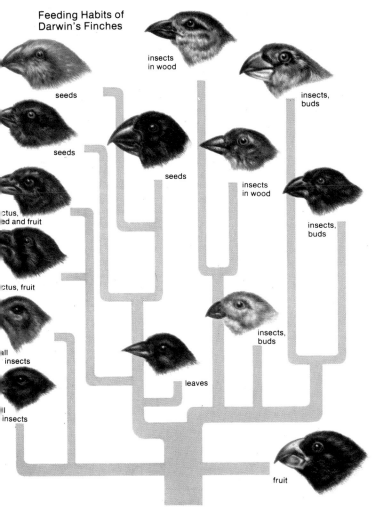

insects in wood

seeds

insects, buds

seeds

seeds

insects in wood

ctus, ed and fruit

insects, buds

ctus, fruit

all insects

insects, buds

ll insects

leaves

fruit

Above: The finches of the Galápagos Islands were studied by Darwin. The various species are closely related but are isolated from each other by feeding behaviour (which has affected the shapes of their bills) and by geography (some species are restricted to just one of the 13 islands). They do not interbreed.

The herring gull (top right), *Larus argentatus*, and the lesser black backed gull (right), *Larus fuscus*, are regarded as separate species for they do not interbreed. In fact, however, they are linked by a chain of intermediate races stretching around the North Pole, and each race interbreeds freely

with neighbouring races. It is therefore difficult to say just where the black-backed gull turns into the herring gull. In this case, the gradual spread of the original population around the Northern Hemisphere has been accompanied by changes in behaviour and two separate species have evolved.

similar to each other than to the males of the same species, yet it would be nonsensical to group the females into one species.

In many plants and animals, there are large genetic differences between species, as is shown, for instance, by the possession of different numbers of chromosomes. These genetic differences normally make hybridization impossible, because the two sets of parental genes do not function correctly when present in the same cells. In certain cases, healthy hybrid offspring are possible, but are infertile. An example of this is the mule, which is the offspring of a cross between a male ass and a female horse.

Where similar species of animals are found together, reproductive isolation is often the result of distinctive patterns of behaviour. Many well-known examples of this phenomenon are found in birds. Several species of European leaf warblers, *Phylloscopus*, are almost impossible to distinguish visually, but have readily identifiable songs. In gulls, *Larus*, the different species have distinctive courtship behaviour in which the sequence of calls and displays varies. The gulls pair off only after a lengthy exchange of such signals, making it unlikely that two birds

of different species will attempt to mate.

In plants, isolation is promoted by insect pollinators which restrict their foraging to one species at a time, and by the inability of pollen to germinate and send out a pollen tube on stigmas of the wrong species. Differences in flowering time make pollination between species unlikely. Where a plant species is restricted to one type of soil or habitat, it is in any case effectively isolated from similar species with different requirements.

Geographical isolation, where different species are separated by physical barriers such as oceans or mountain ranges, is important for both plants and animals. In particular, species on islands are separated from related species on other islands or on the mainland. So, for instance, there' is little likelihood of a Galápagos tortoise, *Geochelone elephantopus*, mating with an Aldabra tortoise, *Geochelone gigantea*. All these mechanisms can serve to maintain the reproductive isolation of particular groups of animals or plants. Isolated groups can probably only *arise*, however, by spatial isolation—on an island or a leaf for example.

An interesting case of species separa-

tion is that known as *ring species*. The herring gull, *Larus argentatus*, and the lesser black-backed gull, *Larus fuscus*, are both found in Western Europe. They are visibly distinct species, with behaviour differences that prevent their interbreeding, although occasionally they do interbreed and produce fertile offspring. Yet the two species are in fact the extreme forms of a chain of ten recognizable races of gulls, which differ mainly in the colour of the leg and back. These races form a ring around the North Pole, from the British Isles through Scandinavia and northern Asia to the Bering Straits, and through Alaska, Canada and Iceland back to northwest Europe.

Inheritance

The evolution of new species is not an automatic result of the reproductive isolation of populations. It also requires an inherited change in the characters of the population. Wallace and Darwin were fully aware of the range of variation in wild species of plants and animals, and of the ways in which breeders had taken advantage of this variation to create new varieties. Unfortunately, their explanation of the appearance of new species in 23

Left: Winners of a Health and Strength League competition in 1961. One of the central tenets of modern inheritance theory is that acquired characteristics, such as physical strength, are not inherited. The genes which control development are passed *unaltered* from one generation to the next.

Below: The classic case of selection in animal species is that of the peppered moth, *Biston betularia*. The dark, *melanic*, form is much fitter than the pale variety in industrial areas blackened with smoke. In Manchester the proportion of the normally rare black form increased to 98% in less than 100 years.

Above: Two red deer males compete for females during the breeding season. Like many animal species, the red deer, *Cervus elaphus*, has developed complex courtship rituals. Behavioural differences help to maintain the isolation of species one from another.

Below: Acts of altruism reduce an individual's fitness and so appear to run counter to evolutionary theory. However, if such behaviour is directed towards a brother, the

ALTRUISM

SELFISHNESS

terms of the inheritance of advantageous characters was muddled by the concept of *blending inheritance*.

This theory, commonly held in the nineteenth century, stated that when two individuals differing in some character, for example size or colour, were crossed, the offspring would always be intermediate between the parents. If this were always the case, it would mean that an advantageous character would tend to be lost in crosses with the normal type.

The modern theory, first formulated by August Weismann (1834-1914) in 1892, is that the genes which control the whole development of a plant or animal are inherited unaltered from one generation to the next. Sexual reproduction, combining genes from two parents, may lead to the appearance of intermediate characters, but the genes are passed on without alteration, so that the original characters can reappear in later generations. The first experimental evidence for this theory was published by Gregor Mendel in 1865, only six years after Darwin published *On the Origin of Species*, but Mendel's work lay unnoticed in an obscure scientific journal for over 30 years.

Genes are now known to be sequences of chemical sub-units along a DNA molecule. (The DNA molecule in a human chromosome contains about 100 million sub-units.) Each gene, or sequence of sub-units, acts as a template for the synthesis of one kind of protein molecule (for example a haemoglobin molecule), and from a small number of DNA molecules the most complex plant or animal can be constructed. The DNA molecule itself is not normally altered by the proteins or other constituents of the cell, so the genes are passed unchanged from one generation to the next.

Molecular evolution

Within a species at any given time, variation in visible characters and in some cases in behaviour can be related to the existence of alternative genes for a character. The alternative genes are the results of *mutations*—changes in the structure of the DNA molecule. The mutations lead to *molecular evolution*, a change in the structure of a protein molecule over long periods of time. For example, haemoglobin is the protein which transports oxygen in the red blood cells of vertebrates, and the sequences of amino acids in haemoglobin from a variety of vertebrates are known. The differences between the haemoglobin molecules of different species parallel the assumed evolutionary relationships of those species; in other words, the more closely related the species, the more similar are the amino acid sequences of their haemoglobin. The study of molecular evolution as much as the traditional studies of fossils and of anatomy in different groups of plants and animals, shows how new species evolve by progressive changes from existing ones.

Discontinuous variation or *polymorphism* results when alternative genes give rise to two or more distinctly different types within a species. More commonly, a character is affected by a number of genes and the existence of alternatives for each gene leads to a range of overlapping types. Characters such as size and

Below: Worker honey bees, *Apis mellifera*, carrying pollen. The members of a colony of bees work towards the survival of common genes rather than individual animals (all are the offspring of a single queen and a single drone). The apparently altruistic worker bees are sterile, but they work to promote the survival of common genes in the eggs laid by the queen.

Right: The world's largest bromeliad, *Puya raimondii*, growing in Bolivia. It has evolved some unusual features which fit it for life in harsh conditions. It can absorb water through special scales on the leaf surfaces.

altruist will still be promoting the chances of his own genes being represented in following generations. This is because a proportion of the brothers' genes will be the same as his own by common descent. This sort of behaviour tends to suggest that the survival of genes may be more important than the survival of individuals. Acts of selfishness and spite may also increase the amount of an individual's genes in the next generation. Following generations are shown at right of each diagram.

SPITE

growth rate normally show this *continuous variation*. Evolution can now be seen as changes in the frequency of alternative genes with a species.

Selection

The study of polymorphism has provided most of the evidence that selection really does take place in natural populations of plants and animals. The classic example is the peppered moth, *Biston betularia*. The normal form is white, speckled with black which provides excellent camouflage when the moth rests on a lichen-covered tree trunk during the day. In industrialized areas with high levels of air pollution, populations of the peppered moth contain a high proportion of the *melanic* form, which is grey speckled with black. The explanation proposed for this

(and later confirmed by experiment) was that air pollution kills the lichens and blackens the tree trunks, so that in polluted areas the light-coloured normal moths stand out against the darkened bark. They would then be more liable to be eaten by birds than the melanic moths, whose dark colouring is now the more effective camouflage. The colour is inherited, and the melanic moths would survive longer and hence lay more eggs. As a result, the melanic form, small numbers of which are found in all populations, would increase in number relative to the normal form.

The selection of different polymorphic forms has also been studied in plants. For example, in some species of grasses there have appeared races which can grow on old mine spoil tips, where the soil con-

tains such high concentrations of lead, zinc and other metals that plants would normally be unable to grow there. These races are descended from the rare individuals found in normal populations, which are able to grow in the presence of these metals.

In any organism, the effect of selection can be understood by measuring the relative *fitness* of different forms. Fitness, in this context, is the average number of offspring which survive to breed themselves; in the peppered moth, the fitness of the melanic form in a polluted area may be up to five times that of normal form. Where two different forms of a species have different fitnesses, selection is taking place, and one would expect the fitter form to become commoner.

The value of a theory

No one example could possibly explain the evolution of every structure and every behaviour pattern found in plants and animals. No theory attempting to explain so much can ever finally be proved true. The value of a theory of natural selection as an explanation for evolution is that it can be tested by experiments and observations in every branch of the science of biology. In Wallace and Darwin's day, sources of evidence for natural selection ranged from fossils to breeds of sheep. Nowadays the same theory is being tested against new evidence from sources as diverse as the structure of protein molecules and the social behaviour of termites. Even if it turns out to be wrong or, more likely, incomplete, it will have stimulated an unparalleled increase in understanding of the natural world, and perhaps of human society as well.

Part II

The World of Plants

Chapter 1 **The Plant Kingdom**

The Plant Kingdom

To help understand the living world it is convenient to divide it into distinct groups of similar organisms; each group having certain combinations of features which are common to it alone and which separate it from all other groups. These groups can then be divided into subgroups or combined to make supergroups—a process which highlights both the similarities and differences between different organisms. The science of classifying living organisms is known as *taxonomy*. Once an organism has been correctly classified it is possible to succinctly summarize a great deal of knowledge about it simply in its name.

The fundamental unit of classification is the *species*. A species is a group of plants or animals which reproduce among themselves to give the same type of plant or animal. Generally the common names used to describe animals and plants refer to particular species such as tomato,

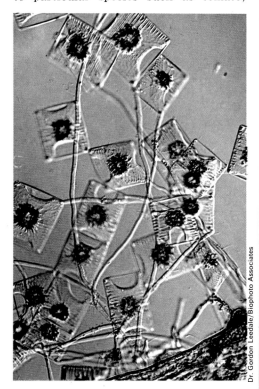

Dr. Gordon Leedale/Biophoto Associates

Lycopersicum esculentum, and man, *Homo sapiens*. Each species is then grouped in larger groups which in ascending order are: *genus* (the first name in the two-part Latin name), *tribe*, *family*, *order*, *class*, *phylum*, and finally *kingdom*. Just two kingdoms are generally accepted—the plant kingdom and the animal kingdom.

Bacteria, blue-green algae and fungi

Although classification is an indispensable aid to study, all divisions above species are entirely artificial. (This explains why whether one group is called, say, a class or a phylum is often in dispute). Many animals and plants are extremely difficult to classify satisfactorily. In particular there are a large number of organisms which cannot be

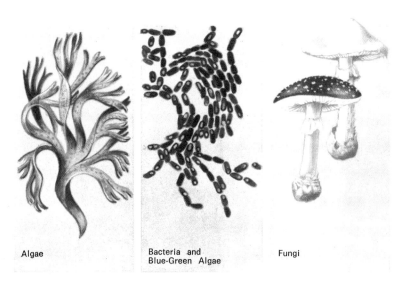

DIVISION 1

Thallophyta

simple plants with no roots, stems or leaves

Algae   Bacteria and Blue-Green Algae   Fungi

DIVISION 2

Bryophyta

plants with leaves and stems but no true roots

Mosses

Left: A group of pennate diatoms, *Striatella*, clustered on the red alga, *Polysiphonia*. Algae are the predominant group of marine plants and vary from simple single-celled species to large complex seaweeds.

Below: *Mycena inclinata*, a fungus, growing on a fallen oak tree. Fungi do not have chlorophyll and are not related to any other plant groups. Some botanists claim they should be classified in a separate kingdom from plants or animals.

Above: The plant kingdom. All life developed originally in the seas and the earliest life forms were probably similar to the *prokaryotic* bacteria and blue-green algae. When the first *eukaryotic* cell (with

specialized organelles) developed is not known, but it is probable that it was much like the simple single-celled algae of today. From the algae all higher plant forms have evolved by improved adaption to life on land.

Heather Angel

28

Pteridophyta

plants with roots, stems leaves and water conducting tissue

rts

Ferns

Horsetails

Clubmosses

Spermatophyta

seed - bearing plants with roots, stems, leaves and water conducting tissue

Gymnosperms (coniferous trees)

Angiosperms (flowering plants)

Below: The Royal fern, *Osmunda regalis*. In many ways ferns resemble higher plants. They have a dominant sporophyte—the gametophyte being an inconspicuous filament many times smaller than the sporophyte.

Right: A species of silver fir, *Abies*, clearly showing the red mature cones. Firs are coniferous trees—the most distinctive group of the *Gymnospermae*, which also includes yews and the tropical cycads and ginkgos.

Giuseppe Mazza

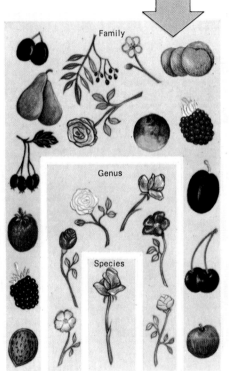

Family

Genus

Species

Heather Angel

Right: Plants are classified into groups each of which has a set of characteristic features which distinguishes it from other groups. The family, *Rosaceae*, illustrated here, includes the *genera*,

Malus (apples), *Pyrus* (pears) and *Rubus* (raspberries and blackberries) as well as *Rosa* (roses). *Rosa* are further divided into species such as *Rosa canina*, the dog rose, and *Rosa odorata*, the tea rose.

conveniently accommodated in either the plant or animal kingdoms. A vast group of such organisms are the *prokaryotes* which includes bacteria and blue-green algae. Their distinctive characteristic— they do not have cells with specialized structures or *organelles*—divides them so completely from all other organisms that many authorities consider them as a kingdom in their own right.

Another group, the *Fungi*, are normally considered to be plants but differ from the majority of plants by one factor—the absence of chlorophyll. Hence, all fungi lack the ability to make their own food. They obtain their nourishment in the same way as animals do by feeding on other living organisms (*parasitism*) or on their dead remains (*saprophytism*).

The three main classes of fungi are the *Phycomycetes*, the *Ascomycetes* and the *Basidiomycetes*. They differ in the way they produce their spores. Some species of phycomycetes have free-swimming *zoospores* though not all do so. The others such as pin-mould, *Mucor*, reproduce by non-mobile spores which are either enclosed inside a spore case (*sporangium*) or are unenclosed so that they can be blown away by the wind. Another characteristic of phycomycetes is that the young cells do not possess crosswalls.

In the *Ascomycetes* the cells have cross-walls and characteristically they also produce eight spores in special sporangia, called *asci*, which are often grouped within cup- or flask-shaped fruiting bodies. Ascomycetes also form

A-Z

Right: Flowers in their many forms are the distinguishing feature of the phylum *Angiospermae*, the flowering plants, which are by far the largest group, in both numbers and species, of plant forms today. These flowers belong to the beech, *Fagus sylvatica*.

Below: *Chionochloa flavescens*, an alpine grass growing in New Zealand. Grasses are a most important family of the sub-phylum *Monocotyledonae*. Monocots have only one seed leaf (*cotyledon*) which develops inside the seed. The cotyledon of grasses absorbs food from another part of the seed (the *endosperm*) and passes it on to the developing plant. In other plants it is a food storage organ itself (as in legumes) or develops with the young plant to become the first green photosynthesizing leaf.

Above: *Quercus*, the oak. There are 450 species of oak—two of which, *Quercus robur* and *Quercus petraea*, are native to Britain and 60 to North America. Before extensive cultivation, oak forest was the dominant vegetation of Europe. The success of oak and other genera of trees relies upon their ability to lay down wood in thickened growths—a process known as *secondary thickening*. Secondary growth allows the tree to produce a tall, dense leaf canopy which suppresses other plants by overshadowing them.

Eric Crichton

the fungal part of the fungus-alga association which comprises a lichen. Two examples of an ascomycete are yeast (*Saccharomyces*) and *Penicillium notatum* from which penicillin is produced.

The third group of fungi, the *Basidomycetes*, includes the mushrooms and toadstools. All these have a spore-bearing structure, called a *basidium*, which swells at the end to form a spore, rather as a glass bulb is blown at the end of a piece of glass tubing.

Algae

The majority of plants, however, differ from animals primarily in their ability to manufacture their own food by photosynthesis. The simplest form of plants which do this are the *Algae*. Algae have no roots, stems, leaves or water-conducting tissue and are all totally dependent on water. Almost all are aquatic.

Colour is the most distinguishing characteristic of algae and the group is divided up into classes according to the predominance of one pigment or another in their cells. In the diatoms (*Chrysophyta*), which constitute the major element of marine plankton upon which all marine life ultimately depends for food, the predominant colour is brown. In the green algae, *Chlorophyta*, however, the green pigment, chlorophyll, is not disguised by the presence of other colouring matter. This class includes the majority of the simple fresh water algae such as *Chlamydomonas* as well as filamentous forms such as *Spirogyra*.

The brown algae, *Phaeophyta*, are almost all seaweeds and are probably the best known algae, owing to the size and complexity which many of them attain

and the extraordinary abundance in which they occur along the coasts. The brown/green colour of their body structure (*thallus*) results from the fact that they contain a brown pigment, *fucoxanthin*, as well as chlorophyll. Treatment with hot water, which dissolves the fucoxanthin, has the effect of turning brown seaweeds green.

Land plants

The simplest land plants are the *Bryophyta* which possesses many features which must have been common to the first land plants. They have an outer layer of cells, the *epidermis*, which surrounds the plants and to some extent prevents drying out. Nevertheless they are highly dependent on water for their reproduction and hence are limited in the habitats they can colonize. Nor do they have a well-developed conducting system for transporting food or water and thus their maximum size is also restricted.

The bryophytes are divided into two classes, the liverworts (*Hepaticae*) and the mosses (*Musci*). In both classes the gamete-producing generation (the *gametophyte*) is dominant over the spore-producing generation (the *sporophyte*). In the liverworts the gametophyte is a flat, green, ribbon-like thallus which grows horizontally with root-like *rhizoids*, while the sporophyte, which develops from a fertilized egg in the gametophyte, remains as a small simple structure dependent on the gametophyte for its nutrition.

The moss gametophyte is not unlike a higher plant. It has a vertical stem with simple leaves, but rhizoids, not roots, anchor it to the ground. Again the

sporophyte is simple, and at least partly dependent on the gametophyte for its food, but it is generally more complex than the sporophyte of the liverworts. Despite this, the structure of the moss gametophyte is quite different from that of the corresponding generation of higher plants, and so mosses and liverworts may be regarded as an isolated group, highly developed in their own way, but with no near affinities to other groups of plants.

This is not true of the ferns (*Filicinae*), the largest class of the phylum *Pteridophyta*. In ferns the situation is reversed with respect to the two generations. The sporophyte is dominant while the gametophyte is small and little more than a structure for producing sex organs and gametes. (Nevertheless it leads an independent life unlike the gametophyte of more advanced plants.) The ferns and their relations, the clubmosses and the horsetails, further resemble higher plants in possessing a sporophyte with roots, leaves and stems and also woody conducting tissue (*vascular tissue*) for transporting water and food. Unlike advanced plants, however, fern male gametes are mobile *spermatozoids*, similar to those of the bryophytes, which must swim to the female sex organs in a water film on the plant surface. Ferns, therefore, are still very dependent on water.

Though they have vascular tissue none of the existing pteridophytes possess the ability to lay down wood in annual rings (*secondary growth*) as do the flowering plants. Secondary growth, however, did occur in pteridophytes of the past and these were possibly related to the early ancestors of the flowering plants.

The *Gymnospermae* are further

A-Z

advanced. In these plants secondary growth is usual, allowing the formation of trees like pine (*Pinus*), fir (*Pseudotsuga*) and spruce (*Picea*). Gymnosperms are also the oldest group of living plants which produce true seeds and in which the male gametophyte is reduced to a nucleus in small wind-borne spores (pollen). Unlike the flowering plants, however, the egg cells of gymnosperms are naked and not enclosed in *ovaries* and gymnosperms do not have flowers. The sporophyte gymnosperms of today are woody trees mostly with evergreen foliage and are particularly abundant as individuals, if not species, in the mountains and cool temperate regions of the world.

Flowering plants

A more recently evolved phylum than the *Gymnospermae* is the *Angiospermae* or flowering plants. This phylum contains the bulk of the present world flora. Like the gymnosperms, angiosperms do not have mobile gametes and hence they are not so dependent on water as the ferns and lower plants. This factor is responsible for their success in a great number of habitats including near deserts.

The characteristic feature of flowering plants is that the egg-bearing ovules are enclosed in an ovary which is usually crowned by a pollen-receiving surface, the *stigma*, borne on a stalk, the *style*. The pollen is produced on nearby reproductive structures called *anthers*. Both the ovary and anthers are then enclosed by special modified leaves, *petals*, and the whole constitutes a flower.

Flowering plants are divided into two sub-phyla: the *Dicotyledonae* which possess two seed leaves (*cotyledons*) and are mainly broad-leaved plants with branching leaf veins, and the *Monocotyledonae* which possess one seed leaf, and have long narrow leaves with parallel veins. Monocotyledons do not undergo secondary growth so all flowering trees are dicotyledons. A major class of the *Monocotyledonae* are the *Graminae*, which include all grasses and cereals.

Classification of the angiosperms is on the basis of the structure of the flowers, fruits and seeds, and a large array of families have been distinguished. Their diversity and adaptability are indicated by the many varied habitats they have invaded. Forms such as cacti and other succulent plants have colonized deserts and the salt sand of sea shores. Water storage tissue and thick wax layers around these plants help to conserve water. Others, such as mistletoe, *Viscum album*, have lost the ability to photosynthesize and have become parasitic.

Finally, a very few angiosperms have returned to the sea from which all plants originated. For example, *Poseidonia* grows on the bed of the sea in warm parts of the world. Thus the group of plants which have become the dominant vegetation of the world because of their success as land plants are now recolonizing the sea and may become a dominant group of marine plants as well. Nevertheless, the dominance of angiosperms cannot be expected to be unending. It is probable that another group of plants, possibly developing from some obscure and unimposing species, will in the future supersede the angiosperms just as they have superseded the ferns and gymnosperms of 300 million years ago.

Above: An example of a monocot flower—the lily, Royal Gold. Monocots are easily distinguished from dicots by their leaves which have parallel veins. Lilies and irises are monocots. Most other flowers are dicots with branched veins on their leaves.

Below: *Papaver rhoeas*, the common field poppy. Poppies are a family of simple dicot flowers with petals which are separated from each other. Some complex flowers, like those of daisies, *Compositae*, consist of many simple flowers fused to form a tube.

Giuseppe Mazza

Chapter 2
Plant Species

Coconut palm (*cocos nucifera*) and young fruit. The sole member of a genus, it has been widely distributed throughout the tropics by ocean currents.

Algae

Algae are simple aquatic or semi-aquatic plants widely distributed in large numbers in most ponds, lakes, streams and the surface waters of oceans. They are perhaps the most numerous of all plants, forming, with small animals, the plankton of the seas which is the primary food source of fish.

They do not possess roots, stems or leaves, yet vary greatly in size from single cells one micron (0.001 mm) in diameter, through colonies and filaments, to large fronded seaweeds which may be up to 100 m (300 ft) in length. In evolutionary terms this variation is thought to indicate the course of the development of the higher plants which are generally supposed to have originated from the green algae.

Colour

Algae are among the simplest plants in which the different functions carried out by the cell occur in specialized structures called organelles—that is they are *eukaryotic*. (Blue-green algae are an exception: they are more closely related to bacteria than to other algae and their cells do not contain discrete organelles.) In particular, algal cells have structures called *chromatophores*, containing various pigments. Most important of these is the green pigment *chlorophyll*, which occurs in chromatophores called *chloroplasts*. Chlorophyll, together with the other pigments, is able to trap the energy of

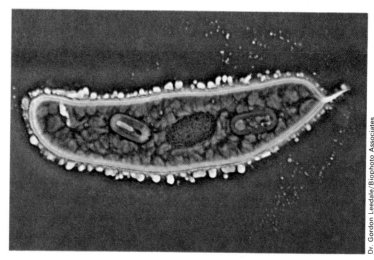

Left: A species of the *Euglena* group of green algae, seen under a light microscope at a magnification of about 1000 times. The plant has been squashed during preparation, causing it to release mucilage which is seen as yellow globules around the edge of the cell. Also visible are the central nucleus, two rings of paramylon —stored carbohydrate— and many green chloroplasts.

Right: *Ptilota plumosa*, a red alga. Red algae are generally small (rarely over a few centimetres in length), many-celled seaweeds with many filaments often arranged in intricate feather-like shapes as shown here.

Right: The single-celled green alga *Chlamydomonas*, found in both freshwater and seawater, showing the organelles within the cell, each with a different function. The centre of the cell is the nucleus containing the genetic material DNA. Around this is the cup-shaped *chloroplast* containing a structure known as a *pyrenoid* in which starch is stored. The *contractile vacuole* is used to force out water which continuously enters the alga from the outside.

Below: Green algae blooming round a soda spring in the Rift Valley of East Africa. The colour is produced by the photosynthetic pigment, chlorophyll.

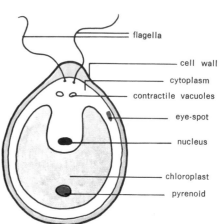

- flagella
- cell wall
- cytoplasm
- contractile vacuoles
- eye-spot
- nucleus
- chloroplast
- pyrenoid

Right: Two different algae taken from the Mediterranean. The long reddish-brown strands are part of a filamentous red alga, *Rhodophyta*, while the circular structure in the centre of the picture is a centric diatom—one of the *Bacillariophyta*. Most oceans, lakes and ponds contain diatoms.

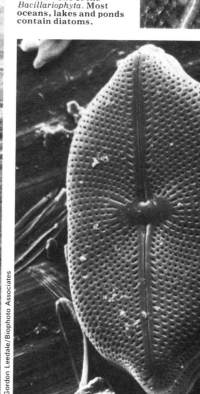

Below: Two types of reproduction in the single-celled green alga, *Chlamydomonas*.
1. Asexual reproduction, in which the cell splits into two halves to produce two identical daughter cells.
2. Sexual reproduction, in which the plant produces several sex cells (gametes) by repeated division. These gametes do not have a thickened cell-wall. When they are released they fuse with gametes, often from another plant, to form first a zygote with four flagella and then a zygospore with a thickened cell-wall able to withstand the cold of winter. On germination the zygospore divides to produce 4 new plants.

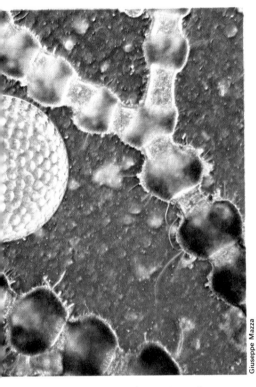

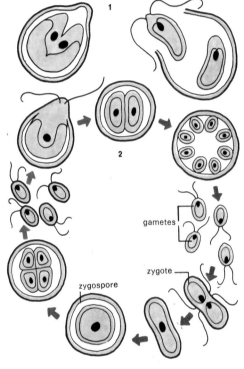

1

2

gametes

zygote

zygospore

Left and below: Two diatoms as seen by the scanning electron microscope—about 1000 times actual size. *Navicula monilifera* (left) is common on sandy beaches around British coasts. Here it is seen in 'valve view' showing the central *raphe* slit. The secretion of mucilage through the raphe is known to produce movement. Because of the silica in the *frustule* ('shell'), it is very long-lasting. The fossil (below), *Melosira sulcata*, is a marine diatom many millions of years old. A gritty deposit, *diatomite*, formed from the accumulation of millions of frustules is used in polishes.

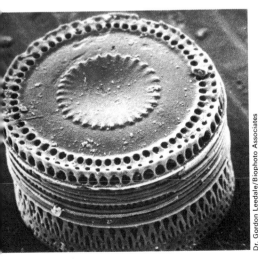

so can live in the soil or on sand, rocks, wood and other plants. The seaweeds anchor themselves to rocks by a structure known as a *holdfast* and are not easily dislodged. Other species intermingle with fungi to form lichens which are composite plants composed of both algae and fungi.

Light is a dominant factor in determining where algae live. The different coloured pigments of the algae trap light of different wavelengths. Water absorbs red light more strongly than other (shorter) wavelengths: only green and ultra-violet light penetrate to any depth. Red algae contain the pigment *phycoerythrin* which absorbs green and ultraviolet light, and so they can live at greater depths—up to 200 m (600 ft)—than green algae. On the other hand, the green algae (which absorb more red light) can live only in the upper or shallow zones.

The chemistry of the water can also determine which species can grow in it. The lack of only one chemical element may be decisive; for example, the single-celled diatoms need a considerable amount of silica. In lakes, during the spring, the light intensity and the temperature increase and algae grow well. If the nutrient content of the lake is high, the growth in the spring may be so great that the water appears to turn green—a phenomenon known as *algal bloom*.

The large seaweeds occupy a unique habitat, the shoreline, part land and part water. The plants must be pliable and resilient, yet tough and leathery to survive beating by the waves and intermittent drying. The height of tides determines how long the algae are dried in the air. To protect themselves in this environment seaweeds often produce large quantities of *mucilage*—a slimy substance secreted by the plant cells. Distinct zones of seaweeds form on the shore—the less adaptable species below the low tide line and the more adaptable higher in the intertidal zone.

Single-celled algae
The green alga *Chlorella* ia a good example of a single-celled alga. It consists of a cell with a nucleus, containing the genetic material DNA, and chloroplasts containing chlorophyll. The cell is surrounded by a cell wall, which in the case of *Chlorella* contains cellulose.

Some single-celled algae are able to move and have one or more *flagella*—whip-like appendages of the cell growing through the cell wall—to propel them through the water. For example, most of the dinoflagellates, present in both marine and freshwater plankton, have one flagellum housed in a transverse furrow and a second flagellum in a longitudinal furrow. Many mobile algae also have an *eye-spot*, an orange-red structure often located near the base of the flagella, usually within a chloroplast. It may be light sensitive and is thought to be used in direction finding.

Diatoms are enclosed in a shell-like case called a *frustule* which is composed of silica and consists of two sections, like the two halves of a box. A special band, the *girdle band*, holds the two halves of the frustule together. The top and bottom sections of the two halves are known as *valves*. When describing a diatom it is usual to say whether it is in 'valve view' or 'girdle view' because the same diatom can look quite different in these two views. Most diatoms look rectangular in

sunlight and use it to build chemicals needed by the cell. This is the well-known process of *photosynthesis*.

The shape and number of chloroplasts varies from one alga to another. For example, *Chlorella*, a unicellular alga, has a single cup-shaped chloroplast. *Spirogyra*, on the other hand, consists of a long filament of cells each having one or a few spiralling, ribbon-shaped chloroplasts. Other algae may have plate-like or star-like chloroplasts.

The colour given to algae by these various pigments is one of their distinctive characteristics. Each group has a particular range of pigments in a particular combination. Because of this, algae have traditionally been divided into groups by colour: the green algae, *Chlorophyta;* the red algae, *Rhodophyta;* and the brown algae, *Phaeophyta*. Other groups include diatoms, *Bacillariophyta*, and dinoflagellates, *Pyrrophyta*.

Ecology
Algae can exist in almost any environment provided it is damp. They occur in salty, brackish and fresh water, though not many species are found in all three. They can grow in hot springs and on snow or ice. Some exist in just a film of water and

Giuseppe Mazza

Heather Angel

Left: A semi-tropical green seaweed, *Caulerpa prolifera. Caulerpa* has many nuclei but is not sub-divided by cell-walls into individual cells. This represents one possible way in which large many-celled plants may have evolved from a primeval, single-celled algal ancestor.

Right: The common shore seaweed, *Fucus vesiculosus*. Male plants have red, while females have dark green, reproductive swellings on the tips of fronds.

Below: Infra-red photography produces a sharp contrast between seaweed (*Fucus*) and surrounding rocks. Chlorophyll in the seaweed appears purple in infra-red light.

Dr. Gordon Leedale/Biophoto Associates

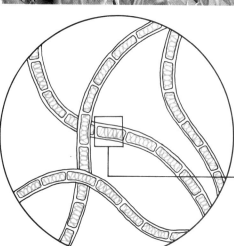

Left and below: The filamentous green alga *Spirogyra*. The bulk of the plant is taken up by a *vacuole*—a large space filled with water containing dissolved substances. Each *chloroplast* is a flat ribbon spiralling round the edge of a cell and dotted with *pyrenoids* surrounded by stored starch.

vacuole — chloroplast — nucleus — cytoplasm

girdle view but appear different in valve view. Diatoms like *Melosira* which are circular, rather like a cheese box, are called *centric*. Others are very variable and can be sausage-shaped, S-shaped, wedge-shaped or broadly oval, and are called *pennate*.

All the diatoms have elaborate and distinctive patterns of pores on the surface of the frustule, but the pennate diatoms often have an additional feature, the *raphe*. This is a furrow extending lengthways through the wall of the valve. Pennate diatoms with raphes are able to move by means of mucilage secreted from the raphe.

The *desmids*, a group of the green algae, also have cells in two halves—though in some species this is not conspicuous—but they differ from the diatoms in having a cell wall which contains cellulose, as in the higher plants. In most desmids the two halves are joined by a narrow neck of tissue, giving the alga a dumb-bell shape. Often the cell wall is decorated with ribs, spines and warts, and the chloroplasts are complex lobed structures, one in each semi-cell.

Many-celled algae

Single-celled algae can clump together to form colonies in which each cell acts more or less independently and there is no specialization of cells within the group to form structures with a specific function, like, for example, reproduction. More complex colonies can be formed by flagellate cells in mucilage. Such colonies have a variety of shapes. For instance, they may be plate-like or spherical. Other algae, particularly the diatoms, form long chains. More genuinely filamentous algae are found attached to rocks, like *Oedogonium*, or are free-floating, like *Spirogyra*.

The larger algae vary considerably in structure. In the common green seaweed *Cladophora* for example, the cells are arranged in highly branched filaments. Red algae are formed of numerous filaments joined together in a wide variety of shapes and structures. And in the common shore seaweeds *Fucus* and *Laminaria* the thalli are formed of many-celled true tissues.

Reproduction

Algae have a great variety of life histories depending on the ways in which they reproduce. In vegetative reproduction new plants are produced by simple fragmentation of the plant into one or more parts. This is different from asexual reproduction where specialized cells or groups of cells produce spores which in turn go on to produce new plants. Many different kinds of spores are involved, in particular the swimming *zoospore*. Zoospores have one, two or more flagella and often contain eye-spots to help them in their direction finding. Their mobility enables them to spread the species throughout any stretch of water. Sometimes a special spore is produced with a particularly thick wall, and this enables the plant to survive harmful conditions such as drought.

Most algae also reproduce sexually. In sexual reproduction, the zygote—formed from the fusion of the haploid male and female sex cells (gametes)—either undergoes immediate reduction division before producing new plants or produces a plant (the *sporophyte*) having a double set of chromosomes in each cell which subsequently produces asexual spores each having a single complete set of chromosomes. (Cells with a double set of chromosomes are known as *diploid*, while those with a single set are called *haploid*.) The asexual spores then go on to produce a second generation of haploid plants, known as *gametophytes*. Two stages of reproduction are therefore involved in the

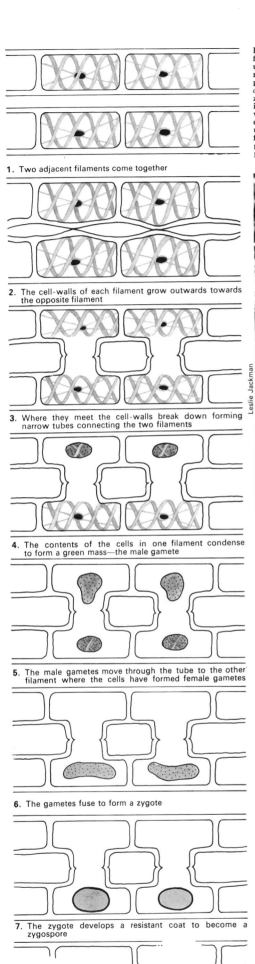

1. Two adjacent filaments come together

2. The cell-walls of each filament grow outwards towards the opposite filament

3. Where they meet the cell-walls break down forming narrow tubes connecting the two filaments

4. The contents of the cells in one filament condense to form a green mass—the male gamete

5. The male gametes move through the tube to the other filament where the cells have formed female gametes

6. The gametes fuse to form a zygote

7. The zygote develops a resistant coat to become a zygospore

8. The filament dies, releasing the zygospore

Left: Two adjacent filaments of *Spirogyra* undergoing sexual reproduction by the process of *conjugation*. The zygospores are covered in a resistant case which can withstand drought, cold and heat until conditions are favourable. Then they germinate, each producing one new plant.

Right: The brown seaweed *Fucus vesiculosus*. It consists of flat blades (*laminae*) attached by a *stipe* to the holdfast which anchors the plant to the sea-bed.

Below: An example of a brown seaweed, 'tangle' (*Laminaria digitata*). The photograph, taken at low-tide, reveals the anchoring holdfasts.

air bladders (to give buoyancy)

reproductive swellings

midrib (to give support and to transport nutrients)

holdfast

Leslie Jackman

Below: One of the uses of algae is the purification of sewage. The sewage is sprayed over beds of clinker on which the algae grow. While the sewage percolates through the clinker it dissolves oxygen produced during photosynthesis by the algae and so allows further purification by bacteria.

P. Morris

latter type of life cycle, as in the higher plants, and the process is called *alternation of generations*.

This occurs in all brown and red algae and a few green algae. In some algae, such as the many celled red algae, these two plant generations are similar in appearance but in others they show marked differences. In the more complex algae, as in higher plants, the sporophyte is dominant and the gametophyte generation is greatly reduced. In the common large seaweed *Laminaria*, for example, the gametophyte generation is reduced to microscopic filaments of a few cells which produce either sperm or eggs. Fertilized eggs develop into the sporophyte.

Algae and man

Despite the great importance of algae as the primary food source of the oceans, their direct use by man is limited. Nevertheless, they can be eaten, for example, *Porphyra*, the lava bread of Wales, or fed to animals. In particular the mucilage from the large seaweeds, such as *Macrocystis*, is processed to make animal foodstuffs. The reproduction of algal cells has been studied to give a guide to the cause of cancer and algae are also used for oxidizing sewage and for pro-

ducing oxygen during space flights.

A jelly, known as *agar-agar*, is produced from some red algae such as *Gelidium*. It is widely used in bacterial and fungal culture, in confectionary, dentistry, in cosmetics and in baked foods. *Carageenin* extracted from the red alga *Chondrus crispus* is used in toothpaste. Other substances, *alginates*, produced from brown algae, are used as emulsifying agents in the treatment of latex for rubber tyres, and in ice-cream, coal briquettes, and paints. The alginates are extracted by disintegrating the plants in acid and then adding calcium carbonate (lime) to settle out the alginate.

Algae are used as food and in the preparation of processed foods. But they can also be harmful. Some are poisonous to animals; more importantly they may produce toxins which can spoil water supplies wanted for domestic use. Alternatively the death and decay of large numbers of algae following an algal bloom can use up all the available oxygen in water turning it fetid and causing fish to die. Despite this, the photosynthesis of the billions of algae in the sea is responsible in no small part for the production of the life-giving oxygen in the atmosphere.

Bacteria and Blue-Green Algae

Bacteria are minute organisms present everywhere, in vast numbers, on the Earth's surface. They live in countless millions in the soil, in the depths of the sea and in the air, in hot springs and in the Arctic. They multiply inside our bodies and on our skins, sometimes causing diseases but often acting beneficially. Some bacteria (*Bdellovibrio*) even prey upon other, larger, bacteria, boring through the cell wall and digesting the contents. Because of their large numbers and the variety of their activities bacteria must be regarded as among the most important of all living organisms.

Bacteria, blue-green algae and a few other similar creatures belong to a group of organisms called *prokaryotes*. The cells of all prokaryotes have an entirely different organization from the cells of the rest of living things (called *eukaryotes*). The most important difference is that the prokaryote cell does not contain the specialized structural components (*organelles*) which are present in the eukaryote cell: there is, for example, no definite nucleus. Specialized functions such as respiration, photosynthesis, secretion and excretion have to be carried on throughout the cell rather than in specially equipped parts of it.

Bacteria

The bacterial cell wall is made of protein; it forms a protective layer and determines the shape of the cell. Bacteria of different groups have characteristic shapes, so *bacilli* are rod-shaped, *cocci* are spherical, *spirilla* are spirally coiled and so on.

As already mentioned, the nucleus of a bacterial cell is not a well defined structure surrounded by its own membrane—the nucleic acid molecules are simply loosely bound together in a network. When the cell is about to divide, the nucleic acids are formed into a single ring called the *genophore* which then splits into two. Once this has happened, the cell itself divides. Given favourable conditions, a typical bacterial cell is capable of dividing once every hour, and if this continues it results in some 17 million cells in 24 hours. That bacteria are capable of very rapid multiplication is obvious to anyone who has suddenly been struck down by blood poisoning from an infected wound or wakened one morning to find that the milk which was reasonably fresh the night before is now undrinkable. One feature of bacteria which certainly contributes to their rapid metabolism and reproduction is their small size, which gives them a large surface area per unit mass. Over this large area a vast number of enzyme molecules can be liberated into the surrounding environment.

Bacteria are capable of using almost any type of animal or plant debris for food; they are rivalled only by fungi in this respect. With a variety of enzymes from a succession of different bacteria, the corpse of a rat or the product of the town sewers is broken down and used, either by the bacteria themselves or by any other organisms which happen to be

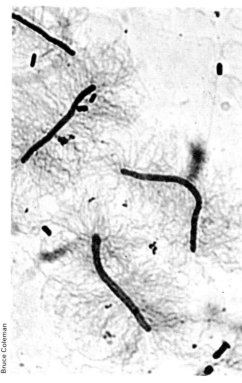

Bruce Coleman

Above: Bacteria are among the smallest of living organisms. These examples of *Bacillus proteus* have been stained with silver and magnified about 2,500 times to make them visible. They are well equipped with flagella.

Below: Tiny helical bacteria seen through a microscope.

Right: A section of a bacterial DNA molecule showing the double helix structure.

Far right: The same as above but with a unit of the antibiotic *actinomycin* incorporated into the structure. The antibiotic is a 'spanner' in the genetic 'works', preventing the bacterium from replicating.

Biophoto Associates

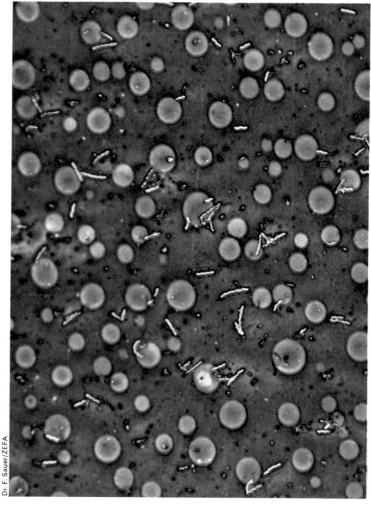

Dr. F. Sauer/ZEFA

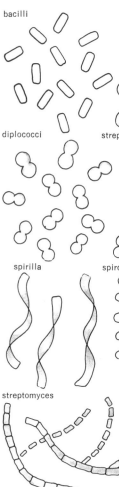

bacilli

diplococci   strep

spirilla   spiro

streptomyces

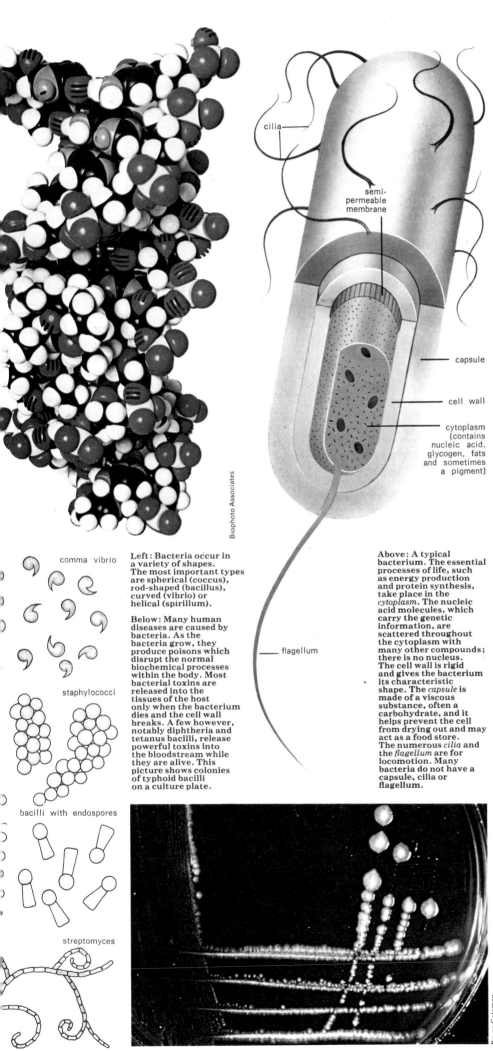

cilia

semi-permeable membrane

capsule

cell wall

cytoplasm (contains nucleic acid, glycogen, fats and sometimes a pigment)

flagellum

comma vibrio

staphylococci

bacilli with endospores

streptomyces

Biophoto Associates

Bruce Coleman

Left: Bacteria occur in a variety of shapes. The most important types are spherical (coccus), rod-shaped (bacillus), curved (vibrio) or helical (spirillum).

Below: Many human diseases are caused by bacteria. As the bacteria grow, they produce poisons which disrupt the normal biochemical processes within the body. Most bacterial toxins are released into the tissues of the host only when the bacterium dies and the cell wall breaks. A few however, notably diphtheria and tetanus bacilli, release powerful toxins into the bloodstream while they are alive. This picture shows colonies of typhoid bacilli on a culture plate.

Above: A typical bacterium. The essential processes of life, such as energy production and protein synthesis, take place in the *cytoplasm*. The nucleic acid molecules, which carry the genetic information, are scattered throughout the cytoplasm with many other compounds; there is no nucleus. The cell wall is rigid and gives the bacterium its characteristic shape. The *capsule* is made of a viscous substance, often a carbohydrate, and it helps prevent the cell from drying out and may act as a food store. The numerous *cilia* and the *flagellum* are for locomotion. Many bacteria do not have a capsule, cilia or flagellum.

within reach. This type of existence, breaking down the products of other organisms, is known as *saprophytism*, and the great majority of bacteria are saprophytes.

But not all bacteria are saprophytes. Bacteria must have played an important part in the early evolution of life on Earth and they could not, at that time, have lived on existing organic products. Almost certainly, many early bacteria were *autotrophic*, capable of synthesis of vital organic materials from simple constituents, and many of them do this today, obtaining the necessary energy by oxidation of inorganic or simple organic materials. A good example is found among the colourless sulphur bacteria, such as *Beggiatoa*, found in stagnant fresh water and marine habitats where hydrogen sulphide is abundant. They are capable of *chemosynthesis* by oxidizing the sulphide to sulphur, which is deposited within the rather large cell.

Thus, by a great variety of processes and under a wide variety of conditions, bacteria are able to degrade and synthesize a range of organic and inorganic substances. In this they are essential to the survival of all other living things: they make available chemicals which would otherwise be locked up in forms which cannot be directly assimilated. A good example of this is seen in the nitrogen cycle. The most satisfactory source of nitrogen for plant growth, on which animal growth also ultimately depends, is nitrate. During the decomposition of nitrogen-containing animal and plant remains by bacterial and fungal saprophytes, large quantities of ammonia are produced. The ammonia is oxidized to nitrite and then to nitrate by the autotrophic *Nitrosomonas* and *Nitrobacter*, and can then be assimilated by the plants. A few prokaryotes, including some bacteria such as the root nodule bacterium *Rhizobium*, have the astonishing ability to oxidize atmospheric nitrogen to nitrate. This process is called 'nitrogen fixation' and is an important part of the nitrogen cycle.

Given the wide variety of forms of nutrition in bacteria it is hardly surprising that they produce a wide variety of chemical by-products, many of which are useful to man. The production of acetic acid (vinegar) from alcohol by *Acetobacter*, and of fermented milk products like yogurt and cottage cheeses by *Lactobacillus*, are well known. Many soil organisms, including bacteria, produce antibiotics. In nature, these highly poisonous substances serve to protect the organism from competitors and predators. Not surprisingly, most of them are as toxic to man as they are to other organisms and hence cannot be used in medicine. Among those produced by bacteria, *tyrothricin* is not toxic to man if applied in small doses and so can be used to kill disease-producing bacteria.

Actinomycetes, or 'star-fungi', so called because they radiate out as they grow, are not fungi at all but organisms closely related to bacteria. Most of them live saprophytically in the soil, among them *Streptomyces griseus*, which produces the antibiotic *streptomycin*. Some are parasitic: *Streptomyces scabies* causes the troublesome common scab disease of potatoes, and *Nocardia* species cause tuberculosis-like diseases and other conditions in man and domestic animals. 39

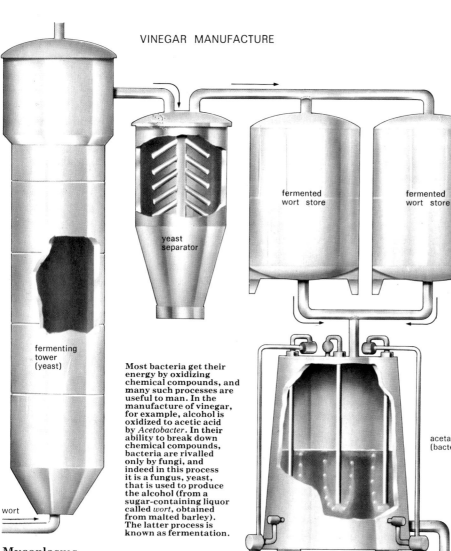

VINEGAR MANUFACTURE

fermenting tower (yeast)

yeast separator

fermented wort store

fermented wort store

wort

acetator (bacterium)

vinegar storage

vinegar storage

filter

pasteurizer

pure vinegar

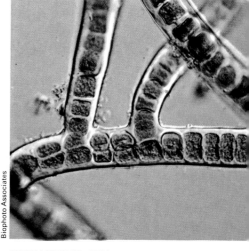

Above: Cultured colonies of bacteria belonging to the genus *Acetobacter* used in the manufacture of vinegar (left).

Below: Filaments of the blue-green alga *Stigonema* magnified 200 times. These organisms contain the green pigment chlorophyll and get their energy by photosynthesis.

Right: Grass fragments being digested in a cow's stomach (the spherical object is a gas bubble). It is the presence of bacteria in the animal's rumen (the first chamber of the stomach) that allows it to digest grass because grass consists largely of cellulose, which can be digested by bacterial enzymes.

Most bacteria get their energy by oxidizing chemical compounds, and many such processes are useful to man. In the manufacture of vinegar, for example, alcohol is oxidized to acetic acid by *Acetobacter*. In their ability to break down chemical compounds, bacteria are rivalled only by fungi, and indeed in this process it is a fungus, yeast, that is used to produce the alcohol (from a sugar-containing liquor called *wort*, obtained from malted barley). The latter process is known as fermentation.

Mycoplasms

Other groups of organisms closely related to bacteria but generally even simpler are known. Among these the *mycoplasms* are specially interesting. They are basically like bacteria except that they are much smaller. It has been estimated that the genophore of an average mycoplasm, though it is structurally similar to that of a bacterium, may only have enough room to contain about 650 genes, one-fifth the number found in a typical bacterium. Because mycoplasms lack a cell wall they can change their shape and so are able to pass through a very fine filter which would retain bacteria.

Some mycoplasms are saprophytic and therefore particularly interesting: they represent the simplest forms of life capable of independent existence. Others are parasitic on man or other animals, causing pleuropneumonia-like diseases. Still others attack plants, including some important crop producers.

Blue-green algae

The chief difference between blue-green algae and bacteria is that the former use the same photosynthetic process as higher plants to extract energy from the Sun. By absorbing sunlight, molecules of the green pigment *chlorophyll* are raised to a higher energy state than usual. These high-energy molecules drive the synthetic process whereby carbon dioxide in the air and water are trapped and gradually built up into more complex molecules useful to the plant. After releasing their energy, the chlorophyll molecules are ready to absorb more sunlight, and so the process continues. Oxygen is a by-product of the process and is released

Right: Typical eukaryote and prokaryote cells in cross-section. There is much more organization in the former: it contains well defined structures (organelles) with specialized functions. The nucleic acid which carries the genetic information is confined to the *nucleus*, energy production is carried out in the *mitochondria*, protein production in the *endoplasmic reticulum* and photosynthesis in the *chloroplast*. The *dictyosomes* are concerned with breaking down waste products.

PROKARYOTE CELL
(BLUE-GREEN ALGA)

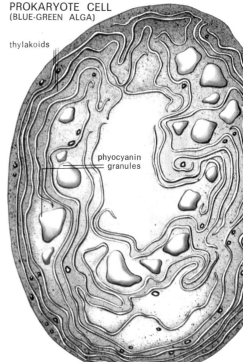

thylakoids

phyocyanin granules

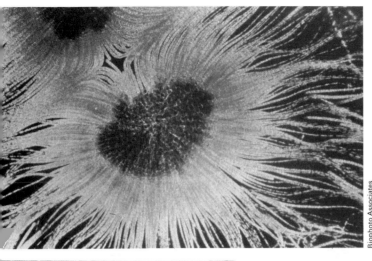

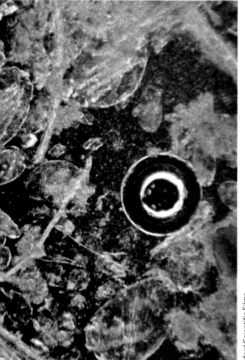

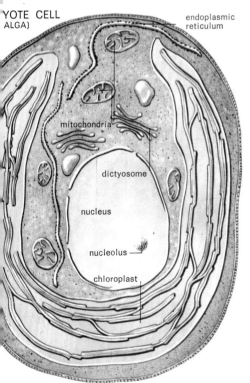

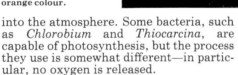

YOTE CELL
(ALGA)

endoplasmic
reticulum

mitochondria

dictyosome

nucleus

nucleolus

chloroplast

Above: A colony of the
blue-green alga
Calothrix magnified
about 100 times.
Filaments of algal
cells radiate out from
a tightly packed
central region.

Right: Blue-green algae
are found in all sorts
of habitats. They occur
as slimy masses in
ponds, on soil and on
the bark of trees, and
they can often endure
extremes of temperature
which would kill higher
plants. This picture
shows blue-green algae
growing on vegetation
near a geyser at
Whakarewarewa in New
Zealand. In this case
the designation
'blue-green' is not
very apt, for the alga
contains a pigment which
makes it a conspicuous
orange colour.

into the atmosphere. Some bacteria, such as *Chlorobium* and *Thiocarcina*, are capable of photosynthesis, but the process they use is somewhat different—in particular, no oxygen is released.

Blue-green algae are so called because a pigment, *phyocyanin*, partially masks the green of the chlorophyll in most species. Blue-green algal cells are usually larger and more complicated than bacterial cells, though they never have flagella of any sort. They often grow in long chains or filaments.

Blue-green algae are found in the same sort of habitats as bacteria. Being mainly photosynthetic, however, they are incapable of secreting the wide variety of enzymes necessary to break down complex organic materials. Nevertheless, many are able to grow under conditions where the light is too dim for photosynthesis, such as the top few millimetres of soil or at the bottom of turbid pools, by absorbing simple organic substances from their surroundings in a process known as *photoassimilation*. Some light is necessary for this process and so active blue-green algae are never found in totally dark environments.

The blue-green algal cell does not contain chloroplasts (the organelles where photosynthesis takes place) as in eukaryote algae, but the pigments are confined to membranous plates called *thylakoids*. The photosynthesis is carried out on these plates and the main storage product, not starch as in higher plants but a glycogen, related to those produced by red algae, fungi and animals, is deposited between the plates.

Soil fertility is known to be closely connected with the activities of nitrogen-fixing blue-green algae. For instance the world's rice production depends to a large extent on the presence of vast numbers of blue-green algae in the water and mud of paddy fields. In many multicellular species of blue-green algae nitrogen fixation is carried on in specialized cells called *heterocysts*. When heterocysts mature they lose most of their pigments, photosynthesis stops and the thylakoids are replaced by a more complicated membrane system where presumably the nitrogen fixation occurs.

Prokaryotic organisms afford a fascinating glimpse of the beginnings of life on this planet. Even among the present day mycoplasms there are forms capable of an independent existence which must resemble closely the first truly living things. The anaerobic bacteria may well resemble organisms which lived when free oxygen was not available. Blue-green algae are all aerobic, and so could not have achieved their present form until free oxygen began to diffuse into the air. Once it did become available, these small and perhaps, to our eyes, insignificant organisms would have nevertheless been responsible for increasing its concentration as a by-product of their new form of photosynthesis.

Today the prokaryotes are still a numerous and important group. The breaking down of organic materials by bacteria and Actinomycetes is essential to the recycling of elements, and the constant nitrogen fixation by a host of prokaryotic cells maintains the fertility of the soil. Its potential for rapid growth combined with physiological diversity, makes the simple prokaryote a useful friend and a formidable enemy.

41

Viruses

Viruses are generally regarded as the smallest of all living things, although whether they are truly 'alive' is very much a matter of opinion. Certainly they are able to reproduce in the sense that they manufacture replicas of themselves from 'spare parts' borrowed from the cells they parasitize, rather as robots might be programmed to make more robots from stolen spares. On the other hand, like most chemical compounds, viruses can be crystallized, and this is certainly not a characteristic normally associated with life. Now that quite logical speculation about the origin of life on the Earth is possible, it has become difficult to draw the line between living organisms and complex aggregations of self-replicating molecules. Viruses plainly lie very close to this line.

Viruses are composed of nucleic acid and protein, and they are small enough to pass through a filter that would retain bacteria—hence their old name 'filterable viruses'. All known viruses are parasitic: they are incapable of an independent existence outside the cells of another living creature, whether animal, plant or bacterium. The diseases which they cause must be as old as man himself, and they include mumps and measles, chicken pox and rabies. Among plants, the striped tulip flowers beloved of Rembrandt, and the degeneration which makes it impractical to go on planting old stocks of potatoes year after year, are examples of virus diseases.

Tobacco mosaic virus

Strangely, perhaps, the virus about which most is known, and on which the first scientific experiments .were done, is a plant virus, the agent of tobacco mosaic disease. At the end of the nineteenth century, Meyer and Ivanovski both showed that the disease could be transmitted by rubbing a healthy tobacco plant with sap from a diseased one. The sap could be rendered uninfective by heating it to 90 °C (194 °F). Ivanovski showed, however, that it was still infective after passing through a bacteriological filter, hence the infective principle could not be a bacterium, but was assumed to be a fluid. Comparable work on an animal virus, that causing foot and mouth disease, was done a few years later by Loeffler and Frosch.

By means of electron microscopy, X-ray crystallography and other methods, the structure of the tobacco mosaic virus (TMV) particle is now well-known. The virus is a narrow rigid rod about 3,000 Ångstrom units long (an Ångstrom unit is one ten millionth of a millimetre). The greater part of it is made up of a protective coat of interlocking protein molecules arranged in a dense left-handed spiral. This spiral fits neatly round a single, helical RNA molecule. It is the efficiency of the sheath which gives the particle its remarkable toughness, but the replicating mechanism, and hence the infectivity, are vested in the RNA molecule. *Ribonucleic* and *deoxyribonucleic acids* (RNA and DNA) are found in all living organisms. Viruses are unique in that they only possess one or the other. The nucleic acids are the

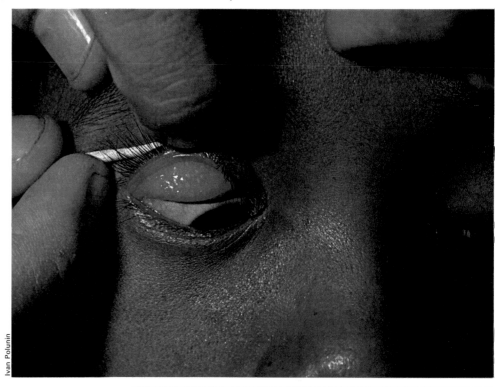

Ivan Polunin

Above: A great many animal and plant diseases are the result of infection by viruses. This picture shows a case of conjunctivitis caused by trachoma virus. The disease is recognized by small spots on the inner side of the eyelid, and it can lead to blindness.

Right: A model of an icosahedral (20-sided) virus. The outer shell is composed of protein molecules (represented here by table-tennis balls) and the core consists of a single molecule of RNA or DNA. Many viruses have this structure, including the polio virus, a very small DNA virus.

Below: Perhaps the strangest-looking viruses are the *bacteriophages*, which attack only bacteria. Shown here is a 'T-2' bacteriophage. Its 'head', shaped like a hexagonal prism, consists of a protein shell enclosing a molecule of DNA. From the base of the prism projects a narrow tube enclosed in a spiral sheath of protein molecules. Six protein 'legs' project from the lower end of the sheath.

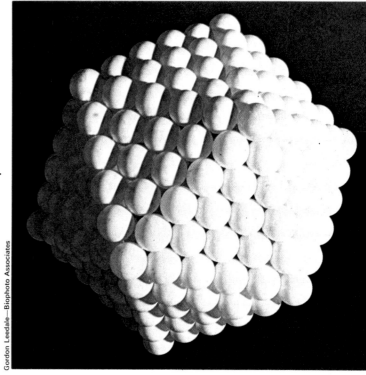

Gordon Leedale—Biophoto Associates

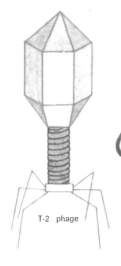

T-2 phage

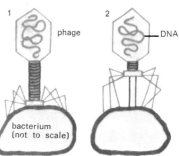

1 phage
2 DNA
3
bacterium (not to scale)
4

T-2 PHAGE ATTACKING A BACTERIUM

Above: A bacteriophage attacks a bacterial cell. The phage settles on the cell wall (1) using its legs to get a firm grip, and the spiral sheath contracts (2) to expose the inner tube. This then penetrates the cell
wall, probably by secreting an enzyme, and the phage DNA enters the bacterial cell (3) where it begins to replicate. The empty and collapsed shell of the original phage remains outside the cell wall. Eventually the
bacterium is killed by enzymes made on the instructions of the phage DNA, the wall disintegrates and the new phage particles are released (4). Rather similar viruses called *cyanophages* attack blue-green algae.

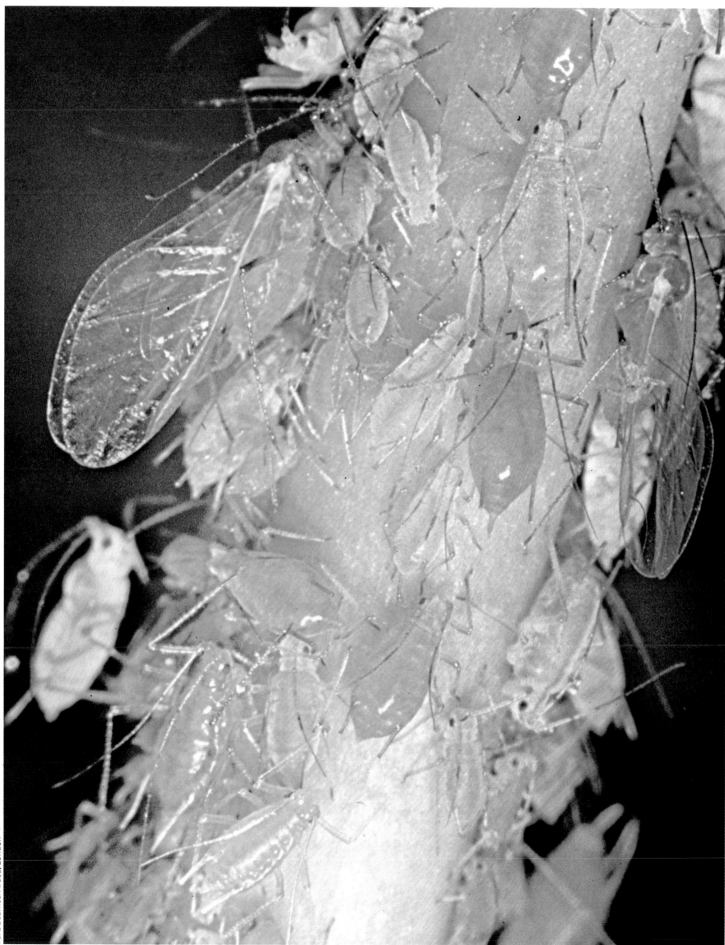

Greenfly aphids may carry viruses from one plant to another, travelling on air currents up to 2,000 feet high.

key to life: they carry the coded information and instructions which determine the shape, the physiology and ultimately the behaviour patterns of living things.

Reproduction

When material containing TMV particles is rubbed on a leaf, the virus enters through tiny wounds, such as broken leaf-hairs, into the cells. (Only a few viruses have a mechanism for boring through an intact cell wall). However, once in the cell the RNA strand quickly sheds its protein coat. The 'bases', which form part of the RNA molecule, are arranged in such a way as to convey an instruction or 'message' to the host cell to produce a particular enzyme. The enzyme in turn lays down a reversed copy of the RNA molecule alongside the original one, obtaining the nucleotide 'bricks' for the new molecule from the host cell. The completed 'negative' molecule then peels off from the original 'positive' and acts as a template for the production of more positives. Finally, the new positives lay down for themselves the protective coating of protein molecules, making use of amino acids and proteins in the host cell.

Though the method of multiplication is apparently similar in all viruses, the structure varies from one group of viruses to another. In many viruses the nucleic acid exists in the reduced form, DNA. The molecule, whether of DNA or RNA, may be either single- or double-stranded. Also, there is considerable variety in the way in which the molecules of the protective coat are assembled. A few viruses have the physical properties of pure nucleic acid and apparently lack a protein coat, but in the vast majority a protein coat is present.

Perhaps the last word in parasitism is a virus which parasitizes another virus. At least one such exists. It is a very small virus particle, known as satellite virus (SV), which is sometimes found associated with tobacco necrosis virus (TNV). Because of their differences in weight, mixtures of the two viruses can be separated in a high speed centrifuge. On its own TNV is capable of multiplication in the tobacco plant, but SV cannot multiply except in the presence of TNV. It is probable that SV does not contain enough RNA to carry the necessary coded information to make all the proteins necessary for its own replication. The protein coat of SV is chemically not related to that of TNV, so it seems possible that the SV makes its own coat. Theoretical considerations suggest that if SV contains the codes for its own coat, it has only enough room on its RNA strand to code for one more protein; not enough to make a complete virus particle. The other necessary protein units appear to be manufactured under 'subcontract' by the TNV.

Pox viruses

Another interesting group are the pox viruses responsible for smallpox, cowpox, fowlpox and so on. One of these, thought to have originated from cowpox, is the *vaccinia* virus. Pox viruses are large as virus particles go, in fact vaccinia virus can be seen in an optical microscope. The virus particle resembles an egg with small tubules projecting inwards from the shell to join up with a central round body which contains the DNA.

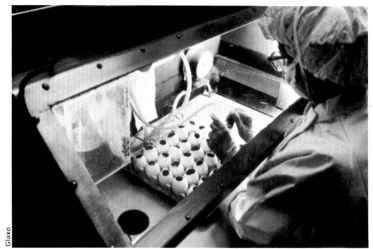

Glaxo

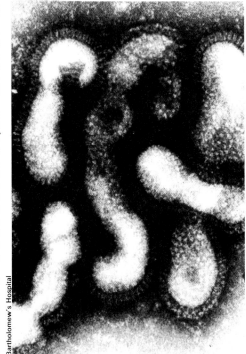

Left and below: Viruses being harvested for the production of an influenza vaccine. Influenza viruses are first injected into fertilized hens' eggs where they develop on the growing embryo and its surrounding membranes. They are then harvested and deactivated to form the basis of the vaccine.

Left: Influenza 'A' viruses seen through an electron microscope. Viruses are responsible for a number of human diseases, including major epidemic diseases like smallpox (now almost extinct) and yellow fever, minor infections like the common cold, and specific diseases like chicken pox and measles.

Below: Normal and yellow-streaked wallflower petals. The streaking is caused by a virus infection. Not all virus infections are regarded as a nuisance: tulip bulbs infected with a virus that causes a particular streaking effect in the flowers can command high prices as new horticultural varieties.

The entire particle incorporates fats and carbohydrates as well as protein in relative proportions similar to those found in bacteria, though it is important to realize that these are not organized in the same way as they would be in the simplest bacterium.

At the end of the eighteenth century, a country doctor called Jenner noticed that patients who were used to handling cattle were seldom infected with smallpox and considered that this might be connected with their having previously been infected with cowpox, which causes only a relatively minor disease in humans. He therefore obtained some serum from cowpox spots and scratched it into the skin of a boy, where it caused only a local infection. After the lesions had healed he subjected the boy to smallpox contagion and was no doubt relieved to find that the boy failed to contract the disease: he had developed a resistance to smallpox.

The vaccinia virus is now propagated only in laboratories and is not known in the wild. It has some of the properties of the original cowpox virus and some of naturally occurring smallpox virus. It can be grown on the membranes of developing hens' eggs by making a small hole in the eggshell, or by vaccinating

Dr. R. G. Milne

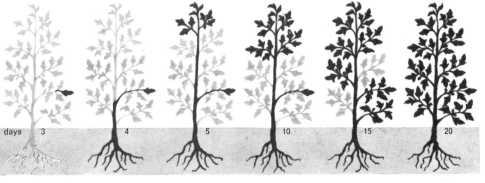

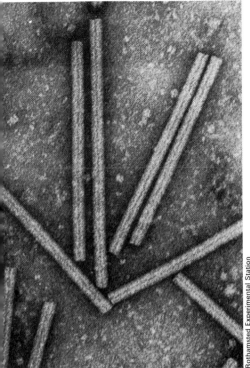

The rod-shaped tobacco mosaic virus (TMV) is one of the best-known of all viruses. Shown here (left) magnified 200,000 times, it causes a mottling of the leaves and a reduction of yield in tobacco plants (right). It also attacks tomato plants (above) causing large yellow or green areas to remain on the fruit after ripening. The virus enters the plant through tiny wounds in a leaf and spreads to the rest of the plant in about three weeks. The virus passes from one cell to the next through *plasmodesmata*, narrow connections that exist between adjacent cells. TMV is very hardy: it can survive in cured tobacco for as long as 50 years.

Rothamsted Experimental Station

Ivan Polunin

Left: Virus diseases that cause mottling of the leaves of a plant are called *mosaics*. This picture shows the leaves of an apple tree infected with a virus. The cells in the affected parts of the leaf contain very few chloroplasts, and those that are present are small. In a healthy plant the chloroplasts are responsible for the vital photosynthetic reactions and they contain the green pigment chlorophyll which is essential for such processes. Consequently, virus-infected areas of a leaf are thin and pale.

Below: Damage done by a stem-pitting virus is revealed after the bark is stripped from a Virginian crab apple.

BASF

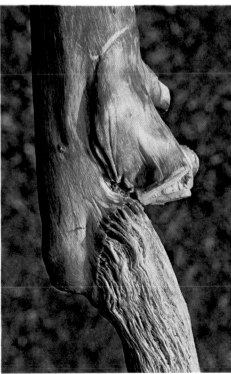

A. G. D. Heath/Heather Angel

rabbits and harvesting the virus from the blood serum. The vaccinia is then purified by centrifugation and can then be used for vaccination against smallpox. The term vaccination is of course now used for preventive immunization against many different diseases.

Animal tissue reacts to the presence of a virus, or any other 'foreign' protein, by producing *antibodies*. Antibodies have the property of neutralizing the specific protein for which they are made, though they have no effect on any other protein unless it has a very similar structure. The antibodies (which are themselves proteins) remain in the bloodstream of the animal for some time after the offending protein has been eliminated. So if the animal is subsequently infected by the same or a closely related virus, antibodies are immediately available, transported to the point of infection by the blood. Thus some degree of immunity is retained by the animal while there are antibodies circulating.

This principle can be extended. Antibodies from animals which have been injected with a virus can be injected into the human bloodstream. If the inoculated person is then infected by that virus the antibodies are available already in his bloodstream and will prevent the infection from becoming established. Alternatively, a suspension of killed or inactivated virus can be injected directly into the human bloodstream so that antibodies will be formed. These antibodies are then able to give protection against attack by a virulent form of the virus.

Since viruses have no means of locomotion, they must rely on outside agencies to carry them from one host to another. Many animal viruses are transmitted by contact or by droplets produced in sneezing or coughing. Some animal and human viruses, including yellow fever, are transmitted by insects, frequently gnats. Insects, particularly leafhoppers and aphids, are also responsible for carrying many plant viruses from one host to the next.

45

Fungi—I

From the bright red 'Fly Agaric' toadstool to the mould growing on an old boot, fungi can be found in practically every environment where life is possible. They are the main rivals of bacteria, in both the variety and the quantity of the materials they decompose.

By far the greatest part of a fungus, called the *mycelium*, remains unseen beneath the surface of the growing medium, be it woodland soil or shoe-leather. The visible parts are merely the reproductive organs of the fungus. The mycelium is a network of narrow, tubular branches, called *hyphae*, which extend in all directions, secreting enzymes to break down organic materials for food. The breakdown products are absorbed into the hyphae along with vital mineral salts and water.

Fungi are unable to build structural materials from simple chemical compounds like carbon dioxide using energy from chemical oxidations or the Sun (photosynthesis). They must, therefore, live on organic material from other living things, whether alive or dead. In other words they are all either parasitic or saprophytic.

Although the mycelium is perhaps the most important part of a fungus, it does not vary much from one species to the next. As a result, the classification of fungi is based largely on their reproductive structures, which are much more diverse. Fungi are usually divided into three groups. The first is called the *Phycomycetes*, literally 'algal fungi', because its members show some similarities to the green algae. The second and third groups have reproductive structures quite unlike anything else known in the plant kingdom. The *Ascomycetes*—cup fungi and their allies—characteristically produce spores, usually in groups of eight, in a special sac, the *ascus*, which explodes violently at maturity, shooting out the spores. The *Basidiomycetes*, to which toadstools and mushrooms belong, characteristically produce four spores on four projections from a special cell, the *basidium*. These spores are shot into the air when they are ripe.

Phycomycetes

The 'water moulds' are among the most interesting of Phycomycetes. Like green algae, most of them live in fresh water or damp soil. *Synchytrium* and *Olpidium* are examples of the simpler type of water mould. They are different from most other Phycomycetes in that they consist of single rounded cells, not of mycelium. Both produce free-swimming spores, *zoospores*, rather like those of green algae, except that they have only a single flagellum. Both are parasitic, either upon algae or on the roots of plants. *Olpidium brassicae* is the fungus whose zoospores transmit virus diseases such as tobacco necrosis virus. *Synchytrium endobioticum* is well known as the organism responsible for the grotesque malformations called 'wart disease' which sometimes afflict potatoes.

Every gardener who raises his own seedlings will be familiar with *damping-off disease*, which causes seedlings suddenly to topple over and die. The disease spreads from plant to plant in a widening

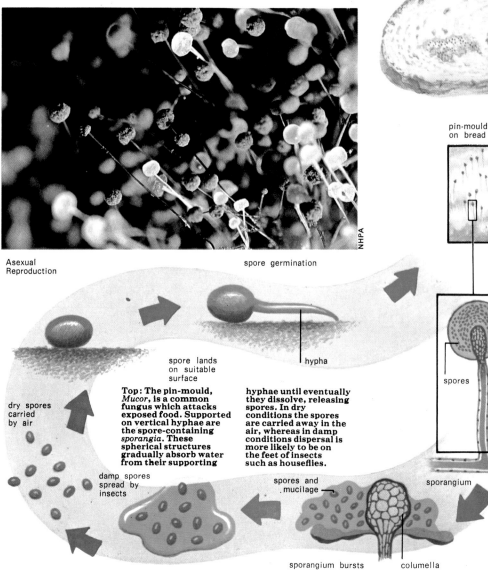

NHPA

pin-mould on bread

Asexual Reproduction

spore germination

spore lands on suitable surface

hypha

dry spores carried by air

Top: The pin-mould, *Mucor*, is a common fungus which attacks exposed food. Supported on vertical hyphae are the spore-containing *sporangia*. These spherical structures gradually absorb water from their supporting hyphae until eventually they dissolve, releasing spores. In dry conditions the spores are carried away in the air, whereas in damp conditions dispersal is more likely to be on the feet of insects such as houseflies.

spores

damp spores spread by insects

spores and mucilage

sporangium

sporangium bursts

columella

Right: Often referred to as 'grey mould', *Botrytis* is a common ascomycetous fungus which attacks a variety of plants including tomato, lettuce and raspberry as well as vines. Nowadays crops are often treated with fungicides to prevent damage such as this.

circle, usually in the centre of the seed-box where the soil tends to be most moist. This damping-off is usually caused by another of the Phycomycetes, *Pythium*.

Pythium mycelium grows between the cells of the seedling and bursts through the skin into the surrounding soil. On the surface of the seedling the tips of the hyphae swell into little sacs surrounded by a cell wall. The multinucleate cell completes its growth and then travels through a germ-tube at the tip of the sac. It remains there surrounded by a very thin membrane while each nucleus, with a small piece of cytoplasm, develops into a separate zoospore with two flagella. The zoospores begin to move about within the membrane, becoming increasingly agitated, until they burst free and swim away, in the soil moisture, in search of other seedlings.

Pythium can also reproduce by a sexual process. Two hyphae fuse together—a small specialized one which is called 'male' and a large, equally specialized one which is regarded as 'female'. A thick wall is then secreted around the fertilized 'egg', which enables it to withstand unfavourable conditions, such as drought and frost. On the arrival of

BASF

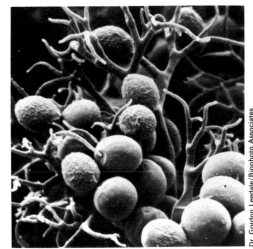

Left: Sporangia of the fungus *Peronospora parasitica* magnified about 400 times. This fungus is a 'downy mildew' which attacks such plants as turnips, cauliflowers, brussels sprouts and wallflowers. The sporangia appear as a white 'fur' on the swollen stems and under the leaves of the afflicted plant. The picture was taken with a scanning electron microscope (SEM) which has a much greater depth of field than other microscopes.

Below: On a forest floor in Thailand, the corpse of a fly is attacked by a fungus (seen as white patches on its thorax and abdomen). Like bacteria, fungi perform a useful function in breaking down dead organic matter.

Dr. Gordon Leedale/Biophoto Associates

C. B. Frith/Bruce Coleman

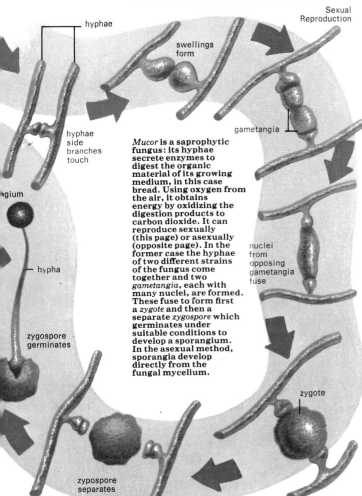

hyphae

Sexual Reproduction

swellings form

hyphae side branches touch

gametangia

Mucor is a saprophytic fungus: its hyphae secrete enzymes to digest the organic material of its growing medium, in this case bread. Using oxygen from the air, it obtains energy by oxidizing the digestion products to carbon dioxide. It can reproduce sexually (this page) or asexually (opposite page). In the former case the hyphae of two different strains of the fungus come together and two *gametangia*, each with many nuclei, are formed. These fuse to form first a *zygote* and then a separate *zygospore* which germinates under suitable conditions to develop a sporangium. In the asexual method, sporangia develop directly from the fungal mycelium.

nuclei from opposing gametangia fuse

hypha

zygospore germinates

zygote

zypospore separates

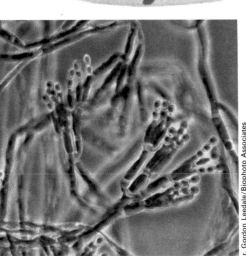

Left: Fungi of the genus *Penicillium* are common on all kinds of decaying animal and plant remains. Seen here (stained blue) is the *Penicillium notatum*, the species which is used commercially to produce the well known penicillin antibiotics. At the tips of the branching hyphae can be seen the *conidia*, which eventually split off and grow into new fungi. Reproduction is always asexual.

Right: Colonies of a bacterium which contains a red pigment when alive. *Penicillium* has been introduced at the centre of the dish: the penicillin it produces kills the bacteria in the central colonies. The outlying colonies are unaffected.

Dr. Gordon Leedale/Biophoto Associates

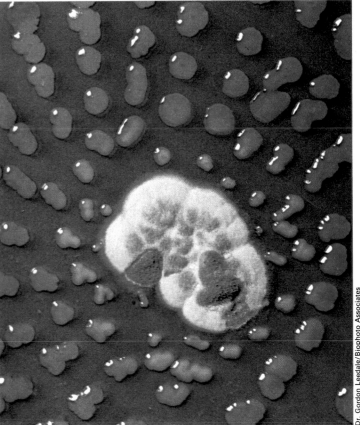

Dr. Gordon Leedale/Biophoto Associates

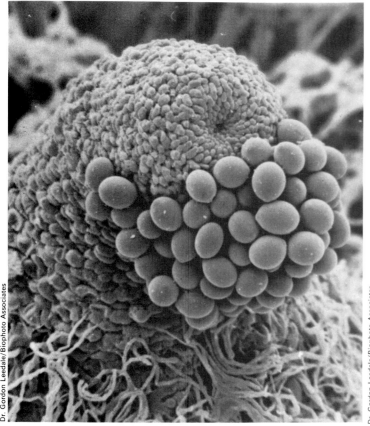

Above: A clump of ascospores on the fruiting body of *Sordaria macrospora*, an ascomycetous fungus. Fungi belonging to the genus *Sordaria* are often found on the dung of plant-eating animals for their ascospores will only germinate readily after passing through the gut of an animal.

Above right: The spore-bearing structure of *Aspergillus niger*, an ascomycetous fungus common in most soils. The spores (conidia) are carried at the ends of the radiating branches. This picture and the one above left were taken with a SEM at magnifications of about 1,800 and 360 respectively.

suitable soil conditions, it germinates to produce zoospores which infect new seedlings.

Among other common phycomycetous fungi are the pin-moulds, such as *Mucor*, the downy mildews, such as *Peronospora*, and the parasitic fungus *Phytophthora*, which is responsible for potato blight, perhaps the most notorious of all plant diseases.

Potato blight

Phytophthora is similar to *Pythium* but is less dependent on moisture. It was introduced into Europe in about 1840 from South America, the original home of the potato, and in the succeeding five or six years spread over the entire continent, including the British Isles.

Whereas the South American native potatoes were resistant to the disease, breeding of the potato in Europe, aimed at giving higher yields, had resulted in loss of resistance in the European varieties. From the appearance of the first few dark green blotches on the leaves of a single susceptible European potato to the time when whole fields were reduced to a blackened mass of rotting vegetation was only a matter of days.

As a direct result of the potato famine, the population of Ireland was reduced from eight million in 1845 to six million a decade later. Many people died and many more were forced to emigrate, mostly to the US. Apart from the direct human suffering, the reduction of the working population was on a scale that no country could afford, and it had long-term economic and political consequences. Fortunately, fungicides are now available to combat potato blight.

Ascomycetes

Ascomycetes and Basidiomycetes, the remaining two groups of the true fungi, are typical land creatures. They can grow and reproduce in the most exposed situations, like the tops of tall trees and the surfaces of rocks. In neither of these two groups is there any free-swimming stage in the life-cycle and the mycelium itself, perhaps from the unique construction of its cell walls, is much better able to resist dry conditions.

Ascomycetes are mostly saprophytic, but an interesting parasitic species is *Taphrina deformans*. This fungus causes the well-known leaf-curl disease of peaches, apricots and almonds. Leaves of peach trees permeated by the mycelium of *Taphrina* swell up and become discoloured and twisted in much the same way as the 'warts' on the potato caused by *Synchytrium*. If examined carefully, the leaves seem to be dusted with a white powder. This discolouration is caused by special spore-containing sacs which protrude through the skin of the leaf. Each of these sacs is a short cylindrical cell, the ascus, formed by the fusion of two cells of the mycelium in much the same way as the sexually produced spore of *Pythium*.

Within the young ascus the male and female nuclei first fuse and then immediately divide again to produce uninucleate spores. When the spores are ripe, pressure generated in the ascus causes it to burst, ejecting the spores. These are then carried by the wind and, if they happen to come to rest on the developing bud of a peach tree, they become trapped between the growing bud-scales where they remain until the spring. They

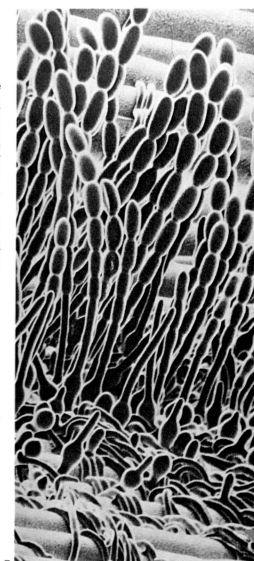

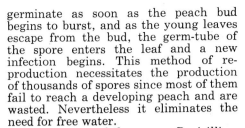

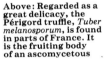
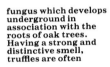
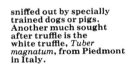

Above: Regarded as a great delicacy, the Périgord truffle, *Tuber melanosporum*, is found in parts of France. It is the fruiting body of an ascomycetous fungus which develops underground in association with the roots of oak trees. Having a strong and distinctive smell, truffles are often sniffed out by specially trained dogs or pigs. Another much sought after truffle is the white truffle, *Tuber magnatum*, from Piedmont in Italy.

Giuseppe Mazza

Above: Commonly called yeasts, the members of the genus *Saccharomyces* are among the most important fungi from a commercial point of view. They are used in both the baking and the brewing industries. By the process known as *alcoholic fermentation* yeast converts sugar into carbon dioxide and alcohol in the absence of oxygen. As shown here, yeasts reproduce by *budding*. A constriction forms in the parent cell, a nucleus moves into the bud and the constriction closes. Sometimes the buds do not separate from the parent cell, so large branching colonies develop.

Left: Powdery mildews can cause considerable damage to crops like wheat and barley. They get their name from their appearance on the surface of the host plant. This SEM picture shows a powdery mildew growing on barley—the hyphae and conidia are clearly visible.

Right: The toadstool-like fruiting body of the ascomycetous fungus *Helvella crispa*. The asci are formed in the 'head' of the fungus.

Dr. Gordon Leedale/Biophoto Associates

germinate as soon as the peach bud begins to burst, and as the young leaves escape from the bud, the germ-tube of the spore enters the leaf and a new infection begins. This method of reproduction necessitates the production of thousands of spores since most of them fail to reach a developing peach and are wasted. Nevertheless it eliminates the need for free water.

Ascomycetes of the genus *Penicillium* are very common on all kinds of decaying animal and vegetable remains. *Penicillium glaucum* is a green mould frequently found growing in these situations. The green colour is not due to chlorophyll, which no fungus contains, but to a non-photosynthetic pigment. *Penicillium glaucum* produces millions of asexual spores, called *conidia*, on special upright hyphae. The tips of these hyphae are repeatedly forked, each final branch ending in a bottle-shaped, spore-bearing cell. The spores emerge in a long chain from the neck of each bottle, so that the whole conidium-producing structure looks like a minute paint brush. Conidia are detached by the wind or other agency and spread all over the Earth's surface and even up into the stratosphere.

On particularly nutritious substrates, *Penicillium glaucum* reproduces sexually as well. A special thin and flexible male hypha grows spirally round a thick female branch. Then a small hole develops in the cell walls at the point of contact of the two. The contents of the male hypha pass into the female, leaving the male as an empty shell. The male and female nuclei move towards each other, but do not immediately fuse. The fertilized female cell then begins to branch and divide and eventually a small knot of cells is formed. In the centre of this knot the asci develop, and at once the descendants of the paired nuclei fuse. The double nucleus immediately divides again to produce *ascospores*, which are spherical with thin flanges around them, reminiscent of the planet Saturn with its rings. If an ascospore encounters suitable conditions it germinates to produce a mycelium with slightly different properties from its parent, and so some variation is maintained within the species.

Many other species of Ascomycetes, however, including most of the penicillia, have lost their ability to reproduce sexually, or do so so rarely that it has never been observed. Some such fungi are used in industrial processes. One of them, *Fusarium graminiarum*, is grown for its high protein content and is used as an additive to human and animal foods —the fibrous texture of the mycelium makes it more acceptable as a human food than other vegetable proteins made from bacteria or soya meal. Another, *Saccharomyces cerevisiae*, is the well-known yeast used in the baking and brewing industries.

One interesting process is concerned with recycling. An enzyme produced by *Trichoderma viride*, another asexual fungus, breaks down cellulose into its constituent glucose molecules. It has been shown that in this way a very high yield of sugar can be obtained from old newspapers. The printing ink and other impurities are not acted upon by the enzyme and are left behind as a black sludge in the bottom of the tank, and the rich syrup can be used without further purification.

Fungi—II

The mushrooms which are sold in markets belong to the group *Basidiomycetes*, generally regarded as the most complex and therefore the most advanced group of fungi. Many Basidiomycetes are large organisms, and cannot easily be called 'microbes' as are other fungi. Nevertheless, however large and complicated their fruiting structures may be, the majority of the fungus is hidden from view in the form of a *mycelium*, permeating the substance on which it lives and behaving in much the same way as other micro-organisms. The mycelium consists of a network of narrow, tubular branches called *hyphae*.

The common mushroom
The mycelium of the common edible mushroom is grown commercially under carefully controlled conditions in beds of horse manure covered with a top layer of soil. A freshly prepared bed of partially rotted manure is 'seeded' with tiny pieces of mycelium grown in the laboratory. If conditions are exactly right, the mycelium spreads rapidly and soon permeates the whole bed.

The mushrooms develop from tiny knots of mycelium under the soil. As the hyphae which make up the knot continue to grow and branch they begin to arrange themselves in a way which corresponds to the arrangement of the tissues in the mature mushroom—they grow vertically in the part which will become the stalk, radiate outwards and downwards in what is to become the cap, and so on.

Still nourished and supplied with water by the myriad hyphae in the bed, the stalk rapidly lengthens, pushing through the soil, and the cap expands. This causes the protective skin or 'veil', which in the 'button' mushroom joins the edge of the cap to the stem, to split and remain as a delicate ring around the middle of the stem. The splitting of the veil reveals the pink 'gills' of the fungus. These are closely packed, evenly spaced, radiating plates which hang down under the cap. They are called gills because they look rather like the gills of fishes. They do not, however, take any special part in respiration: they are the spore-producing organs of the fungus.

Although no longer protected by the veil, the gills are still sheltered from the worst of the elements by the cap. The flat surface of every gill is covered by a densely packed layer of cylindrical cells, the *basidia*, and from the free end of each basidium project two, small, pointed spore-stalks called *sterigmata*. The scientific name of the cultivated mushroom, *Agaricus bisporus*, records the fact that it is unusual in having only two sterigmata on each basidium: most Basidiomycetes have four.

A minute swelling on the tip of each sterigma rapidly enlarges to become a dark brown spore, and it is the presence of millions of spores which turns the gills of the fully grown mushroom from pink to brown. The mature spore is delicately and asymmetrically balanced on its sterigma, its rounded side turned away from the centre of the basidium and its flatter side facing inwards. On the flatter side, just above the point of

Heather Angel

J. Shaw/Bruce Coleman

Mary Evans

Above: One of the most colourful of all fungi is the fly agaric, *Amanita muscaria*. Although poisonous, it is not normally fatal and has been used as a hallucinogenic drug.

Left: In the folklore of many countries, toadstools are associated with fairies. This connection with the supernatural may have arisen from the toadstool's sudden overnight appearance in the fields and woods, or perhaps it stemmed from the effects of eating certain species.

Right: A drop of water sends a puff of dry, powdery spores shooting from a relative of the puffballs, the earth-star, *Gaestrum triplex*. It often grows in beech woods.

Below: Stages in the growth of the deadly death cap toadstool, *Amanita phalloides*. Like its cousin, the fly agaric, it is at first completely enclosed in a 'veil'. As the toadstool grows, the veil splits and the cap separates from the stalk, leaving behind a prominent ring. This toadstool's poison is highly toxic, causing a coma, paralysis and ultimately death. Although antidotes are known, they are virtually useless because the symptoms of poisoning do not appear until about 12 hours after the the fungus has been eaten. It is then too late for treatment.

GROWTH OF DEATH CAP TOADSTOOL

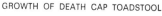
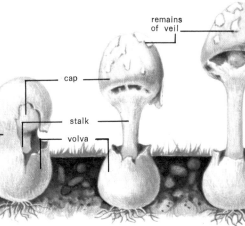

remains of veil

cap

stalk

volva

veil

50

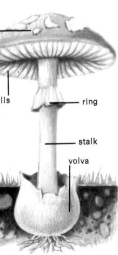

Above left: A toadstool from North America belonging to the genus *Tricholoma*. Other species of this genus are common in Britain.

Above: This fungus, *Laccaria amethystea*, is fairly common in British woodlands—even its mycelium is lilac. The colour fades when the fungus dries.

Below: *Mutinus caninus*, the dog stinkhorn, is found among the dead leaves and treestumps of woodland habitats in the summer and autumn. The spores of the fungus are contained in a green mucus which covers the cap. As its name suggests, it has a distinct and unpleasant odour, though this is much less pronounced **than that of its relative, the common stinkhorn, *Phallus impudicus*. The smell, reminiscent of rotting flesh, performs an important function for it attracts flies to the fungus. The insects feed on the spore-bearing mucus, and so the stinkhorn's spores are spread over the surrounding area.**

gills —

ring

stalk

volva

attachment to the basidium, a swelling develops. This is actually a bubble formed between two layers of the wall of the spore. The bubble grows and finally bursts, propelling the spore a short distance away from the basidium. In the space between the gill on which it grew and the adjacent gill, it falls under the influence of gravity, until, emerging from between the gills, it is wafted away by air currents.

In order to achieve discharge by this method, the spore is precisely balanced on the sterigma so as to fly directly at right angles to the surface of the gill without hitting neighbouring spores. The quantity of energy released when the bubble bursts is exactly enough to carry the spore clear of the gill but not so much as to make it crash into the gill on the opposite side: if the spore touches any object it will stick to it instantly.

For the same reason the gills are absolutely vertical so the spores can fall freely down the narrow gap between them, and they are able to regain their vertical position when the cap moves slightly through growth or drying, or to compensate for movements of the soil. In spite of these remarkable abilities, the mushroom is by no means the most complex example of the kind of precision and elaboration that the Basidiomycetes can achieve.

Other Basidiomycetes

There are thousands of species of toadstools and they grow throughout the world wherever conditions are moist enough, for a few days, to allow their delicate fruit-bodies to grow and discharge their spores. Because of their numbers and their variety they must be regarded as biologically successful, but they suffer the disadvantage that water must always be abundant at the time when they operate their delicate spore-discharge mechanism. So, although successful, they are 'slaves' to the very delicacy of this mechanism.

The larger Basidiomycetes form quite a significant part of man's environment. In autumn, the woods smell of fungi and a glance around is usually sufficient to see how numerous they are in terms of both species and individuals. Each species plays its own role in the economy of nature. Many are saprophytes, playing a particularly important role in breaking down decaying leaf litter and wood. Many others form mutually beneficial associations with the roots of trees. Yet others are specialized parasites of trees.

Among these last, the 'bracket fungi' are specially interesting in that they have been able to conquer the problems of exposure attendant upon life in a treetop. Their fruit-bodies are basically the same as in the mushroom, with the same spore discharge mechanism, but instead of having a stalk, bracket fungi grow directly out of the side of the branch of a tree like a wall-bracket. Instead of being borne on gills, the basidia line the insides of thousands of tiny pores on the underside of the fruit-body. Like their hosts, the trees, these fruit-bodies are woody, some of them being extremely hard. In addition to the usual thin, delicate hyphae, they contain specially toughened, thick-walled ones. They do not produce all their spores at once and then die as do the toadstools, but instead the bracket fungi discharge their spores a few at a time, in moist weather, and the

51

fruit-body lives for several months or even years.

One way of overcoming the need for constant supplies of water is seen in the puffballs and earth-stars. These fungi produce their spores on a basidium, but when they are ripe the basidia simply collapse leaving the dry outer sac full of loose spores like a pot of pepper. When a raindrop strikes the sac, it makes a small depression and a puff of spores is expelled through a small hole in the top of the fruit-body. The wall of the sac is non-absorbent and elastic so that the rain-drop simply bounces off and the sac regains its former shape, awaiting the next raindrop. The fruit-body persists on the ground for many months, releasing some of its spores every time there is a shower of rain.

The fungus with the largest fruit-body known also belongs to this group. The giant puffball, *Lycoperdon giganteum*, grows in gardens and pastures in northern temperate countries, including Britain, and may reach nearly 2 m (6.5 ft) in diameter: it is often mistaken, from a distance, for a recumbent sheep. Even a relatively small one will contain thousands of millions of spores which are dispersed by the wind through rents in the outer sac.

Fairy rings
Because of their method of growth, wild toadstools often produce the 'fairy rings' which are seen on lawns and playing fields. A young mycelium establishes itself from germinating spores and in season duly produces a crop of toadstools. These soon shed their spores and die, but the mycelium continues to grow until it has exhausted the nutrients in that patch of turf. It is then forced to spread outward while the original part of the mycelium dies.

As the dead mycelium is decomposed by other saprophytes, its accumulated supply of nutrients is released into the soil, stimulating the turf into lush, dark green growth. The following year, the crop of toadstools is produced in a ring,

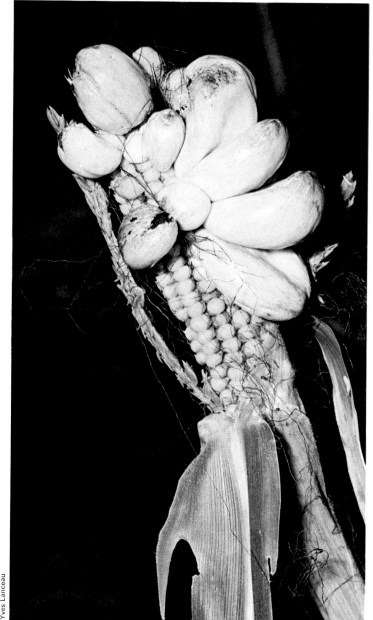

Yves Lanceau

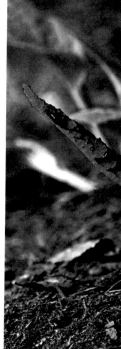

Above: Spore cases (sporangia) of the slime mould *Trichia decipiens* magnified about 30 times. Slime moulds are strange creatures which combine characteristics of animals and plants. Although they produce spores, like a fungus, they spend much of their lives in amoeba-like form, creeping over plants and soil.

Heather Angel

Left: This photograph shows the broad, widely spaced gills of the fungus, *Oudemansiella mucida*, often called 'beech tuft'. It is a saprophytic fungus which grows from the trunk and branches of beech trees, and it is most often found in the autumn. It is pure white and covered with a sticky mucus.

Above: These pale blue galls growing on a cob of corn (maize) are caused by corn smut, *Ustilago maydis*, a parasitic fungus. Smut diseases are of considerable economic importance for they attack the cereal crops, such as wheat, barley and oats, which provide more than 50 per cent of all food eaten by man.

Below: A selection of British grassland and woodland fungi. One of the most distinctive is the shaggy ink cap, which is good to eat when young. Oak trees (far right) act as hosts to several species of parasitic bracket fungi. Perhaps the most striking, though only short-lived, is the 'beefsteak' fungus.

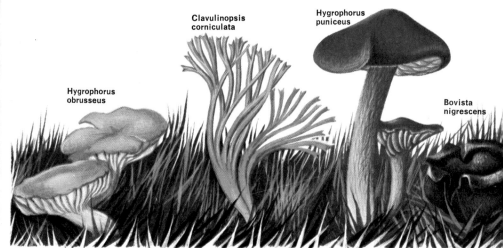

Hygrophorus obrusseus

Clavulinopsis corniculata

Hygrophorus puniceus

Bovista nigrescens

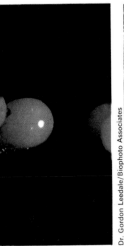

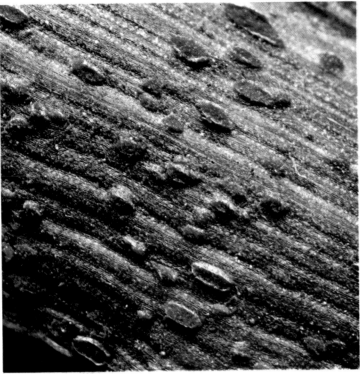

Below: This odd-looking fungus, *Anthurus archeri*, is common in Australia and New Zealand, and it has been introduced to several localities in Europe. At first the arms are joined at their tips, but they separate as the fungus grows. Clearly visible in this picture are the dark green patches of mucus which carry the spores.

Above: Patches of rust, *Puccinia graminis*, on a wheat plant. This parasite can cause serious reductions in crop yields. In 1954, for example, about 70 per cent of the durum wheat crop in Minnesota and the Dakotas was lost as a direct result of rust infection. Fungi are responsible for more plant diseases than any other group of organisms. Among the most important of these are rust, smut, potato blight, ergot (a disease of cereal crops) and Dutch elm disease. In the 1970s thousands of British trees were infected and killed by the last of these. Its spores are spread by a beetle which bores under the bark of the trees.

Fistulina hepatica (beefsteak)

Grifola gigantea

Coprinus comatus (shaggy ink cap)

Agaricus campestris (field mushroom)

where the hyphae are actually growing, around the original patch. The new hyphae compete with the turf for minerals and water and they compact the soil so that the grass roots cannot breathe. The grass in this zone dries up in the sun.

Rusts

Not all Basidiomycetes produce large fruit-bodies; an important group of them, the rusts, are highly specialized parasites of green plants. They are so called because of the little red-brown pustules of spores which they produce on the leaves of the plants they attack. Several kinds of rust attack wheat, and one of them, *Puccinia graminis*, has a particularly interesting life-cycle. The type of spore produced on the wheat plant just before harvest is called the *teliospore*. It is incapable of causing disease directly on another wheat plant; it can only infect the barberry plant.

On the barberry, the sexual stage of the fungus develops, eventually producing pustules of red-brown spores on the underside of the barberry leaf. These spores, the *aeciospores*, in their turn are unable to infect barberry. They can, however, grow upon wheat. Mycelium from these spores permeates the wheat tissues, boring into the cells with minute sucking organs. This of course deprives the grain of its nourishment, and the crop is reduced. The mycelium in the wheat produces two types of spore. The first, called *uredospores*, are round with a short stalk, and they burst in clusters through the skin of the leaf, like little flakes of rusty iron. The uredospores are capable of attacking other wheat plants and serve to spread the infection from one plant to its neighbours.

The second type of spore produced on the wheat plant is the teliospore, which of course, is capable of attacking only barberry. The teliospore is two-celled, with a short stalk and a thick wall. Because the wall is so thick, the spore is able to survive the winter and germinate in the spring, infecting a barberry plant and completing the life-cycle.

Slime moulds

The slime moulds, or *Myxomycetes*, form an entirely different group of fungi from the rest. They are probably not closely related to any of the others, and they have often been classified as animals, hence their alternative name *Mycetozoa* or 'fungus-animals'. Instead of possessing a mycelium they spend most of their lives as amoeba-like masses of protoplasm, creeping about the soil and over plants and ingesting other small creatures in just the same way as does an amoeba. At maturity, however, they become distinctly fungus-like, producing a fruit-body full of dry spores, like a small puffball.

In fact, the 'amoebae' which produce even a fairly small fruiting-body have to be quite large, and one species called 'flowers of tan' frequently causes some consternation to those who witness its fruiting, for its fruit-bodies are sometimes more than 10 cm (4 in) across.

Myxomycetes are easily grown in the laboratory and much of their interest lies in their use as 'laboratory animals' for they resemble the white blood corpuscles of animals, not only in their behaviour, but also in their reaction to various important chemicals.

Mosses and Liverworts

A major step in the evolutionary history of plants from aquatic green algae to the higher flowering plants was the colonization of the land. The exact stages by which this was achieved are not well understood, but a group of simple plants, the *Bryophyta*, which includes mosses, liverworts and hornworts, are probably representative of one stage in this development. In many respects the bryophytes are similar to many-celled algae (seaweeds), having a compact body many cells thick attached by a special structure, the *rhizoid*, (similar to the holdfast of seaweeds) to the underlying surface. Nevertheless, most bryophytes are true land plants. The body is surrounded by a layer of cells, the *epidermis*, which prevents the loss of water from the plant.

There are approximately 14,000 species of mosses and 9,000 species of liverworts. They are all small green plants, usually no more than a few centimetres long, with either a leafy stem, as in most mosses, or a flat, ribbon-like body, called a *thallus*, as in most liverworts. The body is anchored to the soil by the long, thread-like rhizoids.

Although to some extent the bryophytes have adapted to life on land they are still highly dependent on water. They generally have no specialized tissue for the transfer of water and nutrients and, because of this, must necessarily be small so that all parts of the plant are in close contact with water. Their reproduction is also highly dependent on water.

For these reasons the bryophytes are most abundant in, but not confined to, permanently moist places, such as bogs, damp woodlands and the edges of streams. They have their most luxuriant development in tropical climates. They may be found growing in soil, on the surface of other plants, on bare rock, in caves and on the roofs and sides of buildings. Only a few are aquatic and none are marine. One group, known as *copper mosses*, occur only on heavy metal deposits such as copper and antimony. Others occur only on dung.

Reproduction

Like most simple plants, bryophytes reproduce vegetatively by fragmentation —any severed part of the stem, leaf or rhizoid is capable of developing into a new plant. (One of the surest ways of spreading troublesome moss on a lawn is by trying to remove it by raking.) Alternatively they reproduce asexually by special structures, called *gemmae*, which appear on the upper surface of the body. Each gemma, about the size of a pinhead, grows on a small stalk and may be broken off by a small animal or by the wind. If it is carried to a suitably moist environment it will grow into a new plant.

More elaborately, the bryophytes reproduce sexually. As in the more advanced algae and in the higher plants there is a distinct alternation of generations, with two generations of plant, the *sporophyte* and the *gametophyte*. Unlike the higher plants, however, in the bryophytes the gametophyte generation (which develops

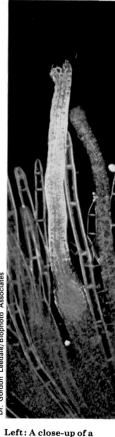

Left: A close-up of a species of the common moss, *Bryum*, found on walls, roofs and rocks. The mosses are the major class of a group of primitive land plants, the *bryophytes*.

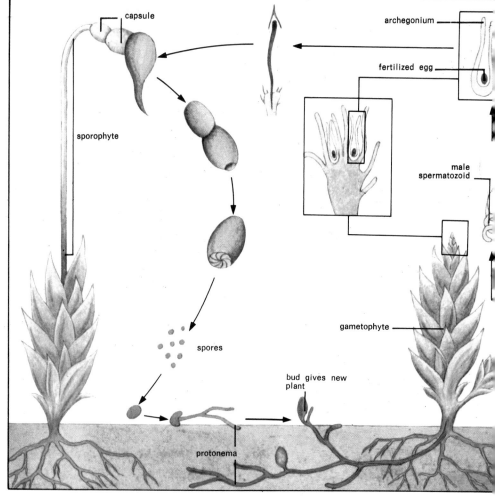

capsule

archegonium

fertilized egg

sporophyte

male spermatozoid

gametophyte

bud gives new plant

spores

protonema

Left: Female sex organs (*archegonia*) of a moss. The older archegonia are open at the top showing the channel down which the sperms swim to fertilize the eggs at the bottom. Among the archegonia are protective 'hairs', the *paraphyses*.

Right: Two kinds of bog moss, *Sphagnum rubellum* (red) and *Sphagnum recuruum* (green). Bog mosses are perhaps more important than all other bryophytes. Starting at the water line they spread by branching and vegetative reproduction to cover completely a stretch of water. In time the resulting bog fills in—gradually converting open water into rich soil composed of the decaying remains of the moss.

Heather Angel

Right: Peat cutting in Donegal, Ireland. Mosses and liverworts are generally of little use to man. Peat, widely used as a fuel source, is a notable exception.

Below: Life history of a moss, showing the two different generations, the *gametophyte* and the *sporophyte*. The gametophyte produces green 'leaves' and both male (*antheridia*) and female (*archegonia*) sex organs. The male gametes swim to the archegonia to fertilize the eggs. The parasitic sporophyte which then develops eventually produces spores which each give a new moss plant from a simple vegetative plant, the *protonema*, which is a green filament when above the ground.

Right: A true Alaskan moss, *Splaknum leteum*. Another northern 'moss', reindeer moss (*Cladonia rangiferina*) is in fact not a moss at all but a lichen.

G. R. Roberts

Bruce Coleman

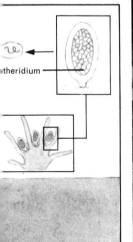

theridium

from asexual spores) is dominant and the sporophyte generation (which develops from a *zygote* after the fusion of sex cells or gametes) is reduced. In this way the bryophytes resemble simple green algae, such as *Spirogyra* and *Chlamydomonas*.

Liverworts

The body (*thallus*) of some of the liverworts (*Hepaticae*) is short and looks like a lobed liver—hence the name for this class of plants. More often it is a regularly branching structure; the form and degree of branching varying as does the complexity of the thallus. In the more complex liverworts, such as *Marchantia*, there are air pores leading inside the body to air chambers where there are photosynthetic filaments and food storage tissue.

The sex organs are either on the upper surface of the thallus or, as in *Marchantia*, on special branches. When they are on the thallus surface, the male organs (*antheridia*) are spaced along the sides of a ridge, running the length of the thallus, while the female organs (*archegonia*) are on a slope facing the growing point at the tips of the thallus. Each antheridium is enclosed in a flask-like sheath with a narrow opening which, when mature, opens liberating the male gametes (*spermatozoids*) which are often spirally coiled cells with two long threads or flagella.

They are attracted by a chemical—the exact nature of which is unknown—which is secreted by the female archegonia and they use their flagella to swim towards this secretion. To reproduce successfully, therefore, the plant body must be covered in a water film; otherwise the spermatozoids are unable to swim to the archegonia.

Each archegonium is shaped like a long-necked jar. The lower part encloses the egg and is called the *venter*, the upper part is a long tube, filled with mucilage, and the spermatozoids swim into this, uniting with the egg. The fertilized egg, the *zygote*, is the first cell of the sporophyte generation. Of all the egg cells in each archegonium which may have been fertilized only one develops, probably because the first one fertilized monopolises all the available food.

The young sporophyte consists of three parts. First there is the foot, shaped like an arrowhead and pushed well into the archegonium for anchorage. Then there is a short stalk, the *seta*, and finally attached to this the *capsule* or *sporangium*. The capsule is normally spherical with a wall several layers thick enclosing the spores. When mature, the capsule bursts releasing the spores.

Mosses

Mosses (*Musci*), unlike the liverworts, all grow vertically. The slender stem may be branched or unbranched but is never more than 3 cm (1.2 in) tall and is anchored by rhizoids to the ground. The small thin leaves (often only one cell thick) are positioned spirally around the stem.

The sex organs are produced at the ends of the main stem or branches and are protected by small leaves and narrow filaments called *paraphyses*. The antheridia, unlike those of the liverworts, are not protected in flasks but stand on short stems while the archegonia, also borne on stalks, have a rather thicker venter than in the liverworts. When the spermatozoids are released the splash of raindrops helps

55

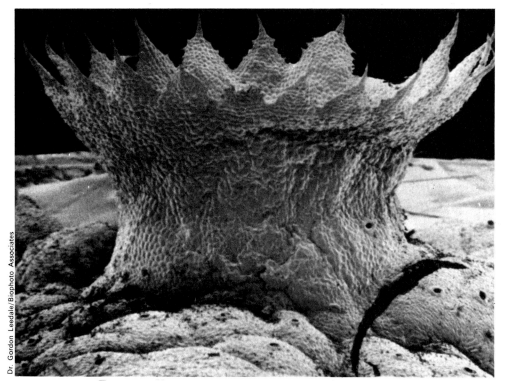

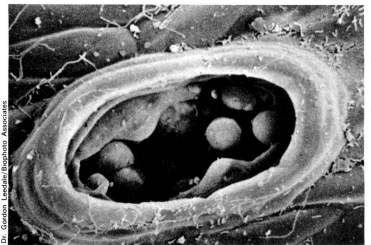

Above: An asexual reproductive structure, the *gemma cup*, seen on the surface of a liverwort (about 200 times life size).

Left: An air pore on the surface of the complex liverwort, *Marchantia polymorpha* (about 2000 times life size). Inside can be seen the tips of photosynthetic tissue. The white dots and lines on the surface are bacteria. The pores of liverworts cannot open and close, unlike the stomata of higher plants and hornworts which shut during times of water shortage.

Below: *Marchantia polymorpha*, common in marshy places. The parasol-like structures are the archegonia, the female sex organs.

to disperse them. Any deposited near the head of a female branch are lured to the neck of an archegonium by a chemical, in this case the sugar *sucrose*. As in the liverworts, the spermatozoids swim towards the secretion by means of thread-like flagella.

Fertilization once again results in a sporophyte with three parts, a capsule, seta and foot. The capsule, however, is a more complex structure than that of the liverworts. Only the upper part is fertile, the lower part is green and synthesizes some of its own food—the sporophyte of liverworts is completely parasitic on the gametophyte. The top half (containing the spores) is a large cavity through which extends a cylinder of tissue, the *columella*. Finally the top of the capsule is closed by a lid.

As soon as the spores are ripe, the capsule begins to dry up and the columella collapses, so the capsule consists finally of only the outside wall and a mass of dark green spores. The lid becomes detached and falls off but the spores cannot freely escape as a double row of 'teeth', the *peristome*, forms from strips of thickened cell-wall. These 'teeth' close over the opening when the air is wet but bend back when the air is dry, allowing the spores to be shaken out by the wind in dry weather when they are most likely to be widely dispersed.

If the spores land on a suitable damp place they germinate to produce a simple plant body called the *protonema*. This may form an extensive green felt, occasionally several square centimetres in size, before it buds to produce the normal leafy stem of mosses. The protonema, like the leafy stem, is the dominant gametophyte generation.

Hornworts

The hornworts (*Anthocerotae*) have a thalloid body similar to the liverworts but are distinguished from them by their capsules which are cylindrical, about 2.5 cm (1 in) long, rather than spherical. When ripe the capsules split from the tip downwards into two halves. Between the two halves is a supporting pillar, the *columella*, similar to that found in the capsule of mosses. In addition the capsules of hornworts have pores, *stomata*, which, unlike those in the liverworts, can open and close and are the same as those in flowering plants.

Economic importance

Mosses and liverworts are of little direct economic importance to man. The bog moss, *Sphagnum*, is used as a soil conditioner or as a lining for hanging baskets because of its water absorbent qualities. For the same reason, it was used as late as the First World War as a wound dressing. *Sphagnum* grows in bogs where acidic conditions and low oxygen availability decreases the rate with which bacteria and fungi can decompose the dead remains. As the remains accumulate they become compacted, forming *peat* which is used as a fuel in some countries.

Occasionally peat is used as a building material. Traditionally, poorer people in many parts of the world have also used some of the larger 'hair' mosses, *Polytrichum*, to make brushes, brooms and lamp wicks. The greatest importance of bryophytes, however, is their ability to grow on bare rock and begin the formation of soil in which all major plant types grow.

PHOTOSYNTHESIS

Above: Apparatus used by Joseph Priestley in his experiments on air.

Below: How light energy is trapped by chlorophyll. A bundle of light energy (a *quantum*) excites an electron of an atom in the chlorophyll molecule by pushing it into an outer orbit. Some of the energy given off as the electron returns to its normal state is used to produce the reactive chemicals which the plant uses to convert carbon dioxide into carbohydrate.

Right: Oxygen being given off by a water plant.

Just by being alive all living things continuously use up energy in the process known as *respiration*. The original source of this energy is sunlight. Green plants alone can trap sunlight and convert it into the complex organic compounds from which plant bodies are constructed and which, when eaten, form the food of animals.

The raw materials used by a plant to manufacture its body are carbon dioxide from the atmosphere and water and inorganic chemicals, such as nitrate, from the soil. These are converted into the plant body by a two stage process which is called *photosynthesis*. In the first stage carbon dioxide and water are converted by light energy into carbohydrates and oxygen; in the second stage the carbohydrates are combined with each other and with inorganic chemicals, such as nitrate and phosphate, to form the proteins, fats, oils and nucleic acids of which the plant body is formed.

Photosynthesis takes place mostly in the *mesophyll* cells of leaves. These cells, which are covered with a thin film of water, form the bulk of the leaf, but between them are numerous intercellular spaces which connect with the outside through pores, the *stomata*. Carbon dioxide diffuses through the stomata into the intercellular spaces, dissolves in the film of water, and diffuses in solution into the mesophyll cells. Oxygen leaves by the same route in reverse. Light is trapped by the green pigment, *chlorophyll*, which is contained within the cells in disc-shaped organelles called *chloroplasts*.

During the middle of the day, plants' consumption of oxygen and production of carbon dioxide by respiration is hidden by the much greater amounts of oxygen produced and carbon dioxide consumed by photosynthesis. As far as the individual plant is concerned oxygen is produced largely as a by-product. Nevertheless this oxygen replaces that removed from the atmosphere by animals. Without it all animal life would cease.

Different kinds of photosynthesis

Photosynthesis is often described in simple terms which make it appear that all plants photosynthesize in the same way. But it is now known that different plants have different kinds of photosynthesis which are adaptations to the environments in which they live. A large number of plants growing in dry tropical environments, including such important crops as maize, *Zea mays*, and sugar cane, *Saccharum officinarum*, have a special kind of photosynthesis using different chemical reactions which allows them to grow faster at higher temperatures.

Research into photosynthesis

Early experiments on photosynthesis were conducted by the English scientist Joseph Priestley (1733-1804). He took a closed jar, burnt a candle in it, and showed that a mouse would die if placed in the exhausted air. However a green plant could still live in this air, and after a few weeks the air was renewed by the plant so that a mouse could again breathe and a candle again burn in it. Priestley's experiments clearly showed the way in which respiration or combustion remove oxygen from air and photosynthesis replaces it. In the twentieth century, the American, Melvin Calvin, was awarded the 1961 Nobel Prize for Chemistry for working out the complex series of chemical reactions, often called the *Calvin cycle*, by which carbon dioxide is incorporated into glucose and other carbohydrates during photosynthesis.

quantum of light

heat energy

light energy

electrical energy

chemical energy

higher energy level

electron

lower energy level

nucleus of atom

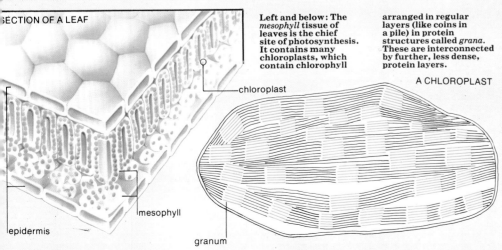

SECTION OF A LEAF

Left and below: The *mesophyll* tissue of leaves is the chief site of photosynthesis. It contains many chloroplasts, which contain chlorophyll arranged in regular layers (like coins in a pile) in protein structures called *grana*. These are interconnected by further, less dense, protein layers.

A CHLOROPLAST

chloroplast

mesophyll

epidermis

granum

Ferns, Horsetails and Clubmosses

As early plants colonized the land, they evolved several features not found in mosses and algae. These features include an outer layer of cells impervious to water (the *cuticle*) and specialized tissue for conducting water and food between the water-absorbing organs, the roots, and the food-producing organs, the leaves.

The first group of plants to develop these features were the *Pteridophyta*: the ferns, clubmosses and horsetails. Though now of minor significance, as the first successful colonizers of the land they were a dominant group of plants for some 100 million years; from their appearance about 350 million years ago to the development of the advanced seed plants of the present day. Particularly in the Carboniferous period (280-345 million years ago) they were extremely abundant, and they grew luxuriantly into many forms in extensive forests. The carbonized remains of these tree ferns contributed to the formation of coal.

Structure

Ferns, *Filicinae*, have leaves, a stem and roots. Of these the leaves are generally the most conspicuous part of the fern. The basic plan of a mature leaf is a central axis, or *midrib*, with smaller side branches. This type of leaf form is called *pinnate* and is common to almost

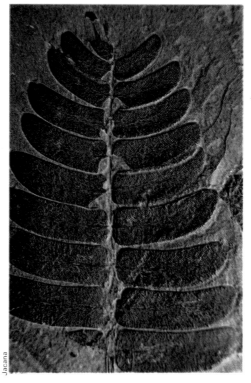

Jacana

Above: A fossil 'fern' leaf. The difficulty of correctly classifying a fossil leaf or stem meant that until 1903 fossil fern-like leaves were wrongly identified as ferns. A large number, however, like *Linopteris* shown here, are not ferns but seed-bearing plants of the extinct group, *Pteridospermae*.

Below: Tree ferns growing at 1,200 m (4,000 ft) in the mountains of Malaysia. Tree ferns have erect, unbranched stems with a crown of palm-like leaves growing from the top. The stems are unlike those of other trees —they have no bark and no secondary wood laid down in annual growth rings beneath the bark.

NHPA

all ferns, though a few, such as *Ophioglossum*, have simple or lobed leaves. A large pinnate leaf is called a frond. The fronds of some species, such as *Cyathea*, commonly grown in conservatories, may reach over 5 m (16 ft) long and 1 m (3 ft) wide.

Fern stems vary from the tall trunks of tree ferns that may be over 70 m (230 ft) tall, down to short, 5 cm (2 in) stems growing horizontally underground like the stems of an iris. Such stems are called *rhizomes*. Although the rhizome is the most common stem form, many ferns are vine-like, shrub-like or tree-like. In the tree ferns the leaves grow directly from the stem and die away leaving leaf bases which help protect the stem and give the surface of tree ferns such characteristic features. In addition to the leaf bases the stems are covered in hairs or scales. These are called *ramenta* and are generally tan or brown in colour.

Internally the stem contains specialized water-conducting tissue (*vascular tissue* or *xylem*) which forms *wood*—a characteristic of higher plants. The wood is arranged in strands like those in a young flowering plant, but in the ferns these interconnect to form a lattice pattern. No *secondary growth* (growth of wood mainly for structural support) occurs, so heavy, strong, wooded trunks are not found in fern trees. Instead fern trees are supported by the thick leaf bases and the high buttressing roots which grow out from the stem above ground level.

The roots of ferns all grow out directly from the stem—that is they are *adventitious*. Otherwise they are similar to the roots of flowering plants. They have central wood for conducting water, and root hairs, when young, for absorbing water. They do not, however, grow in thickness as they grow older.

Life-cycle and ecology

As with the mosses and liverworts, ferns and their allies have a life-cycle with two generations—the *gametophyte*, which is a sexual phase producing gametes, and the *sporophyte*, which is an asexual phase producing spores. The spores germinate to give the gametophyte generation again. In mosses the dominant phase in the life-cycle is the gametophyte, for the sporophyte is parasitic upon the gametophyte throughout its life. But in the ferns the sporophyte is dominant, forming a fern plant with leaves, stem and roots. The gametophyte, by contrast, is tiny and almost never noticed.

In this respect ferns are similar to the flowering plants—in all advanced plants the sporophyte is dominant. Ferns differ from higher plants, however, in that they produce spores and not seeds and do not have flowers or flower-like structures.

In a typical fern, such as *Dryopteris intermedia*, the broad-leafed fern used in flower arrangements, the spore-producing organs, the *sporangia*, are positioned together in groups called *sori* on the underside of the leaf frond. Each sorus is sited on a swelling (the *placenta*) on a leaf vein, and out of the placenta grows a kidney-shaped structure, the *indusium*. The indusium covers the sporangia like an umbrella and protects them when young. Indusia are initially pale in colour but darken with age, conferring a rough brown appearance to the back of a frond.

Left: A fern showing the *epiphytic* life style—using another plant (in this case a tree) for support. This fern, *Platycerium bisurcatum*, the staghorn fern of Australia, has large lobed leaves, in contrast to the leaves of most ferns which have a central midrib with side branches.

Above left: *Salvinia auriculata*, a water fern. Though most ferns are land plants, some, like *Salvinia*, have adapted to live in water. The leaves of *Salvinia* grow from an underwater rhizome and float on the water surface. On the undersurface (shown here) many small sporangia develop.

Below left and below: A young fern plant (sporophyte) developing from the gametophyte generation of the fern, the *prothallus*. The prothallus lies on the forest floor, anchored to the soil by root-like *rhizoids*. The sporophyte is at first parasitic upon the gametophyte and draws nourishment through its 'foot' which is deeply embedded into the prothallus. On producing leaves the sporophyte becomes independent of the prothallus which eventually dies.

TWO GENERATIONS OF FERN

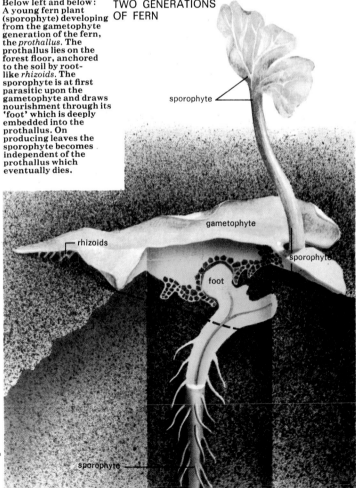

sporophyte

gametophyte

sporophyte

rhizoids

foot

sporophyte

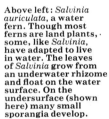

Each sporangium consists of a long slender stalk ending in a spore case or *capsule* which is shaped rather like a watch case, and inside this the spores develop. Around the edge of the sporangium, starting from the stalk and extending over about three-quarters of the capsule, is a row of cells, the *annulus*, which have thickened inner walls. The rest of the capsule is formed of large thin-walled cells and is called the *stomium*.

This rather complex sporangium disperses its spores in an interesting way. By the time the sporangium is ripe the indusium covering it has withered so that it is freely exposed. The cells of the capsule now lose water by evaporation and the annulus begins to dry. As this continues the thin outer walls of the annulus cells are sucked inwards, becoming concave and trying to pull the sides of the cell in on itself. As all the cells of the annulus are trying to do this at the same time, but cannot since each is attached to its neighbour, a strain is set up in the capsule as a whole. The thin cells of the stomium are the weakest point and eventually they rupture. The capsule now curls back like an open watch. Finally, as even more water is lost, the inner walls of the annulus also rupture. Suddenly the bent, thick inner walls of the capsule are released from strain and the whole capsule springs back to its original position, catapulting spores into the air.

On germinating the spores produce the gametophyte generation, called the *prothallus*. In *Dryopteris*, this is a heart-shaped structure no more than 1 cm (0.4 in) long. It is very similar to the gametophyte of mosses. It has no true roots but is anchored to the soil by elongated single cells called *rhizoids*. There are also no woody cells in the gametophyte. Male sex organs, *antheridia*, are found on the underneath part of the prothallus and along its edges while the female organs, *archegonia*, are limited to the thicker end.

The antheridia are very simple, consisting of two ring-shaped cells, one above the other, and covered in at the top by a cell which forms a cap. Inside the antheridia are formed the male gametes (*spermatozoids*), small coiled cells possessing hair-like *flagella* used for swimming. When ripe the antheridia take up water and the increase in pressure bursts the cap, releasing the spermatozoids which swim towards the female archegonia, attracted by the secretion of a chemical, *malic acid*. When they reach the archegonia fertilization takes place, producing the first stage of the sporophyte.

The life-history of ferns, though more advanced than that of mosses—the sporophyte generation being dominant—still includes an independent gametophyte, whereas in the flowering plants the gametophyte is reduced to microscopic proportions and is completely dependent on the sporophyte. Moreover, fertilization in ferns relies on a free-swimming spermatozoid which must swim in a water film on the plant surface. Thus, though ferns were the first successful land plants and were once distributed over the majority of the land surface they are still dependent to a large extent on a moist environment.

This dependence on moisture explains both why they were superseded as the dominant vegetation by the higher plants and their present range of habitats. Their preferred environment in temperate

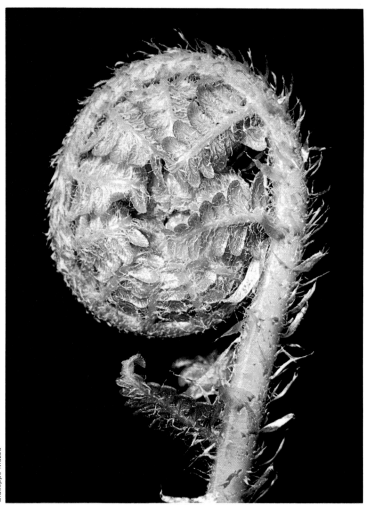

Giuseppe Mazza

regions is a moist, cool, deeply shaded woodland with an abundance of leaf mould. Nevertheless, ferns may be found from Arctic regions to the hot, wet lowlands of equatorial jungles.

Clubmosses

The clubmosses (*Lycopsidae*) are a group of small herbaceous plants growing from rhizomes. In appearance they are small and moss-like, hence their name. They are relatively few in number—indeed only five genera exist today: *Lycopodium*, *Selaginella*, *Stylites*, *Isoetes* and *Phylloglossum*. In the past, however, tree forms were abundant in Carboniferous forests. *Lycopodium* is world-wide in distribution and occurs in almost all climates.

The life-history of clubmosses is very similar to that of the flowering plants, with two types of spores called *microspores* and *megaspores*. The microspores produce gametophytes bearing male sex organs and the megaspores produce gametophytes bearing female organs. The spermatozoids are produced from a few cells inside the microspore and are not released from the spore. They are thus analagous to the pollen of flowering plants. Unlike the flowering plants, however, the megaspores are shed on to the ground before they are fertilized. If the megaspore was not released but developed within the sporangia the lycopod life-history would resemble that of the flowering plants.

Horsetails

The final group of pteridophytes, the horsetails (*Sphenopsidae*), is a very ancient group but has now only one living genus, *Equisetum*, of 25 to 30 species. They are

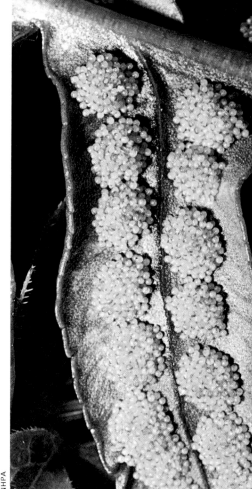

NHPA

Below: The spore case (*capsule*) of a fern. It has been stained to show the spores inside (red), the cells of the *annulus* (left), with their thick inner and thinner outer walls, and the thinner-walled cells of the *stomium* (right).

Right: Catapult-like dispersal of fern spores. As the capsule dries it splits open and folds back. Further drying causes it to spring suddenly shut, throwing the spores into the air where they are caught by the wind.

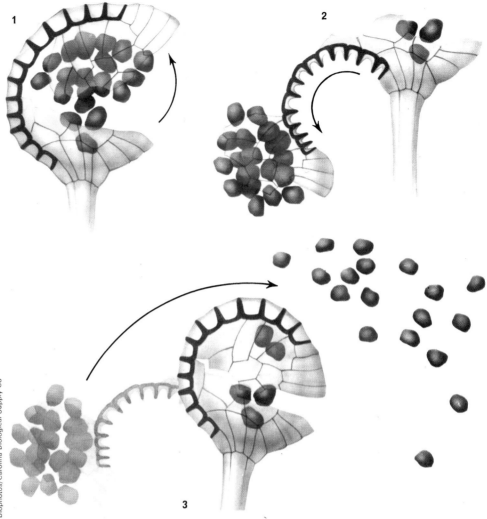

Far left: Underside of the common fern, *Polypodium vulgare*, with its many sporangia clustered together in groups called *sori*.

Left: A species of horsetail (*Equisetum*). Often called a living fossil because of its relation to the giant horsetail, *Calamites*, of Carboniferous times, the horsetail has its sporangia concentrated at the tip of the stem (the flower-like structure shown here) rather than on the underside of leaves as in ferns.

Below: *Equisetum telmateia*, widespread in Britain. The 'cones' at the end of the stems contain the sporangia.

strange-looking plants apparently with no leaves. In fact leaves are present but are scale-like and the manufacture of food that normally takes place in leaves occurs instead in the deeply ridged stem. Because of their scaly leaves the horsetails can be used as scouring pads—and are often referred to as 'scouring rushes'.

Ferns and man

Apart from their invaluable contribution to coal formation, ferns, past or present, are not of much use to man except for decoration. During the last century they were much in fashion and many species, native and exotic, were cultivated in gardens and conservatories. Among the best smaller houseplant ferns are the wood fern, *Nephrolepis*, with bushy rosettes of leaf fronds, the holly fern, *Cyrtomium*, which has rather glossy, leathery, dark leaves, and the leather fern, *Rumohra*, with its leathery, but lacy fronds. In additon to houseplants, most ferns are easy to grow in gardens, and have the advantage that they do well in shady areas where flowering plants would not thrive.

Other uses are few. The potting peat used in orchid potting is usually a mass of fibrous roots obtained from the cinnamon fern, while the trunks of the few remaining species of tree ferns are still used in the tropics for building purposes since they are resistant both to decay and to termite attack.

Nutritionally, ferns offer very little. In Hawaii the starchy pith of tree ferns is baked and eaten while in South America sugar is obtained from species of *Polypodium*. In some parts of the world young uncurled fern leaves are also eaten.

Plant Partnerships

It is often accepted as the 'law of nature' that all living things live directly or indirectly by exploiting others. This is true of all life forms incapable of producing their own food from inorganic substances—that is, of everything except green plants. Nevertheless few plants live entirely independently; each forms part of a living community, the different organisms and species of which are interdependent on one another. The greatest degree of interdependence occurs when two plants of different species live attached to one another in an association known as *symbiosis* which is beneficial to both organisms. Symbiosis is the opposite of *parasitism* in which one partner benefits at the expense of the other.

Lichens

One very common group of plants has been used since the middle of the nineteenth century as an example of symbiosis. These are the *lichens*, the small grey, brown or sometimes brightly coloured plants which grow on walls, rocks and tree-trunks, often appearing as no more than a circular crust 1-2 cm across. Under the microscope a lichen can be seen to be two completely different types of plant—a fungus and an alga—living together in a close symbiotic relationship. The lichen consists of an interwoven network of fungal filaments (*hyphae*) packed together to form a *mycelium*. The mycelium has a number of distinct layers, in one of which, near the upper surface of the lichen, the hyphae are intermingled with cells of an alga which contain chlorophyll and can perform photosynthesis, in which the energy of sunlight is used to produce carbohydrate. Together the fungus and the alga form one unit, the *thallus* of the lichen.

The lichen fungus is usually a member of the group *Ascomycetes*, while the algal partner is most often a species of *Trebouxia*, a green alga, or *Nostoc*, a blue-green alga important because of its ability to *fix* nitrogen from the atmosphere—making it available to the fungus. A few lichens include both green and blue-green algae as well as the fungus, showing that symbiosis may include three types of plant living together.

The fungus and the alga can be seen to be living together in a lichen, but it is more difficult to show that both partners receive some benefit from the association. However, lichens grow on bare rock surfaces or walls where there is no decomposing organic matter, on which fungi normally live. The fungi of a lichen could survive in such conditions only if they obtained carbohydrate from the algae and experiments have verified that this is what happens—up to 70% of the carbohydrate produced by photosynthesis in the alga is released from the algal cells and enters the fungal mycelium. The carbohydrate is usually released as a chemical called a *polyhydric alcohol*, though some types of lichen algae release glucose. The alga benefit by receiving moisture, containing inorganic nutrients dissolved by the fungal mycelium. '

Rod Borland/Bruce Coleman

Above: Lichens growing on rock at Cape Cross, South West Australia. Lichens are most commonly greyish in colour (bottom left of picture) but may be brightly coloured like the orange species here.

Right: *Cladonia sylvatica,* a very common lichen on moorland, on rocks and walls. *Cladonia* produces cup-shaped *podetia*, up to 1 cm in height, around the edge of which are borne small wind-dispersed spores or *soredia*.

There are more than 18,000 species of lichen in the world; about 1,400 have been found in the British Isles alone. They can be divided according to thallus structure into three groups: *crustose* lichens, which form flat, scaly circular thalli, *foliose* lichens, in which the thallus has the form of a leaf, often with root-like structures growing out underneath, and *fruticose* lichens, in which the thallus is branched like a miniature tree. Wall lichens are commonly crustose, while foliose lichens are found on trees or (like reindeer moss, *Cladonia rangiferina*) covering the ground in tundra regions.

Little is known for certain about the reproduction of lichens. Some species of lichen fungi reproduce sexually, by means of *ascospores*, but these contain no algal cells. But an ascospore could grow into a new lichen thallus by combining with cells of the appropriate alga—which would be difficult, since neither fungus nor alga is likely to survive for long by itself. It is more likely that lichens normally reproduce either vegetatively, by *fragmentation*, when small pieces of the thallus break away and later begin to grow by themselves, or asexually by the dispersal of *soredia*, which are small groups of algal cells surrounded by fungal

Jacques Six

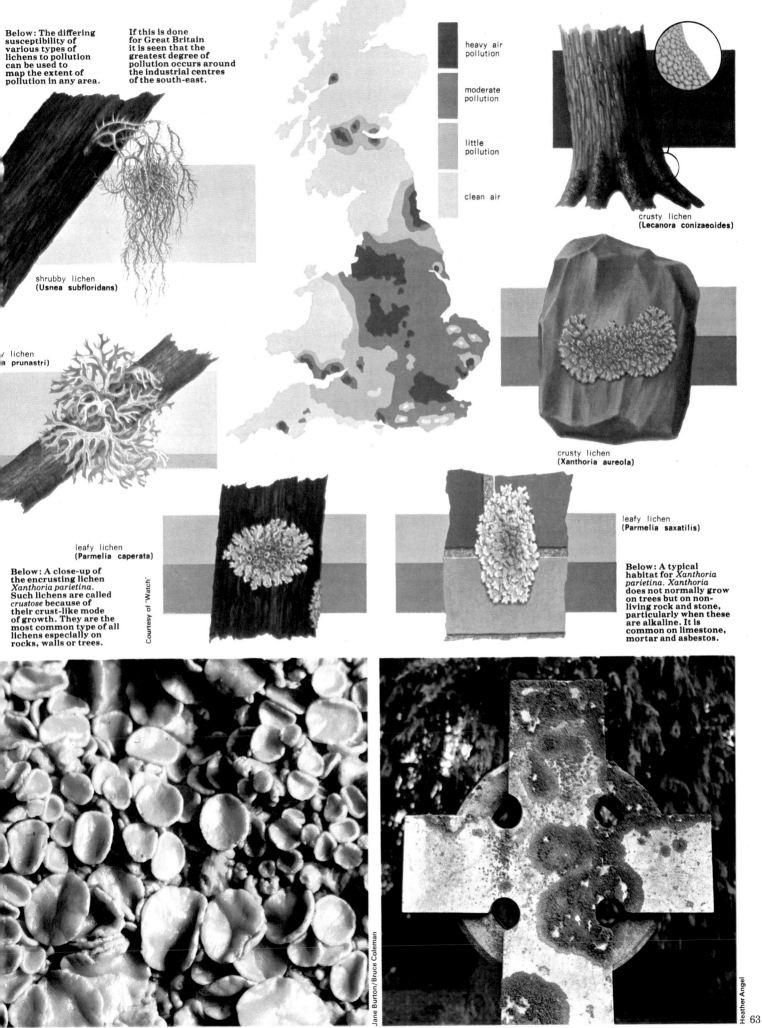

Below: The differing susceptibility of various types of lichens to pollution can be used to map the extent of pollution in any area.

If this is done for Great Britain it is seen that the greatest degree of pollution occurs around the industrial centres of the south-east.

heavy air pollution

moderate pollution

little pollution

clean air

shrubby lichen
(**Usnea subfloridans**)

lichen
(a prunastri)

crusty lichen
(**Lecanora conizaeoides**)

crusty lichen
(**Xanthoria aureola**)

leafy lichen
(**Parmelia caperata**)

leafy lichen
(**Parmelia saxatilis**)

Below: A close-up of the encrusting lichen *Xanthoria parietina*. Such lichens are called *crustose* because of their crust-like mode of growth. They are the most common type of all lichens especially on rocks, walls or trees.

Below: A typical habitat for *Xanthoria parietina*. *Xanthoria* does not normally grow on trees but on non-living rock and stone, particularly when these are alkaline. It is common on limestone, mortar and asbestos.

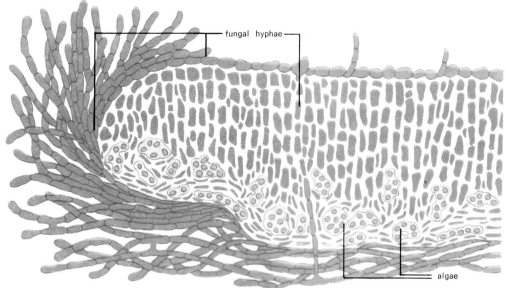

fungal hyphae

algae

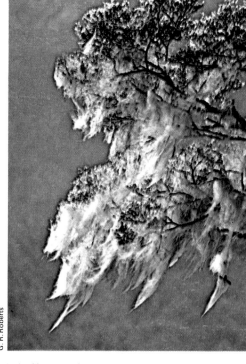

G. R. Roberts

Above: Stylized section through the body of a lichen (the *thallus*) showing the two types of plant—fungus and alga—which together combine to form a third type—the lichen. The alga and fungus do not intermingle randomly in the lichen, but the lichen is divided up into layers which are more or less distinct from one another. Three of these layers are composed of a network of intertwining fungal filaments, or *hyphae*, while the fourth layer contains the algae. The algae contain chlorophyll and can photosynthesize, and a few fungal hyphae grow into the alga layer and obtain carbohydrate produced by them.

Leslie Jackman

Left: Close-up of a *fruticose* lichen. These lichens have a many branched body, producing a shrub-like or antler-like structure. Most are very small—no more than several centimetres in size—but some tropical forms may be up to a metre in length, hanging from trees.

hyphae. Soredia are often visible as a powdery deposit on the surface of a lichen thallus. They are light, and can be blown around by the wind.

In the laboratory, it is possible to grind up the lichen thallus, separate the fungus and alga, and grow them separately. The fungus grows into a simple colony quite unlike the complex structure of a lichen thallus, and the alga no longer releases carbohydrate. The obvious next experiment—taking the separate cultures of fungus and alga and trying to recombine them to form a lichen—has, however, proved to be almost impossible. This may be because it is difficult in a laboratory to simulate the harsh natural environment of a lichen, where growth is limited by low levels of nutrients and the frequent drying-out of the thallus.

Root nodules

Farmers have known for centuries that the fertility of their soils could be maintained by including in their crop rotations a planting of clover or beans. These plants, and others such as the widespread group of tropical trees, *Acacia*, are in a family called *Leguminosae* (legumes). During the nineteenth century it was discovered that the increase in soil fertility was the result of the ability of legumes to absorb nitrogen from the atmosphere and fix it—that is, convert it into the organic forms contained in plant and animal tissues. Later still it was found that this process, called *nitrogen fixation*, is carried out not by the plants alone, but with the help of bacteria present in *nodules* (swellings) on their roots. This is an example of symbiosis involving a higher plant and a bacterium.

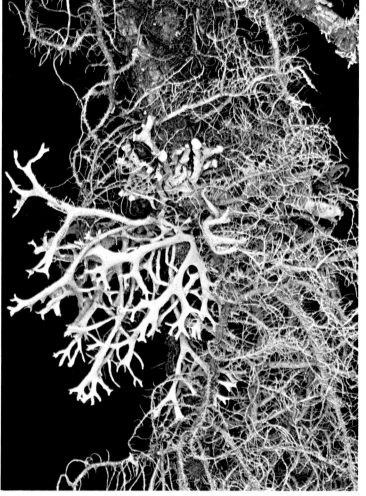

Giuseppe Mazza

Above: An early woodcut of the root of the broad bean, *Phaseolus vulgaris*, showing the nitrogen-fixing nodules on the root. Beans provide a very cheap source of protein because they do not need large dressings of expensive nitrogen fertilizer—nitrogen being provided by the root nodules. In contrast to the action of symbiotic bacteria in root nodules the industrial process used to manufacture nitrogen fertilizer requires a temperature of 450°C and a pressure of 200 atmospheres—and correspondingly consumes large amounts of energy and money.

Above right: Nodules on the root of alder, *Alnus glutinosa*. Unlike the legumes, the nitrogen-fixing organism in the nodules of alder is probably a fungus and not a bacterium.

Left: Two different fruticose lichens of the groups *Evernia* (left) and *Usnea*. *Usnea* lichens form long tangled masses—often up to 15 cm (6 in) long—and are commonly called 'old man's beard'.

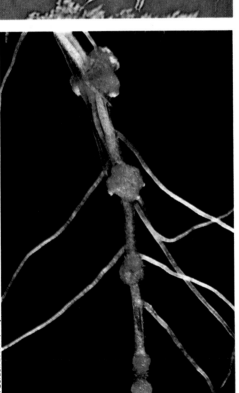

That the bacteria are separate plants from the legumes in which they are growing is shown by the fact that legumes grown from seed in sterile soil do not have nodules and do not fix nitrogen. Instead, nodules develop only after the bacterium, *Rhizobium*, normally present in the soil, infects the roots of the young legume. Inside the nodule the bacteria enlarge to form modified bacterial cells called *bacteroids*.

The bacteroids fix nitrogen using an enzyme called *nitrogenase* which catalyzes the reaction by which nitrogen is converted to ammonia—free-living *Rhizobium* does not have nitrogenase and cannot fix nitrogen. This ammonia is then used by the legumes to synthesize amino acids and ultimately protein used in the construction of plant tissue. Root nodules are thus of great value to the legume as

Above left: Large growth of lichen hanging from a tree in a beech forest in the Eglinton valley of New Zealand. A plant which uses another merely for support, as the lichen does here, is called an *epiphyte*. Epiphytism benefits one partner alone, but only rarely harms the other plant.

Above: The common woodland fungus, the fly agaric, *Amanita muscaria*. Woodland fungi appear to be growing independently but are often in fact symbiotic with the roots of trees such as pine or birch. The fungus is connected to the tree by a mass of fungal filaments in the soil.

nitrogen is an essential nutrient, often in short supply.

Numerous plants other than legumes are now also known to have nitrogen-fixing root nodules. Among these are alder, *Alnus*, sea buck thorn, *Hippophäe*, bog myrtle, *Myrica*, and a tropical tree called *Casuarina*. These plants, however, differ from legumes as the symbiotic organism is probably a fungus and not a bacterium.

Mycorrhizas

A further example of a symbiotic association occurring between the roots of higher plants and fungi is called a *mycorrhiza*. In these, common woodland fungi are connected, through extensive networks of hyphae in the soil, to the roots of trees. Mycorrhizal relationships are in fact extremely common; most common temperate trees including birch, beech, eucalyptus, spruce and larch are known to form mycorrhizas with several species of fungi. Scots pine, *Pinus sylvestris*, forms mycorrhizas with more than 100 species of fungi.

In one type of mycorrhiza, called *ectotrophic*, the fungus forms a sheath of hyphae covering the fine absorbing roots of the tree. This gives the tree a greatly increased area of absorbing root and thus it is able to absorb greater amounts of mineral nutrients such as nitrogen, phosphorus and potassium. Experiments have shown that in its turn the fungus receives a supply of carbohydrate from the tree.

In nutrient-rich soils mycorrhizas are of little value to the tree and the fungus is virtually a parasite on the tree. However, in most soils at least one nutrient is

in short supply and a tree with ectotrophic mycorrhizas will grow faster than an uninfected tree.

A completely different type of mycorrhiza is called *endotrophic*. In this, the fungal hyphae grow inside (instead of outside) the cells of the higher plant. Such mycorrhizas are found in all orchids and in many other plants—indeed possibly in *all* higher plants. In orchids, the mycorrhizal fungus, usually of the group *Basidiomycetes*, infects the roots as they begin to grow from the germinating seed. The hyphae grow into the cells of the root and form coils inside each cell. Later, some of the orchid cells digest the hyphae within them, releasing fungal nutrients for the benefit of the orchid. Because of this a young orchid can grow underground for several years, unable to perform photosynthesis, but obtaining a supply of carbohydrate from its fungal partner.

Eventually most orchids produce leaves and photosynthesize their own carbohydrate, some of which may be passed on to the fungus—a mutually beneficial association. A few orchids, however, never produce leaves and are therefore always dependent on their fungus; in such cases the orchid is a parasite on the fungus.

On plants other than orchids, endotrophic mycorrhizas are often formed with a fungus called *Endogone* from the same group, *Phycomycetes*, as the familiar pin mould, *Mucor*. The fungal hyphae grow into the root cells, branching within them to form structures called *arbuscules* (because of their tree-like appearance) and also thick-walled swellings called *vesicles*. Because of this, this type of mycorrhiza is sometimes called *vesicular-arbuscular*.

Experiments have compared the growth of plants, such as strawberries and tomatoes, with and without endotrophic mycorrhizas, and have shown that the fungus can help to supply the plant with mineral nutrients if these are in short supply in the soil. In most cases the fungus also benefits by receiving a supply of carbohydrate from its partner. This is obviously of vital importance to the most common mycorrhizal fungus, *Endogone*, as it will not grow except as a mycorrhizal partner.

Other kinds of symbiosis

Many other cases are known of associations between different kinds of plant which may be instances of symbiosis. In practice, it is often difficult to discover whether both plants benefit from the presence of their partners, so botanists tend to use the term symbiosis when neither plant is harmed by the other. Examples of possible symbiosis exist between the blue-green alga, *Nostoc*, and cycads (a group of primitive plants like giant ferns) and between green algae and the moss, *Sphagnum*, which forms peat bogs. Much research would be needed in every case to discover whether the association was or was not true symbiosis; whether nutrients are transferred between the two plants, and whether the association is necessary for the survival of either or both partners. Nevertheless, it is clear from an understanding of lichens, root nodules and mycorrhizas that symbiosis is an extremely widespread phenomenon, essential to the normal functioning of nearly all plant communities.

Parasitic and Climbing Plants

Higher plants are generally the *producers* of the world. All other life forms are *consumers*, dependent on the food which plants manufacture during photosynthesis. But in a few species and families of plants this normal pattern is upset. These plants are themselves dependent. They are *parasites* and *climbers*, dependent to a greater or lesser extent upon a host plant.

Parasitic and climbing plants, although different in many ways, have several features in common. Both groups use neighbouring plants to aid them to grow —either as a prop to enable a climber to reach the light, or as a source of food for the parasitic plant. Indeed, many species, like dodder, *Cuscuta*, are both climber and parasite.

Additionally, although particular species in both groups are confined to specific areas of the world, they are all largely non-specific in relation to their choice of host: the neighbouring plant used as a support or food source will simply be that which was nearest to the germinating seed of the climber or parasite. The only exception to this is the observation that parasitic plants, only rarely, and then usually unsuccessfully, parasitize monocot plants. The reasons for this selectivity, however, are not clearly understood.

Parasitic plants

Despite the fact that most plants are producers synthesizing their own food, it is wrong to think that parasitism among plants is rare. Two extremely large and important groups of plants, *fungi* and *bacteria*, are all either parasites or organisms that live on the dead remains of others (*saprophytes*). Even among the higher plants parasites are not all that uncommon, particularly in the tropics. Four families, the *Loranthaceae*, the *Balanophoraceae*, the *Orobanchaceae* and the *Rafflesiaceae* are composed entirely of parasitic plants. Other families, such as the *Convolvulaceae* and the *Lauraceae*, contain both parasitic and non-parasitic members.

Parasitic plants obtain water and food from the host plant through specially developed organs, called *haustoria*, which secure the parasite to the host and grow into the host's tissue, particularly its vascular tissue. Most parasites have a multiplicity of these connections with their host, but some have only a single primary connection. Indeed there are many levels of parasitism in the several families containing parasitic plants, and several forms of growth.

The extent to which a parasite is dependent on its host largely determines its vegetative form. True parasites, such as the dodders, *Cuscuta* and *Cassytha*, are entirely devoid of chlorophyll and rely entirely on the host as a food source. In this case the vegetative parts are very small—the leaves are present only as tiny scales on the thin, weak stem which itself possesses only poorly developed vascular tissue.

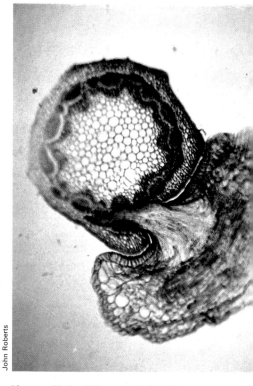

John Roberts

Above and below left:
The common climbing
parasite, dodder,
Cuscuta. Dodder twines
around the plant which
it parasitizes—its
host—and extracts
nutrients and water
from it through
specialized organs
called *haustoria*. These
can be seen (below left)
as small foot-like
pads growing into
the host stem;
one is more clearly
shown in the cross-
section above. Here the
dodder is located
beneath the stem of
the host plant. The
projection from the
dodder into the host
is the haustorium.

Below: The red fruits
of the tropical mistletoe
Viscum minimum.

ZEFA

Dr. G. Leedale/Biophoto Assoc.

Nevertheless, dodders are quite conspicuous, varying in colour from bright yellow to red. After emerging from seed the seedling immediately begins to grow in a circular fashion, searching for another plant around which to twine. Once a suitable host is found, the thin stem of the dodder then twines round the host's stem in a manner similar to that of the related climber, bindweed, *Convolvulus*. Unlike bindweed, however, the dodder stem has haustorial pads which become attached to and grow into the host stem. These pads break through the epidermis of the host stem into its interior, where they branch and form connections with the xylem and phloem. In the mature dodder the initial connection with the ground then withers away. The dodder is then entirely dependent on its host.

Other parasites, such as the toothwort, *Lathrea*, and the broomrape, *Orobanche*, are parasitic on the roots of other plants, rather than their stems. Correspondingly these plants are generally less conspicuous than dodders for most of their vegetative parts are usually below ground. Normally, the only growths above ground are flowering parts. Some root parasites, however, such as *Gaiadendron*, appear as a substantial bush above ground. In such cases the plants are almost certainly not entirely parasitic, but also manufacture some of their own food.

A well known example of a partial parasite is mistletoe, *Viscum*, which grows as a cluster of branches hanging from trees, commonly apple or poplar in Britain. The mistletoe produces a haustorium which connects with the host's xylem and extracts water and mineral nutrients, but it also has green leaves capable of producing much of the food it requires in the same way as other green plants. The host plant is used chiefly as a support but also as a 'root', as the mistletoe has no roots of its own.

In contrast to mistletoe, the tropical *Rafflesiaceae* are completely dependent on their hosts. Although *Rafflesia* bear the largest flowers of all plants, there is virtually no visible trace of the vegetative parts, which are buried in the tissues of the host (normally a liana). These consist of slender filaments, resembling the mycelium of a fungus. Like a fungus, too, these filaments are frequently only single-celled strands. The only large masses of cells are the *floral cushions*, groups of cells which give rise to the massive flowers.

The *Rafflesiaceae* are perhaps the ultimate example of the parasitic tendency to minimize all but the reproductive parts. All that remains of the varied structure of a higher plant is the reproductive apparatus. Such parasitic plants, relieved of the need to produce an elaborate vegetative structure, are able to devote most of the energy extracted from their host to the production of seeds.

Climbing plants

Although climbing plants live on their hosts, and in many cases harm them, they are not, strictly speaking, parasites. They do not obtain nourishment from their host but use it merely as a means of support. Nevertheless, this is no mean benefit. It enables climbers to grow high up in a dense vegetation canopy so that

Above: The bird's nest orchid, *Neottia nidus-avis*, is white because it lacks chlorophyll. It is normally regarded as a saprophyte but, though its food ultimately comes from dead remains in the forest litter, it obtains them parasitically through a mycorrhizal *Basidiomycete* fungus.

Below: The largest flower of any plant belongs to a parasite, *Rafflesia arnoldii* (shown here). The flowers can be up to 1m (3 ft) in diameter and weigh up to 6 kg (15 lb).

Right: The common European mistletoe, *Viscum album*. The white berries ripen in winter and are eaten by birds, especially thrushes, but the sticky seeds cling to the birds' beaks. The birds wipe them off on to the boughs of trees, such as apple, so dispersing them. The germinating seedling then connects itself to the host's water conducting tissue (*xylem*) through a haustorium.

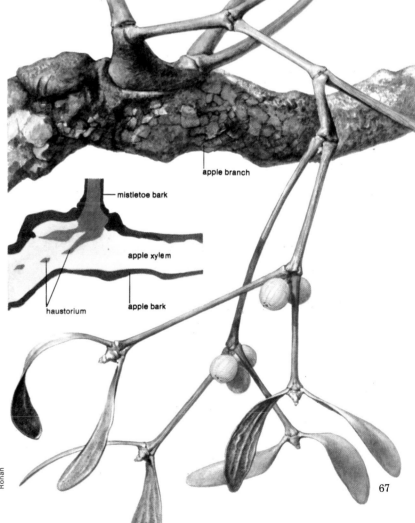

apple branch

mistletoe bark

apple xylem

haustorium

apple bark

Giuseppe Mazza

Heather Angel

Left and above: The climber, honeysuckle, *Lonicera periclymenum*. Because they do not need to expend energy producing supporting tissue climbers often overwhelm their hosts, in this case a young fir tree.

Below left: The sweet pea, *Lathyrus odoratus*, an ornamental climber.

Below: White bryony, *Bryonia dioica*, belongs to the same family, *Cucurbitaceae*, as cucumber and marrow. It produces long, tightly coiled and spring-like *branch-tendrils* which coil around any object with which they come into contact. The result is a very strong yet flexible support.

NHPA

Clematis *'Xerxes'*. The stalk of the leaf, rather than the blade, forms a tendril to cling to the wall, showing off the delicate bloom.

their leaves receive more light and their fruits can be more easily dispersed by the wind.

Climbers have these advantages without the need to produce the structural tissues that their hosts must produce. This enables them both to grow faster than their hosts and to devote more of their energy to the production of flowers and fruits. If a climber fails to find a host, however, it has little chance of survival.

The simplest climbers, such as bramble, *Rubus*, or goosegrass, *Galium aparine*, have stems which are provided with curved hairs, all with tips pointed downwards. These hairs hook the plant on to its support. Goosegrass has single-celled hook-hairs, which are very small and not easily seen, though they are quite effective in aiding the plant to cling to any available support. Brambles, on the other hand, have large multicellular hairs, or thorns.

The hairs of the runner bean *Phaseolus multiflorus* are especially interesting. They do not all grow downwards but are arrayed in all directions. The cells at the base of the hairs are flexible. They allow the hooked tips to twist in different directions around the base, so that purchase may be obtained in several directions at once.

A more specialized method of gaining support is the use of *tendrils*. There are several kinds of tendrils, though most are modified leaves or leaf parts. In the *Leguminosae*, well illustrated by the sweet pea, *Lathyrus odoratus*, leaflets of the compound (*pinnate*) leaf blade serve as tendrils, while leaf-like structures in the bud axils (the *stipules*) are enlarged to compensate for the loss of photosynthetic surface. In extreme cases, as in the meadow vetchling, *Lathyrus aphoca*, the whole of the leaf blade is transformed into a tendril—in which case the large stipules provide the major photosynthetic surface.

A less common form of tendril is produced by old man's beard, *Clematis*. Here the leaf stalk (*petiole*) rather than the leaf blade forms the tendril. In yet another group of climbers, including the virginia creeper, *Ampelopsis veitchi*, and the passion flower, *Passiflora*, the tendril, known as a *branch-tendril*, grows directly from the stem. In virginia creeper the tendrils grow from opposite each leaf, while in the passion flower they grow from the axils of the leaves.

The most tightly attached climbing plants, however, are those in which the plant itself behaves as a 'tendril' and twines about its support. Good examples are bindweed, *Convolvulus*, and honeysuckle, *Lonicera*. Initially the shoots of these plants grow up unsupported, but after some time the tip leans over and begins to revolve until it finds some support about which to twine. The climber then continues to twine up the stem of the support. In most species the direction of twining is always the same. For example, honeysuckle always twines clockwise while larger bindweed, *Calystegia sepium* twines anti-clockwise. A few species, however, like woody nightshade, *Solanum dulcamara*, have no fixed twining habits.

Entwining climbers have one particular adaptation to this life style. The growing point (*apex*) of most plants is surrounded by a cluster of expanding young leaves. These would tend to interfere with the encirclement of the supporting plant. The apex of entwiners, however, is surrounded by only very small leaves and the stem immediately below the apex grows particularly quickly so that there are large spaces (*internodes*) between the leaves.

Disadvantages

The advantage to a plant of the climbing life-style is that it enables it to grow high up in a plant canopy without producing a massive stem. Paradoxically, the lack of a large stem is also a major problem. It is difficult to transport enough water over the often long distances from ground to tip through the thin stem, and consequently small amounts of vascular tissue, of the climbing plant.

To overcome this problem climbing plants have adapted by increasing the efficiency of each individual xylem vessel. Resistance to the flow of water through the xylem is largely caused by the adhesion of water to the walls of the vessels and this is comparatively reduced if the cross-section of the vessels is larger. The vessels in the stems of climbers are very wide in comparison to those of other plants. Indeed they are occasionally visible to the naked eye.

Parasitic plants, dependent as they are on other plants, are of little value to man, but several species of climbers are of major economic importance. These include important pulses, such as peas, *Pisum sativum*, and beans, *Phaseolus*. Other climbers enhance man's enjoyment of life. For many life would not be so pleasant without the grape vine, *Vitis vinifera*, or the hop, *Humulus lupulus*.

Above: An unusual form of support. *Ampelopsis crampons* (shown here) uses *suckers* which grow on a short branch from the stem and hold the plant to its host. Also unusual, and superficially similar, are the *adventitious* roots which grow from the stem of ivy, *Hedera helix*, and hold it to its support.

Below: A more usual way of climbing is by means of downward growing hairs. This electron micrograph (about 50 times life size) is of the stem of goosegrass (or cleavers), *Galium aparine*. Poultry, and geese in particular, like to eat this plant which explains the origin of its name.

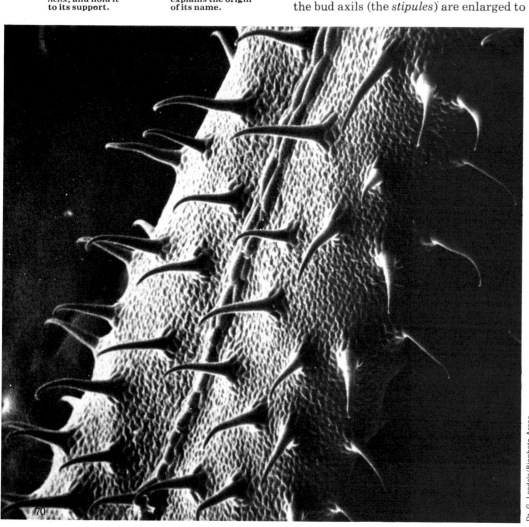

Jean-Pierre Bourret

Dr. G. Leedale/Biophoto Assoc.

Carnivorous Plants

Carnivorous plants live by capturing insects, digesting them and absorbing the products through the leaf surface. By obtaining essential nutrients in this way they are able to grow successfully in poor, mineral-deficient habitats. Carnivorous plants are surprisingly widespread— there are some 450 species distributed between six families—and they grow all over the world and in all sorts of conditions.

The sundew, *Drosera*, and the butterwort, *Pinguicula*, grow in cold acidic bogs, while the Dutchman's pipe pitcher plant, *Nepenthes*, is common in the hot, moist rain forests of South-East Asia. Pitcher plants are not confined to tropical forests. The huntsman's horn, *Sarracenia*, the cobra plant, *Darlingtonia*, of North America and *Cephalotus* of Australia all grow in warm acidic bogs, and *Heliamphora* is confined to mist-enshrouded swamps in Venezuela. Many species of the largest carnivorous plant genus, the bladderworts, *Utricularia*, grow, as does *Aldrovanda*, in pools of slightly acidic water, while several others are found on wet tree trunks in tropical jungle, or in marshy waterlogged soils.

Carnivorous plants have five distinct mechanisms for catching their prey— pitcher traps, snap traps, adhesive traps, suction traps and lobster-pot traps—but there is no correlation between the type of trap and any particular family. Thus, plants with pitcher trap mechanisms are found in three separate families, whereas within one family, *Lentibulariaceae*, four forms of trap occur.

Pitcher plants

Pitcher plants capture their prey by means of modified, cup-shaped leaves or 'pitchers' which contain digestive fluid. Insects are induced to land inside the pitcher where they lose their footing, fall into the pool of fluid below and drown. The traps vary considerably in size and construction. In the genera *Sarracenia* and *Heliamphora*, for example, they are 10 to 60 cm (4 to 24 in) long and are formed from a whole leaf, whereas in *Nepenthes* and *Cephalotus* they are 5 to 40 cm (2 to 16 in) long and are formed by a tendril-like growth from the leaf tip. The simple, conical traps of *Heliamphora* have only a narrow rim, while *Sarracenia* has a wide, decorated lip, the *peristome*.

Both *Nepenthes* and *Cephalotus* have ridged peristomes which may develop vanes, as in *Nepenthes villosa*, or a *cornice* of large, downward-pointing spines inside the pitcher, as in *Nepenthes raja* and *Cephalotus*. In many species the mouth of the pitcher shelters under a lid, while in *Darlingtonia* and *Sarracenia psittacina* the top of the pitcher curls right over forming a hood.

To attract insects, the rim and the inner wall of the pitcher are often a bright red colour, and many pitchers secrete a viscous sugary fluid on to the peristome and the underside of the lid as an added attractant. The lip of *Sarracenia* is covered with long hairs and red veins leading downwards to the mouth of the

Giuseppe Mazza

Heather Angel

Left: A pitcher plant, *Nepenthes pervillei,* from the Seychelles. The pitcher traps, which have lids, form at the ends of the leaves.

Above: A fly in danger of its life at the mouth of a pitcher trap of *Sarracenia drummondii.* All *Sarracenia* species come from N America.

trap. Below the lip is a zone of shorter hairs and then a much smoother area. Just above the water level is another zone of long, downward-pointing hairs. This is all designed to prevent an insect from getting a grip on the pitcher walls.

It is difficult to explain why insects that reach the lip do not fly away before entering the pitcher proper. *Nepenthes*, usually found climbing in forests, catches numerous ants, but the prey of *Sarracenia* is usually winged. Possibly the sugary secretion covering the walls and lip contains a narcotic which drugs the prey, or perhaps the insects become disoriented by the lid overhanging the pitcher.

The lower part of the inner surfaces of the pitchers are lined with small glands which are responsible for the digestive processes. *Nepenthes* secretes a slightly acidic fluid into the pitcher, and this becomes gradually more acidic as the plant matures due to the secretion of hydrochloric acid. The glands also secrete special proteins, called *enzymes*, into the fluid. These compounds speed up the breakdown of the insect bodies, and they function most efficiently in acid conditions. The small molecules produced by the digestion process are easily absorbed by the pitcher wall glands.

One of these enzymes is *nepenthesin*, a protease which breaks down proteins into their constituent amino acids. These compounds provide the pitcher plant with a source of nitrogen which is often lacking in its wet, tropical habitats. Nepenthesin is similar to *pepsin*, which breaks down proteins in the strongly acidic mammalian stomach. The other potential source of nitrogen is the insect's exoskeleton, composed entirely of the virtually indestructible substance *chitin*, and another of the enzymes produced by *Nepenthes* is capable of slowly breaking down this tough material. The digestive fluid of *Nepenthes* also has enzymes to break down fats and nucleic acids.

Despite this prodigious digestive capacity there are some insects which are able to live within the pitchers. Larvae of the mosquito *Wyeomyia smithii* live in the pitcher of *Sarracenia purpurea*, and the adults have no difficulty alighting on the walls or flying out of the pitcher. Other larvae and a host of protozoa all live unharmed within the pitcher fluid, while the spider *Misumenops nepenthicola* spins a web inside the mouth and so is able to move about within the pitcher—an ideal location for catching insect prey.

71

Above: A small frog caught by a Venus's flytrap, *Dionaea*, provides an unusual meal. Although the trap is not designed for such large prey, it will close whenever two trigger hairs inside the leaf lobes are touched.

Right: A Venus's flytrap with both open and closed traps. The inner surfaces of the leaf lobes carry bright red digestion glands. The red colour, caused by an *anthocyanin* pigment, serves to attract insects to the plant.

Above: A fly is trapped by a British species of sundew, *Drosera rotundifolia*. Each unusual-looking leaf carries many slender tentacles, each with a globule of sticky, sugary fluid which sticks to the prey.

Snap traps

The Venus's flytrap, *Dionaea muscipula*, is a small terrestrial plant having rosettes of six to eight leaves bearing traps 1 to 3 cm (0.4 to 1.2 in) long. The trap itself forms on the end of the leaf, the leafstalk forming a hinge and the remainder of the leaf tissue two lobes. The edges of the lobes are equipped with a number of long spines. The spines of opposite lobes intermesh when the leaf closes.

Located in a triangle on each lobe are three stiff hairs. These are about 1.5 mm (0.06 in) long and serve to trigger off the closing of the leaf. An insect moving over the leaf surface will brush against one of the hairs. Movement of the hair compresses a constricted zone of cells at its base causing an electric charge to be established, but the trap remains open. The hinge is activated only when a second hair movement increases the potential to a fixed discharge level.

The electric discharge, which now activates the hinge, moves across the leaf as fast as a nerve impulse, although there is no specialized nervous tissue. Furthermore, the second hair movement can be at the same hair or any one of the other hairs. The Venus's flytrap may have developed this 'double action' trigger to avoid fruitless closing of the trap by, for example, a raindrop. Once triggered, the trap closes very quickly—within one fifth of a second.

When the lobes come together the spines intermesh but do not completely close the gap, and if the trapped insect is very small it can escape and the trap will reopen. In this way valuable digestive fluid is not wasted on prey which will yield less nutrient than is used digesting it. If, however, the prey is sufficiently large the trap closes slowly over several hours, finally crushing it.

BLADDERWORT

Adhesive traps

The traps of the sundews, *Drosera* and *Drosophyllum*, the butterworts, *Pinguicula*, and the rainbow plants, *Byblis*, all use a sticky mucilage to ensnare insects. The leaf surfaces are covered with two types of gland, *stalked* and *sessile*. The stalked glands, in the form of hairs or 'tentacles' secrete a highly viscous sugary fluid which attracts insects and holds them fast once they have landed on the plant. As the prey struggles to escape neighbouring hairs bend towards it and it becomes even more firmly held.

The sessile glands are responsible for producing digestive enzymes. Within one to two days of an insect becoming trapped by the plant, enzymes can be detected and after four days digestion of the prey is at its most active.

Suction traps

The bladderworts, *Utricularia* and *Polypompholyx*, grow free-floating or rooted in ponds and streams. They have branched stems with tight crowns of leaves, and the traps are small bladders from 0.3 to 5 mm (0.01 to 0.19 in) long located on the leaves. The prey consists mainly of water fleas, protozoa and insect larvae.

The pear-shaped bladders are attached to the leaf by a short stalk and have an opening which is closed by a trap door, a free-hanging structure with a hinge at one side and a second hinge three-quarters of the way down. Just below the second hinge are two long, rigid *trigger hairs*. The bottom of the door rests on an inclined semi-circular collar, the *threshold*. A second, much more flexible door rests against the base of the trap door and

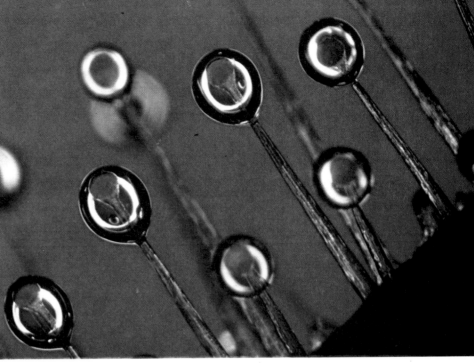

Below: A bladderwort, *Utricularia*. An aquatic plant, it catches its prey, typically water fleas, by means of small bladders carried by the leaves. Each bladder, closed by a hinged 'trap door', is first emptied of most of its water by means of special glands. When trigger hairs near the entrance are touched, the door springs open and water floods in, carrying the prey with it. The door then closes to prevent escape, and digestion begins.

Natural Science Photos

Left: The pink butterwort, *Pinguicula lusitanica*, catches its prey by means of sticky tentacles carried by the upper leaf surfaces. The captured insects supply nitrogen, which is usually lacking in its boggy habitat.

Above: A close-up of the stalked glands of a sundew, *Drosera*. The globules of sticky fluid are plainly visible. Glands on the leaf surface secrete enzymes to digest the prey once it has been caught by these tentacles.

the threshold, thus ensuring a water-tight fit. Two long antennae curve down over the entrance and numerous stiff bristles surround the trap door.

Bifid and *globular* glands, which are located on the inner side of the threshold and on the outer surface of the trap respectively, pump water from the interior of the bladder in order to set the trap. Up to 90 per cent of the original water is expelled so that the door is pressed tightly against the threshold by external water pressure. Glands located on the outer surface of the door and threshold secrete a sugary mucilage which attracts prey and seals the door. The bristles guide prey towards the door until, by pushing against the trigger hairs, the lower part of the door levers open. Within 0.0015 sec the pressure forces the door inwards and both water and prey are sucked in. The door then springs shut, ensuring that the prey cannot escape, and water is pumped out so that digestion can begin.

Lobster-pot traps

Genlisea grows as a small free-floating rosette partially submerged in shallow water and is often found with bladderworts. The trap-leaves, only a few centimetres long, have a short stalk which divides into two tubes. These hang down into the water. A slit runs in a spiral all the way down the tubes, and along the inner edge of this is a row of inward-pointing hairs. The outer edge is covered in glands which secrete mucilage. Small aquatic animals can easily find their way past the hairs and get into the trap, but then cannot find the entrance and are caught. The inner surface has numerous glands similar in appearance to those of bladderworts.

bladder trap (cutaway)

digestive glands

trigger hairs

water flea

entrance

bladder trap (section)

73

Flowering Plants

Over the last 100 million years one group of plants has become dominant on the Earth, both in numbers and species. Called the *Angiospermae*, the flowering plants, the group includes well over 200,000 species, more than a hundred times as many as the next major group, the gymnosperms. It contains most of the trees grown by man for timber and almost all of the plants grown for food.

The dominance and variety of the flowering plants is closely linked with the three features used to distinguish them from other groups, such as the gymnosperms. These features are flowers, seeds enclosed in fruits, and a well-developed conducting system. Flowers encourage *cross-pollination* (fertilization with pollen from another plant rather than the same plant) by insects or other animals; seeds enclosed in fruits encourage widespread dispersal; and a fully developed system of conducting tissues means the efficient transport of water and nutrients within the plant.

Origin of the flowering plants

It is probable that the angiosperms evolved from the gymnosperms, though this can never be known for certain as most species of gymnosperms are known only as fossils. Plants have no skeleton and so plant fossils give only a limited picture of the appearance of the living plant. It is difficult, therefore, to deduce the important details of reproduction and development from a fossil. Nevertheless, it seems that the angiosperms are most like a group called the *pteridosperms*, the seed ferns. These plants, which have been extinct for at least 100 million years, were similar to the *cycads*, a few species of which still survive.

The earliest angiosperm fossils date from the Lower Cretaceous period (100-135 million years ago). Some of these are very similar to present day flowering plants; but the great explosion in the number of species of flowering plants probably took place more recently, during the early Tertiary period (about 80 million years ago). At that time, insects such as bees and butterflies, which are important pollinators, evolved to their present day forms. It is easy to relate the amazing diversity of flowering plants to the equally remarkable diversity of their insect pollinators.

Flowers

Flowers vary enormously in their size, colour and structure. When a flower is described, the first things normally mentioned are the *sepals* and *petals*. The petals are the brightly coloured structures that make flowers attractive to people, and, more important as far as the plant is concerned, to the insects or other animals that pollinate the flower. The sepals are a ring of smaller, leaf-like structures outside the petals. They enclose and protect the flower bud before it opens. All the sepals together are called the *calyx*, and all the petals together the *corolla*. In a few flowers, such as lilies (*Liliaceae*), the calyx is as large and

74

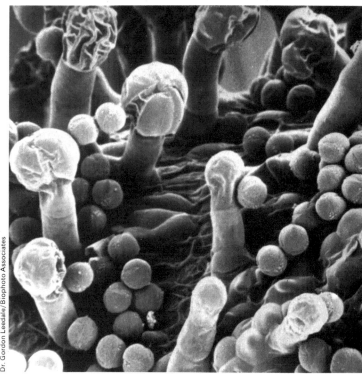

Above: The beautiful forms, colours and perfumes of flowers exist not to be aesthetically pleasing to man but as an attraction to bees and other insects. In their hunt for both pollen and *nectar* (a sugary substance produced by some flowers in glands, *nectaries*, on the petals) insects become covered by pollen produced by the male sex organs (*anthers*). This pollen is then transferred to the female sex organ(s) (*stigma*) of another plant. The pollen of one flower therefore fertilizes the eggs of a second flower—a process known as *cross-pollination*—which produces a plant with characteristics slightly different from either parent and a total population of plants each slightly different from the other. Such a variable population allows the gradual adoption of favourable characteristics by natural selection.

Right: The surface of a stigma (magnification about 500 times) showing *epidermal hairs* and pollen grains between them.

Above: The Swedish botanist, Carl von Linné (1707-78) whose system of classification, based on flower structure, was a great help to early botanists.

Above right: Nodding (or musk) thistle, *Carduus nutans*. Thistles are members of the daisy family, *Compositae*. Each

'flower' is in fact an inflorescence of many small flowers and is called a *capitulum*.

Below right: Flower of the tulip tree, *Liriodendron tulipifera*. Tulip and tulip tree flowers look similar but the plants are not closely related. Tulip trees are dicots, tulips (*Tulipa*) are monocots.

brightly coloured as the corolla, and the term *perianth* is then used to describe both calyx and corolla.

It was realized in very early times that pollination is necessary for seed and fruit production; Assyrian kings performed a ceremonial pollination of date palms. However, the discovery that plants have two sexes is credited to Rudolph Jacob Camerarius (1665-1721). He realized that, less conspicuous than petals and sepals, there are male and female reproductive structures at the centre of a flower.

The male structures are called *stamens*. Each normally consists of a stalk supporting a bright yellow or orange head, the *anther*, which contains thousands of *pollen* grains, inside which are contained the male gametes. The female parts of the flower are more variable. The essential features, however, are the *ovules*, each of which contains one female gamete; the *ovary*, which contains the ovules; and the *style*, an elongated projection from the ovary. The style carries at its tip a flattened, often sticky, surface called the *stigma*.

A flower may have one or several styles and stigmas, and the ovary may be a single structure or be composed of a number of separate parts. When a pollen grain finds its way on to a stigma, it germinates to form a *pollen tube* which grows down through the style and into the ovary where fertilization—the fusion of male and female gametes—takes place. Each fertilized ovule develops into a seed.

The structure of flowers and the details of the reproductive organs in flowering plants are different from anything found in other plants. Flowering plants do, however, have a life-cycle with an alter-

Right: Cross section of a typical flower. *Pollen grains*, deposited on the *stigma*, each produce a *pollen tube* which grows down through the style and into the *ovule* through a small pore, the *micropyle*. Inside the ovule is an *embryo sac* typically containing 8 nuclei—*antipodals, polar nuclei, synergids*, and the *female egg*. The pollen tube discharges two *sperms* which fertilize the ovule—one fuses with the egg, the other with the two polar nuclei. The other nuclei usually disintegrate.

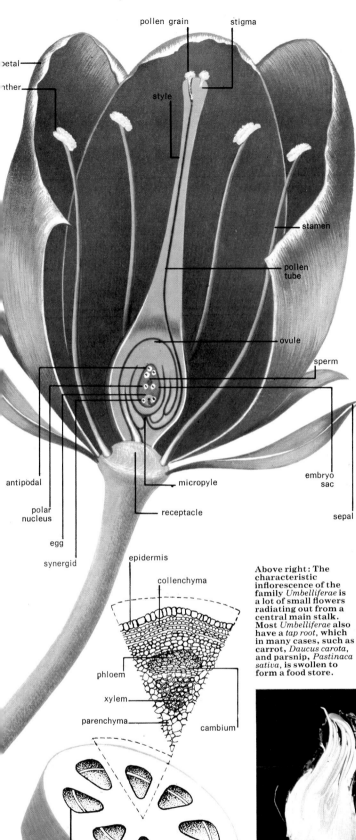

pollen grain
stigma
petal
anther
style
stamen
pollen tube
ovule
sperm
antipodal
micropyle
polar nucleus
receptacle
egg
synergid
embryo sac
sepal

Jean Pierre Bourret

epidermis
collenchyma
phloem
xylem
parenchyma
cambium
vascular bundles

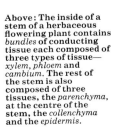

Above: The inside of a stem of a herbaceous flowering plant contains *bundles* of conducting tissue each composed of three types of tissue—*xylem, phloem* and *cambium*. The rest of the stem is also composed of three tissues, the *parenchyma*, at the centre of the stem, the *collenchyma* and the *epidermis*.

Right: Roots differ from stems in having no leaves or buds and in possessing conducting tissue arranged in a central core rather than in vascular bundles. The absorbing area of roots is greatly increased by thousands of tiny root hairs which are in intimate contact with the soil particles.

Above right: The characteristic inflorescence of the family *Umbelliferae* is a lot of small flowers radiating out from a central main stalk. Most *Umbelliferae* also have a *tap root*, which in many cases, such as carrot, *Daucus carota*, and parsnip, *Pastinaca sativa*, is swollen to form a food store.

Below: Flowering plants also reproduce vegetatively. A *bulb* is a modified stem (the darker yellow portion at the base) from which grow fleshy *scale leaves* in which food is stored. An onion, *Alium cepa*, is an example of a bulb eaten for its food. This bulb, however, is the daffodil, *Narcissus*.

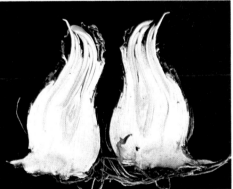

Leslie Jackman

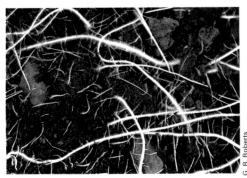

G. R. Roberts

nation of generations, like mosses, ferns and gymnosperms, though one generation is hardly noticeable. The plant as we see it is the sporophyte. The gametophytes are so much reduced in size and complexity that only careful research shows that they are actually present. The male gametophyte, consisting of only three cells, develops inside the pollen grain. The female gametophyte remains buried within the ovule and is never released from inside the sporophyte.

The flower of an angiosperm is different in appearance from the cone of a gymnosperm, but the processes of pollination and fertilization are much the same. The most important difference is indicated by the word *angiosperm*, which means 'covered seed'. In gymnosperms the seed is exposed, whereas in flowering plants it is contained within the ovary. In some plants, as the seed forms, the ovary and other parts of the flower expand to form a *fruit*, surrounding the seed.

Another distinctive feature of many flowering plants is the way the flowers are arranged together in groups called *inflorescences*, giving a large patch of colour which may help to attract pollinating insects. Inflorescences are also useful to the botanist: the different types are often an easy way of recognizing the family to which a plant belongs.

Stems, roots and leaves

Flowers, being conspicuously colourful and varied in structure, are probably the most immediately interesting part of a flowering plant. Nevertheless, the growth and flowering of plants depends on intricate structures and complex processes which occur within stems, roots

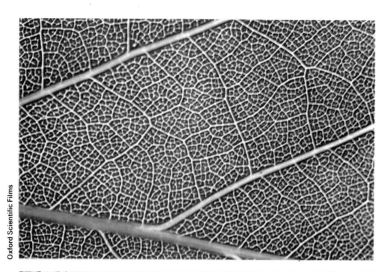

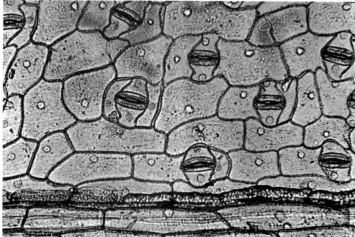

simple lobed
oak

simple
lanceolate
willow

compound
digitate

horse
chestnut

simple
cordate
ovate
lime

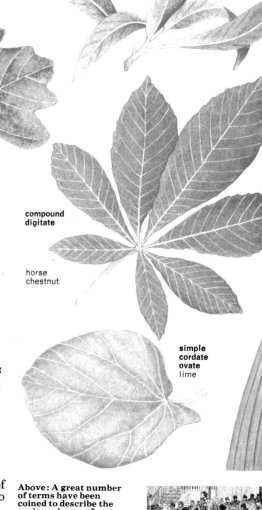

Above left: Intricate pattern of the leaf veins of a tulip tree, *Liriodendron tulipifera*, showing the elaborate branched network of dicotyledons. In monocotyledons the veins are unbranched and parallel.

Left: A close-up of a leaf of *Tradescantia* (x50) showing the small pores, *stomata*, through which water vapour is lost from the plant. The opening and closing of each stoma is controlled by two guard cells at its mouth. These cells respond to changes in the water pressure (*turgidity*) in the cell. As water is lost the pressure falls and the guard cells close the stomata so preventing any further loss of water.

and leaves. The non-flowering parts of plants are by no means always similar: they vary in an almost infinite number of ways.

The stem of a plant provides the framework to which are attached the leaves and flowers. Within it are contained two types of tissue, *xylem* and *phloem*, specially modified for conducting water and nutrients from one part of the plant to another. Xylem consists of long tubes, called *vessels*, formed from dead cells with missing end walls and thickened side walls. It provides the pathway along which water and inorganic nutrients pass upwards from the roots to the leaves. Phloem, on the other hand, consists of two kinds of living cells, *sieve tube cells* and *companion cells*, and is concerned with the transport of organic nutrients—particularly *sucrose* (sugar)—downwards from the leaves to the roots.

Sieve tube cells are elongated cells linked together but separated by perforated end walls to form a tube. The smaller companion cells are arranged alongside the sieve tube cells and apparently control their activity. Additionally, between the xylem and phloem, are a few layers of narrow cells called the *cambium*. Cambium cells continuously form new cells which replace aging xylem and phloem cells.

In the stems of herbaceous plants, xylem and phloem run alongside one another in *vascular bundles*, each of which forms a cylinder of conducting tissue running from the roots up into the leaves. The vascular bundles are either arranged regularly in a ring towards the outside of the stem (in *dicotyledons*), or they are scattered irregularly throughout the stem

(in *monocotyledons*). The number of bundles also varies—from about ten to more than a hundred in some species.

The vascular tissue of roots is not arranged like that of stems. In roots the xylem and phloem are gathered together into a single vascular cylinder running down the centre of the root. Externally, however, root systems vary quite considerably. For example, some plants have a *tap root*, a main root which grows downwards with smaller roots branching off it. A carrot, *Daucus carota*, is a swollen tap root containing a reserve supply of nutrients for the carrot plant. Other plants, such as grasses, have a relatively shallow network of small fibrous roots, which are efficient in extracting water and nutrients from the upper region of the soil.

Leaves are attached to the stem at places called *nodes*: if there is a single leaf at each node the leaves are called *alternate*; if there is a pair of leaves, they are called *opposite*. In either case, each leaf consists of a flat blade attached to the stem by a leaf-stalk, the *petiole*, through which runs a vascular bundle which begins in the stem. (New vascular bundles are created along the length of the stem by the branching of old bundles, thus keeping the total number of bundles in the stem roughly constant.) The vascular bundle of the leaf-stalk branches within the leaf to form *leaf veins*.

Internally, a leaf's structure is related to its function as the main site of photosynthesis. The surface layer of cells, the *epidermis*, is perforated by pores called *stomata*. Stomata allow air, containing carbon dioxide, to enter the intercellular spaces within the leaf, and so reach the

Above: A great number of terms have been coined to describe the various shapes of leaves. Among other things, these terms may describe leaf blade composition, like *simple* (all parts of the blade in one piece) or *compound* (composed of separate leaflets); the general shape of the leaf, such as *linear* (several times longer than broad) or *reniform* (kidney-shaped); or the margin of the leaf, such as *entire* (no indentations) or *serrated* (saw-like indentations).

simple ovate alder

simple triangular lombardy poplar

compound pinnate rowan

simple linear grass

simple ovate-assymetric elm

simple palmate sycamore

simple oval beech

Right: Except for deserts, mountains, towns and coniferous forests, the land surface of the Earth is covered with flowering plants. This is part of a sub-tropical rain forest in Queensland, Australia.

Below right: Another use of flowering plants —Kenyan women picking *pyrethrum* flowers used to make the insecticide, *pyrethrum*. Pyrethrum, in the concentrations used in insecticides, is non-toxic both to plants and higher animals and is widely used on livestock and on edible plants. Though once regarded as a genus in their own right, these plants are now classified as a species of the genus *Chrysanthemum*.

Eric Crichton

Alphabet & Image

Left and below: The importance of flowering plants as food sources is inestimable. They are the basic food of virtually all life outside of the oceans. They are also of major economic importance in other ways. The most significant of these is timber production but other uses include textiles, drugs, dyes, resins, and perfumes. These women (left) are sorting roses for perfume manufacture (France 1891), while (below) vegetable dyes are exhibited for sale in India.

cells where photosynthesis takes place. Stomata may be found on the upper, lower or both surfaces of the leaf, although it is most usual to find them only on the lower surface.

Water is lost from the plant by diffusion from the intercellular spaces through the stomata—a process, called *transpiration*, which can be controlled by opening and closing the stomata. Water loss by evaporation from the epidermis is reduced by a layer of waxes, called the *cuticle*, which extends over the whole of the above-ground surface of the plant.

Monocotyledons and dicotyledons

The English botanist John Ray (1627-1705) was the first person to recognize the fundamental division of the flowering plants into two groups, the *Monocotyledonae* and the *Dicotyledonae*. They are divided by four obvious differences. Firstly, monocots, as their name implies, have only one seed leaf (*cotyledon*), while dicots have two. (Cotyledons are the simple leaves that appear first when a seed germinates, although in some plants they remain inside the seed.) Secondly, monocots have leaves with parallel, unbranched veins while in dicots the veins form a branched network. Thirdly, though the form of the flowers in both groups is very variable, as a general rule monocots have three or six of each flower component, for example three or six petals and three or six stamens, while dicots have their flower parts in fours or fives or in much larger numbers. Finally, although some monocots, such as palms and bamboos, appear woody, none show the *secondary thickening* by which woody dicots increase in girth each year.

As examples, buttercups (*Ranunculaceae*) and cabbages (*Cruciferae*) are familiar plants with obvious dicot features, while lilies (*Liliaceae*) and irises (*Iridaceae*) are monocots. The division into dicots and monocots reflects evolution; the dicots are probably more like the earliest angiosperms than the monocots.

Success of the flowering plants

Flowering plants are successful because of their flowers, their fruits and their efficient water-conducting systems. Many are also successful because they are *herbaceous* (not woody). Herbaceous plants can grow from seed to flower within a very short time—sometimes only a few weeks. This means that they can spread more rapidly than trees which may grow for decades before flowering and producing seed. One extreme example, the herbaceous desert plant, *Boerhaavia repens*, can produce seed eight days after germination. Such adaptation is of great advantage in harsh environments where to survive it is necessary to produce seed quickly before short-lived favourable conditions pass away.

In inhospitable environments the adaptability of the flowering plants has enabled them to grow where other plants would not be successful. In favourable conditions this same adaptability has resulted in a diversity of forms which together dominate the vegetation of the Earth—from tropical rain forest to the upland meadows of the Alps. The scenery of the Earth is largely the scenery of flowering plants. More importantly, they provide food, shelter and clothing for most of the world's population.

Lilies, Irises and Orchids

Few plants are as beautiful as the lilies, *Liliaceae*, irises, *Iridaceae*, and orchids, *Orchidaceae*. These three monocot families have evolved conspicuous flowers with fully developed petals and often other highly specialized structures to promote cross-pollination by insects and other animals. They are probably the most highly evolved of all plants.

Specialization within these families (particularly the orchids) to promote pollination by particular insects has resulted in a large number of species—about 25,000 in all. Also, because of their specialization, most species are confined to very limited habitats. These plants do not dominate large areas as grasses do.

The lily family

In one way the evolution of monocot flower structure parallels that found in the dicots. Lily and iris flowers are *actinomorphic* (symmetrical about more than one plane) while orchids are *zygomorphic* (irregular).

The actinomorphic flowers of lilies typically have petals and sepals that are similar and form a *perianth* with six segments. There are six stamens and the ovary is divided into three compartments —following the general monocot character of having flower parts in multiples of three.

A typical lily is the Madonna lily, *Lilium candidum*, which grows wild around the eastern Mediterranean, and has been cultivated since Roman times. Its large white flowers are often associated in paintings with the Virgin Mary. Other plants in the family include lily-of-the-valley, *Convallaria majalis*, the English bluebell, *Endymion non-scriptus*, and the snake's-head fritillary, *Fritillaria meleagris*. These plants, and most other members of the family, are perennial herbaceous plants which spend part of the year in a *dormant* state, thereby avoiding the need to maintain stems and leaves during seasons when growth is slowed down by low temperatures or lack of rain. They have evolved highly specialized storage organs to enable them to grow quickly once the dormant season ends.

In many genera, such as tulips, *Tulipa*, and lilies, *Lilium*, the dormant plant consists of a *bulb*, which is made up of a number of overlapping whorls of modified leaves. These leaves contain the plant's reserve of nutrients, and are thick and fleshy.

Similar in appearance and function, but structurally quite different, is the *corm*, which is the storage organ in a few

Jean-Pierre Bourret

Right: A wild lily, white asphodel, *Asphodelus albus.*

Below: Arum lilies are not *Liliaceae* **but belong to another family,** *Araceae.* **Most are herbaceous perennials growing from rhizomes. This is an 1891 illustration of** *Amorphophallus campanulatus.*

Below right: Some other plant families have lily-like flowers. One of these, the *Amaryllidaceae,* **includes daffodils,** *Narcissus,* **and snowdrops,** *Galanthus,* **as well as onions and garlic,** *Allium.* **Another family, the** *Agavaceae,* **are mainly tropical woody plants like** *Nolina,* **shown here.**

Ann Ronan Picture Library

Heather Angel

Alphabet & Image

Above: The tiger lily, *Lilium lancifolium* (earlier *Lilium tigrinum*) has been cultivated for centuries in China, Korea and Japan because of its edible bulbs. Many garden lily varieties (the 'Mid Century' group) are derived from crosses of this with other species.

Right: The orchid family, *Orchidaceae*, is a family of remarkably beautiful and highly evolved flowers. Many tropical and sub-tropical species are also *epiphytic*—growing for support on other plants. The genus *Onchidium* (shown here is *Onchidium kramerianum*) are epiphytes from the West Indies and Central America. A few species also occur in Florida.

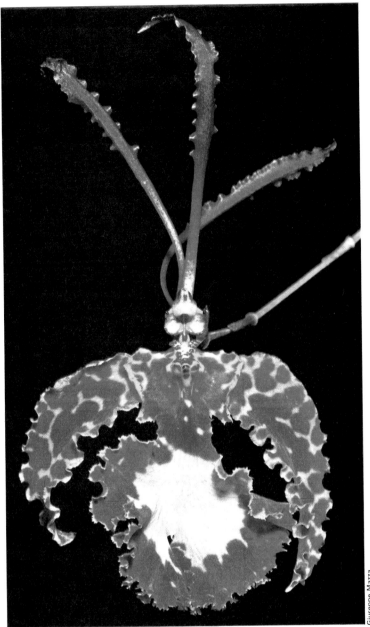

Giuseppe Mazza

members of the family, including the meadow saffron (autumn crocus), *Colchicum autumnale*. Instead of leaves a corm develops from a short section of stem which becomes swollen with nutrients and covered with a single layer of scale-like leaves.

Other plants in the family, such as the bog asphodel, *Narthecium ossifragum*, grow from a creeping underground stem, called a *rhizome*, or, as in *Aloe*, possess whorls of persistent succulent leaves crowded at the base of the plant. These leaves can themselves survive periods of particularly dry weather. Over 300 species of *Aloe* grow in the dry areas of Africa. The relationship of these plants to the temperate herbaceous members of the lily family is not immediately obvious but their flowers, red or yellow in colour and carried in upright spikes, have the characteristic structure of lily family flowers, with a six-segmented perianth and six stamens.

The iris family
The iris family, with only about a thousand species, is not a particularly large family, but it is notable for its spectacular flowers and specialized growth forms. As in the lily family, the flowers typically have an actinomorphic perianth. In irises, however, it is often elongated into a narrow tube with the ovary found well below the opening of the flower. In some genera, *Crocus*, for example, the ovary is below the soil surface.

The iris family are herbaceous plants, often found in areas with Mediterranean-type climates. The plants, like lilies, survive the lengthy dry period in the summer in a dormant state as a bulb, corm or rhizome. For example, the bearded iris, *Iris germanica*, forms a rhizome; *Crocus* species, which grow wild in Southern Europe, grow from corms; while the dwarf *Iris reticulata*, from the Caucasus, forms bulbs.

Many members of the iris family are native to South Africa or America. About a hundred species of *Sisyrinchium*, small grass-like plants with perianths sub-divided into six blue, white or yellow petal-like segments, are found in North America. In South Africa, *Freesia* grow wild, as do less familiar plants, such as *Antholyza*, which are pollinated by sunbirds, *Nectarinidae*. In these plants, the inflorescence incorporates a 'bird-perch', a section of stem so placed that the bird can rest on it while probing into the flowers for nectar.

The orchid family
The most highly specialized flowers are found in the orchid family. Estimates of the number of species of orchids vary from 10-20,000, so that this is either the largest family of flowering plants or the second largest after the *Compositae*, depending on which figure is taken. Whatever the exact number of species, however, all orchids are herbaceous plants, either of tropical or temperate regions. Temperate orchids generally grow in the ground but many tropical orchids are *epiphytes*, that is they grow on the trunks or branches of trees.

Epiphytes are likely to be found in wetter regions, because, as they cannot tap ground water, they must obtain water either from rainfall or from a humid atmosphere. Epiphytic orchids have three types of roots, some for attachment to the tree on which they are growing, others for the absorption of mineral nutrients, and a third kind, *aerial roots*, which absorb water from the atmosphere and, since they contain chlorophyll, act as additional photosynthetic tissue. Mineral nutrients are obtained either from rainwater flowing over the bark of the tree or from the small amount of soil which may accumulate around the plant. Many orchids, both epiphytes and ground orchids, also store nutrients or water in thickened sections of stem called *pseudobulbs*. Alternatively, in some species root storage organs, called *root tubers*, are formed.

The seeds of orchids are generally minute. They contain so little stored nutrient that the development of the seedling depends upon their forming *endotrophic mycorrhizas* in symbiotic association with a fungus, normally a *Basidiomycete*. At this stage the orchid seedling is a *saprophyte*, a plant obtaining its nutrient supply from decaying organic matter, in this case parasitically through the fungus. After a time the orchid produces leaves and photosynthesizes its own carbohydrate, some of which may be passed on to the fungus. Thus the orchid does not normally remain as a parasite but both the fungus and orchid benefit from their relationship. Such an association, which benefits both partners, is called *symbiosis*.

The time during which the orchid is dependent on the fungus may be as little as a few months, or as long as ten to fifteen years, as in the burnt orchid, *Orchis ustulata*. Indeed some orchids never leave this stage. The bird's nest orchid, *Neottia nidus-avis*, for example, never produces leaves and remains as a saprophyte.

In many orchids, flowering, too, is delayed for many years after the seed germinates—and even then may not occur every year. Vegetative reproduction (by spreading rhizomes or the production of several tubers or pseudo-bulbs at the end of the growing season) is therefore important because it allows an orchid to colonize a suitable habitat rapidly without the need for flowering and seedling establishment.

Flowering is more associated with dispersal. The very light seeds can be blown long distances by the wind to spread the species to new sites. Some species, such as the bee orchid, *Ophrys apifera*, normally die after flowering once, but the common twayblade, *Listera ovata*, has been found with as many as twenty-

Oxford Scientific Films

Eric Crichton

four old flowering stalks. Since only one flowering stem is produced each year, and since the species is normally fifteen years old when it first flowers, such a plant must be some forty years old. Plants of some tropical epiphytic orchids have survived, in cultivation, even longer—for more than seventy years.

Pollination in orchids

Many flowers have evolved physiological or structural mechanisms to promote cross-pollination by insects. But it is the orchids which have the most complex adaptations, normally associated with cross-pollination by but one species, or group of species, of insect. The exact mechanism and the insect involved differ from one species of orchid to the next, but there are some features common to all orchids.

Orchid flowers consist of a perianth, one segment of which, the *labellum*, is enlarged and normally has a distinctive shape or colouring. In some species it is also extended as a tube-like *spur* containing nectar. At the centre of the flower, there is only one stamen, which is combined with the ovary to form a structure called the *column*, and two stigmas. The stigmas are separated from the stamen by a projection called the *rostellum*. Both the column and the rostellum vary greatly in shape from one species to another. Pollen grains produced by the stamen are clumped together into one or more bundles, called *pollinia*, and each pollinium has a short stalk, the *caudicle*. Each caudicle is then attached to the rostellum by a sticky disc.

The early purple orchid, *Orchis mascula*, shows a fairly typical version of the

The complex life-histories and the extravagant yet fragile flowers of orchids endear them to botanists. Some of the variation in their flower structure is shown here.

Above: The Australian spider orchid, *Caladenia huegelii*.

Right: The European lady orchid, *Orchis purpurea*, with its human-like flowers.

Below: The Central American epiphytic orchid *Brassia longissima*.

Eric Crichton

82

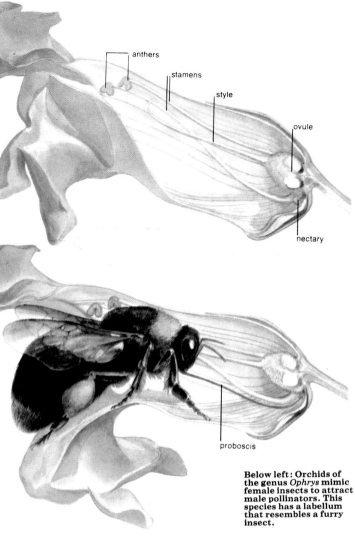

anthers
stamens
style
ovule
nectary
proboscis

Left and below: The purpose of brightly coloured flowers is to attract insects to carry out cross-pollination between different plants. *Antirrhinum* (left, a dicot) shows the general mechanism by which this is done. A bee feeding on nectar at the base of the ovary has pollen dusted on to its back by the anthers. This pollen is then transferred to the stigma of another plant. Below bees are pollinating an arum lily, *Anthurium*.

Bottom: Some flowers attract insects by mimicking the female so that the male attempts to mate with the flower. Here an *ichneumon* wasp 'mates' with the orchid *Cryptostylis leptochile*.

Below left: Orchids of the genus *Ophrys* mimic female insects to attract male pollinators. This species has a labellum that resembles a furry insect.

general mechanism of orchid pollination. The flowers are visited by humble bees, *Bombus*, seeking nectar secreted at the base of the spur. The bee alights on the labellum, which forms a sort of landing-pad, and then pushes its head into the centre of the flower, below the column, in order to insert its proboscis (tongue) into the spur. As it does so, it touches the rostellum and dislodges the sticky discs of the caudicles which immediately become attached to its head—the sticky substance sets like glue in a few minutes —like a pair of horns. Within thirty seconds the caudicles then bend downwards, so that the pollinia are properly positioned for pollinating the stigma of the next flower to be visited by the bee.

Other species of orchids have variations of this mechanism. For example in the

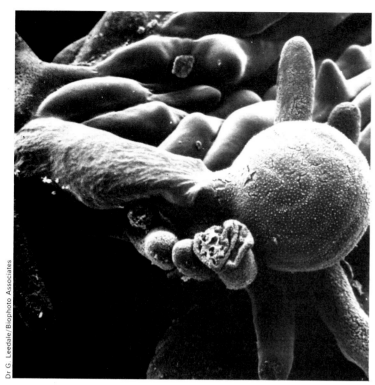

Dr. G. Leedale/Biophoto Associates

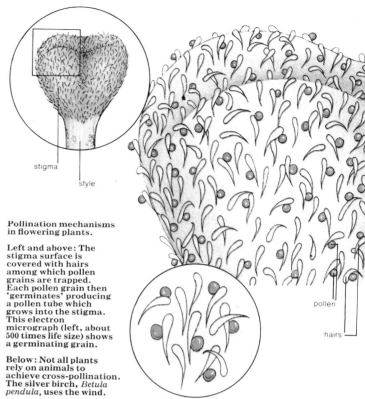

Pollination mechanisms in flowering plants.

Left and above: The stigma surface is covered with hairs among which pollen grains are trapped. Each pollen grain then 'germinates' producing a pollen tube which grows into the stigma. This electron micrograph (left, about 500 times life size) shows a germinating grain.

Below: Not all plants rely on animals to achieve cross-pollination. The silver birch, *Betula pendula*, uses the wind.

stigma

style

pollen

hairs

American epiphytic orchid, *Catasetum*, the rostellum is extended to form two *antennae*, and when these are touched by the bee the pollinia are released; but in this case with such force that they may travel up to 1 m (3 ft) if they are not intercepted by the body of the bee.

Catasetum is also interesting for another reason: the plants are unisexual, and originally, the female plants, whose flowers are very different in appearance, were placed in a different genus, *Monachanthus*. Only by careful observation of the plants in nature, and by experimental cross-pollination, was it possible to show that the male and female plants did in fact belong to the same species.

A particularly variable feature of the orchid flower is the length of the spur. Many orchids, such as the pyramidal orchid, *Anacamptis pyramidalis*, have extra long spurs, and are pollinated by insects such as moths and butterflies, which have longer proboscises than bees. In general, the length of the spur is related to the length of the proboscis of the pollinating insect. Orchids with long spurs and white or greenish flowers, such as the butterfly orchids, *Platanthera*, often emit a powerful smell at night, and are pollinated by night-flying moths.

But perhaps the most remarkable phenomenon in insect pollination, involving the closest adaptation of a plant species to one species of insect pollinator, is the attraction of male insects by orchids which mimic the female insect. This happens in a Mediterranean species, the mirror orchid, *Ophrys speculum*. It has a labellum with a dense fringe of hairs, and a metallic-blue reflective patch outlined with yellow. This apparently deceives the male insect—a *hymenopteran* wasp—into thinking that a female is resting on the flower. He attempts to mate with her; and in doing so at a number of flowers, brings about cross-pollination in the usual way. As well as imitating the female insect structurally, the mirror orchid also emits a *pheromone*, a volatile compound that attracts the 84 male insect to the female.

Heather Angel

Herbaceous Dicots—I

There are well over a quarter of a million species of flowering plants of which the majority (some 340 families) are *dicotyledons*—or more simply, *dicots*. Some of these are trees and shrubs but the majority are *herbaceous* plants. They do not produce lasting woody structures above ground, and in temperate regions the aerial parts generally 'die back' during the autumn. In *annual* plants the plants survive the winter as seeds, in *biennial* and *perennial* plants they survive as underground storage organs.

Among the herbaceous dicots there is a seemingly endless diversity. This is the result of millions of years of evolution during which different species of plants have adapted to differing environments. However, evolutionary trends in the flowering plants are extremely difficult to discover; there are very few useful fossils of herbaceous plants. Furthermore, the flowering plants appear not to have evolved in one straight evolutionary line but in a number of unconnected lines from an obscure common ancestor. This type of evolution can be likened to the spokes of a wheel radiating from a common hub and is called *radial evolution*.

One characteristic has been rather arbitrarily chosen by botanists as the basis by which to classify flowering plants. This is flower structure; and by concentrating on flower structure it is possible to list plant families in a rough evolutionary order. One way of doing this is to assume that the earliest flowering plants had simple regular flowers and that irregular flowers are a characteristic of more recently evolved families.

Regular flowers are called *actinomorphic*. They can be bisected vertically to give two identical or mirror-image halves along two or more planes. Less regular flowers are called *zygomorphic*. They are symmetrical about only one plane, as, for example, in the snapdragon, *Antirrhinum*. Some important regular-flowered families are the buttercup, water-lily, cabbage, hemp, dock, goosefoot, stonecrop, cactus, mesembryanthemum and parsley families.

Buttercups and water-lilies

The buttercup family, *Ranunculaceae*, is a good example of a regular-flowered family. Nevertheless it illustrates that even within families variations in flower structure can be marked. Typically, *Ranunculaceae* have five petals and many stamens but in *Anemone* and *Clematis* the sepals look like petals and the flowers appear to have anything from four to twenty petals. Leaf shape is also very variable, ranging from the large simple leaves of marsh marigold, *Caltha palustris*, to the feathery leaves of water crowfoot, *Ranunculus aquatilis*, which grows submerged in streams with its white flowers emerging above the water.

Another family, the water-lilies, *Nymphaeaceae*, are thought by many botanists to be most similar to the earliest dicots. They have a large indefinite number of petals, the inner of which are

Heather Angel

Above and right: The earliest flowering plants were probably trees with simple regular flowers—but it is flower structure, rather than the presence or absence of wood, that has generally been used by botanists to classify flower families. Many families therefore contain both woody and herbaceous species. Two such families are the *Proteaceae* (above is the evergreen shrub *Protea*) and the mallow family, *Malvaceae* (right is the garden shrub *Hibiscus* 'Douglas Dickins'). *Malvaceae* have stamens which grow in a tuft which appears to stem from the top of the prominent style. The family also includes cotton, *Gossypium*.

intermediate in structure between petals and stamens. It is possible that in early flowering plants petals and other flower structures developed from modified stamens.

The leaves of most water-lilies float on the water surface but the Egyptian lotus, *Nelumbo nucifera*, and its American counterpart, *Nelumbo pentapetala* have flowers which grow on stalks above the water. Buried seeds of *Nelumbo*, estimated to be a thousand years old, have been successfully germinated, illustrating the usefulness of seed dormancy for the survival of herbaceous plants in unpredictable environments. The parent plant may be killed, but so long as its seeds survive the species can re-establish itself when conditions improve—usually, when rain falls after a long interval.

NHPA

Yves Lanceau

Commercially important families

Several families of regular-flowered dicots include commercially important species. Probably the most important of all is the cabbage family, *Cruciferae*, most species of which have a distinctive four-petalled flower, in the form of a Maltese cross, which gives the family its name. The family includes water-cress, *Nasturtium officinale*, mustard, *Sinapis alba*, radish, *Raphanus sativus*, turnip, *Brassica rapa*, horse-radish, *Amoracia lapathifolia*, and cress, *Lepidum sativum*. But perhaps the most versatile species of all crucifers is the cabbage, *Brassica oleracea*. Brussels sprouts, cauliflower, broccoli, kohl-rabi and kale are all varieties of this one species.

Another particularly large family of regular-flowered dicots is the parsley family, *Umbelliferae*. Their characteristic features are their many lobed, often fern-like, leaves and an inflorescence, called an *umbel*, consisting of many small flowers whose stalks radiate from a central point. They are particularly important in north temperate regions, and include some familiar weeds such as cow parsley, *Anthriscus sylvestris* and hogweed, *Heracleum sphondylium*.

One interesting umbellifer weed, the giant hogweed, *Heracleum mantegazzianum*, presents an unusual hazard to humans. It produces sap containing a chemical, *furanocoumarin*, which can sensitize the skin to sunlight and lead to serious burns. It grows to four metres (13 ft) and its enormous creamy-white umbels are a conspicuous feature of stream and river banks in Europe and Britain. Other umbellifers, such as carrot, *Daucus carota*, celery, *Apium graveolens*,

A-Z Collection

and dill, *Anethum graveolens*, are food plants or flavouring herbs.

The hemp family, *Cannabiaceae*, contains only two genera, hops, *Humulus*, and hemps, *Cannabis*, but both are commercially important. Hops are climbing plants, grown extensively as a flavouring for beer. Cannabis, cultivated in Turkey and several parts of Asia, contains both strong fibres, which are used in rope and cloth making, and a resin, from which is produced the drug *marijuana*.

Not all flowering plants produce brightly coloured flowers. Wind-pollinated plants often have inconspicuous green flowers. Two important green, but regularly-flowered, families are the docks, *Polygonaceae*, and the goosefoots, *Chenopodiaceae*. Notable members of the goosefoot family are spinach, *Spinacea*

oleracea, and beet, *Beta vulgaris*, which has two commercial varieties, beetroot and sugar beet.

Sugar beet is a fine example of how, by crossing with wild plants, the yield of commercial varieties can be increased. In 200 years the average sugar content of sugar beet has been increased from 6% to nearly 20%. Sugar beet is biennial; the sugar is extracted from the swollen tap root which acts as a food storage organ during the winter.

Wild goosefoot species include many which are *halophytic*; that is they tolerate high levels of salt in the soil and are common on beaches and salt-marshes. Others, such as fat hen, *Chenopodium album*, are common weeds on waste and cultivated ground. One weed, Good King Henry, *Chenopodium bonus-henricus*, has

Left: Hemlock, *Conium maculatum,* **is an umbellifer which contains a powerful respiratory poison,** *coniine,* **in its leaves. Hemlock is common in ditches, on stream banks and in damp meadowland in temperate regions throughout the world. It grows up to 2 m (6 ft) tall, flowering between May and August.**

Above: The marsh marigold, *Caltha palustris,* **a typical member of the buttercup family,** *Ranunculaceae,* **with five petals and numerous stamens— though it has no green sepals. The name 'marigold' is misleading; true marigolds,** *Calendula officinalis,* **are members of the daisy family,** *Compositae.*

Below: The wild pansy, *Viola tricolor,* **has regular flowers which appear extremely simple. However, the flowers have a specialized structure to prevent self-pollination. The stigma is protected by a valve which can be opened by a pollinating insect but closes again as soon as the insect leaves.**

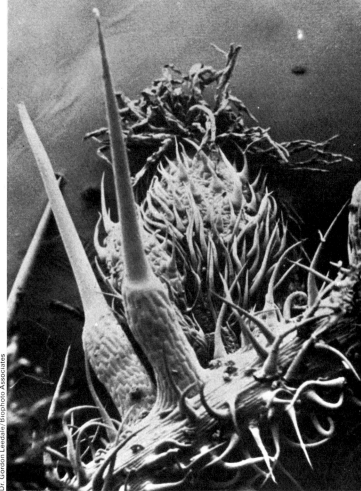

Dr. Gordon Leedale/Biophoto Associates

Eric Crichton

been grown and eaten as a vegetable since prehistoric times, though it is rarely cultivated today.

As well as docks, *Rumex*, the dock family includes rhubarb, *Rheum rhaponticum*. Even edible plants may accumulate toxic compounds in their leaves, and rhubarb leaves contain large amounts of poisonous oxalic acid. Plants store poisons in their leaves either to stop animals eating them or as a way of excreting unwanted substances which are lost when the leaves are shed in the autumn.

Xerophytic families

Another group of regular-flowered dicot families has adapted to a dry desert environment. Plants which can survive in a dry habitat are called *xerophytes* and usually possess succulent stems and leaves containing large quantities of water. More extreme adaptations include the absence of leaves to reduce transpiration, and a wide network of shallow fibrous roots to absorb water from the surface layers of soil immediately following rainfall before the rain can evaporate or run away. They often also have a dense covering of hairs or spines (sometimes both). Spines are to protect the plant from animals; in dry areas where vegetation is sparse, a plant without some means of defence against animals is very likely to be eaten. As further protection, desert and savannah plants often also contain toxic compounds in their leaves.

The stonecrop family, *Crassulacea*, contains many plants that are typical xerophytes. Some, like *Sedum*, are mainly northern hemisphere species, others, such as *Kalanchöe* and *Bryophyllum*, are confined to the drier parts of southern Africa. *Bryophyllum* shows an unusual kind of vegetative reproduction in which small plantlets develop, complete with roots, along the edges of the leaves. Eventually the plantlets drop off and take root in the ground, perhaps some distance off if they are blown by the wind.

The best known family of xerophytes, however, is the cactus family, *Cactaceae*. Cactuses are native to dry areas of North and South America, except for one

Above and right: Nettles, *Urticaceae*, are a green-flowered, wind-pollinated family, many members of which possess stinging hairs upon their stems and leaves. When touched by an animal the hairs break off releasing an acid which causes the sting. In the tree nettle, *Urtica ferox*, (above) which is native to New Zealand, the stings can be fatal. They are less serious in the common stinging nettle, *Urtica dioica*, (right). *Urtica* has single sexed flowers, normally with flowers of only one sex on each plant. This electron micrograph (magnification about fifty times) shows a female flower and several large stinging hairs. There are no brightly coloured petals—these are of no use to a wind-pollinated plant. Male flowers have four stamens which bend inwards towards the centre of the flower. When dried by the sun they suddenly contract catapulting the pollen into the air so that it can be more readily blown away by the wind.

Right: The cabbage—just one variety of species *Brassica oleraceae*.

species, *Rhipsalis baccifera*, which is found in Africa, although nobody knows how it arrived there. Another species, the prickly pear, *Opuntia vulgaris*, though native to the western states of the US, has become a weed in various parts of the world as a result of careless introduction. *Opuntia* was introduced into Australia as a hedge plant in 1839 but by the beginning of the twentieth century it covered four million hectares (ten million acres) making them useless for sheep grazing. By 1925 the infested area had increased to 24 million hectares (60 million acres). However in that year the moth *Cactoblastis cactorum* was released in the infested areas, and its caterpillars, by eating the *Opuntia*, cleared the grazing land so that the cactus now survives in Australia only as scattered colonies. The

use of an animal to control a pest or weed is called *biological control*.

A third family of xerophytes, the mesembryanthemum family, *Aizoaceae*, includes two genera, *Lithops* and *Conophytum*, which are notable for the way that they mimic the stones among which they grow. The chlorophyll bearing part of these plants is below ground level; the plants consist of a few swollen leaves the upper surfaces of which are translucent allowing light to pass down into the lower part of the leaf where the chlorophyll is found. *Lithops* and *Conophytum* can survive years of drought and produce large colourful flowers when rain eventually comes. Mesembryanthemum flowers appear at first glance to be similar to daisies, but are in fact far less complex.

Herbaceous Dicots—II

In adapting to different environments the flowering plants have developed in a bewildering variety of ways, both in growth habit and in structure. Flower structure, in particular, appears to be an extremely adaptable feature. From the earliest flowering plants, with simple regular flowers, evolution has generally been in the direction of increased complexity. Complex flowers tend to be irregular (*zygomorphic*), rather than regular (*actinomorphic*); to be grouped in *inflorescences*, rather than single; and to have flower parts joined together (such as the anthers fused together to form a tube, as in the *Compositae*) rather than separated.

The evolutionary pressure towards flower complexity is associated with the advantages to be gained by *cross-pollination*. Cross-pollination is one way in which plants can produce offspring which show variation in minor details of structure or physiology. Occasionally some of these offspring are better adapted to the environment than their parents. If these adaptations are advantageous enough, and particularly if the offspring are separated from their parents geographically, for example on islands, these adaptations may be incorporated in future generations and a new species may evolve.

Complex regular flowers

The most complex, and therefore the most highly evolved, flowers are zygomorphic, but many plant families have flowers which, though actinomorphic, are highly evolved in other ways in order to promote cross-pollination.

The primrose family, *Primulaceae*, has regular flowers which nevertheless have a complex structure related to their pollination by long-tongued insects, such as bees, and to a condition, called *heterostyly*, which increases the likelihood of cross-pollination. In a typical member of the family, the common primrose, *Primula vulgaris*, there are two slightly different types of flower. In both types the petals are used to make a *corolla* in the form of a tube. However, *pin* flowers have a long, slightly protruding, style with the anthers attached halfway down the corolla tube, while *thrum* flowers have a short style and the anthers are visible at the mouth of the tube. Pollen which is deposited on the back of an insect by the anthers of thrum flowers is liable to be deposited on the long style of pin flowers, while pollen deposited around the head of the insect by the anthers of pin flowers is liable to be deposited on the short style of thrum flowers.

As well as primroses, the primrose family includes a diverse range of flower and plant types, many of which, such as *Cyclamen* and *Dodecatheon*, are well known garden plants. Others are specialized to a particular habitat and are more rarely seen, for example the Alpine plants *Androsace* and *Soldanella*, and *Dionysia* from the mountains of the Middle East.

Another regular-flowered family, with an interesting structure adapted to one particular type of pollinating insect, is the milkweed family, *Asclepiadaceae*, whose common name derives from the milky sap which oozes out of the stems if they are damaged. The special feature of these plants is the pollen grains which are united into waxy bundles called *pollinia*. The arrangement of the stamens and nectaries is such that pairs of pollinia become attached to the legs of visiting insects, particularly flies, which are attracted to the flowers by their smell of rotting flesh.

Perhaps the most important complex-flowered dicot family from an economic viewpoint is the nightshade family, *Solanaceae*. It is a regular-flowered family and includes food plants, such as potato,

Giuseppe Mazza

NHPA

Left: The milkweed family, *Asclepiadaceae*, contains many members which attract pollinating insects (particularly bluebottle flies, *Calliphora*) by emitting a fetid odour. This is especially true of carrion flowers (shown here). This species, *Caraluma lutea*, is common throughout southern Africa.

Above: Cross-pollination is promoted in the begonia family, *Begoniaceae*, by having single-sex flowers which are either male or female. In tuberous-rooted garden begonias (shown here) male flowers are large and conspicuous while female flowers are smaller and are partly hidden by the foliage.

Below: *Thrum* (left) and *pin* (right) flowers of the primrose, *Primula*. Bees, feeding on nectar secreted at the bottom of the corolla tubes, transfer pollen from the long anthers of the thrum plants to the long styles of the pin plants, and from the short anthers of the pin plants to the short styles of the thrum plants.

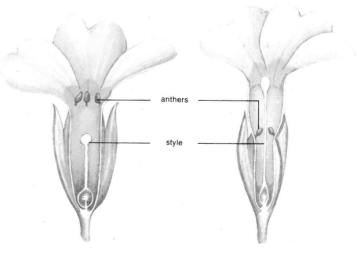

anthers

style

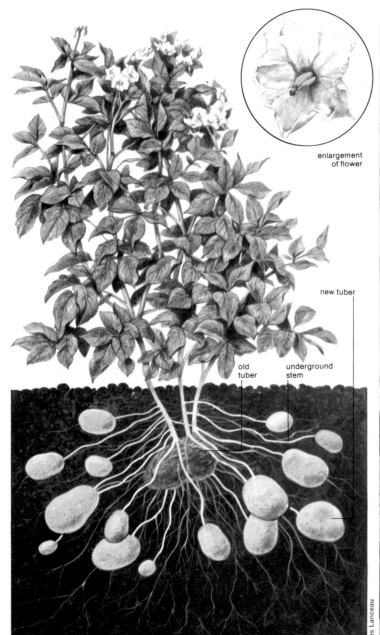

enlargement
of flower

new tuber

old
tuber

underground
stem

Above right: Pumpkins,
Cucurbita maxima, are
members of the cucumber
family, *Cucurbitaceae.*

Above: Potatoes, *Solanum
tuberosum*, are not
roots but swollen
sections of underground
stems, called *stem
tubers*, containing stores
of nutrient which the
plant lays down for its
next year's growth.
The 'eyes' of potatoes
are in fact buds from
which new plants are
produced in the spring.
Potatoes contain a lot
of starch, a little
protein, and a useful
amount of vitamin C
(*ascorbic acid*). Because
of their food value
and because they are easy
to grow, they are a
staple item of diet in
many parts of the world.

Left: Commercial
varieties of potato
produce far more food
than the plants require
for themselves. The
largest potato ever
grown weighed 3.2 kg
(7 lb 1 oz).

Right: Another member
of the same family,
Solanaceae, as the
potato is deadly
nightshade, *Atropa
belladonna*. The plant
contains a poison of
the nervous system.

Solanum tuberosum, tomato, *Lycopersicon esculentum*, and sweet pepper, *Capsicum*; wild plants, such as deadly nightshade, *Atropa belladonna*; and garden plants, like *Petunia*. The flower structure of this family varies but that of the potato is quite typical, with the white petals joined and spreading, and a group of projecting yellow anthers at the centre.

This family also includes the legendary mandrake, *Mandragora officinalis*. This is a perennial with bluish flowers, and fruits not unlike yellow tomatoes. The reputation of the plant derives from the taproot, which may be forked and more than 1 m (3 ft) long, so that it bears a distant resemblance to a human body. The root was valued by medieval herbalists as an anaesthetic and aphrodisiac, and the value of the plant may well have encouraged them to exaggerate the risks involved in digging it up. According to legend, the plant is supposed to shriek as the root is pulled out of the ground and the uprooter to be struck dead, so dogs used to be employed for this allegedly dangerous task. Mandrake grows naturally in southern Europe, in stony ground and neglected fields. It makes an interesting, and harmless, garden plant, notwithstanding its magical reputation.

Mints, figworts and lobelias

Though there are several complex regular-flowered families, most complex flowers are zygomorphic—they are symmetrical about only one plane. Three typically zygomorphic families are the mint family, *Labiatae*, the figwort family, *Scrophulariaceae*, and the lobelia family, *Lobeliaceae*.

The mint family includes familiar plants such as dead nettle, *Lamium*, thyme, *Thymus*, rosemary, *Rosmarinus officinalis*, and lavender, *Lavandula*, as well as many species of mint, *Mentha*. The plants often have stems with a roughly square cross-section and two leaves, or groups (*whorls*) of leaves, at each node. Most of the plants also have glands, sometimes seen as minute translucent dots on the leaves, which secrete volatile oils which give each species its own characteristic smell. The flowers, often called *two-lipped*, have a corolla in which the petals are united into two lobes, above and below the mouth of the flower. Many plants in the family are pollinated by bees. The bees land on the lower lip of the flower before extending their proboscises to reach the nectar deep inside.

The figwort family also has two-lipped flowers, typified by the snapdragon, *Antirrhinum*. Normally the entrance to an antirrhinum flower is completely blocked by the upper and lower lips of the corolla but humble bees, *Bombus terrestris*, are heavy enough to depress the lower lip and open the flower. Pollen is deposited on the bees' hairy backs as they feed on the nectar secreted at the bottom of the corolla tube.

The lobelia family includes many garden flowers, typical of which is the cardinal flower, *Lobelia cardinalis*, with its 1 m (3 ft) spike of scarlet flowers. Other members of the family are even more spectacular although they are never seen in temperate gardens. These are the giant lobelias of East Africa. Many species of these grotesque plants are known, most of them with a very limited distribution. For example, *Lobelia telekii* is found only in one valley on Mount Kenya, and *Lobelia deckenii* grows only on Mount Kilimanjaro in Tanzania. This is probably an instance of that common evolutionary phenomenon—the proliferation of new species on islands. In this case, however, the islands are not surrounded by sea, but are high mountains, above 3,000 m (10,000 ft), separated by lowland areas where these very specialized plants are unable to grow. On each separate mountain, adaptation to the local environment has resulted in a species very slightly different from that growing on the next mountain.

Because the East African mountains are close to the equator they receive a great deal of sunshine by day, but, because of their altitude, they quickly cool at night. Only well adapted plants can survive in these extreme conditions and the

Above left: A member of the figwort family, the foxglove, *Digitalis*. Foxglove leaves contain the chemical *digitalin* which makes the plant poisonous, though digitalin itself is used to make a drug important in the control of heart disease.

Left: Teasel, *Dipsacus*. Plants of the family to which teasel belongs, the scabious family, *Dipsacaceae*, are similar to members of the daisy family, *Compositae*. Both families have a composite flower head (inflorescence) made up of a mass of tiny individual flowers. Teasels can be distinguished from the thistles (*Compositae*) which they resemble by the spines (*bracts*), in a ring called an *involucre*, which surround the flower head.

Right: A typical composite, marguerite, *Chrysanthemum frutescens*. This is a common garden daisy. A wild daisy common by roadsides, the ox-eye daisy, *Chrysanthemum leucantheum*, is also sometimes known as marguerite.

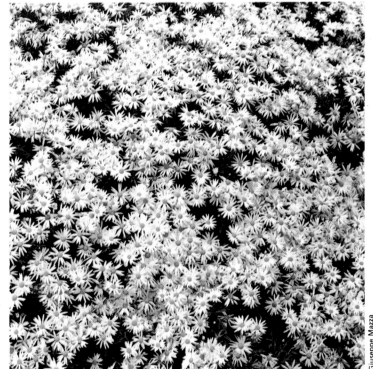

ZEFA

Giuseppe Mazza

91

lobelias have adapted so well that they often grow up to four metres (12 ft) tall, looking like small trees though they are not woody plants.

The stems and growing points of giant lobelias are hidden by a dense growth of leaves, up to 0.25 m (10 in) long, and these leaves protect the stems and growing points by insulating them from the very low night temperatures. For example, in an air temperature of $-5°C$ (23°F) the stem and flower temperature may be $2°C$ (36°F). Arctic and alpine plants of higher latitudes survive much harsher conditions while they are dormant in the winter but, unlike the giant lobelias, they do not experience extreme fluctuations of temperature every day of the year.

Daisy family

The dicot family with the most highly-evolved flowers is also the largest of flowering plant families. This family, the daisy family, *Compositae*, contains at least 13,000 species, about five per cent of all species of flowering plants. A few species are shrubs or small trees, but most are herbaceous and many are found in man-made habitats—as weeds on agricultural land or growing along roadsides and in abandoned pastures. Among these are the dandelion, *Taraxacum officinale*, the common daisy, *Bellis perennis*, the pineapple weed, *Matricaria matricarioides*, thistles, *Cirsium* and *Carduus*, and groundsels, *Senecio*. Like lobelias, giant groundsels, too, are found in East Africa.

Many other members of the daisy family are familiar as garden plants: Michaelmas daisies, *Aster*, and golden rod, *Solidago*, for example, and also *Chrysanthemum* and *Cineraria*. Not surprisingly, the family supplies food plants as well, and these include lettuce, *Lactuca*, and sunflower, *Helianthus annuus*. Sunflowers are grown for their seeds, from which oil is extracted, while the leaves and stems are fed to cattle, either fresh or made into silage. They are widely cultivated in continental Europe and Russia.

It is not easy to account for the huge success, in evolutionary terms, of the *Compositae*. One reason may be the adaptation of the flower and inflorescence for insect pollination. The family receives its name from the composite flower-head, a kind of inflorescence called a *capitulum*. In each flower the anthers are fused into a tube around the style. They shed their pollen into this tube, and the style, which is often ringed with hairs, then grows up and carries the pollen up above the tube. Any visiting insect becomes dusted with pollen, while at this stage the stigma, at the end of the style, is not exposed and self-pollination is impossible. Later on, the tip of the style divides and the two halves curl back to reveal the stigma which can then be cross-pollinated by another visiting insect. But if insects are lacking, the stigma curls back even further, far enough to collect some of the flower's own pollen. In this way self-pollination is virtually certain to take place if cross-pollination fails.

Another reason for the success of the *Compositae* is their seed dispersal mechanism. The sepals of each flower in the capitulum are often modified into a tuft of fine hairs attached to the seed. These are easily caught and blown away by the wind—as dandelion seed-heads show very well.

Above: The mystical and symbolic properties once ascribed to plants often stemmed from improperly understood scientific facts. This seventeenth century illustration describes how the 'magnetism' of the sun makes a sunflower follow the sun—allowing the flower to be used to tell the time of day.

Herbaceous plants are sometimes known simply as herbs, but the word 'herb' is more often used to describe plants whose leaves are used, either fresh or dried, as a flavouring for food. 'Spices' are the dried parts of plants other than leaves.

Right: The seventeenth century herb garden of Altdorf University, Bavaria. The early study of plants was closely associated with their medical and herbal uses.

Basil
Ocimum basilicum

Oregano
Origanum majorana

Coriander
Coriandrum sativum

Below: Fruits of cumin, *Cuminum cyminum*. The plant is a member of the parsley family, *Umbelliferae*. It has finely divided leaves and white or yellow flowers. Cumin is widely used in curry powder and for seasoning bread and cakes. The seeds also yield an oil which is used in perfumery.

Right: Herbs and spices belong to a wide range of plant families but especially to the mints, *Labiatae*. Those here are:
Basil—*Labiatae*
Bay—*Lauraceae*
Mint—*Labiatae*
Oregano—*Labiatae*
Rosemary—*Labiatae*
Cloves—*Myrtaceae*
Coriander—*Umbelliferae*
Ginger—*Zingiberaceae*
Pepper—*Piperaceae*

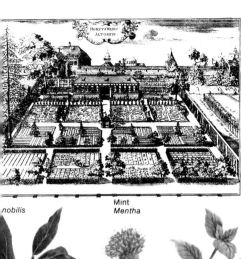

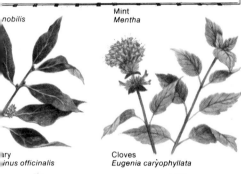

nobilis

Mint
Mentha

ary
inus officinalis

Cloves
Eugenia caryophyllata

officinale

Pepper
Piper nigrum

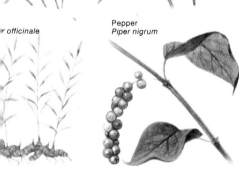

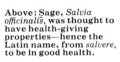

Above: Sage, *Salvia officinalis*, was thought to have health-giving properties—hence the Latin name, from *salvere*, to be in good health.

Left: Nutmeg is produced from the dried seed of *Myristica fragrans*. The seed is enclosed inside a fruit consisting of an outer yellow *pericarp*, an inner crimson *aril*, and a thin shell-like *endocarp*. When ripe the pericarp splits to reveal the aril. The seed and endocarp are removed and slowly dried. The endocarp is then broken and the seed, the nutmeg, removed.

Right: Sieving and refining mustard. Mustard is prepared from the powdered seeds of black mustard, *Brassica nigra*. (White mustard, *Sinapis alba*, is the mustard of 'mustard and cress'.) The seeds are first blended and then crushed to separate the husks from the kernels. The kernels are then ground to a powder on rollers and this powder is refined by passing it through a series of silk screens. *Turmeric*, a colouring agent, is then added.

Flowering Trees and Shrubs

The naturally dominant vegetation of any moderately wet and fertile area is forest. Trees are capable of producing a tall leaf canopy which overshadows other plants. In colder northern regions these trees are normally gymnosperms, but in more hospitable warm temperate and tropical areas they are almost always angiosperms. They are dicots, but have retained the tree characteristics which were probably normal among the earliest flowering plants, rather than evolving into herbaceous forms.

The trunks and branches that form the framework of trees and shrubs are built up over years of growth, with a gradual increase in girth. Typically this increase is about 25 mm (1 in) a year (measuring around the trunk at 1.5 m (5 ft) above the ground.) Some species grow much faster than this, in particular species of *Eucalyptus*. Others, including horse chestnut, *Aesculus hippocastanum*, and the common

Above left: Female catkins of the common sallow (goat willow), *Salix caprea*. Members of the willow family, *Salicaceae*, which also includes poplars, *Populus*, have flowers in catkins but each plant has flowers of one sex only. Willows may be large trees, such as the cricket bat willow, a variety of *Salix alba*; shrubby trees, such as osier, *Salix viminalis*; or dwarf shrubs like creeping willow, *Salix repens*. Poplars are often large, fast growing trees, such as some varieties of black poplar, *Populus nigra*.

Left: Cork oak, *Quercus suber*. Its thick rugged bark is the world's principal source of cork.

lime, *Tilia × europea*, grow more slowly. Young trees usually grow more rapidly than average; old trees more slowly.

The growth of a woody trunk or stem involves a process known as *secondary thickening*. In both dicots and gymnosperms there is a ring of vascular bundles in the stem towards the outer surface. In older stems and branches this ring of individual vascular bundles becomes a continuous ring of conducting tissue, with phloem on the outside, xylem on the inside, and a layer of cambium in between. The cells of the cambium continue to divide to produce new xylem and phloem cells and the stem grows outwards by the laying down of successive layers of xylem tissue. In cold and temperate regions the xylem cells produced in spring are relatively large, with thin walls, but as the growing season progresses the new

cells are smaller, with thicker, darker walls. Thus over a number of years the wood comes to have a series of *annual rings*, each being a band of darker *autumn wood* separated by the lighter *spring wood*. When a tree trunk is sawn across, these rings are clearly visible and by counting them the age of the tree can be found. Trees growing in the tropics, without pronounced seasons, have either irregular rings, corresponding to periods of good and bad weather rather than to years of age, or no rings at all.

Increase in the height or spread, rather than the girth, of a tree or shrub takes place by a different process, called *terminal growth*, which occurs at the tips of the branches. In the autumn, growth ceases and *winter buds* form. Each bud consists of a growing point covered by a number of *bud scales* which are modified

leaves. The bud usually contains part or all of the following year's new leaves and flowers, and the bud scales protect them from the extremes of the winter. In tropical and sub-tropical species whose growth continues throughout the year, winter buds do not form.

Temperate tree families

There is no hard-and-fast dividing line between dicot families which include trees and shrubs and those which include only herbaceous plants. Many families include both—suggesting that, if herbaceous plants evolved from woody plants, then this evolution must have taken place on many separate occasions. Nevertheless, many families consist predominantly of trees and shrubs.

The tree family that contains plants probably most similar to the earliest angiosperms is the magnolia family, *Magnoliaceae*. Like the simple herbaceous family, the water-lilies, *Nymphaeaceae*, they have flowers with many separate petals and stamens. The flowers are valued by gardeners for their large size and delicate pink or cream colouring.

Beeches, *Fagus*, sweet chestnuts, *Castanea*, and oaks, *Quercus*, all belong to one family, the *Fagaceae*. These are mostly

94

Left: The majestic English elm, *Ulmus procera*. Unfortunately elm trees are susceptible to a fungal disease, 'Dutch' elm disease, *Cerotocystis ulmi*, spread by a bark beetle, *Scolytus scolytus*. Periodic outbreaks have killed large numbers of trees. For example, one such outbreak, which started in 1970, killed most of the prominent hedgerow elms in large areas of England. Chemical control of the disease is impracticable for the millions of trees growing in the countryside and in the long term it is probably better to reduce the impact of epidemics by planting different trees to replace the elms.

Right: Common (or European) beech, *Fagus sylvatica*. Beeches, oaks, *Quercus*, and sweet chestnuts, *Castanea*, all belong to the same family, the beech family, *Fagaceae*.

Below: Scanning electron micrograph (about 700 times life size) of the *xylem* (wood) of lupin, *Lupinus*. The thickened rings around the xylem vessels give strength to the wood.

G. R. Roberts

Giuseppe Mazza

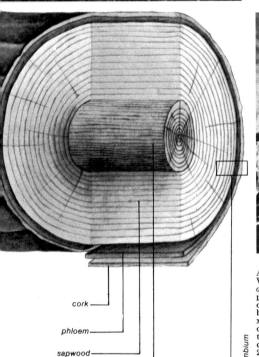

Dr Gordon Leedale/Biophoto Associates

cork
phloem
sapwood
heartwood
cambium

Above left and below: Wood is made up of *annual rings* of xylem produced by a thin layer of cells, the *cambium*, between the phloem and xylem. The cells of the xylem continue to function as water-conducting tissue for 20-30 years. During this time, however, they eventually become *lignified*—filling up with a substance, called *lignin*, which gives strength to the wood but prevents the passage of water. The outer, functional xylem forms a pale zone called the *sapwood*. The central lignified zone, often darker in colour, is called the *heartwood*. The *cork* (bark) is a protective layer of dead impermeable cells.

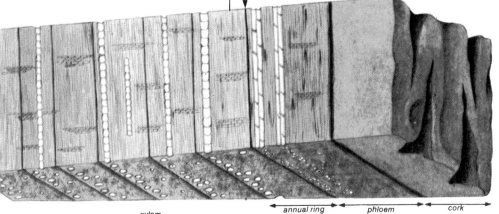

xylem ← annual ring → phloem → cork →

deciduous forest trees, with simple leaves and separate male and female flowers on the same tree. The flowers are grouped into inflorescences of petal-less flowers, called *catkins*, and appear early in the year, often before the leaves. The pollen is carried by the wind from male to female catkins, making cross-pollination very likely where a number of trees of the same species are present. After fertilization the female flowers produce *nuts*, hard-walled fruits dispersed by the animals which use them as a source of food.

Over 450 species of oak grow in Europe, Asia or America. Two are native to Britain and Northern Europe. The sessile oak, *Quercus petraea*, has acorns carried directly on the twigs (which is what the word 'sessile' means), while the pedunculate oak, *Quercus robur*, has stalked acorns. Pedunculate oak is often planted in areas where sessile oak is the naturally occurring wild-growing species and, since the two species interbreed freely, intermediate types are common.

Beeches, *Fagus*, are also widespread. They are particularly common on steep, chalk-based hillsides, such as the Chiltern hills in southern England, although they are found in most north temperate regions; while a related genus, the southern beeches, *Nothofagus*, are common in the southern hemisphere. Beech nuts (*mast*) are enclosed in a prickly husk. 'Copper beech' is a variety of the most common northern species, *Fagus sylvatica*, but has dark, purplish foliage.

Elms, *Ulmus*, belong to another family, the *Ulmaceae*. They are important timber trees but are perhaps more important for their contribution to the scenery in both Europe and North America. They are particularly common hedgerow trees, and, although elm flowers have inconspicuous greenish petals, the stamens have bright red filaments, so that the branches of an elm in flower appear red at a distance. The flowers are wind-pollinated, and the fruits, consisting of a seed surrounded by a circular papery wing, are dispersed by the wind. However, the fruits are often sterile. Most elm trees originate

Sycamore
Acer pseudoplatanus

London plane
Platanus acerifolia

Midland hawthorn
Crataegus oxycanthoides

Above: Trees are capable of enlivening a drab urban scene. These six trees are common in British towns:—
Sycamore is sometimes regarded as an urban weed as it produces masses of winged seeds which often germinate in unlikely places. *Midland hawthorn* is generally planted as a hedging plant, mainly because of its 3 cm (1 in) thorns. *London plane* for many epitomizes the town tree, thriving in central London. Characteristically the dark soiled bark peels off in strips, revealing pale new bark beneath. *Lime*, though often mutilated and 'lollipopped', is in fact a stately tree with yellow-green, heart-shaped leaves. *Flowering cherry* unfailingly produces a mass of colour in the spring. The variety 'Kanzan' is grown by grafting buds on to a rootstock of wild cherry, *Prunus avium*. *Red horsechestnut* is a hybrid between white horsechestnut, *Aesculus hippocastanum*, and American red buck-eye, *Aesculus pavia*.

as suckers thrown up by neighbouring trees.

The family with the hardiest of all flowering trees is the birch family, *Betulaceae*, which includes alder, *Alnus*, and birches, *Betula*. One especially hardy birch is the dwarf birch, *Betula nana*, a small shrub with glossy, circular leaves which grows at high altitudes in northern Europe. Birches generally are small, fast-growing trees which are often the first to colonize open areas of land.

A closely related family to the birches is the *Corylaceae*, which includes hornbeam, *Carpinus betulus*, and hazel, *Corylus avellana*. Hornbeam is somewhat similar in appearance to beech, but its leaves have serrated rather than smooth edges, and the fruit is a cluster of winged seeds rather than a nut.

A final family of temperature woody plants is the heath family, *Ericaceae*, important more for shrubs than for trees. Most members of the family are evergreen shrubs, including *Rhododendron*, and many different kinds of heather, *Calluna* and *Erica*. Heathers and other dwarf ericaceous shrubs are the dominant plants over large areas of heathland, a vegetation type that is widespread in temperate areas and which also occurs on mountains in the tropics.

Tropical food trees

Several woody families include tropical plants from which are obtained food or drinks. Tea comes from the shrub *Cam-*

ellia sinensis of the family *Theaceae*. It has been cultivated in China for at least 3,000 years. Both ordinary black teas and green teas are made from its leaves, but by different processes of withering (drying), roasting, fermentation and pressing. Coffee comes mainly from *Coffea arabica* (family *Rubiaceae*) which originally grew wild in Ethiopia. Another species, *Coffea canephora*, produces the inferior 'robusta' coffee. Coffee plants carry red berries, and the 'coffee beans', which are the seeds, are extracted from inside the berries.

Cocoa, a native of tropical America, but now widely grown in West Africa, comes from a small tree called *Theobroma cacao* (family *Sterculiaceae*). The tree is unusual in that the flowers and fruits grow directly from the trunk and main branches rather than on side

Left: A group of alders, *Alnus*, in their most common habitat—beside water. Alders, which are members of the birch family, *Betulaceae*, have two remarkable features: they are the only flowering trees to produce 'cones', and they have symbiotic nodules on their roots. The 'cones' are not true cones as produced by gymnosperms but fruits which develop from the fertilized female catkins. The root nodules, probably formed by an *Actinomycetes* fungus, provide the alder with a supply of nitrogen which may be in short supply in the poor, boggy soils in which the tree grows.

Below: *Anthocyanins* in the leaves of sugar maples, *Acer saccharum*, turns them golden red in autumn. Maples, *Aceraceae*, occur in America, Asia and Europe. Sugar maples are native to North America, particularly New England. The most common European maples are sycamores, *Acer pseudoplatanus*, and Norway maples, *Acer platanoides*.

Heather Angel

branches. The cocoa beans, of which 40-60% is a fat called *cocoa butter*, are enclosed in red or yellow pods. They can be processed in several ways: to make cocoa for drinking, in which case part of the fat is removed; or to make chocolate, in which case extra cocoa butter, sugar and milk are added.

Many tropical trees yield edible fruits, but the papaya, *Carica papaya* (family *Caricaceae*), is unusual in several ways. The trees grow rapidly from seed and bear fruit in the first year. After 3-4 years they may reach a height of 6 m (20 ft), but their fruit-bearing then declines and they must be replaced. Male and female flowers are borne on separate trees. The female trees produce an edible fruit, something like a melon, which is a greenish-yellow outside but has orange flesh. The sap is also useful. It contains an enzyme, *papain*,

Common lime
Tilia x europea

Flowering cherry
Prunus "Kanzan"

Red horsechestnut
Aesculus x carnea

NHPA

Left: Two ghost gums, *Eucalyptus papuana,* **growing near Alice Springs in central Australia. The name 'eucalyptus' comes from the Greek** *eu,* **well, and** *kalyptos,* **covered. It refers to the cap, formed from the joined sepals and petals, which covers the stamens while the flower is in bud. This cap falls off when the flower opens.**

Right: Two fruits: (top) sweet chestnut, *Castanea sativa;* **(bottom) mango,** *Mangifera indica.* **The sweet chestnut (family** *Fagaceae***) is a common woodland species in north temperate regions but, although once planted it grows well in northern regions, it is really a warm temperate species—it does not produce ripe seed further north than the Midlands of England. The mango (family** *Anacardiaceae***) is a large evergreen tree up to 27 m (90 ft) tall —though cultivated varieties may be smaller—producing the fruit sometimes known as the 'tropical apple'. The fruit is eaten raw, cooked as an ingredient of chutney, or occasionally canned.**

Eric Crichton

G. R. Roberts

which can break down protein. Papain is collected on a commercial scale and used, among other things, to tenderize meat.

Tropical and sub-tropical timber trees
Other tropical families contain species which are valuable for their timber. Among the better known of these timbers are mahogany, from *Swietenia mahogani* (family *Meliaceae*), teak, from *Tectona grandis* (family *Verbenaceae*) and ebony, from *Diospyros ebenum* (family *Ebenaceae*). In sub-tropical areas, species of *Eucalyptus* (family *Myrtaceae*) are becoming increasingly important as timber trees. Eucalypts, or gum trees, are native to Australasia, and are unusual in that they have two kinds of foliage. The foliage found on young plants consists of large rounded leaves clasping the stem. The adult foliage has smaller, lanceolate

(long and narrow), stalked leaves. Eucalypts can grow extremely quickly, up to 10 m (33 ft) a year; one species, *Eucalyptus regnans,* grows to more than 105 m (340 ft), making it the tallest of all flowering trees.

The baobab, *Adansonia digitata* (family *Bombacaceae*) does not grow as fast as *Eucalyptus,* but is one of the oddest-looking trees, having a massive trunk up to 40 m (130 ft) in girth, surmounted by a comparatively sparse crown, as if it had been stuck into the ground with its roots waving in the air. For this reason, it is sometimes called the 'upside-down-tree'. The largest baobabs are around 1,000 years old, and old trees are treated with some reverence—but not by elephants, which frequently kill them. The trunks of baobabs store water and may contain over 100,000 litres (20,000 gallons).

Other uses of flowering trees
Flowering trees are important for food and for their timber. They also have a number of other uses, such as the production of cork, rubber and tannin. Further uses are more exotic. Around the Red Sea, for example, a small twisted tree, *Boswellia thurifera,* (family *Burseraceae*) produces a resin which is collected by making an incision in the tree's trunk. As the resin oozes out it gradually hardens and after about three months can be scraped off as hard, translucent lumps, 1-2 cm ($\frac{3}{8}$-$\frac{3}{4}$ in) across. These lumps are the most important constituent of frankincense, which for thousands of years has been an important item of commerce in the Middle East. It is burnt in houses and churches all over the world. A high-yielding incense tree may be the jealously guarded property of a Somali family.

The Rose, Pea and Spurge Families

It is generally recognized that herbaceous dicots have evolved from woody ancestors. But if this is so it must have occurred on many unrelated occasions, for many dicot families contain both herbaceous and woody species. Three such families are particularly important—both because of the number of their species and economically. They are the rose family, *Rosaceae*, the pea family, *Leguminosae*, and the spurge family, *Euphorbiaceae*.

Within these three families evolutionary adaptation to different environments has produced a diverse range of floral and vegetative structure. This is most conspicuous among the *Rosaceae*, which range from trees with complete flowers and simple leaves, such as the apple tree, *Malus*, to herbaceous plants with compound leaves and small flowers which lack petals, such as the lady's-mantle, *Alchemilla*. Nevertheless, despite this range of structure, it is possible to trace patterns of similarity within each family that confirm its common origin. *Rosaceae*, for example, have leaf-like outgrowths, called *stipules*, at the base of the leaves; most of the *Euphorbiaceae* have systems of vessels in their stems which secrete a milky white liquid, called *latex*; and the *Leguminosae* have root nodules containing symbiotic nitrogen-fixing bacteria.

Fruits and seeds

The *Euphorbiaceae* are economically important mainly because the family includes the rubber tree, *Hevea brasiliensis*, while the *Rosaceae* and the *Leguminosae*

Apple
Malus

Walnut
Juglans regia

Oak
Quercus

Tomato
Lycopersicion
esculentum

Strawberry
Fragaria

Pomegranate
Punica granatum

Whe
Tritic
aest

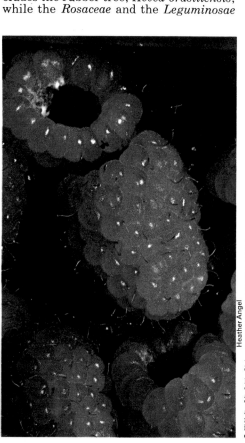

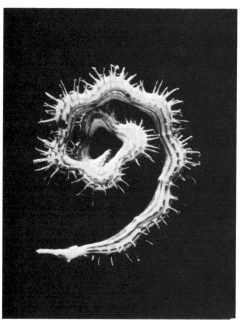

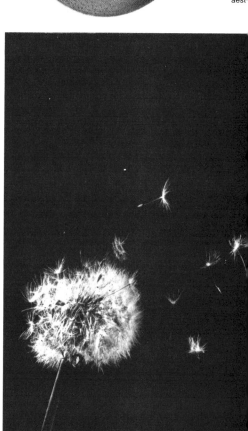

Left, above and right: To be successful a plant species must ensure that its seeds are widely dispersed. Three types of dispersal are shown here. The raspberry, *Rubus*, (left) is a succulent fruit eaten and dispersed by animals. Medick, *Medicago*, (above) is also dispersed by animals—but in this case by hooks that cling to animals' coats. Dandelion, *Taraxacum*, seeds (right) have a tuft of hairs to aid wind dispersal.

Orange
Citrus
sinensis

Sycamore
Acer

Avocado
Persea americana

Left: Fruits are one of the most diverse features of flowering plants. Some of this diversity is shown here. Succulent fruits, which are eaten and dispersed by animals, include *pomes* (such as apple and avocado), *berries* (tomato, grape, orange, melon and pomegranate, *drupes* (almond) and *syconi* (fig). Dry fruits include *samaras* (sycamore), *cypselas* (sunflower), *capsules* (poppy) and *caryopses* (wheat). A wheat grain is both fruit and seed intimately fused together. The syconus of the fig is a particularly complex fruit—it is formed not from a single flower but from an inflorescence of many individual flowers.

Poppy
Papaver

Grape
Vitis vinifera

Fig
Ficus carica

Sunflower
Helianthus
annuus

Water Melon
Citrullus vulgaris

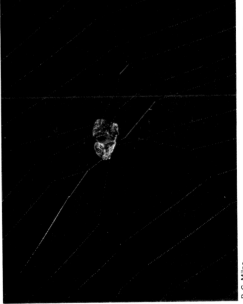

Left: 'Explosive' dispersal. The fruit of the Mediterranean cranesbill, *Erodium botrys*, has a long 'beak' which twists as the fruit ripens. The beak suddenly breaks, throwing the seed at its tip into the air.

Above: Birch, *Betula*, nuts weigh about 0.0002 g (0.000006 oz) and are easily blown long distances by the wind —barring spiders' webs.

Right: A dormouse unwittingly dispersing blackberry, *Rubus*.

Eric Crichton

G. R. Roberts

Left: Plums, damsons, apricots, almonds and cherries all belong to one genus, *Prunus*. The wild species from which thay were originally cultivated is unknown, but a relative is the sloe, *Prunus spinosa*.

Above: The Australian desert pea, *Clianthus formosus*. The plant is specialized to survive in a dry habitat.

Below: In general, rose flowers have five sepals, five petals and many stamens, while the seeds are carried inside a fleshy, urn-shaped *receptacle* at the base of the flower below the sepals. In wild roses, such as *Rosa rugosa x roxburgii*, (shown here) the receptacles turn bright red or orange as the fruits ripen and are called *rose-hips*. Garden roses are often sterile, however, and in these varieties the ripe rose-hips may not form. Garden roses also often have extra petals which obscure the simple regularity of the wild flower. Rose-hips are eaten by birds, so dispersing the seeds which are indigestible.

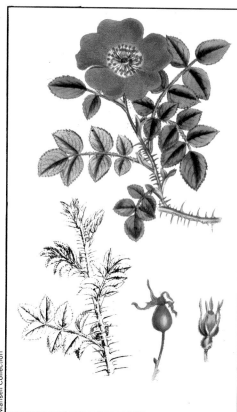

Mansell Collection

100

are important largely because of the use of the fruits and seeds of some member plants as food. Peas and beans (*Leguminosae*) are seeds, while apples and pears (*Rosaceae*) are fruits. There is a distinct difference between seeds and fruits. *Seeds* develop from the female gamete (normally after fertilization) inside the ovary; *fruits* develop from the ovary wall (and occasionally from other parts of the flower as well) outside the seed.

The evolution of fruits is a major reason why flowering plants have become the dominant land vegetation. They have evolved in a number of ways each designed to produce widespread dispersal of the seeds contained inside them. Many have developed wings so that they can be more easily dispersed by the wind; others have developed hooks which attach to passing animals; while a third group, belonging to waterside plants, have developed so that they float on water and can be carried along by water currents.

The most economically important group of fruits, however, produce succulent tissue which is food to animals including man. The seeds, which are normally either inedible or indigestible, are dispersed as the fruits are collected and eaten.

The rose family

The family which is perhaps the most important for its fruit bearing members is the rose family, *Rosaceae*. It includes, among others, apples, *Malus*, pears, *Pyrus*, raspberries, *Rubus*, strawberries, *Fragaria*, plums and cherries, *Prunus*, as well as roses, *Rosa*.

Roses have some of the features which are characteristic of the *Rosaceae*, although few features are common to all of the family's 3,000 species. The only common features, in fact, are leaves with stipules and regular flowers. As well as

these features roses have compound leaves—that is leaves divided into leaflets—and stems which are usually prickly, each thorn being a woody outgrowth of the outer layer of tissue, the *epidermis*. These thorns are modifications of the hairs which are found on the surfaces of most plants. They protect the plant from being eaten by animals.

Roses are most widely grown purely for decoration but they do have a few other uses. Rose fruits, called *hips*, contain ascorbic acid (vitamin C) and are used to make *rose-hip syrup*, and in Bulgaria the damask rose, *Rosa damascena*, is cultivated on a large scale for the manufacture of *attar of roses*, an oil used in perfumery. Some 2,000 rose flowers have to be distilled to yield just 1g (0.03 oz) of the oil.

Brambles, *Rubus*, belong to another genus of *Rosaceae*, and they are often found in habitats similar to those of the roses. Unlike roses, however, they do not have a rose-hip but a composite fruit, typified by the familiar blackberry, which is composed of a lot of small fruits, called *drupelets*.

The common bramble, or blackberry, is also interesting because it shows *apomixis*, a kind of reproduction in which flowers are produced in the normal way but seeds and fruits develop *without* fertilization. This means that the seeds grow into plants that are identical to the parent plant, just as if they had been grown vegetatively from cuttings. In this way minor structural differences between plants are propagated unaltered into succeeding generations. At least 2,000 of these different kinds of blackberries have been given names as separate species, but these names have little meaning or usefulness and the normal practice is to describe the blackberry as an *aggregate species* under the name *Rubus*

G. R. Roberts

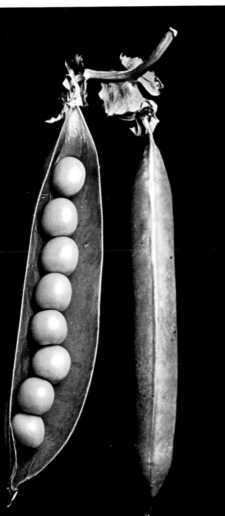

Eric Crichton

Above: A decorative legume—lupin, *Lupinus*. Here garden plants have 'escaped' to grow wild.

Left: The garden pea, *Pisum sativum*. Other cultivated legumes, or *pulses*, are the soya bean, *Glycine max*, chick pea, *Cicer arietinum*, lentil, *Lens culinaris*, broad bean, *Vicia faba*, and several species and varieties of *Phaseolus*, including runner and haricot beans. All are important sources of protein and all, like all legumes, possess symbiotic, nitrogen-fixing bacteria in nodules on their roots. This allows high crop yields to be obtained without expensive dressings of nitrogen fertilizer.

fruticosus. Cultivated brambles include raspberry, *Rubus idaeus*, and loganberry, *Rubus loganobaccus*.

Several other trees and shrubs in the rose family are common wild plants in northern temperate regions. Among these are *Crataegus*, hawthorn, and *Sorbus*, which includes rowan and whitebeam. Herbaceous plants are fewer but one of particular interest is the strawberry, *Fragaria*. Apart from its fruits strawberry can be recognized by its habit of sending out long runners, or *stolons*. The stolons are actually fast-growing horizontal stems which take root and grow into a series of new plants. Cultivated strawberries originated as hybrids between two American species, *Fragaria virginiana* from the east and *Fragaria chiloensis* from the west.

Fruit trees

Like raspberries and strawberries, most common types of fruit tree belong to the rose family. Wild forms of two of these, the crab apple, *Malus pumila*, and the wild pear, *Pyrus communis*, grow wild all over Europe, although the fruits of the wild forms bear little resemblance to the highly selected varieties of apples and pears normally cultivated. These varieties have been developed by gardeners over many thousands of years.

Perhaps the best eating variety, 'Cox's Orange Pippin', was first produced as a seedling from the old variety 'Ribston Pippin' in about 1850. Other old varieties, such as the 'Russets', can also often be bought but modern varieties, such as 'Golden Delicious' and 'McIntosh', crop more heavily, particularly in southern Europe, Australia and North America. Cooking varieties, such as 'Bramley', contain relatively more acid and less sugar, while cider apples have a high tannin content which gives a slight bitterness to the drink.

Plums, damsons, apricots, almonds and cherries all belong to one genus, *Prunus*. As with apples and pears, edible *Prunus* species have been cultivated for at least 3,000 years. Two other small trees in the *Rosaceae* are also cultivated for their fruit, though on a much smaller scale. The quince, *Cydonia vulgaris*, produces a hard yellowish pear-shaped fruit, which is somewhat acid and therefore used for making jam or jelly—the Spanish name of the quince, *marmelo*, is the origin of the word marmalade. The medlar, *Mespilus germanica*, is a small spreading tree with twisted branches. It bears round brown fruits which are eaten when they are half rotten or *bletted*.

The pea family

The most striking characteristic of the pea family is the fruit. It is formed from the cylindrical ovary which splits into two halves to disclose a row of spherical seeds. Typical of such a fruit is the ordinary garden pea pod. The pod is called a *legume*, and plants of this family are often referred to as 'legumes'.

Many crop plants are legumes. Particularly important is the groundnut, *Arachis hypogaea*, which is grown all over the tropics and sub-tropics, and also in the US as far north as Virginia. Sometimes called the peanut or monkey-nut, it is an 101

G. Mazza

G. Mazza

Above: *Acalypha hispida*, an ornamental member of the spurge family, *Euphorbiaceae*. *Acalypha hispida* and its close relative, *Acalypha wilkesiana*, are widely cultivated for their long, flaming red inflorescences. Some varieties also have *variegated* leaves— that is leaves partly lacking chlorophyll.

Above: African acacias, like *Acacia xanthophloea* (shown here), possess spines which develop from modified stipules at the bases of the leaf stalks. Spines protect the acacias from animals such as antelopes. In Australia, however, there are few large grazing animals and Australian acacias, or *wattles*, lack spines.

annual plant which grows either into a small bush, 45 cm (18 in) high, or trails over the ground. It has small yellow flowers, which are usually self-pollinated. After pollination the flower stalks elongate, pushing the developing seed pods into the soil, and the nuts ripen underground.

Groundnuts, removed from their fibrous pods, are an important food in much of the world, because they contain 30 per cent protein and from 40 to 50 per cent oil, as well as vitamins B and E. They can be eaten raw, cooked, or ground to make peanut butter. Groundnut oil is used as a cooking oil and for making margarine.

As well as pulses (legumes with edible seeds, like peas, beans and lentils) the pea family contains about 13,000 other species and is often divided into three sub-families, only one of which, the *Papilionoideae* (meaning 'butterfly flowers'), has the characteristic pea flowers. These irregular (*zygomorphic*) flowers have ten stamens and five petals. The uppermost petal is large and spreading, the two lateral ones are narrower and directed forwards, and the two lowest are partly fused and enclose the ovary and stamens. Nine of the ten stamens are also fused to form a trough surrounding the ovary, but the uppermost one is free.

This distinctive flower structure encourages cross-pollination by long-tongued insects, such as bees, which are also heavy enough to depress and force apart the petals enclosing the stamens. Having done this, a bee can then reach the nectar which is secreted into the trough formed by the fused stamens. In the process, pollen is dusted on to the hairs of the bee's body by the free stamen and is carried to other flowers, so promoting cross-pollination, for most insects tend to visit a number of plants of the same species in succession. Despite this,

Ann Ronan Picture Library

Above: The castor oil plant, *Ricinus communis*, showing flowers and fruit. Inside the fruit are three seeds from which castor oil is obtained. Medicinal castor oil must be extracted from cold seeds, otherwise it is poisonous. The seeds themselves are also poisonous—eating more than three may be fatal. The industrial oil, obtained from heated seeds, is used in hydraulic fluids.

however, many species are self-pollinated.

Pulses belong to the *Papilionoideae* as do several common wild flowers including gorse, *Ulex*, broom, *Cytisus*, and birdsfoot trefoil, *Lotus*. Two other *Papilionoideae*, lucerne (alfalfa), *Medicago sativa*, and clover, *Trifolium*, are common forage plants.

The two other sub-families of *Leguminosae* grow mainly in tropical and subtropical regions and are mostly trees or shrubs. The largest of the two, the *Mimosoideae*, has eight clusters of small regular (*actinomorphic*) flowers, and numerous stamens that project beyond the petals, giving the clusters a feathery appearance. One genus of *Mimosoideae*, *Acacia*, is especially common in South and Central America, Africa and Australia. These trees are interesting because

of the spines which generally develop from modified stipules at the base of the leaf stalks. In some species, called *ant-acacias*, the bases of the spines are inflated and hollow, and inhabited by ants. These ants help the tree to survive. They feed on sugar secreted by the tree but also eat any other plants which grow nearby.

The third sub-family of the *Leguminosae*, the *Caesalpinioideae*, is smaller than the other two sub-families but includes one of the most spectacular tropical flowering trees. *Amherstia nobilis* is a small tree, growing to 10 m (33 ft). It is pollinated by birds which it attracts with clusters of between 20 and 30 large flowers, each about 70 mm (3 in) across.

The spurge family

There are some 3,000 species in the spurge family of which about a third belong to one genus, *Euphorbia*, which contains many plants which contain compounds with a purgative action—hence the name 'spurge'. Most plants in this family are poisonous. Other family characteristics include single-sexed flowers which lack petals, three-celled ovaries, and the production of latex.

Species of *Euphorbia* have several male flowers and one female flower clustered together into an inflorescence, called a *cyathium*, which is surrounded by small flat petal-like structures. The cyathium is the one common characteristic of *Euphorbia*; it links together what is otherwise, both structurally and ecologically, a very diverse collection of plants. For instance, temperate euphorbias, such as sea spurge, *Euphorbia paralias*, which grows on beaches and sand dunes, are mostly herbs or shrubs, while in Africa many *Euphorbia* species in dry areas look like cactuses, having swollen succulent stems with spines and no leaves.

Grasses

About 80 per cent of all known flowering plant species are dicots. The remaining 20 per cent (about 55,000 species in all) belong to the other major group of angiosperms, the *Monocotyledonae*, or more simply the *monocots*. The monocots are generally recognized as being the most highly evolved of all plants and they include orchids, lilies and irises as well as grasses, sedges and rushes. It is the grass family which provides man with his most valuable food and forage crops.

In the 65 million years since they first evolved the monocots have developed along two main and diverging pathways. One of these, typified by the orchids, *Orchidaceae*, is towards extremely elaborate and specialized flower structures to promote cross-pollination by insects. The other, typified by the grasses, *Gramineae*, it towards simplified flowers, often with the petals and sepals missing altogether.

It is the second of these groups, the grasses, which is probably the most important of all plant families. Grasses, either as cereals or as forage for livestock, are the basic source of food for most of the world's population. No other plant family is cultivated to anything like the same extent. The grasses are also one of the larger families of flowering plants, containing more than 8,000 species in over 600 genera. They provide one quarter of the world's vegetation cover.

Despite their importance, however, grasses are rarely conspicuous: different species often look very much the same. The major reason for this uniformity is that grasses have no need for sepals, petals or other brightly coloured structures to attract pollinating insects. Instead the flowers of grasses are very well adapted for wind-pollination. They have three stamens, and a single ovary—containing a single ovule from which develops the *grain*, or seed—with two styles. Each style terminates in a feathery

ZEFA

Above: The most important food crops are cultivated grasses or *cereals*. The most important tropical and sub-tropical cereal is rice, *Oryza sativa*. The rice plant has a loose, open head of many small one-flowered spikelets and is usually grown in flooded fields. The stems are hollow—allowing oxygen to pass

down to the roots which would otherwise be deprived of oxygen by the waterlogging of the soil. These terraced fields are in the Phillipines.

Below: Sugar, *Saccharum officinarum*, is another tropical cereal. This is a 1725 illustration of a West Indian plantation.

stigma which provides the largest possible surface area for catching pollen grains as they blow past in the air.

The individual grass flowers, or *florets*, which are often very small, are grouped into inflorescences, called *spikelets*, containing up to twenty flowers packed tightly together. (Occasionally these spikelets may contain only one flower but they are still normally considered as inflorescences). The spikelets themselves are then arranged in a head which may be very compact, as in the fox-tail, *Alopecurus pratensis*, or loose and widespreading, as in wavy hair-grass, *Deschampsia flexuosa*.

Other characteristics of grasses are their tufted growth style and their hollow circular stems and long narrow leaves. The lower part of each leaf is wrapped around the stem. In many species individual plants increase in size from buds at the base—a process known as *tillering*. Additionally new plants may be produced by spreading horizontal underground stems (*rhizomes*) from which new plants grow up at intervals. It is the ability of grasses to grow from the base, combined with their ability to colonize bare areas rapidly from seed, that has resulted in their extraordinary success. They are able to survive grazing and burning better than any other group of plants.

Cereals

The most important of all food plants are the *cereals*, cultivated members of the grass family. About 12 species of cereals provide the staple diet of most of the world's population. These species have evolved as a result of cultivation and the deliberate selection of characteristics.

Ann Ronan Picture Library

Left, above and right:
Three temperate cereals:
rye, barley and oats.
Rye, *Secale cereale*,
(left) has flower-heads
similar to wheat but
the spikelets contain
only two florets
rather than wheat's
five. There are two
species of barley:
two-rowed, *Hordeum
distichon*, (above)
and six-rowed, *Hordeum
vulgare*. The names
refer to the apparent
number of rows of grain
on the head. Both
species have spikelets
in groups of three in
two rows, one each side
of the flower head. In
six-rowed barley each
spikelet is fertile,
while in two-rowed
barley only one in three
is fertile. Oats, *Avena*,
(right) have spikelets
containing 2-4 drooping
florets.

The most important temperate crop species is bread wheat, *Triticum aestivum*. There are a large number of varieties of this species but most have a spikelet of five florets, of which three are fertile and develop grains. Furthermore, the main stalk of the ear of wheat remains intact while the grains are shed. In related wild grasses, the stalk shatters, making the separation of the grain and chaff much more difficult.

Wheat species are among the earliest plants to have been cultivated by man. A species called emmer, *Triticum dicoccum*, was found by archaeologists to have been cultivated at Jarmo, in Kurdistan, around 5000 BC. It is likely that ancient wheat species originated in this area from artificial crosses between two wild grass species.

The other major temperate cereals are barley, *Hordeum vulgare* and *Hordeum distichon*, grown for animal feed and as a source of malt for brewing; durum wheat, *Triticum durum*, whose flour contains a high proportion of *gluten*, the component of flour which becomes sticky and elastic when wetted, so that it is ideal for making pasta; rye, *Secale cereale*; and oats, *Avena*. Both rye and oats probably grew as weeds in fields of wheat and barley, but were recognized by early cultivators as useful plants in their own right. The wild oat, *Avena fatua*, is still an extremely troublesome weed of cereal crops. It is particularly difficult to eliminate because it is so similar in development and physiology to the cereals among which it grows.

Whereas wheat is the main temperate food species, another grass, rice, *Oryza sativa*, is the staple food for tropical and sub-tropical areas in large parts of Africa and Asia. It is also increasingly grown in other parts of the world, such as Australia and southern Europe. It was first cultivated about 3000 BC, and, because of its value as a food plant, within only 1,000 years was being grown throughout China, India and South-East Asia.

The third major cereal is maize, *Zea mays*. It is the only cereal to have originated in the New World—it was first cultivated between 4500 and 3500 BC—but is now a major crop throughout tropical and sub-tropical areas of the world. It is also quite widely grown in temperate regions. The ripe grain can be ground into meal, or, if grown in countries, such as Britain, where the summer is too short for ripening, the whole plant can be harvested and made into silage.

Other tropical and sub-tropical cereals include sorghum, *Sorghum vulgare*; sugar cane, *Saccharum officinarum*; and many kinds of millet, *Panicum*. A few other rarer cereal species are grown only in one area. For example, teff, *Eragrostis teff*, is the most commonly grown cereal in the upland areas of Ethiopia but is hardly grown at all anywhere else.

Bamboos

Although most grasses are herbaceous, one group of grasses, the bamboos, which grow mostly in tropical and sub-tropical regions, have remained woody. Because of this, and because some species have fleshy fruits, they are regarded as the most primitive kind of grasses. Some species grow tree-like to more than 40 m (130 ft), with stems up to 20 cm (8 in) in diameter, although there is no secondary thickening.

Below: Modern cereals are the result of thousands of years of selection and breeding. In the past this was done with little knowledge of the underlying genetics but in modern times these have been extensively studied. This maize cob is the result of a cross between purple-seeded parents which each contained a recessive gene for yellow seeds. The result is a ratio of three purple seeds to one yellow.

Right: Two other monocot families, rushes, *Juncaceae*, and sedges, *Cyperaceae*, are grasslike. One sedge, papyrus, *Cyperus papyrus*, (shown here) was cultivated in Egypt to make paper.

of day all seedlings have hrome in the form p$_{FR}$

4 normal nights

4 nights with short period far red light- P$_R$ formed

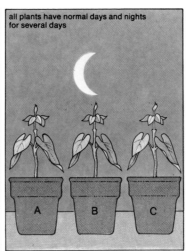

red light reverses the effect of far red - P$_R$ returns to P$_{FR}$

all plants have normal days and nights for several days

no elongation

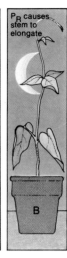

P$_R$ causes stem to elongate

no elongation

Courtesy Scientific American

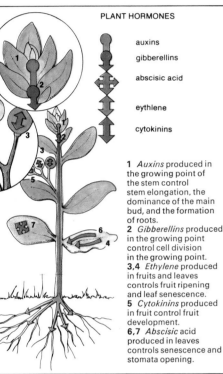

PLANT HORMONES

auxins

gibberellins

abscisic acid

eythlene

cytokinins

1 *Auxins* produced in the growing point of the stem control stem elongation, the dominance of the main bud, and the formation of roots.
2 *Gibberellins* produced in the growing point control cell division in the growing point.
3,4 *Ethylene* produced in fruits and leaves controls fruit ripening and leaf senescence.
5 *Cytokinins* produced in fruit control fruit development.
6,7 *Abscisic acid* produced in leaves controls senescence and stomata opening.

Ann Ronan Picture Library

Left: Some of the effects of hormones. *Ethylene* is a special case. It is unknown whether it is itself a hormone or a by-product of hormone action.

Above: The response of plants to light is partly due to a chemical, called *phytochrome*, which exists in plants in two reversible forms P$_R$ and P$_{FR}$. Red light in daylight converts P$_R$ to P$_{FR}$ but light of a longer wavelength (*far red light*) converts P$_{FR}$ back to P$_R$. One effect of phytochrome (on stem elongation) and the reversible nature of the P$_R$/P$_{FR}$ system are shown here. Three bean seedlings were first grown under normal conditions.

G. R. Roberts

Plant A remained in these conditions but plants B and C were given a period of far red light every night for 4 nights and then normal nights. Plant C was also given a period of red light immediately after the far red light. At the end of the experiment some days later only plant B had elongated. This was due to P$_R$ formed by the far red light. Far red light encourages stem elongation so that plants grow up out of the shade of other plants. Beneath a leaf canopy there is more far red than red light.

Left: The vitality of a growing plant: *Eucalyptus* devouring a fence post.

THE CONTROL OF GROWTH IN PLANTS

The growth of plants from germination to flowering and eventual death is controlled by both genetic and environmental factors. The final shape and nature of an individual plant is the result of the modification of its fundamental hereditary constitution (called the *genotype*) by environmental influences. Exactly how this happens is not fully understood. Nevertheless, it is known that many features of plant growth and development are controlled by *hormones*.

The first plant hormone to be isolated was *indole-3-acetic acid* (IAA), one of a group of plant hormones called *auxins*. It appears to have a general role in controlling the development of plant tissues in conjunction with two other groups of plant hormones called the *cytokinins* and the *gibberellins*. The correct combination of these three hormones can cause isolated plant cells, suspended in tissue culture solution, to develop into complete plants. A fourth plant hormone, *abscisic acid*, is involved in the control of leaf-fall and bud dormancy in deciduous woody plants.

Germination and growth

A seed contains a *dormant* plant embryo in which normal physiological processes, such as respiration, operate at a very low rate while cell division and growth are completely stopped. The seed also contains a store of nutrient, either as *endosperm* or in swollen seed leaves (cotyledons). Until the seedling starts to photosynthesize, it is dependent on its stored reserve.

After the seed is shed from the plant, it remains dormant for anything from a few hours to many years until it receives an external stimulus which triggers germination. This stimulus varies from one species to another, but it is generally a favourable combination of day-length, moisture and temperature, following a suitable additional stimulus, such as exposure to cold, during the dormant period.

When the seed germinates a root grows out first, enabling the seedling to obtain water and mineral nutrients. The cotyledons appear as the first green leaves of the seedling, unless they are swollen with food reserves (as in the runner bean, *Phaseolus coccineus*) in which case they remain below ground.

Growth of the seedling involves a rapid increase in the numbers of cells in localized regions called *meristems* (by the process of *cell division*). The meristems are found at the tips of the stem and roots. After dividing, the cells elongate and *differentiate*, developing the structures, such as vacuoles, which are typical of mature, specialized plant cells. For example some of the cells develop the special features of *xylem* and *phloem*.

Tropisms

The direction in which a plant grows is influenced by light and gravity. The effect of light was first investigated by Charles Darwin. He showed that the *coleoptile* (growing shoot) of a grass seedling bends towards light; this is called *positive phototropism*. Plants also show several other tropisms: stems are *negatively geotropic*, that is they tend to grow upwards against gravity, even in the absence of light, while roots are *positively geotropic*. All these changes in the direction of growth are caused by the cells on one side of the stem or root elongating more than those on the other side as a result of hormone action.

Tropical Monocots

Tropical vegetation contains many strange forms of plant life. This is especially true of tropical monocots, many of which have features of structure or habit unknown in plants of temperate regions. In particular, many grow into tree-like forms superficially more like dicot trees (such as oak or elm) or gymnosperm trees (such as pines) than the herbaceous plants which are the more typical form of monocots.

Palms and screwpines

Although many tropical monocot families have some tree-like species, only two families, the palms, *Palmae*, and the screwpines, *Pandanaceae*, are chiefly composed of large trees. Of these the palm family is by far the larger and more important, containing some 2,500 species. Different species of palm supply food and shelter for millions of people in the tropics.

Palms and screwpines are trees, but their development and structure are quite different from that of dicot trees. A palm seedling grows for several years with its stem *apex*, or growing point, at ground level. This produces leaves but makes no upward growth until the apex has enlarged to a certain width, which varies from species to species. Once this width has been reached, which may take

Above, right and below: Palms, *Palmae*, are most often associated with the desert, camels and oases (right, a Tunisian oasis). However, they are an extremely important tropical and sub-tropical family. The most important cultivated palms are the date palm, *Phoenix dactylifera*, the oil palm, *Elaeis guineensis*, and the coconut palm, *Cocos nucifera* (below), all of which form the basis of major industries. Others are rarer and exotic. The coco-de-mer, *Lodoicea maldivica* (above), whose massive fruits may weigh up to 20 kg (45 lb), is found on only two islands in the Seychelles.

Jean-Pierre Bourret

G R Roberts

Dr Giuseppe Mazza

Left: Many bromeliads, like *Fascicularia bicolor* (shown here), are epiphytes in which the leaf bases form a rosette in which a pool of water collects. The plants use this pool as a supply of water and also the dead leaves and insects, which collect and decompose in it, as a supply of nutrients. Bromeliads can therefore flourish on the branches of trees where other plants would die from lack of nutrients and water.

Above right: The upside-down inflorescence of the banana, *Musa*.

Below: Many tropical monocots are familiar house plants. This is *Maranta leuconeura*.

up to 12 years, no further lateral growth occurs no matter how tall the palm grows. The trunk of a palm is generally the same diameter from base to crown. There is none of the *secondary thickening* that gives strength to dicot and gymnosperm trees.

Despite the lack of secondary thickening, palms can grow to quite considerable heights. One species of wax palm, *Ceroxylon*, which grows high in the Andes, can grow to 60 m (200 ft) or more though most palms only grow to less than half this height. The trunk is supported by the woody, vascular bundles which, as in all monocots, are distributed evenly across the width of the trunk. In the coconut palm, *Cocos nucifera*, there are about 18,000 vascular bundles in a trunk about 30 cm (1 ft) in diameter. For all palms, additional support is provided by fibres which run alongside the vascular bundles.

Other palms, the rattans, such as *Calamus* species, have relatively slender stems and are climbing plants. They are particularly common in South-East Asia and grow up into the forest canopy, attaching themselves by hooks and spines which cover their stems and leaves. This method of growth is an adaptation to the intense competition for light in tropical rain forests.

Palms grow upwards at a rate of anything from 20 cm (8 in) to 1 m (3 ft) per year, producing a succession of new leaves. There are two types of palm leaf. In a *pinnate*, or feather, leaf, like that of the oil palm, *Elaeis guineensis*, the leaflets are attached in pairs at intervals along the axis of the leaf; in a *palmate*, or fan, leaf, the leaflets radiate outwards

from a point. In both cases, in the bud, the young leaves are not divided but folded in a corrugated pattern. As the leaf expands it splits along these corrugations. When a new leaf unfolds the oldest one dies off, so that the total number of leaves on the plant remains the same.

Screwpines, which are not as widely distributed as palms—they are not found at all in America—generally have branched trunks with several heads of undivided leaves. Palm trunks, except in the genus *Hyphaene*, are never branched and palm leaves are normally divided into leaflets.

Flowering and fruiting
The flowering and fruiting of palms can be a spectacular affair. For instance the talipot palm, *Corypha umbraculifera*, cultivated in Ceylon but not found in the wild at all, flowers only once when the tree is 50 to 70 years old, and then dies. This is not surprising as the inflorescence is 6 m (20 ft) high and 10 m (30 ft) across, with half a million fruits ripening as the tree dies.

In other palms the inflorescences are smaller, and many species flower repeatedly. The flowers have three small white, green or yellow sepals, three similar petals, and anything from three to over 1,000 stamens. The ovary has three cells, each containing a single ovule. Sometimes the flowers are unisexual, in which case the male and female flowers may be either on the same tree, possibly in different inflorescences, or on different trees. Little is known about pollination: some species may be pollinated by wind, others by insects.

1(

Palm fruits contain a single large seed, and may be coconut-like, with a dry outer skin covering a thick fibrous husk and the 'nut' within, or date-like, where the stone is enclosed in a fleshy, often brightly coloured, layer containing up to 70 per cent sugar. Succulent, date-like palm fruits are clearly intended for dispersal by animals, which eat them and pass the stones undigested through their guts. Exactly how dry, inedible fruits of the coconut type evolved, however, is not so clear. Many are dispersed by rolling along the ground, or by water, but in some cases, neither of these methods seems very practical. For example, the fruits of the coco-de-mer, *Lodoicea maldivica*, which take six years to ripen and weigh 15 to 20 kg (30 to 45 lb), sink in water and are too heavy to do anything except roll downhill. The distribution of these enormous plants is correspondingly limited. They are found only on two islands in the Seychelles.

Other tropical monocots

Three other important tropical monocot families are the agave family, *Agavaceae*, the bromeliad family, *Bromeliaceae*, and the banana family, *Musaceae*. The first of these, the agave family, includes several species which are fairly characteristic of dry tropical and sub-tropical regions. The plants consist of a clump of many stiff, sword-shaped leaves at the top of a short woody stem. Most members of the family are relatively small, but some species, particularly in the genus *Dracaena*, produce branched stems reaching to heights of 10 m (30 ft) or more.

Agave and *Yucca* species are found from the southern US down into South America. Many species of *Agave* have very long life cycles, growing for 60 to 100 years before flowering and dying, hence their common name of 'century plants'. *Yuccas* have a special pollination mechanism, involving moths of the genus *Pronuba*. The moth lays its eggs in the ovary of the yucca flower, and then deposits pollen, previously collected from another plant, on the stigma. It thus ensures that enough ovules develop both to feed its caterpillars and to perpetuate the yucca, which can only be pollinated by the moth. Neither the moth nor the yucca can survive without the other.

Bromeliads are similar in general appearance to the agave family, but are mostly found in tropical forests in South America. Many are *epiphytes*, growing for support on other plants, but the commercially important pineapple, *Ananas comosus*, is a bromeliad that grows on the ground. Its complex fruit is formed from the amalgamation of all the individual fruits in the inflorescence.

The banana family contains a number of herbaceous plants that build up massive stems and attain the height of small trees. The commercial banana, *Musa*, is fairly typical of these plants. It builds up a tall stem, 3 to 10 m (10 to 33 ft) high, from the overlapping leaf bases. From this a spike of flowers eventually grows out and bends over to hang downwards. The male flowers are at the tip of this 'upside-down' inflorescence, with the female flowers above them. In cultivated bananas the fruits develop from the female flowers without fertilization, so that ordinary bananas for eating are seedless. After fruiting, the whole stem dies and a new one grows up to replace it.

Above: The bird of paradise flower, *Strelitzia reginae* (family *Strelitziaceae*), is so named because the inflorescence is said to resemble a bird's head. It is also remarkable as it is pollinated by sun-birds (*Nectarinidae*) and has two petals fused together to form a 'bird-perch'.

Below: The bromeliad *Tillandsia cyanea*, which is grown as a house plant for its flowers. Another *Tillandsia*, Spanish moss, *Tillandsia usneoides*, grows as a wild epiphyte in the American continent. Its long festoons of thread-like stems and leaves are often seen hanging from telegraph wires.

Pl ·12

Fig: 26.

Fig: 25.

ld you not to overdo the nutrients in the hydroponic garden."

WATER AND NUTRIENT TRANSPORT IN PLANTS

A growing plant needs a constant supply of water and nutrients, which must be transported through the plant to the tissues where they are used. Water has five main functions in a plant. Firstly, all cells need to maintain a certain water content because biochemical reactions take place between compounds in solution. Secondly, the water content of plant cells holds them in shape; a plant that is short of water wilts. Thirdly, a plant must have a film of water over the surfaces of the *mesophyll* cells in the leaves; carbon dioxide dissolves in this water film and diffuses into the cells, where photosynthesis takes place. This water is constantly evaporating and has to be replaced from within the plant. Fourthly, a small amount of water is used up in the basic chemical reaction of photosynthesis. And finally, both organic and mineral nutrients are transported within the plant while dissolved in water.

A plant needs to transport both organic and mineral nutrients. Organic nutrients have to be transported from the leaves, where they are photosynthesized, to other parts of the plant, where they are used either as building blocks in the synthesis of more complex chemicals or as sources of energy. Additionally, in plants with storage organs such as tubers or bulbs, nutrients must be transported to and from these reserves so that they can be mobilized for the rapid growth of new leaves, stems and roots when conditions are favourable. Mineral nutrients, such as nitrate and potassium, are taken up by the roots from the soil, and have to be transported upwards to the above-ground parts of the plant.

Transport in the plant occurs in the *xylem* and *phloem* tissue. Xylem and phloem have different functions related to their different structures. The xylem is concerned with the *passive* transport of water and mineral nutrients up the plant. The plant expends energy to transport mineral nutrients from dilute solution in the soil across the cell membrane into the more concentrated solution within the root cell. Water, on the other hand, enters the roots without the need for the plant to expend energy. This is done by the physical process known as *osmosis* (by which water will pass through a membrane from a weak solution to a more concentrated one).

After entering the root, however, both water and mineral nutrients are then carried up the plant primarily by the suction formed as water is continually *transpired* from the leaves—the xylem acting merely as a pipe. In a tall tree the pressure difference between the crown of the tree and the roots may be as much as 30 bars (430 psi).

As an indication of the quantities of water involved, a large tree may lose 50 kg (110 lb) of water in a day by transpiration. The amount of water lost, and hence the rate of water flow up the xylem, is controlled by the *stomata* of the leaves. If the soil becomes dry, or if the roots cannot absorb water fast enough on a sunny day, the stomata close to prevent the further loss of water. Closure of the stomata is achieved by two cells, known as *guard cells*, which collapse when short of water, so blocking the stomatal pores.

The phloem, unlike the xylem, is concerned with the *active* transport of organic nutrients especially sugars. The nutrients are transported in the *sieve tubes* of the phloem, and although the mechanism of transport remains a mystery, it is likely that the energy required to transport them is obtained by respiration in the *companion cells* adjacent to the sieve tubes. The contents of the sieve tubes, the plant *sap*, consists of water containing a high concentration of sugars, mainly sucrose. This sugar can be used commercially. In the sugar maple, *Acer saccharum*, the bark is tapped in spring when the phloem is carrying nutrients up to the crown, before the new leaves expand. The sap which oozes out is collected and evaporated to yield *maple syrup*.

Below left: Early experiments into the use of water by plants were conducted by Stephen Hales and published in his book 'Vegatable Staticks' 1727. The apparatus at the top here is an early *potometer* which measures the rate at which a plant takes up water. The water taken from the tube on the left is equal to that transpired by the plant through the leaves.

Above: Soil is not necessary for plant growth—it merely acts as a supporting medium from which water and nutrients can be extracted. The growing of plants in a soil-free medium is called *hydroponics*.

Below: Transpiration, and hence the rate of water flow up the xylem, is controlled by the stomata which close when the plant is in danger of wilting so preventing further water loss from the intercelluar spaces in the leaves. Stomatal closing is achieved by *guard cells*. They collapse when short of water and block the stomatal openings.

Below: Plants can have too much water. Some, like maize, *Zea mays* (shown here) excrete excess water through glands (*hydathodes*) on the leaves. This is known as *guttation* and occurs when too much water enters the roots by osmosis.

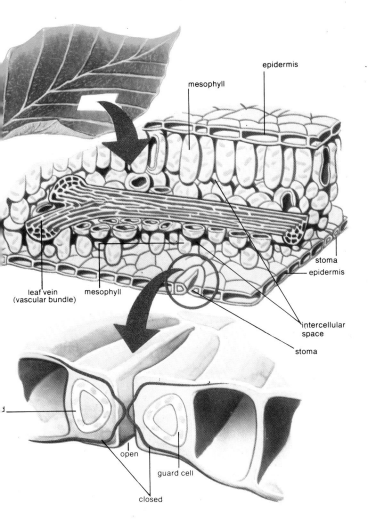

epidermis

mesophyll

leaf vein (vascular bundle)

mesophyll

stoma

epidermis

intercellular space

stoma

open

guard cell

closed

Gymnosperms

Few plants have captured the imagination of botanists as have the maidenhair tree, the dawn redwood of China and the giant coastal redwoods of Pacific California. These exotic trees all belong to a relatively small, but economically important, group of plants known as the *Gymnospermae* or more simply as gymnosperms. This name comes from the Greek *gymnos*, meaning naked, and *sperma*, meaning seed. The gymnosperms are the naked seeded plants.

Most gymnosperms are evergreen trees or shrubs and they characteristically have eggs, *ovules*, which are in direct contact with the air so that pollen can fall directly on to them. Male and female plants are generally separate and typically have reproductive organs borne in cones, *strobili*. The male cones produce great quantities of tiny pollen, some of which is blown by the wind to the cones of female plants to fertilize their eggs.

Many groups of gymnosperms are now extinct and have been so for millions of years. Five groups still have living representatives. These are the cycads, *Cycadales*, maidenhair trees, *Ginkgoales*, yews, *Taxales*, conifers, *Coniferales*, and finally a mixed group, called *Gnetales*, which includes the twitch plants, *Ephedra*, and the extraordinary *Welwitschia bainesii* of the Kalahari Desert in south-west Africa.

Cycads and maidenhair trees

Most cycads are small trees rarely reaching 10 m (33 ft) high. Less commonly they have short subterranean stems with a rosette of leaves at or above ground level. They are sparsely but widely distributed throughout the tropics and the southern hemisphere. Tree cycads closely resemble palm trees at first glance though their reproductive structures are quite different. In most cycads both male and female plants bear cones which are a metre (3 ft) high and 50 cm (20 in) in diameter in some species. The cones are borne in the centre of the plant and are surrounded by palm-like leaves arranged in a spiral from the top of the stem.

Few trees have gained the popularity and mystique reserved for *Ginkgo biloba*, the maidenhair tree, so-called because of the resemblance of its leaves to those of the popular house plant, the maidenhair fern. Extinct, or almost so, in its native China, it was cultivated for its beauty and also for its edible fruits in the royal palace of Peking, from where the first seeds were introduced into Europe in 1762. It is now a prize addition to many parks and large gardens.

Yews and cow-tail pines

Another small, but quite distinct, group of gymnosperms, *Taxales*, includes the yew tree, *Taxus*, and its distant Asiatic relatives, the cow-tail pines, *Cephalotaxus*. One of three gymnosperms native to Britain (the others are the Scots pine, *Pinus sylvestris*, and the juniper, *Juniperus communis*), mature yews have enormous trunks many metres in circumference crowned with a mass of dark green foliage. Yews are unlike conifers in having no female cone. Instead they have a fruit, the *aril*. Female trees in fruit are quite beautiful, as the bright red

Above: Leaves and fruit of a female maidenhair tree, *Ginkgo biloba*. Ginkgo trees may grow to 30 m (100 ft) or more high, are deciduous and characteristically branch low down so that two or more leading shoots are present. Both male and female trees are widely grown, but male trees are more popular as females produce great quantities of olive-like fruits which smell of rancid butter when ripe.

Below: The exception in the cycads, *Cycas* itself. Unlike other cycads, female *Cycas* plants do not bear cones but have reproductive structures which more closely resemble a small leaf. This species is *Cycas revoluta*.

Giuseppe Mazza

Right: The fruit (*aril*) of the yew tree, *Taxus baccata*. The aril is sweet and attractive to birds which eat the fruits whole. The seeds inside the fruits are indigestible and pass through the birds' digestive system unharmed. They may be excreted many miles away, so dispersing the yew trees.

Far right: The biggest trees in the world are the Wellingtonias, *Sequoiadendron giganteum*. One Wellingtonia, known as *General Grant*, is 91.5 m (267 ft) high and 24.3 m (79 ft) in girth 2.4 m (7 ft) above the ground. Coast redwoods, *Sequoia sempervirens*, are generally taller but are not as massive. The tree with the largest girth, however, is a specimen of Spanish chestnut, *Castanea sativa*, which had a girth of 51 m (167 ft) when measured in 1972.

Herve Chaumeton/Jacana

A-Z Collection

The Scots Pine (*pinus sylvestris*) is closely related to the giant redwoods of California, and is one of only three gymnosperms native to Britain.

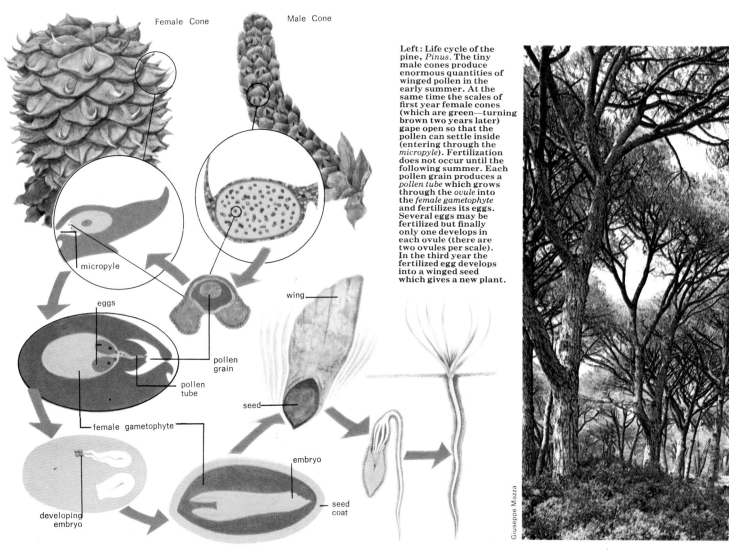

Female Cone   Male Cone

Left: Life cycle of the pine, *Pinus*. The tiny male cones produce enormous quantities of winged pollen in the early summer. At the same time the scales of first year female cones (which are green—turning brown two years later) gape open so that the pollen can settle inside (entering through the *micropyle*). Fertilization does not occur until the following summer. Each pollen grain produces a *pollen tube* which grows through the *ovule* into the *female gametophyte* and fertilizes its eggs. Several eggs may be fertilized but finally only one develops in each ovule (there are two ovules per scale). In the third year the fertilized egg develops into a winged seed which gives a new plant.

micropyle

eggs

pollen grain

pollen tube

female gametophyte

developing embryo

wing

seed

embryo

seed coat

Giuseppe Mazza

Above: A grove of Mediterranean pines, *Pinus pinea*. Unlike most conifers, these trees have branched trunks.

Below: The juniper, *Juniperus communis*, is a small shrub which belongs to the cypress family. Its berries are used to flavour gin.

Herve Chaumeton/Jacana

fleshy aril around each seed contrasts markedly with the dark green leaves.

Conifers

By far the largest living group of gymnosperms is the conifers, *Coniferales*. Not only are there many species of conifers but many have great economic importance. Some may be numbered among the most important cash crops in the world. This is particularly true of many of the species of pine, larch, spruce, fir, podo and monkey-puzzle, all of which are important timber trees often grown in vast plantations.

For convenience, conifers can be divided into two groups, those which are predominantly of north temperate distribution and origin and those which are predominantly from the southern hemisphere. The northern hemisphere group consists of the pine and its relatives, *Pinaceae*, the swamp cypress and its relatives, *Taxodiaceae*, and the cypress and its relatives, *Cupressaceae*.

The red-barked Scots pine, *Pinus sylvestris*, is perhaps the best known member of the *Pinaceae* but it is only one of some 200 species in this family. There are also some 80 species of the genus *Pinus*, one of which, the bristlecone pine, *Pinus longaeva*, is the oldest living tree in the world with a specimen 4,900 years old. Pine species are distinguished by many characters of the wood, bark and cone but particularly by the number of needle-like leaves in the bunches on the short side shoots of each branch. Most species have either two, four or five needles per bunch but higher numbers are known in some species.

Related to the pines are several other familiar plantation trees such as spruce, *Picea*, silver fir, *Abies*, larch, *Larix*, hemlock, *Tsuga*, Douglas fir, *Pseudotsuga*, and cedar, *Cedrus*. Spruces and silver firs are often confused but may be readily distinguished for spruces have pendulous cones and, when their leaves fall, peg-like projections are left behind on the stem, while the cones of silver firs are upright. Larches are easily recognized as, unlike most gymnosperms, they are *deciduous*, that is they lose their leaves in the winter. The Douglas fir, *Pseudotsuga menziesii*, is a superb species with specimens over 90 m (300 ft) tall having been recorded from the Pacific coast of North America.

The largest trees, however, belong to a different group, *Taxodiaceae*, which is a small family, totalling only 14 species, but which includes two of the most famous of all trees, the coastal redwood, *Sequoia sempervirens*, and the legendary dawn redwood, *Metasequoia glyptostroboides*.

The coast redwood, and its close relative, the Wellingtonia or big tree, *Sequoiadendron giganteum*, are both natives of Pacific North America. The former is confined to a narrow coastal belt from Oregon to southern California whilst the latter grows at between 1,500 m and 2,500 m (5,000-8,000 ft) altitude in the Sierra Nevada in California. The tallest living tree in the world is a specimen of coast redwood, 112.4 m (368 ft) high, known as· the *Howard Libbey* tree. Wellingtonias fall a few metres short of this in height but are generally much more massive trees.

Related to the redwoods are the swamp cypresses, *Taxodium*, of the southern USA and Mexico. Growing in swampy ground, such as the Everglades in Florida, these trees develop roots which project, peg-like above the water around the base of the tree. Swamp water contains little dissolved oxygen and these roots, called *pneumatophores*, can absorb oxygen from the atmosphere. The swamp cypresses are also rather unusual among the conifers as they are deciduous.

Another deciduous conifer is the dawn redwood. This extraordinary species was known as a fossil from the Tertiary period before being discovered living in a very restricted area of east Szechwan and north-east Hupeh in China in 1941. Seeds were distributed to European and American botanic gardens and parks in 1948 and its growth has been so rapid that specimens over 27 m (90 ft) tall had been recorded both in Britain and in the USA by 1977. This is an annual increase in height of nearly 1 m (3 ft), an astonishing rate of growth.

A final group of northern hemisphere species is the cypress and its relatives, *Cupressaceae*. Two genera are both commonly given the name 'cypress'; these are the true cypresses, *Cupressus*, and the false cypresses, *Chamaecyparis*. Nevertheless, the two genera can be easily distinguished at a glance, for, despite the characteristic shape of the trees, the true cypresses have branches growing in all planes around the main shoot whilst the false cypresses have their branches all in one plane.

Two families of conifers are native to the southern hemisphere, the monkey-puzzles, *Araucariaceae*, and the podos, *Podocarpaceae*. Both are rarely planted in the northern hemisphere, but one species, monkey-puzzle or Chile pine, *Araucaria araucana*, is very commonly planted in front gardens. Its whorls of slightly drooping branches covered by spirals of triangular, sharply pointed leaves are an exotic sight in many suburban streets. In Chile and Argentina, however, the Chile pine is an important timber tree forming large forests.

The other group of southern conifers is known in the timber trade as *podo*. Their most remarkable feature is the female fruit. In many ways it resembles the fruit of the yew but the fleshy aril is white and the shiny black seed sits on top of it, instead of inside it as in the yew.

History and importance

The gymnosperms are an ancient group of plants, which can be recognized in fossil deposits 300 million years old and are common constituents of the coal measures of the Carboniferous period. For 120 million years, from 220 million years ago to 100 million years ago, they formed the dominant vegetation of the Earth, to be challenged for supremacy only by the rise of the flowering plants during the Cretaceous period. The heyday of the gymnosperms is now over but many species continue to survive, though many are mere relict populations. Others still form the major constituent of the vegetation over great tracts of the Earth's surface. As timber trees they are of massive importance—their straight stems are particularly suitable to the timber industry.

Above: A species of monkey-puzzle, *Araucaria*, showing the classic growth pattern of conifers—one straight, unbranched main stem typified by the Christmas tree spruce.

Above right: Detail of a female cone of Norway spruce, *Picea abies*.

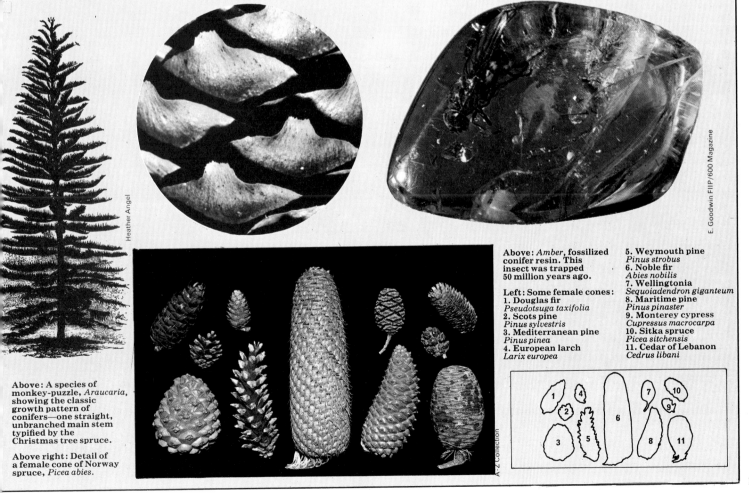

Above: *Amber*, fossilized conifer resin. This insect was trapped 50 million years ago.

Left: Some female cones:
1. Douglas fir
Pseudotsuga taxifolia
2. Scots pine
Pinus sylvestris
3. Mediterranean pine
Pinus pinea
4. European larch
Larix europea
5. Weymouth pine
Pinus strobus
6. Noble fir
Abies nobilis
7. Wellingtonia
Sequoiadendron giganteum
8. Maritime pine
Pinus pinaster
9. Monterey cypress
Cupressus macrocarpa
10. Sitka spruce
Picea sitchensis
11. Cedar of Lebanon
Cedrus libani

Part III

The World of Animals

Chapter 1 **The Animal Kingdom**

The Animal Kingdom

Probably the best known division in the animal kingdom is that between the animals which have backbones, the vertebrates, and those which do not, the invertebrates. The vertebrates claim a larger share of human attention since man himself is a vertebrate—it is easier for us to relate to animals that are built more or less on the same body plan. Also, the vertebrates are the largest of animals.

Whatever the invertebrates may lack in size is more than compensated for in numbers. They are so numerous that their combined weight, or *biomass*, is far greater than that of the vertebrates. As proof of this, it is only necessary to think of the structure of a typical food chain and its associated pyramid of numbers. The organisms at each level of the pyramid, which form the food of those at the level above, must have a greater biomass than their predators. For example, on the African plains the breeding population of antelopes and zebra must have a greater biomass than the population of lions which it supports.

The invertebrates also dominate the animal world in numbers of species. As zoologists tend to disagree about the details of classification their estimates vary, but well over a million species of living animals are known and only about 40,000 of these are species of vertebrates. All the others are invertebrates, including three-quarters of a million arthropods, a group which might be judged the most successful of all. Insects are arthropods and just one group of insects, the beetles, outnumber the living species of vertebrates by over 7 to 1, for almost 300,000 species of beetles are known.

Animal groups

The animal kingdom is made up of 24 or 25 major subdivisions, or *phyla*. The members of a particular phylum will all have certain features in common at one time or another in their life histories, even though they may look very different as adults. It would be hard to imagine two more different animals than men and sea squirts, yet we both belong to the same phylum, the *Chordata*. The tadpole-like larva of the sea squirt has the three typical chordate features: a *notochord* running dorsally along the body, gill slits in the pharynx and a nerve chord lying centrally above the notochord. These features are also observed in the human embryo, but, except for the nerve chord, they do not last for long.

The construction of a family tree to show the relationships between the various phyla and the order of their evolution is bound to be somewhat speculative—evolution is a slow process and has taken place over many millions of years. The family relationships and ancestry of a particular animal may be established by a number of methods. Firstly it must be compared in all stages of development with other animals. If there is a strong similarity between, say, the larvae of two animals this may indicate a close family relationship. On the other hand it may simply mean that the two

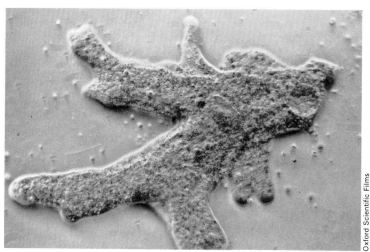

Left: The protozoan *Amoeba*. The first members of the animal and plant kingdoms originated from a common ancestor whose properties can only be guessed at. It probably contained chlorophyll, the green pigment responsible for photosynthesis in plants. At a very early stage in their evolution, almost all animals lost chlorophyll. It is still found in some protozoans such as the colonial *Volvox*. Although the single-celled *Amoeba* is relatively simple it must have undergone many changes in the course of evolutionary history.

Below: Jewel anemones, *Corynactis viridis*. Coelenterates like these probably developed from a group of protozoans.

Below: An earthworm, *Lumbricus terrestris*. In common with other annelids, the earthworm has a segmented body. Although most of the segments are alike, some are specialized for particular functions. The saddle-like bulge (the clitellum) visible in the picture plays an important role in reproduction.

Left: An African grasshopper in mid-air. Along with crustaceans and spiders, insects belong to the enormous phylum *Arthropoda*. Although arthropods have segmented bodies like annelids, specialization is much more extreme. The third thoracic segment, for example, carries powerful legs, and wings.

Below: An edible snail, *Helix pomatia*. Unlike annelids and arthropods, molluscs are not segmented, and it therefore seems likely that they branched off from the evolutionary tree before segmentation arose. There is, however, a striking similarity between the trochophore larvae of molluscs and those of annelids.

A lioness with zebra kill, in South West Africa. The vigilance of the zebra herd forces lions to make combined rushes, or lie in ambush for their prey.

grasshopper

butterfly

beetle

wasp

louse

flea

centipede

bluebottle

peripatus

silverfish

woodlouse

scorpion

spider

mite

man

chimpanz

land snail

jaguar

earthworm

lobster

squid

sea snail

sea slug

syncarida

sea butterfly

agworm

nautilus

copepod

rotifer

cockle

br

leech

chiton

barnacle

nematode worm

brachiopod

deuteros

stony coral

protostomia

tapeworm

turbellaria

gastrula

jellyfish

blastula

graptolite (extinct)

hydrozoan

morula

tabulata (extinct)

simple cell

COELENTERATES   FLATWORMS   ANNELIDS   ARTHROPODS   NEMATODES   MOLLUSCS

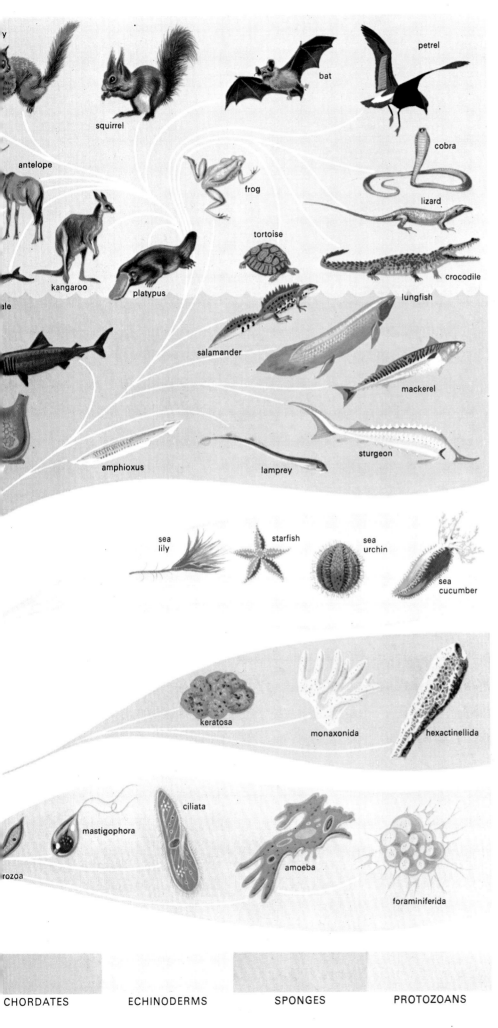

larvae have adapted in the same way to similar living conditions. It is always important to look at all the evidence rather than a single clue. Further indications of an animal's ancestry can sometimes be found in its development from egg to adult, particularly in the way the cells divide and the way the mouth and anus are formed.

Fortunately we do not have to rely only on what we can glean from living species, for fossil remains provide direct evidence of animals which lived in prehistoric times. Indeed fossils provide the most satisfactory evidence of an animal's ancestry. Usually the most ancient fossils are found in the lower rock strata and the most recent ones in the upper strata.

Some of the best fossil lineages are provided by the molluscs. Snails with backwardly coiled shells, straight-shelled cephalopods (related to the present day nautilus) and bivalves were already common in the Ordovician seas of 450 million years ago, and since that time molluscs have been a dominant group in the sea. At one time the sea was populated by great numbers of these early molluscs called *ammonites*, and today their relatives the squids and cuttlefish are important open sea creatures. Sea urchins and starfish have a good fossil history but some other groups, notably the arthropods, are not so well represented and it is more difficult to understand their relationships with the other invertebrates.

Early characteristics

Two important features, observed in almost all animals, probably arose at a very early stage in evolutionary history: bilateral symmetry and the presence of a mesoderm layer between the inner and outer body walls. The former condition may have come about as an adaptation to feeding on the seabed. The development of the mesoderm layer paved the way for the appearance of an internal body cavity surrounding the gut, a necessary preliminary to the development of more specialized organs. The way in which the mesoderm is formed in an embryo or larva provides an important distinction between animals on the two main lines of animal evolution, known as the arthropod and the chordate lines.

The development of the body cavity was a significant improvement in the body plan. Muscles could press against such a fluid-filled cavity to push the animal through the mud without interfering with the operation of the mouth or any other activities of the gut. Organs could become bigger and more complex in an internal body cavity. Several worms evolved with body cavities that fulfilled these functions but they were not identical in structure.

The earthworm's body cavity is called a *coelom*. Its ancestors probably had an open cavity so the animal was just two long tubes, one inside the other. The earthworm, however, is segmented and so the coelom is divided up. The animal

Left: An evolutionary tree of the animal kingdom. The scheme begins with a simple cell, the supposed ancestor of plants as well as animals. The single-celled animals, the protozoans, probably developed directly from this. Cell division led to more complex structures: the morula, blastula and gastrula.

In the last of these an inner wall of cells is present and the animal has developed radial symmetry. It is likely that the ancestors of the coelenterates and the sponges developed from animals modelled on the gastrula plan as did the forerunners of the chordate and arthropod lines. Most extinct animals are not shown.

CHORDATES   ECHINODERMS   SPONGES   PROTOZOANS

119

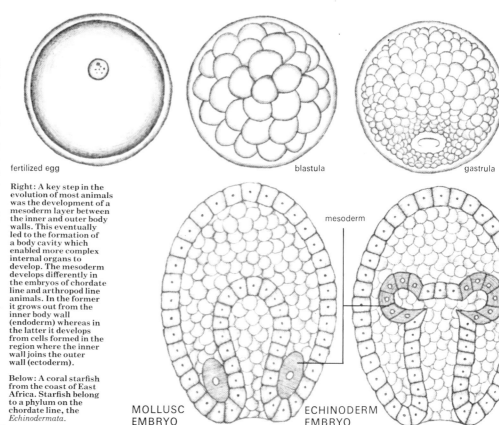

fertilized egg   blastula   gastrula

mesoderm

MOLLUSC EMBRYO   ECHINODERM EMBRYO

moves with one of its pointed ends going first, so the segments at this end become modified so as to become a sort of reconnaissance party, with the main outward-looking sense organs and an important nerve centre. In other words, a simple head develops.

In the arthropods the process has gone further and the head is distinct. So distinct, in fact, that its original segmented nature has been modified almost beyond recognition. Vertebrates, too, are segmented but in a different way. The segmentation can be seen in the repetition of the vertebrate and the spinal nerves.

The arthropod body plan

In the arthropod body plan segmentation is retained and the exoskeleton appears for the first time. In evolving an external skeleton the arthropods have produced an outstandingly effective answer to a number of problems. The arthropod skeleton provides support for the body, protection from enemies and, often, protection against the loss of such important substances as water. As compared with the internal vertebrate skeleton the arthropod skeleton is not only more useful in these ways, but also stronger. As any engineer knows, a hollow tube is stronger than a solid rod of the same material and equivalent weight.

The external skeleton is a major factor in the success of the arthropods, but it also imposes severe limitations upon them. It limits their size and, because an external skeleton cannot grow as easily as an internal one, arthropods must moult as they grow. Moulting is a hazardous process. For a short while, until its new, larger skeleton expands and hardens, the moulting arthropod is defenceless.

Another factor which limits arthropod size is the manner in which they supply oxygen to their internal tissues. In some arthropod groups, including the insects, tracheae—tiny branching tubes—carry air to all parts of the body. Air moves through the tracheae at least in part by diffusion, a process which is inadequate to supply oxygen to the middle of a large organism. The bulkiest insect, the Goliath beetle, uses muscular pumping to help ventilate the tracheae, but even so it is less than 15 cm (6 in) long when fully grown.

Appearing before the vertebrates on the chordate line of evolution are the echinoderms. One reason they appear on this branch of the plan is that, in the embryo, the mesoderm layer develops in the same way as in the chordates.

Vertebrates

By far the most important chordates are the vertebrates—animals with backbones. The first vertebrates probably appeared about 450 million years ago. They were fish which looked rather like an armoured version of the present-day lamprey and they had neither jaws nor pairs of fins. They used the gill slits in the pharynx to strain food from the water. From these early vertebrates fish called *placoderms* developed, which had both jaws and paired pectoral and pelvic fins and sometimes a series of smaller fins between these. The placoderms gave rise to the cartilagenous fish such as sharks. These and the bony fish were able to colonise freshwater and marine habitats as successfully as the molluscs and arthropods. Their shape, pattern and colour was

Right: A key step in the evolution of most animals was the development of a mesoderm layer between the inner and outer body walls. This eventually led to the formation of a body cavity which enabled more complex internal organs to develop. The mesoderm develops differently in the embryos of chordate line and arthropod line animals. In the former it grows out from the inner body wall (endoderm) whereas in the latter it develops from cells formed in the region where the inner wall joins the outer wall (ectoderm).

Below: A coral starfish from the coast of East Africa. Starfish belong to a phylum on the chordate line, the *Echinodermata*.

David C. Houston/Bruce Coleman

Heather Angel

ACORN WORM LARVA

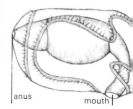

anus   mouth

Heather Angel

Bruce Coleman

Far left: A grass snake, *Natrix natrix*. Snakes are descended from a group of lizards and their ancestors may have been burrowing animals. This is suggested not only by the loss of limbs but also by the structure of their eyes and ears. The remnants of hind legs can still be seen in some snakes such as boas and pythons.

Left: A puffin, *Fratercula arctica*, with two newly caught fish. Like the mammals, birds are descended from reptiles. They developed very rapidly at the end of the Mesozoic era about 65 million years ago. Their success was no doubt helped by the rapid spread of insects and flowering plants at that time. These provided a plentiful supply of food.

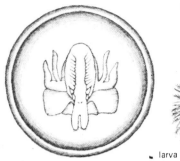
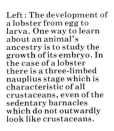

nauplius

larva

Left: The development of a lobster from egg to larva. One way to learn about an animal's ancestry is to study the growth of its embryo. In the case of a lobster there is a three-limbed nauplius stage which is characteristic of all crustaceans, even of the sedentary barnacles which do not outwardly look like crustaceans.

Right: Sea squirts, *Ciona intestinalis.* These are one of the few groups of invertebrate animals to belong to the phylum *Chordata,* which includes all the vertebrates. The relationship between an adult sea squirt and the other chordates is not at all obvious, but chordate features are clearly seen in a sea squirt's tadpole-like larva.

Below: A grayling, *Thymallus thymallus.* Present day fish developed from jawless ancestors which were the first vertebrate animals. The fish's body is supported by its backbone but is able to flex from side to side. It is movements of this sort that propel the fish through the water.

ECHINODERM LARVA

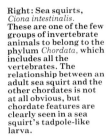

mouth

Left: Although there is hardly any resemblance between an adult chordate and an adult echinoderm, the larvae shown here are very much alike. Acorn worms belong to a phylum which is closely related to the chordates. This sort of similarity often helps to establish relationships between otherwise quite different animals.

Above: A brightly coloured toad, *Bufo periglenes.* Amphibians have changed considerably since they first ventured from the sea about 350 million years ago, but most of them still must return to the water to breed. Amphibians have adapted to many habitats. Some frogs have toe pads for climbing trees.

Below: Cheetahs, *Acinonyx jubata,* are the fastest mammals. They can keep up a speed of about 100 kph (62 mph) over a distance of 600 m (660 yd). Like birds, mammals are warm-blooded and this enables them to lead more active lives than other animals like reptiles whose blood temperature varies with the surroundings.

modified to suit the conditions they colonised, but their success depended in each case on a body plan with an internal supporting skeleton.

The bony fish fell into two groups—those whose bones and muscles remained within the body wall and those whose bones and muscles extended into the fins. A group of these latter 'lobe-finned' fish were probably the first vertebrates to venture on to land: they became the first amphibians. The lobe fins were gradually transformed into legs.

The early amphibians would have been able to feed on a variety of invertebrates which had preceded them on to land, indeed it may have been the presence of this new food source that first attracted them from the water. Amphibians could not, however, stray far from water. They needed a moist environment to keep down the loss of water from their bodies by evaporation and they could not breed in the absence of water. Their larvae were aquatic.

A group of amphibians gave rise to the reptiles which were much better equipped for life on land. A waterproof outer layer of the skin eliminated the problem of water loss and they were able to colonise dry areas of the land. Extra membranes in the reptiles' eggs kept the embryo bathed in fluid and allowed it to develop on dry land.

The Mesozoic era, with the coming of the giant dinosaurs, was the heyday of the reptiles. One such animal, the brontosaurus, must have weighed about 20 tonnes, reaching a length of 18 m (60 ft). It was the largest land animal that has ever lived. By the end of the Mesozoic era, about 65 million years ago, the reptiles were on the decline and the dinosaurs had become extinct.

From two groups of the many reptiles that once existed, the birds and the mammals evolved. Some reptilian features, such as the scaly skin on their legs, are still evident in birds. Both birds and mammals differ from reptiles in one fundamental respect: they are warm-blooded. In order to lead an active life the conversion of food into energy must proceed at an adequate rate in the animal's body. The biochemical reactions involved, like most chemical reactions, are very dependent on temperature—if the temperature is too low they will proceed relatively slowly. Thus reptiles, being cold-blooded, cannot keep moving for long periods even though they can move very swiftly for a short time; at night, when their body temperature is low, they are very sluggish. Birds and mammals, on the other hand, have both developed mechanisms for keeping the body temperature at a suitable constant level and so are capable of sustained periods of activity.

In mammals there are three main structural departures from the reptilian body plan. Firstly, the limbs are rotated so that they become located underneath the body rather than projecting from the sides. This is a much improved arrangement for an animal that lives on land, for much less effort is required to support the body weight—it is transmitted directly through straightened legs to the ground. Secondly, the jaws of mammals are much simpler than those of reptiles and thirdly, the teeth of mammals are divided into three basic types, incisors, canines and molars, while the teeth of a reptile are all very much alike.

Chapter 2
The
Invertebrates

Corals, when formed into reefs, seem
not to be animals at all. Reef building
corals are found north and south of
the equator as far as the 25th line of
latitude. Each begins as a larva, later
changing into a polyp. (see p.132).

Protozoa

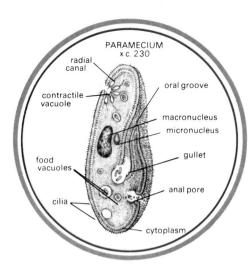

PARAMECIUM
x c. 230

radial canal
contractile vacuole
oral groove
macronucleus
micronucleus
food vacuoles
gullet
anal pore
cilia
cytoplasm

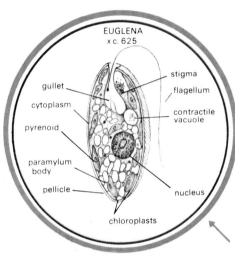

EUGLENA
x c. 625

gullet
stigma
flagellum
cytoplasm
contractile vacuole
pyrenoid
paramylum body
pellicle
nucleus
chloroplasts

Left: *Euglena* is a bright green flagellate often found in the green scum floating on the surface of stagnant ponds. The light sensitive red eyespot on the gullet guides it to the strong sunlight it needs to build its own food from simple chemicals. It bores its way quickly through the water by the spiralling motion of its flagellum.

Above: *Paramecium* is covered by short, motile 'hairs' or cilia which are used for movement and feeding. It is always very active, busily swimming around in search of good feeding grounds and living conditions. It is also one of the speediest protozoa and has been recorded covering about 600 times its own length in a minute.

The Protozoa, 'first animals', are a group of minute, single-celled organisms forming the lowest major division or phylum of the Animal Kingdom. The rest of the Animal Kingdom is composed of multicellular organisms, the Metazoa.

Although there are more protozoa in the world than all other animals put together, their activities generally pass unobserved because they are so small. The majority are smaller than 1mm in diameter and are invisible to the unaided eye. Many have to be measured in microns—1micron, μ (mu)=0.001mm—and can only be seen under a microscope.

The fascinating life of the Protozoa was first seen and studied by Anton van Leeuwenhoek, a seventeenth century Dutch microscopist. About 45,000 distinct forms, or species, both living and extinct have since been identified. These can be divided into four sections, or classes, according to their different methods of locomotion—the Sarcodina, including the amoeba; the flagellates or Mastigophora; the ciliates or Ciliophora; and the spore formers or Sporozoa.

Occasionally numbers increase to such an extent that the protozoa can be seen by the naked eye. A common flagellate, *Euglena,* forms a green scum on the top of stagnant ponds, for example, as large numbers are attracted to the light at the surface. In the Caribbean and off the coast of California, periodic surges in the population of another flagellate, *Gonyaulax,* colour the sea red by day and make it brightly luminescent by night. During these 'red tides', the concentration of toxic waste materials produced by *Gonyaulax* becomes lethal to other marine life. Thousands of fish and shellfish are killed, with serious economic consequences for the local fishermen.

Habitat and ecology

Protozoa are widely distributed throughout the world, living everywhere and anywhere there is fresh or salt water, from the polar regions to hot springs. Since they are microscopic, they are able to exploit situations that are inaccessible to

Structurally a protozoan resembles a single cell, the basic unit from which all plants and animals are made. Three dimensional diagrams of cross sections of a 'model' cell and the various types of protozoa show how each is basically a blob of colourless, gelatinous cytoplasm contained by a cell membrane. In the protozoa the cytoplasm is often divided into a clear, outer ectoplasm and a granular, inner endoplasm. The cell membrane allows simple chemicals to enter and leave the cell yet stops complex proteins in the cytoplasm from escaping. Small units or organelles suspended in the cytoplasm do all the work of the cell under the direction of the nucleus. The

mitochondria are the energy generators of the living cell. The endoplasmic reticulum, a convoluted network of double membranes weaving through the cytoplasm, may serve as a transport system. It also supports some ribosomes, the cell's protein-making factories. These proteins may be stored in the Golgi apparatus. The protozoa have made modifications to the basic cell format. Structures such as cilia, flagella, contractile and food vacuoles, shells and skeletons equip them for life as independent organisms capable of movement, feeding, respiration, secretion, excretion and reproduction, and sensitive to changes in their environment.

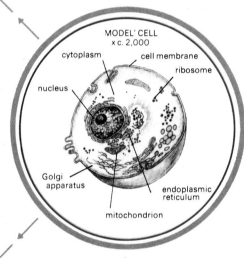

'MODEL' CELL
x c. 2,000

cytoplasm
cell membrane
ribosome
nucleus
Golgi apparatus
endoplasmic reticulum
mitochondrion

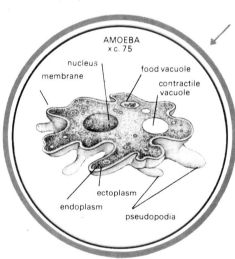

AMOEBA
x c. 75

nucleus
membrane
food vacuole
contractile vacuole
ectoplasm
endoplasm
pseudopodia

Left: The small drop of water on this leaf could contain about 280 amoebas.

Left: *Amoeba* is a pliable mass of animated jelly or cytoplasm surrounded by an elastic skin or membrane which is always changing shape as it moves. One of its favourite haunts is among the rotting weed at the bottom of a pond where it creeps around hunting for the other protozoa, small plants and bacteria which it eats with a voracious appetite.

Below: The sporozoite is the infective stage of the malarial parasite, *Plasmodium.* When a mosquito bites a man, sporozoites are injected into the bloodstream. They travel to the liver and divide. The parasites then invade the red blood cells and digest the blood pigment, producing toxic wastes that may cause the fever associated with malaria.

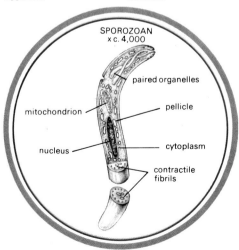

SPOROZOAN
x c. 4,000

paired organelles
mitochondrion
pellicle
nucleus
cytoplasm
contractile fibrils

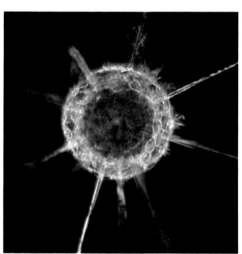

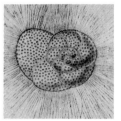

Above: The beautifully delicate glassy skeleton of a radiolarian consists of a holey, central sphere which contains the cytoplasm of an amoeba-like body. The small, thin spikes radiating from the centre bear extremely fine pseudopodia for catching and carrying food. These radial spines also protect the animal.

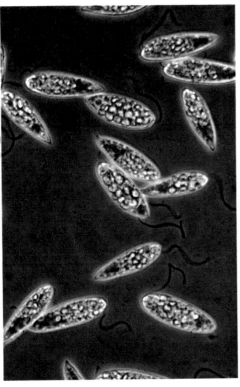

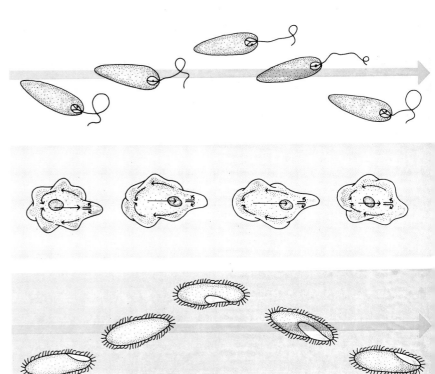

Left and right: *Euglena* and other flagellates move by thrashing the water with their fine, whip-like flagella. In each lash a spiralling wave travels up from the base of the flagellum to its tip. As it unwinds, it spins the flagellate forwards around a spiral course so that the same point on the body always faces the centre.

Right: The amoeba glides forwards by pushing out temporary extensions of the cytoplasm called pseudopodia. The rest of the body then advances by flowing into the pseudopod. It is thought that the endoplasm flows up the centre to the tip of the pseudopod and then back down the sides.

Right: The motion of the cilia is similar to rowing. Each beat has a power stroke and a recovery stroke. Individual beats are coordinated, passing along the body in waves like wheat bending in a breeze. *Paramecium* spins as it corkscrews through the water because its cilia are spirally arranged and beat slightly obliquely.

larger animals. Many are found living in the thin film of water surrounding each soil particle and between the grains of sand on a beach. They are also easily dispersed by water currents, wind and rain. Soil dwellers are often transported in the mud that clings to an animal's feet. To avoid drying up in times of drought, some protozoa such as the amoebae secrete tough, protective envelopes around themselves to form a *cyst* and survive in this dormant state until favourable conditions prevail again.

Other protozoa have become adapted to a parasitic way of life, living in or on the bodies of plants and other animals. These species represent a serious health hazard, especially in the tropics where protozoa are responsible for such diseases as malaria, African sleeping sickness, Chaga's disease and amoebic dysentery.

Protozoa occur at all levels in a community. Some are producers, manufacturing their own food from simple chemicals and light energy like plants; the rest are consumers, either herbivores eating plants or carnivores eating other animals. Since protozoa are present in such vast numbers in marine and fresh water planktons—suspensions of tiny plants (phytoplankton) and animals (zooplankton) floating in the water—they form important links in many food chains. In the summer along the coast of California, the mussel, *Mytilus,* eats such large quantities of *Gonyaulax* that its flesh is tainted with the protozoan's poison. Although harmless to the mussel, it can cause food poisoning in man if mussels are eaten during the summer months.

Plants or animals?

Some flagellates such as *Euglena* and *Volvox* have plant and animal characteristics. Like plants they are green because they have chloroplasts containing the green light-trapping pigment chlorophyll in their cytoplasm. Yet like animals these flagellates are able to move freely.

The existence of these plant-like flagellates causes some confusion about their correct classification. Generally the Protozoa is regarded as an intermediate group in which a sufficient majority is classically animal in form and habit to warrant their position in the Animal Kingdom. The relatively few plant-like forms included in the Protozoa indicate a continuous evolution from plant to animal forms of life.

Movement

There are three methods of locomotion among the Protozoa. The amoeba flows slowly forwards by projecting temporary extensions of the cytoplasm called pseudopodia or 'false feet'. The flagellates move more swiftly by whipping their flagella through the water. The ciliates, the speediest protozoa, swim by beating their cilia against the water. *Paramecium* has been observed covering about 2.5mm per second, or approximately 600 times its own length in a minute.

Feeding

All animals need food as a source of energy and to provide the raw materials for growth, repair and reproduction. Protozoa have two main methods of nutrition. The phytoflagellates such as *Euglena* are autotrophic, producing their own food, as do plants, in a process called photosynthesis. They absorb simple chemicals—water, carbon dioxide and mineral salts—from the surrounding water and build them into more complex sugars using energy from sunlight trapped by the chloroplasts. Oxygen is given off as a by-product. Excess sugar is converted to starch by a structure called a pyrenoid associated with each chloroplast and then stored as an energy reserve in the 125

Left: The Foraminifera secrete multichambered shells with tiny pores through which pseudopodia project for feeding. The White Cliffs of Dover on the south coast of England are built of limestone composed of billions of foraminiferan shells. These were deposited in the sea floor sediment millions of years ago.

Above left and left: Each *Volvox* colony consists of thousands of microscopic green flagellates embedded in a jelly-like sphere. Individuals are linked by protoplasmic threads and show amazing coordination of their flagella. Daughter colonies are released by the rupture of the parent wall.

Above: Clusters of *Vorticella,* a sedentary ciliate, are often found clinging to the weed in fresh water ponds. During feeding the bell-shaped body is extended on a long, thin stalk to trap food particles. If the water is disturbed, the stalk contracts suddenly like a rapidly recoiling spring.

Below: *Amoeba* is adept at capturing *Paramecium*. When *Paramecium* swims imprudently close, the marauding amoeba changes course to intercept it. As it draws nearer to its prey, *Amoeba* extends pseudopodia over, under and around *Paramecium*, embracing it in a food vacuole.

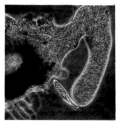

Contractile vacuole fully distended

Contractile vacuoles

Radial canals disappear as vacuole dilates

Radial canals inject contents into vacuole

Contractile vacuole emptying; radial canals filling

Radial canals swell as vacuole continues to empty

Central vacuole almost empty; radial canals full

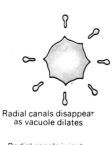

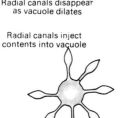

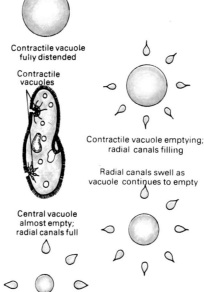

Right: *Paramecium* has two well developed contractile vacuoles, one at the front and one at the rear, maintaining the water balance of the cell. Each vacuole is encircled by a system of radiating canals that collect excess water from the surrounding cytoplasm and siphon it into the central vacuole for expulsion. By pumping water out of the cell at regular intervals the contractile vacuole prevents the cytoplasm from being flooded.

Left: Under the microscope the contractile vacuoles of a paramecium can be seen filling and emptying alternately with a pulsating rhythm. As the main vacuole empties, the radial canals begin to swell with water flowing in from the surrounding cytoplasm. Then the contents of the canals drain into the contractile vacuole, gradually dilating it. When fully distended, the central reservoir suddenly collapses, discharging its contents through a temporary pore in the cell membrane.

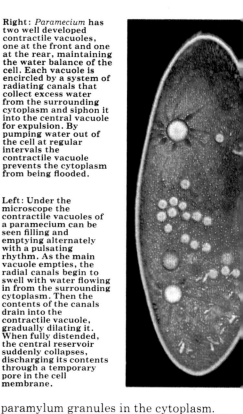

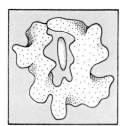

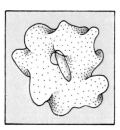

Right: *Stentor* is a large ciliate that can alter its shape dramatically by means of long, elastic fibres in its cytoplasm, from a 'horn' for feeding to a 'megaphone' if threatened. When in danger of being choked by debris a stationary stentor will first try to dodge the deluge by bending from side to side. Then it will reverse the ciliary beat in an attempt to blow the storm away. If this fails it will swim off to a more hospitable location.

Below right: Sometimes *Stentor* looks green because it harbours a green algae, *Zoochlorella*. They share a symbiotic relationship, in which *Stentor* provides shelter while the algae offer extra food and oxygen.

Below: When feeding, *Stentor* anchors itself to a base with its holdfast and beats the elaborate system of fused cilia around its mouth. This creates a swirling water current that wafts food particles into the mouth. They are carried down to the end of the gullet where they are incorporated into food vacuoles.

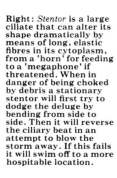

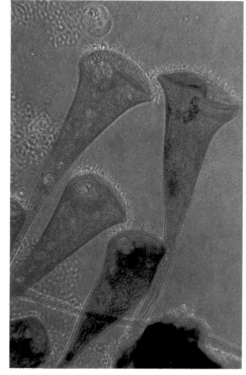

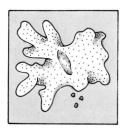

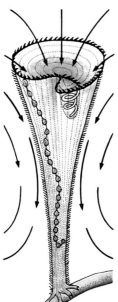

Above: The paramecium may struggle in the food vacuole at first but it becomes quieter when the oxygen supply is used up. The paramecium silhouette grows less distinct as the food particle is gradually decomposed by digestive enzymes. Indigestible remnants are simply left behind as the amoeba advances.

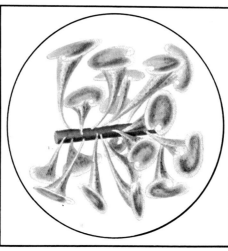

paramylum granules in the cytoplasm.

Photosynthesis becomes impossible in weed-choked ponds where little sunlight penetrates to any depth. Under these conditions, *Euglena* may resort to a saprophytic form of nutrition, obtaining the simple organic materials it needs to sustain itself from the decaying vegetation in the water.

The majority of protozoa, however, are heterotrophic, relying on their skills as predators to capture their food, and their ability to digest it. Clusters of *Paramecium*, for example, can often be found hunting around a decaying morsel of flesh or vegetation where there is a high density of the bacteria that form their staple diet. As the paramecium moves through the water, the special cilia lining the oral groove suck a current of water and food particles into the gullet. They are then incorporated with a small drop of water into a food vacuole, or bubble, in the cell interior.

Digestive enzymes are secreted from the cytoplasm into the vacuole to break down the food particles into simpler units—sugars and amino acids (the building blocks of proteins). These are then absorbed into the cytoplasm. As digestion proceeds the food vacuole moves slowly around the body along a defined path in the cytoplasm. This leads to the anal pore where the indigestible portion of the meal is expelled.

Water control and excretion

Many protozoa, especially those such as *Amoeba* and *Paramecium* living in fresh water, have a special structure in their cytoplasm known as a contractile vacuole which helps to regulate the water balance of the cell. The cytoplasm of the protozoa is vulnerable to flooding as water flows along a natural gradient from the weak environmental solution to the more concentrated cytoplasm in a process called osmosis. The contractile vacuole prevents the cell from bursting by pumping water out at regular intervals.

It is possible that some soluble waste products are also eliminated from the cell

126

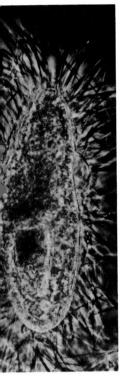

Left: This shaggy paramecium has recently released its trichocysts. These long, spear-tipped filaments are thought to act as defensive weapons. When attacked by a predator, *Paramecium* fires a barrage of trichocysts at it, forcing it away.

Right: Paramecium usually multiplies asexually by binary fission. Sometimes this cycle is interrupted by a sexual phase called conjugation. Two paramecia of different 'sexes' align lengthwise. Upon contact each micronucleus divides twice. Three of the new micronuclei disappear as the fourth undergoes a further division. One product of this division from each individual migrates through the fused oral grooves to unite with the stationary nucleus of the partner to form a zygote. This then divides three times while the old macronuclei disappear. Four micronuclei develop into new macronuclei and are distributed into four new cells by further cell divisions.

cytoplasm divides

two new daughter cells

BINARY FISSION

micronucleus macronucleus — nuclei divide

full grown Paramecium

second cell division

micronuclei divide

first cell division

micronuclei divide again

CONJUGATION

4 micronuclei become macronuclei — exchange of micronuclei

macronucleus disappears

via the contractile vacuole. Protozoa have no special organs of excretion for getting rid of undigested food or harmful waste products from the body. Soluble waste materials are usually excreted by free diffusion through the cell membrane. Solid materials are either ejected through a temporary pore in the cell membrane or left behind as the animal moves forwards.

Growth and reproduction

Growth and reproduction in protozoa are closely linked. In many cases when an individual reaches a certain critical size it simply divides into two new cells, each containing half the nucleus and half the cytoplasm of the parent cell. This asexual division of the parent cell into two daughter cells is called binary fission. It may occur as often as eight times a day in

well nourished protozoa, resulting in very rapid increase in numbers. Sometimes, the asexual cycle in *Paramecium,* for example, is interrupted by a sexual phase called conjugation.

Parasitic Sporozoa, including the malarial parasite, *Plasmodium,* carry out another form of asexual division called schizogony. This is a form of multiple budding in which four to many thousands of new individuals develop as buds on the surface of the parent. Eventually the buds break off and are distributed around the body as spores.

Behaviour

Protozoa are sensitive to many kinds of changes in their environment—light intensity, temperature gradients, chemical and mechanical barriers—and respond to

each stimulus with an appropriate sequence of movements or secretions. Both reception and response seem to be general properties of the cytoplasm. An amoeba, for example, has no nervous system but cringes from bright lights and high temperatures. The only receptor system that has been identified in protozoa is the light sensitive eyespot or stigma of certain flagellates. The red eyespot of *Euglena* directs it towards the strong light sources for photosynthesis. As it moves forwards, its front end sways from side to side, testing the direction of the light.

Most patterns of behaviour are related in some way to the stimulus. Paramecia, for example, are incredibly active little creatures, constantly swimming about in search of food. Any obstacle, extreme temperature change or obnoxious chemical in the path of the paramecium elicits an avoiding reaction. By momentarily reversing the direction of the ciliary stroke it beats a hasty retreat, changing direction slightly as it goes. It then proceeds on a new tack. If it still collides with the obstruction it will continue the 'advance and retreat' policy until it successfully navigates a path around the obstacle. Such adaptive behaviour improves the individual's chances of survival.

Because most of the protozoa do not have shells or skeletons they do not survive well in the fossil record of what animals living hundreds of millions of years ago were like. Consequently, while it is tempting to take the 'first animals' title to its logical conclusion and assume that all other multicellular animals evolved from the simpler single-celled animals, there is no firm evidence to support this. It is only possible to say that the Protozoa are the simplest of living animals.

Despite the apparent simplicity of their structure and organization, however, the protozoa are remarkably successful animals, both in terms of numbers and in the variety of places in which they live. Within the limitations of one cell, the Protozoa have achieved an incredible diversity of form and habits.

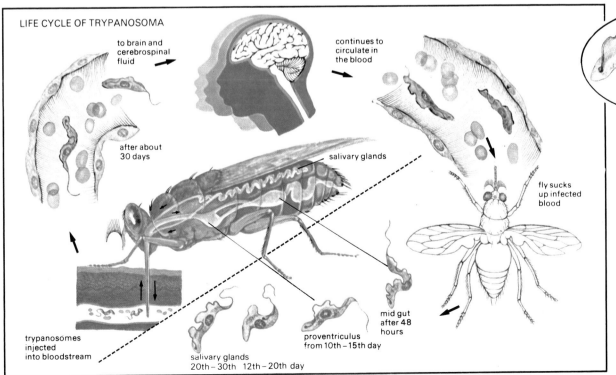

LIFE CYCLE OF TRYPANOSOMA

to brain and cerebrospinal fluid

continues to circulate in the blood

after about 30 days

salivary glands

fly sucks up infected blood

trypanosomes injected into bloodstream

salivary glands 20th–30th 12th–20th day

proventriculus from 10th–15th day

mid gut after 48 hours

TRYPANOSOME x c. 2,500 — flagellum

undulating membrane — pellicle

Above: *Trypanosoma* is a long, slender parasitic flagellate living in the human bloodstream where it causes Africa sleeping sickness. The flagellum is held in an undulating membrane.

Left: Trypanosomes are transmitted by the tsetse fly. If a fly bites an infected man it sucks up some trypanosomes in its blood meal. These multiply in the fly's gut and migrate to the salivary glands. When the fly feeds again, some trypanosomes are injected into the wound with the saliva. They reproduce rapidly in the bloodstream and finally invade the fluid around the brain, producing a characteristic lethargy, coma and ultimately death.

127

Echinoderms

The members of the group *Echinodermata* (the word means spiny-skinned) constitute one of the major groups of the animal kingdom All echinoderms live in the sea and the group contains more than 5,000 living species divided into five classes: the starfish, the brittle stars, the sea urchins, the sea cucumbers and the sea lilies.

Evolution of the echinoderms

The echinoderms are distinctly different from all other invertebrates. They are as complex as the arthropods (the phylum which includes crustaceans, spiders and insects) but their structure and way of life are very different. Because the larval forms of some echinoderms in some ways resemble the most primitive chordates (a phylum which includes some invertebrates and all the vertebrates) it has been suggested that they are distantly related and share a common ancestry. If this is so, then the relationship is remote, for the two stocks must have diverged over 500 million years ago. No fossils giving proof of such a relationship have ever been discovered so its existence remains a matter of speculation.

Certainly there is little resemblance between any particular adult echinoderm and any adult chordate. Like most multicellular animals, chordates are bilaterally symmetrical, which means that basically their bodies consist of two sides, each of which is a mirror image of the other. In mammals, including man, this symmetry is immediately apparent, even though the pattern has been lost in, for example, the positioning of the heart and major arteries. In contrast to the mammals, the echinoderms are built on a radially symmetrical plan, that is, instead of there being only two sections of the body which mirror each other there may be several. This symmetry is usually five-fold in echinoderms.

However, a close examination of the structure of echinoderms shows that certain very primitive features of their anatomy do not correspond with this pattern, indicating that all echinoderms originally developed from creatures with bilateral symmetry.

It is also interesting that radially symmetrical animals are not well adapted for active movement—sedentary creatures like sea anemones, or a passive floating animal like the jelly fish, lack the head and sense organs which play a 'reconnaissance' role in active movement. Most echinoderms do move actively, although never very rapidly. Fossil evidence shows that the kind of echinoderms which are stalked and stay in one place (such as sea lilies) are an extremely ancient group. If all echinoderms were descended from this group it would explain the radial symmetry, which is most suited to a sedentary existence.

Starfish

The best known group of echinoderms is the class *Asteroidea*, containing the starfish. Some forms of starfish live in shallow water and can sometimes be found stranded on the beach near the low tide mark. There are about 1,600 species all of which are all more or less star-shaped,

Above: Not all starfish have well defined arms. The five arms of this cushion star, *Porania pulvillus*, merge into each other.

Left: A starfish, *Fromia ghardagna*, and a bivalve mollusc resting on coral. Like most starfish it has five arms. Starfish commonly prey on bivalves such as oysters.

Above right: As this picture of a sunstar, *Solaster papposus*, shows, not all starfish have, only five arms.

Right: A blue starfish, *Linckia laevigata*. A starfish skeleton consists of a mesh of plates. Unlike an arthropod's exoskeleton, which has to be moulted periodically, it grows with the animal.

Below and right: Diagrams to show the body structure of a starfish. The ampullae which operate the tube feet are connected through valves to radial canals which in turn lead into a central ring canal. This sytem is filled with water which enters through a sieve plate, or madreporite. Two branches of the animal's digestive gland run along each arm from a central stomach. Starfish breathe by means of delicate skin gills (papulae) which project from the body surface between the plates of the skeleton. The skin gills are protected by heavy spines and are kept clean by clusters of tiny pincers called pedicellariae. The five-fold symmetry of the animal is apparent.

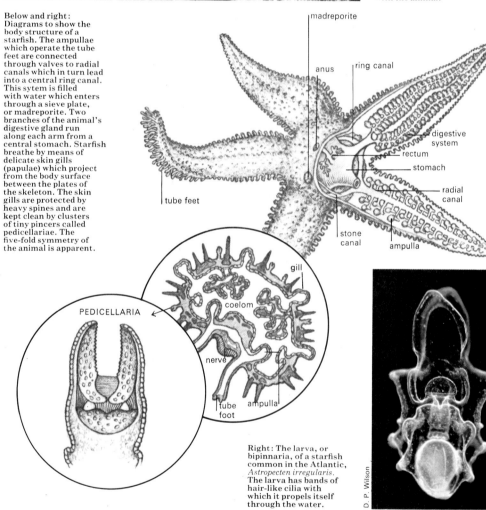

madreporite

anus — ring canal

tube feet

digestive system

rectum

stomach

radial canal

stone canal

ampulla

PEDICELLARIA

gill

coelom

nerve

tube foot

ampulla

Right: The larva, or bipinnaria, of a starfish common in the Atlantic, *Astropecten irregularis*. The larva has bands of hair-like cilia with which it propels itself through the water.

Right: A series of pictures to show how a starfish can regain its 'feet' from an upside down position. Some species take up to an hour to perform the operation. Many starfish can voluntarily turn on their backs. They do this when attacked, especially if the assailant is another predatory starfish.

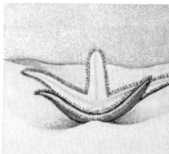

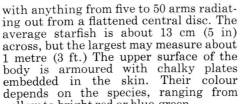

with anything from five to 50 arms radiating out from a flattened central disc. The average starfish is about 13 cm (5 in) across, but the largest may measure about 1 metre (3 ft.) The upper surface of the body is armoured with chalky plates embedded in the skin. Their colour depends on the species, ranging from yellow to bright red or blue-green.

The underside of starfish presents a more varied appearance. In the centre is the mouth, from which grooves radiate out along the length of each arm. On each side of the grooves are numerous mobile, slender tube feet. These are the organs that enable the starfish to move. The ends of the tube-feet are able to grip by suction, being operated hydraulically by an internal system of water-filled tubes. These are connected to the exterior at the *madreporite* which is a large, chalky plate on the upper surface positioned to one side of the central disc. The madreporite is the only visible sign that starfish are not totally radially symmetrical.

The movement of starfish is controlled by nerves radiating from a nerve ring running round the central disc. No one part of this ring is in overall charge and no single arm normally leads the way during movement. In fact when a starfish starts to move, its arms, propelled by their tube feet, sometimes start to move in different directions. Some time may elapse before the central nerve ring manages to co-ordinate the activities of the arms so that the animal moves in one direction. Similarly, if a starfish is turned upside down, when it attempts to right itself each arm initially attempts to do so independently. Since the arms must co-operate to turn the central disc upright, the process is a lengthy one. The disadvantage of not having a single nerve centre or brain is immediately apparent, yet the starfish have survived for many millions of years without one.

Starfish have few sense organs. At the end of each arm, one tube foot acts as an organ of touch and just above is a tiny simple eye. In most circumstances starfish respond mainly to chemical stimuli. For example, if food is near, chemicals from it will dissolve in the surrounding water to be picked up by sensitive cells on the starfish's body. The starfish finds its meal by moving towards these stimuli.

Most kinds of starfish feed on molluscs, often bivalves such as oysters. The starfish straddles the mollusc and, grasping the two halves of its shell with numerous tube-feet, starts to pull. At first the mollusc is able to keep its shell tightly closed, but the starfish has more stamina and after some minutes the mollusc gives way.

Because of their feeding habits starfish can be serious pests at oysterbeds. At one time oyster fishermen dealt with them by hauling them up, chopping them into pieces and throwing them overboard. Despite this, however, the starfish increased in numbers. This was because of their remarkable powers of regeneration. If a starfish loses an arm, not only can it replace it, but the detached arm can also grow a new starfish. One Californian species normally breeds in this way, literally pulling itself apart in order to start the process.

More typically, starfish breed sexually. In the common yellow starfish found off

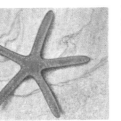

Below: The underside of an arm of a crown of thorns starfish. The thin-walled tube feet which end in yellow suckers are clearly visible: some are extended and some retracted. Expansion or contraction of a water reservoir called an ampulla behind each foot causes it to retract or extend as necessary.

Below: The beautiful crown of thorns starfish, *Acanthaster planci*. These animals feed on coral polyps and have become very common on the Great Barrier Reef, off the coast of Queensland, Australia. So successful have they been that the very existence of the Great Barrier Reef has become threatened.

  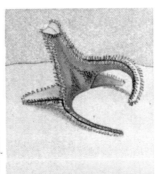 

Above: A starfish, *Marthasterias glacialis*, devours a bivalve. After forcing the two plates of the mollusc's shell apart, the starfish begins to digest its victim by turning the lower part of its stomach inside out and inserting it between the shell plates. The starfish's tube feet can clearly be seen.

129

Above: A brittle star,
Ophiothrix fragilis.
Compared with starfish
these creatures are
fairly agile, using their
arms both for movement
and for catching small
marine animals such as
worms. Most brittle stars
have five arms and these
easily break off when the
animal is attacked.
They do, however,
quickly grow again.

Right: The body plan of
a sea urchin. Although
it does not look much
like a starfish, it has
the same basic structure.
There are five rows of
tube feet which run from
the lower surface, near
the mouth, to the upper
surface, near the anus.
The plates of the
skeleton are joined
together to form a shell
which completely
encloses the soft parts of
the body. A complicated
structure, sometimes
called Aristotle's
lantern, carrying five
teeth for chewing food
surrounds the animal's
mouth. Sea urchins are
mainly scavengers.

Below: An edible sea
urchin, *Echinus
esculentus.* The long,
thin tube feet which
extend beyond the spines
are clearly visible.

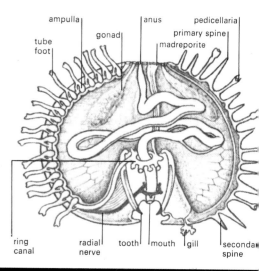

the coasts of Britain all females ripen at
the same time and each produces up to
2.5 million eggs. The release of eggs by
one female stimulates all of the others in
the neighbourhood to do the same, stimulating the males to release their sperms.
For a short time the sea teems with tiny
floating starfish larvae, known as *bipinnaria,* but few survive to settle and metamorphose into small starfish. In some
species females produce only a few very
yolky eggs and on fertilization these
develop directly into starfish.

Brittle stars
Members of the second class of echinoderms, the brittle stars (class *Ophiuroidea*)
are also star-shaped, but have slender
arms which are rounded in section, and
very distinct from the central disc. The
arms are easily detached and this is how
the group gets its popular name. Again,
detached arms can regenerate whole
brittle stars and some species normally
breed in this way. Others breed sexually,
producing planktonic larvae, and in
others the fertilized eggs are retained
within the females' bodies then born as
tiny replicas of their parents.

On the underside of a brittle star's
arms, the tube-feet protrude through
chalky plates. However, the feet are short
and not nearly as useful as those of the
true starfish. A brittlestar gets about by
writhing its way along with its arms.
Living in crowds on the sea-bed, they
feed by scavenging on organic particles
and plankton, carried towards the mouth
by currents set up by cilia in the mouth
region. Brittle stars play an important
role in cleansing the sea: they thrive in
heavily polluted waters.

Above: This sea urchin,
Heterocentrotus, is
equipped with long, thick
spines. To get from place
to place, sea urchins use
both their spines, which
are moved by muscles,
and their tube feet,
which are operated by
water pressure and
muscles. The
spines of some sea
urchins are both sharp
and poisonous.

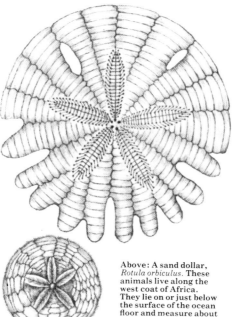

Above: A sand dollar,
Rotula orbiculus. These
animals live along the
west coat of Africa.
They lie on or just below
the surface of the ocean
floor and measure about
7.5 cm (3 in) across.

Left: Top and side views
of the sand dollar,
Echinarachnius parma,
common along the
American Atlantic coast.

Above and right: A heart
urchin, *Echinocardium.*
These animals burrow
under the surface of the
sand feeding on whatever
they can find, usually
small animals or plants.
Heart urchins always
keep clear a channel to
the surface of the sand
for oxygenated water,
and they have specially
modified tube feet for
this purpose.

Sea urchins

Sea urchins and their relations form the class *Echinoidea*. Being either spherical or like thick, flattened discs, they look very different from starfish but are in fact very similar in structure. Although no larger in diameter, sea urchins are also bulkier than starfish. They nevertheless move quite actively using their tube-feet, sometimes assisted by moveable spines and even their jaws. Most live on the beds of shallow seas, but some, including the flattened sand dollar and the heart urchins, burrow in sand. Some species even burrow into rock, using their spines as files.

Echinoids usually breed by shedding eggs and sperms into the water to produce a planktonic larva, the *echinopluteus*, but in some species the young are kept in a special pouch until they emerge as fully formed urchins. Echinoids can replace lost parts of the shell, tube-feet, or pedicellariae, but cannot regenerate themselves as well as starfish do. When full of ripe eggs or sperms, the common urchin of Mediterranean and European coasts has been esteemed as a food by man since at least the time of the Romans.

Sea cucumbers

The sea cucumbers belong to the class *Holothuroidea*. They look rather like large slugs with the addition of a bunch of tentacles surrounding a mouth at one end. Rows of tube-feet run along their bodies, although there are fewer of these on the side of the animal that normally lies uppermost. Some species have no tube-feet at all and move by contracting the muscles of the body which, in fact, is flexible despite the armour embedded in the skin.

Sea cucumbers are found in most seas, sometimes at great depths, and some are active burrowers. The holothurians' powers of regeneration are remarkable; when threatened they eject their internal organs as a kind of organic missile, growing new ones within a few weeks. As an additional defence some species are poisonous to fish.

Some sea cucumbers feed on plankton and other marine animals which they trap with long, slimy feelers, while others scavenge on decaying matter from the sea bed. Reproduction is usually sexual, the planktonic larva being called an *auricularia*. In some species the fertilized eggs develop in special pouches either in the skin or inside the body of the female. Asexual reproduction can also occur in some species, where individuals tear themselves into two parts, each of which regenerates the lost parts.

Sea lilies

Among the strangest and most beautiful of echinoderms are the 80 species of sea lilies and feather stars belonging to the class *Crinoidea*. Sea lilies grow on stalks attached to the bed of deep seas. At the top of the jointed stalk are five branched arms. Each branch has a groove running along it, and in each groove are cilia which catch small floating food particles and pass them on to the mouth. Unusually for an echinoderm, the mouth of the sea lily is on the upper surface. Feather stars are similar but are only stalked when they are young. They live in shallow seas, where they haul themselves along using their arms. Their freely floating larvae are called *doliolaria*.

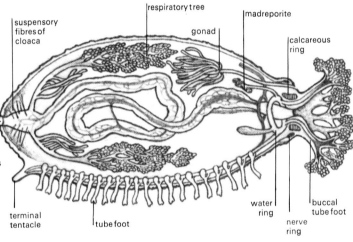

suspensory fibres of cloaca — respiratory tree — gonad — madreporite — calcareous ring — terminal tentacle — tube foot — water ring — nerve ring — buccal tube foot

Above, left and right: A feather star, *Antedon bifida*, and a sea lily, *Pentacrinus*. These animals belong to the class *Crinoidea*. Like other echinoderms they usually have five-fold symmetry although the arms may be branched near their bases. When young, feather stars are stalked like their cousins the sea lilies.

Above: A sea cucumber, *Cucumaria saxicola*. The tube feet and feeding tentacles are visible.

Left and above left: A photograph and a body plan of a sea cucumber. At first sight these animals look quite different from other echinoderms; the body wall, for example, is muscular and has only a few skeletal plates. They do, however, have tube feet and, as in sea urchins, these extend in rows from the mouth at one end to the anus at the other. The system of canals which supplies the tube feet often has five-fold symmetry. Between 10 and 30 tube feet around the mouth are modified as tentacles for feeding. Many sea cucumbers burrow in the sea bed.

131

Sponges and Corals

Corals, sea anemones and jellyfish are members of a primitive group of animals called Coelenterates. Most of them live in the sea—*Hydra* is an exception as it lives in fresh water. Coelenterates have three major characteristics in common: a simple three-layered body-wall; a single body cavity with only one opening or mouth which is an entrance for food, water and oxygen and the exit for wastes and water; and stinging tentacles.

Corals are best known for the massive 'rocky' reefs they build in the tropics. The Great Barrier Reef of Australia is the largest coral reef in the world. It stretches as a giant natural breakwater for 2,012 km (1,260 miles) down the east coast from north of Queensland to just south of the tropic of Capricorn. Occasionally the tip of the reef breaks the surface of the warm, blue Pacific Ocean in a scattering of coral islands and treacherous reef flats. In some places the reef is as much as 457 m (1,500 ft) thick. Yet almost unbelievably the whole of this huge underwater mountain chain has been designed and built by countless billions of industrious little animals called *coral polyps,* each of which is little bigger than a match head.

Each tiny, stony coral polyp looks like a miniature sea anemone sitting in its own private fortress. Small stationary animals like the coral polyp are particularly vulnerable to attack by hungry predators. In order to protect themselves, the stony corals construct hard, chalky skeletons around their bodies into which they can retreat very rapidly in times of danger. It is these white skeletons of the living and, more importantly, the dead coral that form the intricate limestone framework of the reef.

The majority of reef-building corals form large colonies. In some, like the rounded brain coral, the walls of the skeletons merge, creating an intriguing maze of ridges and valleys that meander across the surface of the boulder like the convolutions of the human brain. Others, such as the staghorn coral, are more delicate, with fine branches that create dramatic silhouettes in the water.

In many coral colonies, the neighbouring polyps are only semi-detached. Individuals are linked through holes in the skeletal walls and by body flaps that spread as a thin film across the surface of the colony. Food is shared between polyps via these connections.

Reef corals are typically shy, nocturnal feeders. During the day, polyps are withdrawn into their skeletal cups and the coral looks disappointingly lifeless. But at night, the whole reef comes magically to life. All the coral polyps stretch out their tentacles, probing the waters like fields of hungry flowers. Any small animals that accidentally collide with them are paralysed and trapped by means of powerful stinging cells called *nematocysts*.

While stony corals are the main reef architects and masons, other animals and plants also contribute 'bricks and mortar' to the reef structure. The most important of these are the 'stinging' corals—relatives of the true stony corals that also build heavy, limy skeletons—and the encrusting seaweeds. These stony seaweeds cement loose coral sand, empty snail shells and other rubble into the crevices between the individual coral colonies, binding them permanently together in the massive reef platform.

Growth of the reef

Reef-forming corals are very selective about where they live. They can only grow in shallow, tropical seas where the temperature of the water never falls below 20°C. It is only in these warmer waters that the coral polyps can extract calcium from the sea water and deposit it as chalk, or calcium carbonate, in their skeletons at a faster rate than the waves wash it away again.

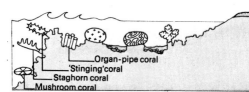

Valerie Taylor, Ardea

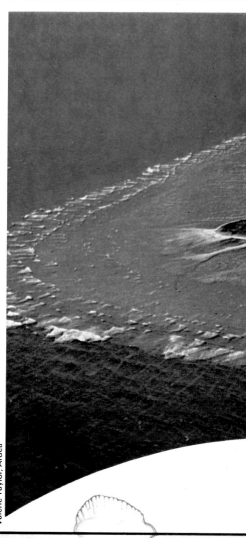

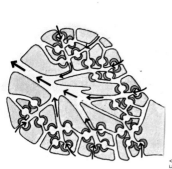

Dr. F. Sauer, ZEFA

Above: Sponges in the phylum *Porifera* are the most primitive multicellular animals. They are aquatic, predominantly marine and sedentary. The surface is penetrated with many inhalent pores through which water laden with small food particles passes into a central cavity, or spongocoel. It leaves by a single inhalent pore. The spongocoel may be folded into many chambers and is lined with collar cells, or choanocytes. Each has a whip-like flagellum surrounded by a sticky collar. Feeding currents are created by the beating of the flagella. Food particles stick to the collar and are ingested by amoeboid cells.

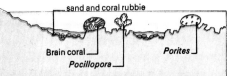

shallow lagoon

sand and coral rubble

Brain coral

Pocillopora

Porites

Left: A slice through a coral reef reveals the zonation of coral growth. The richest growth occurs on the reef cliff. Only the heaviest corals can survive the surf breaking over the reef edge. More delicate forms thrive in the calmer waters of the lagoon.

Left: One Tree Island is a coral island on the Great Barrier Reef. The darker areas of the surrounding reef platform are regions of living coral; the paler patches are coral sand and rubble.

Right: The reef-building stony corals only flourish in shallow tropical seas where the water is always warmer than 20°C.

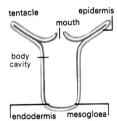

tentacle   epidermis   mouth

body cavity

endodermis   mesogloea

Left and right: The Coelenterates have two body plans. The stationary polyp of the corals and sea anemones is a squat, hollow column topped with tentacles. The free-swimming, bell-shaped jellyfish medusa is basically a squashed upside down polyp with an over-developed middle layer of jelly.

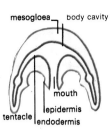

mesogloea   body cavity

mouth

tentacle   epidermis   endodermis

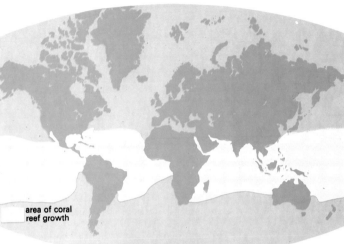

area of coral reef growth

Heather Angel

Silver gull

Above: The pretty little Devonshire cup coral is a hardy, solitary specimen which lives on the rocky shores around Britain. A bird's eye view shows its central split of a mouth surrounded by a perfect ring of tentacles. The bright spots on the tentacles are the stinging cells that stun the prey.

Below: A cut-away section of a stony coral polyp shows it sitting in its chalky skeleton. The body flaps link up with neighbouring polyps for food sharing.

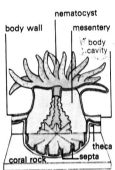

nematocyst

body wall   mesentery

body cavity

coral rock   theca   septa

Bavaria Verlag

Left: The vacant skeletal cups of a dead stony coral colony clearly show the thin radial ridges, or septa.

Below left: A branching 'soft' coral colony grows on the terraces of a reef cliff. 'Soft' corals can live in deeper water than the stony reef-building corals because they do not need sunlight for skeleton formation.

Below: A single 'soft' coral polyp stretches out its eight feathery tentacles for feeding. The individual polyps that build the branches of the colony are linked by a mass of flesh called coenenchyme. The whole colony is stiffened by a hard rod.

SECONDARY CARNIVORES

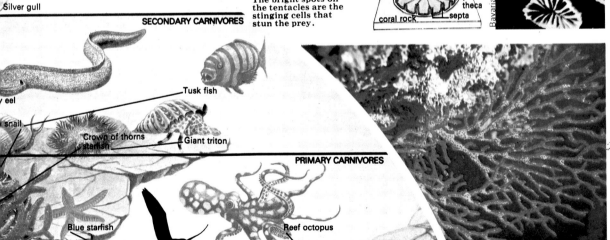

eel   Tusk fish

snail   Crown of thorns starfish   Giant triton

PRIMARY CARNIVORES

Blue starfish   Reef octopus

HERBIVORES

Green turtle   Sea urchin

arrot fish   Sea hare

PLANTS

Seaweed

Crab

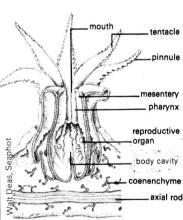

mouth   tentacle

pinnule

mesentery
pharynx

reproductive organ

body cavity

coenenchyme

axial rod

Walt Deas, Seaphot

Left: A coral reef is like a giant, living kaleidoscope, home for teeming millions of brightly coloured animals and plants that find food and shelter in or around its numerous nooks and crannies. Docile sponges, garish sea slugs and venomous snails live side by side on the reef while rainbow

blurs of little fish dart in and out among the coral. A tangled web of 'eat and be eaten' interactions is played out between the members of the complex reef community on a magnificent stage of living coral. Each line on the chart points up from the prey to its predator in the next level of the community.

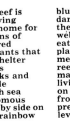

133

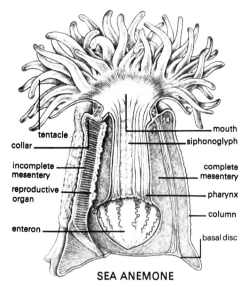

SEA ANEMONE

tentacle
collar
incomplete mesentery
reproductive organ
enteron
mouth
siphonoglyph
complete mesentery
pharynx
column
basal disc

Heather Angel

Top: A sea anemone is divided up internally by soft partitions called mesenteries. These greatly increase the surface area for the absorption of food and oxygen.

Above: The colourful Catherine-wheel of a dahlia anemone's crown of tentacles is a very efficient food trap.

Below: Glistening beadlet sea anemones cling tenaciously to the side of a rock pool at low tide. The column is contracted into a tight little button with the tentacles tucked away inside to protect them from water loss and damage until the tide comes in again. Then the tentacles can expand for feeding.

Heather Angel

Right: A clown fish peeps out from between the tentacles of a sea anemone where it lives, apparently immune to their stings. In return for shelter, the gaily painted little fish probably cleans up the crumbs of waste the sea anemone spits out and may also lure other unwary fish within range of the tentacles.

This does not mean, however, that corals cannot exist in colder seas. The hardy, solitary Devonshire cup coral, *Carophyllia,* for example, is found in British waters at temperatures as low as 3°C, although clearly it cannot participate in reef formation under these conditions.

Corals also only thrive in crystal-clear water. Too much sediment in the water, around the mouth of a river, for example, would smother the tiny coral polyps as it settled. Lots of silt also makes the water murky, which inhibits reef formation by blocking the sunlight.

Sunlight is a critical factor in stony coral growth because of a crucial association between the coral and some minute plants called *Zooxanthella* which live within the cells of the coral tissue. Algal growth stimulates skeleton production, probably by speeding up the chemical process of extracting calcium from the sea water. It may also increase the metabolic efficiency of the coral polyp by using its waste products. The living region of the reef is therefore restricted to the upper reef levels—usually the top 61 m (200 ft) of water—where enough light penetrates to enable algal growth to proceed at an efficient rate.

These small plant 'guests' in the coral tissue contribute to the pastel yellow, brown and green colours of some reef-forming corals. The brighter reds and oranges are created by pigment cells in the body wall. This explains why the corals lose their attractive colours when they die and the living tissue disintegrates. All that remains is the bleached, brittle skeleton, which is itself quickly covered with a 'mossy' film of seaweed growth and becomes a dull, greenish colour.

Building a reef is a mammoth task—coral reefs generally grow very slowly. The corals spread by producing vast numbers of minute 'hairy' larvae called *planulae*. These tiny scouts swim around exploring the reef until they find a hard surface, such as a piece of dead coral, upon which to settle. The sedentary planula then gradually changes into a small polyp, developing a whorl of small bumps or juvenile tentacles around its mouth and the rudiments of a skeleton at its base.

This pioneering young polyp is the founder member of a new coral colony. A miniature polyp sprouts from the side of its column. Gradually as the bud grows bigger it starts to separate from its parent, although they never become completely detached. Budding continues and the colony expands. Thus the reef is built up, layer upon layer, with the skeletons of the ancestors supporting the present generation of living coral.

Life on the reef
Some of the most spectacular reef residents are relatives of the stony corals—the 'soft' corals, sea anemones and jellyfish. These colourful and sometimes bizarre looking creatures are less sensitive about the temperature of the water in which they live than their skeleton-forming cousins. Consequently they are familiar to rock-pool explorers and beach combers around the coasts of North America, Europe and Africa.

'Soft' corals invariably live in colonies, creating fragile, branching formations like bendy sea firs, sea feather and sea whips. In fact the 'soft' corals are not

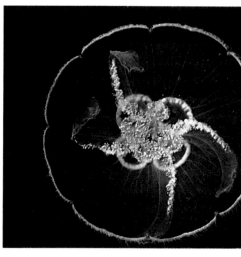

The tiny transparent moon jellyfish, *Aurelia,* floats around the oceans of the world. Viewed from below, the four oral arms around the mouth are clearly visible.—Food raining down on to the top of the bell is swept to the edge where it is 'licked' off by the oral arms and carried to the mouth.

AURELIA

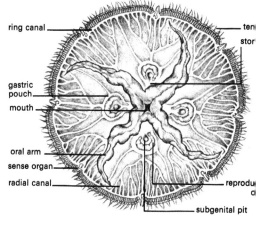

ring canal
gastric pouch
mouth
oral arm
sense organ
radial canal
ten
stor
reprodu o
subgenital pit

Above: Jellyfish are jet propelled. By gently lifting the sides of the bell water is sucked up underneath. When the bell contracts a jet of water is squirted downwards, forcing the jellyfish up into the food-rich surface waters. As soon as the umbrella stops opening and closing, the jellyfish begins to sink.

Below: *Haliclystus* is an unusual, stationary jellyfish. Unlike its free-swimming relatives it lives hanging down by a short stalk from a piece of weed like a tiny orange bell. Each of the eight lobes of the bell is trimmed with a spray of knobbed tentacles which are used for defence and for catching food.

Oxford Scientific Films

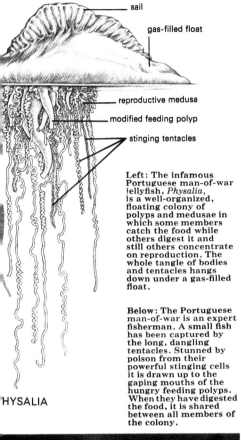

sail
gas-filled float
reproductive medusa
modified feeding polyp
stinging tentacles

PHYSALIA

Left: The infamous Portuguese man-of-war jellyfish, *Physalia*, is a well-organized, floating colony of polyps and medusae in which some members catch the food while others digest it and still others concentrate on reproduction. The whole tangle of bodies and tentacles hangs down under a gas-filled float.

Below: The Portuguese man-of-war is an expert fisherman. A small fish has been captured by the long, dangling tentacles. Stunned by poison from their powerful stinging cells it is drawn up to the gaping mouths of the hungry feeding polyps. When they have digested the food, it is shared between all members of the colony.

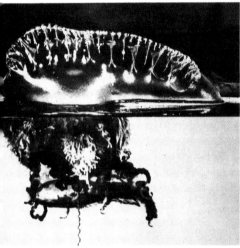

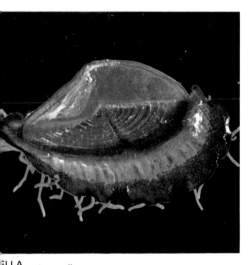

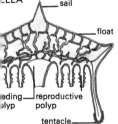

VELELLA

sail
float
feeding polyp
reproductive polyp
tentacle

Above and left: *Velella* is a small colonial jellyfish. Its saucer-shaped float is filled with air chambers for great buoyancy and topped with a high crest to catch the wind as it drifts on top of the sea. This float supports one central feeding polyp surrounded by reproductive polyps and stinging tentacles

really soft at all, but rather leathery to the touch. They are often called 'false' corals because unlike the stony corals they do not build heavy cases around their bodies. Instead they rely on an internal network of coloured rods, spikes or spines to support the mass of soft tissue.

Fortunately, 'soft' corals do not lose their vivid red, orange, yellow and blue colours when they die because this colour is largely part of the skeleton and not of the living tissue. The skeletal rods of the red precious coral, for example, which grows in the Mediterranean and around the Japanese Islands, have been used since Greek times for making jewellery.

The sea anemones are structurally very similar to stony coral polyps, except that they are much bigger and lack a skeleton. One monster sea anemone, the giant barrier reef anemone, can grow as big as 0.9 m (3 ft) in diameter. Most of them also exist independently rather than forming colonies. They spend most of their time anchored to rocks and dead coral by their basal discs, or buried in the sand with their tentacles waving freely in the water, waiting to trap and paralyse passing small fish.

Coelenterates on the move

Although they look permanently anchored on the rocks, most sea anemones are perfectly capable of moving at least short distances, usually by shuffling slowly along on their bases. Some sea anemones will even ride on the back of a hermit crab's shell, an arrangement which seems to work to their mutual benefit. The crab gains camouflage and protection from the sea anemone's stinging tentacles. In return the sea anemone probably collects food floating up as the crab picks over the debris on the reef floor, looking for edible particles.

Sea anemones often reproduce asexually by splitting in half down the middle. They also multiply sexually by producing planulae larvae in much the same way as the coral polyps do.

In complete contrast to the sedate corals and sea anemones, the jellyfish are free to float around the oceans of the world at the whim of winds, tides and currents. Two distinct types of jellyfish frequent the reef—the true, medusoid jellyfish and the colonial jellyfish. The true, free-swimming, umbrella-shaped jellyfish float around in the water, occasionally flapping the sides of the umbrella to lift themselves back into the food-rich pastures at the surface.

Such jellyfish have a complicated life-cycle. Reproductive organs in the mature medusoid jellyfish produce eggs and sperms. The fertilized egg develops into a planula larva that settles and forms a polyp-like larval stage. In spring this polyp undergoes a weird type of segmentation called *strobilation* in which the column of the polyp divides up into a stack of discs. Each disc gradually develops eight radial arms and eventually swims off as a small jellyfish bell.

Jellyfish are notorious for the painful sting they can inflict on unsuspecting swimmers who accidentally brush against the stinging cells on their trailing tentacles. Fortunately, jellyfish stings are rarely fatal to a healthy man. The box jellies, or sea wasps, which appear from time to time around the Australian coast, are an exception however. They are particularly dangerous because the cubes of

Oxford Scientific Films

Heather Angel

Above: A pale forest of *Obelia* grows on a piece of seaweed. The inset shows a detail of a feeding polyp.

Below: Each *Obelia* colony consists of a main stem which grows up from an anchoring 'root' system with feeding and reproductive polyps branching off at intervals.

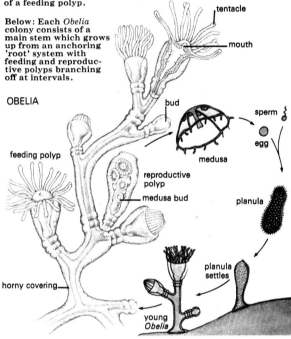

OBELIA

tentacle
mouth
bud
sperm
egg
medusa
feeding polyp
reproductive polyp
medusa bud
planula
planula settles
horny covering
young *Obelia*

Above: In the life cycle of *Obelia*, a tiny medusa buds from the colony and swims off. Its egg, fertilized by a sperm from another medusa, grows into a 'hairy' planula larva which scouts about until it finds a rock or seaweed on which it lands. Then it becomes a small polyp that forms a new *Obelia* colony by budding.

Below: In the colonies of the oaten-pipes hydroid, *Tubularia*, the feeding polyps are perched on top of long stalks. Each one is surrounded by a cluster of reproductive medusae cascading down between the snaking tentacles. *Tubularia* often grows on rocks and seaweed around the coasts of Britain and America.

Heather Angel

135

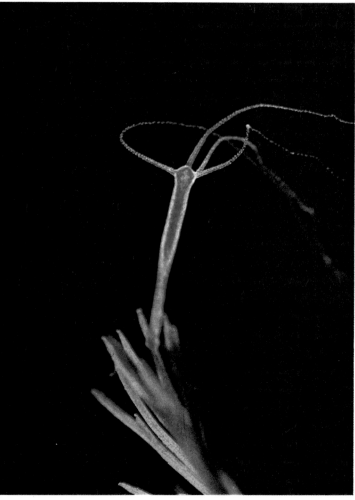

Above left: *Hydra* cartwheels along by repeatedly arching its bendy body over, then flipping its column over its tentacles and swinging back into an upright position again.

Left: *Hydra* lives in fresh water ponds attached to pieces of weed, wood or a stone.

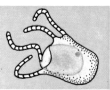

HYDRA

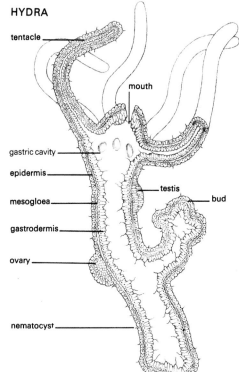

tentacle

mouth

gastric cavity

epidermis

mesogloea

gastrodermis

ovary

testis

bud

nematocyst

basal disc

Right: The waving tentacles of *Hydra* are a death trap for many water fleas. Each one is armed with a battery of stinging cells, or nematocysts. Their poisonous threads kill or paralyse the prey when it swims against them. Then the stretchy tentacles bend over, stuffing the food into the mouth.

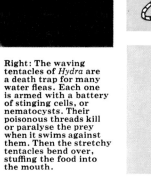

thread

trigger
lid

coiled thread

nucleus

bristle

barb

lid

capsule

nucleus

UNDISCHARGED

DISCHARGED

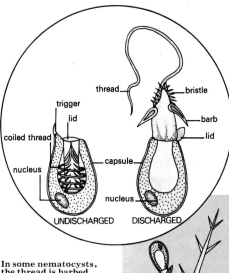

Above: *Hydra* reproduces sexually and asexually. In the autumn, ovaries or testes develop as small bumps on the side of the column. The fertilized egg drops to the bottom of the pond where it overwinters in the mud protected by a thick coat. In spring, a tiny *Hydra* hatches which will multiply in summer.

136

Right: Nematocysts are *Hydra's* deadly weapons. An undischarged nematocyst consists of a tightly-coiled thread wound into a capsule in the tentacle wall. When the prey swims against the tentacles, it triggers a rapid firing of nematocysts, probably by causing a sudden increase in the water pressure of the capsule.

In some nematocysts, the thread is barbed and the tip rotates like a drill as it is ejected. This pierces the prey and injects a lethal poison. In others, the thread is sticky and winds about the prey like a lasso, thus ensnaring it. Each nematocyst is only fired once and then replaced.

jelly are practically transparent and therefore very difficult to see in the water. Their powerful stings cause painful local inflammation and can even be fatal.

The equally infamous Portuguese man-of-war is another stinging visitor to the coral reef. Normally they bob like large, purple-tinged air bubbles on the surface of the water with their tentacles hanging down to trap small reef fish. Sometimes during storms they are washed ashore and left stranded high and dry on the beach, like crumpled plastic bottles.

Threats to the reef

A coral reef behaves like some huge, self-repairing mountain range. Any factor that damages the thin outer 'skin' of living coral exposes the inner, dead regions of the reef to wave action and erosion. Actively budding coral polyps are able to keep pace with a limited amount of damage. If the damaged area is extensive, however, coral regrowth by budding to cover the injury is too slow to prevent serious reef disintegration.

Fortunately, such serious damage has apparently occurred rarely in the long history of the Great Barrier Reef. There is increasing concern, however, about the effect of marine pollution by industrial waste and crude oil spillage on coral growth. Such toxic wastes may either kill the coral polyp by choking or poisoning it, or kill the microscopic animals on which the coral feeds, thus starving it to death.

Another imminent threat to the reef is the amount of dredging, blasting and drilling for valuable deposits of limestone, sand and oil which takes place on or near the reef. The thousands of tourists who visit the reef each year also unwittingly crush large numbers of coral polyps and skeletons as they trample over the reef platform, collecting coral souvenirs.

The most serious attack on the Great Barrier Reef—and other reefs in the Red Sea, the Indian and Pacific Oceans—has occurred in the spiky shape of the crown of thorns starfish, *Acanthaster planci*. This predator is normally found only in very small numbers, feeding at night on coral polyps, particularly those of the important stony corals. Under normal circumstances, coral growth keeps pace with predation. Since the early 1960s, however, there has been a population explosion of *Acanthaster* which has left acres of the reef stripped of living coral and disintegrating.

The reason for this comparatively sudden increase in numbers—whether it is a natural population cycle or triggered off in some way by man upsetting the balance of nature on the reef—is not clear. It has been suggested, for example, that the large scale removal of the only real predator on *Acanthaster,* the giant triton snail, by collectors of its beautiful shell may be one cause.

Urgent control measures are being taken to protect the reef from the onslaught of starfish and man. The crown of thorns starfish has been 'outlawed' and biologists are also experimenting with means of birth control for the starfish, and a careful watch is being kept on the exploitation of the reef's natural resources. In future, strict conservation of the Great Barrier Reef province as a wildlife reserve should help to ensure the survival of one of the great natural wonders of the world.

Sea Squirts Lancelets and Acorn Worms

The chordates are a major division of the animal kingdom that includes not only all the vertebrates (animals with backbones, from fish to man) but also a number of invertebrate, marine animals. The chordates are thus a very diverse group of animals and, no matter how success is measured, the vertebrates are by far its most successful members: they evolved into fish, amphibians, reptiles, birds and mammals, invading the land and developing highly active life styles. But although the more primitive invertebrate chordates remained as relatively inactive marine filter-feeders, they too in their own way are successful.

There are two main groups, or *subphyla*, of invertebrate chordates: the tunicates (sea squirts) and the cephalochordates (lancelets). Along with all vertebrates these animals at some stage in their life cycle share a number of common features.

The first of these is the *notochord* which gives the phylum its name. It is a rod of jelly surrounded by a stiff sheath which provides the chief skeletal support of some invertebrate chordates such as the fish-like animal amphioxus. In vertebrates, the notochord is replaced during development of the embryo by the bony vertebrae which make up the backbone.

The second characteristic feature is the presence of gill slits although in some members of the group, such as the mammals, these are only found in the embryo. Finally, all chordates have a tubular nerve chord which lies close to the upper surface of the body above the notochord.

There is one other small group of animals which is closely related to the chordates. These animals are the acorn

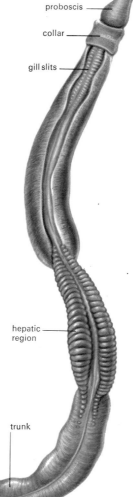

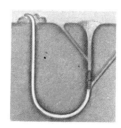

Right: An acorn worm, *Glossobalanus minutus*. These animals live on the sandy bottoms of shallow sea waters. The muscular proboscis and the collar immediately behind it are used for burrowing. The collar can be distended to anchor the animal so that the rest of the body can be pulled forward.

proboscis
collar
gill slits
hepatic region
trunk

Right: An acorn worm living in a U-shaped burrow which it lines with mucus. The animal passes a constant stream of muddy sand through its gut and from this it is able to extract its food. A cast formed of expelled sand builds up around the exit of the burrow. Once installed the worm will rarely, if ever, leave its burrow.

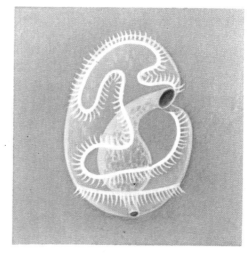

Above: The free-swimming larva of an acorn worm. These larvae are almost indistinguishable from the larvae of some echinoderms (the phylum which includes starfish), and this is good evidence for a fairly close link between the chordates and the echinoderms. The two groups probably had a common ancestor.

Below: An acorn worm, *Glossobalanus sarniensis*, begins to burrow into shell gravel. Acorn worms exhibit many typically chordate features. They have a dorsal nerve chord, which is sometimes hollow, and gill slits. A short projection from the forward end of the digestive tract in some ways resembles the chordate notochord.

Below: The lancelet amphioxus, *Branchiostoma lanceolatum*. Although these animals can swim they spend most of their time buried in the sea bottom with only their mouths protruding. A stream of water is drawn in through the mouth and the tiny marine organisms are filtered out by the gill slits.

Bruce Coleman

Heather Angel

Right: A body plan of amphioxus. The animal has all the typical chordate features: a hollow dorsal nerve chord, a notochord and gill slits. The gill slits are comparable to those found in fish, but in amphioxus they are mainly concerned with feeding rather than respiration. They are supported by gill bars.

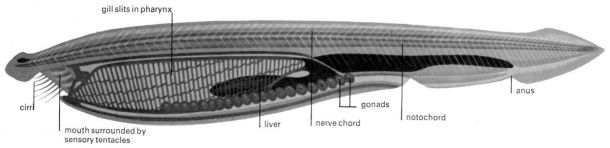

gill slits in pharynx
cirri
mouth surrounded by sensory tentacles
liver
nerve chord
gonads
notochord
anus

Left: Tunicates are usually sedentary and often highly colourful animals. When disturbed the animal rapidly contracts its tough body wall or 'tunic' and water squirts from the two body openings. For this reason they are commonly known as sea squirts. The tunic of a sea squirt varies in texture from one species to another: it may be smooth and slippery, leathery, lumpy or covered with spines. Sometimes the animal has structures resembling roots projecting from its base which help it to cling on to rocks.

Right: This bright red sea squirt, *Halocynthia papillosa*, is found along European coasts, especially where the seabed is sandy.

worms and belong to the phylum *Hemichordata*.

Acorn worms

The elongated animals known as acorn worms are so-called because of an acorn-shaped proboscis at the front end of the body. The proboscis is used in burrowing, and behind it is a fleshy collar from which the worm-like body extends. Into a groove running along this body open numerous gill-slits. Acorn worms, of which there are about 70 living species, live in the sand or mud of the seashore and seabed. Some of them hide in burrows, while others live in slimy tubes of mud or sand. They feed on tiny particles of plant and animal matter obtained either from the mud which they swallow, or trapped from the surrounding water by the sticky mucus on the body surface. This mucus is moved by hair-like cilia towards the mouth which lies between the collar and the proboscis. In the same region is the structure which was once assumed to be the notochord. It now seems very probable that this is no more than part of the wall of the gut.

Also classified as hemichordates are some little known animals of deep seas known as *pterobranchids*. These have shorter bodies, the collar of which bears two branched arms which are used to trap plankton for food. Some pterobranchids live in tubes, and others form branched colonies.

Sea squirts

The most numerous tunicates, with over 1,000 species, are the sea squirts. These show their chordate affinities most clearly when they are in the larval form. Most species are hermaphrodite and the eggs are fertilized inside the body of the parent. In some species the fertilized egg develops directly into a miniature of the adult form which is then born alive. In most cases, however, a superficially tadpole-like larva is formed. This swims by means of a muscular tail which also contains a notochord. Since the larva also has a dorsal nerve cord and gill slits, at this stage of

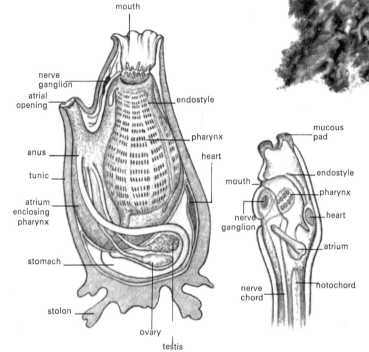

Far left and left: Body plans of an adult sea squirt and the head of a sea squirt larva. In the adult animal, water is drawn in through the mouth, filtered for edible micro-organisms by means of gill slits in the pharynx and then expelled into the atrium, a second body cavity surrounding the pharynx. The water current is set up by the action of cilia on the edges of the gill slits. Sea squirts are often hermaphrodite, having both male and female reproductive organs. Apart from its gill slits, there is little to suggest that a sea squirt is a chordate. With its tadpole-like larva, however, the relationship is much clearer. It has a dorsal nerve chord, a notochord as well as gill slits.

Below: Sea squirts sometimes reproduce asexually. The result is a colony of animals all sharing the same tunic. They arrange themselves in small groups around a central cavity connected to each animal's atrium. The mouths of the various members of the group lie in a circle around the single, central atrium opening.

In this way shells, rock and seaweed can gradually become covered with sea squirts. The normal method of reproduction is sexual. Each animal releases eggs or sperm into the surrounding water and tadpole-like larvae develop from the fertilized eggs. Any one animal will not release eggs and sperm at the same time.

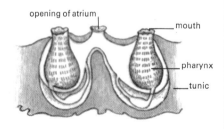

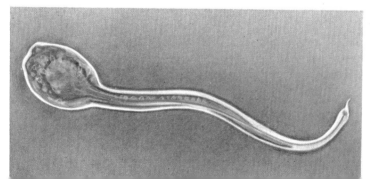

Right: A curious transparent sea squirt, *Clavellina lepadiformis*. One rather unusual feature of sea squirts is the operation of the heart. It reverses the direction of flow of the blood every few beats.

Left: The free-swimming larva of a sea squirt has a long muscular tail for propulsion.

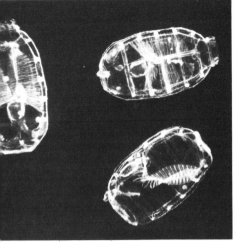

D. P. Wilson

Left: A group of salps, *Doliolum nationalis.* Salps are related to sea squirts, but they float freely in the ocean. The body of a salp is barrel-shaped and at either end are the two body openings. Adult salps vary enormously in size: from 1 mm (0.04 in) to 20 cm (8 in). These particular animals are only about 2.5 mm (0.1 in) long.

Right: Two small inhabitants of the ocean: a salp, *Salpa punctata,* and an amphipod crustacean. The latter is easily recognised by its segmented body and jointed limbs. Salps are filter feeders, water being pumped through the body by muscular action rather than by beating cilia in the gill slits as in sea squirts.

Claude Carre/Jacana

its life it is clearly identifiable as a true chordate.

Settling under a rock, the larva metamorphoses into the sedentary adult animal. In the process its notochord and chordate-like appearance become lost. It secretes a protective covering called the tunic which consists of a substance known as *tunicin.* This is a carbohydrate allied to cellulose, a substance extremely common in plants but unknown in animals. In texture, tunicin is not unlike thick polythene, so the tunic provides tough but flexible protection for the softer parts of the tunicate's body. At the topmost end of the tunic and also slightly lower down to one side are two siphons or openings. Water passes into the first and out of the second, thus supplying the sea squirt with both oxygen and planktonic food.

The related *thaliaceans,* or *salps,* of which there are about 30 species, mostly live in warm seas. Like some sea squirts, they live in colonies, but they differ in that they float freely. One colonial salp, *Pyrosoma,* forms colonies up to nine metres (30 ft) long. *Pyrosoma* also glows in the dark.

Larvaceans

Classified within the same subphylum, but in a class of their own, are the 30 species of larvaceans. In their adult form these resemble the larvae of normal tunicates. However, unlike larvae they have a tunic, although it is not made of tunicin. Movements of a larvacean's tail force water into the tunic which then filters the tiny planktonic plants upon which the animal feeds. Alone among the tunicates larvaceans retain the basic chordate features when they are adult. In the course of their evolution it seems that the original adult form has gradually disappeared as the larval form developed the power to breed. This may also have occurred during the evolution of the vertebrates' ancestors. Perhaps all vertebrates are also precocious larval forms.

Cephalochordates

These animals are in many ways intermediate between the tunicates and the vertebrates. Typically 5-7 cm long (2-3 in), they look rather like caricatures of boneless fish with their elongated form and distinct head end to the body (although such important details as eyes and a heart are absent). The blood is pumped by the muscular action of the walls of the blood vessels themselves. However, the lifestyles of the cephalochordates are more like those of tunicates than fish.

Because of their shape, cephalochordates are often known as *lancelets.* They live buried in the sand of shallow seas and coastal waters. Sometimes, usually at night, they emerge and swim actively. Their bodies are muscular, with the muscles arranged in segmented blocks like those of fish. While swimming, the flattened body ripples in a very fish-like manner since the well developed notochord is flexible. A single fin runs along the back and round the tail. It is strengthened by gelatinous fin-rays. On returning to the sand lancelets wriggle their way in head first, and then turn round so that the mouth protrudes just above the surface of the sea bottom.

Lancelets are by no means uncommon. For example, the species called *Branchiostoma lanceolatum* (known to generations of biology students as amphioxus) inhabits sand banks of the North Sea. The largest lancelets are up to 15 cm (6 in) long and live on the southern coasts of China where they are caught and eaten. All invertebrate chordates are of great scientific interest, but only these Chinese lancelets are of any economic importance.

Lancelets breed during the spring, usually just after a storm. The sexes are separate and eggs and sperms are discharged into the water where fertilization takes place. The manner in which the fertilized egg divides to form a multicelled embryo is very like a simplified version of the same process in the vertebrates. For this reason the embryology of amphioxus has for many years found a place in biology textbooks. The larva hatches when only two segments of the body have been formed. It swims to the surface of the sea by means of the cilia which cover its body at this stage. For a period it floats and swims before becoming adult and returning to the seabed.

Although amphioxus has many features which are no doubt a result of its burrowing way of life, it does provide a basic plan for the other chordates and it may give us an idea of what the early chordates were like. It was first discovered in 1774 by the German scientist Peter Simon Pallas who believed that the animal was a gastropod (the class of molluscs which includes the slugs and snails). About 60 years were to pass before amphioxus received any further attention, this time from the Italian zoologist Costa and the German physiologist Muller. The close relationship between amphioxus and the vertebrate animals was now realised, and amphioxus has been much studied ever since.

tentacle

head lobe

anterior ring of cilia

head lobe

tentacle

tentacle

posterior ring of cilia

tentacle

Left and above: A beard worm and three stages in the development of its larva. The beard worms are a fairly recently discovered group of animals and they fall into a phylum of their own, the *Pogonophora.* Their relationship with the other animal phyla is unclear, but they are usually placed close to the chordates on the evolutionary tree. Like acorn worms they live in burrows on the seabed. One peculiar feature of the beard worms is that they have no digestive tract. The body of a beard worm is typically about 1 mm (0.04 in) in diameter and 30 cm (1 ft) long.

Below: A tiny larvacean, *Oikopleura dioica.* These creatures are chordates which live in the plankton layers of the sea. The adult does not differ much from the tadpole-like larva. The tail is retained through the whole of the animal's life.

tubular covering secreted by worm

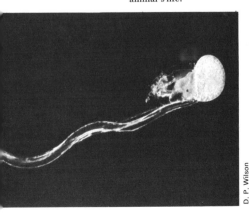

D. P. Wilson

Flukes and Tapeworms

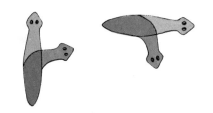

The free-living planarian moves in a zig-zag manner using its rudimentary eyes to detect light. Its normal habitat is under stones and rotting plants at the bottom of ponds and so light indicates danger.

The most familiar of the flatworm group are the tapeworms, the Cestodes, but there are over 7,000 separate species in this important branch of the animal kingdom — phylum Platyhelminthes.

The main groups are the Turbellaria, free-living flatworms; and the parasitic Trematodes, or flukes, and Cestodes, or tapeworms. Each of the classes is highly specialized and well adapted to its particular environment and life style.

The free-living Turbellarian flatworms inhabit damp places — under stones in bogs, in and around ponds, and the majority live in the sea. They are typically small and oval in shape, flattened rather like a leaf. Unlike other types of flatworms they have rudimentary light-sensitive eyes at the front of their body. Their shape seems to change constantly as they move in a zigzag pattern, throwing their head from side to side and gliding over the surface of weeds and stones on beating cilia.

Most Turbellaria feed on worms, protozoa and edible rubbish. They seize any prey smaller than themselves and force it through their primitive gut, digesting it on the way. Larger worms in the group may attack prey bigger than themselves by shooting out a long tube-like extension of the gut called a pharynx which holds and crushes the victim.

The Turbellaria are in their early stages free-living organisms. When they mature, however, they can develop into external, or *ectoparasites,* which live on the outer body wall of an animal, and are found living in association with various types of crabs and small fish.

Members of the other two classes, Trematodes and Cestodes, are *obligate parasites.* This means that they live entirely at the expense of another larger and more highly evolved animal or plant known as a *host.*

The Trematodes, known popularly as flukes, fall into two main groups, those which have a simple life cycle involving only one host, and those which have a more complex life style. The adults of the latter group are parasitic on a vertebrate host and their larvae multiply asexually inside snails which act as an intermediate host. The Trematodes are almost all hermaphrodite, each individual having both male and female sex organs.

Many Trematodes are ectoparasites, living on the scales of fishes. These flukes have developed powerful suckers and hooks with which they cling on to the host and thus avoid being swept away by water currents and the movement of the fish. The endoparasites, which live inside the host, usually have two strong suckers to attach themselves to their base and a simple branched gut with a single opening, or mouth.

The life cycle of the endoparasites is often complex and shows a remarkable degree of adaptation in ensuring transmission to a new host. The first stage of a typical life cycle begins when the larva, the miracidium, hatches from the egg in water. It then attacks and enters a water snail and once established multi-

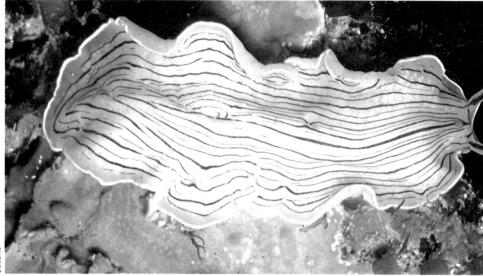

Jacana

Above: A marine polyclad flatworm glides gracefully over rocks on the sea floor. The wavy edges of the body help it to move more quickly in the water. Its tentacles can be seen to the right of the picture at the front end of its body.

Right: Sheep are the final link in the life chain of the liver fluke and are at grave risk from this parasite, particularly during warm, wet summers. Infected sheep have to be destroyed and consequently liver flukes are greatly feared by the farmer.

Bruce Coleman

LIVER FLUKE

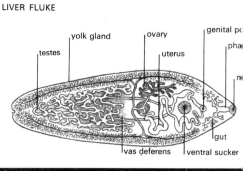

testes — yolk gland — ovary — genital po — uterus — pha — gut — vas deferens — ventral sucker

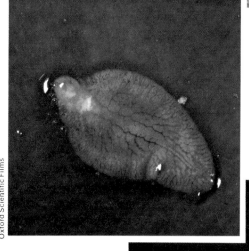

Oxford Scientific Films

Above and above right: An adult liver fluke is firmly attached to a sheep's liver. The fluke weakens its host by draining nutrients from the body and damaging the liver.

Right: The water snail acts as an intermediary host to the vulnerable fluke larva and helps to disperse it to areas where it will be ingested by the sheep.

Oxford Scientific Films

Right: Planaria hunt for food by pursuing the source of a strong chemical attraction, using this rather like a sense of smell. They feed mainly on protozoa and detritus—edible rubbish particles.

Left: A planarian flatworm at rest forms a typically flat, oval shape.

Below left: Stretched out, the worm takes a shape which will prove least resistant to water currents.

Below: A diagram of a planarian flatworm shows its branching blind gut and elaborate reproductive system.

HUNTING

MATING

Above: The planarian glides over the surface of weeds or stones on a film of mucus, brushing water currents past with gently waving cilia. It throws out a pharynx to seize and engulf its food.

Oxford Scientific Films

TURBELLARIAN

genital pore — yolk gland — mouth — pharynx — testes — gut — ovary — nervous system

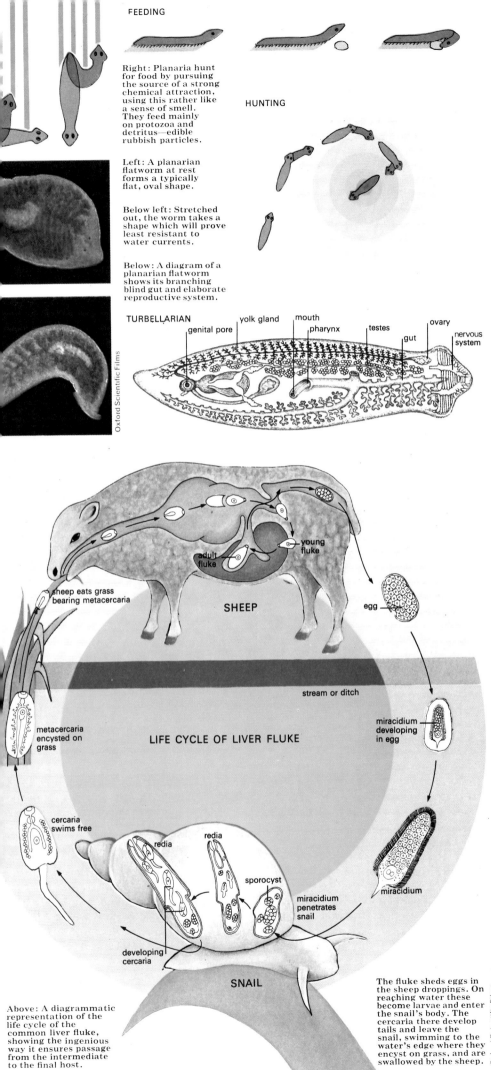

Above: A diagrammatic representation of the life cycle of the common liver fluke, showing the ingenious way it ensures passage from the intermediate to the final host.

sheep eats grass bearing metacercaria

SHEEP

adult fluke

young fluke

egg

metacercaria encysted on grass

stream or ditch

LIFE CYCLE OF LIVER FLUKE

miracidium developing in egg

cercaria swims free

redia — redia

sporocyst

miracidium penetrates snail

miracidium

developing cercaria

SNAIL

The fluke sheds eggs in the sheep droppings. On reaching water these become larvae and enter the snail's body. The cercaria there develop tails and leave the snail, swimming to the water's edge where they encyst on grass, and are swallowed by the sheep.

Oxford Scientific Films

plies asexually inside it. During the next stage, larvae with tails, cercariae, leave the snail, swim strongly to the bank and form cysts on plants, or in fish. When the cyst is eaten by a suitable vertebrate species it develops into a fluke inside the host. The adult fluke then produces eggs to start a new cycle.

The fluke *Leucochoridium* has evolved an ingenious method of ensuring transmission on dry land. The larvae living in the land snail host migrate to its tentacles, causing them to swell. The conspiciously green and brown striped cercariae wriggle around inside the tentacles. The bright colour and movement attract birds, the final hosts, which become infected when they eat the snails. The larvae also apparently alter the behaviour of the snails, causing them to come out in the open instead of hiding in grass, thus making them easier prey for birds.

Adult Cestodes, tapeworms, are parasites that live in the gut of vertebrate animals. A tapeworm has a tiny head, or scolex, with hooks and suckers which is embedded in the gut wall of the host. Behind the head are a series of segments, or *proglottids*, budded off one after the other which make the characteristic tape. There can be up to 3,000 segments in the giant fish tapeworm, *Diphyllobothrium latum*, found in man.

Tapeworms have no gut as they absorb their food, already partially digested by the host, through the body wall. The powerful electron microscope has revealed that the outer body wall has minute finger-like processes which fit between similar projections on the gut wall of the host — greatly increasing the surface area for the absorption of food and also creating a very close contact with the gut wall.

Ronald Sheridan

Oxford Scientific Films

Above: Bathers in the Nile are at risk from *Schistosoma mansonii*, the fluke which causes the tropical disease bilharzia. The larvae enter the body through the feet.

Left: In the blood fluke, *Schistosoma*, the smaller female lives in a groove on the male's underside.

HEAD

hooks
sucker
neck

Left and right: The *scolex* or head of the tapeworm is equipped with hooks and suckers which anchor it firmly to the gut wall of the host. The groove immediately behind the head is the area of growth where new segments, proglottids, are formed to create the characteristic ribbon-shaped body.

MATURE PROGLOTTID

sperm duct
genital pore
vagina
uterus
testes
ovary
vas deferens
yolk gland
excretory canal

As each proglottid matures it becomes capable of reproduction. Each mature segment has male and female sex organs. Cross-fertilization occurs between neighbouring tapeworms in the gut with an exchange of sperms between two segments. The eggs are stored in the segment until when ripe it breaks off in the intestine of the host. A mature tapeworm can have up to 1,000 proglottids and sheds many thousands of eggs a day. Few develop to maturity, but the great numbers increase the chance of at least some succeeding. Such high fertility ensures safe transfer from one host to another.

RIPE PROGLOTTID

uterus full of eggs

A ripe proglottid is basically a bag crammed with fertilized eggs. The two ducts at the left of the diagram are the remains of the female and male openings, while the massed contents of the newly enlarged uterus consist of thousands of fertilized eggs, or zygotes. Each zygote receives a protective shell and begins to develop hooks.

Brian Bracegirdle

Right: The life cycle of the pork tapeworm, *Taenia solium*, involves man as the primary host harbouring the adult form and the pig as intermediate host.
IN PIG
As each segment becomes ripe it drops off from the end of an adult tapeworm in the human gut and passes out in the faeces. The pig picks up the infection when it swallows some mud containing the eggs while foraging in muddy fields where sewage has been spread as fertilizer. As the egg passes along the gut, its casing is digested away, releasing a small onchosphere. Armed with six sharp hooks it burrows through the gut wall into the bloodstream. It is carried along in the blood flow to a muscle where it becomes lodged, forming a cyst called a bladderworm.
IN MAN
When man eats raw or rare pork containing bladderworms, he can become infected with a tapeworm. At first the head of the young tapeworm is tucked into the bladder. During its passage down the gut, however, the small hooked head is pushed out, ready for attachment to the gut.

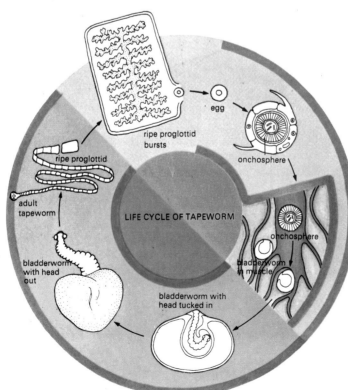

ripe proglottid bursts
egg
ripe proglottid
onchosphere
adult tapeworm
LIFE CYCLE OF TAPEWORM
onchosphere
bladderworm with head out
bladderworm in muscle
bladderworm with head tucked in

Tapeworms have a very poorly developed nervous system and senses and are creamy white in colour. Since they live in the dark in an animal's gut surrounded by food they no longer need eyes to find their way around, or legs to carry them hunting. Nor do they require pigment in their skins to protect them from radiation in sunlight and for camouflage.

There is a dynamic relationship between a parasite and its host involving two opposing biological forces. On the one hand there is the parasite's need to grow, feed and reproduce and on the other the attempt of the host to attack any foreign body which invades its tissues. In the majority of flatworm infections a satisfactory balance is achieved and the host suffers little damage. But when the number of parasites do build up to a high level they can cause disease and sometimes the death of the host.

Host versus parasite

Although the host attacks tapeworms as it does smaller invaders like bacteria and viruses, the large size of tapeworms means that immunity is seldom complete. For instance, larval tapeworms in the tissues often become surrounded by a thick fibrous wall but are able to survive inside it. A very ingenious mechanism for survival against host defences occurs in the schistosomes — parasitic flukes living in the bloodstream of man and domestic animals. The adult flukes coat themselves with host substances, probably derived from red cells, so that they are not recognized as being foreign and are not attacked. However any new invading cercarial larvae, which in these flukes penetrate through the skin, are quickly destroyed. The infection is therefore limited, for the presence of too many worms leading to the death of the host would be of no advantage to a parasite.

Many worm diseases are of great economic and public concern. Parasitic worm infections may be controlled in various ways according to their life histories. Attempts to control fluke infections of man and domestic stock can be made by the use of chemicals to kill the snail intermediate hosts or by preventing eggs in faeces from reaching snails. Tapeworms and flukes are at their most vulnerable when in the process of transferring from intermediate to primary host and so close inspection of all meat freshly killed at abattoirs is essential if worm infections are to be eliminated. In Great Britain such control has been totally effective against the pork tapeworm. Further measures against infection must include thorough cooking of pork and fish — it is interesting to note that in areas where traditional cuisine demands partially cooked or even raw fish the incidence of associated flatworm infection is high. Sanitary disposal of faeces is also effective against Cestodes but is difficult to accomplish for stock or, in many parts of the world, for man because human waste is still the most effective fertilizer available in underdeveloped or remote areas.

Parasites are often regarded as being in some way degenerate organisms but this is far from true. Rather they have become extremely specialized in various ingenious ways in order to cope with an unusual, hostile environment, principally by a great development in the reproductive system.

Roundworms

The roundworms, or nematodes, can be regarded as one of the most successful groups in the animal kingdom, whether success is measured by numbers or by adaptability. One scientist remarked that if all other matter was swept away the outlines of mountains, valleys, lakes, seas and rivers would still be dimly recognizable from a film of nematodes. Even the position of most plants and animals would be indicated by little piles of them.

Large numbers of nematodes are present in all parts of the world, from the polar seas to hot springs, from arid deserts to ocean depths. Several million organisms are present in every square metre of the top few centimetres of the ocean bed. Some nematodes live in very peculiar habitats—there is even a species which has been found only in German beer mats.

One of the most remarkable features of the group is that all forms have the same basic body pattern, whether they are the microscopic free-living nematodes found in soil or water, or the parasitic worms found in plants or animals, which can measure up to 30 cm (1 ft). All nematodes also have the same basic life cycle: egg, four larval stages, and adult form.

Parasitic worms

There is at least one plant-parasitic nematode that will attack almost every crop whether in the field, the orchard, the back garden or the greenhouse. Because of their microscopic size their existence is often not recognized, yet about ten percent of crops grown are eaten by nematodes. In Britain alone it is estimated that more than two million pounds worth of potatoes are lost annually to the ravages of the potato eelworm. Other nematodes are a major cause of illness in domestic animals and in man. The most common is that well-known nuisance the threadworm which, according to one source, is the second most common organism infecting man after the common cold virus. Threadworms are present in the gut in about one third of all children in England and often cause irritation in the anal region.

Hookworms are more actively harmful than most nematodes and are a serious cause of anaemia, particularly in tropical countries. The daily volume of blood lost by sufferers throughout the world is calculated to be about 8,200,000 litres (1,800,000 gallons). The young stages live in soil and actively burrow through the skin of the feet, while the adults live in the small intestine, biting off portions and sucking blood. Once common in the southern United States and in Western Australia, hookworms have become less common since the wearing of shoes became general.

Some parasitic nematodes have a simple life history with only one host. Their eggs are passed out on to the soil where they, or larvae which develop from them, may be eaten by a new host. Others have a second or *intermediate* host in which the young stages develop. All have evolved mechanisms for overcoming the hazards of transmission from one host to another. For instance in the potato eelworm, *Heterodera rostochiensis,* the female be-

Oxford Scientific Films

Dr. J. A. L. Cooke

Left: A nemertine worm. These animals are less complex than roundworms but more developed than flatworms. They all have a long, straight intestine with a mouth at one end and an anus at the other end. The long, thin, retractable tube on the right is used to catch prey, for example protozoa.

London School of Tropical Medicine

Right: Male (left) and female body plans of a generalized roundworm. The male is usually smaller than the female. Roundworms differ fundamentally from flatworms in having an intestinal tube with a mouth at one end and an anus at the other, rather than a single opening. Food is sucked in through the mouth by a muscular structure called the *pharynx.* During copulation sperms are transferred to the female by means of a pair of hard bristles, called spicula.

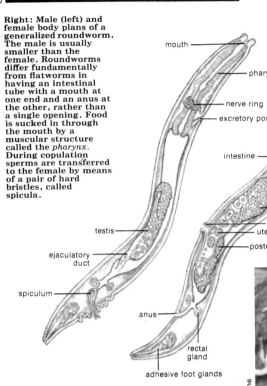

mouth
pharynx
nerve ring
excretory pore
intestine
anterior ovary
vulva
uterus
posterior ovary
testis
ejaculatory duct
spiculum
anus
rectal gland
adhesive foot glands

Top: A long, thin nematode worm of the family *Mermthoidea* emerges from its dead host. These worms spend their early life as parasites of invertebrates such as the spider, but the adults are free-living.

Above: The eye worm, a parasitic nematode common in West Africa.

Below: The life cycle of the human parasite *Ascaris.* The eggs passed out in the faeces hatch in the small intestines of the new host within a few hours of ingestion, and then embark on a 'tour' of the host body. They enter the bloodstream and are carried to the liver, heart and then the lungs where further growth occurs. The worms finally pass into the throat and are carried to the intestine where they mature fully.

Right: Roundworms of the family *Ascaris* taken from the bile ducts of a young pig. Although almost indistinguishable from the parasite of man, *Ascaris lumbricoides* (below), these worms do not normally develop to maturity in a human host. Similarly the human parasite will not infect pigs.

London School of Tropical Medicine

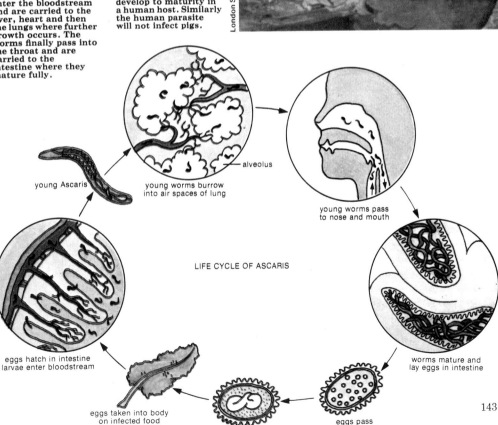

LIFE CYCLE OF ASCARIS

young Ascaris

young worms burrow into air spaces of lung

alveolus

young worms pass to nose and mouth

eggs hatch in intestine larvae enter bloodstream

eggs taken into body on infected food

larva forms inside egg

eggs pass out in faeces

worms mature and lay eggs in intestine

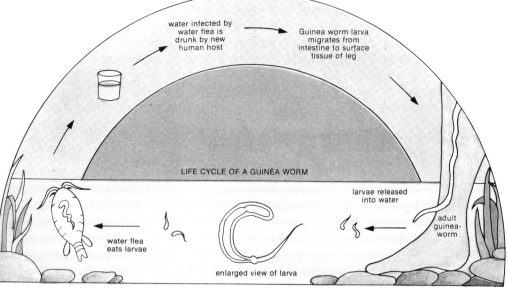

water infected by
water flea is
drunk by new
human host

Guinea worm larva
migrates from
intestine to surface
tissue of leg

LIFE CYCLE OF A GUINEA WORM

larvae released
into water

adult
guinea-
worm

water flea
eats larvae

enlarged view of larva

The guinea worm has
long been one of the
more uncomfortable
features of life in
India and Africa. The
engraving on the left
shows an adult worm,
which can measure more
than a foot (30 cm) in
length, being removed
from the leg of a
sufferer by winding it
out on a stick. This
process is painful and
only successful when
precautions are taken
against infection. When
an infected limb is
bathed in water,
larvae are released
through an ulcer
formed on the skin by
the adult worm. The
larvae are eaten by
water fleas, *cyclops*
(right), and when
infected water is drunk
the larvae pass to new
human hosts where they
develop to maturity.

Above: Hairworms of
the species *Gordius*.
These animals are
found in ponds and
ditches all over the
world, and the adult
worms are free-living.
The larvae, however,
are parasites of
insects and they
emerge fully grown
when the insect
approaches or falls
into a stream or pond.

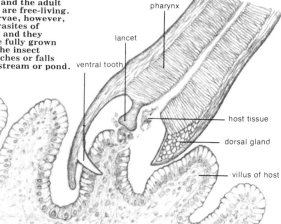

pharynx

lancet

ventral tooth

host tissue

dorsal gland

villus of host

Above: The head of a
hookworm, *Necator
americanus*, showing
the cutting surfaces
or 'teeth' on each
side of the mouth.
These worms infect the
intestines of both men
and pigs. They are
most common in hot
countries, causing
anaemia in the host.

Left: A human
hookworm grips on to a
projection called a
villus in the wall of
the intestine. The
lancet erodes the
intestinal wall so
that the worm can feed
on the blood and
tissue fluids of the
human host.

comes full of eggs and dies in potato roots
left in the soil but her body wall remains
as a protective cyst. The larvae inside the
eggs hatch only when stimulated by a
secretion from another crop of potatoes
and may survive in a dormant state for
many years, making them very difficult to
eradicate.

Each female of the common roundworm
in pigs and man, *Ascaris lumbricoides,*
produces up to 200,000 eggs every day—
the weight of all the eggs produced
annually in China has been computed at
more than 16,000 tonnes. The eggs are
passed out of the host body in the faeces
and must be ingested by a new host before
development can continue, so despite the
vast numbers produced the chances of any
one egg finding a comfortable maternity
home in the human body are infinitesimal.

A striking adaption of life history to
environmental conditions is shown by a
bizarre parasite of man, the guinea worm,
Dracunculus medinensis. The adult female
worms measure over 30 cm (1 ft) and live
beneath the skin, usually in the legs.
When mature the female causes a blister
to form, bursts when an infected limb is
paddled in water. This is the signal for the
head of the worm to burst and release
thousands of minute wriggling larvae into
the water. The portion of the worm still
projecting from the ulcer then dries up
and more larvae are released only when
the limb is plunged into water again. In
this way the parasite is able to exist in
desert areas where oases essential for its
transmission are few and far between.

The larvae resemble free-living
nematodes and only when eaten by water
fleas, *Cyclops,* do they develop further.
Water fleas are tiny crustaceans which
live in ponds or the open wells often used
as sources of drinking water in areas of
the Middle East, Africa and India, and the
parasite enters the body of man when an
infected water flea is swallowed.

An even more specialized life cycle is
shown by the *filariae,* tissue dwelling
nematodes living in all the land dwelling
groups of vertebrates. As their intermediate hosts, filariae have biting insects
which pick up the larvae from the blood
when feeding; the parasites are thus
spared the hazards of exposing their eggs
or larvae to the outside world. A heavy
infestation of these nematodes can cause
elephantiasis in man because the circulatory system is blocked by the worms.

Body structure

Nematodes all have a cylindrical body
shape, pointed at either end and with few
protruberances, apart from extensions at
the tail end of some male parasitic forms
used to clasp the females in copulation.
This uniformity of structure can be
explained to some extent by the great
internal pressure of the fluid filling the
body cavity. This is higher than in any
other group in the animal kingdom and
may reach one and a half times atmospheric pressure. If the body wall of a
nematode is punctured the contents are
expelled with considerable force. The high
internal pressure has also resulted in a
simple undulating mode of locomotion
which is particularly suitable for moving
through a sticky medium and partly
explains their great success as animal
parasites.

Nematodes have an outer impermeable
cuticle which has three layers of fibres
arranged in a spiral trellis pattern. The

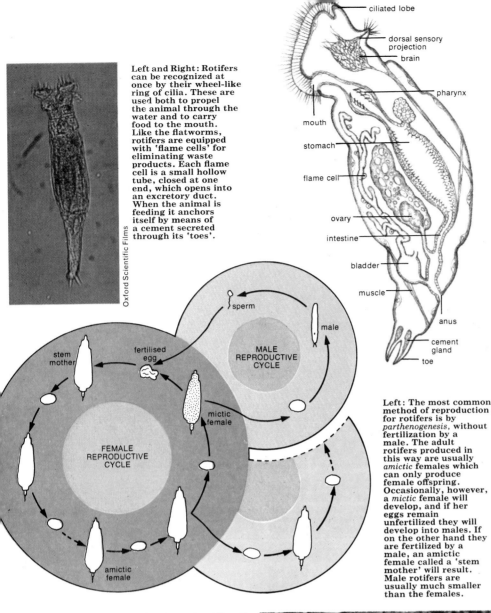

ciliated lobe

dorsal sensory projection

brain

pharynx

mouth

stomach

flame cell

ovary

intestine

bladder

muscle

anus

cement gland

toe

Left and Right: Rotifers can be recognized at once by their wheel-like ring of cilia. These are used both to propel the animal through the water and to carry food to the mouth. Like the flatworms, rotifers are equipped with 'flame cells' for eliminating waste products. Each flame cell is a small hollow tube, closed at one end, which opens into an excretory duct. When the animal is feeding it anchors itself by means of a cement secreted through its 'toes'.

Oxford Scientific Films

sperm

fertilised egg

stem mother

male

MALE REPRODUCTIVE CYCLE

mictic female

FEMALE REPRODUCTIVE CYCLE

amictic female

Left: The most common method of reproduction for rotifers is by *parthenogenesis*, without fertilization by a male. The adult rotifers produced in this way are usually *amictic* females which can only produce female offspring. Occasionally, however, a *mictic* female will develop, and if her eggs remain unfertilized they will develop into males. If on the other hand they are fertilized by a male, an amictic female called a 'stem mother' will result. Male rotifers are usually much smaller than the females.

fibres in each layer are arranged in two sets that diagonally cross over each other, enclosing minute diamond shapes. They can be compared to 'lazy tongs', the contraction of the longitudinal muscles making the worm shorter and fatter and the internal fluid pressure making it longer and thinner when the muscles relax.

A specialization present in the mouth cavity of some plant-parasitic nematodes is a spear which can be protruded like a miniature hypodermic needle to penetrate the cellulose wall of plant cells and suck up the contents. Some animal-parasitic forms have a large mouth cavity with cuticular 'teeth' for cutting off portions from the gut wall of their host.

Related animals

There are other little-known groups of animals which are near or distant cousins of the nematodes. The spiny-headed worms, or *acanthocephalans*, are all parasitic, mostly in the guts of birds or fish. They have no digestive tract, food being absorbed through minute canals in the thick wrinkled body wall, but all have a fearsome looking proboscis (a long muscular projection) which is armed with rows of hooks and can be withdrawn into the body. The hooks provide a firm anchorage to the gut wall of the host. These worms are very much adapted to a parasitic mode of life as the only free-living stage in the whole life cycle are the eggs, which are passed out in faeces and eaten by an intermediate host, usually an insect.

The hairworms, or *nematomorphs,* are a small group of freshwater animals which are not hermaphrodite but exist in separate sexes. While the adults are free-living the young live parasitically in insects such as grasshoppers or dragonflies. If the host insect falls into water the young hairworm will emerge. It is remarkable that the fully developed juvenile in the insect may be many times the length of its host. The long threadlike adult, which may be up to one metre or yard long but only 3mm (0.12 in) wide, swims like a miniature snake in the water. A typical example is *Gordius,* so named because the loosely tangled masses of adults in water are reminiscent of the Gordian knot of mythology. Its unexpected appearance in cattle troughs after an insect had fallen in led to the belief that it developed from horse hairs.

Rotifers and *gastrotrichs* are common all over the world but because of their microscopic size are rarely recognized. The rotifers or 'wheel animals' live in water and soil, and their most characteristic feature is the unique organ at the front of the body which in some forms looks like a rotating wheel. It has many hair-like structures, *cilia*, which by their beating can either form a whirlpool drawing particles into the rotifer's mouth or can act like a propeller, driving the animal forward. Rotifers of one species or another are present in almost every wet or damp spot and there are even forms which can withstand complete drying and extreme temperatures—above boiling point or below −200°C (−328°F)—for many years. The gastrotrichs are a related group of miscroscopic worm-like organisms without a wheel organ. They are found in seas, lakes and ponds, often anchored to stones by means of adhesive glands at the tail end of the body.

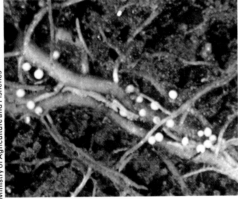

Above: The small white cysts of the potato eelworm. The eggs inside each cyst will only hatch when a new potato crop is planted to act as host for the larvae.

Ministry of Agriculture and Fisheries

Left: A plant parasite feeds on a fungus. This roundworm, a female, has the typical nematode shape, a cylindrical body pointed at each end. The mouth is at the top left and the anus close to the tail at the bottom right.

Right: The gall-like swellings on the roots of this plant are caused by the root knot nematode. Melons, tomatoes, cotton and even orchard trees may be attacked by this parasite.

C. C. Doncaster, Rothamsted Experimental Station

Ministry of Agriculture and Fisheries

145

Annelid Worms and Leeches

The common earthworm, *Lumbricus terrestis*, is the most familiar of all segmented worms, or *annelida*. It has been estimated that every acre of grassland contains about three million earthworms and that as much as 8 to 18 tonnes of new soil per acre are brought to the surface each year by these animals.

The earthworm belongs to the annelid class *oligochaetes* which includes about 3,000 terrestrial and freshwater species. Many members of the class are very similar to the common earthworm and they vary in length from a few millimetres to two metres or more. The common earthworm reaches a length of 20 cm (8 in) when fully grown and lives in permanent burrows about a metre deep. Other closely related species live in shallow temporary burrows. They move through the soil by anchoring the rear of the body with short bristles, called *setae* or *chaetae*, sticking out singly from the body wall, and forcing the head by muscular movement through the gaps in the soil. They then retract the rear setae and anchor the front ones, pulling the rear of the body up after them. In order to force through more compact ground they eat the soil as they go. Some species leave their burrows at night to gather leaves which they drag back and consume. The soil particles and any remnants of organic matter in the gut are excréted as 'casts'.

The digestive system of the earthworm is divided into three main sections: a crop, a gizzard and an intestine. Food is drawn into the mouth by means of a muscular *pharynx* and then proceeds to the crop. This seems to serve little purpose except as a storage cavity, for the food undergoes little change in it. Next, the food passes to the gizzard where it is ground into very fine particles by the thick muscular walls aided by small abrasive particles such as sand swallowed with the food. Finally, the food passes into the intestine where digestion proper takes place. The intestine extends to the anus, and digested food is absorbed into the blood by means of blood vessels in the intestine wall. These vessels are in turn connected to main blood vessels above and below the digestive tract, and circulation is maintained by five primitive hearts.

The sexually mature earthworm has a saddle-like bulge in the body wall called the *clitellum*. The worms mate by lying head to tail, their sexual organs held pressed together by the setae and by belts of mucus. After the mutual exchange of sperm and separation of the worms, a mucus band secreted by the clitellum is passed along the body collecting eggs and sperm. Fertilization takes place and the band slips off the head and forms a cocoon containing about 20 eggs. The worms hatch between one and five months later although often only a few escape being eaten by their fellows. If it survives this initial hazard an earthworm can live for up to ten years.

The freshwater oligochaete *Tubifex* is also familiar. This is the blood worm,

Heather Angel

Above: This earthworm, *Eisenia Foetida*, is a close relation of the commonest earthworm, *Lumbricus terrestris*. It is a nocturnal animal, remaining in the safety of its burrow during the day. It feeds on decaying organic matter such as leaves and is found all over the world in moist soils.

Right: During the mating of earthworms, which possess both male and female sex organs, sperms are passed from each worm to the other. The eggs are not fertilized until after the worms have separated. The swollen ring, called the *clitellum*, of each animal can be seen in the picture.

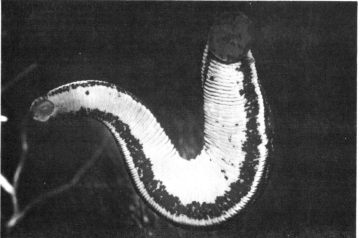

Heather Angel

Left: A medicinal leech. The larger sucker is used for clinging on to the host animal while the smaller one surrounds the mouth and jaws. In some parts of the world leeches are still used to draw colour out of bruises. A leech can remove several times its own weight of blood.

Right: A body plan showing the general characteristics of a leech. The digestive tract has numerous branches, called *diverticula*, which allow the animal to ingest large amounts of blood. Like the earthworm, leeches have both male and female sex organs.

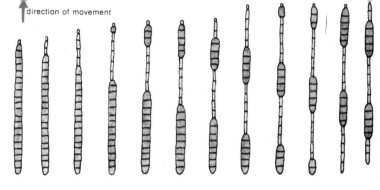

direction of movement

Right: This diagram shows how an earthworm moves. The segments alternately extend and contract under the influence of circular and longitudinal muscles. Contraction of the circular muscle and relaxation of the longitudinal muscle in a segment causes extension. The reverse leads to contraction.

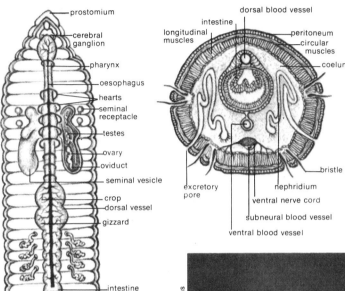

prostomium
cerebral ganglion
pharynx
oesophagus
hearts
seminal receptacle
testes
ovary
oviduct
seminal vesicle
crop
dorsal vessel
gizzard
intestine
ventral vessel
ventral nerve cord

dorsal blood vessel
intestine
longitudinal muscles
peritoneum
circular muscles
coelum
bristle
nephridium
ventral nerve cord
subneural blood vessel
ventral blood vessel
excretory pore

Left and far left: A cross-section and a plan of the 'head' end of an earthworm. Four pairs of bristles, or setae, extend from each segment. These act as anchors during locomotion, allowing the animal to pull itself along through the soil. Blood is distributed to the body through the lower, or ventral, blood vessel and is returned to the five hearts (little more than muscular tubes) through the upper, or dorsal, blood vessel. The digestive system includes a crop, chiefly a storage cavity, a gizzard where food is ground up and a long intestine where the food is digested.

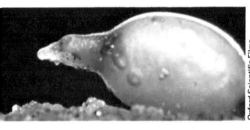

Left: A close up of an earthworm showing setae projecting from successive segments of the body.

Below: A writhing mass of bloodworms, Tubifex tubifex. These worms live in the bottom mud of poorly aerated water and are often sold as live food for tropical fish.

Oxford Scientific Films

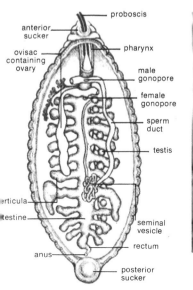

Above: A young earthworm beginning to hatch out from its cocoon. The cocoon is formed from a mucous ring secreted by the clitellum after mating. The ring moves along the body of the worm collecting the eggs and sperm as it goes. Once free of the worm, the ends of the ring close together.

Below right: A young trout killed by a fish leech. Fish leeches are one of the few groups of leeches that remain attached to their prey for long periods. They leave the host fish for only a short while in order to breed. Unlike the other annelids, leeches are not equipped with setae.

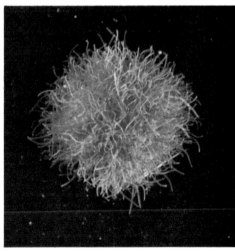

Oxford Scientific Films

Heather Angel

proboscis
anterior sucker
ovisac containing ovary
pharynx
male gonopore
female gonopore
sperm duct
testis
articula
testine
seminal vesicle
rectum
anus
posterior sucker

Heather Angel

coloured bright red by the haemoglobin in its blood. It is often used to feed tropical fish and is a characteristic member of the animal community living in the bottom mud of poorly aerated waters. Blood worms thrive in what are often the foulest of conditions, reaching a population density of up to 8,000 individuals per square metre (6,700 per square yard). Like earthworms, they feed on organic matter found while burrowing in the bottom mud.

There are two other important annelid classes: the *polychaetes* and the *hirudinae*. The polychaetes are almost exclusively marine, over 4,000 species having been described, many of them burrowing in the intertidal sand mud. Like the oligochaetes they are equipped with setae, but instead of being mounted singly these are carried in bundles on extensions of the body wall called *parapodia*. Fishermen use two of the burrowing species as bait, the lugworms, *Arenicola*, and the ragworms, *Nereis*.

The polychaetes class is arbitrarily divided into two groups, the errant or free-swimming worms and the sedentary worms. The errant group contains many species like *Nereis* that burrow but which are usually predatory and free moving. Externally they are divided into numerous and essentially similar segments. The sedentary worms like *Arenicola* are nearly all tube-dwellers or burrowers, and the group includes many filter-feeding fan worms and tentacle feeders. In these animals the body is divided into two or more distinct regions some of which have become specialized, for example to act as gills. The parapodia in the sedentary species are reduced or modified for burrowing. The errant species often have well-developed eyes, tentacles and parapodia adapted for swimming.

One common species of lugworm, *Arenicola maronie*, reaches a length of about 25 cm (10 in) and a thickness of one centimetre (0.4 in). It has 13 pairs of red gills and irrigates its burrow to maintain a supply of oxygenated water by gentle undulations of its body. The burrow is made of sand or mud and is essentially a U-shaped tube, one end being funnel-shaped and the other usually marked by a cast. The funnel is at the front end of the worm and is produced by the constant swallowing of mud and sand which is rich in the organic matter upon which the worms feed. With remarkable precision they void their waste to form a cast once every 40 minutes.

In October they release their eggs and sperm on to the incoming tide, and the eggs form a mucus mass that sticks to the surface of the sand. The eggs are fertilized and hatch as free swimming larvae called *trochophores*. On finding an appropriate environment these metamorphose into the adult form and burrow into the sand.

The nereid ragworms live in mucus-lined burrows, and some are equipped with sufficiently powerful jaws to inflict a painful bite. These jaws are not always indicative of a carnivorous life-style. Some nereids are herbivores, using the jaws to tear off small pieces of algae, while others do use them to catch small invertebrates. The largest British nereid is *Nereis virens*, a large bright green and pink worm that lives under the rocks of some muddy northern shores. Another species of ragworm is *Nereis fucata* which

Right: A ragworm, *Nereis.* This is a typical member of the annelid class *polychaetes.* The segmentation of the body is clearly visible, and the setae are carried in bundles on the end of body extensions called *parapodia.* These are used both for crawling and swimming.

Below: Another common marine annelid, the lugworm. It lives in a burrow and feeds on organic matter in the sand. To get enough food, the lugworm passes large amounts of sand through its digestive system. The 'casts' visible in the picture are formed of the unwanted sand excreted by the worm.

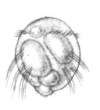

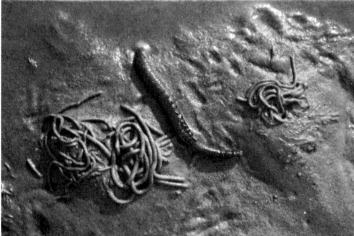

Right: Stages in the development of a ragworm larva. Eggs released by the adult worm are fertilized near the surface of the sea. The newly hatched larvae are sometimes called *trochophores.* The top diagram shows a trochophore prior to hatching, while in the bottom diagram it is about three weeks old and clearly becoming segmented.

Far right, above: A close-up view of the head end of a ragworm. The jaws are clearly visible.

Far right, below: A ragworm larva taken from plankton. It can be compared directly with the bottom of the four diagrams.

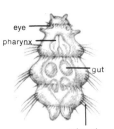

eye

pharynx

gut

setae of parapodium

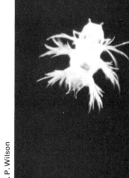

lives in the spirals of hermit crab shells, and feeds by stealing from the crab.

Before mating some nereid species swarm, the worms rising to the surface in large numbers, vigorously discharging eggs and sperm into the water through a rupture in the body wall. In most species swarming occurs irregularly throughout the summer months, but in others a remarkable rhythm has developed.

The palolo worm, *Eunice viridis,* of the southern Pacific demonstrates a remarkable lunar rhythm. On the dawning of the last quarter of the October-November moon the palolo worm breaks in half. The front end of the worm remains in its burrow on the sea bed while the other half, which is extremely light sensitive, rises to the surface with its eggs or sperm. The number of worms is so enormous that the sea appears to boil, and turns milky white with the eggs and sperm released. The spent end of the worm falls lifeless to the bottom while the front end begins to regenerate the missing half. Swarming then does not occur for another year.

The class hirudinea is composed of about 300 species of leech. The body of a leech always consists of 34 segments although this fact is hidden by the presence of secondary rings. The majority of leeches are only a few centimetres in length but one American species, *Americobdella valdivania,* has been reported to reach a length of over 40 cm (16 in). The front of the body is marked by a small sucker around the mouth, while the hindermost seven segments are fused to form a powerful sucker. All members of the class are hermaphrodites with several pairs of testes and a single pair of ovaries.

Right, left and far left: *Sabellaria alveolata,* the 'honeycomb worm', is found on seashores near the low water mark. The worm lives in a smooth round tube made of fine mud particles. When the tube is covered by the tide, the worm expands its tentacles into the water. These act as a sophisticated filter feeding mechanism and extend the surface area available for respiration. The picture on the left shows the worm removed from its tube and on the right is a colony showing the mouths of the tubes. When the tide is out the worms remain withdrawn inside their tubes. (Far left) This picture shows a group of *Sabellaria* larvae about seven days old.

Right: This marine worm, *Chaetopterus,* has developed a remarkable mechanism for filtering food particles from the water. The animal lives in a U-shaped burrow through which it draws a constant stream of water by means of modified parapodia acting like fans. Food particles are collected by two wing-like scoops and are trapped in a mucus bag. Periodically, this bag is rolled up in a cup-shaped structure and passed forward along a groove to the mouth. The water current not only serves to draw in food particles, it also introduces oxygen needed for respiration and carries away waste products.

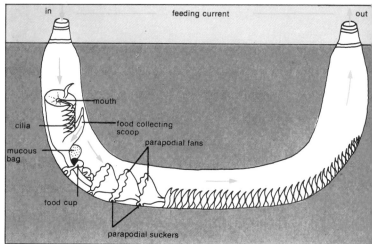

in   feeding current   out

mouth

cilia

food collecting scoop

parapodial fans

mucous bag

food cup

parapodial suckers

first parapodium

palp

eye

nd podium   first elytron   'felt' setae

Above: This curious looking annelid, *Aphrodite*, is often referred to as the 'sea mouse'. It owes its strange appearance to the presence of a blanket of threads extending over its back. It burrows in the mud, feeding by drawing water through the blanket into a space over its back. In this space are two plate-like extensions of the body wall called *elytra* which may act as respiratory surfaces. Food particles ingested from the currents of water are passed to the gut.

Left: The head of a sea mouse viewed from above. The two long *palps* are sensory organs.

P. Morris, Ardea

In some species the sperm are transferred to the vagina by means of a penis, but others lack a penis and vagina and instead have remarkable 'hypodermic' sperm. The sperm are deposited on a special patch on the body wall and punch their way through into the *coelom*, the cavity between the gut and the body wall, and from there to the ovaries. Cocoons are produced as they are in earthworms, and these are buried or hidden among stones and vegetation.

All leeches are either blood-sucking or predatory, some having adopted a parasitic life-style, remaining with a specific host throughout their lives. Blood-sucking leeches can sometimes remove enormous meals from their victims without being noticed. They owe this ability to the production of an anaesthetic substance and an anti-coagulant called *hirudia*. After they have sliced a hole in their victim the blood flows freely and does not clot for some time after the leech has gorged itself and left.

Freshwater and marine species often attack fish, as does the common marine leech *Pontobdella muricata* which feeds on skates and rays. Other species such as the large medicinal leech, *Hirudo medicinalis*, feed on cattle that come down to the water to drink. Most of terrestrial species live in the tropics, dropping off vegetation on to their prey as it passes by. The temperate species *Trocheta*, however, hunts earthworms at night.

The annelids are characterized by a segmented body structure. Each segment comprises two concentric tubes of muscles, the outer tube contracting circularly and the inner one longitudinally. The leeches have two extra sets of muscles, a double layer of diagonal muscles between the circular and longitudinal ones, and bands of muscle linking the flat top and bottom surfaces. In all groups these muscle layers are covered by an epidermis and a thin cuticle.

The gut is not segmented and lies within a fluid-filled space, the coelom. The coelom is separated into sections by membranes along the same segmental lines as the body wall. The incompressible fluid lying within the muscular tube acts as a hydraulic skeleton conveying the forces produced by muscular contractions. Contractions of the circular muscles are compensated for by a change in the length of the longitudinal muscles, causing the worm to lengthen. Waves of contraction and elongation passing down the length of the worm enable it to crawl when the front and back ends are alternatively anchored by the setae. The extra muscles of the leeches allow them to rear and loop.

Earthworms are famed for their ability to regenerate lost parts. The earthworm cannot regenerate to form two worms if cut in half, but can produce a new head or tail if only a short length is severed. This capacity to regenerate is accompanied in some species by the ability to reproduce asexually. The polychaetes demonstrate a variety of asexual proliferation techniques, some budding off new individuals and some spontaneously falling to pieces, each piece becoming a new worm. The polychaetes also reproduce sexually and are *dioecious*, that is to say there are separate male and female individuals. The oligochaetes, like the leeches, on the other hand, are all hermaphrodites.

COELENTERATES

ectoderm
endoderm
mesogloea
digestive cavity

FLATWORMS

ectoderm
endoderm
mesoderm
digestive cavity
nerve cord
excretary ducts

NEMATODES

ectoderm
endoderm
mesoderm
digestive tract
pseudo coel
nerve cord
excretory ducts

ANNELIDS

ectoderm
endoderm
mesoderm
digestive tract
coelom
nerve cord
blood vessel

Heather Angel

Above: The 'peacock worm', *Sabella*, is a fan worm found along the British coastline.

Left: A common European annelid worm, *Eulalia viridis*, which belongs to the class *Polychaetes*. These are found on rocky shores and can often be seen among clumps of weed when the tide is out.

Jacana

The diagrams on the left show the characteristic features of four of the animal phyla. The coelenterates can be regarded as the most primitive phylum and the annelids the most advanced. The first two phyla, the coelenterates and flatworms, have a single opening in the digestive cavity and this serves both for the ingestion of food and the excretion of waste. The nematodes and annelids have a much more efficient system with a mouth and an anus at either end of a digestive tract. In the annelids there is a cavity, called the *coelom*, lined with a layer called the *mesoderm* between the digestive tract and the body wall. In the nematodes the cavity is not fully lined and is called the *pseudocoel*. It is absent entirely in the two most primitive phyla. The flatworms and both subsequent phyla have excretory and nervous systems. Neither are found in the coelenterates. Of the four phyla only the annelids have a circulatory system with blood flowing in blood vessels. Division of the body into segments is first apparent in the annelids and it is seen in more advanced phyla such as the *arthropoda*, which includes crustaceans such as crabs and lobsters, and insects. In the arthropods, however, segmentation is not so regular.

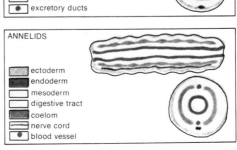

149

Crustaceans

Crustaceans range from the microscopic transparent organisms that form a major part of plankton in the sea, to the much larger and more familiar shrimps, crabs and lobsters. It is a large class of animals and, indeed, although most crustaceans live in the sea, there are many freshwater and land-dwelling varieties as well. Woodlice, for example, are found under stones and rotting wood in most back gardens, and the 'water flea', *Daphnia*, is present in most ponds and lakes.

The crustaceans belong to the *Arthropoda* (a name which means 'jointed legged'), the largest and most successful of the animal groups. Out of a total of over one million known animal species, more than three-quarters are arthropods. As well as crustaceans, the group encompasses four other major animal classes: the centipedes, the millipedes, the arachnids (spiders) and, the largest class of all, the insects.

Before considering the particular features of the crustaceans, it is worth looking at the general characteristics of the arthropods. Firstly, almost all have segmented bodies like the annelids, but in the higher arthropods the various segments are markedly different from each other and serve specialized functions. Secondly, as anyone who has eaten crab or lobster will know, they have a hollow shell-like skeleton, called the *exoskeleton*, which acts as a framework for the body. Unlike the skeleton of a vertebrate animal, the arthropod exoskeleton encloses the soft parts of the body, and the various sections are moved by means of internal muscles.

The exoskeleton is formed by the outer layer of the body, called the *cuticle*, which is made up of a substance called *chitin* and protein. It is segmentally hardened to act as a skeleton. Once the cuticle has been formed, it cannot increase in size and so arthropods have to moult in order to grow. Useful calcium salts and other material are withdrawn from the old cuticle while the new soft, larger cuticle forms underneath. The animal takes in water or air, swells up and splits the old cuticle along the lines of weakness. It then takes in still more water or air and increases further in size before the new cuticle hardens.

Most crustaceans are aquatic, and they can grow much larger than terrestrial arthropods. This is probably because the buoyancy of the water permits a larger body weight to be supported when the cuticle is soft, just after moulting, and the animal is lacking its skeletal support. Like other arthropods, the body is segmented and can be divided into three regions: the head, the thorax and the abdomen. In some crustaceans, however, the head and thorax are joined to form a single *cephalothorax* region covered by a large shield of cuticle called the *carapace*.

Again, like other arthropods, crustaceans show a basic arrangement of a pair of limbs per segment and, unlike the insects and arachnids, retain these limbs in most species. The adaptations of these limbs are often exquisite and they are rewarding subjects to study. The basic equipment is a pair of antennae, which are primarily sensory but sometimes serve

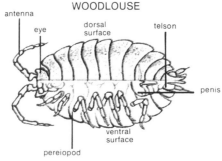

WOODLOUSE

antenna · eye · dorsal surface · telson · penis · ventral surface · pereiopod

Above: A body plan of a woodlouse, split to show the upper and lower body surfaces.

Below: The under surface of a pill woodlouse showing the brood pouch with young. These crustaceans are well adapted to life on land; their bodies are shaped to resist drying by evaporation.

Right: Common woodlice on the underside of a piece of tree bark. These animals are usually found in damp places because their gill-like breathing organs must be kept moist. Woodlice are the most common land crustaceans. They are found all over the world and feed on rotting vegetation.

J. A. Grant/Natural Science Photos

Heather Angel

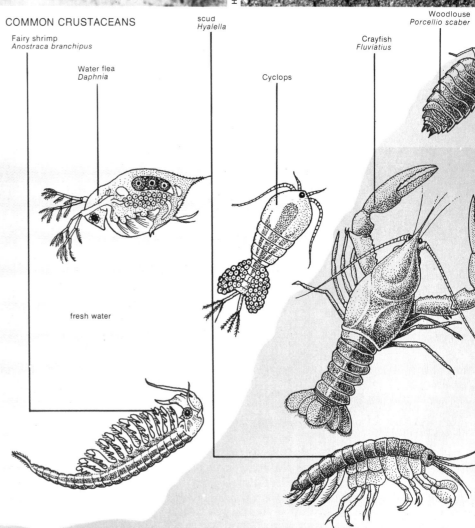

COMMON CRUSTACEANS

Fairy shrimp
Anostraca branchipus

Water flea
Daphnia

scud
Hyalella

Cyclops

Crayfish
Fluviatius

Woodlouse
Porcellio scaber

fresh water

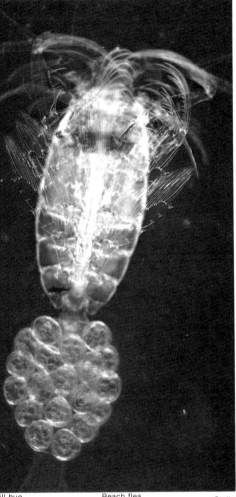

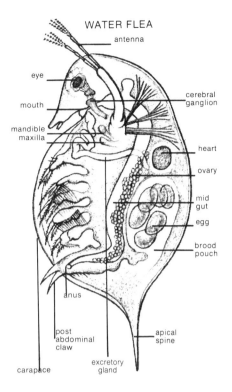

WATER FLEA

antenna

eye

mouth

mandible
maxilla

cerebral
ganglion

heart

ovary

mid
gut

egg

brood
pouch

anus

post
abdominal
claw

carapace

apical
spine

excretory
gland

Jacana

Left: A marine copepod with a bulging egg sac. The copepods are the most important of all crustaceans since they are a major constituent of the plankton which provides food for many sea creatures. The plankton consists of all sorts of small animals and plants carried along by sea currents.

Above: A body plan of the water flea *Daphnia*. These animals belong to the branchiopods, a group of freshwater crustaceans. They are about 1.6 mm across and live in ponds and ditches. A carapace formed of two plates encloses most of the body. They swim by jerking the large branched antennae.

Pill bug
Ligia oceanica

Beach flea
Orchestia ganmarella

Stalked barnacle
Lepas fascicularis

Fiddler crab
Portunus puber

Spiny lobster
Palinusus vulgaris

Edible crab
Pagarus

Hermit crab
*Eupagurus
bernhardus*

Acorn barnacle
Balarius perfurates

Shrimp
Crangon vulgaris

marine

other purposes as well, a pair of chewing mandibles and two pairs of limbs, called *maxillipeds*, for transferring food to the mouth. These are followed by other limbs for feeding, respiration, swimming, walking and reproduction.

The crustacean groups

The primitive *Branchiopoda* (the name means 'gill legs') are a group of freshwater crustaceans which exhibit many features typical of the class. They have leaf-like limbs used for feeding and often for swimming and respiration as well. Like most crustaceans, these animals are filter feeders; as the legs swing forwards, water is sucked in between them and food particles are filtered off on fringing hairs. As the legs swing back stiffly to propel the animals through the water, a small leakage washes the food from the hairs forwards to the mouth. Here the particles are stuck together with a sticky fluid and manipulated into the mouth by the mouthpart limbs. Some branchiopods have stouter, more bristly limbs that are used to stir up detritus lying on the pond bottom or to scrape algae off pond weeds.

Smaller animals of the group, like *Daphnia* and its close relatives, live in ponds while others are successful planktonic species in large lakes. The branchiopods succeed in avoiding competition with other animals by appearing early in the spring with the bloom of algae and then declining again.

Crustaceans move through water in many different ways. For example, many row themselves along by their limbs. In the primitive brine shrimps and fairy shrimps all the limbs beat fore and aft in what is called *metachronal rhythm*—each one slightly ahead of the one behind. The limbs are straight on the back stroke and flexed on the recovery stroke so as to propel the animal along. At the same time food is collected by the limbs.

Crustaceans, being essentially aquatic animals, use gills carried on limbs for respiration. In small species the general body surface may be used, or, in the branchiopods, the thin-walled limbs themselves. These thin-walled regions usually have special respiratory currents directed over them.

The nervous system and sense organs of crustaceans are typically arthropodan —sensory hairs for mechanical and chemical sensation, simple and compound eyes for light perception and vision. Some advanced species may recognize their prey visually. Many planktonic species migrate vertically each day; they swim down during the daylight hours and rise to the surface at night covering distances of as much as 600 ft (200 m). This is thought to be important in increasing the feeding range of the animals.

The sexes are separate in most crustaceans, and some structure for transferring sperm to the female is present in most males. Fertilized eggs typically develop into a series of larvae, often planktonic in the case of non-planktonic adults, thus avoiding competition with the adult population and aiding dispersal of the species. The first larval stage is called the *nauplius* and this has an oval body carrying three pairs of limbs. The nauplius larval stage is a fundamental characteristic of crustaceans; animals which are very different when adult (barnacles and copepods, for example) often have remarkably similar nauplius larvae. Even when

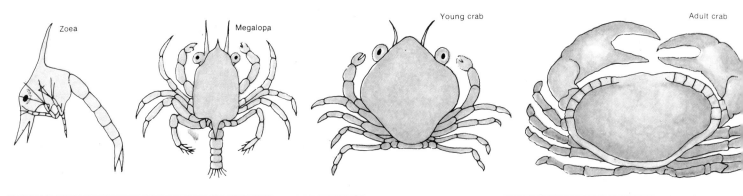

Zoea   Megalopa   Young crab   Adult crab

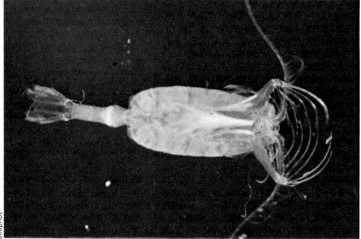

Above and left: Plankton is composed of a variety of small animals and plants. Among the crustacean members are the copepods (left) and newly hatched larvae of crabs (top left). These young larvae are called zoeae. The series of pictures above shows the other stages in the development of the edible crab, *Cancer pagurus*. The zoea is free-swimming, and about three or four weeks after hatching it changes into a megalopa larva which sinks to the sea floor. This becomes a young crab with a shell width of about 2.5 mm after a few more days. An adult crab can measure as much as 30 cm (1 ft) across.

Seaphot

Far right: The European crayfish, *Astacus astacus*. This animal only lives in very clean water and is therefore susceptible to pollution. It is not surprising that these creatures are becoming less common.

Right: A diagram showing the internal organs of a lobster. The stomach is divided into two sections separated by a strainer. Food is ground up in the cardiac stomach and then passes to the pyloric stomach where it is mixed with the digestive fluids.

Below: A marine shrimp *Stenopus hispidus*.

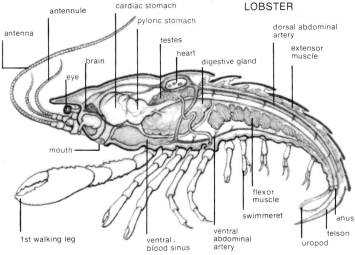

LOBSTER

antenna — antennule — cardiac stomach — pyloric stomach — testes — heart — digestive gland — dorsal abdominal artery — extensor muscle — brain — eye — mouth — 1st walking leg — ventral blood sinus — ventral abdominal artery — flexor muscle — swimmeret — uropod — telson — anus

Dr. F. Sauer/Bavaria

Bavaria

the eggs hatch into a different larval form, as in the case of the crayfish, there is often evidence of a nauplius-like embryonic stage in the egg before hatching.

Resistant, heavily-shelled eggs are produced by many branchiopods. Brine shrimp eggs have been experimentally exposed to severe drying and temperatures of 100 °C and still remain viable. Some animals like *Daphnia* produce eggs early in the season which do not require fertilization by a male and so the population can increase rapidly. In the summer and autumn they produce fertilized, resistant eggs to survive the rigours of winter.

Crustaceans in the food chain

The *Copepoda* are a group of small crustaceans which occur in immense numbers in marine and freshwater plankton. They are of enormous importance to all marine life, because they are one of the first links in the food chain. It has been estimated that there are more marine copepods than all other animals put together, and they constitute the world's largest stock of animal protein. (Plankton is basic to the feeding of animals like herring, sardines, whales and basking sharks; a whale can reach maturity and a weight of between 60 and 70 tonnes within two years just by straining plankton from the sea.) Not all copepods, however, are planktonic; *Cyclops*, for example, is a familiar form found in ponds and ditches.

Like the branchiopods, most copepods are filter feeders but they use different methods. Vortices generated by swimming bring particles towards the animal and these are then collected by the bristly mouthparts which create their own feeding current by rapid vibration.

Many copepods have evolved towards parasitism, and some are highly adapted for this way of life. Less modified forms are external parasites such as the fish lice which are flattened and have clawed limbs for clinging to the host. A more advanced state is seen in animals like the gill maggot, *Chondrochanthus*. With its loss of limbs, it hardly resembles a copepod apart from the sucking mouthparts embedded in the blood-rich gill tissue of the fish host.

Most crustaceans have several methods of travelling, although one may be dominant. In the copepods, the limbs near the head are rotated rather than rowed, and this creates a vortex on either side of the animal, driving it slowly forward. This type of movement is closely

Above: A slipper lobster, *Scyllarus*. These animals are easily distinguished by their flattened second antennae.

Left: A hermit crab occupies the shell of a whelk. As the crab grows, it periodically replaces its home with a new, larger one.

Right: The top two diagrams show the difference between the skeleton of a vertebrate animal and the exoskeleton of an arthropod. The bottom diagram shows the structure of the cuticle of an arthropod. The waxy outer layer prevents water from penetrating the layers underneath.

muscles

skeleton

exoskeleton

muscles

waxy layer

rigid chitinous layer

flexible chitinous layer

epidermis

Left: A male and female masked crab, *Corystes cassivelaunus*. The smaller animal is the female.

Right: A painted crayfish, *Panulirus longipes*. This animal is only about 7.5 cm (3 in) long, but it shows many of the features common to both lobsters and crayfish. The body is divided into two distinct regions; the cephalothorax and the segmented abdomen. The cephalothorax has a single shield-like covering, the carapace, while each of the five abdominal segments has its own covering, called a somite. The abdomen ends in a fan-like tail called the telson.

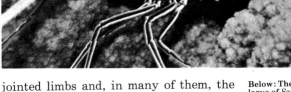

linked to the way the animal feeds, but the forked trunk limbs may also be used in rowing fashion for more rapid movement.

Barnacles

If one considers the barnacle zone of a rocky shore, it is as if a coat of living tissue had been painted on the rocks, so numerous and so close together are they packed. The barnacles, or *Cirripedia*, are also filter feeders, but as adults they remain attached to rocks, relying on the sea to bring food to them. Enclosed in their shells they can resist drying at low tide but open up to feed when the tide is in. This way of life is one commonly adopted by many different animals, from sponges to sea squirts.

The barnacles have been aptly described as lying on their backs, kicking food into their mouths. They are highly modified animals, with six pairs of curved hairy legs called *cirri* which are repeatedly thrust out of the shell cavity in subtly different ways, to form an effective net with which to catch suspended food.

Another group of crustaceans are the *Ostracoda*, tiny animals which mostly live in freshwater habitats. They do not have an obviously segmented body, but are recognized as crustaceans by their jointed limbs and, in many of them, the characteristic nauplius larva.

Lobsters, crabs and shrimps

These, the best known crustaceans, belong to the great group called the *Malacostraca*. Among them, the essential model is a shrimp-like swimming animal, but this has been modified to form bottom-living and burrowing animals as well. All the familiar forms of crab, crayfish and lobster are bottom-living forms. Terrestrial or semi-terrestrial woodlice (or sow bugs) have evolved here as well. A carapace joining the head to the thorax and enclosing this region is especially characteristic of the *Malacostraca*, although not peculiar to them. While the more primitive members of the group are filter feeders, specialization of limbs allows feeding upon larger prey or food masses. The characteristic pincers for manipulation of food become developed in this group.

In prawns and shrimps, the limbs on the abdomen, called *swimmerets*, row the animal along. In bottom-living forms, like crayfish and lobsters, the swimmerets are small and incapable of propelling the animal; they are nevertheless important in making a pouch for their brood and

Below: The nauplius larva of *Sacculina carcini*. The adult is shaped like a sack and is parasitic on crabs, extracting nourishment by means of 'roots' growing into the host's body. A nauplius larva with three pairs of limbs is characteristic of many very different crustaceans.

Heather Angel

Left: The common prawn, *Leander serratus*. Like their crayfish cousins, shrimps and prawns can move very rapidly backwards to escape from danger, by flexing their powerful abdominal muscles. Shrimps and prawns are common in many parts of the world. They are usually found in shallow coastal waters.

Right: A vividly marked painted shrimp, *Hymenocera picta*. These animals feed on starfish which they attack with their pincers. Bright colours and bizarre markings to warn off predators are particularly common in animals which live in tropical marine environments.

1st and 2nd pereiopods

antennule

artery to head

antenna

heart

gills

ventral abdominal artery

dorsal abdominal artery

COMMON PRAWN

Left and below: A stretch of the Welsh coastline showing the barnacle line along the rocks. Barnacles like the acorn barnacles (below) cling to the rocks. They close up when above the water line at low tide, but when submerged they extend their thoracic limbs to search for food.

Above: The body plan of a prawn. The walking legs are modified thoracic limbs and are called pereiopods. The limbs on the abdomen are called swimmerets or pleopods and they are used to propel the animal through the water. The gills are situated underneath the carapace where they are protected.

Heather Angel

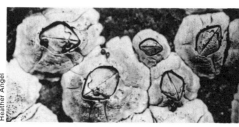

Heather Angel

thoracic limbs

penis

anus

oesophagus

testes

adductor muscle

seminal vessel

digestive gland

stomach

stalk

ovary

cement gland

BARNACLE

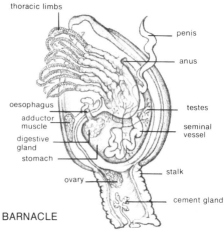

Heather Angel

Above: Goose barnacles, with their limbs extended for gathering food. These animals get their name from the ancient belief that they were the young of barnacle geese. The supposed marine origin of these birds once allowed them to be eaten during religious fasts when meat was banned.

Right: A body plan of a barnacle. These animals live attached to rocks by means of a cement gland. They are hermaphrodite, having reproductive organs of both sexes. Early zoologists thought these animals were molluscs, like oysters, but their first larval stage is clearly a crustacean nauplius.

may be retained solely for this purpose as in crabs.

The legs on the thorax of *Malacostraca* are relatively strong, often unforked, and used for walking. Though slender in animals like prawns, which can swim well, these walking legs are very strong in species like lobsters, crawfish and crabs, or in semi-terrestrial or terrestrial forms like sand hoppers and woodlice.

The swimming crabs are bottom-living animals, with small swimmerets and abdomens, that have acquired an ability to swim. The last pair of walking legs of swimming crabs are flattened so that they can be used as paddles to propel the animal.

Many crustaceans make use of the abdomen for swimming, most commonly as an escape mechanism. In animals like the freshwater crayfish the last pair of swimmerets are broad and form a tail fan with the end of the abdomen. When the abdomen is suddenly bent under the body this shoots the animal backwards through the water. Anyone who has tried to pick up a crayfish will be well aware of this effective mechanism.

Many of these animals collect food particles by rotary movements of parts of the thoracic limbs, as in the *Euphausids* (the 'krill' that whalebone whales feed on). Alternatively, some animals like the fiddler crabs may collect food from mud or from sand grains picked up and carefully searched by the mouthparts. Most of the larger *Malacostraca*, however, are predators and scavengers, feeding on relatively lethargic prey.

The gills in advanced *Malacostraca* are protected by a downgrowth of the carapace, and water is drawn through the gill chamber by specially modified limbs. Species living in muddy or tidal conditions may have the openings of the gill chamber guarded by hairs; indeed, in a crab they are hard to detect. The blood is circulated by a heart after oxygenation in the gills, the usual respiratory pigment being haemocyanin.

The crustaceans are of great zoological interest as well as being economically important. They provide food vital to life in the sea and, to a lesser extent, are a source of food for man. On the negative side, some copepods transmit human parasites like the guinea worm of the tropics, and barnacles have long been a problem for shipping. Another crustacean pest is *Limnoria lignorum*, a tiny marine animal which bores into wood. If present in large enough numbers these animals can destroy wooden jetties and wharves.

154

Slugs and Snails

Snails and slugs are molluscs belonging to the class *Gastropoda*. This is the most successful of the mollusc classes, containing as it does some 35,000 living species most of which are marine. The sea shore limpets and winkles, the land dwelling snails and slugs, and the fresh water pond snails are well known to all while many of the beautiful marine forms are familiar only to specialists.

From their outward appearance it is hard to imagine that molluscs could have anything in common with the segmented worms *(annelids)*, but the two groups are quite closely related. The likeness is only clearly apparent in the embryonic and larval stages; the early embryos of the two groups are almost identical and the larvae, called *trochophores*, are very similar to each other. Molluscs, however, do not have the segmented structure of the annelids; it is thought that they must have branched off from the evolutionary tree just before the annelids, the first group to show segmentation.

The gastropods most commonly encountered are the garden slugs and snails. These are very abundant; many hundreds of slugs can be removed each night from a half acre garden without markedly affecting the total slug population. Although the common terrestrial slugs and snails are often rather drab, other members of the class can be vividly coloured. These include the yellow, pink and brown periwinkles found on rocky sea shores, green sea hares, iridescent blue winkles and ormers, and blood-red freshwater snails. In contrast to many of their terrestrial cousins, the sea slugs exhibit an astonishing variety of colours and markings.

Although gastropods do not generally form an important part of the human diet, several species can be eaten. Indeed, the gastronomic possibilities of the species *Helix pomatia*, the 'edible' snail, are directly responsible for its presence in Britain; it was introduced by the Romans who obviously considered it a delicacy. In certain regions of Africa the large land snail, *Achatina*, is an important source of food, and various marine species such as the periwinkle, *Littorina littorea*, found on European shores, and the conch, *Strombus gigas*, common in the West Indies are also eaten.

The shells of certain snails have long been admired for their iridescent colouring, and they are nowadays collected by the ton for use in the jewellery trade. *Trochus* shells, for example, are widely used in Japan to make decorative buttons.

The body of a gastropod is divided into three parts: the head, the foot and the *visceral mass* which contains most of the internal organs. This arrangement is typical of molluscs. In snails, the visceral mass is covered by a single coiled shell, often of great complexity and beauty. Coiling is an ancient gastropod feature, probably associated with making the visceral mass more compact. As well as being coiled, the visceral mass is twisted during development of the *veliger*, one of the larval stages of a gastropod. To begin

Heather Angel

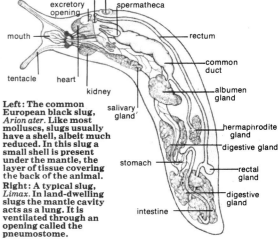

Left: The common European black slug, *Arion ater*. Like most molluscs, slugs usually have a shell, albeit much reduced. In this slug a small shell is present under the mantle, the layer of tissue covering the back of the animal. Right: A typical slug, *Limax*. In land-dwelling slugs the mantle cavity acts as a lung. It is ventilated through an opening called the pneumostome.

Anthony Bannister/NHPA

Left: A giant land snail, *Achatina maculata*. These animals are found throughout most of southern Africa, and in some places they are an important source of food. This one is about seven inches (18 cm) long.

Below: A series of diagrams to show how a snail moves along. Bands of contracted longitudinal muscle are lifted up and moved forwards while the regions in between are held to the ground by a mucous slime. This results in the 'waves' o contraction which are observed to move along the foot of the animal. Snails can typically move at a speed of about 2 inches (5 cm) per minute.

Right: The mating of two Roman snails. *Helix pomatia*. Although these animals are hermaphrodites, mating is essential because they cannot fertilize their own eggs. During copulation sperms are passed from each animal to the other by means of a penis. A 'love dart' made of a substance containing lime is discharged by each snail into its mate at the culmination of courtship. This unusual behaviour is thought to stimulate effective mating of the animals.

NHPA

P. Morris/Ardea

Below and left: The shell of the giant African snail *Achatina*. The picture on the left is an X-ray photograph.

Heather Angel

Left: Giant pond snails, *Limnaea stagnalis.* These gastropods are *pulmonates,* which means they have a lung cavity, rather than gills, and breathe air. A string of eggs surrounded by transparent gelatinous material have been laid on the shell of the nearer animal by another snail.

Right: A body plan of a land-dwelling snail. Blood is supplied to the various organs through an aorta leading from the heart. The aorta has two branches, one supplying the head and foot, the other supplying the visceral mass. The blood is oxygenated directly by air in the lung.

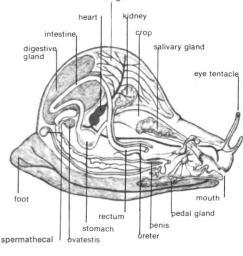

Left: Two views of a shell of the freshwater snail *Helisoma trivolvis.* The shell of a living snail is lined with a layer called the mantle which thickens into a collar where it joins the foot of the animal. Most of the shell is formed by a secretion from this mantle collar.

Right: A whirlpool ramshorn snail, *Planorbis vortex.* These snails are found in ponds and lakes. They can withstand a high level of pollution because, unlike other gastropods, they have haemoglobin in their blood. This improves respiration, making lower oxygen levels acceptable.

Heather Angel

with, the veliger is symmetrical so that one side matches the other and it has a foot, a head with a mouth, and a digestive tube leading through the visceral mass to the anus at the back.

During development the visceral mass twists round through 180° while the head and foot of the animal remain stationary so that the anus comes to be positioned above the head of the animal. The string of faeces coming from under the front of the shell of a snail is outwardly visible evidence of this twisting. Possibly as a result of the coiling and twisting processes, the organs on one side of the body do not develop fully. Usually it is the organs on the right side of the adult (the left side of the larva) which are reduced.

While many gastropod species remain twisted throughout their lives some untwist later, but usually some sign of their earlier twisted condition remains. No one is sure what advantage twisting gives gastropods or their larvae, and it is strange that the most characteristic feature of the group should remain so little understood.

Gastropod groups

Gastropods show a wide range of form and adaptation to different ways of life, and they are divided into three groups: the *prosobranchs,* the *opisthobranchs* and the *pulmonates.* The prosobranchs have gills at the front of the body and well developed shells. They are mostly marine and exhibit the characteristic twisting as in winkles and top shells. The opisthobranchs have gills at the back of the body, reduced shells and a more streamlined shape. Like the prosobranchs they are marine, but the gills are less well developed or even

absent, and the twisting is less marked or lost. Examples include the sea hares and sea slugs. Finally, the pulmonates are land or freshwater species without gills. They breath air in a lung cavity and show the characteristic twisting of the visceral mass. Garden slugs and snails fall into this class.

In most molluscs the foot is highly muscular and this is certainly true of the gastropods which are active animals, albeit slow moving. If a snail's foot is observed while the animal is moving on a piece of glass, about eight darker bands moving forward can be seen. These are bands of contracted longitudinal muscle lifted up and moved forwards before being put down, while the regions in between are held down by mucus secreted from a gland at the front of the body. Variations of this musculature allow greater mobility or speed, or dogged adherence to resist wave action or predators. In contrast, forms such as the sea butterflies 'fly' under water using lateral flaps of the foot in a most graceful way. Swimming forms of this sort show great reduction of the shell which may even be absent altogether and a general lightening of the body.

Some gastropods, such as limpets, are adapted to withdraw under their shell by means of a shell muscle and cling to rocks, while others, like winkles, retreat entirely within the shell and close the opening with a plate, the *operculum,* carried on the back of the foot. This is especially important in shore-dwelling species as it prevents them from drying out at low tide as well as helping them to resist predators. In land snails a horny cover sealing the shell entrance may be formed, especially when the animal hiber-

nates, to isolate the animals from the hostile outside world. Their ability to resist drying out has been an important factor in the successful adaptation of many gastropods to a terrestrial existence.

Feeding

Primitive gastropods show the basic method common to many molluscs of more or less continuous feeding. The food-collecting structure, the *radula,* is a continuously growing flexible strip bearing rows of teeth which is moved over the ground to collect particles of food. It is flanked by horny jaws and moved by a muscular region of the gut called the *buccal mass.* Particles of food are drawn in a mucus string to the stomach by the *style,* a secreted rod which is rotated by hair-like structures called *cilia.* The food is sorted out by cilia in the stomach, fine particles being carried into a large digestive gland where digestion and absorption takes place. The intestine leads from the stomach to the rectum which discharges into the *mantle cavity,* a region located above the head of the animal under the shell which also houses the gills. This kind of general arrangement is seen in ormers and slit limpets, but evolution has also developed the feeding mechanism and gut in a number of other directions.

In limpets and many winkles the radula has fewer but stouter teeth for rasping algae from rocks and is very long to compensate for rapid wear. As food is not mixed and feeding is intermittent, the stomach lacks the continuously winding style and the complex sorting areas and simply forms a storage region. Forms such as the slipper limpet and chinaman's hat collect fine food particles in mucus on an

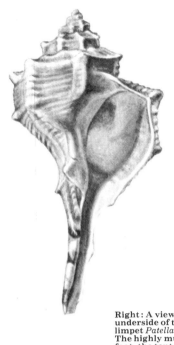

Left: The shell of the marine snail *Murex* found along the shores of the Mediterranean. In the time of the Phoenicians many thousands of these snails were killed annually for the purple dye they produce. Huge deposits of such shells have been found at Tyre, Sidon and other former Phoenician cities.

Right: Coloured varieties of *Nucella lapillus*, the dog whelk, lying on an Atlantic shore. Like *Murex*, these snails produce a purple dye which was once extracted and used. Egg capsules, each containing as many as 1,000 eggs, can also be seen in the picture.

D. P. Wilson

Right: A view of the underside of the limpet *Patella vulgata*. The highly muscular foot, the tentacles and, between the tentacles, the mouth can clearly be seen. The large foot allows the animal to cling tightly to rocks on the sea shore, thus preventing it from becoming dislodged by the action of the waves.

Left: A shell of the marine limpet *Acmaea*.

Far right: A body plan of the marine limpet *Acmaea*. Water circulates under the shell to supply oxygen to the gills and to carry away waste products.

Alison Wilson

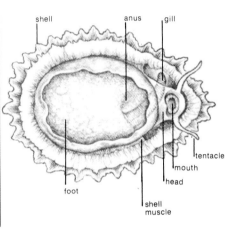

Left: The veliger larva of a gastropod. This stage of development is intermediate between the first larval stage, called the trochophore, and the adult snail. The veliger is free-swimming, propelling itself through the water with the hair-like cilia plainly visible in the picture.

Right: A violet snail, *Janthina globosa*, floats on a raft of air bubbles. These snails are found along the east coast of Africa.

Below: Stages in the development of a veliger larva. To begin with the veliger (left) is symmetrical with one side of the animal matching the other. The shell is very small and the foot has hardly begun to develop. In its most advanced stage (right) the veliger has a well developed shell and foot and the visceral mass has become twisted so that the anus comes to lie above the animal's head.

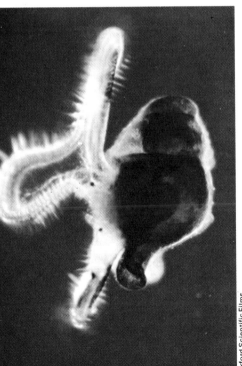

Oxford Scientific Films

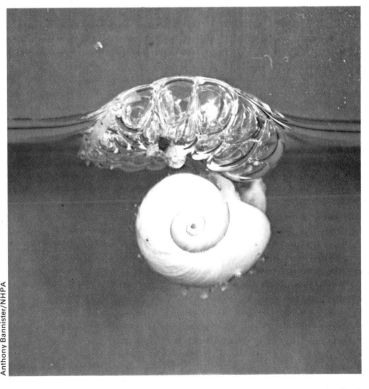

Anthony Bannister/NHPA

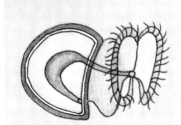
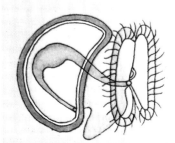
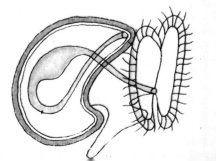

157

Below: A sea slug, *Glossodoris capensis*, crawling on a gorgonian coral. As well as a pair of tentacles on the head, the animal has a feathery secondary gill projecting from its back. Sea slugs are usually quite small. This one is only about one inch (25 mm) long.

Right: A sea slug crawling on an African coral reef. The remarkably vivid colours and the strange shapes of the sea slugs serve as a camouflage to protect them against predators. In deeper water where there is less light, these animals lose much of their brilliant colour.

Anthony Bannister/NHPA

enlarged gill. A string of food and mucus is then pulled into the mouth by the simple radula and buccal mass, but the stomach and style are well developed to deal with the continuous supply of particles.

In herbivores, like the snails and sea-weed-feeding forms such as the sea hare, the radula has rows of small teeth for breaking up the food which is bitten off in pieces by the jaws. Many gastropods have become carnivores, and in such forms the radula is short with reduced rows of sharp teeth. Salivary glands become large and secrete enzymes capable of digesting proteins, while the forward gut region may be developed so that the buccal mass can be brought to the tip of an elongated proboscis. Such a proboscis is often developed as a 'drill' for penetrating the shells of bivalve molluscs such as mussels or oysters. The shells are neatly drilled by the radula, with the help of acid secretions in some species, so allowing entry of the proboscis. Drilled bivalve shells can often be picked up in large numbers on sandy shores at low tide. Less specialized carnivorous gastropods feed on stationary animals such as sponges and coelenterates.

Some sea slugs which feed on coelenterates show a most extraordinary adaptation. While most of the victim's body tissue is digested in the normal way, stinging capsules, called *nematocysts*, remain intact and eventually find their way to projections called *cerata* in the slug's body surface. Here they mature and come into action if the animal is attacked for example by a predator. Associated with this remarkable mechanism is the bright colouration of these sea slugs which presumably acts as a warning to predators.

Right: A series of diagrams of *Limacina*, a shelled sea butterfly, to show how it moves through the water. The animal has two wing-like parapodia which push it along.

Below: A sea butterfly, *Cavolinia*, found along the coast of the Atlantic ocean.

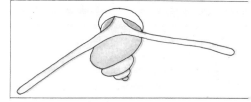

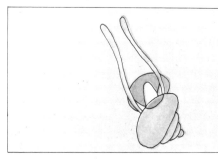

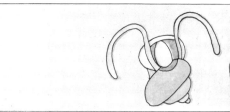

158

Left: A sea slug, *Cyerce nigra*. The shield-like structures covering the animal are modified gills, called cerata, and contain outgrowths of the liver.

Above: A sea slug, *Chromodoris coi*. The sea slugs belong to the *opisthobranch* group of gastropods.

Below: A sea hare, *Aplysia punctata*. In the background is sea lettuce, *Ulva*, which is eaten by sea hares. The animal swims along by means of two flap-like parapodia, one on each side of the body.

Bottom: Another species of sea hare, *Aplysia sowerbyi*.

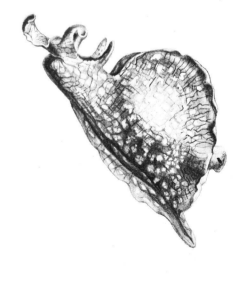

Most terrestrial snails and slugs are herbivorous, but some prey on animals such as earthworms. Perhaps the most advanced carnivores are the marine cone shells. Here the radular teeth are reduced to a single pair in each row. They are very large and pointed, and have a groove that carries a nerve poison secreted by the salivary glands. A single radular tooth is suddenly struck into the prey, rapidly paralysing it with the salivary poison. One Australian species of this group has even proved fatal to man.

Respiration

The mantle cavity of all molluscs is vitally important, but in the gastropods with their diversity of form and habits, it shows much variation. It is most important as a respiratory area protecting the delicate gills. In the primitive ormers and their relatives, water is brought in over the two gills and then out through a series of apertures along the mid-line of the shell, carrying away with it waste products from the anus and the kidney ducts. This irrigation is brought about entirely by the action of cilia. In more advanced gastropods the gill and kidney of the right hand side are lost and water can flow in an efficient U-shaped path, in at the left hand side, across the single gill and out at the right hand side. The mantle cavity opens at the front of the animal as a result of the twisting process, and the flow of water through it may be assisted by the animal's forward movement. In the sea slugs and their relatives respiration takes place through the general body surface or by means of secondary gills. The pulmonates such as garden slugs have a single small opening called a *pneumostome* leading into

the mantle cavity which acts as a lung; the anus, kidney and genital ducts open outside the mantle cavity.

In all gastropods the heart drains blood from the respiratory surface and distributes it by means of arteries throughout the body from where it drains into the main body cavity. Haemocyanin is the respiratory pigment and its general efficiency is low, but this is unimportant in view of the low level of activity of the animals. Unlike haemoglobin, the red iron-containing respiratory pigment of human blood, haemocyanin is very faintly blue and contains copper.

In reproducing their kind, gastropods show remarkable diversity. In the most primitive species, reproductive cells, or *gametes*, are shed through the mantle cavity into the sea where fertilization takes place and the larvae develop. During their life some gastropods show a change of sex. In a group of slipper limpets, *Crepidula farnicata*, sitting one on top of the other it is observed that the sexes range from a young male on top, through hermaphrodites to the largest female on the bottom. Most gastropods have very complex hermaphrodite reproductive systems that allow internal fertilization, and they may produce hard shelled eggs or even live young. This is another factor that has been important in colonising difficult non-marine habitats.

With terrestrial life and hermaphroditism a complex courtship is often seen. Common garden snails for example indulge in a remarkable courtship which culminates in the shooting of lime-containing 'love darts' into each other, followed by copulation and the mutual exchange of sperm.

159

Octopuses, Squid and Oysters

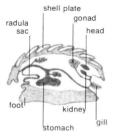
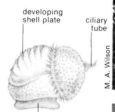
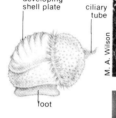

radula sac — shell plate — gonad — head — foot — kidney — gill — stomach

developing shell plate — ciliary tube — foot

shell plate clearly defined

There are more than 80,000 living and 35,000 fossil species of the molluscs. As a large and successful group of the animal kingdom, they inhabit a wide range of ecological niches, and are found on land, in freshwater and in the sea.

The group can be divided into seven classes, three of which contain fairly common animals. The mussels, oysters, cockles, clams, scallops and razor shells belong to the Bivalvia class and are typically rather slow-moving creatures, often found buried in sand or mud on the sea bed or firmly attached to rocks. In contrast, squid, cuttlefish and octopus are active swimmers belonging to the class Cephalopoda. This class contains the largest known invertebrate animal, the deep sea squid, *Architeuthis*, which can reach a length of more than 15 metres (50 ft). The class Gastropoda contains the slugs, snails and limpets. Somewhat less familiar are the 'coat of mail' shells or chitons of the class Placophora, and the specialized, often worm-like and burrowing, deep water species in the class Scaphopoda.

The final class, Monoplacophora, contains the primitive *Neopilina* which looks rather like a limpet and was first discovered in 1952, dredged up from deep water off the Pacific coast of Mexico.

Molluscs and Man
A number of molluscs, particularly bivalves, are of economic importance, usually as a source of food. Oyster cultivation has been recorded from Roman times, and the presence of quantities of oyster, mussel and scallop shells in archeological excavations emphasizes the importance of shell-fish in the diet of prehistoric man. British oyster beds were once the largest in Europe, but have greatly declined in extent and productivity over the last century. The accidental introduction of oyster predators such as the American oyster drill (a marine snail) as well as the arrival of competitors for food or space such as the American slipper limpet, *Crepidula*, and the barnacle, *Elminius*, have all contributed to the decline of the British oyster beds. On top of this, there has been over-fishing, pollution and, in 1962-63, a particularly severe winter. Most commercial beds today are stocked with the faster growing but gastronomically inferior Portuguese oyster, *Crassostrea angulata*. This warmer water species rarely breeds in Britain, and so young oysters are imported from abroad for sowing in British beds.

Also of considerable economic importance, albeit adverse, are the shipworms, *Teredo*. These are specialized bivalves that can bore into wood using their shells and feed off the wood cellulose. They can cause extensive damage to wooden jetties and piers.

Mollusc characteristics
All the mollusc classes, despite apparently having a great diversity of structure, have certain basic molluscan features in common. One of the most obvious is the possession of a hard external shell for the

160

Left and below: Chitons or 'coat-of-mail' shells are perhaps the most typical of all molluscs. They have a soft body, a muscular foot and a hard covering shell. They are found on rocks along the seashore where they feed on algae and other vegetable matter. In some chitons like the one on the left, *Acanthochitona crinita*, the fleshy mantle grows over the outer edge of the shell and carries nine pairs of tufts of bristles. These bristles are extremely sensitive to touch. Chitons are most active at night, returning during the day to a particular home location. If disturbed they cling tightly to the rock.

M. A. Wilson

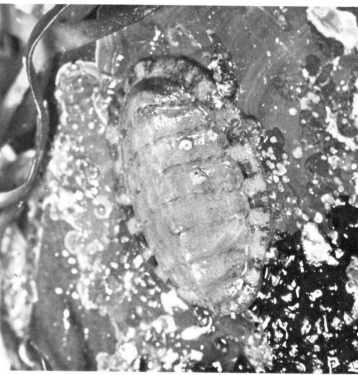

Jane Burton/Bruce Coalman

Above: The top diagram shows the positions of the main organs of a chiton. The eight shell plates are secreted by the mantle which covers the upper part of the body. Chitons breathe by means of gills which lie on both sides of the animal between the mantle and the foot. The centre diagram shows a free-swimming chiton larva with the shell plates just beginning to develop. The ring of cilia around the middle of the animal enables it to move through the water. The bottom diagram shows a later stage of development. The cilia have been lost, and the foot and the shell plates are much more clearly defined.

Jacana

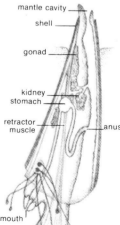

mantle cavity — shell — gonad — kidney — stomach — retractor muscle — anus — mouth — foot — captacula

Above: If it is disturbed a chiton will roll itself up so that all the soft parts of the body are enclosed within the protective shell.

Left: A photograph and a body plan of tusk shells. These molluscs have almost tubular shells, with an opening at both ends. They spend their lives almost completely buried in the sand with only the top of the shell projecting. Currents of water flowing in and out of the upper shell opening permit respiration and the excretion of waste products. The head has a large number of sense organs, called *captacula*, which help in capturing prey.

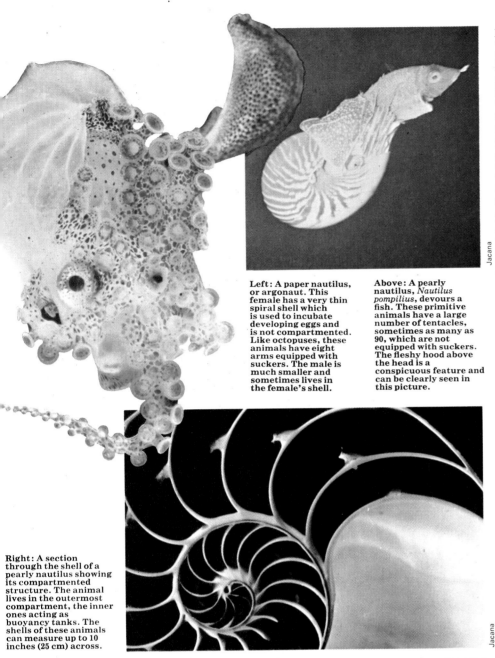

Left: A paper nautilus, or argonaut. This female has a very thin spiral shell which is used to incubate developing eggs and is not compartmented. Like octopuses, these animals have eight arms equipped with suckers. The male is much smaller and sometimes lives in the female's shell.

Above: A pearly nautilus, *Nautilus pompilius*, devours a fish. These primitive animals have a large number of tentacles, sometimes as many as 90, which are not equipped with suckers. The fleshy hood above the head is a conspicuous feature and can be clearly seen in this picture.

Right: A section through the shell of a pearly nautilus showing its compartmented structure. The animal lives in the outermost compartment, the inner ones acting as buoyancy tanks. The shells of these animals can measure up to 10 inches (25 cm) across.

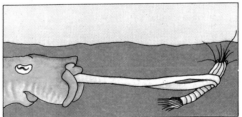

Above and left: The common cuttlefish, *Sepia officinalis*, is another member of the mollusc family. These creatures catch their prey by shooting out a pair of tentacles at the unsuspecting victim. The tentacles are usually retracted in a cavity underneath the eyes and are not normally visible. The shell of the cuttlefish, called the cuttlebone, is covered by the mantle and is often given to cage birds as a source of calcium. When attacked, the animal releases an inky fluid which contains the brown pigment *sepia* used by artists. Most of the time cuttlefish remain partly buried on the sandy ocean floor, lying in wait for prey.

protection of the soft body (the Latin word *mollis* means soft). The shell is of particular importance to biologists as it helps to identify the species. The innermost layer of the shell, the nacreous layer, is iridescent and is the commercially valuable mother of pearl. It is composed of flat horizontal plates of aragonite crystals, one of the crystalline forms of calcium carbonate. Outside the nacreous layer are two further layers. The middle layer is again composed of calcium carbonate crystals, but here they are arranged perpendicularly to the shell surface. The outermost layer, called the *periostracum*, is a thin horny covering which prevents the two calcium carbonate layers from being attacked if the water is acidic.

In the common sea mussel, *Mytilus edulis*, and other bivalves the shell takes the form of two plates or 'valves' almost completely enclosing the body and held firmly together by strong *adductor* muscles. The valves are joined at their upper edge by an elastic ligament 'hinge', and controlled relaxation of the adductors causes the valves to open. Shells can reach gigantic proportions. For example, the giant clam, *Tridacna*, living in shallow warm water on the coral reefs of the Indian and Pacific Oceans, has a shell over a metre across, weighing up to a quarter of a tonne (250 kg).

Cephalopods like the squids usually have a very small shell. In the squid, *Loligo*, and the cuttlefish, *Sepia*, the shell is internal, forming the 'pen' and 'cuttlebone' respectively. In the octopus, however, it is completely absent. Fossil cephalopods such as *Belemnites* and *Ammonites* have a large, chambered shell and such a condition is still seen in the pearly nautilus, a primitive member of the group found in the surface waters of the south-west Pacific. The shell is spirally coiled and new chambers are added as the nautilus grows; the animal lives in the largest, most recently formed chamber. The other chambers are kept filled with a gas to neutralize the animal's weight in the water, like the buoyancy tanks of a submarine, so that the nautilus can move up and down through the water at will.

The papery nautilus or argonaut is only distantly related to the pearly nautilus. Here only the female produces a shell which is paper-thin and fragile. It is held by two racquet-shaped arms and is used as an incubation chamber for the developing eggs. Sometimes, however, the much smaller, shell-less male has been known to inhabit it.

The chitons, a small group of marine molluscs, have a somewhat flattened body covered by a shell of eight overlapping plates. A well developed foot enables the chiton to attach itself, limpet-like, to rocks in the inter-tidal zone. If detached it can curl itself up like a wood louse because of the freedom of movement between the shell plates, and in this way it protects itself from possible injury by wave action. It is a herbivore, rasping seaweed from rocks with a well developed 'tongue', the *radula*, which acts like a chain saw.

Structure

The molluscan body is divided into three parts: head, foot and visceral mass. The head is particularly obvious in cephalopods where in addition to the mouth there is a pair of eyes comparable with those of the vertebrates, having an iris diaphragm,

161

a movable lens and a curved retina. This gives the cephalopods the ability to discriminate colour and fine detail. In bivalves, probably because they lead a much less active life, the head region is absent. The foot, however, is well developed, being muscular and plough-like in shape, and can be protruded between the two valves for digging or burrowing. In mussels the foot has a gland which produces a mass of extremely tough protein threads, the *byssus*. These are used to attach the animal to rocks in the intertidal zone, so overcoming wave action. The cephalopod foot has become modified to form a circle of eight or ten arms—an octopus has eight, squid and cuttlefish ten—surrounding the head and also a funnel which connects the mantle cavity with the exterior. In squids two of the arms are particularly long and prehensile and can be retracted. They are known as the tentacles and are used for catching prey.

The visceral mass contains the main body organs and is surrounded by a thick flap of rather muscular tissue known as the *mantle*, the edge of which produces the major part of the shell. The mantle forms a skirt around the visceral mass, being attached to it only at the top. The cavity so formed between the mantle and the body is known as the *mantle cavity* into which open the anus, the kidney and reproductive ducts. Contained within the cavity are the respiratory organs, the gills or *ctenidia*.

Since many bivalves lie buried at considerable depths, the gills are supplied with water by means of two extendable tubes or *siphons*: an inhalant siphon which conducts oxygenated water and food into the mantle cavity from above the surface, and an exhalant siphon which removes the partially deoxygenated water together with any waste products. The mussel possesses a pair of gills each of which has undergone folding to produce a large surface area for respiration and also food collection. Small planktonic organisms and organic debris entering the mantle cavity are sieved off by cilia on the gills, trapped in long strings of mucus, and transported by other cilia to the mouth.

A rotating rod, the crystalline *style*, is present in the stomach. It acts as a capstan, winding in the long mucus strands, but it also releases enzymes vital for digestion. Large particles that could clog the filtering apparatus are removed by ciliary rejection currents and periodically the shell valves are clapped together. The increase in mantle cavity pressure shoots the debris out through the inhalant siphon.

In cephalopods the gills are supplied with water by muscular activity. The mantle muscles relax, increasing the volume of the mantle cavity, and water enters between the mantle and the base of the funnel. The modules then rapidly contract, causing the water to be violently expelled through the funnel. By pointing the funnel in different directions cephalopods, particularly the very active ones like squids, can move at considerable speed in any direction by a water-jet propulsion mechanism. Normally, however, a squid swims forwards by undulating the fins on either side of its body. In times of danger a black pigment, *melanin*, can be liberated into the water, producing a 'smoke screen' to confuse predators.

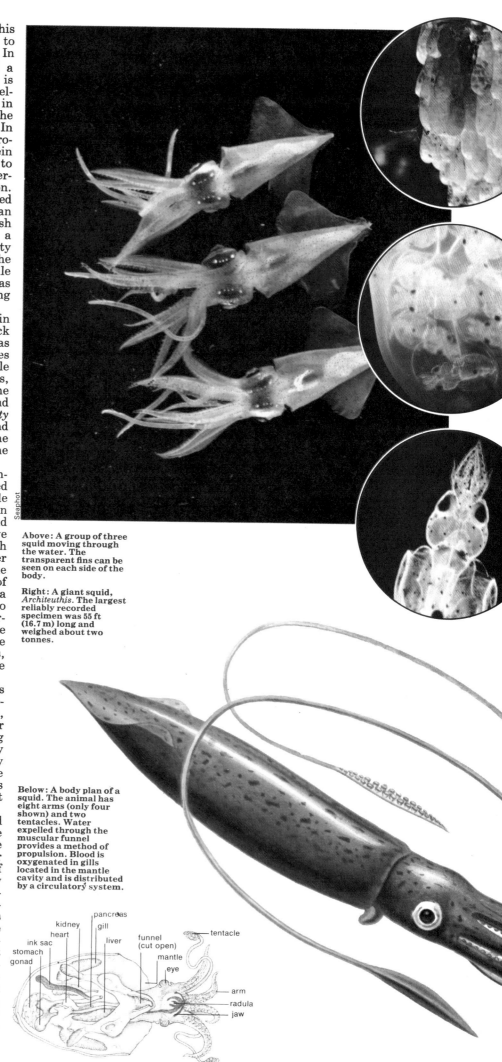

Seaphot

Above: A group of three squid moving through the water. The transparent fins can be seen on each side of the body.

Right: A giant squid, *Architeuthis*. The largest reliably recorded specimen was 55 ft (16.7 m) long and weighed about two tonnes.

Below: A body plan of a squid. The animal has eight arms (only four shown) and two tentacles. Water expelled through the muscular funnel provides a method of propulsion. Blood is oxygenated in gills located in the mantle cavity and is distributed by a circulatory system.

pancreas
kidney
heart
gill
liver
funnel (cut open)
tentacle
ink sac
stomach
gonad
mantle
eye
arm
radula
jaw

162

Left: A series of pictures to show the development of the dwarf squid, *Alloteuthis subulata*. Each of the transparent egg capsules shown in the top picture contains many eggs. The centre picture is a close-up of one of the capsules showing the embryos in the eggs in a fairly advanced state of development. The bottom picture shows a newly hatched young squid. The two eyes and the heart are plainly visible.

Right: A young deep water squid. A squid has ten arms provided with suckers. Two of the arms are elongated to form tentacles for catching prey such as fish.

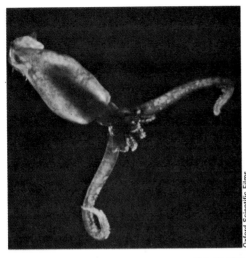

Oxford Scientific Films

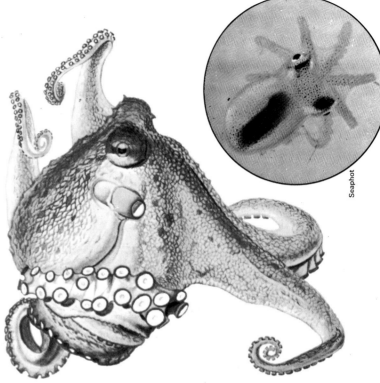

Seaphot

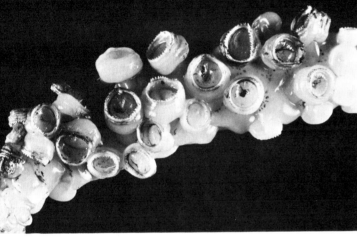

Above: A close-up of the suckers of the squid *Loligo forbesi*. The tiny hooks on the rim of each sucker help to grip the prey. Both the arms and tentacles have suckers.

Right: Apart from its unusually long neck this strange looking deep sea squid shows most of the features seen in other species.

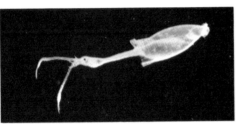

Seaphot

Above: The common octopus, *Octopus vulgaris*, and (inset) a newly hatched octopus. These animals do not have a larval stage: the young hatch directly from the egg capsules. Unlike most other molluscs, octopuses have no trace of a shell, not even an internal one.

Heather Angel

Right: A lesser octopus, *Eledone cirrosa*, with a captured shore crab. The octopus is biting through the shell of the crab with its beak. Octopuses exhibit considerable skill and perseverence in hunting their prey, sometimes even following crabs on to dry land.

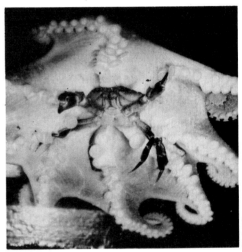

D. P. Wilson

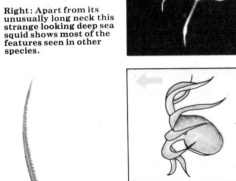

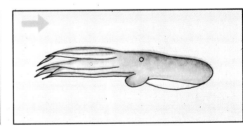

Above and right: The three diagrams above show how an octopus escapes from an enemy. On being disturbed the animal moves rapidly 'backwards', helped by a jet of water from its funnel. The opening of the funnel is clearly visible in the photograph of *Octopus vulgaris* on the right.

P. Morris/Ardea

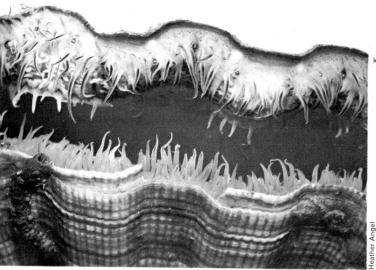

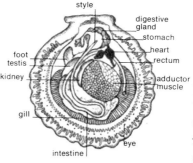

Above: A body plan of a scallop. Blood is circulated through blood vessels by the heart and is oxygenated in the gills. The gills are covered with cilia which maintain a current of water through the valve plates. This carries food particles to the animal's mouth.

Above: A close-up of the giant scallop, *Pecten maximus*. The edge of the mantle carries numerous tentacles as well as a series of eyes which look rather like pearls. The eyes are fairly well developed and can detect motion, so helping the animal to escape from its predators.

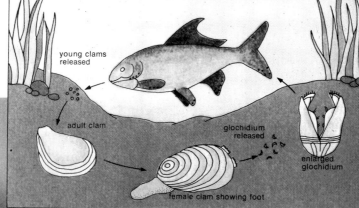

Left: A queen scallop, *Chlamys opercularis*, escapes from one of its predators, the common starfish, by clapping together its valve plates. Although these animals can swim they are often found anchored to rocks by means of *byssus* threads. Queen scallops are common in the Mediterranean.

Above: The life cycle of the freshwater clam. Fertilized eggs develop into larvae called *glochidia* in the gills of the female clam. These are released into the water and attach themselves to the gills or fin of a fish. Here they develop into young clams which then leave their host.

Left, right and below: Three different bivalve molluscs. On the left is a spiny cockle, *Acanthocardia echinata*, with its foot protruding from between the two valve plates. Right is a mussel, *Mytilus edulis*, lying open in sea water, and below is an American spiny oyster, *Spondylus*.

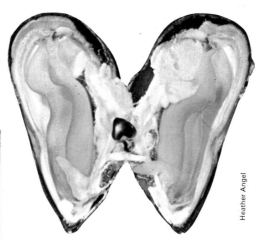

Right: The formation of a pearl by an oyster. This is a protective mechanism to prevent parasites such as fluke larvae from harming the animal. The outer layer of the mantle, the *epithelium*, secretes layers of pearly substance around the parasite to isolate it.

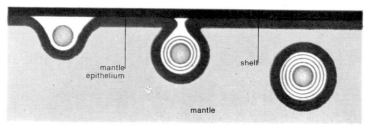

Cephalopods are carnivorous, feeding on fish and the larger crustacea. Food i captured by the long tentacles which, lik the arms, are equipped with numerou powerful suckers. Living food is killed b a pair of strong beak-like jaws. Th salivary glands produce enzymes calle *proteases* which allow food to be par tially digested before it reaches th stomach. In species like *Loligo*, th salivary glands also produce a powerfu poison.

As might be expected from their activ way of life, the cephalopods have a ver well developed nervous system. The brai possesses higher intelligence centers s that sensory information can be memor ized and used to modify behaviour. Lead ing from the brain are giant nerve fibre capable of rapidly transmitting impulse at up to 20 metres per second. This allow the animal to contract all the mantl muscles almost instantaneously.

Many deep sea squids are luminescent Often the light-producing organs ar highly complex, having lens tissue and reflector cells as well as the light-generat ing cells themselves. It may be that thes cells enable the squid to pick out its pre in the darkness.

Reproduction

The bivalves usually reproduce by re leasing enormous numbers of eggs and sperm into the water. External fertili zation results in the development of ciliated larvae called *trochophores*. The trochophore, together with the next larval stage, the *veliger*, floats in the plankton and distributes the species before settling on a suitable surface and developing into an adult. In the fresh water swan mussel, *Anodonta*, and the European flat oyster, *Ostrea edulis*, how ever, fertilization is internal: sperms are released into the water and then carried into the mantle cavity to fertilize the eggs. In *Ostrea* clouds of veligers are liberated about eight days after fertilization.

It has been estimated that *Ostrea* can incubate up to a million eggs at a time, but even this number is small compared with the reproductive potential of the American oyster, *Crassostrea virginica*, where eggs are released in masses of 100 million at a time. Oyster veligers settle down after between one and two and a half weeks, but they are capable of swim ming off again if they find the surface unsuitable. Eventually, however, the veliger cements itself to a surface, ideally a flat rock. This is done with a secretion from a cement gland in the foot which is a modification of the byssal gland found in mussels. At this stage the young oysters are about 1.2 mm (0.047 inch) across and are known as *spat*.

In cephalopods, fertilization usually follows an elaborate courtship often in volving complex colour changes. The eggs are generally fertilized internally, one of the arms of the male, the *hectocotylus*, being specialized for transferring packets of sperm, known as *spermatophores*, into the female mantle cavity. Squids lay their eggs in clusters on the sea bed where they are left to develop. Eventually the eggs hatch directly into young squid. Unlike most other cephalopods, however, the octopus exhibits very little preliminary courtship behaviour, but the female takes great care of the eggs, flushing them with water and cleaning them with the tips of her arms.

Spiders and Scorpions

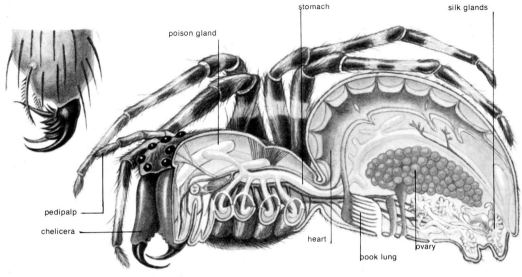

Spiders are often wrongly thought of as insects. In fact they belong to a quite different arthropod class, the *Arachnida*, which also includes such animals as scorpions, harvestmen, mites and ticks.

Arachnids are animals with four pairs of jointed legs (except for some mites, which only have three), and segmented bodies divided into two main parts, the cephalothorax, consisting of the combined head and thorax, and the abdomen. Arachnids can therefore usually be distinguished without difficulty from insects, which always have three pairs of legs and a head separated from the thorax by a narrow neck.

Arachnids and insects have both evolved from some type of aquatic segmented, worm-like ancestors, but they have done so separately. In fact the arachnids have invaded the land independently of the insects, so the two groups provide an interesting example of parallel evolution. Arachnids and insects nevertheless do have features in common: for example, dorsal main blood vessels, ventral nerve cords and, most obviously, tough external skeletons which provide excellent support and protection, but act as something of an impediment to growth. However, in the course of their long history, the ancestors of the two groups have sometimes evolved very different answers to the same problems.

Unlike insects, arachnids never have antennae. Their mouthparts, originally derived from the limbs of the segments which have joined together to make up the head region, always include paired structures known as the *chelicerae* and the *pedipalps*. The structure of these is important in classifying arachnids into groups. They have, at the most, simple rather than compound eyes. Their sense organs also include at least some hair-like projections of the skeleton, to be found on the outside of the body. While insects breathe by means of an internal system of air-pipes, known as the *tracheal* system, the smallest of arachnids have no special respiratory system at all. They simply pick up oxygen from the air at the external surface of the body. Arachnids like scorpions have paired gill-like book-lungs on their abdomens, while others, such as harvestmen, have book-lungs modified to form a tracheal system very different from that of insects. However, the arachnids' respiratory systems are never efficient enough to permit continuous and strenuous activity. If running hunters, such as the wolf spiders, do not catch up with their prey within the first few feet, they have to stop in order to get their breath back.

Most arachnids are carnivorous predators, hunting other small arthropods. They often kill by means of venom delivered through hollow fangs, and feed by sucking the juice from their prey. With the exception of some kinds of mites, arachnids can take food only in liquid form. The prey is therefore partly digested by means of enzymes which the arachnid pumps into it, before sucking out the semi-digested contents. They leave behind

Above: A diagram to show the body structure of a spider, and a detail of the tip of a spider's leg. The body is divided into two regions, the abdomen and the cephalothorax. The animal breathes by means of a 'book lung', so called because it consists of a number of 'leaflets' which resemble the pages of a book. The lung is situated at the front of the abdominal surface. The front two limbs are called chelicerae which carry poison ducts. Next come a pair of pedipalps whose bases, called maxillae, act as jaws. These are followed by four pairs of long, jointed walking legs.

Above: The head of a wolf spider showing the pincer-like chelicerae. The fangs at the end of the chelicerae are used like hypodermic needles to inject poison. Spiders have eight simple eyes, six of which are visible here.

Above right: Scorpions engage in an elaborate courtship dance prior to mating.

Right: Young scorpions ride about on their mother's back for about a week after birth. Unlike most arachnids, which are egg layers, scorpions produce live, well-developed young.

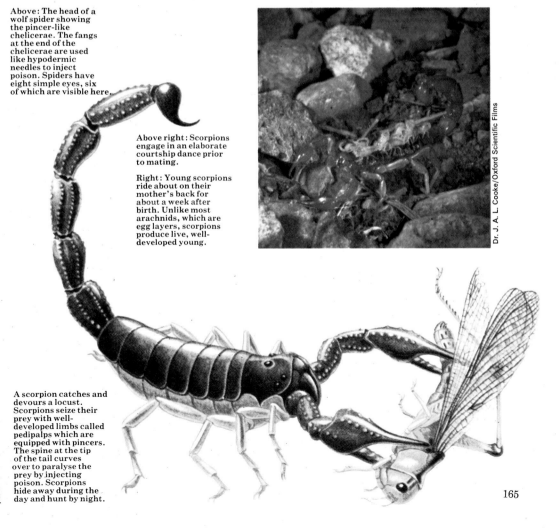

A scorpion catches and devours a locust. Scorpions seize their prey with well-developed limbs called pedipalps which are equipped with pincers. The spine at the tip of the tail curves over to paralyse the prey by injecting poison. Scorpions hide away during the day and hunt by night.

165

sea scorpion
(extinct)

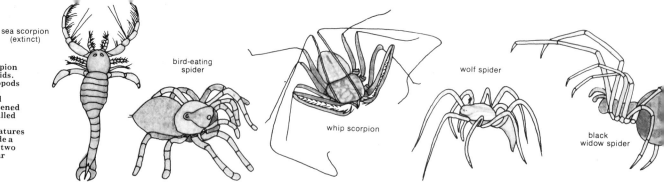
bird-eating
spider

whip scorpion

wolf spider

black
widow spider

Right: A sea scorpion
and some arachnids.
Like other arthropods
they have jointed
limbs, segmented
bodies and a hardened
outer covering called
the exoskeleton.
Characteristic features
of the class include a
body divided into two
main regions, four
pairs of legs and
simple eyes.

Heinz Schrempp/Frank Lane

Left: A European wasp
spider waits for
insects to blunder
into its web. These
animals are easily
recognized by their
characteristic black
and yellow markings.

Right: A water spider
grabs and kills a
water louse (a fresh-
water crustacean).
Like their land-
dwelling cousins, water
spiders construct webs
to catch their prey.
Visible in the picture
is a bubble of air
trapped by the hairs
on the spider's
abdomen. This bubble
provides the essential
supply of air for
breathing and must be
refilled periodically
at the surface. These
animals are found
among the plants at
the bottom of ponds.

only the empty external skeleton which
can often be seen near spiders' webs, just
as empty soup cans might be seen near the
dwellings of untidy humans. Many kinds
of mites and ticks are parasitic, feeding
on the living tissues of plant and animal
hosts.

Scorpions
Scorpions are not only the most-feared,
but often among the largest of the arachnids. The biggest scorpions may be as
much as 18cm (7 inches) long. Their
history as fossils goes back for 400 million
years and they must have been among the
earliest of land-living arthropods. Today
there are about 600 species; they are
found in all tropical regions and other
warm areas including southern Europe
and the western coast of Canada. They
are shy in habit and are mainly nocturnal.
By day they hide away beneath stones, in
crevices and in other suitable hiding
places. It is this habit which accounts for
the tales of travellers who have found
scorpions hiding in their shoes in the
morning.

Among scorpions the mouthparts,
known as *pedipalps*, bear pincers not
unlike those of crabs (which belong to
quite a different group of arthropods, the
crustaceans). Even more prominent is the
sting, which is situated on the last slender
segment of the abdomen and curves over
the back. The scorpion's venom is a nerve-
poison, and is produced by paired glands
at the base of the sting.

The severity of a scorpion's sting
depends very much on the particular
species. Most scorpions are relatively
harmless to humans, their sting being
more painful than deadly, but some

Above: A male jumping
spider performs a
courtship dance before
mating. Male spiders
often perform some
sort of courtship
ritual to prevent the
females from regarding
them only as prey.

Right: A female wolf
spider, *Lycosa
piratica*, with young
clinging to her back.

Above: A tarantula.
The name is applied to a
variety of large,
usually hairy spiders
which hunt their prey
by night and hide
under logs or stones
during the day.
Although painful, their
bite is not dangerous
to man. A large
tropical tarantula may
measure as much as
18 cm (7 in) across.

Near right: Spider's
silk is spun from
three pairs of minute
pores called spinnerets
at the back of the
abdomen.

Far right: Three
diagrams show stages
in the construction of
a spider's web. The
signal thread lets the
spider know when a
fly or other prey
strikes the web.

Natural Science Photos

166

mping spider

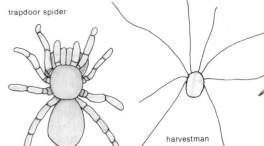
trapdoor spider

harvestman

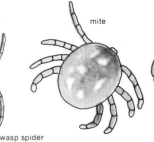
wasp spider

mite

book scorpion

ght: An orb web spider
ith a grasshopper it
as caught in its web.
he body of this spider
about two centimetres
).8 inch) long. The
eb was spun between
ow bushes and was
bout five metres (5.5
ards) in diameter.

elow: A diagrammatic
iew of a spider's
helicera. The fang
trikes at the prey,
sually an insect, and
oison is injected
rom a duct leading
from the poison gland.
The fang is 'hinged' so
hat it can be folded
lown when not in use.

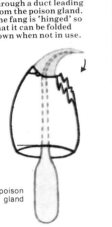

poison
gland

NHPA

Anthony Bannister/NHPA

Above and below:
Spiders catch their
prey by a variety of
different methods. The
yellow crab spider
(above) waits
camouflaged on a
flower until a fly
unwittingly approaches.
Other species like the
garden spider (below)
build elaborate 'orb'
webs to catch flying
insects.

tropical species, like the Egyptian scorpion, *Leiurus*, can be very dangerous, particularly to children and old people. The poison acts by paralysing the nerves of the heart and chest muscles.

Although they look like smaller versions of scorpions, pseudoscorpions have no tail stings. They are found in most parts of the world but are seldom noticed because they are shy and well camouflaged. Many of the 1,100 species live under bark or in the leaf litter on top of the soil. One very widely distributed species, *Chelifer cancroides*, is found in houses.

Pseudoscorpions all have two pairs of pincers. Both the pedipalps and the chelicerae bear claws. The pedipalps also bear poison glands (although these animals are too small for their poison to be any kind of threat to man) and the chelicerae contain silk glands, which produce silk very like that of spiders. This silk is used to make a cocoon into which the eggs are laid on the undersurface of the female. Female pseudoscorpions have glands comparable to the mammary glands of mammals with which they produce a secretion upon which their newly-hatched young feed.

Even less conspicuous and less well known are the members of a number of other groups of arachnids. These include the camel spiders, of which there are 500 species living in warm, dry habitats like deserts. They have pincers on their chelicerae and leg-like pedipalps. Characteristically, a camel spider will run for a short distance with its pedipalps stretched out in front of it, and then will stop to hunt for prey.

The 20 species of micro-whip scorpions are small and live in the soil of warm countries. Their mouthparts resemble those of camel spiders, but their abdomens end in slender tails. A similar feature is also found in the true whip scorpions, which are larger and widespread in the tropics (although not in Africa or the Middle East). There are about 100 kinds of whip scorpions, with toothed chelicerae and thick, often pincer-like pedipalps.

Brian Hawkes/NHPA

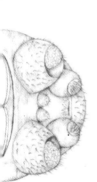

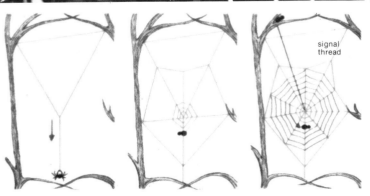

signal
thread

Left: A female harvestman or 'daddy-long-legs' devours a male of the species. These animals are recognized by their very long legs and the absence of a waist. The adults die in the autumn after laying their eggs. These will survive the winter to hatch out in the following spring.

Right: Bright scarlet velvet mites. These creatures live in the upper layers of the earth and feed on such things as insects' eggs. As their name implies, mites are very small, often having a body length of less than one millimetre (0.04 in). Often they are parasitic on animals or plants.

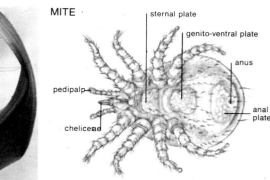

MITE

sternal plate

genito-ventral plate

anus

pedipalp

chelicerae

anal plate

Far left: A harvestman clings to the underside of a leaf.

Left: The lower surface of a parasitic mite. Unlike most arachnids, the heads, thorax and abdomen of a mite are joined together to form an unsegmented body. The egg of a typical mite hatches into a larva having only three pairs of walking legs. A fourth pair of legs is acquired when the larva moults to become a nymph. Finally, the nymph moults to become a fully-developed adult animal.

Far right: A burnet moth infested with tiny mites. One species of moth mite, *Pyemotes herfsi*, exhibits bizarre mating behaviour. The animals are born live, the newborn males acting as 'midwives' for their sisters. As soon as the females are born mating occurs.

Right: Velvet mite larvae on a scorpion. Mites are found in the most unlikely places, both as parasites and free-living. Some are even adapted to life under water.

Another group, the tailless whip scorpions are up to 45 mm (1.75 inches) long and found in warm parts of America and Africa. Their pedipalps are long and barbed, and are used in seizing the prey. There are about 50 species.

Harvestmen, mites and ticks

Harvestmen have very long, slender legs and for this reason they are sometimes called 'daddy-long-legs', a name which they share with the equally long-legged crane flies, which are insects. Their chelicerae bear small pincers, and their pedipalps are leg-like and equipped with poison glands. The cephalothorax and abdomen are joined together so as to give the entire body a unified, rounded appearance. Harvestmen live in most parts of the world, usually in rather damp places. There are over 3,000 species, and of all arachnids they are the least fussy of feeders. They eat dead animal and plant material as well as smaller invertebrates which they hunt for themselves. Female harvestmen deposit their eggs in the soil or in decaying wood by means of an elongated *ovipositor*.

Mites and ticks are mostly small but very widespread. Many of them are parasitic, but there are also numerous free-living forms which live in such habitats as leaf-mould. Some of them even live in water, and one species lives inconspicuously in mattresses and bedding. It is very common and does humans no obvious harm. Altogether over 10,000 species are known, but many more must remain to be discovered.

Many kinds of mites are destructive, some attacking cultivated plants like fruit trees, while others, like *Sarcoptes*, cause mange in domestic animals. The effects of some of the blood-sucking ticks can be even more serious. They are responsible for transmitting diseases from one human host to another. Spotted fever, *tularemia* and relapsing fever are all spread by ticks. By contrast the activities of the European harvest mite, *Trombicula autumnalis*, appear trifling, for it usually causes only itching to its human hosts.

Spiders

As a group the spiders do not vary as much as the mites and ticks, but in sheer numbers they are unrivalled. There are over 40,000 species, and it has been calculated that no less than 5 million spiders live in a single hectare of temperate grassland (2 million to every acre). The hordes of spiders, some of them almost microscopic in size and others up to 10 cm (4 inches) long, are primarily predators of insects.

Some of the largest tropical species including various species known as 'bird eating spiders,' do sometimes feed on small vertebrates such as birds. They kill by means of poison injected through their fangs and then suck the juices from their prey. But even these giant spiders most often feed on insects. The total amount of insects eaten by spiders is vast. It has been calculated that within the British Isles the weight of the insects killed and eaten by spiders in the course of a year must be greater than the total weight of the country's human population.

Spiders are insects' greatest enemies by far. Insects have evolved various defences against the spiders' attack, including thicker armour, unpleasant tastes and evil-smelling glands, and it may well be that the insects' power of flight evolved partly for the same reason. However, as in modern technological warfare, for every form of defence there is an appropriate answer, and for all kinds of living insects there are still spiders lying in wait. The power of flight cannot save an insect that blunders into the sticky silk of the spider's web.

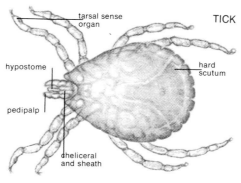

TICK

tarsal sense organ

hypostome

hard scutum

pedipalp

cheliceral and sheath

Above left, above and left: Ticks feed on the blood of reptiles, birds and mammals, and the limbs around their mouths are modified for penetrating and clinging to the skin of the host animal. They can live for long periods without food, and are the carriers of several diseases which infect domestic animals. Usually a tick bite will cause only local irritation to humans, but sometimes the disease 'relapsing fever' may be transmitted. The two sexes are often quite distinct because the male tick (the animal illustrated above is a male) has a hard covering called the *scutum* which extends over almost the whole of the upper body surface. In females the scutum is much smaller. The photograph above left shows a tick on the base of an eagle's beak, while the one on the left shows three ticks on the underside of a hedgehog.

Almost all spiders have venomous glands, normally used only to paralyse and kill the normal small prey species. There are, however, several notorious species (sometimes vaguely referred to as *tarantulas*) with powerful venom which is sometimes used to ward off the attentions of large vertebrates, including man. Best-known is the black-widow spider, *Latrodectus nectans*, which is widely distributed in many parts of the world, including North America. One regrettable habit of this species is the way in which it frequently seeks peace and quiet under lavatory seats, emerging to bite when its peace is disturbed.

Cocoons and webs

All spiders have the ability to make silk. It is produced in liquid form by large abdominal glands. A spider has several of these glands, each producing a slightly different kind of silk. The glands open on the surface of the spider's abdomen at the *spinnerets*. As the silk is drawn out it solidifies because of the stretching it receives in the process.

The ancestors of the spiders almost certainly produced their primitive silk as a waste product. The first use to which it was put was in the construction of cocoons to protect the spiders' eggs from predators. To this day all female spiders construct silken cocoons. However, silk has now been adapted for several other purposes.

The best-known of these is the construction of the elegant orb webs which act as stationary trawls to trap flying insects on their sticky strands. Many kinds of spiders, however, construct different webs. Some build formless, tangled webs while others make funnel-shaped webs, examples of which are often to be found in the corners of garden sheds. Some spiders live inside silk-lined tubes, seizing and biting their prey through the walls; others live in similarly lined tunnels with well-concealed, hinged lids.

Many spiders, on the other hand, make no use of silk in catching their prey. Jumping spiders stalk and pounce, and wolf spiders chase their prey. Crab spiders patiently wait for their prey to come within reach on flowers where they are well camouflaged. These groups have other uses for silk. Many of them trail a strand of it behind them wherever they go as a kind of safety-rope.

Mating

Silk also plays a vital part in the mating of spiders. As a preliminary the male spins a very small web upon which he deposits a drop of sperm. This he takes up into special receptacles on the ends of his pedipalps. He then searches for a female into whose genital opening he places his pedipalps.

Once fertilized, female spiders are able to produce eggs for a year or more without further mating taking place. The eggs are laid in batches, always into a silken cocoon. In some species female spiders go to great lengths in caring for their young. Some kill prey for them, and others feed their young from their own mouths.

During their growth spiders moult an average of eight or so times. Most spiders are mature by the time they are a year old. Females often live longer than males, the females of some of the largest species living for 20 or more years. By contrast, adult males of some smaller species have a life expectancy of only a few weeks.

Right and below: A shore-dwelling horse-shoe crab. In spite of their name, these animals are not crustaceans. They are related to the arachnids but fall into a separate arthropod class called the *Merostomata*. The extinct sea scorpion which sometimes reached a length of two metres (six feet) also belonged to this class.

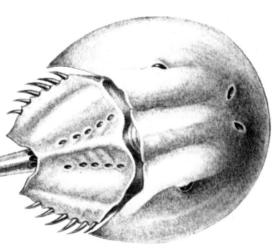

HORSESHOE CRAB

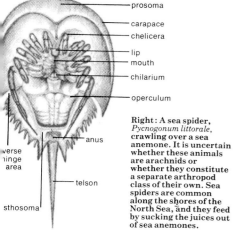

- prosoma
- carapace
- chelicera
- lip
- mouth
- chilarium
- operculum
- anus
- verse hinge area
- telson
- sthosoma

Right: A sea spider, *Pycnogonum littorale*, crawling over a sea anemone. It is uncertain whether these animals are arachnids or whether they constitute a separate arthropod class of their own. Sea spiders are common along the shores of the North Sea, and they feed by sucking the juices out of sea anemones.

169

Insects

The insects are undoubtedly the largest and one of the most successful groups of animals. There are more than 750,000 species inhabiting a vast range of habitats on land and in water. The only environment that insects have failed to colonize to any great extent is the sea; they are completely absent from deep sea water. In the air, on the other hand, they are present up to heights of 2,000 metres (6,600 ft), forming an aerial 'plankton' on which many birds depend for food.

Insects owe their success to a number of features, perhaps the most important of which is the development of a waterproof layer on the outside of their hardened cuticle. This has liberated them from the restrictive damp environments of the onychophorans, centipedes and millipedes and, coupled with the development of flight, has enabled them to escape more easily from predators and to explore and colonize new habitats. Another important feature of the insect success story is their tremendous reproductive potential.

Insects are built on the basic arthropod design. The body is divided into three quite distinct regions. A head of six joined segments bears the feeding and sensory apparatus and is connected by a very short 'neck' to a thoracic region of three segments which bear the wings and three pairs of walking legs. The third region is an abdomen of eleven segments, either with no limbs at all or with small specialized limbs for purposes other than walking.

Wingless insects

Not all insects have wings, and they are thus divided into two groups: the wingless *Apterygota* and the winged *Pterygota*. The former contains those groups like the springtails, *Collembola*, and the bristletails, *Thysanura*. In these species some of the other features typical of insects are also poorly developed.

The springtails are small cosmopolitan, insects with a unique forked jumping organ at the bottom end of a short abdomen of five or six segments. They have a 'spring' fastened to the end of the abdomen by a 'catch' which when released allows the spring to move suddenly downwards, striking the ground and throwing the insect into the air. Since their cuticle is not waterproofed they only thrive in damp environments, in leaf mould, soil and rotting wood. It has been estimated that in an acre of English meadowland there may be as many as 250,000,000 rounded green springtails, *Sminthurus viridis*.

Bristletails derive their name from three bristle-like projections at the end of the abdomen and their long bristle-like antennae. They are about 2 cm (0.8 in) long and their legs are well developed for swift running. Although they are found throughout the world, they also are restricted to damp environments. The best known bristletails are the silverfish, *Lepisma*, and the firebrat, *Thermobia domestica*. The silverfish is so called since the division of the body into three parts is not obvious, giving a fish-like form and the body of the adult is covered with silvery scales which easily rub off. They are frequently found in larders, cup-

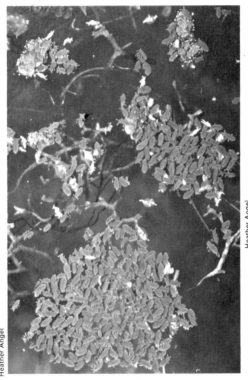

Heather Angel

Heather Angel

Left: Springtails, *Podura aquatica*, clustering on the surface of a pond. Springtails are primitive wingless insects which are usually very small. They have a spring mechanism formed from a pair of abdominal limbs. On each side of the head there is a group of simple eyes rather than the compound eye of most insects.

Above: Well camouflaged bristletails, *Petrobius maritimus*, on a stone. These animals get their name from the three jointed filaments at the tail end of the abdomen. Like the springtails, bristletails are primitive insects and cannot fly. They are usually found among rotting wood or leaves and under stones.

Below: The mating of two damselflies. The male grasps the female's thorax with claspers at the end of his abdomen. Like most insects damselflies have two pairs of wings carried on the second and third thoracic segments. Damselflies carry their wings parallel to their abdomens when they are not in flight.

Right: A close-up of the head of a dragonfly, *Aeshna cyanea*, showing the enormous compound eyes. They are composed of almost 30,000 separate light-sensitive units and cover most of the head. Compound eyes are found in most insects although in some (infants, for example) they may be composed of as few as 50 units.

Jane Burton/Bruce Coleman

Anthony Bannister/NHPA

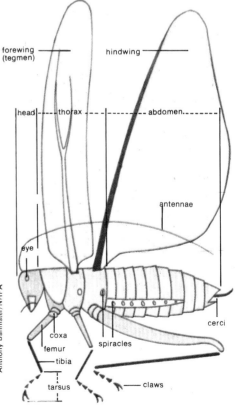

forewing (tegmen), hindwing, head, thorax, abdomen, antennae, eye, coxa, femur, tibia, spiracles, tarsus, claws, cerci

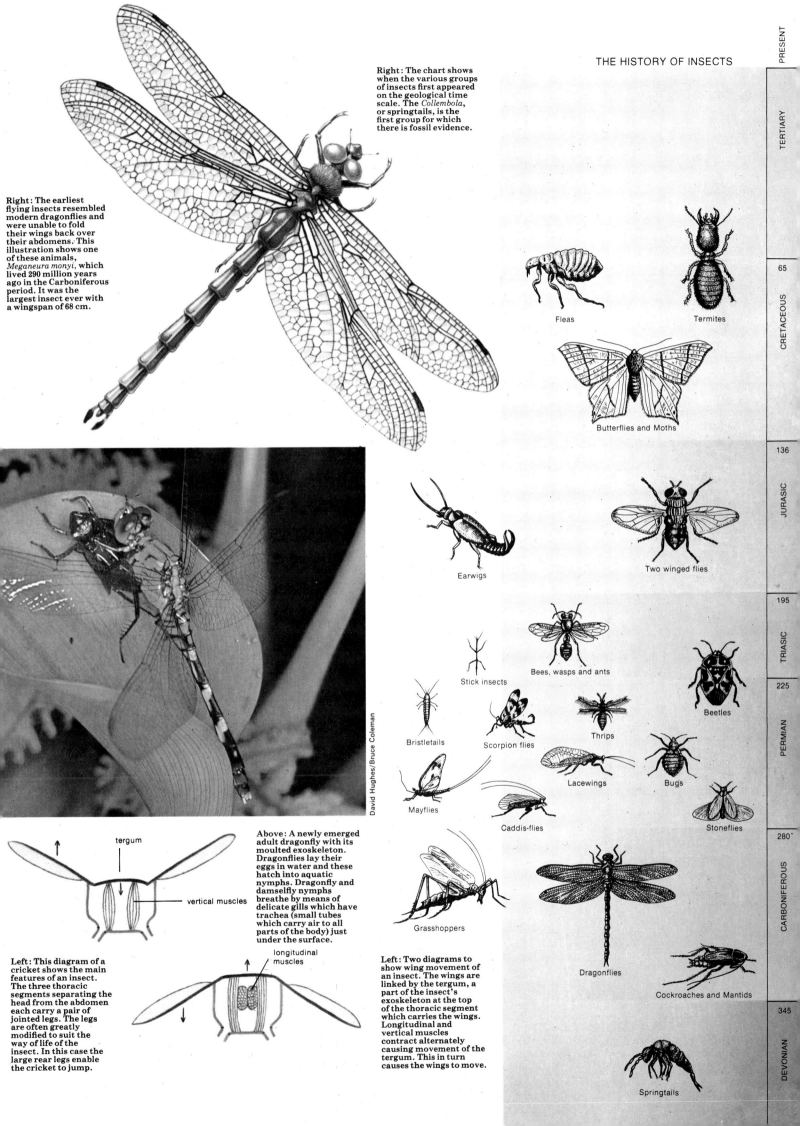

Right: The chart shows when the various groups of insects first appeared on the geological time scale. The *Collembola*, or springtails, is the first group for which there is fossil evidence.

Right: The earliest flying insects resembled modern dragonflies and were unable to fold their wings back over their abdomens. This illustration shows one of these animals, *Meganeura monyi*, which lived 290 million years ago in the Carboniferous period. It was the largest insect ever with a wingspan of 68 cm.

David Hughes/Bruce Coleman

Above: A newly emerged adult dragonfly with its moulted exoskeleton. Dragonflies lay their eggs in water and these hatch into aquatic nymphs. Dragonfly and damselfly nymphs breathe by means of delicate gills which have trachea (small tubes which carry air to all parts of the body) just under the surface.

Left: This diagram of a cricket shows the main features of an insect. The three thoracic segments separating the head from the abdomen each carry a pair of jointed legs. The legs are often greatly modified to suit the way of life of the insect. In this case the large rear legs enable the cricket to jump.

tergum

vertical muscles

longitudinal muscles

Left: Two diagrams to show wing movement of an insect. The wings are linked by the tergum, a part of the insect's exoskeleton at the top of the thoracic segment which carries the wings. Longitudinal and vertical muscles contract alternately causing movement of the tergum. This in turn causes the wings to move.

Fleas

Termites

Butterflies and Moths

Earwigs

Two winged flies

Stick insects

Bees, wasps and ants

Bristletails

Scorpion flies

Thrips

Beetles

Mayflies

Caddis-flies

Lacewings

Bugs

Stoneflies

Grasshoppers

Dragonflies

Cockroaches and Mantids

Springtails

PRESENT

TERTIARY

65

CRETACEOUS

136

JURASIC

195

TRIASIC

225

PERMIAN

280

CARBONIFEROUS

345

DEVONIAN

boards and behind skirting boards of houses and in books where they can cause damage to the binding material. Firebrats occur in large numbers around fireplaces, boilers and bakery ovens.

It is probable that the winged insects arose from a bristletail-like stock 400 million years ago in the Devonian era. The first winged insects could not fold back their wings over their abdomen when at rest. These insects are known as the *Palaeoptera* and are represented by the present day dragonflies and damselflies (the *Odonata*) and mayflies (the *Ephemeroptera*).

Dragonflies, damselflies and mayflies

Dragonflies, or 'devils daring needles' as they are sometimes known, derive their name from their long, brilliantly coloured scaly body. They are completely harmless to man although males patrolling their territory can be a nuisance when they try to drive away human intruders. They are among the largest living insects; a Borneo dragonfly, *Tetracanthagyna plagiata*, has a wing span of 18cm (7.1 in) and a length of about 13 cm (5.1 in). A 300 million year old fossil dragonfly from the Carboniferous era had a wing span of about 68cm (26.8 in) making it the largest known insect. The *Odonata* have two pairs of large wings with a complex system of veins supporting the wing membrane. Although the wings are only capable of simple up and down movements, dragonflies can travel at speeds estimated at up to 96 kph (60 mph) which makes them one of the fastest flying insects. Damselflies, however, have a much slower, fluttering flight which, with their more slender body, easily distinguishes them from dragonflies.

Both dragonflies and damselflies mate near water, and the males are distinguished from females by their colour. In some damselflies there is even a form of courtship. The method of mating is unique among insects. The male transfers sperm from the opening of the male glands at the end of the abdomen to an accessory organ near the front of the abdomen. He then alights on the back of a female and holds her head (male damselflies hold the female's thorax) with a pair of claspers at the end of his abdomen. The female curls her abdomen round so that her posterior reproductive opening is in contact with the male accessory organ and sperm is transferred.

Damselflies and some dragonflies insert their eggs into the stems of water plants and some dragonflies bury them in sand or gravel at the water's edge. Most dragonflies, however, shed the eggs directly into the water while flying over it with the tip of their abdomen under the surface. The eggs hatch into nymphs which, like the adults, are carnivorous. Young fish, other aquatic insects and tadpoles are caught by a unique method. The lower lip, the *labium*, is enlarged and is rapidly extended to seize the prey in its pincer-like hooks. The labium is then retracted bringing the victim within reach of the jaws.

Damselflies spend at least a year and dragonflies two years as nymphs. In this time they form a very important source of food for fresh-water fish. After this they climb up a water plant into the air and undergo a final moult to become winged adults which live for only a few summer months.

Left: An adult mayfly, *Ephemera danica*. The larvae of these insects are aquatic and breathe by means of gills.

Below: A diagram to show how the song of a male cricket is produced. One of the front wings has a series of ridges near its base while the other front wing carries a projection coupled to a

membrane. When the wings are rubbed together the projection is drawn across the ridges so generating the characteristic song which is amplified by the membrane.

Right: The head of a bush cricket. These insects have mouthparts which are designed for biting and chewing.

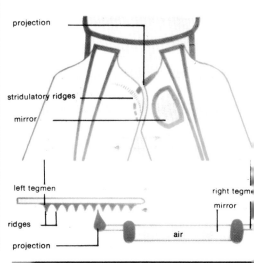

projection

stridulatory ridges

mirror

left tegmen

right tegmen

mirror

ridges

projection

air

Below: The nymph of a stonefly. These animals are aquatic and only live in clean water. Their presence therefore means a low level of pollution. They breathe by means of gills. The adult flies have two pairs of large membranous wings but are poor fliers and usually prefer to run from place to place.

Right: A lubber grasshopper, *Phymateus purpurascens*, displaying the vivid colours of its hind wings.

Far right: The bizarre toad grasshopper is wingless and normally well camouflaged against its background. It is found in the dry and semi-desert regions of Southern Africa.

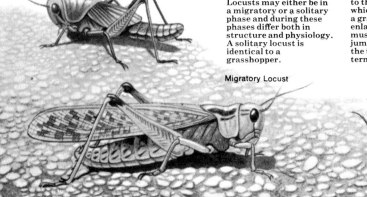

Grasshopper

Migratory Locust

Hopper

Below: Locusts often migrate in enormous numbers either on the ground as bands of nymphs, called hoppers, or as flying insects. Locusts may either be in a migratory or a solitary phase and during these phases differ both in structure and physiology. A solitary locust is identical to a grasshopper.

Right: A front leg (above) and back leg (below) of a grasshopper. Insect legs have four main sections: the coxa which connects the leg to the thorax; the femur which in the back leg of a grasshopper is enlarged to contain the muscles needed for jumping; the tibia, and the tarsus which terminates in claws.

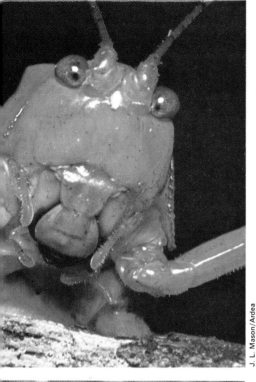

The group known as *Ephemeroptera* to which the mayflies belong, is so called because of the 'ephemeral' life of the adult fly. It usually lives only long enough to reproduce. This may take a few hours or at the most a few days after the transition from an aquatic nymph stage that may last for up to four years. The adult has two pairs of finely veined wings; the first pair is larger than the hind pair which may be absent in some species. The legs are small and weak; the abdomen ends in three, or sometimes two, long filaments or *cerci*. The antennae are greatly reduced but the compound eyes are very well developed, suggesting great dependence on sight. This also seems to be the case in the free-swimming nymphs which orientate themselves by the direction from which light reaches their eyes. If illuminated from below they will swim upside down. The nymphs breathe by means of gills along each side of the abdomen and are herbivorous. The mouth parts of the adult, however, are rudimentary and the adult is incapable of feeding. The front part of the gut can be filled with air to reduce the body weight and make flight easier.

The aquatic nymph of a mayfly first changes into a terrestrial *subimago* stage whose wings are dulled by a covering of extremely fine hairs. After a few hours this stage moults to the true adult, or *imago*, stage. The emergence of adults is synchronized so that great numbers appear together, the males gathering in large dancing swarms which attract the females. The male dies immediately after mating and the female soon after dropping her eggs into the water. Adult mayflies are a favourite food of fish, especially trout, and artificial flies are made by anglers as lures to catch them. The sub-imagos are called 'dun' and the adults 'spinners'.

From the original *Palaeoptera* there also arose insects, probably in the early Carboniferous era, which were able to fold their wings over the abdomen when at rest. They are called the *Neoptera* and were able to explore such new environments as areas of dense foliage, to hide under stones and logs, and even to burrow. The early *Neoptera* were probably similar to the present day stoneflies and give rise to the group containing the grasshoppers and crickets, the *Orthoptera*. In this group the immature forms are known as nymphs and generally resemble the adult form except in size and degree of wing development. They gradually change into the adult imago stage through a series of up to twenty moults. They also inhabit the same general environment as the adult and eat the same type of food. Insects with this development are *exopterygote* insects.

A second more specialized evolutionary line from the early neopteran stock led to the flies, butterflies, bees and beetles where the young, known as *larvae*, do not resemble the adult and usually occupy a very different environment, feeding on different foods. After a number of moults the larvae pass through a quiescent *pupal* phase where extensive alteration of larval tissue precedes the emergence of a winged adult. These are the *endopterygote* insects to which about 80 per cent of present-day insects belong.

Grasshoppers, crickets and cockroaches

The *Orthoptera* include such insects as grasshoppers, katydids, crickets, cock-

Above: A desert locust just after moulting. Locusts are a type of grasshopper and sometimes migrate in swarms causing enormous damage to the surrounding countryside and crops. A medium sized swarm may contain 1,000,000,000 insects and consume as much as 3,000 tonnes of vegetable material in a single day.

Below: Front and side views of the head of a grasshopper. The animal has three simple eyes (ocelli) as well as the two large compound eyes. The mouthparts, designed for biting and chewing, are equipped with two pairs of sensory organs, or palps, which help the insect to distinguish one sort of food from another.

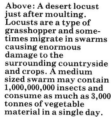

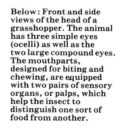

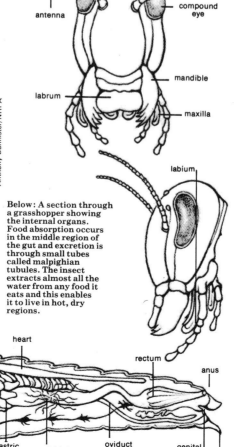

Below: A section through a grasshopper showing the internal organs. Food absorption occurs in the middle region of the gut and excretion is through small tubes called malpighian tubules. The insect extracts almost all the water from any food it eats and this enables it to live in hot, dry regions.

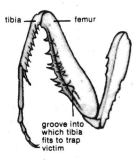

tibia — femur

groove into which tibia fits to trap victim

Right and above: A praying mantis and a diagram of one of its forelegs. The leg is specially adapted for seizing prey. The leg is grasped between the femur and the tibia which have spiny inside edges for the purpose. The innermost section of the leg, the coxa, is much larger than that of a grasshopper.

Below: A well camouflaged praying mantis eating a fly. These insects lie in wait for their prey, seizing the victim very rapidly when it strays within reach of the forelegs. These insects get their name from the way they carry their forelegs (see the picture on the right) which looks rather like an attitude of prayer.

Jacana

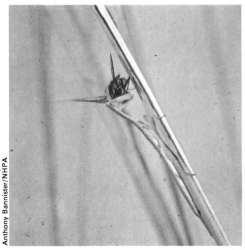

Anthony Bannister/NHPA

Below and right: It is often almost impossible to see stick insects in their natural habitats, so well do they blend in with their backgrounds. The stick insect in the photograph on the right even has spines resembling the prickles of the bramble on which it lives. Stick and leaf insects are sluggish animals, often remaining stationary for long periods. They are herbivorous, usually feeding on leaves. The longest living insect is a tropical stick insect which can grow to more than 30cm (1 ft). Because female stick insects can produce fertile eggs without mating, males are very rare and possibly do not exist in some species.

Natural Science Photos

roaches, mantids and stick insects. Cockroaches and mantids however are now generally placed in a separate group, the *Dictyoptera*, and the stick insects in the *Phasmida*. Typically, they have two pairs of wings although they may be reduced or absent as in some crickets and the common British cockroach. The male of this cockroach has reduced wings, the female is almost wingless, and both sexes are incapable of flight. The fore wings of orthopterans are leathery and when folded cover and protect the delicate membranous hindwings which are the flight wings. The large head has well developed compound eyes and strong chewing mouth parts.

There are about 3,500 species of cockroaches living mostly in the tropics but some have been accidentally transported throughout the world and are now cosmopolitan. In Britain there are six such imported species; the most common are the brown-black common cockroach, *Blatta orientalis*, the yellow brown German cockroach, *Blatta germanica*, and the reddish brown American cockroach, *Periplaneta americana*.

Cockroaches are nocturnal scavengers feeding on a very wide range of dead animal and plant material. In houses they will devour any kind of human food and although the amount eaten is relatively small the remainder is fouled. Females lay 16 eggs enclosed in a hard dark brown purse-like capsule, the *ootheca*, which is deposited in crevices. The eggs hatch after about two to three months, the ootheca splitting to let out the white wingless nymphs. As they grow, they become brown in colour and reach maturity in 6 to 12 months. In the German cockroach the ootheca contains up to 45 eggs and is carried by the female until about a day before hatching.

Grasshoppers are the most numerous of the *Orthoptera*. They prefer a grassy habitat and have greatly enlarged hindlegs which enable them to jump considerable distances when disturbed. The male attracts the female to mate by rubbing a row of very small projections on a hindleg joint against the veins of the forewing to produce the familiar chirping song, or *stridulation*, of grasshoppers. The song varies from species to species. Eggs are laid in pods in the soil, each pod containing up to 14 eggs. Grasshoppers are herbivorous, and when they occur in very large numbers can cause damage to crops.

Crickets and bush crickets, sometimes known as 'long-horned grasshoppers' or in America 'katydids', are cosmopolitan and resemble grasshoppers in possessing long, though less powerful hind legs for jumping. Their antennae, however, are long, they stridulate by rubbing the wing edges together and are nocturnal. Specialized organs, the *tympani*, are developed to receive soundwaves. Grasshoppers have a pair on the first abdomenal segment but in crickets they are on the forelegs. Crickets are herbivorous but bush crickets can be carnivorous. Eggs are laid singly in slits made in plant stems by a well developed blade-like or tubular organ called an *ovipositer*. Like grasshoppers there is one generation a year. Of particular interest is the mole cricket which is now rare in Britain. It does not have jumping legs, but the forelegs are powerful and armed with cutting edges which enable it to tunnel through the soil in a mole-like fashion.

Centipedes, Millipedes and Onychophora

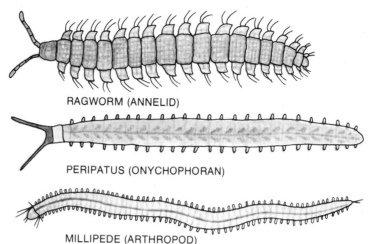

RAGWORM (ANNELID)

PERIPATUS (ONYCHOPHORAN)

MILLIPEDE (ARTHROPOD)

The *Onychophora* are one of the most extraordinary groups of animals alive today. They are of great zoological interest because they are believed to represent an evolutionary bridging group between the soft bodied annelids and the hard bodied arthropods. The members of the group are primitive land-dwelling animals which look rather like caterpillars. There are only about a hundred structurally very similar species in the class, and their distribution is limited to the damp forests of Australia, the Malayan archipelago, South America, South Africa and India.

The onychophorans exhibit a mosaic of structural features, some typically arthropodan, some primitively arthropodan, others in common with annelids and some which are specializations to their mode of life. The body is composed of up to 43 similar segments, tapering towards the body of the animal and capable of an extraordinary degree of contraction and extension. Movement is sinuous and the head region is not very distinct.

Onychophorans are nocturnal. They feed on small arthropods such as termites and woodlice. Prey is sensed by antennae which feel the ground as the animal moves and may be trapped by the ejaculation of a milky fluid from the slime glands. The food is first tasted by sensory *papillae* on the tongue and circular lip which surrounds the mouth. If it is found acceptable the lip extends to form a tube which fastens on to the prey by suction. The food is then converted into a semi-liquid form by the mechanical action of the jaws and muscular rasp-like tongue and the chemical action of salivary enzymes, all acting within the confines of the lip. The annelid-like simple eyes at the base of the antennae probably play no part in food detection and are thought incapable of image formation. Scattered over the body surface are papillae, each ending in an elaborate sensory spine sensitive to air movement, vibrations and touch.

Reproduction in onychophorans has some curious features. Typically the male deposits spermatophores into the female genital aperture, and fertilization occurs internally. In the African species *Peripatopsis capensis*, however, the male places spermatophores anywhere on the female's body surface. White blood cells travel to these areas and cause the wall and cuticle to disintegrate so that the sperm can enter the body and travel to the ovary. In a few Australian species the fertilized eggs are well supplied with yolk and laid in moist conditions. In other onychophorans the eggs develop in the uterus, the female giving birth to live young after a thirteen-month pregnancy. In the South American species *Peripatus trinitatis*, however, the eggs have little yolk and a placenta develops between the embryo and the uterine wall through which food passes from the mother to the developing embryo. This is a specialized and unusual condition in invertebrates.

As in other arthropods the cuticle

covering the body is hardened. In spite of this, however, it is flexible because it is very thin and furrowed—there is a lot of 'slack' in all directions. The body is able to bend at any point, and has no joints like those between the hardened plates of the exoskeleton of other arthropods. The absence of joints has resulted in the virtual loss of external evidence of segmentation.

The extreme and spectacular deformations of which the body is capable has enormous survival value for it enables onychophorans to squeeze into minute crevices to escape predators.

On either side of the body are twenty or more pairs of short, conical, unsegmented limbs, each ending in a spinous pad and a pair of claws. The limbs are essentially extensions of the body wall and are frequently equated with the *parapodia* of annelids such as the ragworm *Nereis*. In annelids, the body wall and parapodia function as a unit when the animal is moving quickly. In onychophorans and all other arthropods, however, the limbs can move independently of the body wall muscles. Movement is slow and the gait primitive. Typically in arthropods the effective length of the leg in locomotion can be altered by the bending of its joints, but in onychophorans the whole leg is retracted or protruded. A leg is swung forward and protruded until it contacts the ground which is gripped by the claws and spinous pads; the leg then retracts pulling the animal forward. The hold on the ground is released as the leg is retracted further and finally it starts to swing forward again and protrude. In normal movement protrusion and retraction strokes occur

Above: An onychophoran giving birth to its young. Fertilized eggs develop within the female and are fed through a special organ rather like the placenta in mammals.

Right and below: An underside view of the head and a body plan of an onychophoran. The internal anatomy has features resembling both annelids and arthropods. Respiration is by means of air tubes called trachea and this is typically arthropodan. The excretory system, however, is much closer to that of the annelids.

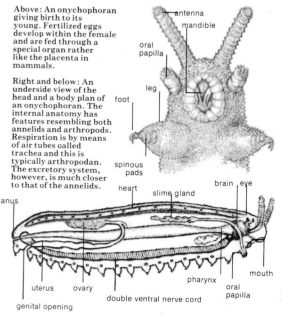

antenna
mandible
oral papilla
leg
foot
spinous pads
heart
brain
eye
slime gland
anus
uterus
ovary
genital opening
double ventral nerve cord
pharynx
oral papilla
mouth

Oxford Scientific Films

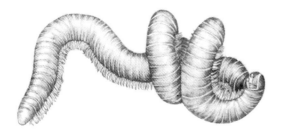

Left: Millipedes mating. The reproductive organs of millipedes open near the front of the body, close to the second pair of legs. After fertilization the eggs are laid in batches below the surface of the ground. The female often guards the eggs until the larvae, which have six legs and look rather like insects, hatch out.

Above: A common millipede. These animals have two pairs of legs on each body segment. Although millipedes do not have as many as a thousand legs, one South African species has been reported with 710 legs.

N.H.P.A.

Left: A forest millipede from Southern Africa. Millipedes usually feed on dead vegetable matter.

Left: A millipede shedding its old skin. Like all arthropods, millipedes have to moult in order to grow. The hardened cuticle splits and is cast off allowing a new cuticle to form underneath. Insects usually only moult as they progress from the larval to the adult animal. Millipedes, however, continue to moult throughout their adult life, as do centipedes, crustaceans such as crabs, and arachnids.

Frank W. Lane

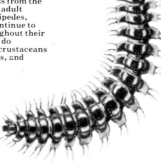

Left: A common black millipede crawling over a piece of wood covered with a yellow fungus. In spite of their large number of legs, millipedes can only move very slowly. They have eyes which look rather like the compound eyes of insects, but are in fact composed of clusters of simple eyes called ocelli.

Heather Angel

Above: A member of the millipede family *Polydesmida*. These animals are all blind. Some tropical species can reach a length of several inches.

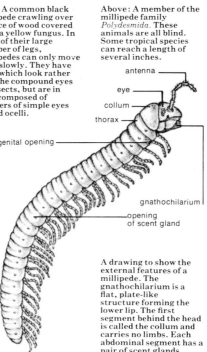

antenna
eye
collum
thorax
genital opening
gnathochilarium
opening of scent gland

A drawing to show the external features of a millipede. The gnathochilarium is a flat, plate-like structure forming the lower lip. The first segment behind the head is called the collum and carries no limbs. Each abdominal segment has a pair of scent glands and two pairs of segmented walking limbs.

alternately down the body.

The structure of onychophorans has been shown to be more generalized than that of the majority of arthropods. They cannot, however, be regarded as ancestral to other arthropod classes principally because of the structure and mode of action of their jaws. The class *Onychophora* probably arose from the main arthropodan stem at a very early stage in their evolution from the annelids. This view seems to be substantiated by the 500 million year-old marine Cambrian fossil *Aysheaia* which is remarkably like present day onychophorans in its body form.

Millipedes

Superficially centipedes and millipedes appear to resemble the onychophora. They usually have a long body with many similar walking limbs. Like the onychophorans they are nocturnal animals and because their cuticle is not waterproofed they are restricted to damp environments, for example under leaves, stones and rotten wood. The head region, however, is distinct and the limbs are jointed as in typical arthropods like insects or spiders. In millipedes most trunk segments have two pairs of legs due to the joining of segments in pairs, hence the name *Diplopoda*, meaning 'paired legs', for the millipede class. Since the maximum number of trunk segments in millipedes is about a hundred, the name millipede (a thousand legs) is obviously a misnomer.

Most millipedes are burrowers, their mobile and powerful legs pushing them head first through the soil. Their eyes are small or completely absent, probably as a consequence of their life in the dark. Typically arthropodan compound eyes are, however, found in early fossil millipedes. When walking, each leg is a little out of step with the one in front so waves of movement appear to pass back along each side of the body.

The body varies in length between 2 and 300 mm (0.08 inch to 1 foot), and in cross-section it tends to be half cylindrical in shape with a flattened lower surface. This allows an animal like the pill millipede, *Sphaerotherium*, to roll itself into a ball for protection. In smaller millipedes the cuticle is soft and very flexible but in most species it is hardened, as in crustaceans like the wood louse, by the deposition of calcium carbonate. Additional protection is given by poison and stink glands down each side of the trunk, which release toxic chemicals such as chlorine, cyanide iodine and quinine when the animal is disturbed. Some large tropical millipedes

Right: A house centipede, *Scutigera coleoptera*. These animals are easily recognized by their very long legs which enable them to move extremely quickly. They are found in southern Europe in damp parts of houses and in vineyards. They feed on insects such as cockroaches and silverfish. These animals only have 15 pairs of legs, so the name centipede (a hundred legs) is hardly appropriate. Some centipedes, however, belonging to the family *Geophilomorpha* can have 177 pairs of legs.

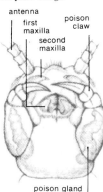

Above: A detail of the head of a centipede (seen from below) to show the poison claws which are used to catch and disable prey.

Right: A body plan of a centipede. There are two legs on each body segment except for the first, which carries the poison claws, and the last two.

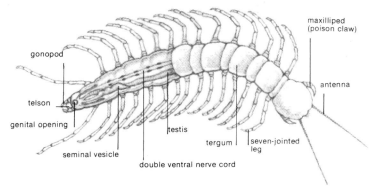

Below: Almost all centipedes are carnivorous. This animal, however, known as *Haplophilus*, is found in grassland and sometimes eats living plants. It has as many as a hundred pairs of legs and is relatively slow moving. Like many centipedes *Haplophilus* is blind, relying on its sense of touch for guidance.

Right: A centipede, *Lithobius*, hurries over the forest floor looking for suitable shelter. Centipedes hunt their prey by night, remaining under cover during the day for fear of drying out. They feed on soft insects, earthworms and slugs.

can discharge these chemicals in the form of a fine spray for a distance of about a metre. Many of these tropical forms also possess bright warning colours and a few, such as a 40 mm (1.6 inch) long millipede from Sequoia Forest, California are luminescent.

Millipedes are herbivorous, typically feeding on decaying vegetable material they have little economic importance apart from attacking certain plants in dry conditions to obtain water. The spotted snake millipede *Boniulus guttolatus*, for example, attacks potatoes but it is believed that such attacks occur only after the potatoes have been damaged by other pests.

The eggs of the female millipede are usually fertilized by indirect insemination. In *Lithobius piceus*, for example, the male deposits a spermatophore on a small web and this is taken up when the female places her genital aperture over it. Eggs are laid in batches of 25 to 50 and hatch into six-legged larvae which add double segments during development. Some species may live for up to seven years.

Centipedes

Centipedes are another class of arthropods. The technical name for the class is *Chilopoda* which refers to their poison jaws. Like millipedes, centipedes have a distinct head followed by a long body of similar segments. The body length is usually between 3 and 275 mm (0.12 to 10.8 inches). The exact number of segments is variable even within a species. Most trunk segments have a single pair of legs and those on the first segment form characteristic poison jaws. The cuticle is never hardened with calcium salts and the body is flattened and ribbon-like. There are four different types of centipede. The *Scolopendromorpha* and *Lithobiomorpha* are like millipedes, living under stones, wood and leaves, and are active, stout-bodied animals. The *Geophilomorpha* are slender, burrowing animals with up to 177 pairs of legs, justifying the name centipede. The *Scutigeromorpha*, on the other hand, have a cigar-shaped body with only 15 pairs of very long slender legs which enables them to move with great speed and agility.

Centipedes feed on slugs, earthworms and insects such as locusts and are therefore beneficial to agriculturalists as predators of some plant pests. They catch and then kill their prey with the poison jaws, and cut it up with powerful mandibles assisted by *maxillae*. The bite of a large centipede such as *Scolopendra gigantea* from Trinidad which can catch and devour small mice, is very painful to man but few fatalities have been recorded.

In centipedes the male inseminates the female directly, and the fertilized eggs are then laid in the soil and left to hatch In the *Scolopendromorpha*, however, the female protects the eggs, which are usually laid in a depression in rotting wood, by winding herself around them. The young either hatch as miniature adults or as larvae with seven pairs of legs; additional legs appear during development until they reach maturity within about three years.

The centipedes and millipedes are sometimes classed together with two groups of tiny centipede-like animals, the *Pauropoda* and the *Symphyla*, into a single large class, the *Myriapoda*. All four groups are, however, quite distinct. 177

Beetles

There are enormous differences in the size of beetles, from the tiny winged beetles a fraction of an inch long to the enormous Hercules beetle, which can reach a length of 18 cm (7.1 in). Easily recognized by their 'armoured' bodies, beetles also differ in colour, from the sober black of the stag beetle to the brightly coloured ladybird. Altogether there are something like 250,000 species of beetles (*Coleoptera*), more than any other group of insects.

Beetles occur in almost all possible habitats and are especially successful as fresh water animals. Many beetles are of ecological importance, feeding upon dung or carrion and upon rotten wood. From such forms have arisen the many pests of stored food and the timber of furniture and buildings. Some beetles like the Colarado beetle, *Leptinotarsa decemlineata*, which attacks potato plants, cause serious damage to agricultural crops while others have been of immense value in controlling pests.

Apart from being heavily armoured, or *sclerotised*, beetles have biting mouthparts and forewings which are hardened to act as wing covers called *elytra*. These characteristically fit closely together down the mid-line when they are closed over the folded hindwings. It is these features which distinguish a beetle from any other insect.

The general body shape of beetles varies from group to group and depends on the particular way of life. It is compact and athletic in the ground beetles, stout and lumbering in the dung beetles and chafers, cylindrical in many woodborers and comfortably rounded in some leaf beetles. Rove beetles, which belong to the family *Staphylinidae*, have very short elytra and a very long body. This gives them a curous shape, superficially like that of an earwig, but without the pincers. In weevils the head is elongated to form a snout giving an immediately recognizable appearance.

Beetles have large compound eyes, sometimes of rather odd shape. In the aquatic, surface-dwelling, whirligig beetles each eye is divided into two separate parts: an upper part for aerial vision and a lower part for seeing under water.

The antennae of beetles vary greatly. For example, they may be long and thread-like as in ground beetles, or with the end segments like the leaves of a book as in stag beetles and chafers. In weevils and some other beetles they are bent into an elbowed form. As well as acting as 'feelers', antennae are receptors of smell and may be essential in determining the humidity of the surrounding air.

Adult beetles have well-developed mandibles for siezing and cutting up their food. In some cases the mandibles are much larger in the male than the female. This is very apparent in members of the family *Lucanidae*, the stag beetles and their relatives, but its significance is not really clear. The male beetles show great variation in size of their antler-like mandibles as well as in total size. This is thought to be a result of their diet when young, and it is sometimes argued that the larger male beetles with larger mandibles

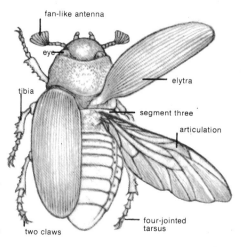

fan-like antenna
eye
tibia
elytra
segment three
articulation
two claws
four-jointed tarsus

Left: A drawing of a cockchafer or May beetle showing the main features of the *Coleoptera*. Like other insects they have three pairs of legs carried by the three thoracic segments, and two pairs of wings carried by the second and third thoracic segments. The first pair of wings, however, has become hardened by impregnation with a plastic-like substance called sclerotin to form wing covers (elytra). The flying wings are articulated about half way along their length to allow them to be folded away under the elytra when not in use. The beetle's head has a set of biting mouthparts, two compound eyes (each with about 5,000 light-sensitive units) and two antennae.

Right: A male Hercules beetle, *Dynastes hercules*. These beetles are easily recognized by their two long, forward pointing horns, the smaller one on the head and the larger one on the thorax. Female Hercules beetles look quite different from their male counterparts: they are considerably smaller and have no horns.

Below: A rhinoceros beetle, *Oryctes nasicornis*. The three horns (there are two smaller ones behind the prominent front one) are carried on the thorax which overhangs the head. These beetles are surprisingly good fliers, in spite of their heavily armoured exoskeleton.

Frank Lane

ZEFA

Below: Two male stag beetles fighting. The females are slightly smaller and lack the enormous antler-like jaws. These are the largest British beetles, sometimes reaching a length of 7.5 cm (3 in). In spite of their fearsome appearance, the jaws cannot inflict such a painful bite as those of many smaller beetles.

Right: A cockchafer, *Melolontha melolontha*. These beetles feed on the leaves of trees such as oaks and chestnuts. They remain out of sight for most of the day and are most commonly seen on warm spring evenings flying from tree to tree. Their chief enemies are large birds like rooks which feed both on the larvae and the adults.

Anthony Bannister/NHPA

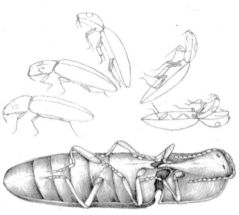

Left: To escape from a predator, a click beetle may release its hold on its perch and fall to the ground on its back. To right itself, the beetle bends its thorax back until a spine engages in a notch on its abdomen. On releasing the notch, the thorax jerks forwards away from the ground throwing the beetle into the air. The operation is repeated as often as necessary until the insect finally lands on its feet. This unusual 'click' mechanism may also be used by the beetle to startle predators.

Above left: Egyptian scarab beetles, *Scarabaeus sacer*, rolling a ball of dung. The ball is rolled around to increase its size, like a snowball, and then buried in a burrow. The female lays her eggs in the dung ball which acts as a food store for the larvae when they hatch.

Left: A leaf beetle lays its eggs on a leaf. Like many other members of the family *Chrysomelidae* this beetle has smooth, brightly coloured wing covers.

Right: An East African Cardinal beetle, *Cissites cephalotes*, taking off from a leaf. The way in which the wing covers, or elytra, are lifted well clear of the hind, flying wings can be clearly seen in this picture. The elytra may act like the fixed wings of an aircraft to give the beetle extra lift during flight.

ZEFA

Jane Burton/Bruce Coleman

Frank Lane

Above: A net-winged beetle, *Lycus trabeatus*, from South Africa.

Anthony Bannister/NHPA

are more successful in competing for food and mates. Despite their large mandibles, stag beetles feed upon vegetable fluids such as sap, sucked up with the aid of the hairy maxillae.

Feeding

The fierce-looking cutting mandibles of carnivorous beetles do not always operate in the obvious way. For example, it has recently been shown that tiger beetles, the beautiful jewel-like inhabitants of sandy heaths and sand dunes, do not swallow solid food at all. The large mandibles seize and pierce the prey (other insects), then the maxillae rake out the soft contents of the victim to be cut up by the bases of the mandibles. Only the fluids and very fine particles are actually ingested. In a number of ground beetles digestive fluids are pumped into the prey so that what is actually eaten is a sort of half digested soup. This 'external' digestion is employed more by larvae than adults. In the water beetles *Dytiscus*, both the adult and the larva are voracious carnivores, but the larva is even more ferocious than the adult, having long curved, hollow mandibles which pierce the prey. Digestive enzymes flow into the prey and external digestion results.

A recent study of four species of S. African ladybirds, found that while the two larger species of ladybird could seize and hold an aphid by its leg or body, the two smaller ones had considerable difficulty in doing so. It was discovered, however, that these smaller species inject a poison when they bite, which rapidly immobilises the aphid. Ladybirds have been of the greatest importance in controlling pests, especially scale insects. The classic case of biological control was the control of fluted scale insect, *Icerya purchasi*, in Californian citrus orchards nearly a hundred years ago by the ladybird *Rodolia cardinalis*. This ladybird has since been used to control the scale in other parts of the world.

Most beetles and their larvae are active feeders, but a few wait for prey to come to them. The tiger beetle larva is an example. From the top of its tunnel it can leap out suddenly to seize passing insects. Only one or two parasitic beetles are known, such as *Platypsyllus castoris* which is parasitic on beavers. A number of beetles live in ants' nests, scavenging or feeding on eggs and larvae, and sometimes producing secretions attractive to the ants.

A beetle's leg gives a clear indication of its owner's way of life. Ground beetles and tiger beetles (super-family *Caraboidea*) have long and slender legs, and the animals are very rapid runners catching their prey by speed and endurance. The *Scarabaeoides* have stout legs armed with spines which make them efficient for digging. Water beetles show special adaptations for swimming: the end segments of the legs are flattened and fringed with hairs. On the power strokes the legs present the flat surface with hairs erect, but on the recovery stroke the leg is feathered and the hairs passively folded back. The front legs are usually little modified because they are used for seizing prey or anchoring the animal. The legs of plant-dwelling species are usually short, even in predators like ladybirds, and this allows the insect to maintain a close hold on the plant. The hind legs of flea beetles are swollen at their bases to house the muscles used in jumping. These beetles are well-known to farmers as serious pests of plants such as turnips, belonging to the family *Cruciferae*.

Flight

Among all the invertebrates, true flight has been achieved only by the insects. This has certainly been a major factor in their success. Beetles however, are often more reluctant to fly than dragon-flies, moths or flies. This is perhaps because they have to raise the elytra and unfold the hind wings before take-off. The tiger beetles are probably the quickest off the ground and are difficult to catch. When a beetle is flying the elytra may be held in one of two ways. Either they may simply be lifted enough to allow the hind wings to come out, as in the rose chafer *Cetonia*, or they may be lifted high so as to act like the wings of an aircraft giving lift, as in the stag beetles. It does not, however, seem that this extra lift is needed in all heavy beetles, as the goliath beetle, *Goliathus giganteus*, only raises the elytra slightly. One specimen of this beetle was 14.8 cm (5.8 in) long and weighed 98 g (3.5 oz). Some beetles have lost the power of flight altogether. Their wings are small, or even absent, and the elytra cannot be lifted.

Protection

As the elytra cover most of the dorsal surface of a beetle their colour is very evident. This colour may be dull or black in the many beetles that lead incon- spicuous lives but may be brilliant as in the beautiful metallic green of the rose chafer. Beetles like ladybirds which have an unpleasant taste are often brightly coloured to act as a warning to their pre- dators, particularly birds. Some beetles are protected by their colour and shape. Tortoise beetles, for example, are green and look like part of the plant they are living on. Their larvae disguise them- selves by carrying detritus on their backs. Some beetles gain protection when dis- turbed by making squeaking sounds, often by rubbing the abdomen against the elytra as in the screech beetle, *Hygrobia*.

Some beetles have very bizarre methods of protecting themselves from their enemies. For example, when the bom- bardier beetle, *Brachinus crepitans*, is disturbed it ejects a highly volatile acrid fluid from its anus with a small jet of smoke and a slight explosion. The brightly coloured blister beetles secrete an oily fluid from the joints of their limbs. The fluid contains a chemical which raises blisters on the skin of predators.

Below: Diagrams to show how a beetle breathes. As in all insects there is a network of branched air tubes, called trachea, which lead to openings along the abdomen called spiracles. Each segment of the abdominal exoskeleton consists of two parts: an upper, dorsal plate and a lower, ventral plate which are connected by a flexible section so that they can move relative to each other. To expel air from the trachea, the abdominal muscles contract, drawing the upper and lower plates together. This compresses a number of small air sacs which are connected to the trachea, thus forcing air out of the system.

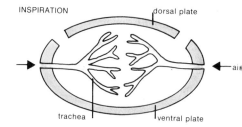
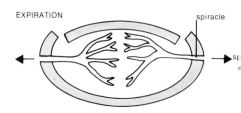

Left and above, left to right: A series of four pictures illustrating the life history of the voracious Colorado beetle, *Leptinotarsa*. After mating (left) the female lays a batch of bright yellow eggs and these hatch into a very distinctive red and black larva. As with many beetles, the larva does not resemble the adult. After a number of moults, the larva passes through an outwardly quiescent pupal phase (far right) during which there is extensive alteration of the larval tissue to give the adult beetle. The Colorado beetle was once a harmless insect living on the eastern slopes of the Rocky Mountains in the USA. When settlers began to inhabit the area in the 1860s, however, the beetle changed its diet from the desert buffalo burr to the newly-introduced potato plant, and rapidly spread eastwards across the continent. With improved communications, it was not long before the beetle made its way to Europe.

Right: A series of drawings showing the metamorphosis of a beetle. Beetles are endopterygote insects, which means they undergo complete metamorphosis through larval and pupal phases from the egg to the adult. Less specialized insects like dragonflies or grasshoppers develop in a different way: the immature insect is called a nymph and broadly resembles its parent. These are called exopterygote insects. Beetle larvae can be as destructive as the adult insects. The larvae of deathwatch beetles, for example, damage timber structures and Colorado beetle larvae have almost as large an appetite as their parents for the foliage of potato plants.

METAMORPHOSIS OF A BEETLE

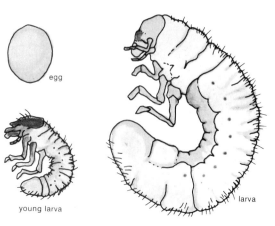
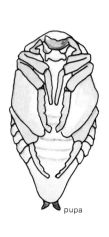
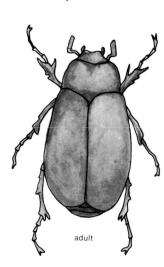

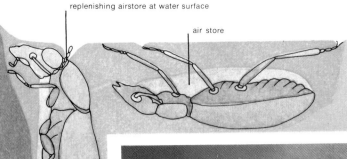

replenishing airstore at water surface

air store

Below: A larva of the great diving beetle, *Dytiscus marginalis*, devours a tadpole. These larvae, sometimes called water tigers, are one of the most aggressive members of the underwater community. They digest their prey externally by injecting digestive enzymes through their hollow curved mandibles.

Natural Science Photos

Above: Despite their name, fireflies are beetles and not flies. The glowworm pictured above feeding on a dead snail is a larva of the firefly *Lampyris noctiluca*. The females of the species do not have wings and are also generally referred to as glow-worms. Not surprisingly, these insects are nocturnal.

Right: A water beetle belonging to the family *Hydrophilidae*. In order to breathe underwater the beetle carries a store of air trapped around its body by the effect of surface tension. These insects can walk upside down under the surface of the water (above right), their weight counteracted in part by the air store.

Bavaria

Bavaria

Heather Angel

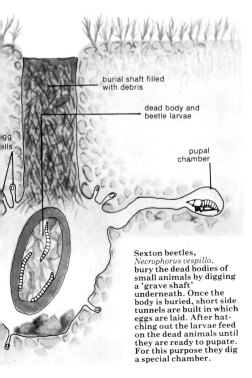

burial shaft filled with debris

dead body and beetle larvae

egg cells

pupal chamber

Sexton beetles, *Necrophorus vespillo*, bury the dead bodies of small animals by digging a 'grave shaft' underneath. Once the body is buried, short side tunnels are built in which eggs are laid. After hatching out the larvae feed on the dead animals until they are ready to pupate. For this purpose they dig a special chamber.

Life history

The life history of a beetle shows the typical stages of a fully-metamorphosing insect: first the egg, next the active larva, then an outwardly inactive pupa and finally the adult. As has already been mentioned, the adult males and females of some species are strikingly dissimilar, but this is unusual. The egg may give rise to an active larva preying on other insects or scavenging on carrion, or there may be a relatively fleshy, almost immobile larva as in wood-boring beetles.

In burying beetles (genus *Necrophorus*) the adults are attracted to carrion where mating takes place. The carrion is gradually buried in an underground chamber by digging soil from underneath it, and then a side passage is constructed by the female in which some fifteen eggs are laid. She returns to the carrion and is joined by the larvae which hatch out after a few days. Here they are fed by their mother with regurgitated food until they are old enough to feed for themselves. At each moult the larvae change considerably in appearance, and finally burrow off to pupate.

This changing of larval form is especially evident in the oil beetles. These insects lay thousands of eggs in batches.

The eggs hatch into small active larvae which climb flowers and sieze upon hairy insects and are carried away by them. If, by chance, they have chosen a bee of the correct species they will be carried to the bee's nest. Here the larva feeds on a bee's egg before moulting to an entirely different immobile type which feeds on pollen and nectar. Other moults and changes follow before pupation.

Food serves to bring carrion and dung feeding beetles together, but in bark beetles (*Scolytidae*) some species produce a scent. Many bark beetles are serious timber pests, such as *Scolytus scolytus*, producing burrows under bark from which the larval galleries radiate. Fungi are often associated with bark beetles: *Scolytus scolytus* carries the fungus which causes Dutch elm disease.

In the death watch beetle, *Xestobium*, the larvae feed in fungus-affected timber for three years before pupating in the autumn near the surface of the wood. The pupae soon moult to become adults, but these do not emerge from the wood until the following spring. The young adults tap upon the wood with their heads, signalling to each other, and bringing fear to the silence of the Tudor or Elizabethan sickroom.

181

Butterflies and Moths

Of all the insects the butterflies and moths have been the most admired and popular. Butterflies are large and very beautiful but although we can understand the functioning of their colours it is difficult to explain why they should be so bright and exuberant. While the butterflies belong to a single well defined group, the popular name 'moth' covers a diversity of insects both large and small. Most moths are sombre-coloured and nocturnal although there are some that resemble butterflies inasmuch as they are brightly coloured and are active during the day. Butterflies and moths belong to the insect order *Lepidoptera*, a name which refers to their scaly wings, and there are about 100,000 different species.

The scales which are characteristic of butterflies and moths are hollow, flattened hairs covered with minute grooves and ridges. They usually contain pigment or give colour by reflecting and scattering

S. Bisserot

Above: Three pictures showing the egg, larva (caterpillar) and pupa (chrysalis) of a swallowtail butterfly.

Left: The caterpillar of a swallowtail butterfly. It has a curious forked organ behind its head which it shoots rapidly in and out to disperse an unpleasant smell when disturbed.

Above: A swallowtail butterfly, *Papilio machaon*, newly emerged from its chrysalis. This is the only member of the *Papilionidae* family which is a permanent resident in Britain.

Above right: A swallowtail with its wings spread out. More usually they are held vertically.

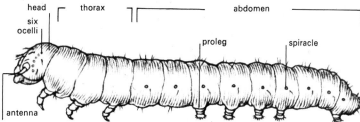

Above: A diagram to show the main features of a caterpillar of the cabbage white butterfly. Each of the thoracic segments carries a pair of legs, and five of the abdominal segments have pairs of fleshy extensions called prolegs. The outermost layer of the body, the cuticle, is quite soft but is able to act as an exoskeleton because the caterpillar's blood pressure is sufficiently high to keep it taut. The head does not have antennae or compound eyes. There are six simple eyes (ocelli) on each side. The animal has strong biting mandibles for chewing cabbage leaves.

light. Sometimes the scales are shed, leaving the wings transparent as in the clearwing moths, which look like wasps or other members of the insect order *Hymenoptera*.

The colours of lepidopterans serve a number of purposes, for example to help members of the same species recognize each other and to camouflage them against predators. Butterflies carry their wings vertically when they are at rest, and the undersides of the wings are often coloured in such a way as to conceal the insect. For instance, the underside of the wing of the Indian leaf butterfly, *Kallima*, looks remarkably like a dead leaf and the grayling butterfly, *Eumenis semele*, even leans to one side when it is on the ground so that its shadow is minimized.

Unlike butterflies, most moths hold their wings flat over their backs when at rest, but these are also often cryptically patterned so that the moth blends into its background. Such moths as the yellow underwings, *Triphaena comes*, for example, have brightly coloured hind wings which provide flashes of colour as the insect flies along. When the moth settles the flashing suddenly stops and this can be confusing to predators as well as entomologists. Another method of defence

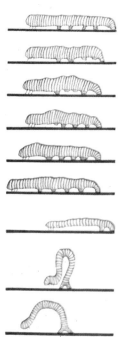

Left: Diagrams to show how two different types of caterpillar crawl along. The most important organs are the prolegs which are alternately retracted and extended by contracting and relaxing 'locomotor' muscles. The lower diagrams show how caterpillars of the family *Geometridae* (the name means 'earth measuring') proceed by looping movements.

Right: The eggs of a privet hawk moth.

Heather Angel

against predators is shown by the peacock butterfly, *Nymphalis io*, and the eyed hawk moth, *Smerinthus ocellatus*. These insects have markings on their wings called 'eye spots' which look rather like the eyes of mammals. The eye spots are suddenly displayed when the insect is disturbed and may confuse or frighten off a predator.

Some of these insects, like the burnet moths, have bright colours to advertise the fact that they are unpalatable or poisonous and in many cases other, palatable species very closely resemble them, so gaining protection. It was from such observations a century ago that the British naturalist H. W. Bates first put forward his theories on the phenomenon of mimicry, now known to be widespread among insects. The milkweed butterflies, which belong to the family *Danaidae*, are distasteful and are very widely mimicked by other palatable butterflies. For the mimic to gain protection it has to be less common than the model, otherwise birds will learn that the common pattern means palatable rather than unpalatable prey. In the swallowtail butterfly *Papilio dardanus* there are five different-looking varieties of female, and four of these mimic four different species of distasteful butterfly. By this means the species maintains a larger population than if it mimicked only a single species.

Some butterflies show colour variations according to the season. The comma butterfly, *Polygonia c-album*, in Britain shows different colours in spring and summer broods, the spring generation being much paler and brighter than the summer one. The African butterfly *Precis octavia* is also well known for its marked seasonal forms. Some moths, particularly those species which rest during the day on rocks or soil, show variation in colour with geographical area. The peppered moth *Biston betularia*, for example, has a normal pale speckled form in rural areas, while a black, or *melanic*, form has become common in industrial areas where the lichens on trees have been killed and soot deposited. Experiments have shown that birds will mainly feed on the more conspicuous form: in cities the speckled form and in the country the black form. This phenomenon of industrial melanism has been much studied in the last 20 years or so and has given valuable information about how evolution takes place in nature and the rate at which it can become effective.

Migration

Butterflies and moths are usually strong fliers, although they may not always travel very far. Marking experiments in the Scilly Isles demonstrated that meadow brown butterflies remained in their own area of bramble and bracken and did not even fly the short distance across a grassy area to another bracken and bramble area inhabited by other meadow browns. In a few species such as the early moth, *Theria rupicapraria*, and the winter moth, *Operophtera brumata*, the male is normally winged but the female has very small wings or, in some species, none at all. After emerging from the pupa the female has to climb up the trunk of a tree to lay her eggs. In spite of these flightless varieties, however, the *Lepidoptera* contains some of the most powerfully flying insects and a number are known to be migratory.

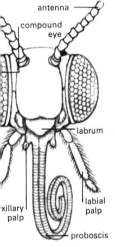

antenna
compound eye
labrum
xillary palp
labial palp
proboscis

Right: A map to show the migrations of the bath white butterfly, *Pontia daplidice*, and the silver Y moth, *Plusia gamma*, in Europe.

Left and bottom left: Drawings of the heads of a butterfly and a moth. These insects feed on nectar and their mouth parts are specially adapted for this. The two maxillae are much longer than in other insects and they are joined together by a series of hooks and spines to form a tube called the proboscis through which the nectar is drawn. Feeding on fluids, butterflies and moths have no need for the cutting mandibles of insects like locusts, and these organs are very small or absent.

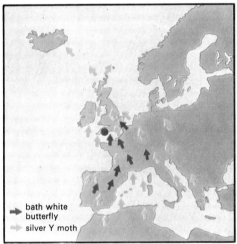

→ bath white butterfly
→ silver Y moth

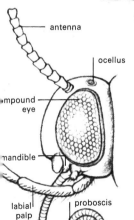

antenna
ocellus
mpound eye
mandible
labial palp
proboscis

Above and right: A privet hawk-moth, *Sphinx ligustri*, and its caterpillar. The bodies and wings of butterflies and moths are covered with scales which not only give rise to the characteristic iridescent colouring of the wings, but also serve to conserve body heat by enclosing an insulating layer of air.

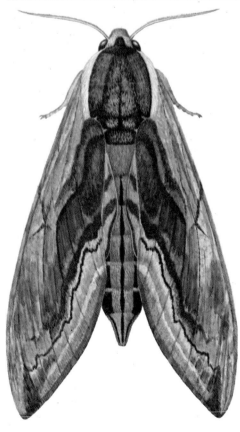

Heather Angel

183

Heather Angel

Anthony Bannister/NHPA

Left: A pearl-bordered fritillary butterfly, *Argynnis euphrosyne*. In order to show the wing markings, the picture was taken with the insect's wings in the uncharacteristic spread position. This butterfly, like most others, has antennae which are enlarged, or 'clubbed', at their tips. Both butterflies and moths have a well developed sense of vision and can distinguish one colour from another. This is important in feeding and mating for both flowers and potential mates are recognized by sight.

Right: An African butterfly, *Charaxes saturnis*.

Below: The beautiful golden emperor moth of India.

Stephen Dalton/NHPA

Heather Angel

In recent years it has been shown that the other two great migratory groups of insects, the locusts and the aphids, are both passively carried along with the prevailing wind, even though some of their short term flights appear oriented. The situation with butterflies and moths is far from clear. Pioneer work on butterfly migration was carried out by C. B. Williams who showed that many of the butterfly species that migrate to the British Isles in the summer return in the autumn, although it is the offspring of the original migrants that make the return. The red admiral, *Vanessa atalanta*, was the first species that was shown to make this return, but since then it has been demonstrated that other species do the same. It is characteristic of most butterflies when migrating to fly in a constant, clearly oriented direction. They do not seem to fix their direction by reference to wind, temperature or magnetic factors, and it has recently been argued that the Sun is the reference point. This is by no means impossible since other insects navigate by reference to the Sun.

The best known migratory species is the milkweed butterfly *Danaus plexippus*. It breeds in the northern USA and Canada during the summer and then migrates south in swarms in the late summer to California, Florida or New Mexico. Marked individuals have been recovered that have flown nearly 3,200 km (2,000 miles). The butterflies spend the winter in trees, using the same ones year after year, forming something of a tourist attraction. In the spring a northerly journey begins. As with other butterfly migrations the return flight is more scattered, with individuals flying singly rather than in a swarm. On the way back the insects lay their eggs and the species becomes spread throughout the northern part of its range. A number of moths also migrate, notable visitors to Britain being the humming-bird hawk moth, *Macroglossum stellatarum*, and the silver Y moth, *Plusia gamma*. The latter seems to show oriented flight early in its adult life when it flies by day, but later, nocturnal flights are downwind. It seems likely that prevailing winds bring it all the way from North Africa. The humming-bird hawk moth is an immigrant to Britain from southern Europe, and arrives from June onwards.

Flight

Moths and butterflies have their fore and hind wings coupled together, though the method of coupling varies from species to species as does the rate of wing beat and speed of flight. The wings of moths are typically linked by a bristle which projects from the hind wing and engages a hook from a vein of the fore wing. Wing speed and flight may be quite rapid: a hawk moth may beat its wings 70 times a second and reach a speed of 55 kph (35 mph). In butterflies the wings merely overlap at the base. They flap about 12 times every second, giving the insect a top speed of about ten kph (six mph). Large butterflies can glide quite effectively, especially in the sheltered conditions of woodland.

A remarkable feature of some nocturnally flying moths is their ability to avoid bats. Bats detect their prey by an 'echo sounding' system of ultrasonic squeaks that reflect from any object such as a flying moth. Some moths have a pair of hearing organs called *tympanal organs* set at the sides of the base of the abdomen which can detect these ultrasonic signals. Thus the moth can tell when a hunting bat is nearby and even determine its angle of approach. Different moth species respond in different ways—some swing violently off course, some zig-zag and others drop to the ground. This manoeuvring brings to mind the technological warfare of our own species.

A very few moths can make audible sounds—the death's head hawk moth, *Acherontia atropos*, for example, squeaks when disturbed—but this is rare. Sight is important to most butterflies and moths, and the compound eyes are well developed. Antennae act as smell receptors and in some species the front legs are used for tasting. Many butterflies have small forelegs which are no use for walking but are important organs of taste.

Above: The caterpillar of a puss moth, *Cerura vinula*, in its defence posture. Normally the caterpillar is well camouflaged against its background, and irregular purple markings on its green back break up the body outline. When attacked, however, the animal rears up to expose the vivid 'face' markings seen in the picture and lashes out with the threads attached to its tail. If this fearsome display is not enough to deter the predator, the caterpillar will squirt strong formic acid from a gland in its thorax.

Above right: A convolvulus hawk moth, *Herse convolvuli*, feeding on tobacco flowers. The long, uncoiled proboscis can be seen probing one of the flowers for nectar. There is a slight bend in the proboscis about one third of the way along its length, and this 'knee joint' allows the insect to feed whatever the angle of the flower. A moth picks out flowers by sight rather than smell, and the accuracy with which it can 'aim' its tongue shows just how good its sight must be.

184

Left: A scarlet windowed moth which lives in the Himalayan region of India is well disguised as a leaf. There is even a dark line running from one wing tip to the other to represent the mid-rib of the leaf.

Right: The broken irregular pattern and colour of this hawk moth, *Deilephila merii,* camouflage it against a background of foliage. The outline of the insect is broken by the pale band which extends across both wings and the front of the abdomen.

Below: The head of a buff-tip moth, *Phalera bucephala.* When at rest with its wings folded back, this insect looks exactly like a freshly broken twig covered with lichen.

Stephen Dalton/HNPA

W. Harstrick/Bavaria

Anthony Bannister/NHPA

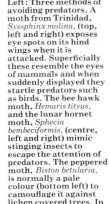

Left: Three methods of avoiding predators. A moth from Trinidad, *Syssphinx molina,* (top, left and right) exposes eye spots on its hind wings when it is attacked. Superficially these resemble the eyes of mammals and when suddenly displayed they startle predators such as birds. The bee hawk moth, *Hemaris tityus,* and the lunar hornet moth, *Sphecia bembeciformis,* (centre, left and right) mimic stinging insects to escape the attention of predators. The peppered moth, *Biston betularia,* is normally a pale colour (bottom left) to camouflage it against lichen covered trees. In smoke-blackened industrial areas, however, a black variety (bottom right) has become common.

Right: The small yucca moth, *Pronubia yuccasella,* is vital for the survival of the yucca plant (and itself depends on the plant) in the southern parts of North America. The moth pollinates the plant, and in return the plant produces enough seeds both to feed the moth's larvae and ensure its own survival.

Life history

The life history of lepidopterans is well-known: the egg, a plant-eating caterpillar (the larva), an immobile chrysalis (the pupa) and finally the adult insect. In some species the virgin female produces a scent which attracts males from a considerable distance. The French entomologist J. H. Fabre described this phenomenon, and Victorian collectors used it to collect large numbers of lepidopterans like male emperor moths. Today a similar method is used to control populations of the gypsy moth, a forest pest; a synthetic female scent attracts males to a death by insecticide.

Caterpillars are soft-bodied and mostly found on plants; they are an important source of food for birds. Caterpillars protect themselves against their predators in a number of ways. Some are camouflaged by their green body colour while others resemble twigs. Several caterpillars are distasteful to birds and they generally have bright and characteristic markings to advertise the fact. The cinnabar moth, *Hypocrita jacobaeae,* for example, is marked with vivid black and yellow bands along its entire length, and birds soon learn to avoid the hairy caterpillars (often called 'woolly bears') of the tiger moth, *Arctia caja.* Many caterpillars suffer from parasites like ichneumon flies or other parasitic members of the insect group *Hymenoptera.*

W. Harstrick/ZEFA

Some moths are of considerable economic value to man. The silk from the pupal cocoon of certain species has been used to produce the fabric of that name from ancient times. Indeed, the silk moth, *Bombyx mori,* is a highly bred flightless species not found in the wild. However, wild silk is produced from such species as the giant atlas moth, *Attacus atlas.* Some species are also economically valuable because they pollinate night scented flowers like tobacco, a crop of immense commercial importance.

Conversely, caterpillars can cause enormous agricultural losses by feeding on crops. For example, the caterpillar of the codling moth, *Cydia pomonella,* damages apple orchards, the pink bollworm, *Platyedra gossypiella,* can reduce the yield of a cotton crop by as much as 25 per cent, and the maize stem borer, *Busseola fusca,* can completely destroy African maize crops. In marked contrast, the well named *Cactoblastis cactorum* was instrumental in the destruction of the great cactus plague in Australia. The *Lepidoptera* are an order that touches man in many ways.

Flies

Flies probably affect man more than any other group of insects. Among the many diseases which they transmit are elephantiasis, yellow fever, dengue, malaria, sleeping sickness and river blindness. In addition to these, a host of diseases which infect domestic animals such as cattle are spread by flies. It is not therefore surprising that an enormous amount of research has been done on the control of fly pests and that so many insecticides are available today.

Flies are extremely adaptable insects and they are found in all sorts of different habitats. One species of fly, *Psilopa petrolei*, even lives in pools of crude oil. Their survival is due in no small measure to their adaptability, as can be seen today in certain species which have developed resistance to man-made insecticides.

The word 'fly' is commonly used to cover a whole variety of flying insects, but when an entomologist uses the word he is referring to members of the order *Diptera*. These insects are sometimes called 'true flies' to make the distinction clear. The *Diptera* is one of the six *panorpoid* orders of insects. The others are the *Mecoptera* (scorpionflies), the *Neuroptera* (alder flies, lacewing flies and ant lions), the *Trichoptera* (caddisflies), the *Lepidoptera* (butterflies and moths) and the *Siphonaptera* (fleas). The group gets its name from one of its members, *Panorpa*, a scorpionfly.

Panorpoid insects are *endopterygote*, which means that they change completely as they pass from egg to larva, larva to pupa, and pupa to adult. The larvae are soft bodied and often equipped with fleshy *prolegs*, like caterpillars. The adult insects typically have mouthparts specially modified for feeding on fluids, and the fore and hind wings (where two sets of wings are present) are coupled together by a system of lobes and bristles. In spite of these broad similarities, there are considerable differences between the six groups of panorpoid insects.

True flies

The true flies (*Diptera*) outstrip all the other panorpoid orders in their diversity, success and impact on man. Altogether there are some 80,000 living species and they are found almost everywhere: along the sea shore, associated with fresh water, in open country, woodland and in the home. They feed on organic fluids of all kinds, from nectar to blood. Their larvae also have diverse habits, but they mostly feed on decaying organic matter such as leaf-litter or carrion. Some, however, will eat the living tissue of plants or animals. The larvae of flies do not have legs, but they are not all typically maggot-like; some have well developed heads and prolegs. Evolution is proceeding very rapidly in many families and this has been especially evident in the development of resistance to insecticides.

No other insect order is such a threat to health. Well over 30 major viral, bacterial, protozoan and nematode diseases are transmitted by blood-sucking flies alone. Despite intensive studies, control of the tsetse fly, *Glossina*, which carries sleeping sickness, remains remote and river blindness, carried by blackflies, affects some 20 million Africans today.

Stephen Dalton/NHPA

N.H.P.A.

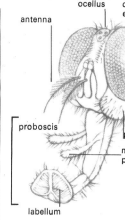

Above: The mouth of a blowfly consists of a proboscis which carries a spongy pad for tasting food. The proboscis houses a tube formed of two parts, the labrum and the hypopharynx, for sucking up liquid food.

Above: An alder fly resting on a leaf with its wings folded like a roof over its back. Alder flies are neuropterans, and they are usually found on waterside vegetation. Their larvae are aquatic and prey on other small water animals.

Right: A scorpionfly, *Panorpa communis*. These insects belong to the order *Mecoptera*. They get their name from the way in which, in some species, the end of the male's abdomen curves forwards to resemble the sting of a scorpion. Clearly visible in the picture are the large, well-marked wings and the curious beak-like face. Scorpionflies feed during the day, mostly on carrion and dead insects.

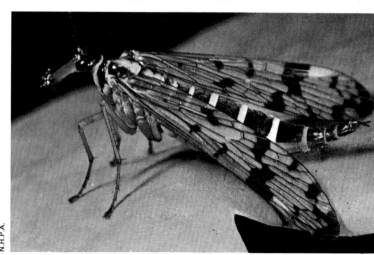

N.H.P.A.

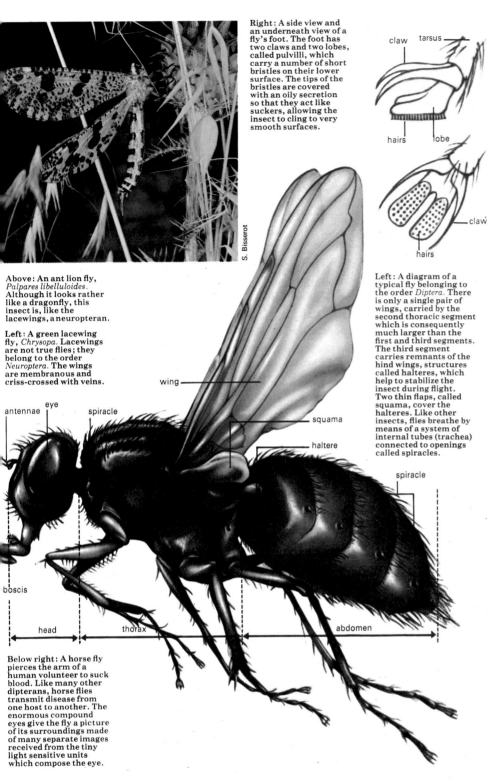

Right: A side view and an underneath view of a fly's foot. The foot has two claws and two lobes, called pulvilli, which carry a number of short bristles on their lower surface. The tips of the bristles are covered with an oily secretion so that they act like suckers, allowing the insect to cling to very smooth surfaces.

S. Bisserot

Above: An ant lion fly, *Palpares libelluloides*. Although it looks rather like a dragonfly, this insect is, like the lacewings, a neuropteran.

Left: A green lacewing fly, *Chrysopa*. Lacewings are not true flies; they belong to the order *Neuroptera*. The wings are membranous and criss-crossed with veins.

Left: A diagram of a typical fly belonging to the order *Diptera*. There is only a single pair of wings, carried by the second thoracic segment which is consequently much larger than the first and third segments. The third segment carries remnants of the hind wings, structures called halteres, which help to stabilize the insect during flight. Two thin flaps, called squama, cover the halteres. Like other insects, flies breathe by means of a system of internal tubes (trachea) connected to openings called spiracles.

claw tarsus

hairs lobe

claw

hairs

wing

antennae eye spiracle

squama

haltere

spiracle

boscis

head thorax abdomen

Below right: A horse fly pierces the arm of a human volunteer to suck blood. Like many other dipterans, horse flies transmit disease from one host to another. The enormous compound eyes give the fly a picture of its surroundings made of many separate images received from the tiny light sensitive units which compose the eye.

Below: The compound eye of an insect consists of many tiny units which are sensitive to light. Each unit points in a slightly different direction and sees only a small part of the 'scene' with clarity.

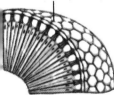

compound eye

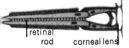

SECTION OF SINGLE UNIT

retinal rod corneal lens

Dipterans have only a single pair of flying wings. The head is typically large and mobile, with large compound eyes. In many males the eyes are larger than those of the female and meet on top of the head. The antennae may be fairly simple in more primitive flies such as crane flies, or of a characteristic three-segmented bristle-bearing form in the higher flies such as house flies. As well as being sensitive to smell, the antennae of certain species are important to the male in recognizing the pitch of the hum of the female in flight (mosquitoes) or for detecting wind speed (blowflies).

Feeding
The mouthparts of dipterans are very varied in form and function although they all show modification to fluid-feeding. The most important parts are the *labrum*, *hypopharynx* and *labium*. The labrum and the hypopharynx together form a canal up which fluid food is sucked and down which saliva flows. This double-channelled structure may be dipped into the fluid being ingested, or the fluid may first be 'sponged' up by two minutely-grooved lobes on the end of the labium, then passed into the food channel between the labrum and the hypopharynx.

Female mosquitoes, blackflies and horseflies possess mandibles and maxillae which can pierce or cut into the skin of a warm-blooded animal. In mosquitoes and blackflies the blood is sucked up directly, but in horseflies the labium is used to sponge up the blood exuding from the wound. Blood is needed by the female for development of the eggs, but the males of these groups do not have mandibles or maxillae and they feed upon nectar, which is also an additional food source for the females. In houseflies and blowflies the labium is developed for sponging up surface liquids. The fly regurgitates drops of vomit on to the food to digest and dissolve it before sucking it up. A little often remains and may be full of bacteria from the last meal.

The stable fly, *Stomoxys*, looks like a house fly but bites by means of cutting teeth on the end of its labium which has only very small sponging lobes. The labium of tsetse flies, *Glossina*, is like a slender stiletto to be thrust into game, cattle or humans to take blood directly. The saliva of most blood-sucking species contains an anti-coagulant to ensure a free flow of blood.

Vision is known to be important to blood-sucking flies in detecting their prey, but carbon dioxide concentration, warmth and humidity are often important factors as well.

The dipterans can be divided into three natural groups. The first of these is the *Nematocera*, slender, long-legged and primitive flies. The crane flies (often called 'daddy-long-legs') are perhaps most primitive of all, being large, slow flying and feeding little as adults. Their larvae, called 'leatherjackets', have biting mouthparts and feed on the roots of grass; they can cause considerable damage to the turf of sports grounds. Mosquitoes are well-known as blood-sucking disease-carriers that have aquatic larvae.

The larvae are active-swimmers and feed on particles by vibrating tufts of bristles termed 'mouth brushes'. Some species live in relatively large bodies of stagnant water, while others prefer rain-filled holes in tree stumps and similar

N.H.P.A.

187

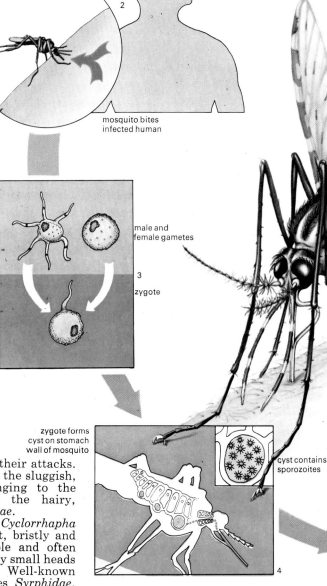

Above: Hoverflies belonging to the family *Syrphidae* mating on a birch leaf. These insects are frequent visitors to flowers (such as ivy flowers) whose nectar is easy to obtain. They feed not only on the nectar but also on the pollen grains. Their wasp-like appearance deters potential predators.

Right: Malaria is caused by certain protozoa of the genus *Plasmodium* which are carried by the *Anopheles* mosquito. The mosquitoes breed in swampy ground (1). On biting a person infected with malaria (2), the insect picks up two types of malarial cell from the victim's blood. Once in the mosquito, the two cells combine

(3) to form a worm-like *zygote* which forms a cyst in the insect's stomach (4). Eventually the cyst bursts, releasing many spores which migrate to the mosquito's salivary gland. When the insect bites another person (5), the disease is transferred and symptoms such as temperature fluctuation develop (6).

mosquito bites infected human

male and female gametes

zygote

zygote forms cyst on stomach wall of mosquito

cyst contains sporozoites

crevices. As mosquito larvae and pupae are air-breathing, a film of oil on the water surface has long been an effective control measure against disease carrying species. Small fish also feed on mosquito larvae.

Midges which belong to the family *Chironomidae* are non-biting and have aquatic larvae, some of which live in stagnant water. The adults may form immense clouds over lakes and are often considered a nuisance. In East Africa midges are collected in their millions and pressed together to form a food called Kungu cake.

Midges which belong to the family *Ceratopogonidae* are biting insects. The blood-sucking females attack a variety of animals including other insects. The genus *Culicoides* is a persistent attacker of man in the evening, choosing the head especially, and clouds of these tiny flies are familiar to gardeners, ramblers and tourists, particularly in Scotland.

The blackflies, which belong to the family *Simulidae*, are an important group. The larvae live in the most rapidly flowing regions of streams, attached to rocks by a sucker and filter-feeding by mouth brushes. The adults fly in clouds around humans or other mammals and the females feed by sucking blood. These flies carry river blindness and other human diseases; sheer weight of numbers can drive agricultural workers from the fields.

The best known members of the second dipteran group, the *Brachycera*, are the blood-sucking horseflies. They are perhaps the fastest flying dipterans, being capable of speeds of about 50 kph (31 mph). Like black flies, horse flies can be a great annoyance to people living in the

country by the intensity of their attacks. Other brachycerans include the sluggish, metallic soldier-flies belonging to the family *Stratiomyidae* and the hairy, predatory robber-flies *Asilidae*.

The last group of flies, the *Cyclorrhapha* or 'higher flies', are robust, bristly and aggressive, highly adaptable and often small. Their larvae have very small heads and are typical maggots. Well-known examples are the hover-flies *Syrphidae*, which mimic wasps and bees and in some cases live as larvae in the nests of the insects they resemble as adults, the familiar house flies and tsetse flies. Some members of the group have evolved to feed on wounds and to invade living tissue as parasites as in the notorious screw worm fly and the sheep blowflies. Finally, there are several groups whose members are truly parasitic, either as larvae or as adults.

Lacewings

The Neuroptera includes more than 4,000 different species and is often divided into several separate orders. Neuropterans have large gauzy wings and they are not usually strong fliers. The fore and hind wings are alike, but the coupling structures are not well developed. Their larvae prey on other insects and they have piercing and sucking mandibles and maxillae with which they suck up the juices of their prey. Lacewing larvae, sometimes called 'aphis lions', are important as predators of aphids.

The larvae of *Myrmeleon* are called 'ant lions'. They dig pits in sandy ground and lie half buried at the bottom of the pit waiting for unsuspecting insects such as ants to fall into their clutches.

Below: Blowflies, *Calliphora*, feeding and laying their eggs on the head of a dead snake. Blowflies (bluebottles) are a familiar household pest. Their eggs are laid on a suitable supply of food for the larvae (maggots)—often uncovered meat intended for human consumption. They can be seen at all times of the year.

Below right: A South African robber fly, *Promachus vagator*, stands astride its victim (a hoverfly) as it sucks up the body juices through its piercing proboscis. Robber flies will attack quite large insects including bees and wasps, so the hoverfly's wasp-like markings have not helped it.

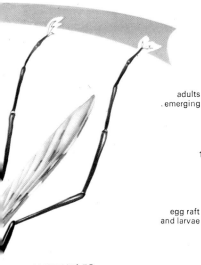

ANOPHELES

THE MALARIA MOSQUITO

adults emerging

1

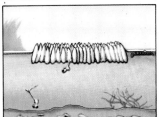

egg raft and larvae

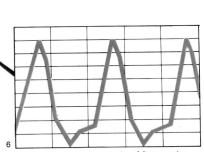

6

victim suffers regular attacks of fever and temperature fluctuation as organisms develop in liver and bloodstream

Right: The larva of a lacewing fly feeding on aphids. Like the larvae of all neuropterans, these insects are carnivorous, and they are equipped with long curved mandibles for seizing their prey. The larva is quite different from the adult insect, and this is typical of insects which go through larval and pupal stages.

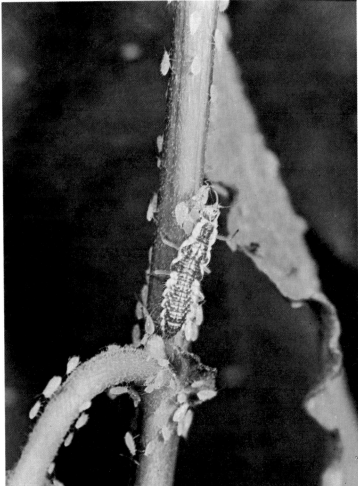

Heather Angel

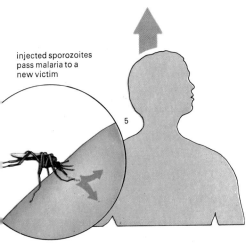

injected sporozoites pass malaria to a new victim

5

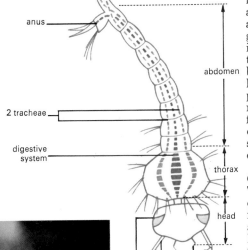

siphon

anus

abdomen

2 tracheae

digestive system

thorax

head

feeding brushes

antenna

eye

N.H.P.A.

Above: A mosquito larva. After a meal of blood, female mosquitoes lay their eggs in stagnant water. The eggs hatch out into larvae which hang upside down at the water surface by the effect of surface tension. The larvae breathe by means of trachea leading to the siphon tube which breaks the water surface.

Scorpionflies

The scorpionflies (*Mecoptera*) get their name from the way in which the prominent genitalia of the male curves over the abdomen giving a scorpion-like appearance. The most familiar member of the group is *Panorpia*, a common woodland insect with speckled wings and a projection on its head which looks rather like a beak. Mecopterans are predatory and so have biting rather than sucking mouthparts. The slender fore and hind wings resemble each other and are coupled by a full complement of two lobes and two sets of bristles. The larvae of scorpionflies are soil-dwelling. At this stage they look like caterpillars.

Caddisflies

The caddisflies (*Trichoptera*) are very closely related to the moths and butterflies and like them have mouthparts adapted to fluid feeding. Rather than having a long proboscis for reaching into flowers for nectar, caddisflies have elongated mouthparts designed for surface feeding. They are similar to butterflies and moths in their wing structure. The wings are very hairy and often there are primitive scales as well. The coupling of fore and hind wings is generally like that of the *Lepidoptera*.

Caddisflies are nocturnal and are found near water in which their caterpillar-like larvae live. Some larvae are vegetarian and build cases, made of material appropriate to the species' habitat, to protect themselves. Other larvae, however, spin silken nets in which prey may be caught. Larvae of this latter type live in rapidly flowing streams rather than ponds or lakes.

189

Bugs, Fleas and Lice

There are many parasitic insects, all of which are very specialized in their feeding mechanisms, their reproduction and their general behaviour. Those attacking man, domestic animals and crops are of particular importance because, in addition to nuisance and economic factors, they frequently act as carriers for dangerous diseases such as typhus and plague, and virus diseases of crops, for example, potato leaf roll.

Most parasitic insects fall into one or other of the following seven insect orders: *Siphonaptera* (fleas), *Mallophaga* (biting lice), *Anoplura* (sucking lice), *Thysanoptera* (thrips), *Hemiptera* (true bugs) and *Homoptera* (plant bugs). The order *Dermaptera* (earwigs) also includes some parasitic insects which, like the others, live and feed on the outside of their hosts; they are called *ectoparasites*. The order *Psocoptera* (book lice) contains insects which are closely related to the sucking and biting lice, but they are not parasitic. A final order, *Strepsiptera*, contains a number of insects which spend at least part of their lives as internal parasites (*endoparasites*) of certain other insects.

Lice

Of all insects the lice are the most completely commited to parasitism. All stages from egg to adult are spent in close association with a warm blooded host. In sucking lice this host is always a mammal but in biting lice the host is typically a bird, although a few mammals can also become infested. Transfer of lice to new hosts occurs only when members of the same species are close together, such as in feeding the young, copulation or overcrowding in refugee camps and prisons. Indeed lice soon die if separated from a living host.

As their names suggest, the main difference between sucking and biting lice is their mouth parts. Sucking lice have mouth parts modified to form a hollow tube which can pierce the host's skin and through which blood can be sucked. It functions in much the same way as a hypodermic syringe. Biting lice have a pair of large toothed mandibles for chewing the feather or hair of the host, although blood produced by scratching and dead skin cells may also be eaten.

Lice eggs, called nits, are laid singly or in groups of up to ten, cemented on to hairs or feathers. They require body warmth to develop and hatch in about a week. Although adult life is short (only 4 to 7 weeks) the constant conditions of the body allow continuous breeding through the year so very large louse populations can rapidly be built up. A single shirt has been recorded as bearing 10,428 individuals of the human body louse.

Humans can be infested with three kinds of sucking lice (no biting lice have been recorded on humans). The human louse, *Pediculus humanus*, has two varieties, the body louse, found in clothes next to the skin, and the head louse, found amongst hair on the head. The third type, found among the pubic hair, is the crab

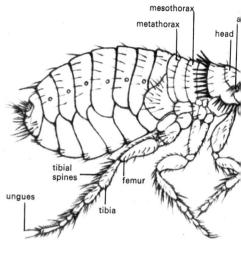

Above and above right: A photograph and a body plan of a flea. Fleas have mouthparts capable of piercing the host's skin and sucking blood, a tough cuticle to prevent damage from scratching and claws for clinging on to the host. The backward-pointing bristles help prevent the host from dislodging the flea during preening.

Right and far right: A human body louse and details of the large claws which enable the insect to cling to its host. Lice are wingless, and their bodies have become flattened so that they can lie close to the skin of their host. Like fleas, lice have a tough, leathery cuticle to prevent injury from the host's scratching.

louse, *Phthirus pubis*.

Crab lice do not transmit disease, but the human louse carries relapsing fever and typhus, also known as gaol fever, ship fever and trench fever, which afflicted soldiers in the First World War. Typhus is caused by a virus-like micro-organism, *Rickettsia*, which is transmitted into the body through skin lacerations that become infected with louse excrement or the body fluids of squashed lice.

The book-lice are closely related to the insects discussed above but are neither true lice nor parasitic. They are very small, sometimes winged, insects which reach a maximum length of only 2 mm (0.08 in). They live on the bark of trees, particularly where there are lichens and fungi, and in old bird nests. They are also found infesting stored cereals, museum specimens and old library books where they feed on binding materials.

Fleas

Fleas, like lice, are wingless ectoparasites feeding on the blood of the warm blooded animals and, although highly specialized for a parasitic life, they can spend considerable periods away from their host. Fleas are endopterygote insects and therefore have a larva totally different from the adult. Eggs are laid a few at a time loosely amongst hair or feathers of the host. They fall out into the host's nest or lair where they hatch in 2 to 4 days into white, legless, eyeless larvae. The larvae have strong biting mandibles for feeding on organic debris, particularly the excrement of adult fleas. Just prior to laying eggs, the adult female feeds rapaciously so that large amounts of

Right and below: A few hemipterous bugs are aquatic. The backswimmer or water boatman (below) has large bristly hind legs with which it rows itself upside down through the water. They cannot walk on land but are good fliers and so quickly colonize new areas of fresh water. The water scorpion *Nepa cinerea* (right) gets its name from the large front legs which are used for grasping prey. It spends much of its time on the bottom and sides of muddy ponds and ditches, and when submerged it looks like a dead leaf. Some water scorpions can inflict quite a painful bite: in Australia they are known as toe-biters or needle bugs. They feed on small aquatic animals such as tadpoles.

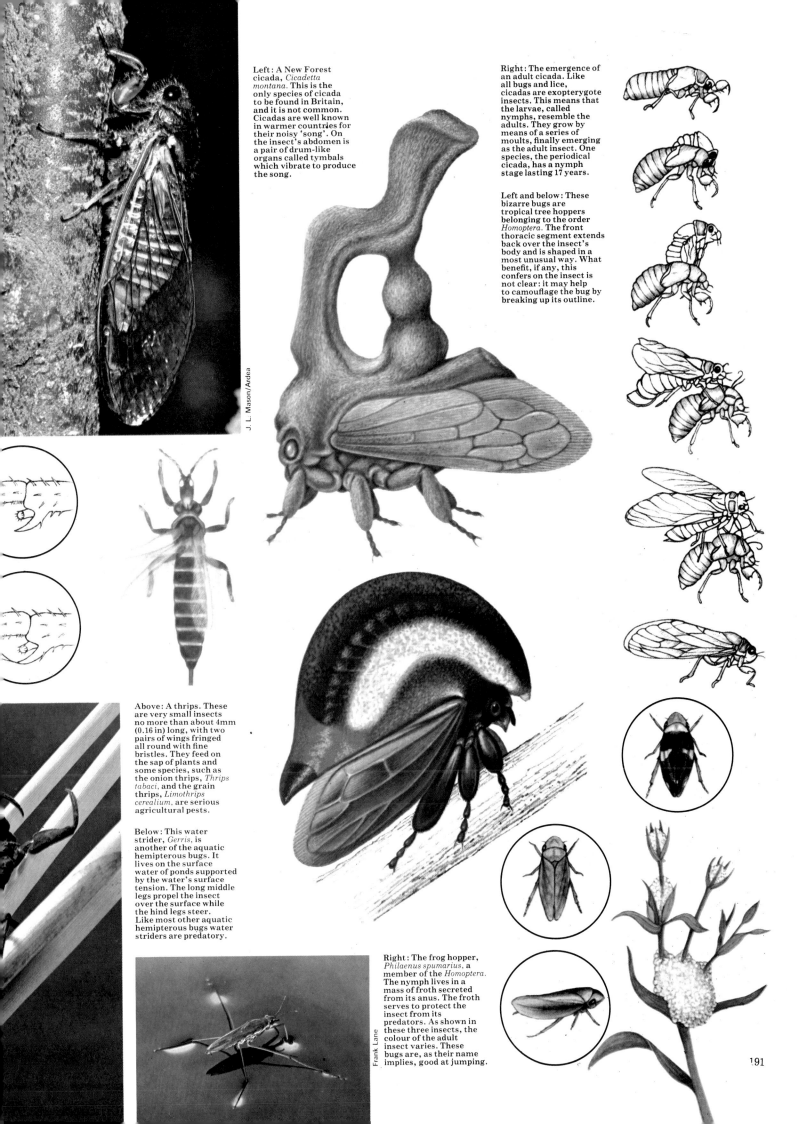

Left: A New Forest cicada, *Cicadetta montana*. This is the only species of cicada to be found in Britain, and it is not common. Cicadas are well known in warmer countries for their noisy 'song'. On the insect's abdomen is a pair of drum-like organs called tymbals which vibrate to produce the song.

J. L. Mason/Ardea

Right: The emergence of an adult cicada. Like all bugs and lice, cicadas are exopterygote insects. This means that the larvae, called nymphs, resemble the adults. They grow by means of a series of moults, finally emerging as the adult insect. One species, the periodical cicada, has a nymph stage lasting 17 years.

Left and below: These bizarre bugs are tropical tree hoppers belonging to the order *Homoptera*. The front thoracic segment extends back over the insect's body and is shaped in a most unusual way. What benefit, if any, this confers on the insect is not clear: it may help to camouflage the bug by breaking up its outline.

Above: A thrips. These are very small insects no more than about 4mm (0.16 in) long, with two pairs of wings fringed all round with fine bristles. They feed on the sap of plants and some species, such as the onion thrips, *Thrips tabaci*, and the grain thrips, *Limothrips cerealium*, are serious agricultural pests.

Below: This water strider, *Gerris*, is another of the aquatic hemipterous bugs. It lives on the surface water of ponds supported by the water's surface tension. The long middle legs propel the insect over the surface while the hind legs steer. Like most other aquatic hemipterous bugs water striders are predatory.

Frank Lane

Right: The frog hopper, *Philaenus spumarius*, a member of the *Homoptera*. The nymph lives in a mass of froth secreted from its anus. The froth serves to protect the insect from its predators. As shown in these three insects, the colour of the adult insect varies. These bugs are, as their name implies, good at jumping.

191

semi-digested blood pass out in her excrement which on falling to the ground forms an abundance of food for the larvae when they hatch. The larva of the human flea, *Pulex irritans*, however, is not dependent on such a parental food supply and can live off a variety of organic materials which enable it to live in relatively clean surroundings.

After about a week the larva spins a cocoon around itself and pupates to the adult, emerging in one to four weeks. In some circumstances, however, flea pupae can remain dormant for considerable periods of time, and it is believed that one of the factors causing emergence is vibration caused by a nearby host. In this way an immediate food supply is available to the newly emerged adult.

Fleas are more active than lice and the body is laterally compressed to enable them to pass easily between the hairs or feathers of the host. Their legs are long and powerful and they can leap considerable distances to escape danger or infest a new host. The human flea is able to jump over 30 cm (1 ft) horizontally and nearly 20 cm (8 in) vertically; this is equivalent to a man jumping 150 m (165 yd) and 90 m (100 yd) respectively. Fleas jump by suddenly straightening their hind legs, but the energy required is far in excess of that which could be supplied by direct muscle action. The extra energy is supplied by a rubber-like protein, *resilin*, which stores energy when compressed and can suddenly release it to power a jump.

One of the most dreaded human diseases, bubonic plague or Black Death, is transmitted by rat fleas, such as *Xenopsylla*. Plague is caused by a bacterium, *Pasteurella pestis*, which is passed into humans with the anticoagulant saliva that fleas inject before sucking blood. Normally *Xenopsylla* infests rats but, when rats die of plague, the flea seeks a new host. In overcrowded populations where hygienic standards are so low as to allow rat infestation, the rat fleas pass to human hosts, carrying the plague bacterium with them. In the Middle Ages conditions of this sort were not uncommon, and plague epidemics caused millions of deaths.

Bugs

Only two groups of the true bugs, *Hemiptera*, are parasitic on man, the bed bugs and the assassin bugs. The common bed bug, *Cimax lectularis*, is flightless, oval in shape, a reddish brown colour and covered with fine bristles. It has well developed legs for fast running and the eyes are well developed. Bed bugs do not live on their host but at night emerge from cracks in furniture, walls and bedding to feed. They are not known to transmit diseases to man, but their bite causes considerable irritation.

The assassin bugs *Rhodnius* and *Triatoma* can transmit the protozoan, *Trypanosoma cruzi*, which causes Chagas disease. *Triatoma* can also transmit encephalomyelitis virus which causes inflammation of the brain. Most assassin bugs, however, feed on invertebrates, particularly insects, and only some of the tropical types attack vertebrates, including humans. They are often well camouflaged and can also squirt a toxic saliva at would be predators.

The plant feeding shield or stink bugs are also members of the *Hemiptera*. Crops

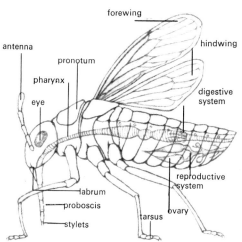

Left: A body plan of a bug belonging to the order *Hemiptera*. Like lice and fleas, these insects have piercing and sucking mouthparts. They can be distinguished from the plant bugs, *Homoptera*, with which they used to be grouped, by a thickening at the base of each forewing. The hind wings and the end parts of the forewings are completely membranous. As in other insects, the body is divided into three regions: the head, the thorax and the abdomen. Three pairs of legs and two pairs of wings are carried by the three thoracic segments.

Above right: The gradual metamorphosis of a chinch bug nymph is typical of an exopterygote insect.

such as wheat are attacked in the USSR and Near East by the tortoise bug, *Eurygaster integriceps*, and beans and tomatoes are attacked in tropical and subtropical countries by the green vegetable bug, *Nezara viridula*. A North American species, however, is beneficial to agriculture since it attacks the Colorado beetle.

Plant bugs

The *Homoptera* include such insects as greenfly (aphids), froghoppers, leafhoppers and cicadas. They cause a great deal of damage to crops by transmitting virus diseases and by sucking their sap, so weakening the whole plant by depriving it of some of its nourishment.

Aphids are small, soft bodied insects with piercing and sucking mouth parts similar to the true bugs. Control of these delicate insects is difficult because they often migrate at certain seasons from wild vegetation to crops. The black bean aphid, *Aphis fabae*, spends the early stages of its life on the guelder rose or spindle tree and subsequently migrates to bean crops. Even if only a few aphids reach a bean they can breed at a tremendous rate to form huge colonies since they can reproduce without fertilization of the eggs by a male; this process is called *parthenogenesis*. Generally parthenogenetic offsprings are wingless but, under certain conditions of light, temperature, overcrowding and food availability, winged offspring develop which migrate to fresh hosts. Ultimately a winged generation is produced which returns to the primary host plant, producing fertile males and females which lay eggs capable of surviving the winter.

Above: An assassin bug, *Nularda nobilitata*, from Nigeria. Assassin bugs are sometimes called kissing bugs because of their habit of biting people on the face. Their extremely painful bite has been likened to an electric shock and can cause severe allergic reactions. Some assassin bugs are transmitters of disease.

Above: Looking just like thorns, these tree hoppers, *Umbonia crassicornis*, are well concealed from their predators. As with the tree hoppers illustrated on the previous page, the thorn-like projection is an outgrowth of the front thoracic segment. Here it has an obviously useful function.

The hind legs of this strange South American bug are flattened into leaf-like structures. The purpose of these brighly coloured appendages is not known.

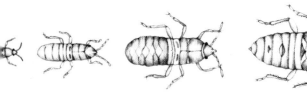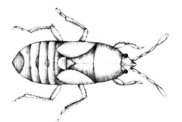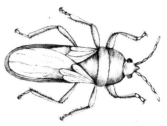

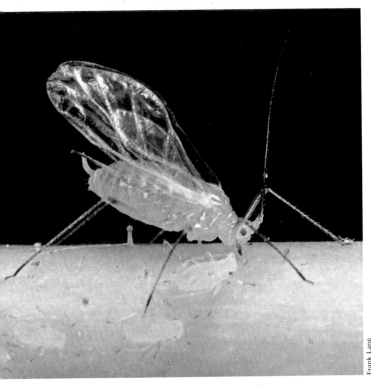

Above left: An aphid (greenfly) surrounded by young. Aphids feed on plant sap, and in order to extract enough protein for growth they must ingest large quantities of the sap. The excess carbohydrate is excreted as 'honeydew', a food much sought after by ants. Some aphids spend their lives in ants' nests.

Above: These lantern bugs, *Laterinaria candelaria*, are so called because they were once thought to be luminous. They are tropical insects belonging to the order *Homoptera*. The long 'nose' is a hollow projection from the front of the insect's head and is typical of this and other members of the family *Fulgoridae*.

Like aphids, froghoppers and particularly leafhoppers are serious crop pests in many areas of the world. The cicadas of the tropics however, although they suck the sap from plants, are not serious pests. Cicadas are large insects—the Malaysian empress cicada has a wing span of more than 20 cm (8 in).

A further small order of insects that suck plant juices and are therefore agricultural pests are the thrips. They often occur in very large numbers on a wide range of plants including cereals and have peculiar asymmetrical, sucking mouthparts.

A few members of the order *Dermaptera* are parasitic. The insect *Hermimerus*, for example, lives in the fur of African rats. The most familiar dermapteran, however, is the common earwig, *Forficula auricularia*, which lives in gardens all over Europe and in America. Although it rarely, if ever, flies, the earwig does have wings which are quite different from those of other insects. The fore wings are short, hardened structures (*tegmina*) which act as covers for the hind wings. The latter are semicircular in shape and can be folded up rather like a fan to be tucked under the tegmina. The 'pincer' at the hind end of the abdomen is used in defence and to help fold up the wings.

The final group, the *Strepsiptera*, are parasites of wasps, bees and plant bugs. The females, which are little more than sacks of eggs, and the larvae spend their lives inside the host insect. The males are flying insects having large quadrant-shaped hind wings. The fore wings are no more than tiny club-shaped structures reminiscent of the halteres found in true flies of the order *Diptera*.

Right: This beautiful insect is a shield bug, *Sphaerocoris annulis*. Shield bugs are sometimes called 'stink bugs' because they have special glands which secrete an unpleasant tasting fluid. The vivid markings on the insect's back act as an outward warning to potential predators that it is unpalatable.

193

Social Insects

Some species of insects associate together in hundreds, thousands or even millions to form colonies whose members all contribute in some way to the overall success of the community. Such insects, known as social insects, are found in the insect orders *Hymenoptera* (bees, wasps and ants) and *Isoptera* (termites).

It is the sharing of labour for the common good that distinguishes a true insect society like a colony of bees or an ants' nest from a collection of insects living in close proximity, such as a swarm of locusts. In some insect societies the individuals responsible for a particular task are structurally different from other members of the colony: worker ants, for example, can easily be distinguished from soldier ants.

In other insect societies most 'citizens' are virtually indistinguishable from one another and the division of labour is according to age. The worker honey bee acts as a nursemaid to the developing larvae for the first two weeks of its life. During the third week it is occupied in building and repairing the nest and converting collected nectar into the honey which is stored in special honey cells. Finally, after a spell of duty guarding the nest, it leaves the colony to forage for nectar and pollen.

Social insects plainly benefit by living together in a large community: the whole is stronger than its individual parts. For such a system to be successful, however,

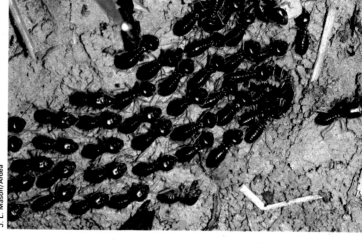

J. L. Mason/Ardea

Below: The nests of African termites, *Macrotermes bellicosus*, can reach skyscraper proportions. A nest six metres (20 ft) high is not uncommon. The nests have rock hard, water-tight walls of earth and plant material bound together with saliva and excreta. The walls help to insulate the nest from extremes of temperature.

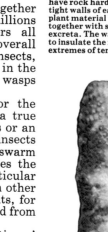

male

worker

soldier

queen

Above: The four castes of the North American termite, *Termes flavipes*. Winged termites develop only at certain times of the year. They soon leave to found new colonies.

Above: A column of foraging termites, *Macrotermes*, from Malaysia. Termites feed on wood and other vegetable matter. They can severely damage wooden constructions such as buildings, but can also serve a useful purpose in increasing the aeration and drainage of soil. These are worker termites.

Dr. F. Sauer/Bavaria

Below: a thick-walled nest belonging to a species of South African termite. Air circulates constantly through the living area of the nest and this keeps the temperature, humidity and oxygen concentration at the correct levels. The atmosphere in some termites nests contains enough carbon dioxide to make a man unconscious.

Anthony Bannister/NHPA

Above: A termite queen, *Macrotermes bellicosus*, her abdomen grossly distended with eggs, being tended by worker termites. Soldier termites, with enlarged heads and jaws stand guard. The queen lives in a 'royal chamber' deep within the termitaria. She may lay as many as 36,000 eggs in a single day.

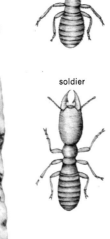

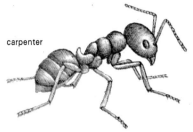
carpenter

legionaries

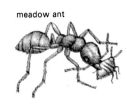
meadow ant

Left: Weaver ants build their nests in trees and shrubs by joining leaves together with silk secreted by their larvae. The worker ants grasp the larvae in their jaws and pass them back and forth between the leaves to bind them together.

Above and right: The way of life of ants varies from species to species. Carpenter ants will bore long galleries in rotting wood. Legionary ants are nomadic; they move in single file and hunt other insects. The meadow ant farms aphids for the sweet fluid called 'honeydew' which they secrete. Leaf cutter ants chew leaves to a spongy mass which acts as compost for a fungus, the ants' staple diet. Thief ants scavenge from other ants.

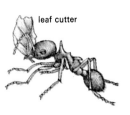
leaf cutter

Bruce Coleman

Left: Worker garden black ants, *Lasius niger*, tending the larva of a queen ant. These common ants are often a pest in kitchens and larders. They live under stones or logs or in the walls of buildings.

Right: Leaf cutter ants, *Atta*, from Trinidad. The queen is being tended by the much smaller workers. These insects are sometimes called parasol ants because they carry cut pieces of leaves above their heads like banners or parasols back to the nest. Compared with a bee's or wasp's nest, an ant's nest is fairly simple consisting of a series of excavated galleries and chambers. Ants do not build cells for their larvae or pupae, so these can easily be moved.

thief ant

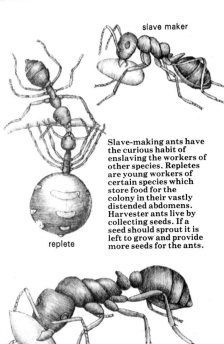
slave maker

replete

harvester

Slave-making ants have the curious habit of enslaving the workers of other species. Repletes are young workers of certain species which store food for the colony in their vastly distended abdomens. Harvester ants live by collecting seeds. If a seed should sprout it is left to grow and provide more seeds for the ants.

there must be a complex communication and control network so that members of the community can respond quickly to tackle problems which are bound to arise from time to time.

One such control mechanism involves chemicals called *pheromones* which act rather like hormones to influence the behaviour of the colony members. A good example of this control is the rapid reaction to the loss of a queen in a colony of bees. The queen bee secretes a material known as 'queen substance' which contains the pheromone *oxodecanoic acid*, which becomes spread all over her body during grooming. The workers who constantly attend the queen pick up the material from her body and pass it to other bees. In this way traces of the pheromone are passed throughout the hive so that every bee 'knows' that the queen is present.

If the queen is removed, the behaviour of the workers changes: within 24 hours 'queen cells' are being built to make good the loss of the queen, and the ovaries of worker bees have developed so that egg-laying can resume as soon as possible (normally egg-laying is the sole responsibility of the queen). This dramatic change in behaviour is at least partly the result of the sudden interruption to the supply of queen substance. This and other control mechanisms are constantly in operation in social insect colonies to ensure that the tasks necessary for the continued well-being of the community are carried out.

Termites

Termites are pale-coloured, soft-bodied insects living mainly in the tropics with a few inhabiting southern Europe and the USA. They are not found in northern Europe. Termites are sometimes referred to as 'white ants', but this is a misnomer since they are more closely related to cockroaches than ants. Like cockroaches, they are exopterygote insects.

The more primitive termites build nests called *termitaria* in decaying wood, often underground, but more advanced species can build huge mound-like nests.

A new nest is started at certain times of the year when winged males and females develop, leave the nest and mate. They break their wings off and both male and female start to excavate a new nest. The 'royal pair' as they are known constitute a king and queen whose only function is to produce young, so all members of the colony are derived from them. The queen's

Above: Pupae of the wasp *Vespa germanica* in their cells. The cells are made of a papery material. The first larvae of the year are tended by the queen who feeds them on the juices of captured insects. As soon as the first workers appear, however, her function is limited to egg-laying. The workers tend the nest.

Below: A series of diagrams showing the operation of a wasp's sting. The sting is a modified ovipositor (egg-laying organ) and once it has penetrated the skin of the enemy, poison is injected as in a hypodermic syringe. The poison contains the chemical histamine and can be countered by antihistamine tablets.

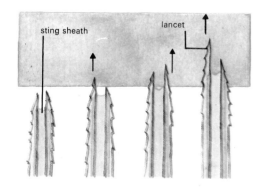

sting sheath

lancet

abdomen becomes very large, particularly in mound-building termites, for the continuous production of eggs. A queen *Macrotermes* increases in length from 3.5 to 14 cm (1.4 to 5.5 in) and can produce 36,000 eggs a day; an average of one every two seconds. The royal pair are groomed and fed by worker termites and have a very long reproductive life, probably at least 15 years in *Amitermes*. Their eggs hatch into nymphs of four different types, known as *castes*.

The wingless soldier caste have large heads and jaws. They defend the nest against intruders, particularly ants. The worker caste are also wingless and serve to maintain the colony, foraging at night for food, cleaning the nest and feeding the soldiers and reproductives. Flightless but fertile secondary reproductives are also produced, which can take over from the royal pair if they die or their egg production decreases with age. They are stimulated to egg laying activity through special feeding by the workers and in this way a nest might last for up to 40 years or more. The fourth caste is produced at certain times of the year and consists of winged fertile males and females which disperse and form new colonies.

196

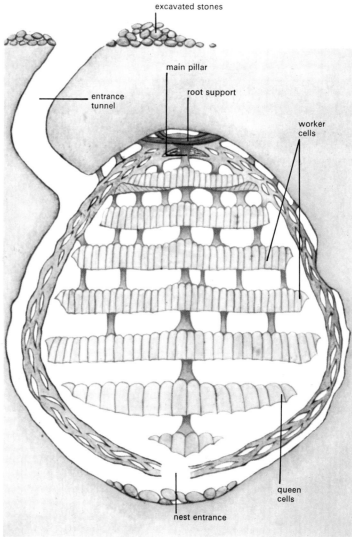

excavated stones

entrance tunnel

main pillar

root support

worker cells

queen cells

nest entrance

Left: A section through the nest of a common wasp, *Vespula vulgaris.* By the end of the summer the nest may measure 23 cm (9 in) in diameter, contain ten stories of nest cells and house 5,000 wasps. In the autumn fertile males and females are produced. After mating the males die and the females hibernate to start new colonies the following year.

Below: A female solitary wasp, *Ammophila campestris,* captures a caterpillar, paralyzes it by stinging, and places it in a prepared nest. She then lays an egg on the caterpillar and closes up the nest entrance with stones. When the larva hatches it will feed on the paralyzed caterpillar.

Left: An ichneumon wasp, *Psilimastrix,* on the chrysalis of a swallowtail butterfly, *Papilio asterias.* Ichneumons are parasitic insects. They lay their eggs in the larvae or pupae of other insects, particularly butterflies and moths. When the parasite's larva hatches it feeds on the body tissue of the host.

Below: A queen wasp, *Vespa media,* feeding the first larvae of the year. Like bees, wasps lay their eggs in hexagonal cells. The eggs hatch after three to four weeks into sterile female worker wasps which forage for food and extend the nest. Hornets are considerably larger than wasps, but they have a similar life history.

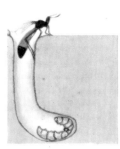

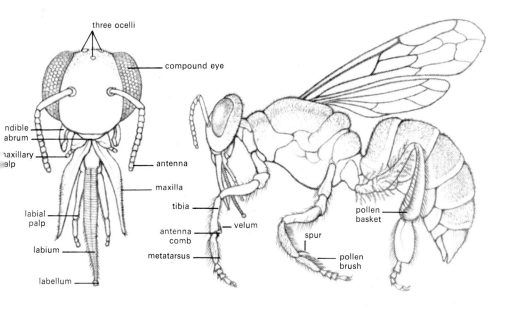

three ocelli

compound eye

ndible
abrum

maxillary
palp

antenna

maxilla

tibia

labial
palp

antenna
comb

velum

labium

metatarsus

spur

labellum

pollen
basket

pollen
brush

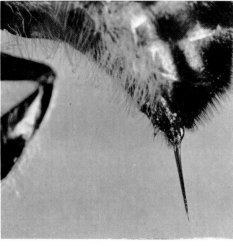

Frank Lane

Above: The sting of a bee. It consists of two barbed darts guided by a sheath. After initial penetration by the two darts, the sheath is inserted into the wound and poison is injected. The barbs hold the sting in position. After stinging, the sting and part of the intestine are usually pulled away and the bee dies.

Above: Diagrams showing the head and legs of a honeybee. The legs are specially modified for collecting pollen. The hind leg is equipped with long hairs forming a 'pollen basket' which carries most of the pollen load. The joint between the tibia and the metatarsus of the front leg is modified to act as an antenna cleaner.

Below: A honeybee, *Apis mellifera*, with the 'pollen baskets' on its hind legs full of pollen. Pollen and nectar are stored in special cells in the nest. A worker draws nectar into its crop where the action of saliva converts it into honey. The honey may then be regurgitated to provide the community with a food store.

Below: A swarm of honeybees clinging to a bush. Normally a colony of bees will contain only one queen, but in exceptional circumstances a new queen may appear. The old queen will leave the nest with an entourage of workers. A queen cannot found a colony on her own since she cannot forage for food or build a nest.

Frank Lane

Ants

Ants can easily be distinguished from termites by the presence of a narrow waist between the thorax and abdomen, an abdominal sting, a thick, dark cuticle and larval and pupal stages in the life cycle. Ants, like all *Hymenoptera*, are endopterygote insects. There are over 6,000 different species of ant and although cosmopolitan they are largely restricted to the tropics.

Ants usually inhabit a more or less permanent subterranean nest, but the tropical army ants of South America and driver ants of Africa are nomadic; a temporary nest is made each day by masses of ants coming together and hooking on to each other with their legs, leaving spaces for the queen and juvenile stages. Such 'nests' may be formed in a hollow tree hanging from a branch or simply in a depression in the ground. The common European wood ant, *Formica rufa*, builds huge mounds of twigs and pine needles which may be 150cm (five feet) high and 300cm (ten feet) in diameter, over its underground nest. This thatching to the nest helps to waterproof and insulate it.

Each nest, depending on species, may contain anything from 10 to several million adults. The nest is founded by a single reproductive queen, the male dying after mating. Normally there is no more than one queen ant in a nest, but wood ant nests may contain two or three queens. In all hymenopteran colonies, including those of ants, there are two main castes besides the queen.

The worker caste are flightless, infertile females which develop from fertilized eggs and are specialized for food foraging, care of larvae and nest building. Some workers of species such as army and harvester ants develop into large soldier ants with big heads and jaws. They function to guard the nest or, in army ants, the marching columns.

The second caste are the winged males that develop at intervals from unfertilized eggs and serve to fertilize the queen on her nuptial flight. In wood ants, however, although both sexes are winged, mating takes place on the ground near the nest, and the queen may re-enter the nest where she lived as a larva or found a new nest.

Army ants have a definite cycle of reproductive behaviour. Every 30 to 40 days the column stops marching and forms a more permanent nest where the queen produces up to 35,000 eggs over a period of 2 days. The eggs hatch into larvae at the same time as the pupae of the previous generation of larvae 'hatch' into adult ants.

Wood ants and army ants are fierce predators. The marching columns of army ants contain millions of ants and at night constantly scour large areas, attacking and eating every living thing in their path; a tethered horse is soon reduced to a skeleton. Soldier scouts march ahead and lay scent trails for the main columns to follow.

Wasps

Ants together with bees and wasps belong to a subdivision of the *Hymenoptera*, the *Apocrita*, whose members are characterized by the presence of a narrow waist between thorax and abdomen and the absence of legs on the maggot-like larvae. Generally the *Apocrita* are beneficial to agriculture. Bees, for example, pollinate flowers, and many insect pests are 197

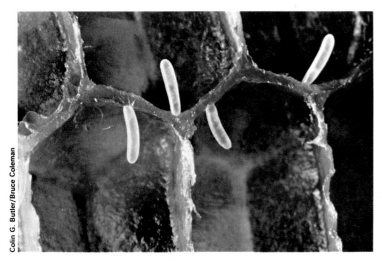

Left: Newly laid eggs of the honeybee, *Apis mellifera*, in their hexagonal cells. When they hatch, the larvae will be tended by young worker bees who feed them on regurgitated food and a jelly-like secretion called 'royal jelly'. If large amounts of royal jelly are fed to a larva, it will develop into a queen rather than a worker. This will be done if, for example, the queen of the colony should die. The cells in which the eggs are laid and the larvae develop are made of wax produced by a special abdominal gland. All the egg-laying in a colony of bees is done by the queen. She has a useful life span of three or four years after which time she is ruthlessly killed.

preyed on by wasps and parasitized by ichneumon and chalcid 'flies' which, in spite of their names, are types of wasp. The other subdivision of the *Hymenoptera*, the *Symphyta*, which is considered to be the more primitive, contains woodwasps such as sawflies whose thorax and abdomen are broadly joined and whose caterpillar-like larvae have legs.

Sawflies have an extremely long egg-laying organ called the ovipositor and are sometimes mistaken for common wasps, particularly since their bodies are also coloured yellow and black. Their adult life is very short, for the male dies after mating and the female soon after laying her eggs (in slits made in wood or leaves) with her saw-like ovipositor.

The chalcid 'flies' are minute insects and one of their close relations, the fairy 'fly' *Alpatus magnanimus*, is the smallest known insect, being only 0.12 mm (0.0047 in) long. Many chalcids are parasitic on moths and butterflies, laying minute eggs in their eggs and pupae.

The ichneumon 'flies' are also parasitic on insect larvae. The largest British ichneumon, *Rhyssa persuasoria*, lays its eggs in the larva of the sawfly, *Sirex*, which burrows in pine trees, ruining the timber. The female ichneumon has an extremely long ovipositor, which is capable of boring through a few inches of solid wood to reach the sawfly larva.

Many wasps such as the hunting wasps are solitary in their nesting habits, laying a single egg in a nest and leaving it to develop. Hunting wasps hunt other insects, paralyze them with their sting and place them in their nest to serve as a fresh but immobile food store for the

Above: The brood cells in a colony of honeybees. At the bottom of the picture is the queen. The remaining insects are workers and drones. There are normally only a few drones in a nest. They are males whose only function is to fertilize the queen on her mating flight. Like the queen and the larvae, they are fed by the workers.

Below: A carpenter bee, *Xylocopa*, from Malaysia. This is a solitary bee which bores into wood to build its nest and so can damage wooden structures. Solitary bees do not have castes such as queen, worker and drone. Eggs are laid in cells which are separately provisioned with pollen and honey for the larvae.

developing larva. Numerous separate nests are constructed, some no more than burrows in sandy soil.

Some species of wasp, however, such as the European hornet, *Vespa crabro*, the common wasp, *Vespula vulgaris*, and the paper wasp, *Polistes*, are social insects living in a nest of papery material. Hornets will build their nests above the ground in trees or buildings but wasps nests are often found below ground. The paper wasp builds a small nest above ground which is unusual since the egg cells are not covered with a papery cap as in other wasps but are left open. Wasp colonies last for only a single year. The only wasps to survive the winter are young fertilized queens.

Bees

The bees, like wasps, are cosmopolitan and only some bees such as the bumble or humble bee and the European honey bee are social insects. The bumble bee, *Bombus*, closely resembles the honey bee except that it has a larger body covered in stiff yellow, orange and red hairs, also its sting is not barbed so it can be used again and again, unlike the honey bee that can sting only once. In general the social life of bumble bees resembles that of the common wasp. The nest may be below ground or on the surface and is usually constructed from very fine grass and other vegetation. Eggs are laid in hexagonal egg cells constructed from wax produced by a special abdominal gland. On hatching the larvae are fed on a mixture of pollen and nectar, collected by worker bees from flowers.

The nectar is sucked up through a special extendible tube leading from the mouth and stored in the crop. Pollen, deposited on the bee's hairy body when it forces its way into a flower for nectar, is scraped off by the second pair of legs into pollen baskets attached to the outer face of each hind leg. On returning to the nest, pollen is removed from the baskets by the forelegs and placed in an egg cell as a food store for the developing larvae. Surplus nectar is placed in a large 'honeypot' cell near the nest entrance to serve as a food store for workers when the weather is too bad for foraging. It is during food collection that the cross pollination of flowers occurs.

When food is located by a foraging bee, its position is indicated to other workers in the nest by a complicated dance accompanied by wagging of the abdomen and a vibration of the wings. In this way information is given relating the food source to the position of the sun. On cloudy days the pattern of polarized light in the sky is used as a reference source.

There are four species of honey bee, one of which *Apis mellifera*, is the western European domestic bee. Unlike other social insects in temperate climates, honey bee colonies can survive the winter because of extensive food reserves in the form of honey that are built up during the summer months. The value of this reserve honey as a human food has made the honey bee economically important.

In midsummer a colony of bees may contain about 60,000 workers, a few hundred males known as *drones*, whose only function is to mate with the queen, and one queen. In winter the bees enter into a semidormant condition huddled together in the centre of the nest for warmth.

Honey bees removing pollen from their storage baskets into the pollen store. The brood cells provide food for the developing larvae.

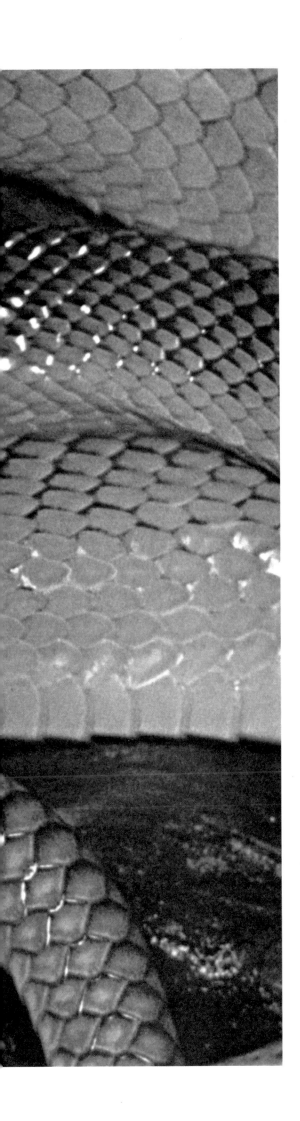

Chapter 3
The Vertebrates

Snakes are an excellent example of
adaptation in nature – elongation of
the body has led to an increase in the
number of vertebrae, and articular
surfaces between them ensure that
the vertebral column is flexible and
strong.

The Bird Kingdom

Before studying any group of animals, particularly a group as large and diverse as the birds, it is helpful to put the various members into subgroups which reflect evolutionary trends and affinities. Unfortunately, the fossil record is frequently far from complete so that the reconstruction of the various branches of the evolutionary tree must to some extent be a matter of guesswork. Although this is certainly true of the bird kingdom, it is nevertheless possible to classify birds in a reasonably satisfactory manner.

Where the classification of animals or plants is concerned, much is owed to the great Swedish naturalist, Carl von Linné (1707-1778), often known as Linnaeus, who introduced what is known as the binomial system of scientific or Latin names. His system involves the use of two Latin names—one for the genus and one for the species. The genus is a purely artificial concept whereby species which are assumed to be close relatives are grouped together under a single name. Most surface-feeding ducks, for example, are put together into the genus *Anas*. The species, on the other hand, is a fundamental unit because it refers to a particular animal that exists in nature, for example *Anas platyrhynchos*, commonly known as the mallard.

Families and orders

Higher classification involves the grouping of genera into families and families into orders. For completeness the name of the first person to describe the animal scientifically may be placed after the name of the species. Thus in the case of the mallard (which was described by von Linné) its classification would be given as follows: order *Anseriformes*, family *Anatidae* (which is simply the Latin name for the duck family), genus *Anas* and species *Anas platyrhynchos* Linné. If the describer's name is shown in brackets the species has been transferred from the genus in which it was originally placed. For example the rock thrush, was first named by von Linné as *Turdus saxatilis* Linné, but further study showed that it resembled birds in the genus *Monticola* rather than those in the genus *Turdus*. The same bird is now known as *Monticola saxatilis* (Linné).

Both internal and external features of a species are taken into account when classifying it into a particular genus, family or order. Often, though by no means always, members of the same order are so very alike, for example the owls (order *Strigiformes*), that classification presents few difficulties.

Just as no two humans are exactly alike no two specimens of a species are ever exactly alike, although no one would doubt that they are of the same kind and should be classified together. How then is a species to be defined when individual characteristics vary? A suitable definition might be that it is a group of similar animals occupying a well defined geographical area and breeding with each other but not with those that differ from them either physically or in behaviour.

Jacana

Hans Reinhard/Bruce Coleman

Left and above: A purple heron, *Ardea purpurea*, with its young, and a bluethroat, *Luscinia svecica*. The herons constitute one of six families belonging to the order *Ciconiiformes*, the others being the shoebills, the storks, the hammerheads, the ibises and the flamingos. All these birds have long legs and live close to water. They move about in the shallows with slow, deliberate steps. The bluethroat is a typical member of the order *Passeriformes*, the perching birds.

Below: A blue-footed booby, *Sula nebouxii*, with its young. These birds belong to the order *Pelecaniformes*. One of the features which characterize members of this order is the curious structure of their feet which, in addition to being webbed, have a forward pointing hind toe. This is a clear distinction from ducks and geese. Most *Pelecaniformes* are large or medium-sized birds which obtain their food from the sea, often by diving. Gannets may dive from heights of 15 m (50 ft) or more.

Right: A peregrine falcon, *Falco peregrinus*, with its young. Birds of prey belong to the order *Falconiformes* and they are easily distinguished from other birds by their short, hooked beaks and powerful talons. They have very keen eyesight. These characteristics are adaptations for seizing and feeding on living prey. Peregrine falcons are perhaps the most effective of all birds of prey. They can reach speeds of nearly 320 kph (200 mph) when swooping on their prey.

Eric Hosking

R. Fieselmann/Bavaria

Emperor Penguins, the largest of the spheniscifformes, stand waist high to a man. They gather in April and May to begin courting, displaying their orange ear patches.

The ostrich is the
largest living bird,
often growing to 8 feet,
of which nearly half is
neck. Only one species
now survives of the nine
in existence during the
Pliocene era.

Left: A bird of paradise, *Diphyllodes magnificus,* from New Guinea. These are perching birds belonging to the order *Passeriformes.* In the classification of birds, genera with very similar features are placed in the same family, and families which broadly resemble each other will belong to the same order. Sometimes members of the same order may look so very different from each other that it is difficult to see how they can be related. They will, however, have at least one characteristic in common, perhaps the structure of part of the skeleton, which to a scientist definitely relates them. Passeriformes have feet designed for perching. Four toes project from the same point of the leg—three forwards and one backwards. The design of the bony palate is characteristic of the order, and is only rarely seen in other birds. More than a fifth of all living bird species are *Passeriformes.*

Right: The brown pelican, *Pelecanus occidentalis.* Pelicans belong to the order *Pelecaniformes* as do a number of other sea birds, such as gannets and cormorants, which nest in colonies.

Marc Lelo/Jacana

Okapia

Bavaria

Right: The razor-billed auk, *Alca torda,* is a sea bird which inhabits the shores and islands of the North Atlantic. It belongs to the order *Charadriiformes* along with a wide variety of wading birds, gulls and terns. Although members of this order come in many different forms and sizes, they are related by internal similarities and by the composition of their blood albumin. The auk family, which also includes the guillemots and puffins, feeds mainly on small fish and invertebrates.

Below: The golden eagle, *Aquila chryseatos,* is the most powerful of all birds of prey. Its victims include other birds, young deer, foxes (as in this picture) and even wolves. It is a typical member of the order *Falconiformes.* Eagles of the genus *Aquila* (there are nine different species) are found in all parts of the world except South America. The largest of these, the golden eagle, has a wingspan of about 2.1 m (7 ft), the females being slightly larger than the males.

This is by no means a perfect definition, but it is perhaps the closest to the facts as they are observed in nature.

Sub-species

Within any individual species, particularly one with a wide distribution, a further problem may be the existence of separate, distinctive populations. These are called sub-species or geographical races. They are distinguished by the addition of a third scientific name added to the name of the species. Thus it has been shown that the mallard of Greenland is slightly different from that found in Europe. The form occurring in Europe is therefore named *Anas platyrhynchos platyrhynchos* Linné while the Greenland variant is called *Anas platyrhynchos conboschas* Brehm. The naturalist C. L. Brehm was the first to distinguish the Greenland mallard from the common European variety.

In most cases sub-species of birds differ from each other only in slight variations in their colour and size. It is often necessary to examine a specimen very closely before it can be distinguished from allied races with any degree of certainty. Indeed, there are some ornithologists who do not consider that these minor differences should be recognized by name, in the belief that it is quite enough to note the localities where the variants live.

Excluding the various sub-species, there are something like 8,600 species of birds living in the world today. Ornithologists hold diverse opinions as to the number of orders and families that these represent, but the system of classification most widely adopted today is that of the American ornithologist J. L. Peters, based on the system of his fellow American Alexander Westmore. This system recognizes 27 orders and about 150 families. In the chart that follows the English equivalent of the family name is used.

Visage/Jacana

Ostrich
Struthioniformes

Rhea
Rheiformes

Cassowary
Casuariiformes

Albatross
Procellariiformes

Pelican
Pelecaniformes

Flamingo
Ciconiiformes

Parrot
Psittaciformes

Crane
Gruiformes

Gull
Charadriiformes

Pigeon
Columbiformes

Mousebird
Coliiformes

Humming bird
Apodiformes

THE 27 ORDERS OF
LIVING BIRDS

Kiwi
Apterygiformes

Tinamou
Tinamiformes

Penguin
Sphenisciformes

Diver
Gaviiformes

Goose
Anseriformes

Grebe
Podicipediformes

Secretary bird
Falconiformes

Turaco
Cuculiformes

Curassow
Galliformes

Owl
Strigiformes

Roller
Coraciiformes

Frogmouth
Caprimulgiformes

Toucan
Piciformes

Crow
Passeriformes

...niformes

Columbiformes
1. Sandgrouse
2. Pigeon

Psittaciformes
Parrot

Cuculiformes
1. Turaco
2. Cuckoo

Strigiformes
1. Barn owl
2. Typical owl

Caprimulgiformes
1. Oil bird
2. Frogmouth
3. Potoo
4. Owlet frogmouth
5. Nightjar

Apodiformes
1. Swift
2. Crested swift
3. Humming bird

Coliiformes
Mousebird

Trogoniformes
Trogon

Coraciiformes
1. Kingfisher
2. Tody
3. Motmot
4. Bee-eater
5. Cuckoo roller
6. Roller
7. Hoopoe
8. Wood hoopoe
9. Hornbill

Piciformes
1. Jacamar
2. Puffbird
3. Barbet
4. Honeyguide
5. Toucan
6. Woodpecker

Passeriformes
1. Broadbill
2. Woodhewer
3. Ovenbird
4. Antbird
5. Antpipit
6. Tapaculo
7. Pitta
8. Asity
9. New Zealand wren
10. Tyrant flycatcher
11. Manakin
12. Cotinga
13. Plantcutter
14. Lyrebird
15. Scrub bird
16. Lark
17. Swallow
18. Wagtail
19. Cuckoo shrike
20. Bulbul
21. Leafbird
22. Shrike
23. Vanga
24. Waxwing
25. Palmchat
26. Dipper
27. Wren
28. Mockingbird
29. Accentor
30. Thrush, gnatcatcher,
    warbler and babbler
31. Tit
32. Nuthatch
33. Treecreeper
34. Flowerpecker
35. Sunbird
36. White eye
37. Honeyeater
38. Bunting
39. American warbler
40. Honeycreeper
41. Vireo
42. Oriole
43. Finch
44. Weaver finch
45. Weaver and sparrow
46. Starling
47. Drongo
48. Wattlebird
49. Magpie lark
50. Wood swallow
51. Magpie
52. Bowerbird
53. Bird of paradise
54. Crow

207

Bird Anatomy

The dinosaurs which once populated much of the earth's surface belonged to the reptile group *Archosauria*, and it was from a two-legged member of this group that the first birds evolved. In the course of evolution a considerable number of internal and external changes took place to equip the animal for life in the air. The heavy reptilian scales became feathers, the fore-limbs developed into wings and the bones of the skeleton were reduced both in numbers and weight. At the same time features evolved which are also observed in mammals. In particular birds became warm-blooded and their arterial and venous circulation in the heart were separated. This allowed them to adopt the active lifestyle so characteristic of the group today.

External features

A bird's feathers determine the contours and colour of its body. This unique covering, which is both flexible and light, protects the skin, provides insulation against heat loss and supports the bird in flight. Feathers grow only on certain areas, or feather tracts, of the skin. Between the feather tracts are bare spaces (*apteria*) which can be clearly seen if the feathers of a bird are parted. Penguins are an interesting exception in that their feathers grow all over the skin, presumably as a special protection against the extreme cold of Antarctica.

The feathers are periodically replaced by moulting, a process made necessary by wear, fading and loss. All birds moult at least once a year and some undergo a second and even a third moult. To ensure that large areas of the body are not left bare at any one time, moulting takes place gradually and, in the case of the flight feathers, is usually accomplished by shedding symmetrical pairs so that flight is not greatly impeded. Notable exceptions are geese and ducks, many of which undergo a large scale moult of the flight feathers in a relatively short time, leaving them flightless for a period of weeks.

The colours and patterns of a bird's plumage are often very vivid: they may provide concealment, a means of recognition and also a form of sexual stimulation. The colours are produced, as in other animals, partly by pigments and partly by the reflection and diffraction of light falling on the feather. The most usual pigments are yellows, browns and black, called *melanins*, which are produced by special cells in nipple-like structures on the skin called *papillae*. The melanins are incorporated into the feather during early formation and growth. The red colour of species like flamingos is produced by the pigment *zooerythrin*, whereas blue is often a reflection from a porous layer overlying melanin pigment. White is simply the result of reflection.

The absence of teeth and the development of the forelimbs as wings means that a bird's bill must serve both as a mouth and as hands. It is thus used for a range of functions including the capture and eating of food, gathering and arranging nest material, preening and defence. The bill is a development of the horny covering of the jaws and it grows continually to

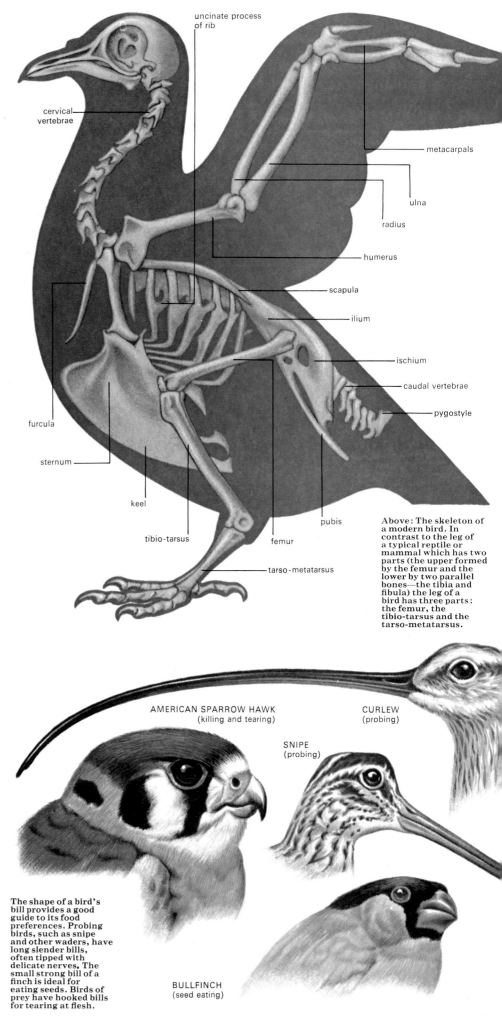

Above: The skeleton of a modern bird. In contrast to the leg of a typical reptile or mammal which has two parts (the upper formed by the femur and the lower by two parallel bones—the tibia and fibula) the leg of a bird has three parts: the femur, the tibio-tarsus and the tarso-metatarsus.

AMERICAN SPARROW HAWK
(killing and tearing)

CURLEW
(probing)

SNIPE
(probing)

BULLFINCH
(seed eating)

The shape of a bird's bill provides a good guide to its food preferences. Probing birds, such as snipe and other waders, have long slender bills, often tipped with delicate nerves. The small strong bill of a finch is ideal for eating seeds. Birds of prey have hooked bills for tearing at flesh.

Left: This blue and yellow macaw, *Ara ararauna*, from South America has the short hooked bill typical of parrots. The bill is used not only for feeding (macaws can crack open very hard nutshells) but also as a means of getting about. The birds spend much of their time climbing in trees and the bill is a useful 'third foot'.

Right: The puffin, *Fratercula arctica*, uses its beak both for catching fish and excavating the burrow in which it builds its nest. As with most birds the eyes are set at the side of the head. This provides a very wide field of view but only very limited binocular (3-D) vision.

NHPA

P. Morris

Left: The spoonbill, *Platalea leucorodia*, has a long flat bill which it uses to sieve food organisms from the water. The two nostrils (called nares) can be seen at the upper end of the bill. The sense of smell, however, is only poorly developed in birds, and in some species it is absent altogether.

Right: A long-eared owl, *Asio otus*. As well as having upper and lower eyelids, birds possess a third eye covering, called the nictating membrane, which keeps the eye clean. In this picture the nictating membranes can be seen half way across the owl's eyes. With forward pointing eyes, owls have good 3-D vision but a poor field of view.

Frank Lane

Tierbilder Okapia

make up for wear and tear. The type of bill usually provides a good indication of food preferences. Compare, for example, the flat laminated bill of a duck adapted for straining organisms from water with the curved bill of a bird of prey, adapted for seizing and tearing flesh.

The foot of a bird generally has three toes in front and one behind, but they are modified according to their owner's way of life. Woodpeckers, for example, which can climb vertically up a tree trunk have two toes in front and two behind, and in some game birds and wading birds (including gulls), which only infrequently perch on branches, the hind toe is small or absent altogether.

The skeleton

As in most vertebrates the skeleton of a bird consists of cartilage and bone, with the latter predominating. In birds, however, lightness and strength is achieved by the presence of tubular bones which may be strutted or contain air sacs (*pneumatization*). The two limb girdles are strongly built so that each can support the entire weight of the bird—the *pectoral girdle* during flight and the *pelvic girdle* when walking or perching.

The neck is long and flexible and is usually composed of 16 cervical vertebrae, the exact number depending on the species. This arrangement allows free movement of the head for feeding and other activities. In contrast, the trunk vertebrae are close fitting and nearly rigid. The strong ribs, some possessing small projections called *uncinate processes*, which overlap to strengthen the rib cage, carry the large *sternum* and *keel* to which the main flight muscles are attached.

The skull of an adult bird is a continuous thin-walled bone structure enclosing the brain and sense organs and carrying the bill. The individual bones (which can be identified in young birds before their bones join together) show a similar arrangement to those of the archosaurian reptiles from which birds evolved. The very large sockets at the side of the skull are needed to accommodate the highly developed eyes, and the jaws are characteristically long and slender.

The internal organs

As in most vertebrates the digestive system of birds consists of a coiled tube leading from the mouth to the anus, along which food passes during digestion. Food is collected by the bill and swallowed whole with little or no mechanical break-

GOLIATH HERON
(fishing)

SHOVELLER
(sifting)

EURASIAN WIDGEON
(grazing)

down. The size and function of the tongue varies from species to species: woodpeckers and humming birds, for example, have long pointed tongues for obtaining food whereas parrots have short fleshy tongues. In some birds the tongue is almost absent. From the mouth the food passes down the long oesophagus into a distensible crop (if present) to be stored. After that it enters the stomach, which consists of a soft *proventriculus* secreting digestive juices and a muscular *gizzard* where the food is ground up into small particles. Finally, a long coiled intestine leads from the gizzard to the rectum.

The nervous system of a bird resembles that of a reptile (particularly certain lizards and crocodiles) but the brain is proportionately about ten times larger. Not surprisingly the regions of the brain responsible for co-ordination, the *cerebral hemispheres*, are usually conspicuously large, especially in parrots, crows and owls. Exceptions are the game birds, plovers and pigeons which have only relatively small cerebral hemispheres. Birds have very keen sight but a poor sense of smell, and this is reflected in the size of the optic and olfactory lobes of the brain.

Birds, like mammals, possess a highly efficient circulatory system which undoubtedly plays an important part in controlling body temperature. An efficient four-chambered heart provides completely separate systems for the circulation of blood round the body and circulation through the lungs. The lungs, though relatively small, have a large internal surface for gaseous interchange. They are augmented by air sacs, thin-walled reservoirs which extend from the bronchi (the bronchi are tubes leading from the windpipe to the lungs) into the body cavity and the bones. The wings also form a significant part of a bird's respiratory apparatus, for the movement of wing-beats greatly assists in breathing out.

Senses
Sight is extremely well developed and highly efficient in birds, enabling them to locate food and mates, to navigate, to return to their nest site and to warn them of approaching danger.

The general structure of the eye is similar to that of other vertebrates—a lens situated within the large cavity (*vitreous body*) of the eye protected by a transparent *cornea*. Light entering the eye through the cornea is focused by the lens on to a large, light-sensitive screen, the *retina*, at the back of the eye which

Above left: A black swan, *Cygnus atratus*, from Australia. Birds have keen eyesight, so it is not surprising that the colour and pattern of their plumage plays an important part both in recognition and sexual stimulation. Black and brown colours are produced by pigments called melanins.

Above: A purple gallinule, *Porphyrula martinica*, holds water weed in its foot while feeding. The centre of gravity of a bird's body lies directly over its feet. This enables it to balance without needing the complex system of back muscles found in other vertebrates to support the front of the body.

Above: A malachite kingfisher, *Corythornis cristatus*, from Africa with a newly caught fish. Kingfishers' eyes are equipped with two foveas (regions of the retina where vision is most distinct). When they dive under water, the image simply transfers from one fovea to the other and so remains in focus.

Above: A shoebill, *Balaeniceps rex*. These normally solitary birds live in the marshlands of tropical Africa and feed on such things as fish, frogs and snails. To help them hold on to slippery prey the inside of the bill is serrated.

Left: A greater flamingo, *Phoenicopterus ruber*, straining algae, small crustaceans and other aquatic organisms from the water. Its bill is specially modified for feeding in this way. Water is pumped through the inside of the beak by forward and backward movements of the bird's fleshy tongue. Food particles are filtered out as the water is expelled over ridged filtering areas inside the beak.

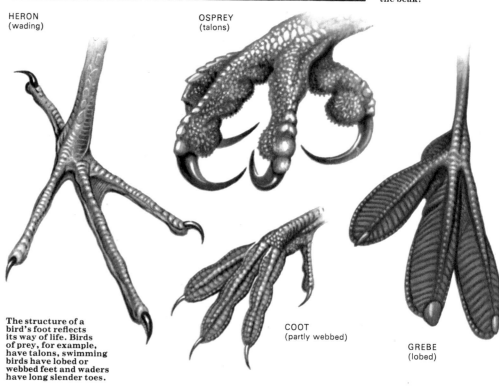

HERON
(wading)

OSPREY
(talons)

COOT
(partly webbed)

GREBE
(lobed)

The structure of a bird's foot reflects its way of life. Birds of prey, for example, have talons, swimming birds have lobed or webbed feet and waders have long slender toes.

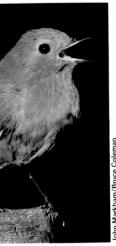

Left: The Eurasian robin, *Erithacus rubecula*, is a typical perching bird. When perching on a branch a bird usually 'squats' with its legs folded under it. The result of this is a tightening of the tendons in the leg which causes the toes to wrap around the branch so that the bird becomes 'locked' on to its perch. In this way it can sleep without danger of falling.

Below: The lappet-faced vulture, *Torgos tracheliotus*, is an inhabitant of central and southern Africa. Vultures perform a useful function in disposing of the remains of dead animals. Dangerous bacteria are destroyed in their digestive systems.

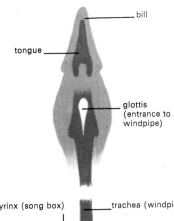

bill

tongue

glottis (entrance to windpipe)

syrinx (song box)

trachea (windpipe)

bronchi

cervical air sac

lungs

abdominal air sac

thoracic air sacs

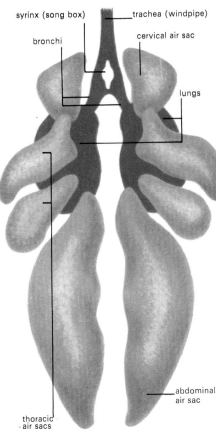

Above: A bird's vocal cords are situated in a special box, the syrinx, which lies at the junction of the windpipe and the two bronchi. The bronchi pass through the lungs (which are fairly small) and have side branches not only to the lung tissue but also to the large air sacs which help respiration.

Below: A section through the eye of a bird. The pecten is a structure peculiar to birds; it may help them to detect movement. A hawk's eye is about eight times better than the human eye at distinguishing detail because its retina has many more visual cells. The most sensitive parts of the retina are the foveas.

MALLARD (webbed)

WOODPECKER (climbing)

RAVEN (perching)

cornea

iris

lens

vitreous body

fovea

pecten

optic nerve

retina

fovea

passes visual information to the brain along the optic nerve. A feature peculiar to the eye of birds is the *pecten*, a structure located at the back of the vitreous body and composed almost entirely of blood vessels.

Birds have relatively large eyes compared to other vertebrates. The eye almost fills the entire space available in the skull, so that movement of the eye within the socket is very limited. The most extreme example is to be found in the nocturnal owls which cannot move their eyes at all. To compensate for this, a bird's head is extremely mobile. Birds that are active during the day can distinguish colours, but nocturnal birds cannot. The range of colour vision is similar to that of man. In nocturnal species such as owls increased sensitivity for night vision is obviously helpful; they have a large cornea and lens which allows more light to enter the eye.

All the evidence suggests that the hearing abilities of birds are similar to those of man, although the range of audible frequencies is reduced by one or more octaves at each end of the range. Within that reduced range, however, their hearing is considerably more acute than human hearing: they can separate sounds which to the human ear appear as one continuous note. Two genera, the oil birds, *Steatornis*, and the swiftlets, *Collocalia*, have developed an echo-location system (rather like an aircraft's radar) which enables them to fly about in the dark caves where they breed.

The sense of smell is only poorly developed in birds, and in some species it may be absent altogether. The olfactory organs are situated in paired nasal cavities at the base of the bill, opening to the exterior through two nostrils, *nares*.

Bird song

The sounds of birds are a familiar and enjoyable feature of the countryside, particularly in spring, for their principal function is associated with breeding. Bird calls are usually very distinctive and so they provide a good method of identifying different species.

The vocal cords are situated in a special box, the *syrinx*, at the base of the windpipe where it divides into two bronchi. This contrasts with mammals whose vocal cords are at the top of the windpipe in the larynx. In fact birds do have a larynx but it is voiceless. The syrinx has a bony framework and forms a sound box within which membranes vibrate when the bird exhales, producing all the varied sounds of bird song. The structure of the syrinx varies from species to species and seven different types have been recognized.

A few birds such as cormorants and pelicans are voiceless, others have a simple call, while birds belonging to the sub-order *Oscines* (the so-called 'songbirds') have a definite song. The song of these birds has a pitch of about 4,300 Hz, which is above the highest note of the piano. Simple bird calls vary from the deep pitched hoot of owls to the very high notes of some small birds which are scarcely audible to the human ear. Songs and calls are an important method of communication among birds. They are used in the breeding season to attract mates, to warn other birds of danger from predators and to establish home territories.

211

Bird Flight

In conquering the air birds have set themselves apart from all other vertebrate animals. Although some other groups have developed the power of flight, notably the now extinct pterosaurs (reptiles) and the present day bats (mammals), none has achieved the mastery displayed by birds. Their flying ability meant that they could colonize previously inaccessible habitats and enabled them to escape easily from most ground-based predators. With these advantages, birds rapidly spread into many different regions all over the world.

More than any other single feature it was the development of feathers that gave birds their advantage over other flying animals. Just how or why feathers first evolved is a mystery: possibly they developed as an insulating layer when the ancestors of birds became warm blooded. Whatever the reason it was a development that led to a highly successful class of animals; there are more than 8,000 species of birds living today.

Feathers

There are three principal types of feather: contour feathers called *pennae*, down feathers called *plumulae* and hair-like feathers called *filoplumes*. Most of the body is covered with contour feathers, the most noticeable being the flight feathers, or *remiges*, on the wing and the tail feathers, or *rectrices*. Most birds only possess down feathers when they are young, these being shed before the young bird leaves the nest. The filoplumes are usually hidden underneath the other feathers, but they can be seen in some birds, such as thrushes, at the nape of the neck. They are plainly visible on a chicken or turkey which has just been plucked.

The growth of a feather begins with the formation of a conical projection of soft tissue under the outermost layer of skin (the epidermis). The base of this 'feather bud' then sinks down to form a follicle which will hold the feather firmly in position. The outermost epidermal cells develop into a smooth, hardened sheath within which the feather proper begins to form. A large central rib of epidermal tissue inside the sheath eventually forms the shaft of the feather while smaller ribs on either side of it form the *barbs* which make up the two vanes. As it grows the feather is fed by a network of blood vessels in the shaft, but these dry up as soon as growth is complete. Once the feather is fully formed, the sheath is no longer needed; it splits and breaks and is removed by preening.

The main feathers of the wing are the flight feathers, divided according to position into *primaries*, *secondaries* and *tertiaries*. The primaries (there are usually 11 of them) are attached to the outer part of the wing which is supported by the *metacarpal* and *phalanx* bones. The more numerous secondaries are carried by the *ulna* which, together with the *radius*, forms the central part of the wing skeleton. The inner section of the wing skeleton, the *humerus* bone, carries a small number of tertiary feathers. The bases of the large flight feathers are protected by smaller feathers called *coverts*. On the upper side of the wing these form three

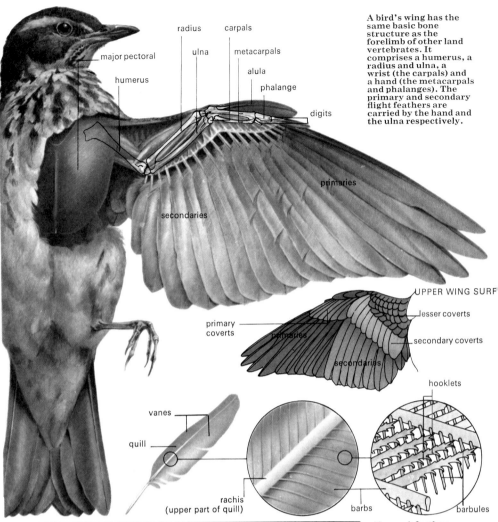

radius · carpals · ulna · metacarpals · alula · phalange · major pectoral · humerus · digits · primaries · secondaries

A bird's wing has the same basic bone structure as the forelimb of other land vertebrates. It comprises a humerus, a radius and ulna, a wrist (the carpals) and a hand (the metacarpals and phalanges). The primary and secondary flight feathers are carried by the hand and the ulna respectively.

UPPER WING SURF
lesser coverts
primary coverts
primaries
secondary coverts
secondaries

vanes
quill
hooklets
rachis (upper part of quill)
barbs
barbules

Above: A feather consists of a central quill and two vanes. Each vane is composed of a network of criss-crossing barbs and barbules. The forward pointing barbules are equipped with small hooks which catch on to the backward pointing barbules so as to hold the whole structure of the vane together.

Left: The 'eye' marking on the end of a peacock's tail feather. It is only in this region of the feather that the barbs cling closely together. Perhaps the most well known of ornamental birds, peacocks are admired in their native India not only for their beauty but also because they eat young snakes, notably cobras.

rachis
aftershaft
calamus

Giuseppe Mazza

212

Above: A watercolour of a bird's wing by Albrecht Durer and dated 1512. Like his contemporary Leonardo da Vinci, Durer was very interested in the workings of the natural world. This picture is almost scientific in its detail, and the primary, secondary and covert feathers are plainly visible.

distinct rows known as the greater, median and lesser coverts, but underneath the wing they cannot be distinguished from one another and simply form a general lining.

Part of the outer section of the wing (the second digit) carries a small number of feathers and can be moved independently of the main wing. This structure is known as the bastard wing, or *alula*, and it serves an important function in preventing stalling. Along the front and rear edge of each wing is a flap of skin called the *patagium* which prevents the feathers from twisting during flight.

The tail feathers are supported by a bone called the *pygostyle*. Normally there are between six and 30 tail feathers, the most common number being 12. The length of the tail varies from species to species and may even be absent altogether. The bases of the tail feathers are, like the flight feathers, protected by coverts. These are usually quite small but in some species, notably the peacock, *Pavo cristatus*, they are long and brightly coloured.

Aerodynamics of bird flight

A bird, like an aircraft, must overcome three forces in order to fly: gravity, air resistance and air turbulence. Gravity is overcome by an upward force (lift) which results from the flow of air past the curved wing surfaces. The upper wing surface is convex (outwardly curved) while the lower surface is concave (inwardly curved), which means that air flows faster over the upper surface than the lower surface. This in turn causes a reduction of air pressure above the wing so that the wing is pushed upwards by the relatively higher air pressure underneath it. Air resistance opposes the forward movement of the bird through the air and is counteracted by muscular energy in flapping the wings or, when gliding, by losing height. To reduce air resistance to a minimum birds have developed a smooth, elongated body and thin, tapering wings. Turbulence is controlled by forming 'slots' in the wing surfaces. This is done by fanning out the primary feathers at the wing tips and by moving the bastard wing away from the front edge of the wing proper.

To provide the mechanical energy needed for flight birds have two large flight muscles, the major and minor *pectorals*. Half of the total muscle tissue of a bird is concentrated in these two muscles. They are anchored to the breast bone (the *sternum*) and the collar bone (the *furcula*), the former having a broad extension called the *keel* for the purpose. In the wing the end of the major pectoral is attached to the underside of the humerus by a tendon which passes through a hole in the pectoral girdle.

A bird does not use its wings to 'swim' in the air, rather the ends of the primary feathers are bent back and function like the blades of a propeller to pull the bird forwards. The primaries are responsible for movement through the air while the secondaries provide most of the lift. As the wing flaps up and down, the wing tips follow a figure-of-eight path, the lower loop being much smaller than the upper one. On the down stroke the feathers are flattened against each other and form an unbroken, air-resistant surface, while on the up stroke they rotate and allow air to pass between them with relatively little resistance. The downward stroke, driven

PTERODACTYL

membranous flap

BAT

PERMANENT DOWN FEATHER

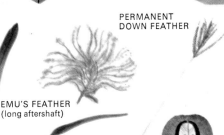

EMU'S FEATHER
(long aftershaft)

FILOPLUME

NESTLING'S DOWN FEATHER

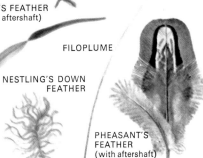

PHEASANT'S FEATHER
(with aftershaft)

Left: The wing of a pterodactyl (an extinct reptile) and a bat are each quite different from that of a bird. The working surface of the wing is made up of a membranous flap which extends from an elongated digit or digits on the forelimb to the hind limb. Neither pterodactyls nor bats have feathers.

Above: Because it is so heavy, this whooper swan, *Cygnus cygnus*, has to paddle clumsily over the surface of the water before it can take off. Its webbed feet serve both to push it along during take-off and to slow it down on landing. Swans cannot obtain the lift needed for take-off simply by flapping their wings.

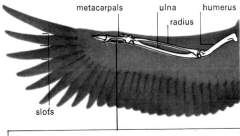

metacarpals   ulna   humerus
radius

slots

Left: Various different types of feather. Some are distinguished from normal feathers by having barbs which are not coupled to each other. The aftershaft branches from the junction between the upper and lower sections of the quill (the rachis and the calamus). Some feathers have no aftershaft.

Above: A section through a bird's wing bone shows that it is hollow and reinforced by a number of bony struts. This makes the bone both light and, for its weight, very strong. Hollow bones are a characteristic feature of birds: they are not found in other flying vertebrates such as bats.

213

Left: A razor-billed auk, *Alca torda*, coming in to land. The bird spreads its wings, legs and tail against the direction of flight to slow itself down before reaching the ground.

Right: The great crested grebe, *Podiceps cristatus*, is designed for strong, fast flight and streamlining is very marked. The eleven primary flight feathers can be clearly seen at the end of each wing.

Far right: A brown pelican, *Pelecanus occidentalis*, from the Pacific coasts of North and South America comes in to land at its nest. It uses its wings, tail and feet to slow it down in much the same way as the razor-billed auk (left).

Left: A Galapagos hawk, *Buteo galapagoensis*, hovers in mid-air as it scans the ground for prey. To counteract the effects of air turbulence, the ends of the wings are deeply slotted and the small bastard wing, or alula, projects from the front edge of the wing. The tail feathers, or rectrices, prevent forward movement and help the hawk to hold a constant position.

Right: The shape and size of a bird's wing is a good indication of how the bird flies. For example, soaring birds like vultures have long broad wings whereas fast fliers like swifts have thin swept-back wings. Gliding birds like fulmars have long thin wings.

VULTURE

(soaring)

BUZZARD

FULMAR (gliding)

(high speed)

HOBBY

HAWK

Below: An eagle owl, *Bubo bubo*, in flight. Owls hunt their prey by night, and their plumage is specially adapted to this way of life. Long bristles extending beyond the feathers eliminate flapping sounds so that the bird can pounce silently on its prey. The colour and pattern serve as camouflage.

by the major pectoral muscle, is thus the power stroke.

The weight supported by a given area of wing, called the 'wing loading', varies from species to species and is greatest in large birds. Each square centimetre (there are 6.5 square centimetres in a square inch) of a swan's wing supports two grams (0.07 oz) of the bird's weight whereas the same area of a goldcrest's wing supports only 0.1 gm.

Take-off and landing

A bird cannot fly unless air is flowing over the wing surfaces because this is how it obtains lift. The simplest method of take-off is for the bird to spread its wings and drop from an elevated perch, or to take-off into the wind. If, however, it is on the ground on a still day it must set up an artificial airstream by flapping its wings. To get the maximum possible lift (the faster the airflow the greater the lift) heavy birds often run along the ground or paddle along the water surface during take-off. Small birds do not normally need to do this and simply leap into the air. A few long-winged species such as swifts cannot take off from the ground, so they must always land on a perch above ground so that they can drop into flight.

A bird has to reduce its speed very rapidly when landing. To do this, most birds make a sudden glide upwards just before reaching the ground. The wings are spread out to act as air brakes and may be flapped against the direction of movement. The bastard wing is extended just before the stalling speed is reached and the legs are extended to absorb the shock of landing. Spreading the tail feathers also helps to reduce speed for landing. Landing

on water is easier than on land because the bird's speed at the moment of touch-down can be relatively high, the water itself being used as a brake. The large webbed feet of species such as ducks are important in landing: they act as brakes, both when the bird is still in the air and when it first touches the water.

Types of bird flight

The shape of the wing and tail of a bird is a good indication of the way it flies and this in turn is related to its way of life. Large, heavy, soaring birds, such as vultures and buzzards, have large broad wings, prominent bastard wings, deeply slotted wing tips and a broad tail. Fast gliding birds, such as albatrosses and gulls, have long narrow wings and only limited slotting. The high speed powered flight of swifts and falcons requires long swept back wings with little or no slotting. A number of birds, such as pheasants and hawks, are capable of short bursts of speed and have a considerable man-oeuvring ability. Short broad wings and long broad tails equip them for this sort of flight. Some birds, particularly birds of prey, are capable of hovering but only one group, the humming birds, can fly backwards. They do this by swivelling the wings at the shoulder.

To reduce the amount of energy needed to remain aloft, birds make extensive use of air currents. Soaring birds can often be seen rising and circling in columns of warm air (thermals). Species which live on coastal cliffs make use of the air currents created by both on-shore and off-shore winds—the former give rise to updraughts while the latter create rolling eddies as they pass over the cliff edge.

Above: Humming birds' wings are almost rigid but are connected to the 'shoulder' by a remarkable swivel joint which allows the leading edge of the wing to point forwards during the forward wingbeat and backwards during the backward wingbeat. This enables the bird to hover, fly straight upwards or backwards.

Frank Lane

W. Fuchs/ZEFA

M. Morecombe/NHPA

MAGPIE   PHEASANT

(bursts of speed)

Above: A hermit humming bird, *Phaethornis*, feeding on nectar. The human eye is unable to perceive the movement of a humming bird's wing—there are between 50 and 75 wingbeats per second in hovering flight. Being so small and so active, humming birds feed constantly—mainly on insects and nectar.

Above: A crimson rosella, *Platycercus elegans*, about to land on a tree. Its clawed toes reach forwards to grasp the tree trunk.

Below: A blue tit, *Parus caeruleus*, frozen by the camera in mid-flight. These birds have small rounded wings and cannot fly for long distances.

The most effective use of air currents, however, takes place over the sea. Because of frictional resistance between the air and the sea surface, the air in a wind travels slower the closer it is to the sea. Large gliding birds, such as albatrosses and fulmars, use these conditions to sail in a series of regular circling movements. They move down-wind losing height and then turn up-wind to gain height by entering a faster moving layer. This all takes place within 20 m (65 ft) of the surface of the sea and can continue for many hours with only occasional wing beats. Gulls following ships also make use of the local upcurrents created by the movement of the vessel.

Accurate determinations of the speed of bird flight are hard to obtain. The smaller perching birds such as sparrows fly at between 30 and 50 kph (18 to 31 mph), while migrating ducks may reach speeds of around 80 kph (50 mph). The normal speed of a racing pigeon is also thought to be around 80 kph. The fastest of all birds is said to be the peregrine falcon, *Falco peregrinus*. An experiment carried out in Germany has shown that a peregrine reaches speeds of between 270 and 320 kph (167 to 198 mph) when swooping on prey.

As a result of sighting from aircraft and radar, there is more information available about the heights at which different birds fly. Most birds keep well below 150 m (500 ft) during normal local movements, but they may fly much higher during migration. Migrating wading birds have been observed at heights of at least 6,000 m (20,000 ft). Smaller migrants, such as perching birds, cannot reach such heights —they rarely fly above 1,500 m (5,000 ft).

Stephen Dalton/NHPA

215

Bird Migration

Migration is fairly common in the animal kingdom—some species of fish, whales, turtles, insects, bats and land mammals (including man) all migrate. But birds are unique among the migratory animals; their powers of flight give them exceptional mobility and they have a remarkable ability to navigate over immense distances.

Bird migration is a seasonal shift in the centre of gravity of a population; a regular move both in season and direction involving a 'round trip'. In many cases the entire population of the species moves from a winter to a summer range separated by hundreds or even thousands of kilometres: these are called total migrants. Sometimes, however, the summer and winter ranges overlap or only part of the population migrates. Birds which follow this pattern of migration are known as partial migrants.

Some groups that regularly disperse at a particular season are not, strictly speaking, migrants at all because there is no mass movement in any particular direction; the population simply becomes more scattered. Some British seabirds arrive with great regularity each spring at their coastal colonies and depart again when breeding is over, but during the winter they wander widely. Kittiwakes, *Rissa tridactyla*, for example, range extensively over the Atlantic, reaching as far south as 40°N (the latitude of Madrid), westwards to the Grand Bank of Newfoundland and north to Greenland, while others may remain in home waters.

The reasons for migration

Apart from the enormous physical demands they make, these journeys can only be hazardous—they lead birds across hostile environments and, especially in the case of young birds, to unfamiliar habitats. For those species which do migrate, however, the risks involved in doing so are clearly less than those involved in staying put; were it not so, natural selection would have eliminated the migrating habit.

Migration is therefore concerned with survival and with food supply, and in the case of those species such as swallows, *Hirundinidae*, swifts, *Apodidae*, and flycatchers, *Muscicapidae*, which feed on flying insects, to remain in colder climates in winter would be impossible. Because the long cold winter night of the Arctic is an impossibly harsh environment for all but a very few highly specialized birds, many residents migrate southwards after feeding on the myriads of insects which flourish in the short summer.

The reasons for some migratory patterns, however, are less obvious. Many European swallows winter north of the equator, where there is evidently an adequate supply of insect food. Yet British breeding swallows fly on for thousands of kilometres to winter in the extreme south of Africa. What benefit they derive from this further journey is a mystery.

Equally perplexing is the case of the lapwing, *Vanellus vanellus*. This familiar bird is a partial migrant which suggests that the balance of advantage between staying put and migrating is a delicate

one and not yet firmly resolved one way or the other. Each year countless lapwings from northern and central Europe come to winter in Britain and Ireland, escaping the snow-covered landscape which deprives them of access to food. In Britain, and especially in Ireland, the snow cover is usually brief, so the advantage to the immigrant lapwings is obvious. The odd thing is that perhaps half of all British lapwings migrate to spend the winter in the south of France and Spain, their places being taken by the immigrant lapwings from the North.

The evolution of migration

The wheatear, *Oenanthe oenanthe*, is one of the clearest examples of the evolution of migration. Primarily a bird of rocky uplands, the population breeding in western Europe has a relatively simple journey southward into Africa, where it winters in semi-desert country to the south of the Sahara. At some time after the last ice age, however, the species colonised first Iceland, then Greenland, and finally northeast Canada. Remarkably, these pioneering populations retained the same winter home in Africa, their migratory journeys getting longer and longer with each stage. In the process of evolution these northern birds have grown bigger and longer winged than their southern relatives, so becoming better equipped to face the long overseas flights.

It seems probable that a number of species originally made rather short simple migratory journeys which subsequently became much longer as they extended their range. The pied flycatcher, *Ficedula hypoleuca*, appears to have evolved in the west of Europe; it migrates from there southwards to Spain and Africa each autumn. A successful species, it has spread eastwards in the course of history and now breeds well to the east of Moscow. One might suppose that these eastern birds would follow a simple southward route into Africa, yet ringing has shown that they travel in a south westerly direction and first fly to the

Right: One of the most remarkable migrants is the wheatear, *Oenanthe oenanthe*. Colonies are found in Alaska and Greenland, and both groups spend the winter in Africa. Curiously they migrate to their winter home by quite different routes. The Alaskan birds travel westwards across Asia while the Greenland group travel eastwards by way of Iceland and western Europe.

Below: It is not only large species like the pintail duck, *Anas acuta*, that are capable of migration. The tiny ruby-throated humming bird, *Archilochus colubris*, migrates each year across the Gulf of Mexico from the eastern United States to central America.

D. N. Dalton/NHPA

Pintail duck

Ruby-throated humming bird

Below: Golden plovers, *Pluvialis apricaria*, on migration. The golden plover nests in northern Europe and Canada, migrating to southwest Europe, North Africa and South America for the winter. It is a wading bird but prefers drier land than its cousins the curlews, sandpipers and snipe.

Frank Lane

216

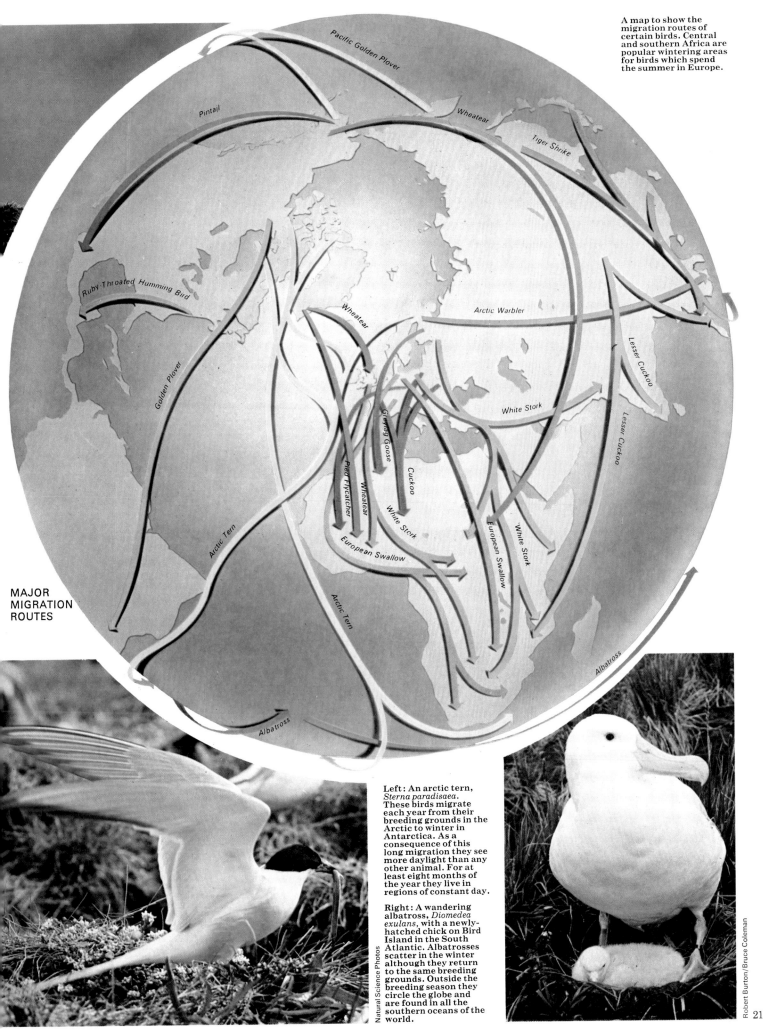

MAJOR
MIGRATION
ROUTES

A map to show the
migration routes of
certain birds. Central
and southern Africa are
popular wintering areas
for birds which spend
the summer in Europe.

Pacific Golden Plover

Pintail

Wheatear

Tiger Shrike

Ruby-Throated Humming Bird

Wheatear

Arctic Warbler

Lesser Cuckoo

Golden Plover

Greylag Goose

White Stork

Lesser Cuckoo

Pied Flycatcher

Wheatear

Cuckoo

Arctic Tern

White Stork

European Swallow

European Swallow

White Stork

Albatross

Arctic Tern

Albatross

Albatross

Left: An arctic tern,
Sterna paradisaea.
These birds migrate
each year from their
breeding grounds in the
Arctic to winter in
Antarctica. As a
consequence of this
long migration they see
more daylight than any
other animal. For at
least eight months of
the year they live in
regions of constant day.

Right: A wandering
albatross, *Diomedea
exulans*, with a newly-
hatched chick on Bird
Island in the South
Atlantic. Albatrosses
scatter in the winter
although they return
to the same breeding
grounds. Outside the
breeding season they
circle the globe and
are found in all the
southern oceans of the
world.

coast of Portugal before heading south.

Migration is, of course, part of an annual cycle. Into each twelve month period every bird must fit a breeding season, rarely lasting less than six to eight weeks and sometimes many months. There is also a period of moult, during which the bird replaces all its worn plumage with a new set of feathers. Then, for the migrants, there has to be time for two travel seasons.

The timing of migration

Most birds moult immediately after breeding is completed but some migratory species postpone the process until they have reached their winter quarters. In just a few species which breed in the extreme north, where the summer season is very short, the moult starts on the breeding grounds, is suspended for migration and is then resumed and completed further south. One species, the tiny willow warbler, *Phylloscopus trochilus*, actually undertakes two complete moults in the year, one immediately after breeding in the autumn and one in Africa before the start of the spring migration. A moult may last for six weeks or even longer in some species and, since birds normally do not moult and migrate at the same time, migration has to be fitted into those parts of the year not affected by breeding and moulting.

A migrating bird covers its long journey in a series of stages, and the time spent feeding at each 'staging post', and therefore the amount of fat deposited seems to depend on the length of the stage ahead. Thus a small insect-eating bird might leave southern Britain (most departures occur at dusk) with sufficient reserves for a flight of several hundred kilometres. There may be two or more such stages, but then for migrants travelling to tropical Africa comes the critical phase of the journey across the Sahara—a flight stage of not less than 1,600 km (1,000 miles). Remarkable though such a flight may seem, there is strong circumstantial evidence that many species take off from Spain or even from France, flying over both the Mediterranean and the Sahara in a single stage. Since their flying speed in still air is generally between 30 and 40 kph (20 to 24 mph) it is evident that many of them must fly uninterruptedly for 60 hours or more—a prodigious feat of endurance.

Navigation

One fascinating aspect of migrating birds is their ability to navigate with great precision. Using identification rings, it has been established that adult swallows and swifts, which winter south of the Sahara, tend to return to the same nest each year throughout their lives, while young ones normally return at least to the district of their birth. By taking the eggs of migratory species from the wild, hatching them in incubators and hand rearing them in isolation from others of their kind, it has been proved that young birds inherit not only a knowledge of the direction in which they must fly in autumn, but also the ability to determine that direction. Young cuckoos, *Cuculus canorus*, also travel alone to southern West Africa, departing a month or two after the adults.

Navigators require some means of holding a steady course across the featureless ocean and, before the invention of the

Above and right: The greylag goose, *Anser anser*, lives in central and northern Europe, migrating to southern and western Europe and Africa for the winter. As in other birds, the yearly cycle of migration is controlled by a biological 'programme' in each bird. This releases into the bloodstream at the correct times of year the hormones responsible for migration, breeding and moulting. The V-shaped flight formation is typical of many wild geese. The leading birds will probably have been on several previous migrations, so they will have learnt to recognize landmarks on the route. Younger birds will lie at the back of the group.

Left: A North American screech owl, *Otis asio*. A European owl belonging to the same genus, the scops owl, *Otis scops*, is a night migrant. Each year it makes its way under cover of darkness to winter in equatorial Africa.

Below: A curlew sandpiper, *Calidris ferruginea*. Many birds interrupt their long migratory journeys to build up strength for the next stage. Curlew sandpipers can be seen feeding around the coasts of Britain in the spring and autumn as they break their northerly and southerly journeys. Staging posts of this sort are vital to migrants which have to fly long distances over sea or desert. Many species seem to use traditional 'fattening areas' in southern Europe in the autumn and central Africa in the spring. These areas are vital for their survival.

Above: Starlings, *Sturnus vulgaris*, depend at least partly on the sun for their navigational skill. When the sun is shining they are able to orient themselves without difficulty, but on an overcast day their movements are much more random. Pigeons also need to see the sun for accurate navigation.

cuckoo

white stork

swallow

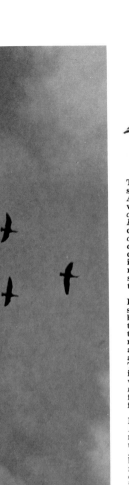

Three species which spend the winter in Africa: the European white stork, *Ciconia ciconia*, the swallow, *Hirundo rustica*, and the cuckoo, *Cuculus canorus*. The swallow is common in Britain during the summer but in the winter months it may be found as far south as the southern tip of Africa.

Right: In order to study the movements of birds it is necessary to mark individuals and this is usually done by means of light aluminium rings fixed around the right leg. The bird being ringed in this picture is a whinchat, *Saxicola rubetra*, which migrates from Europe to Africa for the winter.

Below: Adelie penguins, *Pygoscelis adeliae*, move each spring from the pack ice to the Antarctic mainland for breeding. They not only return to the same colony each year but individual birds even occupy the same nest site year after year. Among other penguin migrants are the crested penguins, *Eudyptes*.

Frank Lane

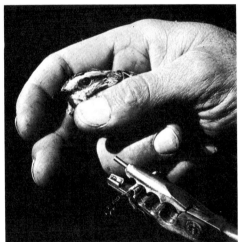

Eric Hosking

Ardea

compass, primitive man made use of both the sun and the stars. Many years ago it was noted that migrating birds tend to become disoriented when the sky is totally overcast, and this observation prompted experiments which proved that birds, too, make use of the sun to set their course. However, many migrants set off at dusk and must be able to steer in darkness. At first it was thought that they might somehow 'remember' the position of the setting sun, but the true explanation proved more remarkable. It was discovered that birds kept in a windowless room could, when taken outdoors, nevertheless 'read' the night sky. This observation led to a series of studies involving placing living birds in planetaria, from which it was deduced that while they may recognize certain constellations, they make use of the north-south axis about which the night sky appears to rotate.

Thus it seems that in determining direction birds primarily use celestial clues. Recently, however, it has been discovered that some species are apparently able to use the earth's magnetic field to guide them. Even more surprising is an Italian discovery that some birds' ability to orientate is impaired if their olfactory nerves are severed. This new evidence presents two difficulties. Firstly, because the olfactory lobes in the brains of birds are very poorly developed it has always been thought that they have very little sense of smell; secondly, even if they do have a sense of smell, it is very difficult to see how it could help them navigate.

One feature which is undoubtedly important in helping birds to navigate is their 'built-in clock'. (Human navigators need chronometers to determine the exact longitude of any position.) This clock is so accurate that even if a bird is confined for several weeks in a cellar, whose lighting bears no relation to that outside, they still follow a normal 24-hour rhythm.

Although birds do inherit a sense of direction, their navigational ability also depends to some extent on learning details of the migratory route. It is significant that most young birds fly in the company of adults; this ensures that they will arrive safely at their destination in spite of their inexperience. On the way they learn to recognize landmarks, feeding grounds and the position of their winter home. In this way some essential aspects of navigation and the geographical positions of their summer and winter homes are passed on from one generation to the next.

Bird Mating and Breeding

One of the most familiar signs of spring is the change in the behaviour of the local bird community: the winter routine of food-finding gives way to one designed to produce and care for eggs and young. Just what causes the change is not fully understood but no doubt the increase in daytime temperature, lengthening of daylight and increasing food supply from growing vegetation all play a part. Internally, hormones released into the bloodstream lead to development of the reproductive organs, which are small and inactive outside the breeding season. The combined effect of all these factors is to ensure that birds breed at the time of year when there is cover for the nest, a mild climate and abundant food.

Most birds pair off in the breeding season, the two partners co-operating in essential activities such as nest building and feeding the young. A few species, however, (particularly game birds) are polygamous, a single male bird having a number of mates. After mating, the duties of parenthood are sometimes undertaken by just one of the birds: for example, among the tinamous of South America the males are solely responsible for incubating the eggs and raising the young. Breeding normally begins with the male establishing a breeding territory.

Territories

Breeding territories are important not only as nesting sites but also as feeding grounds. In solitary species each bird may have quite a large territory—as much as several thousand hectares for a large bird of prey. Most song birds have breeding territories which extend for a few hectares. Of course in species such as gannets, *Morus bassanus*, which gather in colonies, the breeding area is tiny, just enclosing the nest and the area immediately around it. In such cases the feeding area is obviously separated from the nest and it may be shared with the rest of the colony, as with the rook, *Corvus frugilegus*, and many coastal species, or territorial as with the oystercatcher, *Haematopus ostralegus*.

Territorial rights are usually proclaimed either by calling, by a visual display or by a combination of both. Bird song is the most familiar example of territorial calling; it is carried on most energetically at dawn and dusk, giving rise to the well known dusk and dawn 'chorus'. Each species has its own distinctive song which it can recognize easily, so that males of the same species can avoid each other and females are attracted to the appropriate mate.

Generally speaking the less conspicuous the bird, whether because of the dullness of its plumage or the density of the vegetation in its habitat, the louder and more distinctive is its song. Many birds sing from prominent perches such as a fence post or the top of a tree or bush. Other birds have a song flight. This may simply consist of a short flight into the air, returning to the same or a nearby perch, or it may involve a prolonged flight, as with the famous song of the

Above: The embryo of a chick is almost fully formed after 15 days. It draws nourishment from the shrunken yolk through blood vessels.

Below: A chick hatches from its egg. To break the shell it uses an 'egg tooth'— a blunt horny projection on the upper surface of the tip of the bill.

Right: A male frigate bird, *Fregata minor*, inflates its bright red throat sac in a courtship display. Like many other seabirds, frigate birds nest in colonies. The female lays a single egg which is incubated for about 45 days. The young depend on their parents for at least six months after hatching.

Below: A one day old chick is already in a fairly advanced state of development and can search for food itself. The common domestic chicken has been bred by man for many hundreds of years: it is descended from the red jungle fowl, *Gallus gallus*, which is still an inhabitant of South-East Asia.

Right: The reproductive organs of a female bird are only developed on the left side. The rudimentary right ovary will grow if the left one is destroyed by disease or removed but it then forms a testis, not a mature ovary. A complete change of sex from female to male (but not male to female) is therefore possible.

Below: A diagram to show the main features of a bird's egg. The yolk is the food source for the growing embryo; it contains protein, fat and water. The albumen is mostly water but contains some protein: it protects the yolk and prevents it from drying out. The yolk is supported by two strands called chalazae formed from the vitelline membrane.

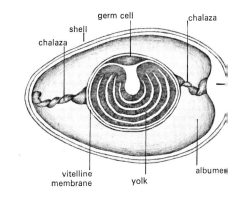

shell
chalaza
germ cell
chalaza
vitelline membrane
yolk
albumen

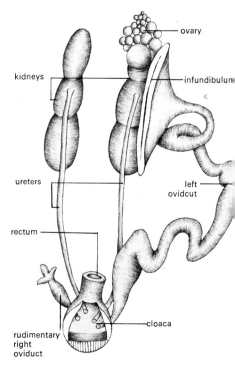

kidneys
ureters
rectum
rudimentary right oviduct
ovary
infundibulum
left oviduct
cloaca

Left: A pair of wandering albatrosses, *Diomedea exulans*, performing their strange courtship 'dance'. Many patterns of behaviour observed in birds seem to derive from some normal activity such as feeding. In this case there is a resemblance to taking off.

Right: The courtship display of the peacock, *Pavo cristatus*. The fan is formed of elongated upper tail coverts supported by the relatively short tail feathers. The peacock usually attracts several females by his display, but as soon as any one of them approaches he turns his back. The reason for this peculiar behaviour is not at all clear.

Jacana

Heather Angel

PENGUIN DANCE

DISCOVERY RITUAL

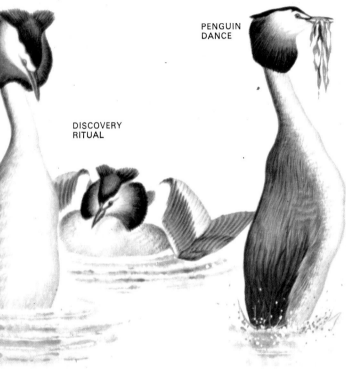

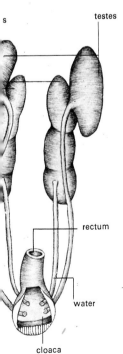

s

testes

rectum

water

cloaca

Left: The reproductive system of a male bird. As with the female, both the reproductive organs and the excretory organs open into a single chamber, known as the cloaca. The testes are normally quite small, but in the breeding season they become as much as a thousand times heavier than usual.

Above: Pairs of great crested grebes, *Podiceps cristatus*, perform a series of elaborate courtship rituals. In the 'discovery' ritual one bird dives and rises up in front of the other which partly spreads its wings. In the 'penguin dance' each bird faces the other, its beak full of weed.

Below: The nest of a little tern, *Sterna albifrons*, is simply a hollow in the sand. These birds breed in small colonies, each nest being about 10 m (30 ft) from the next. From a distance, the colour and the pattern of blotches on the eggs makes them very hard to see against a sandy background.

Dr. R. Skiba/Bavaria

skylark, *Alauda arvensis*. Although less melodious, the hooting of owls and the booming of the bittern, *Botaurus stellaris*, are equally effective ways of proclaiming breeding territories.

Large birds living in the open, or predators covering huge territories in mountainous or wooded regions, rely on sight rather than sound in establishing their breeding grounds. Eagles and falcons soar over their territories, perching on prominent rocks or branches, and hawks wheel over their forest homes. A bird noted for its combined calling and visual display is the African snipe, *Capella gallinago*. The males fly over their territories interrupting their flight with short steep dives during which the outermost tail feathers are extended and vibrate in the air, making a drumming sound which carries a considerable distance. Once a territory has been established the occupying male will repel any other males entering the area by fighting if necessary but more usually by aggressive display.

Courtship

Once a male has attracted a female to his established breeding territory a period of courtship begins. This serves two purposes—to overcome the natural aggression of the male in defending his territory and to strengthen the pair bond, often to the extent that both birds will defend the territory.

Many birds have special plumage or other adornments which appear, or become particularly pronounced, in the breeding season to increase the visual impact of their courtship displays. The blackheaded gull, *Larus ridibundus*, for example, has a 'hood' of feathers which appears in the early spring and is moulted out at the end of the breeding season. Often the bills and wattles (fleshy lobes hanging from the throat of some birds) become more vividly coloured.

Courtship displays are ritual forms of functional activities such as feeding, drinking, preening and flying. Thus a common form of display, seen in birds like terns, is the passing of food from one bird to the other. The ritualization is so advanced in some species that the birds go through the movements of feeding each other but no food is involved.

The head, tail and wing movements so common in courtship displays are reminiscent of postures adopted just before flight; in some species the take-off and landing movements have become ritualized into elaborate courtship dances. Flocks of African crowned cranes, 221

Balearica pavonia, divide into pairs and then the males, with crests erect, bow to the females before leaping several times into the air and making a trumpeting call. The females then join in the dance, making it a most spectacular event.

Courtship displays are sometimes interspersed with apparently pointless activities. A herring gull, *Larus argentatus*, for example, may suddenly start furiously to tear up the grass in its territory. This sort of behaviour is called 'displacement behaviour' and appears to indicate frustration.

The simple one male to one female relationship is sometimes replaced by communal displays involving many individuals of both sexes. This sort of behaviour is seen most often in game birds and wading birds; their display areas are called *leks*. In the breeding season male European ruffs, *Philomachus pugnax*, have exotic neck collars and ear tufts of varying colours, and each bird occupies a small area within the lek. When a female arrives the males display by squatting down and turning on the spot, the female then selects a male and mates with him.

One of the most extraordinary courtship rituals is that performed by the satin bower bird, *Ptilonorhynchus violaceus*, of Australia. Having established his territory by calling, the male bird proceeds to build two parallel walls out of small branches or twigs. He then decorates the ground at one end of the construction with small coloured objects such as feathers, flowers and even glass or paper if they are available. He seems to prefer the colour blue for these adornments. Once the 'bower' is complete he displays to the female bird by rapidly beating his wings and leaping into the air.

Mating

The sexual organs of both male and female birds lead into a chamber called the *cloaca* which has an external opening. During mating the cloacae of the male and female birds are pressed together and turned inside out so that sperm can pass from one to the other. Only a few birds, such as ducks and ostriches, have penises. The sperm finds its way into the left oviduct of the female (the right ovary and oviduct do not normally develop) where fertilization of the egg occurs. By this stage the egg is already surrounded by a large yolk, and it now begins to gather layers of albumen (the familiar 'egg white') secreted by special glands in the oviduct. Next it is enclosed by two membranes, the inner one being quite smooth and the outer one rough so that it will cling to the eggshell. Finally the eggshell is formed in the uterus and receives its characteristic colour and pattern. As the egg is laid, through the cloaca, it cools and draws in air through pores in the shell. The air collects at the broader end of the egg between the two membranes and forms a small air pocket.

The largest known egg was laid by the Madagascan elephant bird, *Aepyornis* (now extinct). It measured about 33 cm (more than 12 ins) from end to end and had a capacity of about nine litres (two gallons). In proportion to its body weight the ostrich only lays a relatively small egg, but it is nevertheless the largest bird's egg found today, being about 17 cm (7 in) long. The smallest eggs, 1.3 cm (0.43 in) long, are laid by humming birds.

222

John Markham/Bruce Coleman

Above: A cuckoo's egg closely resembles that of its reed warbler host. This helps to ensure that it will be accepted by the foster parent. Other cuckoos, which lay their eggs in meadow pipits' nests, have differently coloured eggs which once again match those of their hosts.

Above: A young cuckoo, *Cuculus canorus*, swamps the nest of its foster parent, a reed warbler, *Acrocephalus scirpaceus*. Female cuckoos lay their eggs in other birds' nests after first removing one of the original eggs. No more than one egg is laid in any one host nest. The incubation period is shorter than that of the host bird, so the cuckoo hatches first. It then instinctively throws all other eggs out of the nest to ensure its own survival.

Below: A hoopoe, *Upupa epops*, feeds a caterpillar to its young. Although the eggs are incubated by the female alone, both parents provide food for the young birds.

ZEFA

Above: Sociable weavers, *Philetairus socius*, of southern Africa build their nests clustered together in trees. These communal nests are used again and again, being enlarged each year. One group of nests, reputedly more than 100 years old, measured 5 m (16 ft) by 3.5 m (11 ft) and had 125 separate entrances.

Right: The Baya weaver, *Ploceus philippinus*, builds a hollow nest with a downwardly directed entrance. This design provides maximum protection for the occupants of the nest. The Baya weaver goes one step further than most of its cousins by constructing a long entrance tunnel.

Above and right: A village weaver, *Textor cucullatus*, builds a hollow nest in a tree by weaving palm fibres together. It first constructs a ring which acts as a perch. Next the roof and the walls are built up and finally the entrance is formed. These birds are common throughout tropical Africa.

M. F. Soper/Bruce Coleman

Above: A grey-headed albatross, *Diomedea chrysostoma*, with its chick. Some young albatrosses spend as long as eight months on the nest before they are abandoned by their parents and have to fend for themselves. In that time they grow to a considerable size. Because of the long nesting period, albatrosses breed only once every two years, each pair laying a single egg.

Below: The tailor bird, *Orthotomus sutorius*, of India, Sri Lanka and South-East Asia builds a remarkable nest. First it bends one or more living leaves into a roughly cone-shaped container. Then it pierces the leaves near their edges with its beak and sews them together with lengths of spider's web, hair or whatever is available. Finally it builds the nest proper inside the container. The tailor bird is related to the warblers and some members of this group also join leaves together when building their nests. Their efforts, however, are clumsy when compared with the tailor bird.

Some birds' eggs are almost perfectly spherical, many are oval while yet others are pear-shaped, with one end considerably larger than the other. Birds like guillemots, *Cepphus*, which lay their eggs precariously perched on bare cliff ledges, usually lay pear-shaped eggs which will not roll around too freely. The eggs may be white, blue, green, red-brown or yellow and they are often covered by a pattern of spots, blotches or streaks. The differences in appearance are hard to understand, but in ground-nesting species the colour and pattern often camouflage the eggs.

Nesting and rearing young

The most important function of a bird's nest is to keep the eggs and the featherless young warm. Without the insulation provided by the nest the fledgelings would lose body heat rapidly whenever the parent left the nest to forage for food, which would be dangerous for a warm-blooded creature. The nest also serves to conceal and shelter the eggs, the young and the brooding bird.

Most bird species have a characteristic type of nest. Twigs and pieces of grass are the most popular building materials, but mud, saliva and stones may also be used. The effort involved is considerable—a single nest may be built of several thousand separate pieces. A few birds manage to raise their young without resorting to a nest. Penguins, for example, incubate their eggs between their feet which are well supplied with blood vessels so that they can warm the eggs. Some birds use holes in trees or earth banks while others take over old nests.

Some birds, such as the common cuckoo, avoid the chores of parenthood by laying their eggs in other birds' nests. In Africa the honeyguides, *Indicatoridae*, lay their eggs in the holes of woodpeckers and starlings, and in North America the cowbirds, *Molothrus*, make use of a wide variety of unsuspecting hosts. Not all of these social parasites are as specialized as the cuckoo, for many will only make use of foster parents if the opportunity presents itself, being perfectly capable of building nests of their own when circumstances demand it. In all there are about 80 species which use other birds to raise their young.

Depending on the species, incubation is carried out by one or other of the parents, or by both the male and female birds. It lasts for between 10 and 80 days. Many birds develop bare 'brood patches' on the breast to transfer body heat directly to the eggs. Some young, such as ducklings, hatch in an advanced state of development and soon learn to feed themselves: these are termed *nidifugous*. Shortly after hatching the young birds become 'imprinted' on their parents and thereafter recognize them immediately and remain close to them. Other birds, called *nidicolous*, are born naked and sometimes blind, and they remain in the nest for several weeks.

Young birds often have highly coloured and distinctive markings inside their mouths which trigger the feeding instinct in the parent birds. Another way of stimulating feeding is by pecking or pulling at the parent's bill; the young herring gull pecks at a red spot on the adult's bill. Parents usually continue to be attentive until their young are fledged, but shortly afterwards they must leave to fend for themselves.

223

Bird Ecology and Conservation

One of the most common birds in North America during the eighteenth century was the passenger pigeon, *Ectopistes migratorius*. Larger than many pigeons, millions of these birds roamed the forests in the east of the country throughout the summer months. The American naturalist J. J. Audubon estimated that on a single occasion one spring he saw more than a million passenger pigeons migrating eastwards. The species is now extinct—it was slaughtered for food by man in the last century. The last surviving individual died in Cincinnati zoo in 1914.

The case of the passenger pigeon is, unfortunately, by no means unique. The dodo, *Raphus cucullatus*, the great auk, *Pinguinus impennis*, and many other species have been exterminated by man in relatively recent times, and today the pressure is as great as ever. Uncontrolled killing, pollution and the destruction of habitats all play a part in reducing bird populations: some species such as the oriental white stork, *Ciconia boyciana*, the California condor, *Gymnogyps californianus*, the Japanese ibis, *Nipponia nippon*, and the short-tailed albatross, *Diomedea albatrus*, have considerably less than 100 members still living. About 150 species throughout the world have populations of less than 2,000. If the variety of birds in the world is to be preserved, positive steps must be taken for their conservation.

Before anything can be done to save a threatened animal species, it is essential to know the precise reason for its decline. Often the cause is not at all obvious and so the first task of the conservationist is to study in detail the relationship between the animal, its neighbours and its surroundings—in other words how it fits into the natural order of things, the ecosystem. The science of ecology is concerned with relationships of this sort. In the case of a bird, its food, its predators, its nesting sites and all the other factors which influence its survival must be considered.

As far as its animal life is concerned, the world may be divided into six main geographical regions, each having an animal community peculiar to itself. The six regions are known as the Palearctic (Europe and Asia), Ethiopian (Africa), Oriental (India and South-East Asia), Australian, Neotropical (South America) and Nearctic (North America) zones. These 'faunal zones' are separated from each other by major barriers such as oceans, mountain ranges, deserts or differences in climate. These barriers keep the various animal species in each zone distinct from those of others although a certain amount of overlap does occur. Birds, for example, being highly mobile, are more difficult to relate to geographical regions than other animals—many birds occupy completely different ranges in winter and summer, migrating between the two in spring and autumn.

Because evolution has produced many species which are specially adapted to feed on particular food sources, the birds found in any of the six faunal zones are not evenly distributed, but are confined

Right: The short-tailed albatross, *Diomedea albatrus,* **breeds only on the Japanese island of Torishima. Volcanic activity at its breeding place combined with merciless hunting in the past for its feathers has reduced the total world population to no more than about ten pairs. The Palearctic and Nearctic zones are often regarded as subdivisions of a larger zone, the Holarctic zone. Loons,** *Gaviidae,* **accentors,** *Prunellidae,* **auks,** *Alcidae,* **and grouse,** *Tetraonidae,* **are typically Holarctic bird families.**

SHORT-TAILED ALBATROSS

Right: In 1968 the total population of the American whooping crane, *Grus americana,* **was estimated at less than 70. The birds are now carefully protected—both their winter and summer homes, in Arkansas and Canada respectively, are wildlife reserves. The bird has a remarkably long windpipe, often measuring as much as 1.5 m (5 ft), and this no doubt contributes to the characteristic call which gives it its name. Although they are more widely spread nowadays, turkeys,** *Meleagrididae,* **dippers,** *Cinclidae,* **and waxwings,** *Bombycillidae,* **probably originated in the Nearctic zone.**

This map shows how the world can be divided into six 'faunal zones'. Between the Palearctic zone and the Oriental and Ethiopian zones there are fairly wide areas of overlap where the animal communities blend together.

Right: A very rare turaco, *Tauraco ruspolii,* **from the Great Rift Valley of Ethiopia. The turacos constitute one of the bird families found only in the Ethiopian faunal zone. Others include the ostriches,** *Struthionidae,* **the whydahs,** *Viduinae,* **the secretary birds,** *Sagittariidae,* **the guineafowl,** *Numididae,* **the hammerheads,** *Scopidae* **and the mousebirds,** *Coliidae.* **Because it has been separated from the African mainland for so long, the island of Madagascar has a distinctive animal community of its own.**

Right: The Chinese egret, *Egretta eulophotes,* **is an endangered species from South-East Asia. It is closely related to the eastern reef heron,** *Egretta sacra,* **a coastal bird found from Burma to New Zealand. The Oriental zone blends both with the Australian and the Palearctic zones. Of its resident bird families only the leaf birds,** *Irenidae,* **are not found elsewhere.**

PRINCE RUSPOLI'S TURACO

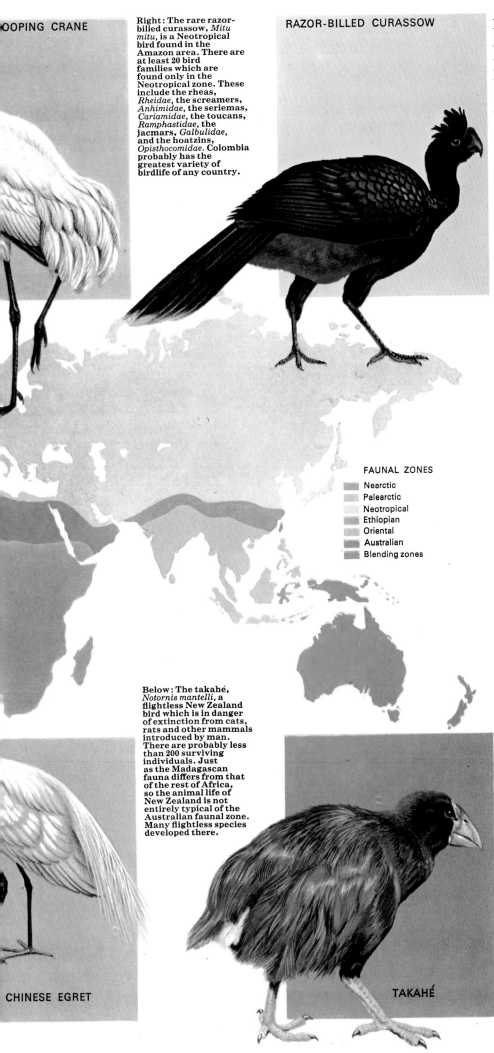

OOPING CRANE

RAZOR-BILLED CURASSOW

Right: The rare razor-billed curassow, *Mitu mitu*, is a Neotropical bird found in the Amazon area. There are at least 20 bird families which are found only in the Neotropical zone. These include the rheas, *Rheidae*, the screamers, *Anhimidae*, the seriemas, *Cariamidae*, the toucans, *Ramphastidae*, the jacmars, *Galbulidae*, and the hoatzins, *Opisthocomidae*. Colombia probably has the greatest variety of birdlife of any country.

FAUNAL ZONES
- Nearctic
- Palearctic
- Neotropical
- Ethiopian
- Oriental
- Australian
- Blending zones

Below: The takahé, *Notornis mantelli*, a flightless New Zealand bird which is in danger of extinction from cats, rats and other mammals introduced by man. There are probably less than 200 surviving individuals. Just as the Madagascan fauna differs from that of the rest of Africa, so the animal life of New Zealand is not entirely typical of the Australian faunal zone. Many flightless species developed there.

CHINESE EGRET

TAKAHÉ

to particular habitats. Thus, wading birds, which have long bills to reach organisms in the mud, live on marshes and mudflats; perching birds, which feed on insects, inhabit woods; aquatic birds, which filter food from water, occupy lakes and ponds.

Even within one such habitat there may be a further separation of species. A single broad-leafed tree, for example, provides food for several different kinds of birds: some will feed on insects on the upper surfaces of the leaves, while others feed on the undersides of the leaves; some extract insects from the bark, or feed on debris which has fallen to the ground under the tree and still others catch flying insects among the branches. Preservation of a wide variety of habitats within a particular faunal zone is therefore a vital factor in successful conservation.

Threats to survival

The main threat to the continued survival of many animal and bird species comes from man. He endangers them in two ways: firstly by direct extermination and secondly by altering or destroying their environment. For thousands of years birds have been hunted for their feathers, their eggs or simply for their meat. Feathers have long been in demand for decorating women's clothes and until recently thousands of birds, such as egrets and birds of paradise, were destroyed for this purpose. Fortunately, early legislation put a stop to much of this. A more recent problem is the export every month of thousands of live wild birds to be kept as pets. A high proportion of these perish in transit before reaching their destination because of unsuitable containers or lack of food. Hopefully, the Washington Convention, an international agreement prepared by the United Nations, will restrict the import and export of endangered species, but much has still to be done to stop the needless death of the more common species still being traded. The collection of birds' eggs, though often illegal, is a further burden on threatened bird species and, inevitably, the rarer the bird the more highly prized are its eggs.

In some parts of the world birds are slaughtered in large numbers for sport, for food or because they are considered (often wrongly) to be pests. In southern Europe and Mediterranean countries such as Italy and Malta very large numbers of birds of all kinds, from song birds to birds of prey, are shot, trapped and netted during their autumn migration. Without proper control this sort of indiscriminate killing is bound to reduce the chances of survival of some bird species.

A far more serious threat to birds is the destruction or alteration of their home territory. The destruction of such habitats can be seen all over the world as the human population increases: forests are felled, marshes are drained and the countryside vanishes under bricks and concrete. In Europe, many small animals and birds are deprived of their homes each year as miles of hedges are cut down to create the ever larger fields demanded by modern farming methods. In every instance the original occupants must find a new home or perish.

Less obvious, but no less damaging, is the slow transformation of animal habitats by man. Often this happens quite unintentionally as a consequence of some other

225

Left: The owl parrot, *Strigops habroptilus*, is an extremely rare flightless bird from New Zealand. It has been driven to the brink of extinction by animals such as cats, dogs and foxes unwittingly introduced into the country by man. Little is known about the bird and it probably cannot now be saved.

Above: The magpie lark, *Grallina cyanoleuca*, is widely distributed in Australia but is not found in any of the other faunal zones.

Right: The splendid parakeet, *Neophema splendida*, is another species found only in Australia. It is threatened by man for it is a popular pet.

human activity. For example the use of insecticides on nearby crops may destroy the insects which form the staple diet of one bird or another. Naturally the bird will then be eliminated from that environment unless it can adapt to a new source of food. In New Zealand it was the introduction of rats and cats by man which caused the extinction of the Auckland rail, *Rallus muelleri*, and has almost exterminated its relative the takahé, *Notornis mantelli*. Both birds were flightless and were able to survive only because predatory mammals were absent from the islands, until man arrived.

A more recent hazard facing many birds is the increasing use of pesticides in agriculture. These synthetic chemicals, which contain carbon and usually chlorine as well, are highly toxic to many birds. Aldrin, dieldrin, heptachlor and DDT are among those which are particularly harmful. Not surprisingly thousands of grain-eating birds such as finches, pigeons and pheasants are poisoned each year when they feed on seeds dressed with insecticide. Unfortunately birds have no biochemical mechanism for breaking down and excreting these poisons, so they gradually build up in the body tissues, especially the fat reserves. This means that a great many birds carry potentially dangerous insecticides in their body tissues, even though the concentration may be too low to cause any direct harm.

These apparently harmless amounts become highly significant, however, when contaminated individuals are eaten by predators: with each bird eaten more insecticide is ingested and it very quickly builds up in the predator's body. Eventually the predator will begin to suffer from

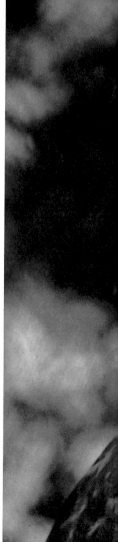

Left: A male turkey, *Meleagris gallopavo*. Turkeys are typical birds of the Nearctic zone; originally they were found throughout North America except in the west, but today they are much less common. The familiar domestic turkey is descended from these wild birds.

Right: Livingstone's turaco, *Tauraco persa livingstonii*, from East Africa. The turacos constitute a family of birds, *Musophagidae*, which are found only in Africa. They are quite common and live in pairs or small groups.

Below: A male (left) and female pheasant, *Phasianus colchicus*. These birds developed in the Palearctic zone, occupying a similar ecological niche in Europe and Asia to the turkeys (left) in North America. They have been introduced to America and New Zealand by man.

Eric Hosking

Su Gooders/Ardea

Above and left: Keel-billed toucans. *Ramphastos sulfuratus*, and a yellow-knobbed curassow, *Crax daubentoni*. Both these species inhabit the richest faunal zone, the Neotropical (South America). As many as half of all the world's bird species live in the Neotropical zone or visit it annually.

Right: The blue-tailed pitta, *Pitta guajana*, inhabits the Oriental zone—it is found in Thailand, Malaysia and Indonesia. Pittas live in dense forests, usually keeping close to the ground where they feed on snails, worms, insects and even lizards. They have short rounded wings and are poor fliers.

Tierbilder Okapia

Ron Boardman

the poison and may even die. The species most seriously affected in this way was the peregrine falcon, *Falco peregrinus*. It was wiped out in the eastern United States, brought to the verge of extinction in Sweden and greatly reduced in Norway and Finland. In the British Isles it was wiped out throughout most of England, Wales and Ireland and only survived in Scotland. Even here, however, its breeding success was greatly reduced, with the birds laying thin-shelled eggs (an effect of the insecticide) which they often destroyed themselves. Many countries now operate strict controls on the use of agricultural insecticides, and in Britain the peregrine population is recovering. In the eastern United States and Sweden attempts are being made to reintroduce the bird.

Conservation

The aim of conservation is not only to prevent the extinction of bird species but also to minimize any decline in their number and variety. The benefits of conservation are many. To begin with, birds give pleasure to an increasingly large section of the human population: they are watched, recorded, studied, photographed and painted, and game species provide food and sport. Perhaps more importantly, they are a vital part of the ecosystem and the balance of nature would undoubtedly be upset without them.

Conservation is best achieved by legislation providing protection for a species throughout its range, and by establishing reserves which afford safety for individuals in particular areas. Legislation imposes penalties for killing or taking birds and for collecting or destroying their eggs and young. The most effective legislation protects all wild birds and their eggs but makes exceptions in certain cases. Usually these exceptions are for game species during designated 'open seasons', and pest species which may be killed by land owners and farmers to prevent damage to their crops or property.

Conservation measures for migrating species must operate in both the breeding areas and the wintering sites, and must provide sanctuaries along the migration routes. For example, no matter how carefully the Arctic breeding areas of wild geese are protected, this is to no avail if they are shot in excess during their migrations or on their winterings grounds further south. The International Council for Bird Preservation (ICBP), with its headquarters at the British Museum in London, co-ordinates the work of the national conservation organizations, but a great deal of work remains to be done before it can be claimed that effective worldwide conservation of birdlife has been achieved.

When setting up new nature reserves it is important to remember that even the richest habitat can only support a limited number of individuals. The factors which regulate bird populations are numerous, and they include such things as climate, cover, food, nesting sites, predation, disease and the behaviour of the birds themselves. Unfortunately, for many species detailed information about their ecology is still scarce in spite of a great deal of research, and conservation can only begin to be effective when all the many factors which influence the survival of a threatened species are known and taken into account.

Monotremes

First discovered towards the end of the eighteenth century, the duck-billed platypus is a curious aquatic animal with beaver-like fur and a bird's bill, and is found only in Australia and Tasmania. Its habit of laying eggs (a characteristic of reptiles) greatly baffled the early zoologists and some even doubted the animal's existence: indeed the first complete platypus skin to reach the British Museum in London in 1798 was thought to be a hoax. The remoteness of Australia in those days made it difficult to study the animal properly—many sightings were unconfirmed and specimens reaching Europe arrived in poor condition. It was not for some years, and only after careful dissection of specimens, that the platypus was finally recognized as a mammal.

The duck-billed platypus is the best known member of the order *Monotremata*, a group which includes another animal with certain reptilian characteristics—the spiny anteater. The presence of hair and of milk glands on both animals are the most obvious mammalian features, yet monotremes are of particular interest to zoologists because they provide clues to the evolution of mammals from their reptilian ancestors. The clearest affinity with reptiles is the egg-laying habit, and indeed this distinguishes them from all other mammals. Closely connected with this method of reproduction is the fact that both the rectum and the reproductive organs lead into a common opening called the *cloaca*. The yolky eggs measure between 14 and 19 mm (0.5 to 0.75 in) in diameter and have a whitish shell.

Spiny anteaters transfer their eggs to a special pouch on their abdomen as soon as they are laid and it is here that they are incubated. The incubation pouch is only present in the breeding season. The platypus, on the other hand, incubates its eggs in a nest chamber lined with wet leaves. Like reptiles, young monotremes have a

Bruce Coleman

Left: A young spiny anteater, *Tachyglossus aculeatus*. The animal is completely naked for six to eight weeks until its spines begin to develop, and for most of this period it remains in its mother's abdominal pouch.

Below: Monotremes and marsupials (for example kangaroos and koalas) each have a different method of reproduction from most animals, called placental mammals. Placental mammals give birth to well developed young after a prolonged period of gestation. While in the uterus the embryo receives oxygen and nourishment from its mother by means of a connecting organ called the placenta. Monotremes, however, lay eggs which are incubated on the ground or in a pouch; the embryos feed on the yolk of their eggs before hatching. Marsupial embryos feed on the yolk-sac while in their mother's uterus, and they are born in a very immature state of development when this source of food is exhausted. Monotremes and marsupials both possess cloacae.

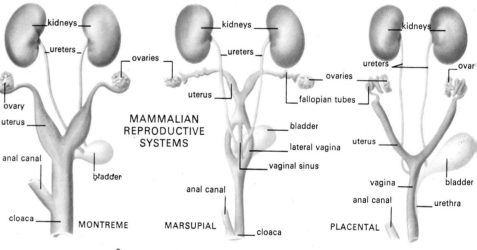

MAMMALIAN REPRODUCTIVE SYSTEMS

MONTREME — kidneys, ureters, ovaries, ovary, uterus, anal canal, bladder, cloaca

MARSUPIAL — kidneys, ureters, ovaries, uterus, fallopian tubes, bladder, lateral vagina, vaginal sinus, anal canal, cloaca

PLACENTAL — kidneys, ureters, ovar, uterus, vagina, anal canal, bladder, urethra

A chart to show how the mammals have evolved. The first mammals probably developed from carnivorous therapsid reptiles at the end of the Triassic period. The time of greatest expansion, however, was the early Tertiary.

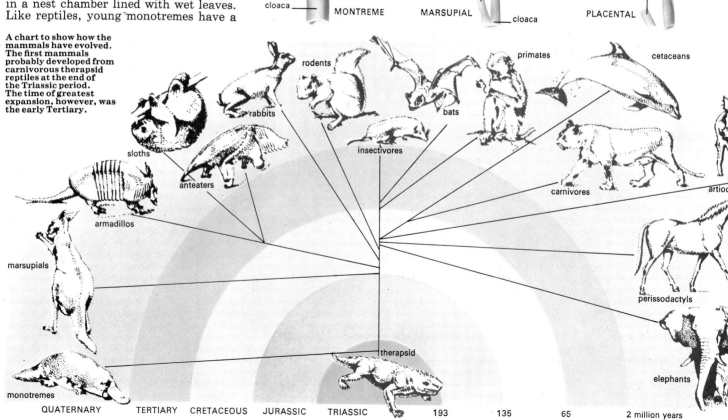

sloths, anteaters, armadillos, marsupials, rodents, rabbits, insectivores, bats, primates, cetaceans, carnivores, artiod, perissodactyls, elephants, therapsid, monotremes

QUATERNARY   TERTIARY   CRETACEOUS   JURASSIC   TRIASSIC   193   135   65   2 million years

Above: An adult spiny anteater, *Tachyglossus aculeatus*. Monotremes are considered to be mammals because they have warm blood, body hair, unnucleated red blood corpuscles, a single dentary bone in the lower jaw and a number of other typically mammalian features. The structure of the brain and heart are also mammalian. Their skeleton and method of reproduction, however, are reptilian in character.

Right: A map to show the distribution of monotreme species in Australasia.

Below: Spiny anteaters share with European hedgehogs the ability to roll themselves into a ball when threatened.

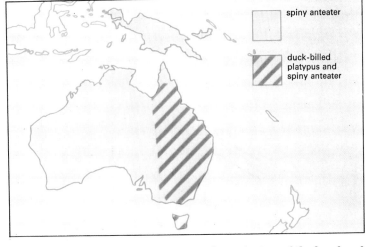

spiny anteater

duck-billed platypus and spiny anteater

hard outgrowth on the top of the head and an egg-tooth to help them break out of their eggs. Once they have hatched, however, they lap up milk which is exuded from specialized sweat glands on the female's belly.

Other reptilian features are less obvious and involve the structure and arrangement of the bones in the skeleton. Many of these similarities stem from the fact that both monotremes and reptiles have legs which project from the side of the body (the legs of other mammals are situated underneath the body). This makes the bones and muscles in the lower part of the body of a monotreme reptilian rather than mammalian in character. Further resemblances to a reptile are seen in the backbone and the skull. The condition of the skeleton and recent fossil evidence suggest that monotremes diverged from the main mammalian line of evolution some 200 million years ago during the Triassic period.

Spiny anteaters
Spiny anteaters, sometimes called echidnas, look like small porcupines with long tapering snouts. When standing, they turn their front toes inwards and their hind ones out, giving them a rather ungainly and awkward appearance. There are five species altogether, divided into two genera, *Tachyglossus* and *Zaglossus*, and they are found throughout Australia, in Tasmania and in New Guinea.

The compact body is covered with hair and numerous long pointed spines. The fur is dark brown or nearly black with the spines yellowish near the base and darker at the tips: the short stumpy tail is also covered with long spines. Both the hands and the feet have well developed claws, which the spiny anteaters use for digging and tearing open the nests of ants and termites on which they feed. The particularly large claws on the second digit of the hind feet are turned inwards, and are used for grooming. In the male these enlarged claws are connected to poison glands whose function is still uncertain but presumably has to do with self defence. The mouth, situated at the end of the naked snout, is a small slit through which the long, sticky tongue continuously darts in and out. The animal has no teeth; its insect prey is chewed between the horny ridges at the back of the palate and the tongue.

The genus *Tachyglossus* comprises two short-nosed species whose snouts are slightly upturned at the tip. The Australian short-nosed spiny anteater, *Tachyglossus aculeatus*, is found in Australia and New Guinea and the Tasmanian short-nosed spiny anteater, *Tachyglossus setosus*, lives in Tasmania and the islands of the Bass Strait. The more bizarre looking long-nosed spiny anteaters, the *Zaglossus*, are larger, have longer legs and fewer spines. The three known species are confined to New Guinea, although one species also lives in the Salawati Islands.

Although spiny anteaters can dig with their stout fore-claws, they do not excavate their own burrows, but live in hollow logs, among roots or crevices in rocks. They burrow only in emergencies and can do quite a spectacular 'disappearing act' when threatened. They do not burrow head first, but bury themselves by digging with all four feet and sinking straight down. If the ground is too hard, they either curl up like hedgehogs or wedge themselves securely between rocks or in undergrowth. The ability to burrow also helps them regulate their body temperatures especially in intense heat. They do not have such an efficient internal temperature regulating mechanism as other mammals and to survive they must avoid extremes of temperature by burying themselves.

The short-nosed spiny anteaters feed mainly on termites and ants, especially the meat-ants, *Iridomyrmex*, which they devour in large quantities when the nests are swarming with highly nutritious virgin queens. The long-nosed echidnas probably feed more on earthworms and other soft invertebrates which they probe for in the moist earth of the forest floor.

Spiny anteaters are secretive, nocturnal animals with few enemies. Aborigines and the natives of New Guinea however consider them a delicacy and cook them wrapped up in clay over hot coal fires. Curiously, this is the very same method used by gypsies to cook another spiny creature, the European hedgehog.

The duck-billed platypus
The platypus, *Ornithorhynchus anatinus*, is the only member of the monotreme family *Ornithorhynchidae*. It inhabits 229

creeks and rivers of eastern Australia and
Tasmania from sea level up to 1,500 m
(5,000 ft). The platypus is quite unlike its
spiny anteater relatives both in form and
habits. It grows up to 60 cm (two feet) in
length, has thick dense fur and a characteristic large naked snout resembling a
duck's bill in shape. The bill is covered
with delicate skin that acts as a sensitive
organ of touch for detecting prey. Unlike
spiny anteaters the platypus does have
teeth, though these are very simple in
form: the three hardened teeth of the
young animal are, in fact, soon replaced
by two horny plates on each side of each
jaw.

The animal is a versatile swimmer and
has a streamlined appearance when underwater. The webbed hands are used for
propulsion, while the hind legs seem to be
used more for balancing and steering.
Both the eyes and the ears are protected
by a fold of skin when swimming. The
platypus is very buoyant and so when
diving for food it has to swim actively
downwards to prevent itself from floating.
Platypuses seldom stay submerged for
more than a couple of minutes; their
underwater activities consist of frantic
searches for food—usually insect larvae,
crustaceans and molluscs. Small prey is
eaten underwater but larger game like
crayfish are first hauled on to land. When
alarmed the animal smacks the water
with its flat tail, like a beaver.

The platypus can dig as well as it can
swim. Burrows up to 12 m (40 ft) long are
excavated along the banks of streams,
with the entrance little more than 30 cm
(one foot) above the level of the water.
The female platypus is a diligent mother;
wet leaves used to line the nest chamber
are carried between the belly and the
underside of the tail, which is tucked
forwards. The powerful fore-claws do
practically all the digging and the
excavated earth, instead of being thrown
out of the burrow, is pressed down and
flattened with the tail. The wet vegetation
and the habit of plugging the nest burrows
help to maintain a constant humidity and
so prevent the eggs from drying out. The
female lays two or three eggs which she
incubates by curling round them. The
newborn young are blind and naked and
remain in the burrow for four months
being suckled, after which time they start
foraging for their own food.

Platypuses have been successfully kept
in captivity both in Australia and North
America. It is by no means an easy task
to keep these animals as they are always
on the move and have an enormous
appetite. A captive platypus at Bronx
Zoo consumed 540 earthworms daily as
well as 20 to 30 shrimps, 200 meal-worms,
two small frogs and two eggs. Special
artificial burrows also had to be built so
that the animals could squeeze out the
surplus water in their fur as they entered
the burrow. This was necessary because
free-living platypuses dry their fur in
their earth tunnels.

The platypus was once hunted for its
rich fur, but this practice is now prohibited under Australian law. Unfortunately, some still die needlessly by
suffocating in fish traps. Spiny anteaters
have received full protection since 1905
and they are much more common than the
platypus, especially the short-nosed form
from Tasmania, which is found quite
frequently even near the suburbs of
Hobart, the Tasmanian capital.

Above: The duck-billed
platypus, *Ornithorhyncus,
anatinus,* is an expert
swimmer as its
streamlined shape and
webbed feet suggest.
The broad, flat tail
helps it to move up or
down in the water when
swimming. Platypuses
breed between the
months of August and
November, and mating
takes place in the
water. They conduct an
elaborate courtship
ritual during which the
male takes hold of the
female's tail while the
pair swim in circles.
The female usually lays
two soft-shelled eggs
about two weeks after
mating. They are kept
moist by the wet leaves
which line the nest
chamber.

Below: A platypus about
to enter the water.

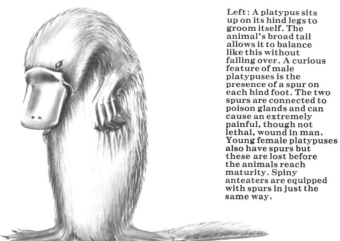

Left: A platypus sits
up on its hind legs to
groom itself. The
animal's broad tail
allows it to balance
like this without
falling over. A curious
feature of male
platypuses is the
presence of a spur on
each hind foot. The two
spurs are connected to
poison glands and can
cause an extremely
painful, though not
lethal, wound in man.
Young female platypuses
also have spurs but
these are lost before
the animals reach
maturity. Spiny
anteaters are equipped
with spurs in just the
same way.

The long nosed spiny anteater (*zaglossus*) can grow to 39 inches in length and weighs up to 21lbs. It has an extremely long tongue and much longer legs than the *tachyglossus* species.

Marsupials

The largest and best known members of the order *Marsupialia*, or pouched mammals, are the kangaroos of Australia. They were first discovered by a Dutch explorer, Francisco Pelsaert, in 1629 but his report of strange new animals did not arouse much interest in Europe. It was not until more than 140 years later, in 1770, when kangaroos were rediscovered by Captain James Cook, that naturalists first took notice of the new family of animals. Several years later the first live specimens to reach Europe caused a considerable stir when they were put on show in London. Although their upright gait and powerful hind legs immediately distinguish kangaroos from other animals, it is their unusual method of reproduction —the young develop in a pouch on the mother's abdomen—that makes them fundamentally different from non-marsupial animals.

The offspring of most mammals (placental mammals) reach a fairly advanced stage of development while still inside the mother's womb. The growing embryo receives oxygen and nourishment from its mother's bloodstream by means of a connecting organ called the *placenta* and the umbilical cord. Kangaroos, however, like most other marsupials, have no placenta and the embryo feeds on the yolk-sac of the egg. Although the marsupial egg is much larger than that of placental mammals, the food supply provided by the yolk-sac does not last for very long, and so marsupials are born at a very early stage in their development. The embryonic kangaroo when born is extremely small and hardly resembles its parent at all, but it is nevertheless able to crawl to its mother's pouch and there to find one of the nipples.

This is a remarkable feat for an animal which weighs only 0.9 gm (0.03 oz) at birth as compared with 25 kg (55 lb) for an adult kangaroo, and not surprisingly the newly born animal is specially adapted for the climb. Its fore limbs and shoulder region are relatively well developed and the digits are equipped with sharp curved claws for clinging to its mother's fur.

Once in the pouch the young animal finds the nipple by trial and error; as soon as the teat is touched it stops moving and takes hold. If it fails to find a nipple to supply it with milk, as may happen if there are already other young in the pouch, the young kangaroo is doomed to starvation. Once on the nipple the young does not release its grip and, because it is unable to suckle by itself, the muscles of the mother's mammary gland regulate the flow of milk. The epiglottis, which in placental mammals covers the trachea (the tube leading to the lungs), is extended upwards to form a tube leading into the nasal chamber. Thus a continuous passage is formed from the nostrils to the trachea so that air passes down to the windpipe as milk flows to the gullet.

All marsupials share the kangaroo's basic method of reproduction, with only minor variations from species to species. The group includes the wombats and marsupial moles, which are tunnellers, the gliding possums which are the only aerial representatives, the tree-dwelling

Rat opossum

Above: A South American marsupial, the Ecuador rat opossum, *Caenolestes fuliginosus.*

Right: A view inside the pouch of an Australian brush-tailed possum, *Trichosurus vulpecula*, shows a young possum clinging to its mother's teat. The picture clearly shows how undeveloped newly born marsupials are. As soon as it is born the tiny and virtually helpless animal crawls into its mother's pouch to suckle. At this stage it is unable to feed for itself and muscles in the mother's milk gland control the flow of milk to her offspring. The young possum will remain in its mother's pouch for about five months.

Left: The common opossum, *Didelphis marsupialis*, lives in both North and South America. It was the first marsupial to be discovered by Europeans (in 1520) and in the years after its discovery its then unique method of reproduction aroused considerable interest.

Below: A ringtail possum, *Pseudocheirus*, from Australia. The animal usually curls the end of its tail into a ring, and this accounts for its name. Ringtail possums are nocturnal animals and they feed on fruit and leaves as well as small vertebrates such as lizards. They are solitary animals and, as this picture suggests, they live in trees.

koala bears and a variety of surface land animals ranging in size from the marsupial mice to the kangaroos.

The ancestors of the marsupials separated from the main evolutionary line of mammals about 100 million years ago. Since then both marsupials and placental mammals have evolved a wide variety of adaptations to different ways of life, and it is surprising how similar these adaptations are. The kangaroo, for example, is the marsupial equivalent of the antelope. There are also marsupial versions of the mouse, the wolf, the mole, the cat and the anteater, and these animals look remarkably like their placental mammal counterparts. Although today most marsupials are quite small, this was not always the case: one extinct marsupial, *Diprotodon*, was as big as a rhinoceros.

Right: The koala bear, *Phascolarctos cinereus*, is one of the most familiar marsupials. It feeds exclusively on eucalyptus leaves and this makes it a difficult animal to keep in captivity outside Australia. A curious feature of this diet is that young eucalyptus leaves and shoots often contain lethal amounts of hydrogen cyanide, especially in winter, and this accounted for many deaths among the first zoo animals in Australia. In the wild, koalas avoid the young shoots, feeding almost exclusively on the more mature leaves. Only a century ago there were many millions of koalas in Australia, but today the total population must be measured in thousands. They have completely disappeared from southern and western Australia, exterminated by hunting and by natural epidemics. In 1927 alone more than half a million koala furs were exported from the state of Queensland. Fortunately the animals are now protected and the population is on the increase. Koalas have been reintroduced in some areas.

NHPA

Left: A female rabbit bandicoot, *Macrotis leucura*, with her young. These animals get their name from their long rabbit-like ears and their habit of building long burrows to a depth of 1.5 m (4.8 ft) or more. They are beneficial to man because they have a large appetite for pests such as insect larvae and mice.

Below: A young long-nosed bandicoot, *Perameles nasuta*, climbs into its mother's pouch. Most burrowing marsupials, like the bandicoots, have pouches which open to the rear. Bandicoots are found in most parts of Australia and some species, such as the spiny bandicoots, live in New Guinea.

Long-nosed bandicoot

NHPA

The geographical distribution of the marsupials is unusual—they are found only in Australia and South America (except for a few opossums which have spread to North America relatively recently). The reason for this odd distribution is obscure—possibly Antarctica once formed a bridge between the two continents so that their animal populations merged. At any event it seems likely that competition from placental mammals drove them out of all other regions of the world (fossils of marsupials have been found in both North America and Europe). Marsupials were most successful in Australia where such competition was least.

Australian marsupials

Of the nine marsupial families, seven are exclusively Australian: the kangaroos, *Macropodidae*, the carnivorous marsupials, *Dasyuridae*, the phalangers, *Phalangeridae*, the wombats, *Vombatidae*, the bandicoots, *Peramelidae*, the marsupial anteaters, *Myrmecobiidae*, and the marsupial moles, *Notoryctidae*.

The word 'kangaroo' is often restricted to the three members of the genus *Macropus* (the word means great foot): the red kangaroo, *Macropus rufus*, of the plains, the great grey kangaroo, *Macropus giganteus*, of the open forests, and the stocky, powerful wallaroo, *Macropus robustus*, of the rocky mountain ranges. The many smaller species of the kangaroo family are usually called 'wallabies'.

Kangaroos and wallabies occupy the same ecological niche as the grazing animals such as deer and antelopes of other lands. Like ruminants (animals which chew the cud) they have specialized bacteria in their stomach to break down the cellulose in the sparse vegetation which forms their diet. Some species have even developed the ability to regurgitate food and chew the cud like cattle. Because they can digest plant material efficiently kangaroos and wallabies can survive in the most inhospitable environments.

The long tapering tail is used as a balance and rudder for leaps and turns. At high speed the tail does not hit the ground with every bound, but is used more to help turning. The tail is so powerful that the animal may actually stand upon it and take its hind legs off the ground. Large kangaroos can achieve speeds of about 50 kph (30 mph) for short bursts and can sustain a speed of 40 kph (25 mph) for some time. An adult grey kangaroo may stand over two metres (seven feet) tall and weigh 90 kg (200 lb) or more.

The family *Phalangeridae* contains a wide variety of marsupials, including the koala, *Phascolarctos cinereus*, the slow moving cuscuses, *Phalanger*, with prehensile (grasping) tails and big eyes, the flying possums, *Petaurus*, which glide from tree to tree like flying squirrels, and the doormouse possums, *Cercartetus*. The solitary koala 'bear' is one of the most interesting and attractive of all marsupials. It is rarely seen in zoos outside Australia because it thrives only on a diet of leaves from the native eucalyptus tree, which have a high oil content. Koalas seldom drink water, apparently deriving sufficient moisture from the eucalyptus leaf diet and dew. The reproductive rate of koalas is low. The female produces a single young every two years 233

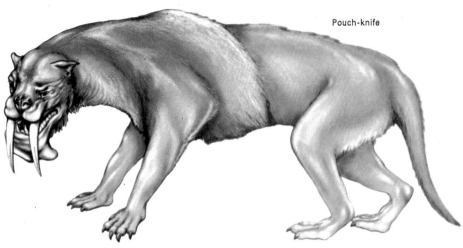

after a pregnancy of about a month. At birth the young koala weighs only about five grams (0.2 oz) and, after reaching its mother's pouch, it remains there for six months being suckled. As in many other marsupials such as the Tasmanian wolf and the wombats the koala's pouch opens to the rear. After weaning, the young koala clings to its mother's back until it is able to fend for itself.

Bandicoots are shy nocturnal animals which inhabit New Guinea as well as Australia. They range in size from that of a rat to that of a badger and have pointed noses. They feed on insects and roots which they scratch from the ground. Wombats are stocky rodent-like animals which live in burrows; they are solitary and feed mainly on roots.

Marsupial moles have adapted to a burrowing existence in just the same way as the placental mammals of the same name, and this has resulted in a striking resemblance between the two groups. Although they are quite unrelated the marsupial mole, *Notoryctes*, is outwardly very like the African golden mole, *Chrysochloris*; it has fine silky fur varying in colour from white to a rich golden red.

Carnivorous marsupials

The largest and rarest of the flesh-eating marsupials is the marsupial wolf, *Thylacinus cynocephalus*, which lives in caverns among the rocks in the most mountainous part of Tasmania. Very few of these creatures survive today and unless drastic steps are taken to protect them they will shortly become extinct. The animal looks like a dog with chocolate coloured stripes across its lower back. Most of the day is spent in a lair from which it emerges at dusk in search of prey, hunting either singly or in pairs. Its natural food consists of wallabies and smaller marsupials, rats and birds.

Another carnivorous marsupial is the Tasmanian devil, *Sarcophilus harrisi*, which is still quite common in Tasmania. It received its unfortunate name after early reports of its aggressive temperament. In fact it is no more aggressive than many other animals, but it will use its powerful jaws to defend itself if attacked. The Australian native cats, *Dasyurus*, are slender carnivores which look rather like martens and feed on birds, small mammals and lizards.

The rare marsupial anteater or numbat, *Myrmecobius fasciatus*, is sometimes placed with the marsupial carnivores in the family *Dasyuridae* rather than in a separate family of its own. It has a pointed

Above: *Thylacosmilus*, a large carnivorous marsupial which once roamed the forests of South America. Its similarity to the sabre-toothed tiger is remarkable because the two animals were quite unrelated. Evidently both animals evolved in the same way to meet similar environmental conditions.

Right: An albino brush wallaby, *Wallabia*. Members of the kangaroo family normally produce only a single young at a time, and twins, as seen here, are rare. Albinism, the absence of body pigmentation, is a genetically produced condition and, although not common, it occurs in many mammals, including man.

Douglas Baglin/NHPA

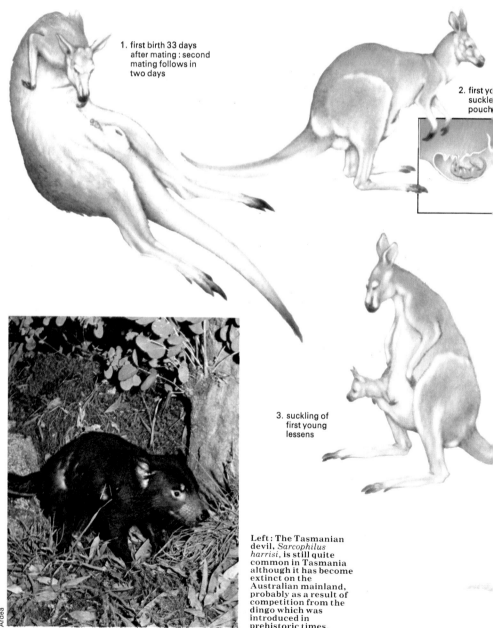

1. first birth 33 days after mating : second mating follows in two days

2. first yo suckle pouch

3. suckling of first young lessens

Left: The Tasmanian devil, *Sarcophilus harrisi*, is still quite common in Tasmania although it has become extinct on the Australian mainland, probably as a result of competition from the dingo which was introduced in prehistoric times.

Ardea

Len Robinson/Frank Lane

Above: Matschie's tree kangaroo, *Dendrolagus matschiei*. This strange animal lives in the forests of northern Australia and New Guinea feeding on fruit and leaves. It is not at all well adapted to its tree-dwelling existence, but this does not seem to matter because it has no natural enemies and food is plentiful.

Right: An Australian 'tiger cat', *Dasyurus maculatus*, devouring a crimson rosella parrot. These carnivorous marsupials are excellent climbers and they prey on lizards, fish and small mammals as well as birds. They were once slaughtered in large numbers for raiding chicken coops and are now quite rare.

NHPA

4. second birth after first young has left pouch : about seven months after second mating

second young suckles in pouch and first young returns to suckle occasionally

Left: A typical breeding sequence for the red kangaroo, *Macropus rufus*. After the first young is born (the mother leans back as the tiny embryo crawls up into her pouch) mating takes place for the second time. The fertilized egg, however, only begins to develop when the suckling of the first young has lessened. By the time the second animal is born, the first will have left the pouch, although it may still return to suckle occasionally.

snout, long hair and a long bushy tail. Its diet consists mainly of termites which it extracts from crevices and rotten wood with its long tongue. It lives only in a few small regions of central and southern Australia.

American marsupials

The two American marsupial families are the rat opossums, *Caenolestidae*, and the opossums, *Didelphidae*. There are only three species of rat opossums. They are small animals found in the forests of the Andes from Venezuela to southern Chile. Fossil evidence suggests that they are the survivors of a much larger marsupial group which flourished in the Tertiary period.

The most widely distributed member of the opossum family is the common opossum, *Didelphis marsupialis*, which is found from Argentina to Canada. It inhabits forests at all altitudes, feeding on insects and small mammals, but avoids grasslands and the high plains of the Andes. Opossums are solitary, nocturnal animals; they spend the hours of daylight in dens or nests taken over from other species. Despite their fairly large size—about 75 cm (2.5 ft) from head to tail—opossums do not live long. The average lifespan from weaning has been estimated to be only 1.3 years and the longest four years, so few opossums live beyond the summer following their birth. Even though females become mature at six months, they rarely breed more than once in a lifetime.

The water opossum, *Chironectes minimus*, of South America has the distinction of being the only marsupial adapted to an aquatic existence although its cousin the thick-tailed opossum, *Lutreolina crassicaudata*, is also a good swimmer. It lives on the banks of ponds and rivers feeding on shellfish, spawn and crayfish. The pouch of the water opossum, which opens to the rear, is equipped with a muscle so that it can be closed off when the animal dives, ensuring that the young remain dry while their mother searches for food.

Hedgehogs, Moles and Shrews

Hedgehogs, moles, shrews and a number of other small insect-eating mammals all belong to the order *Insectivora*. The grouping is largely one of convenience because its various members do not have many structural features in common: they are linked more by their way of life than anything else. Insectivores are small animals—none is larger than a rabbit and most are considerably smaller—which lead secret, often nocturnal, lives hidden in the undergrowth and the earth. It is not therefore surprising that although they are quite common they are only rarely seen.

The insectivores are placental mammals: they differ from both monotremes (such as the duck-billed platypus) and marsupials (such as kangaroos) in a number of important ways. The main distinction is that the young are retained within the mother's womb until an advanced stage of development and are nourished through a connecting organ called the placenta, a complex system of blood vessels and tissue. This arrangement provides maximum protection and a controlled environment for the growing embryo. Another important feature seen in placental mammals but not monotremes or marsupials is the *corpus callosum*, a bundle of nerve fibres which connects the left and right cerebral hemispheres of the brain providing improved co-ordination.

Hedgehogs and moles

Altogether there are more than 350 known species of insectivores and these are normally divided into eight families. The family *Erinaceidae* contains the hedgehogs and the moon rats. Hedgehogs are found throughout Europe, Africa and Asia, north to the latitude of Oslo and east as far as Borneo. They will inhabit any region where they can find food and dry shelter: hollow trees, the bases of hedges and cavities underneath farm buildings make popular living quarters. They line their nests with moss, leaves and grass but only rarely dig burrows of their own.

The most familiar feature of the hedge-

Above: A group of young European hedgehogs, *Erinaceus europaeus*, at the base of a tree. Hedgehogs are most active in the evening and early in the morning, probing among leaves and moss and under stones with their sensitive noses. They feed on insects, snails and even mice. In the autumn when the outside air temperature drops to around 10°C (50°F) hedgehogs begin their hibernation. First they burrow into their nest material and roll themselves into a ball to minimize heat loss. Then the body processes slow down: the breathing rate falls to about seven per minute and the heart rate to 20 per minute. The blood temperature falls dramatically although it is never allowed to drop below about 2°C (36°F). With the onset of warmer weather in the spring, the animal 'wakes' and immediately begins feeding.

Right: A common mole, *Talpa europaea*, feeding on an earthworm.

Below: The bizarre star-nosed mole, *Condylura cristata*, from North America.

Right: When alarmed a hedgehog rolls itself up into a ball, presenting a mass of sharp spines to its attacker.

Left: The bones in the hand of a mole are specially adapted to equip the animal for its burrowing way of life.

Below right: The lesser tenrec, *Echinops telfairi*, from Madagascar is a typical insectivore. It lives in gardens, the drier forests and sandy areas where it forages for snails, worms, insects and lizards. The sense of smell is well developed and the animal uses its long snout as well as its claws to uncover food.

Below: An elephant shrew, *Elephantulus brachyrhynchus*, eating an insect. Most elephant shrews, which inhabit central and southern Africa, have longer trunk-like snouts than this species. Their long hind legs enable them to jump and hop rapidly for considerable distances, and this, together with their long snouts, distinguishes them from other insectivores.

Left: The bicoloured white-toothed shrew, *Crocidura leucodon*, is common in central and southern Europe. It inhabits the undergrowth of hedges, fields and gardens, and like most insectivores it feeds mainly on invertebrate animals such as insects and earthworms. The smallest of all mammals is a shrew—Savis' pygmy shrew, *Suncus etruscus*—which measures only about 7 cm (2.7 in) from nose to tail.

Right: A Cape golden mole, *Chrysochloris asiatica*. It belongs to a different family from the European moles but has a similar way of life, constructing long burrows just below the surface and feeding on insects and earthworms.

hog is its covering of spines—as many as 16,000 extend over the animal's back and sides from its forehead to its rump. On the face and underside of the body is a covering of soft hair. The spines provide an almost impregnable defence against possible predators such as foxes, for when a hedgehog is alarmed it curls up into a tight ball by contracting its well developed skin muscles so that the soft parts of the body are protected and the spines point outwards. Hedgehogs are fairly agile and will eat almost anything, from insects, slugs and snails (their preferred diet) to fruit and berries, the young of nesting birds and amphibians and reptiles.

Some of the stranger habits of hedgehogs are not fully understood, including the peculiar habit of anointing the spines with saliva when chewing strong-smelling food, be it a toad or carrion. This behaviour may be to do with grooming or it may simply be a way of disguising the animal's own scent. Not surprisingly the many spines make grooming a difficult operation, and as a result hedgehogs are frequently plagued with parasites. Almost all wild hedgehogs are infested with fleas, *Archaeopsylla erinacei*, and many also carry ticks, mites and nematode worms.

Hedgehogs are remarkably resistant to poisons that would prove deadly to other mammals. It is well known that the European hedgehog will tackle a large adder; the snake has little chance of biting because of the hedgehog's spines and defence tactics. Hedgehogs eat blister beetles, which contain the powerful poison cantharidin, with no harmful effect and reputedly can tolerate 7,000 times as much tetanus toxin as a human. In the same family as the hedgehogs are the moon rats which are large opossum-like insectivores with striking black and white markings. They are nocturnal creatures and live in the lowland and mangrove forests of Malaysia.

The moles are classified in the family *Talpidae*. Among the several sub-families are the shrew moles of South East Asia, the desmans of east and southwest Europe, the Old World moles of Europe and Asia and the star-nosed moles of North America. The diversity of animals within one family is typical of the insectivores.

Moles, especially those of the genus *Talpa*, are well adapted to an underground life. The forelimbs and the hands are specialized; in the most extreme types, like the European mole, *Talpa europaea*, the shoulder girdle is shifted close to the neck and the front joint of the breast plate is prolonged forward and broadened to give a large area for the attachment of digging muscles. The size of the hand is increased by a special sickle-shaped bone and there is an equivalent bone in the feet which probably helps the animal to get a grip on the sides of its burrow. Most species of mole throw out the excavated earth from their burrows as 'molehills', pushing it up from below with the palms of the hands. The nest, made of dry leaves and grasses, is usually below ground and covered with a particularly large mound of earth known as a 'fortress'.

Most moles eat earthworms, and stocks of immobilized worms with their heads cut off are often kept as a food store. This diet is supplemented with insects while some of the North American moles eat large quantities of vegetable matter. Although moles have a poor sense of smell and poor eyesight, they make up for this by having extremely sensitive tactile organs located on the snout, as well as sensitive hairs on the nose and wrist. The extraordinary star-nosed mole of North America has a ring of 22 fleshy tentacles surrounding its nostrils. No doubt these help the animal to feel its way through the earth and locate its prey.

Shrews

The shrews form the largest family of insectivores (*Soricidae*) with over 300 species. They are found in most parts of the world, being absent only from Australasia and the southern part of South America. Shrews forage in and under the leaf litter and undergrowth of woods where they construct runs and shallow burrows. They are forever on the move and are extremely aggressive little animals, communicating with each other by high-pitched squeaks and twitterings. Like bats, they probably use echo location to help detect each other and their prey. Although they eat all kinds of insects, shrews will also tackle any other prey that they can overpower. The European common and pygmy shrews appear to favour woodlice, while the diet of some North American shrews includes a high proportion of vegetable matter.

To maintain their high metabolic rate, shrews have to eat a great deal of food, indeed their life is one continuous meal. The food consumed each day often exceeds the animal's body weight and digestion is very rapid, the gut being emptied in three hours. Common shrews are often found lying dead during the autumn; the cause of death most probably being cold and starvation. The reason why so many are found is that their skin contains strong-smelling glands which make them unpalatable to most carnivorous mammals which would otherwise eat them. The main predators of shrews are birds of prey, particularly owls.

It is easy to think of shrews as typical of European woodlands but they have an immense range and the 300 forms are spread throughout most of the world, with many species confined to the remote mountain streams of Tibet and eastern Asia. The strangest of all are the armoured shrews of tropical Africa. These medium-sized shrews show no outward appearance of anything unusual but their internal anatomy is quite extraordinary; the details of the vertebral column are like nothing found in any other mammal. The dorsal and many of the lumbar vertebrae are large and have a complex system of extensions, so that most of the backbone

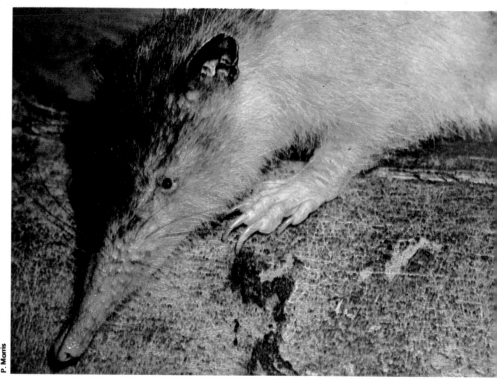

P. Morris

MOLE'S NEST COMPLEX

Tony Bemish/Ardea

forms a strong braced girder. The purpose of this strange fortified backbone remains a mystery but illustrates the unusual make-up of many insectivores.

The elephant shrews belong to a separate insectivore family, the *Macroscelididae*. They look like long-nosed rodents, and have large eyes, long legs and a stance and way of moving that is unlike other insectivores. Most elephant shrews (they get their name from their long, mobile snout) are about the size of a mouse and they live in the rocky scrub areas of northern Algeria and Morocco as well as in central and southern Africa. Some members of the group, like the giant elephant shrews, *Petrodromus* and *Rhynchocyon*, are forest dwellers and differ from the others in having only four toes on the hind feet. Elephant shrews feed almost exclusively on ants which they prise out of rotting wood and other crevices with their long snouts.

Other insectivore families

The smallest insectivore family, the *Solenodontidae*, contains only two rare species which are found on the islands of Cuba and Hispaniola (Haiti and the Dominican Republic) in the West Indies. Solenodons are odd-looking mammals about the size of a guinea pig, with long pointed snouts bristling with sensitive hairs. They have large naked ears and an equally naked rat-like tail. Solenodons live in rocky, wooded country where they hunt smaller mammals, reptiles and ground-nesting birds as well as the more usual insect diet.

Another group of island insectivores is the family *Tenrecidae* found only in Madagascar and the nearby Comoro Islands in the Indian Ocean. Most of the twenty or so species are nocturnal and dig their own burrows and nests. The tenrec, *Tenrec ecaudatus*, is the largest living insectivore and the most widely distributed and commonest member of the family. It has a long snout and a coat of mixed hairs and spines. The spines, mostly on the nape of the neck, are raised when the animal is alarmed giving this small mammal a ferocious appearance.

Closely related to the large family of tenrecs are the otter shrews of the family *Potamogalidae* which live on the mainland of Africa. As their name suggests, these aquatic insectivores look and behave like miniature otters. There are only three species of which the giant African otter shrew, *Potamogale velox*, is the largest. It inhabits lowland equatorial West Africa whereas the other two species (of the genus *Micropotamogale*) live only in the mountain streams of West Africa. All have a broad, flat head, small eyes and short soft fur, and they feed on a variety of prey such as fish, amphibians and crustaceans.

The golden moles make up the final family of insectivores, the *Chrysochloridae*. Although looking superficially like the true moles, these animals are more exotic in appearance: their fur is thick with a dense soft underfur and has an iridescent bronzy sheen of green, violet, yellow or red. The forelimbs are very powerful and have four digits, the outer ones small but the central two very large and armed with huge pointed claws. There is a hard leathery pad on top of the snout. They live in Africa south of the equator where they feed on insects, earthworms and lizards. The prey is held by the long fore-claws while being eaten.

Left: A solenodon, *Solenodon paradoxus*, from Haiti. Solenodons are not as defenceless as they look for they have very large incisors and also poisonous salivary glands (an unusual feature for a mammal) which they use to subdue large prey such as rodents. They are now quite rare and face extinction.

Above: A colugo, *Cynocephalus volans*, from the Philippines. Unlike other mammals which have developed the ability to glide, these animals have a web of skin stretching between the hind legs and the tail. Often misleadingly called 'flying lemurs', they are classified in an order of their own, the *Dermoptera*.

Below: All insectivores have much the same way of life. They live under the ground or on the surface sheltered by the undergrowth, feeding mainly on small invertebrates such as insects and earthworms. In this illustration of a typical insectivore habitat can be seen a European hedgehog, *Erinaceus europaeus*, a common mole, *Talpa europaea*, and its young, and a common European white-toothed shrew, *Crocidura russula*. Many beetle grubs lie buried in the ground—they will probably fall prey to moles. The inset shows how a mole's nest is surrounded by a network of tunnels. It often lies under a large mound of earth,

Bats

Bats inhabit almost every corner of the globe. Only in Antarctica, the Arctic tundra and a few remote islands are they unknown. The total number of individuals runs into tens of billions and there are more than 1,200 known species and sub-species. They belong to the order *Chiroptera* and, second only to the rodents (order *Rodentia*), constitute the largest population of mammals on earth.

Their small furry bodies and large membranous wings make bats instantly recognizable. They are the only mammals that can fly, although a number of creatures, such as the flying squirrels of West Africa, are able to glide from tree to tree. In most respects bats are typical placental mammals: their young are born alive and feed on their mother's milk. The group is divided into two sub-orders: the *Megachiroptera*, fruit-eating bats with large eyes, a clawed thumb and second finger and a small or non-existent tail, and the *Microchiroptera*, mainly insect-eating bats with claws only on the thumbs, a tail forming part of the wing and the ability to find their prey by echo location, or 'sonar'.

Bats are nocturnal, and this way of life suits them in several respects. Firstly, most species are tropical so daytime activity would expose the thin skin of their wings to the harmful effects of the ultra-violet radiation in sunlight. Also, the heat would increase the rate of water loss from these large surfaces, and so would restrict bats to feeding grounds close to water sources. For most bats, however, the most important advantage of a nocturnal lifestyle is that it makes available the enormous food supply of night-flying insects. During the day bats roost in caves or trees, hanging upside down from suitable perches.

Bats usually mate in the autumn before hibernating. The sperm from the male remains in the female's fallopian tubes

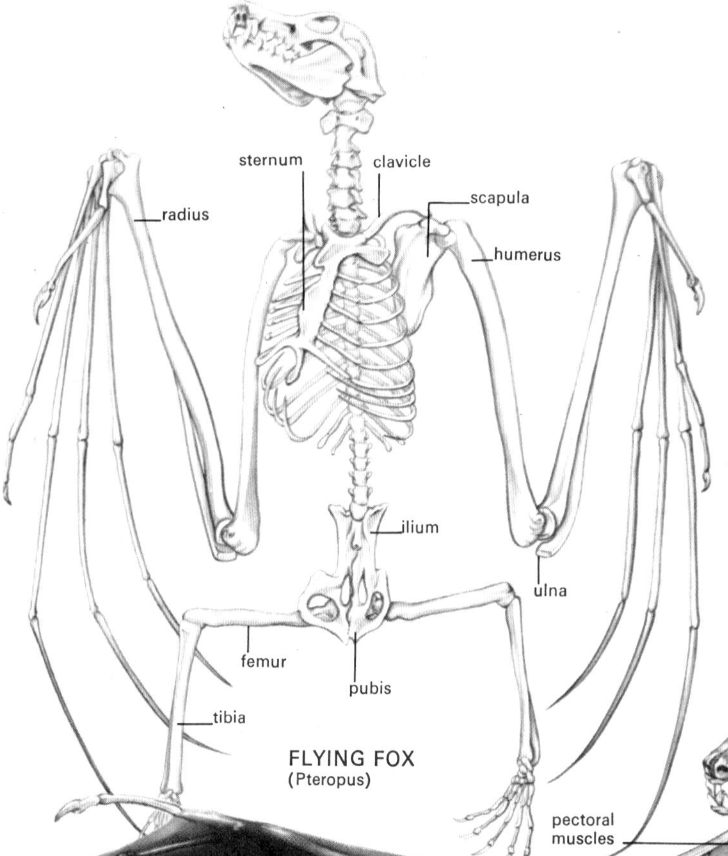

FLYING FOX
(Pteropus)

Labels: sternum, clavicle, radius, scapula, humerus, ilium, ulna, femur, pubis, tibia

Left: The skeleton of a flying fox, *Pteropus*. It has long arms and particularly long fingers for supporting the wings. The breast bone (sternum) has a keel to which the powerful flight muscles are attached. Ignoring those features which are special adaptations for flight, bats resemble the insectivores, such as shrews and moles.

Right: A nectar bat, *Leptonycteris sanborni*, feeds on the pollen and nectar of an agave flower and pollinates the plant. These bats have long tongues for probing flowers, but they also feed on insects. During the day they cluster together in groups in the hollows of cliffs and trees.

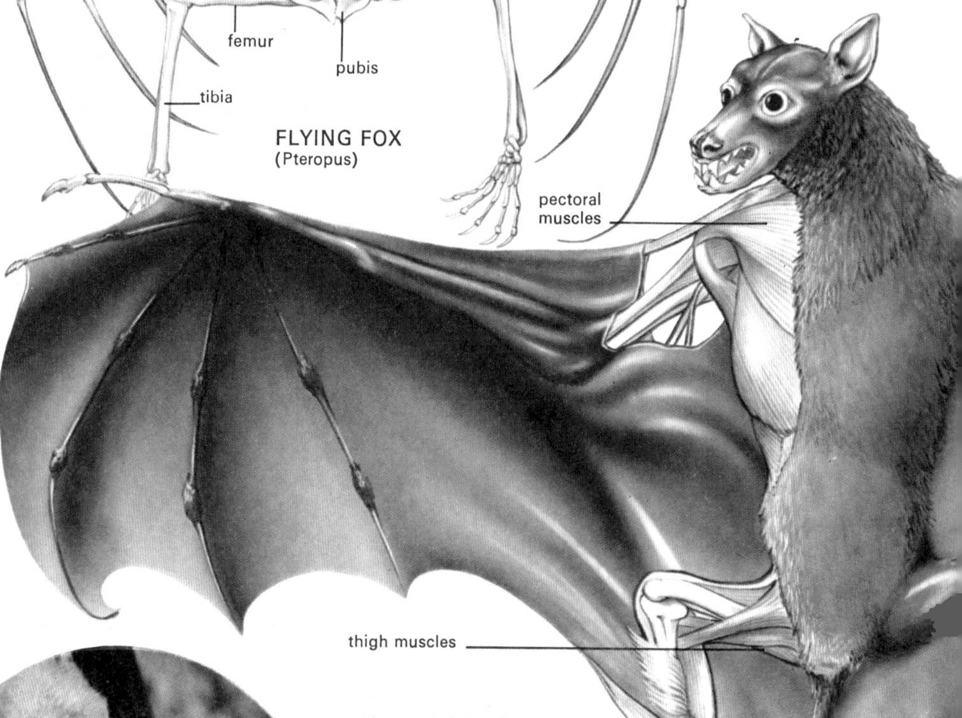

Labels: pectoral muscles, thigh muscles, calcar, tail, foo[t]

Above: A flying fox, *Pteropus*, partly cut away to show the wing structure and the arrangement of the muscles. The short first digit, or thumb, can be seen projecting from the front edge of each wing. The animal uses these for climbing. The wing membrane, or patagium, is joined to the fore and hind limbs.

Above: A long-tongued fruit bat, *Macroglossus logichilus*, from South East Asia. This species is the smallest of all fruit bats, having a body length of only about 6 cm (2.4 in).

Left: A flying fox, *Pteropus*, from the Seychelles. During the day, fruit bats like the flying fox roost in trees, wrapping their wing membranes around their bodies.

Right: An Indian short-nosed fruit bat, *Cynopterus sphinx*, feeds on a banana.

Heather Angel

S. C. Bisserot/Bruce Coleman

ZEFA

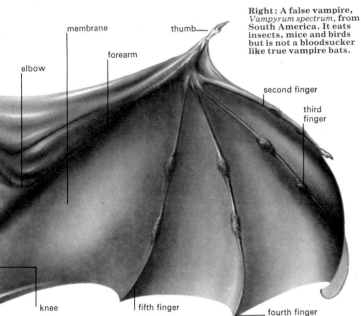

elbow
membrane
forearm
thumb
knee
fifth finger
second finger
third finger
fourth finger

Right: A false vampire,
Vampyrum spectrum, **from
South America. It eats
insects, mice and birds
but is not a bloodsucker
like true vampire bats.**

until the following spring, when the first egg is produced. A single foetus develops from the fertilized egg and the baby is born in the summer. At birth the young bat is naked and blind, and it clings to its mother's body to keep warm, travelling with her when she leaves the roost at night to feed. As the bat grows older it becomes less dependent on its mother, flying behind her at night and hanging next to her during the daytime rest period. Insect-eating bats develop quickly and are able to fly at an early age; they are fully grown in no more than eight weeks. Unlike birds, young bats seem to inherit their skill at flying, for they fly well from the beginning without any practice flights.

Flight

The wings of a bat are formed of skin and in this respect they resemble prehistoric flying reptiles like the pterodactyl more than birds. The design of the wings is essentially the same in all bats: there is a short, stout upper arm, a long, slender forearm and extremely long fingers which support the skin of the wing. The second finger extends along the leading edge of the wing; immediately behind it is the third and longest finger; and behind that are the fourth and fifth fingers, which are

well spaced out and serve as 'struts' to support and control the shape of about half of the wing membrane. The wing extends between the fingers and continues beyond the fifth finger to the side of the body and leg. It consists of upper and lower layers of skin enclosing a network of fine blood vessels. The animal's thumb, or first finger, projects from the front edge of the wing and carries a claw; it plays no part in supporting the wing.

Bats usually roost upside down. As they approach a landing they flip over in full flight, throw their hind claws against the roost, grasp it and hang. To take off they simply release their grip, fall for a short distance and begin to fly. A few heavier bats, such as the flying foxes, flap their wings to raise the body to a horizontal position before releasing their hold. Many bats do not fly more than two kilometres or so from their roost, although some species may cover 100 km (60 miles) or more on a round trip. A few species are known to migrate; the nectar bat, *Leptonycteris*, for example, travels from Mexico to Arizona for the summer. Bats fly at altitudes of anything up to about 300 m (1,000 ft); insect-eaters will naturally tend to fly at the same height as their insect prey.

Senses

The expression 'as blind as a bat' is very much misplaced. Many bats can see very well, and their eyes have become adapted to operating in extremely dim light. Bats that feed on fruit or flowers no doubt also use their sense of smell to detect their food. One of the most remarkable features of bats, however, is their sonar system which enables them to catch their prey and avoid obstructions such as trees and buildings when it is almost completely dark. Only one genus, *Rousettus*, of the sub-order *Megachiroptera* possesses it, but all members of the other sub-order *Microchiroptera* have this ability.

The bat sends out a series of high-pitched squeaks as it flies along, and the pattern of sounds in the echo tells it what objects are ahead, how far away they are and whether or not they are moving. The squeaks are short and intense, but their pitch (wave frequency) is too high to be heard by the human ear. However, bats also emit audible sounds as they fly about at dusk catching their prey. These sounds lie at the high frequency end of the human hearing ability and are more easily heard by children than adults. The sounds are emitted through the animal's mouth or nostrils, depending on the species. Those 241

Above: Common pipistrelle bats, *Pipistrellus*, **clinging to a wall. Insect-eaters are smaller than fruit-bats, and they have the advantage of a 'sonar system'.**

Left: A long-eared bat, *Plecotus auritus*. **These creatures belong to the largest of the bat families, the** *Vespertilionidae*, **and they are common throughout Europe. The enormous ears help give the animal the keen sense of hearing needed for its sonar system.**

Right: A tomb bat, *Taphozous melanopogon*, **from Malaya. The genus was first discovered in ancient Egyptian tombs by French naturalists in the late 18th century.**

bats that emit sound nasally usually have a large nose 'leaf' which probably acts rather like a reflector to 'aim' the sound in a particular direction. Bats which emit sound orally, on the other hand, usually form their mouth and lips into a megaphone shape to project the sound. The squeak of a bat is not a continuous sound but rather a series of individual sound pulses and the pitch of each pulse varies depending on whether the animal is cruising or closing in on a target.

Flying foxes

The largest of all bats are the flying foxes, *Pteropus*, from India, South-East Asia and Australia, which can weigh up to 1.5 kg (3.3 lb) and have a wingspan of up to 1.5 m (5 ft). They have a fox-like face and long sharp canine teeth, but despite their forbidding appearance they are strictly vegetarian. They use their teeth for tearing husks or even cracking coconuts. Flying foxes belong to the sub-order *Megachiroptera* and they have prominent well-developed eyes but no sonar system. Flying foxes live in colonies of many thousands of individuals. They roost in high trees during the day, moving to food trees, which they detect mainly by smell, in the evening. After returning to their roost the following morning they fly noisily around for several hours before settling down for the day. The roost is not a permanent site, for the bats will always rest close to a suitable source of food.

Insectivorous bats

Insect-eating bats are smaller than fruit bats. One of the smallest, *Pipistrellus nanulus*, from West Africa, has a body length of only four centimetres (1.6 in) when fully grown. Among the larger families of insect-eating bats are the horseshoe bats, *Rhinolophidae*, which are found from Western Europe across Asia to Australia; the Old World leaf-nosed bats, *Hipposideridae*, of Africa, southern Asia and Australia; and the New World leaf-nosed bats, *Phyllostomatidae*, of the southern United States and northern South America. The largest family of all

A BAT IN FLIGHT

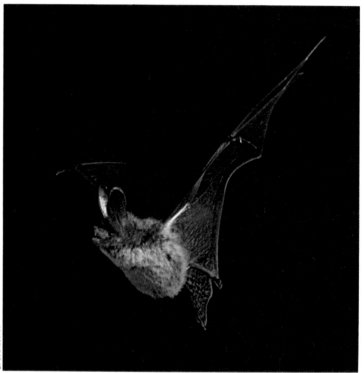

Above: A series of illustrations of a bat in flight.

Left: A Bechstein's bat, *Myotis bechsteini*, **is frozen by the camera in mid-flight. This is one of about 60 species of mouse-eared bats (genus** *Myotis*) **which are found in most parts of Europe. This particular species has larger ears than most other members of the genus. Mouse-eared bats roost together in large colonies, and their summer and winter quarters may be separated by as much as 200 km (120 miles). They hibernate in natural or artificial chambers such as caves and buildings.**

Right: A diadem round-leaf bat, *Hipposideros diadema*. **The strange shape of the nose has to do with the transmission of the ultrasonic 'squeaks' of the animal's echo location system. As with other leaf-nosed bats, the squeaks are emitted from the nostrils and not the mouth. Closely related to the leaf-nosed bats are the horseshoe bats which also have nostrils surrounded by skin growths.**

Below: A bat emits 'squeaks' at frequencies of up to 100,000 Hz (the limit of human hearing is 20,000 Hz) and the character of the echoes reflected back provides information about what lies in its path— how far away it is, its size and so on.

A BAT'S 'SONAR SYSTEM'

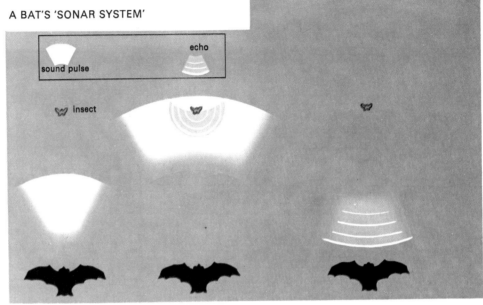

sound pulse

echo

insect

Left: A dog-faced fruit bat, *Cynopterus brachyotis*, roosting in a tree. As its name suggests, this bat's diet consists mainly of fruit: figs, bananas, guavos and mangos are popular food items. It inhabits the forests of India and South-East Asia. Very few predators feed on bats to any great extent; one that does is the bat hawk, *Machaeramphus alcinus*, from the tropics. Occasionally a bat will be taken by an owl, a mammal predator or a snake, but this is rare. Bats do, however, suffer from the attentions of parasites, particularly fleas, lice, ticks and mites. One family of wingless insects is found only on bats.

is the *Vespertilionidae* which is world-wide in its distribution.

Many insect-eating bats have adapted themselves to other food sources in order to supplement their diet. One of the most remarkable examples of this is the fishing bulldog bat, *Noctilio leporinus*, of Mexico and Central America. It uses its echo location system to detect fish under the water and then flies down to the surface and rakes the water with its long claws. In this way it usually succeeds in impaling a fish which it transfers to its mouth while in flight. If it is a long way from its roost the bat may chop up the fish with its teeth and store the pieces in its cheeks until it can eat them at leisure.

Another curious group of bats are the false vampires of the family *Megaderma-tidae*, which are strongly built animals with long, razor-sharp teeth. In addition to their normal diet of insects they prey on birds, smaller bats (though never their own species) and other small mammals. The African species *Lavia frons* is a dove-grey colour with pink wings and nose while the ghost bat of Australia, *Macroderma gigas*, has white wings, large white ears and a very pale body. These creatures are far removed from the popular conception of bats as dark, sinister animals.

Vampire bats

The notorious vampire bats belong to the family *Desmodontidae* and are related to the leaf-nosed bats. They are found only in the tropics and sub-tropics of the Americas and feed exclusively on the blood of vertebrate animals such as cattle, horses, dogs, poultry and even humans. Their prey is almost always warm-blooded. They are not particularly large bats, but have a broad skull and enormous incisor and canine teeth. The two upper incisors are curved and extremely sharp, the upper canines are large and pointed and the back molar and lower teeth are small.

The common vampire, *Desmodus rotundus*, lives in darkened caves which shelter many other kinds of bats. It feeds at night on the blood of cattle, landing very lightly on its victim. First of all it licks the spot it intends to bite, and this may serve as an anaesthetic since animals rarely stir when they are bitten. If the animal does wake the bat will immediately fly off. The wound is made by the front incisors and the tongue is extended and curled over at the edges. In conjunction with a deep groove in the lower lip, this forms a sort of 'straw' through which the blood is channelled. An anticoagulant in the bat's saliva prevents the blood from clotting while it is feeding.

The usual nightly consumption is about 30 g (1 oz). This may be taken from a single animal such as a cow, which may be bitten on the neck, ears or anal region, or from several smaller animals. Small birds are known to have been drained of blood by a vampire bat and so killed. Although the amount of blood taken by a single bat is relatively little, even quite a small colony may consume a considerable amount: 1,000 bats will need about 70 litres (15 gallons) of blood every night. Humans are attacked only rarely and when they are, the fingers, toes, ears, forehead or lips are usually the areas singled out. The loss of 30 g of blood is very unlikely to be serious, but vampire bats are carriers of the deadly disease of rabies and so a bite can be dangerous.

Elephants and Hyraxes

Man's association with the elephant dates from the earliest times. Many thousands of years ago the elephant and its relatives were a prized source of food: if a band of Paleolithic hunters could kill an elephant or a mammoth they would not need to hunt again for many days. More recently elephants have been hunted for their tusks, and countless animals were slaughtered in the 18th century and the first half of this century. Fortunately the ivory trade is now strictly controlled in most countries, so the pressure on the elephant population has been eased.

The Carthaginians were probably the first people to train elephants—they were used in the Punic Wars against the Romans. The Carthaginian general Hannibal took 38 elephants with him when he crossed the Alps with his army in 218 BC. Trained elephants are still used today in the forests of India and Burma for handling timber.

The elephant's closest living relatives are much less familiar creatures. They are the hyraxes, which belong to the order *Hyracoidea*, and the sea cows, which belong to the order *Sirenia*. The hyraxes are small furry animals looking rather like large guinea pigs, while the sea cows are aquatic mammals which resemble seals. From its outward appearance the hyrax would seem an unlikely relative of

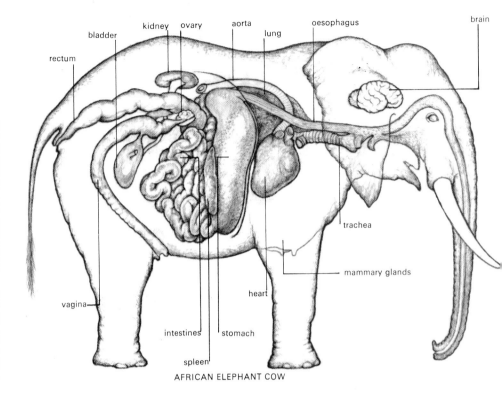

AFRICAN ELEPHANT COW

Above: A body plan of a female African elephant, *Loxodonta africana*, showing most of the main body organs. The brain is larger than that of any other land mammal, and research has shown that elephants have a well developed learning ability. There may therefore be some truth in the saying 'elephants never forget'.

Below: Only rarely will elephants charge in earnest; usually they halt or veer off before reaching their target, but wounded animals can be very dangerous. The African elephant was once found throughout Africa, but the ivory trade drastically reduced the population and now they are rarely found outside reserves.

Above: An Indian elephant feeding on bamboo in the Chitwan National Park of Nepal. An elephant's digestive system is inefficient; about half of what it eats is excreted undigested. To allow for this, elephants must eat even more food than the already enormous amount their bodies actually need.

Below: The great weight of an African elephant enables it to fell sizeable trees without much difficulty. It does this to get at the leaves near the top of the tree, which would otherwise be out of reach. A herd of elephants can quite quickly demolish whole stands of trees in this manner.

Left: An Indian elephant, *Elephas maximus*, at work lifting rocks. Although the species is in decline, wild Indian elephants are still hunted and put to work in such countries as Burma. The hunt, called a *khedda*, may involve as many as 2,000 drivers and 50 tame work elephants. A herd of wild elephants is slowly surrounded by this army of hunters and driven into a strong wooden enclosure. Once caught, the elephants are easily trained, and each animals will have just one keeper and driver, the *mahout*, throughout its working life.

Below: A herd of African elephants on the march. These animals can migrate hundreds of kilometres to escape from regions of drought, often negotiating formidable obstacles in their path. They have been known to swim across more than one kilometre of open ocean to get from one island to another—they swim with their trunks held above their heads like a snorkel. Steep slopes present few problems for elephants; even large bulls are surefooted.

Sylva/Tierbilder Okapia

Des Bartlett/Bruce Coleman

mature cow

immature cow

immature bull

young

mature bull

Left: A herd of elephants has a well defined structure. The main part of the herd is led by a large cow elephant and is composed only of females, immature animals and calves. Mature bulls live apart from the herd, and the oldest bulls, which are often very bad tempered, are completely solitary.

the elephant, but scientists have shown that the two animals must have had a common ancestor in comparatively recent times. Skeletal features such as the crossing of the bones of the forelimb and the flattening of the bones below the wrist are shared by animals in both groups.

Evolution

Elephants are descended from a small animal, *Moeritherium*, which lived in what is now Egypt about 45 million years ago. This creature was only about 60 cm (2 ft) high and had no trunk. In the course of time its descendants grew larger and developed long trunks and tusks. They colonised all the continents of the world except Australia, Antarctica and much of South America.

The closest and most recent of the elephant's ancestors were the mammoths, *Mammuthus*, and the mastodons, *Mammut*. Mammoths flourished only in cold climates: during periods of glaciation they inhabited central and southern Europe, but during interglacial periods they would retreat northwards with the ice. The largest of these creatures was the mammoth *Mammuthus imperator*, an enormous animal with a shoulder height of around 4.5 m (15 ft), which roamed the southern half of North America.

We know a considerable amount about the woolly mammoth, *Mammuthus primigenius*, which inhabited Europe and Asia and probably died out less than 10,000 years ago in Siberia. Paintings of the animal, made in French caves by its Paleolithic hunters, show a creature outwardly like an elephant but with very long hair, long curved tusks and a huge hump at the back of the neck. These drawings are now known to be remarkably accurate, for the remains of complete animals 'deep frozen' in the Siberian ice have the same features. The excellent state of preservation of many of these frozen mammoths has allowed a detailed study of them—even the contents of their stomachs have been found intact.

The evolution of the hyraxes has been much less varied than that of the elephants. The group probably branched from the same evolutionary line as the elephants in the late Paleocene epoch about 55 million years ago. Fossils found in Africa show that hyraxes have existed in more or less their modern form at least since the Oligocene epoch 35 million years ago.

Hyraxes

Hyraxes are alert, energetic animals, rather fat with pointed muzzles and small rounded ears. They are about the same size as a rabbit and have brown fur with a patch of yellow, white or black fur surrounding a scent gland in the middle of the back. Like elephants they are herbivores and feed on leaves, climbing trees to reach them, and grass. There are eleven species divided between three genera. The members of two genera (*Heterohyrax* and *Procavia*) are called rock hyraxes while the members of the third (*Dendrohyrax*) are known as tree hyraxes. Hyraxes are found only in Africa, Arabia and Syria.

Rock hyraxes live in colonies of from 30 to 60 individuals. They are found in the dry, semi-arid areas bordering deserts and also high up mountains, such as Mount Kenya, in the rain and mist. They are unable to burrow for themselves and make their homes in existing holes beneath the

Left: A group of
African elephants (cows
and young) leaving a
water hole. A young
elephant is protected
not only by its own
mother but also by other
cows in the herd.
Sometimes 'kindergarten'
groups composed of
several young animals
and one or two adult
cows will split off
from the main body of
the herd.

Right: An Indian
elephant bathing in a
river. Elephants
usually bathe several
times each day; it
helps them to cool off
as well as providing an
opportunity to drink.
They can drink about 50
litres on each occasion,
sucking the water up
into the trunk and
then squirting it
into the mouth.

Below: A newly born
African elephant is
helped to its feet for
the first time by its
mother. It weighs about
100 kg (220 lb) and is
about 1 m (3 ft) tall.

rocks. Normally they are careful to choose
holes with small entrances so that they
can escape from their chief predator, the
leopard. As its name implies the tree hyrax
is arboreal—it inhabits the great rain
forests of West Africa. It is a solitary
animal, an extremely agile climber and
lives in hollow trees.

Elephants

Only two species of elephant (order
Proboscidea) survive today: the Asiatic
elephant, *Elephas maximus*, and the
African elephant, *Loxodonta africana*.
The African elephant is the larger of the
two, a mature bull standing 3.4 m (11 ft)
or more at the shoulder and carrying
tusks between 1.8 and 2.4 m long (6-8 ft).
The largest elephant ever recorded was
shot in Angola in 1955: it measured 4 m
(13 ft) at the shoulder and weighed nearly
11 tonnes.

The Asiatic elephant seldom stands
more than three metres (10 ft) at the
shoulder and its tusks are usually between
1.2 and 1.5 m long (4-5 ft). While female
African elephants have long, if slender
tusks, females of the Asiatic species are
either tuskless or have very small tusks,
known as 'tushes', which do not project
beyond the jaw. The females of both
species weigh between one and two tonnes
less than the males.

In side view the two species look very
different. The ears are the most obvious
distinguishing feature, being so large in
the African species that they cover the
whole of the neck and shoulders and
reach as low as the breast; the ears of the
Asiatic species are relatively small. The
back of the African elephant has a marked
dip between the fore and hind quarters,

Left: The woolly mammoth, *Mammuthus primigenius*, was one of the more recent relatives of the modern elephant. It flourished in the late Ice Age and had a thick coat of long hair to resist the cold. It was hunted by prehistoric man for its flesh and hide, and died out less than 10,000 years ago.

Above: An African elephant dusting itself. This behaviour may help to keep down the number of insects, such as elephant lice, which live in the many folds of the animal's skin. An elephant's skin is quite sensitive and the animal quickly feels uncomfortable if it is carrying too many parasites.

whereas the back of the Asiatic elephant tends to be slightly humped. The trunks of the two species are also slightly different: in the African elephant it is marked by horizontal ridges and ends in two fleshy outgrowths or 'fingers', but in the Asiatic species it is relatively smooth and has only a single outgrowth.

Next to its size the elephant's most distinctive feature is its trunk. This is an extremely sensitive organ both of touch and smell, and is ideally suited to searching for food. It has evolved from the animal's upper lip rather than its nose, although it does enclose the nostrils which open at its tip. An elephant uses its trunk not only to search for food but also to transfer the food to its mouth. It grasps leaves and grass by coiling its trunk around them or by holding them between the fingerlike outgrowths at the tip of the trunk. When drinking, water is sucked into the trunk and then squirted into the mouth. The trunk also acts as an amplifier for a variety of different sounds expressing pleasure, dislike, apprehension and so on. Elephants produce a distinctive trumpeting sound when they are excited and this is actually created in the trunk itself rather than the larynx.

Elephants have to learn how to use their trunks; it is not an instinctive skill. Baby elephants evidently find their trunk a considerable inconvenience—not only do they have no use for it at first (they drink and feed with their mouths) but also it gets in their way and they tend to trip over it. They solve the problem by curling it up or holding it to one side.

Feeding
Elephants are herbivorous animals, feeding mainly on grass and leaves. As with other plant-eating mammals their molar teeth are particularly suited to grinding vegetable material. During its life an elephant develops 24 of these molars, although only one or two on each side of each jaw are ever in use at the same time. While the first group of four are being worn down, four new teeth are growing behind them; these gradually move forward to replace the old teeth, which are eventually shed. Each successive tooth is larger than the last, and when the sixth and largest tooth, which may be 30 cm (one foot) long and weigh 4 kg (9 lb), has passed through each half of each jaw no further teeth can be grown. It is the rate of deterioration of these final teeth that determines an elephant's maximum lifespan, for it cannot survive without them. Normally

they will be very worn by the time the animal is 60 and elephants rarely live beyond this age.

Not surprisingly, elephants eat an enormous quantity of food. A fully grown elephant in a zoo will eat about 45 kg (100 lb) of hay every day. Zoo animals are usually females, however, and a large bull might be expected to eat twice as much. An elephant's thirst matches its appetite; the daily water intake for an adult animal is between 130 and 230 litres (30 to 50 gallons).

Social behaviour
Elephants are gregarious animals and live in herds. The herd is composed of a number of distinct family groups, each consisting of a matriarch, her daughters and her grandchildren. Males, except for the younger ones, are not normally tolerated within these groups and they spend much of their time alone or in small groups some way off from the rest of the herd. For communal activities such as bathing or drinking, however, the herd becomes more integrated, while females will temporarily leave the family group for mating. Bull elephants become bad tempered and unpredictable in their old age and they then live entirely alone.

Pregnancy in elephants lasts for between 19 and 22 months, and at birth the calf weighs about 100 kg (220 lb) and is about 85cm (34 in) high. Sometimes other females in the family group assist the birth by removing the foetal membrane and then helping the calf to its feet. After about 20 minutes the baby elephant can stand on its own. The mother will help her clumsy offspring while it is very young by moving obstacles such as fallen trees out of its way or even lifting it over them. All the cows in the family group are attentive to the young; they fondle them, wash them and protect them from danger. The bulls rarely come into contact with the calves and have nothing to do with their upbringing.

When the herd is on the move the elephants travel in single file. The cows usually go first, their calves trotting behind, while the young males form separate contingents. Normal marching speed is about 10 kph (6 mph) but this can be raised in an emergency to a fast shuffle of 25 kph (15 mph) or more. An elephant walks on its toes—its 'knee' joint is really the equivalent of our wrist—and its legs are ideally adapted to support its vast bulk. Elephants can neither trot nor gallop, but they can move through the jungle very quietly.

Left: A group of Cape hyraxes, *Procavia capensis*, resting on a rock. They live in small colonies and one or two animals act as guards while the remainder of the group feed or rest. The main predators are eagles and leopards. Cape hyraxes feed on grass and shrubs during the day, spending the night in holes and crevices among the rocks.

Right: A common tree hyrax, *Dendrohyrax arboreus*, from East Africa. Unlike rock hyraxes, tree hyraxes are nocturnal and solitary animals. They proclaim their territory at night by loud and penetrating calls each consisting of a succession of screams.

Rhinos and Tapirs

The largest living land mammal after the elephant is the rare square-lipped rhinoceros of Africa: adult males may stand over 1.8 m (6 ft) at the shoulders and weigh more than three tonnes. Their huge size and strange 'armoured' appearance have long fascinated Europeans: Dürer's well known woodcut of an Indian rhino, executed in 1515, aroused a great deal of interest. The large pointed horn on the rhino's snout has earned the animal an undeserved reputation for fierceness—in fact this timid creature will charge an intruder only if suddenly alarmed.

The rhino's nearest relatives are the tapirs. They have much the same body shape as rhinos, but are considerably smaller, lack the rhino's horn and have a generous coat of hair. Rhinos and tapirs, together with their more fleet-footed cousins the horses and zebras, belong to the order *Perissodactyla*. Members of this group have a number of important features in common: they are all plant-eaters and have noticeably elongated skulls to accommodate the continuous row of broad cheek teeth needed to cope with their diet of grass and leaves. Their feet have an odd number of toes, the weight of the body being carried mainly or entirely by the third toe of each limb, which terminates in a hoof.

Tapirs

The tapirs living today are the survivors of a much larger group, which in its heyday populated much of the globe. Fossil remains from that time (the Miocene epoch, which began about 26 million years ago) show that tapirs have remained almost unchanged for many millions of years: the modern species look very much the same as their ancestors must have done. But they are now found only in Central and South America and Malaya.

Tapirs are solitary jungle animals with short legs, rounded ears, small eyes and a short proboscis or trunk formed by an extension of the upper lip and the nose. They are animals of habit, keeping to well-used paths through the thick undergrowth where they browse on leaves and shoots. Like many forest dwellers they have poor eyesight, but make up for this by good hearing and an acute sense of smell.

Tapirs are particularly fond of water and frequently wallow in river shallows. Bathing probably helps them to get rid of irritating parasites such as ticks and other biting insects. In the wild tapirs often defecate in or near their favourite water hole; possibly this serves as a recognition signal to others of the species. Rhinos behave in the same way. There is only one genus of tapirs, *Tapirus*, with four species of which one is Asiatic and three South American.

The Malayan tapir inhabits the Malay peninsula and the island of Sumatra and is the largest of the four species, having a nose to tail length of around 2.5 m (8 ft). The body markings of the adult animal are unusual: the head, shoulders, limbs

Left: Albrecht Dürer's famous woodcut of an Indian rhinoceros, executed in 1515. Dürer clearly shows the heavy 'armour' of this huge beast which, unlike the African rhinos, normally has one horn only. Dürer cannot have drawn from life, for he also shows a small extra horn on this rhino's back.

Right: A young black rhino, *Diceros bicornis*. The two large horns characteristic of this species are only partly formed. Black rhinos are found only in Africa, where they were once widely distributed. Today their numbers are seriously depleted—a 1967 estimate gave a total of about 12,000, of which almost one-third were in Tanzania.

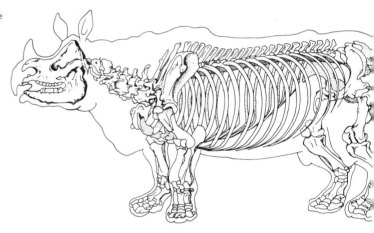

Right: The skeleton of an Indian rhinoceros. The anatomical structure has changed very little in the last million years. The vertebral column acts like a girder balanced on the front legs, and the weight of the body is carried almost entirely by the third toe of each foot, which ends in a kind of hoof.

Below: Black rhinos rarely travel in groups of more than five; when two are found together they will usually be a bull and a female, or a mother and her young. It was once thought that the birds which follow rhinos picked the ticks from their skin, but it now appears they are interested only in the insects stirred up by the animals walking.

Tierbilder Okapia

Left: Black rhinos mating. During their courtship, the animals sniff at each others' mouths, frequently uttering gurgling noises. The female will often charge the male, butting hard into his flanks. Black rhinos can conceive at any time of year; the gestation period is about 15 months.

Below: Black rhinos are mainly nocturnal, and spend most of the day sleeping in sand or dust-filled hollows. Sometimes seen in mountain forests as high up as 2,100 m (7,000 ft), their normal habitat is the open plain, with mixed vegetation. Their pointed upper lip is used for stripping foliage from shrubs and bushes. They have no incisors or canine teeth.

Jacana

Frank Lake

and belly are black, while the back and flanks are white. The young, like those of all tapirs, are strikingly marked with a series of horizontal stripes and dots. Both the adult's body pattern and that of the young has a camouflaging effect, breaking up the animal's outline and making it difficult to detect in the changing light and shade of the jungle.

The three South American tapirs all have a uniform brownish coat with slight differences in shade, thickness and texture between the species. The Central American tapir is the largest mammal of the American tropics and also has the distinction of being one of the rarest. The second species, the lowland tapir, is the most common, and inhabits the forests of the northern part of South America. The mountain tapir is the rarest of all and lives in the northern Andes at altitudes between 1,800 and 3,600 m (6,000 to 12,000 ft). It has a thicker coat than its lowland relatives to protect it from exposure and extremes of temperature.

Being solitary and rather shy animals, tapirs avoid areas which are inhabited by man, retreating further into the forest whenever a part of their territory is cleared for cultivation. Consequently, the populations of all tapir species are declining as their jungle habits are eroded, and this trend will only be halted if areas of tropical forest are set aside as sanctuaries, free from development by man.

Rhinos

The rhinos are the only surviving large perissodactyls. Like tapirs they are mainly nocturnal and timid creatures, though they will charge when threatened, especially when protecting their young. The skin is characteristically thick and has little hair. The horns are composed entirely of hair-like growths set above thickenings of the nasal bone and (in two-horned species) the frontal bones. They are not attached to the skull, and may even be torn off in fighting; when this happens they quickly grow again.

The largest rhinoceros is the square-lipped rhino, *Ceratotherium simum*, from Africa. The upper lip is very broad, having evolved to equip the animal for grazing. This rhino is a gregarious creature, living in small herds on the open savannah, and at one time it occupied most of the open grassland south of the Sahara. In the Pleistocene epoch, about one million years ago, it could be found as far north as Algeria and Morocco.

There are two surviving races of square-lipped rhino, separated by more than 1,200 miles (2,000 km). The northern race lives in southwest Sudan, Uganda and Zaire, and it is seriously threatened with extinction—only about 300 individuals still survive in the wild. Early white settlers pursued the animal for its tasty flesh and for its hide, and nowadays it is poached for its horn, which the Chinese value for its undeserved reputation as a powerful aphrodisiac. The southern race, which lives in Natal, South Africa, is more fortunate. Although it is found only in a relatively small region, it has been protected there since 1897 and its future seems assured.

The black rhino, *Diceros bicornis*, is smaller than the 'square lip', standing less than 1.5 m (5 ft) at the shoulder. It is a browser rather than a grazer and has a prehensile upper lip which it uses for reaching and stripping off foliage from

249

Above: *Dicerorhinus sumatrensis*, the Sumatran rhino, is the smallest and hairiest species. It is now extremely rare and expected to become extinct, for its natural habitat is being destroyed by the timber and rubber industries. Moreover, the Chinese believe powdered rhino horn to be aphrodisiac, and poaching has proved impossible to reduce significantly.

Left: The great Indian rhino, *Rhinoceros unicornis*, is found today only in protected areas. Large folds divide the skin into sections marked by flat bumps which look like rivets. Despite its appearance, the skin is not very thick, and many bulls carry large scars caused by fighting.

Above: Four related species of perissodactyls. Remains of the whoolly rhino (1), now extinct, have been found as far apart as China, Russia and Spain. The Javan rhino, (2) *Rhinocerus sondaicus*, is practically extinct. (3) *Tapirus bairdi*, the Central American tapir. (4) The mountain tapir, *Tapirus pinchaque*.

Left: *Ceratotherium simum*, the square-lipped rhinoceros, is better known as the 'white' rhino—a mistranslation of the Afrikaans work *wijde*, meaning 'wide'. The largest of all rhinos, they reach a height of some 2 m, and weigh up to 3 tonnes. Their horns are attached rather loosely to the skin and are easily torn off, but quickly grow again.

Right: *Tapirus terrestris*, the most common of the tapir species. All young tapirs have horizontal stripes and dots on their coats; these usually take about a year to disappear. The projecting upper lip is adapted for tearing off leaves and shoots from trees and bushes.

Left: The Malayan tapir, *tapirus indicus*, is easily identified by its distinctive markings. These are ideal for camouflage in the changing patterns of light and shade of its natural forest habitat. They break up the outlines of the body so that, lying down in the daytime, the tapir looks just like a pile of stones.

Below: Past and present distribution of tapirs and rhinos. The South American lowland tapir and the African black rhino are the only species with a good chance of survival, although both their populations have been seriously reduced in recent years. Rhinos are hunted for their meat and their horns, which are prized for their supposed medicinal properties. The animal is rarely found today outside protected areas. Tapirs live mainly in forested regions and their habitats are being progressively destroyed by timber companies and rubber plantations. They are hunted for meat and for their skins, which can be tanned and cut into long straps for reins and whips. They are often killed as pests.

Bruce Coleman

T DISTRIBUTION OF
S

PAST AND PRESENT DISTRIBUTION OF
RHINOS

AFRICA

INDIA

SOUTH-EAST
ASIA

SOUTH
AMERICA

BORNEO

MALAYA

SUMATRA

SUMATRA

JAVA

Lowland Tapir
Mountain Tapir
Central American Tapir
Malayan Tapir

● Present populations
Javan Rhino
Sumatran Rhino
Great Indian Rhino
African Rhino

shrubs and bushes. It was once widely distributed in Africa, from Cape Province to eastern Africa and as far north as the Sudan, but only scattered populations remain today. Although not classed as endangered its status is vulnerable.

The black rhino spends much of its life within a well defined home range which may vary from 8 to 50 sq km (3 to 20 sq miles) in area and changes according to the seasons and consequent food supply. When they meet their neighbours in overlapping parts of their ranges black rhinos are not usually aggressive, but determined trespassing is not tolerated and a large intruder may be suddenly charged.

The largest of the Asiatic rhinos is the great Indian rhino, *Rhinoceros unicornis*, which can approach the size of a square-lipped rhino. Unlike its African relatives it has only a single horn. The upper lip is prehensile and the lower jaw contains a large pair of incisor teeth which have developed into tusks and are used with great effect for self-defence.

The Indian rhino once inhabited a wide tract of country in northern India and Nepal, from the foothills of the Hindu Kush to the Burmese border, but today less than 1,000 individuals remain in eight reserves in India and Nepal. This impressive animal lives a slow and quiet existence in secluded swampy areas where there is an abundance of tall grass and reeds. Its diet includes a large number of food plants, including many agricultural crops.

The Javan rhinoceros, *Rhinoceros sondaicus*, is the rarest of all rhinos. It looks like a smaller version of the Indian rhino, but the skin folds are slightly different and the male's horn is shorter—it is absent altogether in females. The Javan rhino's favourite food has been reported to be the peculiar 'tepus' plant, one of the ginger family which throws up 5.5 m (18 ft) broad-leaved spikes but carries its red flowers at or below ground level. The horn trade has wiped out all but a few of these creatures and it seems likely that the population of Javan rhinos is now too small for the species to survive, and it will probably soon be extinct.

The smallest and hairiest rhino is the Sumatran rhino, *Dicerorhinus sumatrensis*. Small isolated populations occur in widely separated areas of Asia from Burma southeast through Thailand to Sumatra and Borneo. It has two horns—the front one reaches a length of up to a foot (30 cm) while the back one is usually no more than a slight hump.

Sumatran rhinos favour forested hill country and are extremely agile: they can climb up steep mountain slopes with no apparent difficulty. They browse on twigs and leaves, invariably feeding in virgin forest or very old regenerated jungle. Like the Javan rhino they are very rare and the principal cause of their decline has been over-hunting. In 1972 a single rhino carcass was worth more than 2,000 US dollars, many times the annual earnings of most local farmers, so it is hardly surprising that the animals are so ruthlessly hunted.

Responsibility for the survival of both rhinos and tapirs rests with man. Conservation areas, such as the famous Chitwan National Park in Nepal (where there is now a good stable population of Indian rhinos), are likely to play an increasingly important role as the animals' natural habitats are destroyed.

Bruce Coleman

Horses, Asses and Zebras

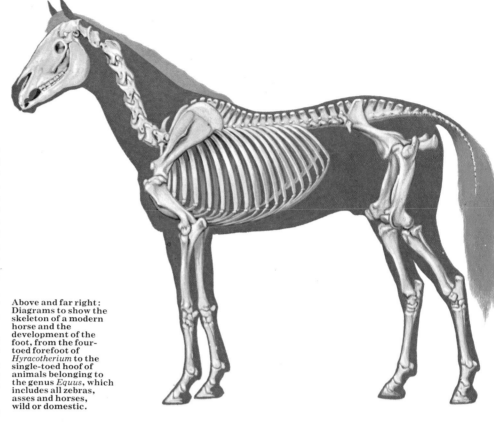

The horse family, together with the rhinoceros and the tapir, belongs to the order of mammals known as *perisso-dactyls*—hoofed animals with an odd number of toes on each foot. Their most important feature is not that they have an odd number of toes, but that the weight is borne by the middle toe. The toes on either side—numbers one and five, and sometimes numbers two and four as well—are very small or absent altogether, to make the foot lighter for fast running. The perissodactyls move on tiptoe, and in the case of the horse family only the hoofs (which are modified claws) touch the ground.

Speed is very important to the horse and its relatives for they are grazing animals and need to be able to escape from predators on the open plains where they feed. Horses are the most lightly built of all the perissodactyls; they have only one toe left on each foot and are the fastest members of the group. The Asian wild ass has been clocked running at 50 kph (31 mph). Racehorses are appreciably faster than this, reaching nearly 64 kph (40 mph), but they would be too delicate to survive on their own in the wild.

Evolution

The history of the perissodactyls goes back 55 million years to *Hyracotherium*, a plant-eating animal the size of a terrier which lived in Europe and North America, then tropical and densely forested. By 35 million years ago many very varied forms existed, but since that time the perissodactyls have been in decline. The position they once occupied as the most widespread large, plant-eating mammals has now been taken by the even-toed hoofed animals, or *artiodactyls*, such as deer, antelopes and cattle. It is not known for certain why artiodactyls should be more successful, but it is probably connected with their ability to chew the cud: this not only makes digestion more efficient but also allows them to eat their food in a place of safety.

All these modern members of the horse family have long heads, allowing ample room for the battery of grinding teeth, deep-chested bodies with plenty of space for the lungs and for digesting the bulky

Above and far right: Diagrams to show the skeleton of a modern horse and the development of the foot, from the four-toed forefoot of *Hyracotherium* to the single-toed hoof of animals belonging to the genus *Equus*, which includes all zebras, asses and horses, wild or domestic.

Hans Hinz

Jacana

Above: Cave painting showing a horse. Such early Stone Age paintings may have had a magic purpose: to ensure success in hunting or to provide dwelling places for the spirits of slain animals.

Left: Przewalski's horse, *Equus przewalskii*, having almost entirely disappeared from the wild, now exists mainly in zoos. Although in captivity, it retains its old modes of behaviour. The stallion, for instance, still stands apart from the herd which, when feeding, faces him. If the herd becomes scattered when in an open space or when being exercised, he will bring it together again, and will defend it against intruders.

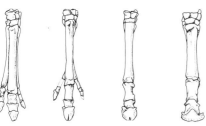

Above: Mustangs, found mainly in south-west US, are the descendants of imported European domestic horses, *Equus caballus*, who went wild. Large numbers were caught and tamed by later colonists and by Indians, notably the Mohawks, who used them to develop the Indian Pony. Today, only about 20,000 mustangs survive.

Above: A palomino mare and foal. Palominos derive mainly from domestic horses of Arabian origin, and their typical adult colouring is pale tan, yellow or gold with a white or silver mane and tail.

Left: Modern thoroughbreds such as this one are the result of crossbreeding between pure Arabian horses and other thoroughbreds. The type was specifically bred for speed and endurance to produce potential racehorses. Suitability for the racetrack is still one of the criteria needed to earn the title thoroughbred, as is an unbroken line of descent in the stud book. All thoroughbreds have narrow heads and are quite tall, reaching 160-180 cm (64-72 in) at the shoulder.

Below: Shire horses are strong, draught animals, once bred chiefly in the Midland shires of England. These and similar breeds are larger, heavier and more docile than other types of horse, and probably all originate from a subspecies of the wild horse, *Equus przewalskii robustus*, which died out in the Middle Ages.

diet, and long, very slender legs. Zebras are in several respects most like the ancestors of the group, and it may be that all living forms are descended from striped animals; there is no way of being certain, however, for fossils very rarely retain their natural colours. Certainly all the living forms are quite closely related, for they can all interbreed, although with the possible exception of a very few female mules (the offspring of male domestic donkeys and female horses) the progeny of these hybrids are invariably sterile.

Horses

Although the domesticated horse, *Equus caballus*, has run wild in several parts of the world—examples are the mustangs of North America, the brumbies of Australia, and the Dartmoor ponies of Great Britain —almost all genuine wild horses have been killed by man within the past few thousand years. The only survivors became known to European naturalists in 1879 when a Polish explorer, Przewalski, discovered them on the steppes of Mongolia.

Today very few of this type, known as Przewalski's horses or *Equus przewalskii*, survive in the wild, but the species breeds well in zoos and is in no immediate danger of extinction. Przewalski's horse is stockily built and tan in colour, the legs and the short, stiff mane being somewhat darker. In appearance it differs only slightly from cave paintings of the wild horses that lived in western Europe perhaps 20,000 years ago.

The wild tarpan belonged to a smaller, greyer race of Przewalski's horse which lived on the Russian steppes of Europe until at least the 18th century. It disappeared gradually by interbreeding with escaped domestic horses. In Roman times there were still several types of wild horses in Europe, inhabiting plains, swampy areas, and forests. It seems likely that domestic horses are descended from several of these forms producing the variety of size and shape displayed by, for example, a racehorse and a Shetland pony.

253

Donkeys and asses

The origins of the domestic donkey are clearer. It was bred perhaps 5,000 years ago from the African wild ass, *Equus africanus*, of which two races survive. Both inhabit hot, dry, hilly areas, the Somali wild ass being found in Somalia, and the Nubian wild ass further north in areas between the Red Sea and the Nile and also in parts of the Sahara Desert. The Somali race is distinguished by stripes on all four legs, and all African wild asses are very lightly built with donkey-like ears.

Opinions are divided as to whether Asia holds one species of wild ass or two; perhaps most experts would say that there is one species, *Equus hemionus*. If so, it is a very variable species, with a number of races, found from Mongolia to Syria. Each of these races has its own common name or names, the variety of which can be somewhat confusing. The *dziggetai* inhabits the Gobi Desert and Mongolia, and in colouring is most like the larger, broader hoofed *kiang* of Tibet, the form sometimes regarded as belonging to a separate species.

The *kulan* inhabits Turkestan, the *khur* the borders of Indian and Pakistan, the *ghor-khan* Iran, and the *achdari* Syria. A popular name sometimes applied to all of these forms (with the possible exception of the kiang) is *onager*. Asiatic wild asses are reddish-brown in colour, the longer winter coat being paler in shade. In ancient times Asiatic wild asses were domesticated, as shown in the royal standard of Ur of the Chaldees, which depicted onagers pulling chariots.

Zebras

There are three living species of zebra. The most widely distributed, *Equus quagga* is known either as the common zebra or as the plains zebra, and inhabits eastern and southern Africa south of Ethiopia, where its range partly overlaps that of Grevy's zebra, *Equus grevyi*, which also lives in Somalia. Grevy's zebra is the largest species, and has numerous thin stripes and very large ears.

The common zebra, like many other widely distributed animals, occurs in different forms in different parts of its range. These have been named as separate sub-species, but in fact they form a continuous series or *cline*. The most northerly have very distinct stripes, and the populations to the south tend to have increasing numbers of indistinct stripes between the more definite ones.

The third surviving zebra species is the mountain zebra, *Equus zebra*, which has numerous narrow stripes over most of the body except for the hindquarters, where they are broader. On the rump the stripes form a distinctive gridiron pattern. Alone among members of the horse family, the mountain zebra has a fold of skin hanging down from the throat. There are two races: a small number of the first race to be discovered survives in reserves and protected areas of Cape Province in South Africa, and the slightly larger Hartmann's mountain zebra lives in the mountains of Namibia (South West Africa) and Angola.

A fourth species may once have existed. The quagga, named after its barking cry, was a zebra with stripes only on its head, neck and shoulders. At the beginning of the last century it was common south of the Orange and Vaal rivers in South Africa, but it was hunted

Left: Kulans, *Equus hemionus kulan*, are a subspecies of the Asiatic wild ass, *Equus hemionus*. Still found in small numbers in parts of the USSR, they have been protected there since 1919.

Below: Mules, the offspring of female horses and male donkeys, first appeared centuries ago. Their size depends on the characteristics of their parents and the conditions in which they were reared.

Right: Two common zebra stallions fight. Normally the stallion's presence alone will suffice to keep other males away from the herd, and defence of a mare is only necessary when she is in season.

Below: Donkeys, *Equus asinus*, were domesticated long before the horse and are still popular working animals. Their virtues include a high resistance to disease, a long working life and a need for comparatively little food. Here, they are used to carry peat in Donegal in Ireland.

254

Left: *Equus quagga antiquorum*, the Damara zebra or Chapman's zebra, is one of the surviving forms of the common zebra. It inhabits an area from Angola and southwestern Africa to the Transvaal.

Right: Mare and foal of Grant's zebra, *Equus quagga boehmi*, a northern race of the common zebra living in Tanzania. Studies of this group showed that they live in very stable herds. Breakaway bachelor groups are formed by young stallions who later start their own family groups when five or six years old. Mares are fertile at about two years, the age for first foaling being three. Most foals are born between October and March.

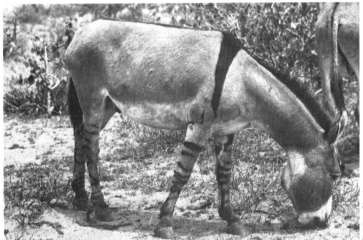

Above: The common patterns of stripes on different forms of zebra. From left to right these are Grevy's zebra, Hartmann's mountain zebra, Damara zebra and Grant's zebra. Within these groups, however, the stripes can vary widely and be as individual as human fingerprints. This may help members of a herd to distinguish each other. It has also greatly aided scientific observation.

Left: In areas such as northern Ethiopia the Somali wild ass, *Equus africanus somalicus*, and the Nubian wild ass, *Equus africanus africanus*, have interbred to produce hybrid forms such as this, exhibiting both the typical Somali leg stripes and the shoulder cross of the Nubian.

mercilessly by the Boers for its meat and its skin, and finally became extinct in about 1880.

Since there are three separate, living species of zebra, all with stripes, it is reasonable to suppose that the stripes must in some way help their owners to survive. But no simple, clear-cut explanation of their function can be given with certainty. A number of theories have been put forward, and any or indeed all of them may have some validity. The stripes may create a 'dazzle pattern', making it difficult for a lion to judge the distance before pouncing. Another suggestion is that the stripes are disruptive, breaking up the outlines of zebras as individuals when they are bunched together at a water-hole, and therefore making it difficult for a lion to single out a victim.

Social behaviour

All members of the horse family feed chiefly on grasses and other low-growing herbs which they gather into the mouth by means of their mobile lips and crop with their sharp incisor teeth. All live in herds, and tend to roam widely in search of food. The typical herd of Przewalski's horses consists of one adult male and about five females. Male Asiatic wild asses, on the other hand, tend to live on their own outside the breeding season, so the typical herd (up to 500 strong) consists of females and immature males only.

African wild asses live in small herds, and here again adult males tend to live apart. The social organization of the common zebra is closer to that of the wild horse than the wild ass. The typical herd consists of one male, up to six females, and their immature young. Surplus males live together in small herds of their own. Members of the same herd know and respond to each other as individuals even when food is abundant, at which time many herds may mingle, together with large numbers of wildebeest, *Connochaetes taurinus*, forming what has the superficial appearance of a much larger herd. Mountain zebras never come together in such numbers, but otherwise their behaviour is very similar.

When male horses fight they use their hooves and their teeth, especially the canines of the lower jaw, which are reduced in size or absent in females. Wild stallions of all horse species often bear bite-marks acquired in combat over females, which come into season several times in the course of the breeding season.

The gestation period varies between 300 days (the minimum figure for the mountain zebra) and 390 days in the case of Grevy's zebra. The domestic horse, with a gestation period of about 330 days is therefore average for the family. Usually one young is born at a time, although twins do occur. The young totter to their feet in order to suckle within minutes of birth, and can run within hours.

They grow rapidly, reaching the normal adult height within a year or so. Sexual maturity is reached a little more slowly, and full adult strength is not reached until three or four years of age. Nevertheless, for such large animals they mature remarkably quickly.

We know very little about the life-span of horses in the wild. Zoo specimens are not typical, for they never starve and are never killed by predators. A common zebra has lived to the age of 25 years under zoo conditions, which suggests that other members of the family are potentially as long-lived as domestic horses, among whom very exceptional individuals live to be over 50, although the average is much lower. Wild members of the group lead dangerous lives, and are normally killed by predators before they reach old age.

Hippos, Pigs and Peccaries

The most prolific large mammals living today are the members of the order *Artiodactyla*. These are hoofed animals with an even number of toes on each foot and they rely on speedy running or sheer bulk as a defence against predators. The group includes the camels, deer, antelopes, cattle, goats and sheep, as well as pigs, peccaries and hippopotamuses. One of the key factors in their success is the ability to make efficient use of the most readily available of all food sources—plants.

All artiodactyls have highly developed digestive systems which can break down cellulose, the main structural material of plants, and most have evolved the habit of ruminating, or chewing the cud, which further improves the digestion process. Pigs, peccaries and hippopotamuses, however, are non-ruminants and they have changed relatively little since the first artiodactyls appeared about 45 million years ago.

Pigs

The artiodactyls' remote ancestors were not plant-eaters, but were related to the ancestors of the modern carnivorous mammals. With this ancestry it is not surprising that the surviving members of the pig family are by no means purely herbivorous. Their molar and premolar teeth have low, rounded cusps not unlike those of other omnivorous mammals, such as man, and certainly pigs have omnivorous tendencies, feeding on such things as small animals, roots and fruit. Most omnivorous mammals, such as brown rats or bears, are basically either herbivores or carnivores but are simply not very fussy about what they eat. Pigs, however, like our own order, the primates, seem to have been omnivorous throughout their history.

For hoofed animals, pigs have relatively short legs. They have four toes on each foot, the thumb and big toe being absent as is always the case in artiodactyls. The two middle toes are the largest and usually carry all the weight, the hoofs on the outside toes coming into use only on marshy ground or very uneven surfaces. Pigs are not very fleet-footed: the wart hog, for example, has a maximum speed of about 18 kph (11 mph). Because they are not very tall, however, pigs are able to run beneath branches, and their heavy bodies are ideal for crashing through thick undergrowth. This is more important to them than sheer speed, for pigs are typically inhabitants of forests and bush. They are also good swimmers.

One rather unusual feature of the pig family is the way in which they keep their bodies warm. Almost all land mammals are kept warm by their hair, the skin being only loosely joined to the body, rather than bound to it by layers of fatty tissue. But examination of a rasher of bacon reveals that immediately beneath a pig's skin there is a great deal of fat, an excellent insulator but more commonly found in aquatic mammals such as seals and whales. Apart from pigs the only other land mammals primarily insulated

Bruce Coleman

Above: A female wart hog, *Phacochoerus aethiopicus,* **with her young. The wart hog inhabits the savannahs and bush country of Africa south of the Sahara. Unlike most members of the pig family, wart hogs are only active during the day; at night they sleep in dens which are usually the abandoned homes of other animals such as aardvarks. The long curved canine teeth are formidable weapons and can inflict very severe injuries on predators such as lions and leopards.**

Right: A wild boar, *Sus scrofa,* **in a West German forest. In cultivated areas the wild boar can cause considerable damage to crops by its continual rooting in the ground, but in forests it assists growth by feeding on tree parasites such as sawfly larvae and by loosening the soil.**

Below: Two African bush pigs, *Potamochoerus porcus.* **Like most pigs, these creatures eat a wide variety of both animal and plant food. In South Africa they sometimes damage peanut and fruit crops.**

ZEFA

Keith Dowson/Natural Science Photos

Above: The breeding capacity of the pig was undoubtedly one of the factors which led to its domestication. A Danish sow is on record as having given birth to as many as 34 young in a single litter, the largest number for any mammal. In the wild, where infant mortality is high, large litters are a great advantage.

Above: In France the keen sense of smell of a trained domestic pig enables it to sniff out truffles. All domestic pigs are descended from wild boars.

Below: The babirusa, *Babyrousa babyrussa*, is a strange-looking pig from the Celebes Islands of South-East Asia. In males the canine teeth of both the upper and lower jaws are particularly long and curved. The survival of the species is threatened by the clearing of forested areas for cultivation.

Above: Although these collared peccaries, *Tayassu tajacu*, from Texas look like the wild pigs of Europe, Asia and Africa, they are only distant relations.

by subcutaneous fat are human beings. In each case the reason is obscure.

Wild pigs usually feed by rooting in the ground and they have a keen sense of smell. The domestic pigs in France which are trained to smell out truffles (rare fungi considered a delicacy since classical times), which grow beneath the ground, behave in a very natural way for members of the pig family. The only thing that they have to be taught to do is to indicate the presence of truffles to their human trainers, rather than digging them up and eating them on their own account.

Wild pigs root in the ground for fungi, roots, bulbs, tubers and earthworms, and also eat leaves, fruits and nuts, and sometimes small vertebrates and carrion. They are gregarious animals, living in herds of up to 50, although male wart hogs are often observed on their own. When not feeding or resting, they often wallow in mud to keep their skins in good condition. Contrary to popular belief, wild pigs (and properly kept domestic ones) are clean in their habits, and not notably greedy.

Wild boars
There are eight living species in the pig family, and by far the most widely distributed of these is the wild boar, *Sus scrofa*. Before man reduced its range the wild boar was found in most parts of Europe; it only became extinct in Britain in the early 17th century. It still inhabits parts of central Europe as well as North Africa and Asia, from its western border to Java, Sumatra, Formosa and Japan. A male wild boar may weigh as much as 200 kg (440 lb) and, although flight is its normal defence, it can be a fierce adversary. Hunting wild boar with lances, as was once the custom in India, was by no means a one-sided sport. A wounded or cornered wild boar uses its teeth in self-defence, and they are formidable weapons. The constantly growing tusks, which are canine teeth, are razor sharp, and the molar and premolar teeth have great biting power. A bite from a wild boar is said to be worse than a bite from a lion.

Wild boars are prolific breeders, and the female may have up to 12 young in a litter. They are born after a pregnancy of about 115 days and, in contrast to the brindled brown appearance of the adults, have boldly striped markings which provide good camouflage in dappled shade. No doubt it was the wild boar's breeding capacity combined with its ability to thrive on almost anything edible that caused man to domesticate it.

The domestic pig is so similar to the wild boar from which it was derived that it is regarded as belonging to the same 257

Heather Angel

hippopotamus

Left: A hippopotamus, *Hippopotamus amphibius*, wallowing in mud. These creatures spend much of their time lying on the muddy shores of lakes and rivers or standing almost entirely submerged in the water. In this way the animal's legs are spared the effort of supporting the enormous body weight (it is not uncommon for a hippo to weigh as much as three tonnes).

Right: A pygmy hippopotamus, *Choeropsis liberiensis*. As its name suggests, it is a much smaller animal than its more abundant relative. Being very shy, the pygmy hippo is difficult to study in its swampy forest homeland and little is known about its way of life in the wild.

Below: A herd of hippos in the Virunga National Park, Zaire. Within the herd mother and child groups live slightly apart from the other animals, and young hippos usually stick very close to their mothers. Old aggressive males live very much on their own.

Bruce Coleman

Bruce Coleman

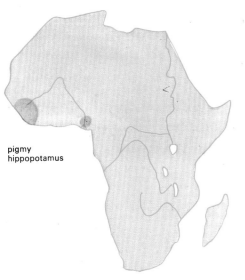

pigmy
hippopotamus

Above left and above: Maps to show the distribution of the hippopotamus and the pygmy hippopotamus (brown areas). Although pygmy hippos inhabit only small areas and are regarded as rare, it may be that they were never very common. Hippos were found in Egypt up to the early 19th century.

Right: A hippo's lower canine teeth grow throughout the animal's life, to become formidable tusks. A male animal threatens its rivals by opening its mouth to display these enormous teeth. Fights between males are not uncommon and sometimes one of the combatants is killed by his opponent.

species, *Sus scrofa*. However, selective breeding by man has resulted in greater efficiency in producing meat. The heaviest domestic pig can weigh twice as much as a wild boar, a large part of this increase being in the form of fat, and domestic sows have even larger litters than their wild cousins.

Closely related to the wild boar and very similar in appearance, are three Asian species which are much less widely distributed. These are the rare pygmy hog, *Sus salvanius*, of southern Asia, the Javan pig, *Sus verrucosus*, of Java, Celebes, and the Philippines, and the Bornean pig, *Sus barbatus*, of Borneo and the Philippines.

Another species from the same part of the world, the babirusa, *Babyrousa babyrussa*, of Celebes and neighbouring small islands is remarkable for the development of the canine tusks of the males. In addition to the lower tusks which emerge from the side of the mouth and curve upwards, the upper tusks protrude from the top of the snout and curve upwards and backwards. These tusks are too long to be kept sharp by wear and have no apparent function except as distinguishing characteristics of males. The native legend that babirusas sleep hanging from branches hooked on by means of their tusks is certainly untrue.

The remaining species of wild pigs live in Africa. The most common is the wart hog, *Phacochoerus aethiopicus*, which owes its popular name to thickenings of the skin in front of the eyes of males. Unlike most other pigs, wart hogs are mainly active by day, and they live in grasslands as well as the open forests of Africa south of the Sahara. The giant forest hog, *Hylochoerus meinertzhageni*, inhabits only thick equatorial forests. This is the only kind of pig with glands on the face, immediately in front of the eye. These glands are probably scent glands, used in signalling. The bush pig, or water hog, *Potamochoerus porcus*, usually lives in long grass of southern Africa and Madagascar. It is the hairiest of the pigs, has extremely sharp canine teeth and long ear tufts.

Peccaries

Wild pigs have never existed in America. Here their place is taken by the peccaries, which have evolved from the same ancestors as the pigs but have a long history of their own; they have evolved their pig-like characteristics quite separately as an adaptation to much the same way of life. They are therefore placed in a different family. They look very much like small, rather densely-haired pigs but have shorter tusks, those of the upper jaw growing downwards rather than upwards or outwards.

There are two species. The collared peccary, *Tayassu tajacu*, is distinguished by a band of lighter hair round the neck, and inhabits semi-deserts and dry woodlands from Texas to Patagonia, while the white-lipped peccary, *Tayassu pecari*, lives in rain forests from southern Mexico to Paraguay. Peccaries have scent-glands producing a strong musky odour on their backs. They breed less prolifically than pigs, usually only having two young at a time, and rarely more than four.

Hippopotamuses

Although fossil hippopotamuses occur in Europe, parts of Asia including Sri Lanka (Ceylon) and Madagascar, the surviving members of the family are found only in Africa. In many ways they are like large pigs, but in order to support their weight on soft ground they have four large toes on each foot and, because of the difference in their feeding habits their muzzles are not at all like pigs' snouts. Both their incisor and canine teeth grow continuously throughout life, the incisors pointing forwards and being rounded in section, while the canines, especially the lower canines, form formidable, sharp tusks. They have three-chambered stomachs, but do not chew the cud.

The common hippopotamus, *Hippopotamus amphibius*, can weigh over four tonnes, and is therefore one of the heaviest of all land animals. However, common hippos are amphibious, spending much of their time in the water where they are almost weightless, and perhaps

should be judged among such aquatic mammals as the whales: in this company they are but small fry.

The position of the eyes, ears and slit-like, closeable nostrils on the upper surface of a hippo's head is typical of the way these organs are placed in amphibious animals, permitting breathing, seeing and hearing when the animal is almost completely submerged. Hippos spend much of the day in rivers and lakes, diving for as long as ten minutes at a time in search of the water plants on which they feed. When they surface they expel the air from their lungs with a snort that can be heard many hundreds of metres away. They have huge appetites and in order to satisfy them they also feed for part of the night, coming ashore to graze. Although hippos are normally placid animals, they will sometimes attack humans; old hippos are notoriously bad tempered and aggressive. Attacks usually occur when the animals are grazing on land and suddenly find their retreat to the water cut off.

Hippos live in herds of up to 40 animals. Large male hippos defend territories, scent-marking by means of their faeces, which are scattered by vigorous wagging of the short brush-like tail, in order to warn rivals to keep clear. When necessary they fight, using their bulk and their tusks. Females have only one young at a time, giving birth in the water after a pregnancy of up to 240 days. Young hippos weigh about 40 kg (90 lb) at birth, and can swim before they can walk. They are mature at about 3 years, and may live to be 40 or 50.

The pygmy hippopotamus, *Choeropsis liberiensis*, is less aquatic in its habits, and is found only in the dense forests and swamps of Ivory Coast, Liberia and Sierra Leone in West Africa. Apart from having a rounder head and circular nostrils, it looks very much like a smaller version of the common hippo, but is no bigger than a large pig, weighing up to 240 kg (540 lb). Pygmy hippos seem to live singly or in pairs, but they are shy and partly nocturnal in their habits and difficult to study in the wild.

Camels and Llamas

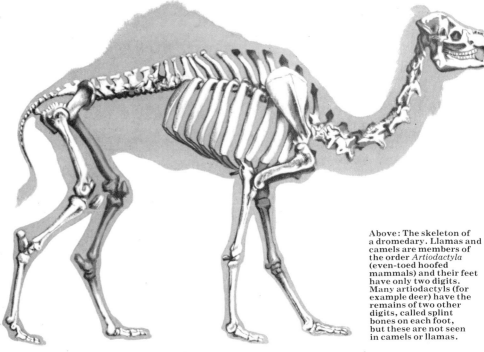

The camels of Africa and Asia and the llamas of South America belong to the same family, the *Camelidae*. At first sight the close relationship between the two genera is surprising considering their wide geographical separation, but fossil evidence shows that both camels and llamas once flourished in North America where indeed they evolved as long ago as the Eocene epoch more than 50 million years ago. The camels moved across the land bridge (now the Bering Straits) into Asia about two million years ago, and the llamas travelled south.

The camels and llamas belong to the great order of even-toed hoofed mammals, the *Artiodactyla*. Their feet have two toes and an elastic cushion covered with a single horny sole. The ends of the toes have large nails on their upper sides, but these are much smaller than the well developed hooves of animals such as deer. In common with other artiodactyls (including deer, antelopes, sheep and cattle) camels and llamas have complex chambered stomachs, and they chew the cud. This enables them to digest plant material very efficiently and so survive in areas where vegetation is sparse. When food is abundant a camel will build up a store of fat in its hump to provide energy in leaner times. Contrary to popular belief, the hump does not contain a reservoir of water.

Camels

The two species of camel are the Arabian camel or dromedary, *Camelus dromedarius*, and the two-humped Bactrian camel, *Camelus bactrianus*. They are so similar in anatomical detail that some zoologists consider there is just one species—the two types readily interbreed, producing a one-humped form. In fact both species have two humps, but the dromedary's second hump is very small and positioned over the shoulders in front of the main hump. The Bactrian camel is also identified by its thick shaggy coat, a protective measure against the cold Asian deserts, whereas the dromedary has thin soft fur.

Both species have been domesticated for thousands of years, but two remnant wild colonies of the Bactrian camel remain—one in south-west Mongolia and the other in north-west China. These last wild survivors are able to drink the brackish water of the Mongolian steppes which is unpalatable to most other animals. The dromedary inhabits much of the arid land from northern Africa through the Middle East to India, and has been introduced to North America and the Canary Islands.

The way in which the camel's body has adapted to extremes of drought and high temperature has only recently been properly studied. Most animals cope with high temperatures by sweating—the body surface is cooled as water evaporates from the skin. Of course this means that body moisture is constantly being lost, and it must be replaced regularly by drinking. But the camel can tolerate a much higher body temperature (up to 42°C, 108°F)

Above: The skeleton of a dromedary. Llamas and camels are members of the order *Artiodactyla* (even-toed hoofed mammals) and their feet have only two digits. Many artiodactyls (for example deer) have the remains of two other digits, called splint bones on each foot, but these are not seen in camels or llamas.

Right: A young dromedary, *Camelus dromedarius*. The camel's mating season lasts for only a short time, usually from early February to late March. During this period the males are extremely aggressive and may inflict severe injuries with their teeth if approached. A single young is born after a pregnancy of about 400 days. The newborn animal can walk within three hours of birth and is perfectly surefooted after two days.

Below: A group of dromedaries beside a stream in Kenya. These creatures can drink prodigious amounts of water very quickly after a long spell in the desert—as much as a third of their body weight in about ten minutes. In central Asia where the ranges of the dromedary and the Bactrian camel overlap hybrids are common. They are often stronger than their parents.

Jacana

Mirella Riccardi/Bruce Coleman

260

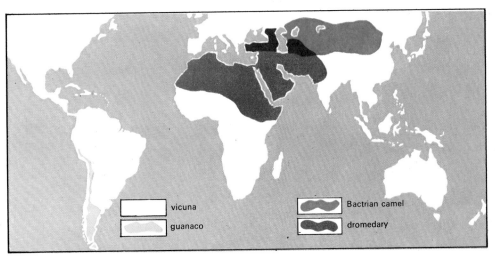

Above: Members of the camel family are found only in Africa and Asia (camels) and South America (llamas). Both groups originated in North America and migrated to their present homes within the last two million years when there was a land bridge between the American and Asian continents.

Below: A camel's foot consists of two widely spread toes and an elastic cushion-like pad covered with a single horny sole. This gives solid support on soft sandy surfaces and provides effective insulation against the very high desert temperatures and the winter cold of the Asian steppes.

Above: A Bactrian camel, *Camelus bactrianus*, in Mongolia. The species is so-called because it was once thought to come from Bactria—an area near what is now the Soviet border with Afghanistan. Bactrian camels can tolerate both extremely hot and extremely cold weather. In their natural habitat the temperature may reach 50°C (122°F) in summer and —25°C (—13°F) in winter. The camel can go for long periods without food or drink: it breaks down the fat in its humps to provide water and energy.

Below: Camels spend much of their time in hot sandy areas and many of their anatomical features reflect this. Long eyelashes protect the animal's eyes, and hairs cover the ear openings to prevent dust and sand from entering. Strong muscles in the animal's nose allow it to close its nostrils tightly when necessary. Although wild Bactrian camels still exist in remote parts of central Asia, they seem to be on the decline and could well become extinct in the wild before long.

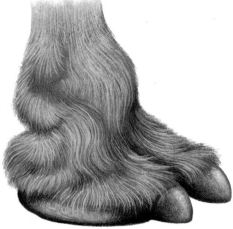

than most other animals. At this higher temperature the camel's body can lose more heat to the air by the normal process of radiation and therefore does not need to sweat so much. In this way precious body fluid is preserved.

During the short wet season in the desert, camels eat all they can of the sparse vegetation, particularly the shrub known as camel's thorn, and this vegetable food is efficiently converted to water and fat. The camel can also quickly make up reduced water supplies; it can drink up to 135 litres (30 gallons) of water at a time. A further advantage is the production of very concentrated urine. A part of the nitrogen-containing waste excreted by the liver is recycled to the stomach instead of passing through the kidneys.

Camels are temperamental animals and are liable to sudden fits of bad temper—especially the males, who generally snort and bellow when handled or loaded as though protesting against any form of work. When they make these noises, the back of the palate is inflated from behind and blown into the mouth. This peculiar structure, known as the *palu*, is extended outside the mouth like a small balloon when the animal is sexually excited.

The camel has a very long history of domestication. The earliest record of the dromedary is contained in the stories of Genesis. From such biblical references and from middle Bronze Age remains, it seems that the dromedary was a domesticated animal used for traffic across the deserts in the border lands of Arabia as far back as 1,800 BC. Camels also appear on rock carvings, on Roman coins and on tile mosaics over large areas of the Middle East and North Africa. The history of the Bactrian camel is less well known, but it appears that the Persians and their northern and eastern neighbours were familiar with the species by 1,000 BC.

As beasts of burden camels are unrivalled for strength and stamina. Until they were domesticated, man was unable to penetrate the interiors of hostile desert regions. In addition their flesh and milk provide food, their hide is used for making tents and their hair for weaving cloth.

Llamas

Llamas look like small humpless camels but have comparatively larger ears and straighter necks. Also the feet are slightly different; they have a deeper cleft between the toes and the foot pad is less well developed. There are two wild species: the guanaco, *Lama glama guanicoe*, and the vicuna, *Lama vicugna*. The guanaco, the larger of the two species, has dark and light parts to its rather shaggy coat. It lives in an area extending from southern Peru to Tierra del Fuego at the very southern tip of South America. It inhabits semi-desert areas from sea level up to 4,000 m (13,000 ft) in the Andes.

Guanacos live in small herds of four to ten females led by one male. Alternative herds are made up only of males, both young and old, and these usually contain up to 25 individuals. Guanacos are extremely aggressive during the mating season: males fight each other by trying to bite into the opponent's front legs, which involves striking each other neck to neck. It may be that the partly ritualized 'neck fighting' which is observed in many artiodactyls originated from genuine fighting of this sort. Guanacos also kick with their fore-feet and spit.

Members of the camel family reproduce only slowly, a factor probably connected with their scant food supply and the harsh conditions under which they live. The guanaco, for example, has a gestation period of 11 months and the female normally gives birth to only one young—twins are extremely rare. The guanaco once inhabited a much wider area than it does today; it was particularly common 261

Left: A vicuna, *Lama vicugna*, in the Urubamba Valley of Peru. The characteristic mane of white hair at the front of the animal's chest is plainly visible. These creatures are under pressure not only from poachers, who can obtain enormous sums of money for their skins, but also from their own cousins, the domestic llama and the alpaca. In areas where both vicunas and the domestic breeds are found, the vicunas, which are smaller and weaker, are usually ousted from the best grazing areas.

Below: A group of llamas, *Llama glama glama*, in the ruins of a border fortress above Cuzco, the ancient Inca capital of Peru. Llamas were once of great economic significance as beasts of burden, but nowadays their role has been taken over by mechanized transport except in the remoter regions. Alpacas were bred mainly for wool.

over much of the central and western plains of South America.

There are two domestic types of llama: the common llama, *Lama glama glama*, and the alpaca, *Lama glama pacos*. Both of these are sub-species of the guanaco and were first domesticated by the Incas or their ancestors. Bones of domestic llamas have been found on a site in the Virzu valley in Peru dating from between 2,500 and 1,250 BC. The heavily built common llama, the largest of all South American members of the camel family, has always been predominantly a beast of burden. The alpaca, on the other hand, was chiefly kept for its fine wool.

Large herds of both breeds were owned by private individuals and by the Inca state; a man's wealth depended on the number of llamas he owned. Herds of common llamas roam the plains and foothills of the southern Andes. Alpacas tend to inhabit the mountain regions between the haunts of the guanaco on the lowland slopes and those of the vicunas below the snow line.

The vicuna is an animal of the high Andes, found at heights of 3,500 to 5,000 m (11,500 to 16,500 ft), south through Argentina and Peru from Bolivia to Chile. Smaller and more graceful than the guanaco, it has a shorter head and longer ears. There is also a distinct mane of soft white fur at the base of the neck and the front part of the chest. In summer vicunas feed on the succulent vegetation just below the snow line, while at other times they range extensively over the high grassy plateaux or *puna*. Vicunas have a similar herd structure to guanacos, and males defend their territory vigorously.

Left: A group of guanacos, *Lama glama guanicoe*, in the Andes. The guanaco is one of the two wild species of llama (the other is the vicuna), and it inhabits semi-desert areas from sea level to an altitude of 4,000 m (13,000 ft). The common domestic llama and the alpaca are both descendants of the guanaco.

Below: A female alpaca, *Lama glama pacos*, with her offspring. The alpaca was once thought to be derived from the vicuna, but because its brain is larger than that of the vicuna such an ancestry is unlikely. Domestic animals almost always have smaller brains than their ancestors who lived in the wild.

At the very high altitudes at which vicunas live, breathing is particularly difficult because the atmospheric pressure is low and oxygen is consequently scarce. Other mammals, like man and sheep, adapt slowly to these heights by increasing the number of red cells in the blood (these are responsible for carrying oxygen from the lungs to the rest of the body). In the vicuna, however, the oxygen capacity of the blood hardly alters at all with altitude; instead the blood is specially adapted for efficient oxygen uptake by having a very high number of small red blood cells, which present a large surface area for absorbing oxygen in the lungs.

The vicuna is an endangered animal. The total world population has been estimated at less than 20,000 individuals, with half this number confined to Peru, especially the Pampa Galeras reserve 480 km south-east of the capital Lima. In the past decades tens of thousands of these beautiful animals have been slaughtered for their highly prized wool, which is twice as fine as the finest merino wool and extremely light and warm. Mass killings were started by the Spaniards and reached a peak in recent years as the demands of the luxury market grew. Most of the killing is done by poachers who come from the cities and camp in the vicuna areas until they have killed virtually every vicuna.

The World Wildlife Fund has joined with other wildlife organizations to support the government of Peru in its efforts to conserve the remaining vicuna population and build up herds again. Conservation in this case has proved to be a dangerous business, for only a few years ago a reserve guard was killed by poachers in their desperate efforts to obtain skins.

NHPA

ZEFA

Bruce Coleman

Bruce Coleman

Bears

The Kodiak bear of Alaska is the largest of all land carnivores, weighing up to three quarters of a tonne and reaching a height of 3.3 m (11 ft) when it rears up on to its hind feet. With its bulky body and enormous strength this formidable creature is a typical member of the bear family, *Ursidae*. Not surprisingly, man has had a high regard for the bear since the earliest times—bear cults have existed from the early Stone Age to modern times, and the image of the bear has been incorporated into many heraldic designs as a symbol of power.

The combination of size and strength has given the bear an unjustified reputation for fierceness. In fact most bears are shy animals and, with the exception of the polar bear, they favour a diet of berries, nuts, leaves and grass supplemented only occasionally with fresh meat or carrion. They are the least carnivorous of the carnivores.

Bear ancestors lived about 26 million years ago. They were an offshoot from the carnivore family *Canidae* (wolves, dogs and foxes) that turned towards a mixed and mainly herbivorous diet and developed teeth better suited to crushing and grinding vegetable food than slicing meat. Early bears were probably very similar to today's small black bears and fossil remains suggest that they evolved in the Old World, only later reaching the Americas. One early species was the forest-dwelling Etruscan bear, *Ursus etruscus*, which was eventually replaced by the Asiatic brown and black bears and the extinct cave bear, *Ursus spelaeus*, a contemporary of early man. About 500,000 years ago black bears spread into North America, followed later by brown bears, which reached most parts of North America from Alaska.

Modern bears—the black and brown bears of North America, Europe, and Asia, the polar bears of the Arctic, the spectacled bears of South America, and the sun and sloth bears of Asia—have suffered from contact with man, as have many other carnivores. Primarily forest animals they are now found only in remote pockets of forest, often high in the mountains, or in cold barren areas free from human habitation, or in National Parks.

In the forests they have some protection from man, shelter for hibernation and a good supply of vegetable food. They live a solitary existence, except for brief pairing in the mating season and the bond between mother and cubs. A complex set of communications ensure that there are very few encounters, aggressive or peaceful, between bears at any other times. Like other carnivores of the forest, they have short legs, walk on the soles of their feet, have acute hearing and sense of smell and are expert tree climbers. In the trees they find sleeping quarters and safety, particularly as cubs. Those species which spend most time in trees, the sun, sloth and Asiatic black bears, are equipped with large, naked, rough foot pads and long curved, non-retractible claws for shinning up trees. In contrast, grizzly bears, which are too heavy to climb, and polar bears, which have little to climb but ice floes, have hairy foot pads.

Above: The cave bear, *Ursus spelaeus*, must have been a formidable adversary of prehistoric man. It flourished in the Ice Ages and was even larger than the modern Kodiak bear.

Right: For centuries Asian black bears, *Selenarctos thibetanus*, have been trained to 'dance' for the benefit of their owners. Dancing bears can still be seen in some Middle Eastern countries.

Below: The bear has long had an undeserved reputation as an aggressive animal, as this 19th century illustration shows. In fact it is a relatively shy animal and only attacks when cornered; it normally flees when danger threatens.

Der Baer.   DE BEER.   THE BEAR.

Bavaria Verlag

Above: The polar bear, *Thalarctos maritimus,* is a good swimmer and is quite capable of crossing stretches of ocean 35 km (22 miles) or more across. The front legs provide propulsion while the back legs are reserved for steering. Polar bears are able to close their nostrils when they submerge.

Below: The largest living bear is the Kodiak bear, a race of the brown bear, *Ursus arctos.* Nearly as big are the polar bear and another North American brown bear, the grizzly. Asian and European brown bears are generally smaller than their American cousins, and black bears are smaller still.

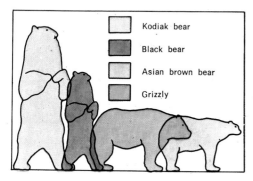

Kodiak bear

Black bear

Asian brown bear

Grizzly

Some forest bears, with plenty of food to hand, remain active throughout the year while others, facing low temperatures or lack of food in the winter, must hibernate. They feed heavily during the plentiful summer and autumn months in order to lay down a thick layer of fat as a winter food store. Then, depending on the species and weather conditions, they 'den-up' during a particular winter month. Some species use natural dens while others dig their own, and they always, with the exception of females with cubs, hibernate on their own.

Unlike most hibernating animals, which become torpid (a state in which the body temperature drops considerably and the animal is difficult to rouse), bears only become dormant and are easily woken. Their body temperature drops only slightly and their hot breath keeps the tiny den warm. However, their heart rate can fall to one fifth of its original rate, and they do not eat, drink, urinate or defecate for the entire six or seven months in the den.

Female American black and brown bears, having mated in the summer, give birth in early spring to two or maybe three or four cubs. To prevent the cubs being born in the harsh and barren midwinter, the fertilized eggs do not implant in the uterus until November, a process known as 'delayed implantation', and the cubs are born after a gestation period of between one and two months. At birth they weigh only about $\frac{1}{200}$ th of their mother's weight (for a human baby the figure is nearer $\frac{1}{20}$ th), and they are blind and hairless for the first few weeks of life. They then leave the den, closely guarded by their mother in case of attack by male bears, which may even eat them.

Black bears push their cubs up into trees at the approach of danger. In the tropics the sloth bear's cave, or earth, and the sun bear's hollow log or tree-platform gives the cubs shelter from the sun or

Above: A polar bear swimming in icy Arctic waters. In such cold conditions a human would last for only a few minutes. The bear, however, is protected from the cold by its dense fur and a thick layer of fat.

Right: The fur trade once threatened the survival of the polar bear. Fortunately in 1973 an international agreement came into force prohibiting the killing or capturing of bears except for research purposes or by Eskimos using traditional methods.

Below: Most polar bears build dens for the winter, and the young are born in them. The newborn cubs weigh less than 1 kg (2.2 lb).

Fred Bruemmer

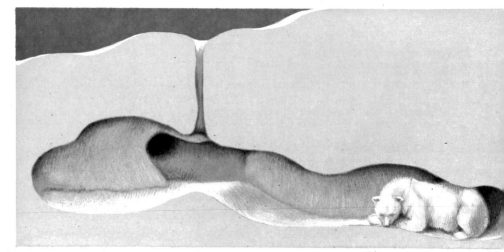

Above: A Malayan sun bear, *Helarctos malayanus*, displays the long flexible tongue which it uses to extract bees and other insects from their nests. In some ways these bears resemble the sloth bears, *Melursus ursinus*, of India, and in 1966 a hybrid between the two was born in a Japanese zoo.

Above: Fights between polar bears are rare occurrences. A female will defend her young, and sometimes males fight with competitors during the mating season, but otherwise these bears rarely come into contact with one another as they roam the Arctic ice.

Left and right: The spectacled bear, *Tremarctos ornatus*, lives in high forested regions of the Andes, from Venezuela to northern Chile. It gets its name from the rings round the eyes of some individuals—in fact the face markings vary considerably from one animal to the next (left). Adult males weigh about 130 kg (286 lb) but the females are much smaller, rarely exceeding 65 kg (143 lb). The spectacled bear is an accomplished climber and spends much of its time in trees eating fruits and leaves. It is the rarest and least carnivorous of all bear species. Because their natural habitat is so remote and inaccessible, spectacled bears are difficult to study in the wild and little is known about their way of life.

heavy rain. The cubs are looked after for between one and two years and so they sometimes den-up with their mother the following year. Females are ready to breed when they are about three years old and do so every other year. The average bear life span is probably between 15 and 34 years.

Being so heavily built and strong, bears have few enemies. They are occasionally killed by wolves and pumas, and smaller bears may be eaten by larger species, but their only real enemy is man. However, even though they have been hunted throughout history, it is only since the invention of guns, and with the massive destruction of their forest habitat to accommodate man, that their numbers have seriously declined. Some species are undoubtedly doomed but others, thanks to some long overdue conservation measures, may survive a little longer. One case in point is that of the polar bear.

Polar bears

Although polar bears, *Thalarctos maritimus*, still range all around the North Pole, trophy hunters, fur traders, the sealing industry (seals are their staple diet) and marine pollution have taken a vast toll since the turn of the century. The remaining population is probably no more than 10,000 animals. In 1956 they were totally protected in Russia, and in 1973 an international agreement prohibited the killing or capturing of bears except for research purposes, or by Eskimos using traditional methods. Nevertheless, hunting with the use of aircraft continues in Alaska and large numbers of bears are killed annually. Fortunately conservation measures have

Below: A Kodiak bear with a freshly caught salmon. In the spring salmon provide a valuable addition to the bear's diet as they swim up-river to spawn. The bear wades into the river and flips the fish out of the water with its paw. Grizzly bears, which also live in Alaska, catch fish in much the same way.

Above and right: Kodiak bears are the largest subspecies of brown bear, *Ursus arctos*, and they get their name from an island off the coast of Alaska, their home territory. Like most bears they feed mainly on grass, nuts, roots and fruit and, unless threatened or alarmed, they are harmless to man. The brown bear has no fixed breeding season, but cubs are not normally born in mid-winter. At birth the cubs (there are usually two or three) are hairless, blind and extremely small, sometimes weighing as little as 450 g (1 lb). The mother vigorously defends her cubs, and when they are older she chases them up a tree if danger threatens.

Below: A brown bear. Although the bulk of the brown bear population is found in Asia and North America, some animals still live in eastern European countries such as Poland, Hungary and Romania. In Sweden the species survives thanks to conservation and a shift of the human population to cities.

Right: A brown bear rubs itself on a tree as if to relieve an itch. In fact the purpose of this behaviour is to mark out the creature's territory—other bears will be able to smell the owner's scent on the 'marking tree'. In addition pieces of bark are often torn off with the teeth and claws.

ensured that substantial populations still exist.

Polar bears roam for miles across the tundra, sailing on icebergs and drifting from Arctic islands to the mainland feeding on seals. In the summer months they may turn to other food—berries, mosses, lemmings, shellfish and so on. Sometimes they kill narwhals trapped close to the shore by the rapidly freezing ice. Their 720 kg (1,580 lb) body weight gives them the strength to drag the 360 kg (790 lb) whales out of the water and on to the ice. Ringed seals, however, form the major part of their diet. The seals are hauled out of holes in the thick winter ice as they surface to take air, and the bear can gorge up to 18 kg (39 lb) of blubber in one meal. Males sometimes hunt seals all year round, but pregnant females invariably hibernate. They dig an oval den in a deep snow drift and the temperature inside is kept up by the bear's own body heat.

Brown bears

Brown bears, *Ursus arctos*, have the widest distribution of all bears: they are found throughout most of Asia, eastern Europe and North America. There are various races (subspecies), including the Kamchatkan bear from eastern Siberia,

the Kodiak bear from Alaska, the grizzly bear from North America, the red bear from the Himalayas and the Syrian bear from Syria, Iran and eastern Turkey. In the days before firearms they ranged from deciduous forests into the tundra, but they now have a much narrower range.

Since the beginning of the 19th century North American grizzlies have been under threat of extinction by hunting and by the destruction of their habitat by ranching, the construction of commercial fish canneries, and logging, and their total population is probably no more than 30,000. There are something like 12,000 Alaskan grizzlies living in the forested mountains, but the barren-ground grizzlies of the Yukon and North-West Territories may number as little as 500. Even in such inaccessible areas as Mount McKinley Park more than 30 may be illegally killed each year. Of the grizzlies left in the US one third live in the protection of Yellowstone National Park.

Asian brown bears are mountain dwellers most of the year. Like the grizzlies they descend in early summer to feed on young grass. They are also very adept at digging out small rodents and turning over stones for insect food. For at least one of the summer months Pacific

Left and above: The bear's size and strength made it popular with designers of coats of arms in the days before the lion was well known. It still appears in many European heraldic devices, and Bern, the capital of Switzerland, not only has a bear in its coat of arms but keeps a number of living bears as mascots.

Above: A female grizzly bear and her cub probing a dead tree-trunk for insects.

Left: A black bear, *Ursus americanus*, begging for food in the Yellowstone National Park, Wyoming. The establishment of national parks and the regulation of hunting has led to an increase in the black bear population. Slowly they are beginning to return to old, long abandoned haunts. The black bear is smaller than the brown bear and a better climber—it inhabits many of the forest regions once occupied by grizzly bears. In the last century grizzlies were hunted almost to extinction in the belief that they were major predators to cattle.

brown bears romp in the rivers feeding on spawning salmon and at this time of the year they can be seen in quite large numbers. Idaho grizzlies dash into the water and flip the salmon on to the bank, often burying them as a food store, and Alaskan grizzlies seize the fish with their mouths and paws. The salmon, together with red-currants, crowberries and blue-berries, help build up a layer of fat for the winter. All grizzlies dig their own hiber-nating dens: an entrance passage three metres (ten feet) long leads to a round chamber lined with grass which usually faces north for maximum snow cover and insulation. When they emerge in March or April they eat fibrous roots, and mosses which possibly act as purgatives.

Black bears

American black bears, *Ursus americanus*, are smaller than brown bears weighing up to 159 kg (330 lb). They are also less aggressive and more numerous—there may be 200,000 left in the US and as many again in Canada. Although described as black there are several colour forms from cinnamon and maltese-blue to the silvery-white Kermode bears. They feed in the daytime and so avoid dangerous contact with evening-feeding brown bears. Their

diet ranges from acorns, beechnuts, leaves and grass to insects, frogs and even young deer. Their constant raids on domestic beehives proves the popular notion that bears do like honey. Like grizzlies they den-up in the winter, but sometimes only in shallow depressions filled with moss.

The Asiatic black bear, *Selenarctos thibetanus*, is about the same weight and the same height (up to 90 cm, 35 in, at the shoulder) as the American black bear and it has a pale V-shaped mark on its chest. It spends much of its time sleeping in nests which it builds in trees about 5 m (16 ft) from the ground and it feeds during the day. Numbers are declining as their forest homeland is destroyed, and they are shot as vermin in areas where they prey on domestic stock. There is also a constant market for the cubs as performing bears.

Tropical bears

The stocky, short-haired Malayan sun bear, *Helarctos malayanus*, is one of the few bears to live in tropical forests. It is also the smallest bear weighing no more than 65 kg (143 lb), with a body length of about 1.5 m (5 ft) and a shoulder height of 70 cm (28 in). It is an expert climber

and spends most of the year searching in the trees for birds, lizards, fruit and above all honey. Sometimes called the honey bear, it has a long tongue for licking honey and grubs from wild bees nests and appears to be undisturbed by the stings.

A close neighbour, the sloth bear, *Melursus ursinus*, of India and Sri Lanka has similar habits but is more aggressive and is feared by local people. Slightly larger and heavier than the sun bear, it has longer hair and a V-shaped chest mark like the Asiatic black bear. Its preferred food during the day is social insects such as bees or termites. The nests are torn apart with its huge, curved claws; its long, mobile snout is inserted into the nest; its nostrils are closed and the insects are noisily sucked up through a gap in the front teeth. The sloth bear is now very rare due to poaching for fat and the destruction of its forest home. Unless steps are taken to protect the sloth bear in India it is unlikely to survive.

The most elusive species of bear is the South American spectacled bear, *Trem-arctos ornatus*, so named because of the white rings encircling its eyes. It is now a rare animal, found chiefly high up in mountain forests away from easy access by hunters.

Deer

Deer belong to the mammalian order *Artiodactyla*. Like their cousins the cattle and sheep, they have an even number of hoofed toes on each foot and a complex four-chambered stomach for digesting plant food efficiently. They are easily distinguished from other artiodactyls: in almost all species the males bear antlers for most of the year. The exceptions are the musk deer and the Chinese water deer, which never have antlers, and the reindeer or caribou, in which both sexes have antlers.

Antlers differ from the horns of cattle, sheep and antelopes in a number of ways: in particular, they are branched and they are shed and replaced each year. Once antlers are fully grown, and the skin and blood vessels which cover them during growth have died and fallen away, they consist only of bone, while horns consist of the protein *keratin* covering a bony core.

In northerly, temperate climates, where most deer live, the males cast their antlers in late spring and new ones start to grow almost immediately. The new antlers are covered with skin from which fine hair grows, and at this time a stag is said to be 'in velvet'. The antlers of a large species such as the wapiti, *Cervus canadensis*, may weigh as much as 18 kg (40 lb) when fully grown, and not surprisingly the formation of this much bone requires a large amount of calcium. At this season stags have been seen gnawing at old, cast antlers, apparently obtaining by instinct the minerals that they need, and which their normal diet lacks.

The materials necessary for bone formation are carried to the new antlers by the blood vessels lying under the covering skin, and the antlers grow fast during the summer months. By the autumn they are fully grown and the dying skin is rubbed off as the stag 'frays' his antlers against branches. This is the beginning of the breeding season or 'rut', when rival stags clash antlers in trials of strength, fighting for the possession of the females. Antlers are ideally suited to bloodless combat; their branching shape allows them to interlock as the stags strain against each other. The loser usually escapes unscathed by pulling back, turning quickly, so that his vulnerable flanks are exposed for as short a time as possible, and making a run for it.

Only mature, strong stags are successful in combat of this kind. This benefits the species, for it means that the fathers of the next generation are the fittest of their own generation, passing on their qualities to their offspring. In the large deer species with spreading, handsome antlers, such as the red deer, *Cervus elaphus*, males take about six years to reach their prime. A young stag will grow a larger set of antlers each year until he reaches maturity, beginning with a simple unbranched spike in the first year. In each succeeding year larger antlers are produced with more branches or 'points'.

It is sometimes believed that each point represents a year in the animal's age, but this cannot be so because a really fine stag perhaps eight years old may have as many as 12 points on each antler. Once mature, a stag will grow antlers of about the same size for several successive years, but as old age approaches he will produce smaller ones. Few deer reach 20 years of age.

Most deer are gregarious creatures, living in herds and most often in forested or bushy country. The combined vigilance of the herd provides their first line of defence against predators: when danger threatens, they run. Only when exhausted or cornered do they turn, fighting for life with their hoofs and antlers. One of the most detailed studies ever made of deer and their predators was made on a population of elks, *Alces alces*, which are hunted by wolves. Out of a total of 131 animals detected by wolves only six were killed and one other was wounded, but escaped. The moose killed were usually either immature or old specimens.

All deer are plant-eaters, most species browsing on the bark, buds, shoots and leaves of bushes and trees, and it is for this reason that foresters tend to regard deer as enemies. However, most deer are by no means fussy feeders, and will also eat grass and growing food crops. The reindeer has the most specialized diet, feeding on lichens of a kind known as 'reindeer moss'. In captivity reindeer must be given some of this food if they are

EUROPEAN GIANT DEER (extinct)

Above: The extinct European giant deer, *Megaloceros giganteus*, was the largest of all deer. It roamed the open country during the early Ice Age, about two million years ago. Its antlers were huge, having a span of 3.5 m (11.4 ft) or more. Just why the giant deer became extinct is something of a mystery.

Possibly the strain of replacing such enormous antlers each year simply became too much for it. More likely, perhaps, is that the antlers severely restricted the creature's movement as its habitat became covered with forest when the ice retreated. The largest deer today is the elk, *Alces alces*.

Above: Two fallow deer stags, *Dama dama*. Fallow deer are hardy animals and they are common in European parks. Like most deer they have a keen sense of smell and good hearing, but while most deer have rather poor eyesight, the fallow deer can see well. It is hardly surprising therefore that a healthy adult fallow deer has little difficulty escaping from predators.

Right: An elk, *Alces alces*, in a typical stretch of grazing land along the shores of a lake. These creatures inhabit northern Asia and Canada (where they are called 'moose') and their antlers are short but broad and flat with many points.

Left: A muntjac, *Muntiacus munjak*. These deer are small solitary animals which inhabit the thick forests of India, China and South-East Asia. They are active only at night and so are rarely seen. There have been reports of escaped muntjacs thriving in other parts of the world, including Britain.

Below: Stages in the development of a fallow deer's antlers from early spring to autumn. Stags grow new antlers each year, the size of the new set depending on the animal's age and physical condition. As the new antlers grow they are fed by a network of blood vessels which lie beneath a covering of velvety skin.

ANTLER DEVELOPMENT OF EUROPEAN FALLOW DEER

to thrive, but the constituents of the moss which are so important to them have yet to be identified.

Musk deer and muntjacs

The deer family comprises about 40 living species and is usually regarded as consisting of four sub-families. The first of these, *Moschinae*, contains only one species, the musk deer, *Moschus moschiferus*, which inhabits the forests and brush of Asian plateaux from China and Korea to Siberia and Mongolia. They are no larger than big dogs and live rather solitary lives, more like hares than typical deer.

The musk deer lacks antlers, but the upper canine teeth—absent in most deer—form long, downward-curving tusks. In males these are about 7.5 cm (3 inches) long. The males also have abdominal scent glands producing the substance which gives the species its name.

The muntjac or barking deer and its relative the tufted deer make up another sub-family, *Muntiacinae*, inhabiting southern Asia from Nepal to Formosa and Borneo. In several respects this group is intermediate between the primitive musk deer and other deer. There are several species of muntjac and two of these, the Indian muntjac, *Muntiacus muntjak*, and Reeves' muntjac, *Muntiacus reevesi*, have been introduced to Britain.

Muntjacs are small, slender deer with greyish or brownish fur. The males' antlers are very short, rarely exceeding 15 cm (6 in), usually with only two points on each. To make up for their short antlers males have large canine tusks, and use them in combat. Muntjacs live alone or in pairs, and are mainly active at night—their alarm call, like the bark of a dog, is often the only indication of their presence. Tufted deer, *Elaphodus cephalophus*, are very similar in their

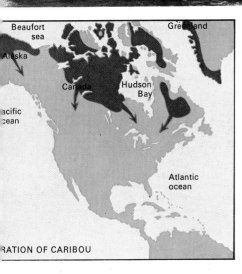

RATION OF CARIBOU

Above: A group of wapiti hinds, *Cervus canadensis*. Wapitis are close relations of the European red deer.

Left: A map to show the migration of caribou, *Rangifer tarandus*. During the brief arctic summer they feed on the Canadian tundra, but as winter approaches they move south to warmer latitudes where they can continue to feed.

Right: A herd of reindeer crossing a lake in Norway. Reindeer are of great economic importance to the Lapps, who follow their herds as they migrate in search of food. Although the animals are partly domesticated, the urge to migrate remains and so the herdsmen are always on the move.

Left: A red deer stag, *Cervus elaphus*, roaring to attract a mate.

Below: Two red deer stags fighting. The combat is more of a pushing contest than a genuine fight because the animals' antlers interlock and this usually prevents any serious damage to either contestant.

Above: One of the few species of South American deer, the southern pudu, *Pudu pudu*. These creatures live only in the extreme south of Chile and Argentina. Horned artiodactyls, such as antelopes, sheep, goats and cattle, are absent from the sub-continent altogether, except for domesticated forms.

habits, but are slightly larger, and inhabit Burma and southern China.

Fallow deer and red deer

Most European and Asian deer belong to the sub-family *Cervinae*. Among the members of this sub-family are the fallow deer, *Dama dama*, which originally lived in lands bordering the Mediterranean, but which have been introduced by man to other areas: the ancestors of the fallow deer now found in Britain are believed to have been brought here by the Romans.

In winter the coat of this species is grey, but in summer it is brown with white spots —excellent camouflage in dappled forest sunlight. Among deer spotted coats are most often found in juveniles, but the chital or axis deer, *Axis axis*, of India and Sri Lanka is spotted throughout life. This medium-sized species is very gregarious and lives in herds of up to 100, although its relation the hog-deer, *Axis porcinus*, of India and Indo-China is usually found only in groups of two or three. Perhaps because they sometimes inhabit thick forests these deer have only three main points on each antler; more points might become entangled too easily.

Belonging to the same sub-family, but with larger antlers, are the members of the genus *Cervus*, of which the red deer may be taken as typical, although a variety of other species are common in Asia. Red deer are really inhabitants of deciduous forests, although in Britain, where all of the primaeval forests have been felled and most of the large wild animals killed off by man, they now survive only on moorland such as Exmoor and in parts of the Scottish Highlands. Under these rather unnatural conditions they do

Right: A Père David's deer hind, *Elaphurus davidianus*. The first European to see these strange animals was a French priest, Armand David, in 1865. At that time the only surviving members of the species were the property of the Chinese emperor and they lived in a game park south of Peking. A flood in 1895 reduced the population to only a few animals which soon died, but fortunately by then there were several of the deer in European zoos. These survivors were all transferred to Woburn in England where it was hoped that a breeding herd could be established. The experiment was a success, and Père David's deer is no longer on the verge of extinction.

Above: A young roe deer is well camouflaged against the forest undergrowth.

Left: Roebucks, *Capreolus capreolus*, have relatively small antlers with knotty protuberances near the base. The animal shown in this picture has three points on each antler and this is typical for the species. Roe deer belong to the American deer sub-family *Odocoileinae* although they are now found only in the northern forests of the Old World, including Britain. Another species which belongs to the same sub-family but is no longer found in America is the Chinese water deer, *Hydropotes inermis*. These animals are very small and have long canine tusks instead of antlers so that they rather resemble chevrotains (below left). In the wild, water deer live solitary lives on the shores of the Yangtse River in China.

Below: A Malayan chevrotain, *Tragulus napu*. These creatures are often called 'mouse deer' although they do not belong to the deer family. They are only about 30 cm (1 ft) tall, have no antlers and live a secretive life in the dense undergrowth of tropical forests. Of all the ruminants (animals which chew the cud), chevrotains probably most resemble the ancestors of the group which lived in the Eocene epoch about 50 million years ago. As can be seen in this picture, the upper canine teeth of the male chevrotain are very long and curve down below the animal's lower jaw. The females do not have these long teeth.

not grow as large as the red deer still surviving in the forests of eastern Europe.

The wapiti (usually known as 'elk' in the US) is the only North American representative of this sub-family and it is very closely related to the red deer; it is regarded by some experts merely as a giant race of the same species. For much of the year female red deer and their young live in herds, while the males form smaller, more loosely-knit groups. Only during the autumn rut are the stags rivals, competing for dominance of the herds of females. Normally a single calf is born early the following summer after a pregnancy of about 8 months.

With its spreading hoofs, long tail and deeply forked antlers Père David's deer, *Elaphurus davidianus*, is in some respects the most distinctive of the Eurasian species. The animal became extinct in China at the beginning of the 20th century, and it was only the swift action of European zoo keepers in setting up a breeding herd at Woburn in England that saved the deer from extinction.

American deer

The fourth sub-family, *Odocoileinae*, contains the typical deer of the Americas, although some species of this group have found their way into the Old World. Some members of the group look like Eurasian deer, but they are not usually so gregarious. In North America the solitary white-tailed deer, *Odocoileus virginianus*, and the mule deer, *Odocoileus hemionus*, were the animals which furnished North American Indians with buckskin clothing.

The largest South American deer, the swamp deer, *Blastocerus dichotomus*, also lives in very small groups, inhabiting swampy grasslands from Guyana to Uruguay. The brockets, *Mazama*, of tropical American forests are smaller, and have antlers that are mere spikes, as are those of the pudu, *Pudu pudu*, which inhabits the forested slopes of the Andes. The pudu is no larger than a medium-size dog but is quite heavily-built.

In contrast, the elk, *Alces alces* (called 'moose' in the US) is the largest of all deer, with a shoulder height of about 1.7 m (5.6 ft), and the bulls have huge, flattened antlers. Inhabitants of the marshy northern forests, of America, Asia and Europe, elk are often seen standing along the edges of lakes, browsing on water weed. Another species of this group, the reindeer (known as 'caribou' in the US), *Rangifer tarandus*, also occurs in Europe and Asia as well as North America.

Some experts believe that the caribou is a separate species, because it is much less easily domesticated than the European reindeer, and for this reason reindeer from Lapland have been introduced to Alaska. Reindeer live in huge herds and their antlers (borne by both sexes) are thin but long and highly branched. The splayed hoofs support reindeer equally well on snow or the marshy tundras of summer.

At one time deer were widely hunted for their meat (venison), their skins and even their antlers, which were used as tools by prehistoric man. A few species are still economically important to man: one of these is the musk deer whose sweet-smelling glandular secretion, musk, is used to make expensive perfumes and soaps. Nowadays, however, hunting is mostly done for 'sport' and it is usually carefully controlled so that the deer population does not decline. The main threat to deer species is not from hunting but from the erosion of their habitats by the clearing of land for cultivation.

Cattle

Cattle have been valued by man since prehistoric times as a source of meat and milk and as beasts of burden. They are particularly useful as draught animals, capable of working in hot and humid climates which would be unsuited to the horse. Nowadays, however, in most of the developed countries, cattle are used almost exclusively as a source of food because they have been superseded as draught animals first by the horse and then by machines.

Cattle belong to the mammalian order *Artiodactyla* and, like other members of that order, they have an even number of hoofed toes on each foot. The horned artiodactyls (cattle, antelopes, sheep and goats) are placed in a family of their own, the *Bovidae*. Apart from the familiar domestic breeds of cattle there are various wild and semi-wild species such as the yak, the banteng and the gaur as well as the closely related buffalo and bison. The word 'ox' simply means a member of the cattle subfamily—it is not restricted to any particular species although it usually refers to draught animals rather than food producers.

All cattle are plant-eaters with front teeth or incisors designed for cropping grass. The incisors are present only on the lower jaw; on the upper jaw there is simply a hard palate against which the incisors bite. The canine or 'eye' teeth typical of flesh-eating animals are absent altogether. The jaw is designed to allow a circular grinding motion so that grass can be thoroughly crushed between the animal's large cheek teeth.

The structural material of plants is cellulose, a carbohydrate which many animals, including man, cannot digest. Ruminants, however, such as cattle, antelopes and deer, have developed a complicated digestive system which allows them to break down cellulose and use it for food. Ruminants possess four stomach chambers: the *rumen*, the *reticulum*, the *omasum* and the *abomasum*. Large quantities of grass are chewed and swallowed to the rumen to be moistened, and here the cellulose begins to break down by the action of bacteria. From the rumen the food passes to the reticulum where bacterial digestion of the cellulose continues.

In between periods of eating the animal regurgitates portions of the partly digested food from the reticulum back into the mouth where it is rechewed and again swallowed. This process, known as 'chewing the cud', ensures that the grass cells are thoroughly pulverized before digestion proper occurs in the omasum and abomasum. The abomasum is the 'true' stomach where the ordinary digestive enzymes comes into play.

Domestic cattle

The ancestor of all modern domestic cattle was the aurochs, *Bos primigenius*, an animal which originated in northern India. The earliest aurochs were very large animals at least two metres (six feet) high at the shoulders and bearing massive horns, very like those of the present day highland cattle.

The early domestic cattle were quite unlike those of today, and by modern

Left: The ancestor of all modern domestic cattle was the aurochs, *Bos primigenius*. By modern standards aurochs were very large creatures, the bulls (above) standing as much as two metres (over six feet) at the shoulders. The cows (below) were slightly smaller and had shorter horns. The last true aurochs survived in Poland until the beginning of the 17th century.

Right: This fresco from an ancient Egyptian tomb of 1,400 BC shows domesticated cattle being inspected by herdsmen. There is a striking resemblance between these cattle and their aurochs forebears.

Below: Highland cattle are a domestic breed native to the western Scottish hills. They are very hardy animals, able to endure bad weather and thrive on poor pasture. The long horns and hair of this animal are typical of the breed. Highland cattle are kept for beef. Other beef breeds include the Shorthorn, the Hereford, the Aberdeen Angus and, in the southern US, the Santa Gertrudis.

Bryan Alexander

Michael Holford

Jen & Des Bartlett/Bruce Coleman

Above: The water buffalo, *Bubalus bubalis*, **is an important domestic animal in India. This particular beast provides milk for a family of the Toda tribe from southern India. It will not be slaughtered for its meat because Todas are vegetarian. The water buffalo is not considered a sacred animal by Hindus so it is an important source of meat elsewhere in India. It is also widely used for pulling ploughs and carts.**

Left: A zebu bull. These domestic cattle are common in Africa and India, and in the US they have been used extensively for crossing with other breeds. Although it cannot match European breeds for meat or milk production, the zebu is a good draught animal. To Hindus it is a sacred animal, the so-called 'sacred cow', and cannot be killed. Zebus are sometimes called Brahman cattle.

Below: A Hereford bull. This is an important beef-producing breed. Dairy breeds include the Friesian, the Ayrshire, the Jersey and the Guernsey.

Heather Angel

standards they would be considered to be of poor quality. The Romans were probably the first to attempt to improve cattle by selective breeding, but little success was achieved until recent times. The first 'modern' cattle breeder was an Englishman, Robert Bakewell, who developed the highly successful longhorn breed during the eighteenth century. Important advances were also made in France, Holland and Switzerland.

British breeds of cattle, such as the Hereford, the Aberdeen Angus, the Shorthorn and the Polled Hereford are the major beef breeds in the world today. The most important beef-producing countries are those which have large areas of grazing land, with a light population and a soil or climate which is not suited to the cultivation of crops—the United States, Argentina, Uruguay, Australia, New Zealand, South Africa and Mexico are among the major exporters of beef.

Veal is produced from calves restricted to a liquid diet. They are usually slaughtered when they are between 12 and 13 weeks old and weigh only 115 to 135 kg (250 to 300 lb). Sometimes they are slaughtered even earlier, weighing only about 40 kg (90 lb).

Unlike the mare or ewe, the cow does not have a clearly defined breeding season. However, during the summer months breeding activity is higher than in the winter and, since pregnancy lasts about 285 days, a high proportion of cows tend to give birth in the spring. To counteract this natural tendency in dairy herds, heifers (young cows) are mated so that they calve in the autumn thus ensuring a good supply of winter milk. Nowadays conception is often achieved by artificial insemination, which makes genetic selection easier and the farmer can be certain which of his cows has been fertilized. The semen collected from a bull on just one occasion can be used to fertilize some 400 cows.

Wild Cattle

Inhabiting South-East Asia are two species of wild oxen, the gaur, *Bos gaurus*, and the banteng, *Bos banteng*. The gaur is a heavily built animal with comparatively short legs and a deep chest, and lives in the hilly forests of India, Burma and Malaya. The general colour is dark brown with paler underparts and white 'socks'. The gaur is normally a timid and inoffensive animal, and a semi-domesticated version, the gayal, yields good milk and beef. The banteng resembles the gaur in many respects but it is not

Giuseppe Mazza

Left: An African buffalo, *Syncerus caffer*. The large curved horns are formidable weapons as many people have discovered to their cost—more hunters have been killed by African buffalos than by any other species of game. In fact buffalos are not particularly aggressive, but they will attack if provoked.

Below: A banteng cow, *Bos banteng*, from South-East Asia. Bantengs are wild cattle which shelter in the shade of forests except when grazing. The rare kouprey from Cambodia looks somewhat similar and is probably a cross between a zebu and a banteng. It may, however, be a separate species.

Below: The American bison, *Bison bison*, (often wrongly referred to as buffalo) provided the Plains Indians with many of their needs. Bison once roamed the plains in enormous numbers, but they were brought very close to extinction through indiscriminate killing by European settlers in the last century.

Right: Musk oxen, *Ovibos moschatus*, from the Arctic. Although they are the size of cattle, these creatures are actually more closely related to sheep and goats than oxen. They can survive in the extreme cold of northern Canada and Greenland by virtue of their thick coats of long hair.

found in India. Mature bulls are black with white socks and a white patch on each buttock; the cows and calves are bright chestnut.

Related to these is the yak, *Bos grunniens*. Yaks are heavily built cattle with a fringe of long hair on the shoulders, flanks and thighs as well as over the whole tail. There are domesticated and wild forms, the latter living at heights of 4,250 to 6,000 m (14,000 to 20,000 ft) in the Himalayas of eastern Tibet and western China. Yaks are large animals and the bulls may reach a height of two metres (six feet) at the shoulders although the domestic form is usually rather smaller. They are used as beasts of burden in much the same way as oxen in India, but they can only survive in the cool of the mountains.

Buffalos

One of the most imposing animals of the African forests and grasslands is the buffalo, *Syncerus caffer*. African buffalos usually live in herds of about 40 animals, each herd inhabiting an established range which includes a grazing area, cover and, most important, a water hole. In times of drought, when water holes are few and far between, several smaller herds may amalgamate to form a single large herd of several hundred animals.

In the mating season the bulls are constantly trying to assert their superiority over rival bulls for the possession of cows. They charge each other from a distance of about nine metres (30 ft) with horns lowered, and their heads crash together with such violence that the sound can be heard a considerable

distance away. Surprisingly these contests

rarely result in any serious injury. In the end one of the combatants simply runs off when he has had enough.

The water buffalo, *Bubalus bubalis*, is a large creature—it is almost as big as the African buffalo which it resembles. It lives in India and South-East Asia and, as its name suggests, lives close to rivers and swampy areas. Nowadays the population of wild water buffalos is declining for they are hunted for their meat, hide and even horns. Not only this but constant interbreeding with escaped domestic water buffalos has weakened the strain. There are several breeds of domesticated water buffalo and they are, along with the zebu, the most important domestic animals of the tropics.

Another species of Asiatic buffalo is the anoa, *Bubalus depressicornis*, a rare animal from the Celebes Islands. It is much smaller than most oxen and looks rather like an antelope. Unfortunately anoas are in danger of extinction because they are mercilessly hunted for their meat, skins and horns, a problem which has only arisen since the introduction of firearms.

Bison

The largest mammal of the American continent is the bison, *Bison bison*, a creature which is easily distinguished from other wild oxen by its large maned and bearded head and small curved horns. At one time bison roamed the American plains in enormous numbers—it was said that a large herd could take as long as five days to pass a given point. Although the Plains Indians depended on the bison for food and skins, their hunting was never on a large enough scale to affect the population of the species.

It was with the colonization of central and western America by European settlers that wholesale slaughter began. Bison are easy prey to men armed with rifles, and they were killed in huge numbers whenever their natural inquisitiveness led them near to human settlements or crops. Many thousands more were killed when the Union Pacific Railroad was forged across the continent in the 1860s. The result of all this carnage was that a population of some 60 million bison in 1700 was by 1890 reduced to just 840 individuals. Fortunately steps for conservation of the species were taken just in time, and there are now herds of bison living in various parts of the US and Canada. The total population today is probably in excess of 30,000.

The European bison, *Bison bonasus*, which looks much like its American cousin, has had a no less colourful history. By the beginning of this century it was found only in the forests of Bielowecza in Poland, although it had once inhabited most of Europe and Asia as far east as Siberia. This time the drastic fall in the population was the result of clearing land for cultivation, rather than senseless massacre, but the effect was the same.

The First World War reduced the population of the Polish herds even further, and by 1921 the species had become extinct in the wild. Fortunately there were by that time a few animals (about 50) in European zoos and these formed the basic stock for a last ditch conservation programme. In spite of setbacks the conservationists succeeded, and there are something like 1,000 European bison living today. Some of these animals have been reintroduced to their forest homelands in central Europe.

Above: A domestic yak, *Bos grunnieus*. The yak lives in Tibet where it provides the inhabitants with milk, meat, wool and hides. In a country where roads are few and far between, the yak is a valuable beast of burden—it is the only pack animal which can work efficiently at altitudes as great as 6,000 m (20,000 ft).

Below: The European bison, *Bison bonasus*, looks much the same as its American cousin, but it does not have such a thick mane. Both species originated in northern India. One group of animals travelled west to Europe while another migrated east across a land bridge (now the Bering Straits) into America.

Antelopes

Antelopes are among the most graceful and handsome of the even-toed hoofed mammals which make up the order *Artiodactyla*. They range in size from the tiny royal antelope, only 25 cm (10 in) high, to the giant eland, an ox-like animal standing about 2 m (6 ft) at the shoulder and weighing 450 kg (1,000 lb). Antelopes originated in southern Europe and spread east into Asia and south into Africa, where the greatest variety of antelopes is found today.

Like many artiodactyls such as cattle and deer, antelopes have four-chambered stomachs and are able to chew the cud. This means that they can digest the cellulose in their plant diet with great efficiency. Along with cattle, sheep and goats they belong to the family *Bovidae* whose members are distinguished from other artiodactyls by having horns. A deer's antlers are normally branched, present only in the males and shed and replaced every year. In contrast, the horns of antelopes, cattle, sheep and goats are unbranched, possessed by both sexes and permanent. Also, the composition of horns differs from that of antlers: horns are formed of a sheath of the protein *keratin* surrounding a bony core, while antlers are solid bone.

Antelopes live in a variety of habitats—they are found in dense forests, open plains, swampy areas and even deserts or mountainous rocky regions. A few species are solitary but the great majority live in herds, sometimes numbering as many as 10,000 animals. Antelopes are not found in the Americas, although the pronghorn, *Antilocapra americana*, is sometimes called the 'American antelope'.

In fact the pronghorn is not closely related either to antelopes or to any other living hoofed animals, and so it is placed in a family of its own. It is about the size of a deer, with a predominantly brown coat and a white rump. The forked outer sheath of its horns is renewed every year. Pronghorns were once almost as common as the bison on the central American plains until, like the bison, they were slaughtered in larger numbers and almost became extinct.

Kudu, bushbuck and eland

There are about 100 species of antelopes living today and these are divided between four sub-families: *Bovinae* (which also includes the oxen), *Cephalophinae*, *Hippotraginae* and *Antilopinae*. Among the antelopes belonging to the *Bovinae* are the kudus, bushbucks, elands and bongos; all these animals have some oxen-like features. The greater kudu, *Tragelaphus strepsiceros*, is sometimes called the 'king of the antelopes' although it is not the largest species. It is a tall animal with magnificent horns shaped like huge open corkscrews and it can run very swiftly to escape predators.

The bushbuck, *Tragelaphus scriptus*, is smaller than the kudu but has longer fur and a crest of long, stiff hair running down the middle of its back. When it encounters a rival, a male bushbuck will lower its head and erect the crest of hair on its back as a threat display. There are various subspecies which vary in colour from grey-brown to red; they are fairly

276

ROYAL ANTELOPE

REEDBUCK

SPRINGBOK

PRONGHORN

Left to far right: The heads of these six antelopes are roughly to scale, from the tiny royal antelope to the huge eland. Although the pronghorn is often referred to as an antelope, it belongs to a family of its own and is not a true antelope like the other animals shown here. The most obvious difference is seen in the horns which, in true antelopes, are not branched. The reedbuck, *Redunca arundinum*, is a relation of the kob and the waterbuck. It lives in grassy or reedy country close to water. Unlike most antelopes reedbucks live alone or in pairs and when they are disturbed they lie still on the ground, only fleeing when in extreme danger.

Below: A gerenuk, *Litocranius walleri*, feeding on the leaves of a tree. Gerenuks have such a good sense of balance that they can stand on their hind legs with hardly any support from the front legs. They are gazelle antelopes and inhabit Kenya and Ethiopia, usually living in herds of about 12 animals.

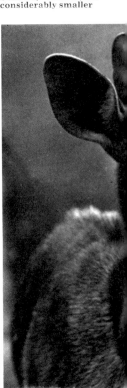

Below: Delamere's bushbuck, *Tragelaphus scriptus*, is a shy forest dweller from East Africa. This particular animal is a young male (the females do not have horns), and its short conical horns and large ears make it look rather like a duiker, *Cephalophus*. Duikers, however, are considerably smaller

Jacana

Giuseppe Mazza

Frank Lane

Left: Dorcas gazelles, *Gazella dorcas*, live in North Africa and Saudi Arabia, and they have been known to Europeans since ancient times. Sadly, these graceful creatures are now in danger of extinction. They suffer not only from the attentions of their natural predators (lions, leopards, wild dogs and jackals) but also from widespread hunting by man. Fortunately the range of the dorcas gazelle hardly overlaps at all with that of the cheetah, the most specialized of gazelle hunters. The cheetah relies on sheer speed to overtake its prey. It then knocks the animal over with a blow of its forepaw and kills it by biting at the throat.

ELAND

NILGAI

Below: An oryx, *Oryx gazella*. There are various subspecies of oryx, the East African race (pictured here) and the South African race being the commonest. The Arabian oryx, which inhabits a small region of Saudi Arabia and Oman is very rare in the wild although a breeding herd now exists in the US.

than bushbucks, rarely exceeding a height of 75 cm (2 ft 6 in). The horns of an antelope often provide a good way of identifying the species: they may be short and conical (as in this picture), long and straight, twisted like a screw, lyre-shaped or sickle-shaped. They never form the tight curl of rams' horns.

Giuseppe Mazza

well camouflaged in the African forest and bush where they live.

The eland, *Taurotragus oryx*, is the largest living antelope. It is a heavily built ox-like animal, with thick folds of skin hanging from the neck and short hair varying in colour from fawn to red-brown. Like most antelopes elands live in Africa, and both the males and the females have spirally twisted horns about 90 cm (3 ft) long. Because they are so like cattle, efforts have been made to domesticate elands but without much success: oddly enough one of the most successful attempts took place in the Ukraine at the end of the last century. In Africa elands would theoretically be a much better source of meat and milk than cattle, and they would cause less damage to the countryside (constant grazing by cattle is turning grassland into desert in many places), but domestication remains an elusive goal.

In addition to the African representatives of this sub-family there are two Asian species: the nilgai, *Boselaphus tragocamelus*, and the four-horned antelope, *Tetracerus quadricornis* (the only species of antelope to have four horns). The nilgai inhabits the open plains of India and it has short, conical horns about 25 cm (10 in) long; the coat of male animals is a blue-grey colour. The four-horned antelope is a shy jungle dweller little more than 60 cm (2 ft) high at the shoulder.

Duikers

The second sub-family, the *Cephalophinae*, is a small group comprising the so-called 'duikers'. The name comes from the Dutch word for 'diving', a reference to the way these antelopes dive for cover when surprised. Duikers live in the forests and bush of central and southern Africa where they feed on grass and foliage. The horns, which are rarely grown by females, are short and straight.

Most antelopes are extremely agile, and the duikers are no exception. When pursued by a predator they can move very swiftly, zig-zagging from side to side and flicking their tails up and down over their white rumps. This behaviour, interspersed with occasional high leaps, confuses the pursuing animal, making it difficult for him to launch an attack.

The sub-family *Hippotraginae* contains a large number of antelope species including the waterbuck, kob, reedbuck, roan, sable, oryx (gemsbok), wildebeeste (gnu) and hartebeeste. The waterbuck, *Kobus ellipsiprymnus*, and kob, *Adenota kob*, are known as marsh antelopes for they never stray far from water where they take refuge when pursued. They are found throughout central Africa and their ringed or knotted horns form the outline of a lyre. The kob is the more gregarious of the two species; it lives in groups of between 10 and 12 individuals.

The roan and sable are often called horse antelopes. Both live in herds, the roan, *Hippotragus equinus*, in groups of about 15 and the sable, *Hippotragus niger*, in groups of 50. The roan is very horse-like, having large, long ears with tufts of hair at the tips. It roams the plains and rolling hills of Africa north of the Orange River. The sable looks much like the roan but it also has a mane along the back of its neck. In contrast to the females, which are chestnut, male roans are a deep blue-black colour. Both

Giuseppe Mazza

Keystone

Left: A herd of brindled gnus, *Connochaetes taurinus*. These odd-looking antelopes live on the plains of eastern and southern Africa. Their herds often intermingle with those of other plains animals such as zebras.

Right: A baby brindled gnu with its mother. The behaviour of very young antelopes usually conforms to one of two patterns, referred to as 'stay put' or 'follower' behaviour. In the former case the young animal lies hidden in the grass or under a tree while its mother grazes some distance away and it only runs to her when she approaches to within a few metres. Young blackbucks, impalas, gazelles and duikers behave in this way. Young 'followers', on the other hand, stick close to their mothers at all times. Brindled gnus fall into this category.

Below: The impala, *Aepyceros melampus*, is one of the most agile of all antelopes—it runs by a succession of bounds, covering as much as 10 m (33 ft) in a single leap.

Bruce Coleman

Left: A female nilgai, *Boselaphus tragocamelus*, chewing the cud (ruminating). This process of re-chewing food which has already been partly digested means that ruminants are fast eaters for they do not need to chew the grass very thoroughly as they graze. Chewing the cud is often done in places where the animal is safe from predators, away from the open grazing areas.

Below: One of the most striking antelopes, the greater kudu, *Tragelaphus strepsiceros*. The fur is deep blue and there are from four to nine vertical white stripes down each side of the body. Kudus live in small groups of up to eight animals.

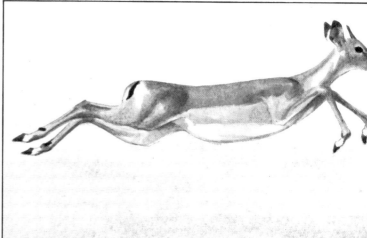

sables and roans have large ringed horns, each curved like a scimitar.

Oryx, hartebeeste and gnu

The oryx or gemsbok, *Oryx gazella*, is a large antelope with long rapier-like horns almost 1.2 m (4 ft) in length. There are various subspecies which inhabit the Sahara, eastern and southern Africa and a small region in eastern Saudi Arabia. They live in troops of 10 to 15 animals and travel very quickly across the vast dry plains of their homelands. The Arabian subspecies is probably better adapted to desert life than any other antelope—when water is scarce it eats the succulent roots of the sparse desert vegetation. Some other antelope such as the dik-diks and the duikers can also obtain some water in this way, but they are not so well adapted as the oryx. Mating also follows a pattern typical of many antelopes. After fighting off rival males, the successful combatant will chase or 'drive' the female, often for a considerable distance. Just before he mounts the female, the male kicks her with his front leg, a habit which is also seen in some other antelopes such as the gerenuk, the dibatag and the duikers. This curious ritualized behaviour prob-

278

Frank Lane

Below: The bongo, *Taurotragus euryceros*, lives in the tropical forests of central and western Africa. Mature males and females have horns about 90 cm

(3 ft) long which make one complete spiral turn. The bongo is the rarest of the large antelopes and little is known about its way of life in the wild.

Jacana

ably derives from a fighting kick.

One of the strangest looking antelopes on the African veldt is the hartebeest, *Acelaphus buselaphus*. It has an exceptionally long face, with lyre-shaped horns each supported on a bony base. This sand-coloured antelope lives in herds of up to several hundred animals on open grassland and plains. Closely related to the hartebeest are the wildebeests, or gnus. There are two species: the white-tailed gnu *Connochaetes gnou*, which has a brown coat and, as its name suggests, a white tail, and the brindled gnu, *Connochaetes taurinus*, which has a grey coat with dark vertical bars. Both animals have horns like those of a buffalo, a long face like a hartebeest and a horse-like body and tail. They also have a mane of short hair along the top of the neck. The combination of all these features results in an odd-looking animal, not at all the graceful image the word antelope conjures up.

Gnus occupy much the same habitat as hartebeests and for the most part they behave in a similar manner. However, they react to danger in a different way, for when a herd is disturbed, gnus move away at a fast trot rather than a gallop and in a column two abreast. When the leader of the herd judges that they have moved sufficiently far to be safe, he will turn around and trot back towards the source of the disturbance. The remaining members of the herd carry on forward, each pair turning at the precise spot where the leader turned. As soon as the last pair has turned the herd comes to a standstill as if by command and the leader checks that there is no further danger.

Gazelles

The final sub-family, the *Antilopinae*, includes the pygmy antelopes and the gazelle antelopes. Of the pygmy antelopes, the royal antelope, *Neotragus pygmaeus*, has the distinction of being the smallest of all antelopes. It is hardly larger than a hare and inhabits the hot and humid coastal forests of West Africa. It is a timid animal and emits a high-pitched scream when alarmed.

The gazelle antelopes are perhaps the most graceful of all antelopes. They include the springbok, *Antidorcas marsupialis*, the impala, *Aepyceros melampus*, the blackbuck, *Antilope cervicapra*, the dibatag, *Ammodorcas clarkei*, and the gerenuk, *Litocranius walleri*, as well as various species of true gazelles, *Gazella*. They are slender, agile animals adapted for speed and life on the hot arid regions of Africa and Asia.

The blackbuck is the fastest antelope of the Indian plains: it can run at speeds of up to 80 kph (50 mph) and only the cheetah in its initial burst of speed can overtake it. In gazelle antelopes speed is matched by agility: the impala runs in a succession of huge bounds, covering as much as 10.5 m (35 ft) with each leap and reaching a height of 2.5 m (8 ft). This jumping prowess is matched by other members of the tribe, particularly the springboks which once inhabited the South African plains in herds of thousands but are now much less common. They have the peculiar habit of making sudden leaps into the air if they are alarmed, possibly to get a better view of their surroundings, and it was this behaviour that gave them their name.

Left: Huge herds of brindled gnus live in the Serengeti National Park of Tanzania and they migrate across the plain twice a year in search of fresh grazing. Unfortunately one end of the migration route lies outside the protection of the park and so thousands of animals are killed each year by farmers.

Above: The brindled gnu has keen eyesight and an acute sense of smell which help it to avoid predators such as lions, but when 'kneeling' to drink it is especially vulnerable. Most at risk in a herd of gnus are the baby animals which have to keep up with their mothers from within about 15 minutes of birth.

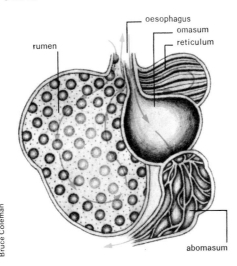

oesophagus
omasum
reticulum
rumen
abomasum

Above: A ruminant's stomach has four chambers: the rumen, the reticulum, the omasum and the abomasum. Grass is partly digested by bacteria in the rumen and reticulum, then regurgitated and chewed again. It is swallowed for the second time, and passes to the omasum and abomasum where digestion proper occurs. This rather complicated system enables the animal to digest cellulose, one of the chief constituents of plants.

Left: Male hartebeests, *Alcelaphus buselaphus*, fighting during the breeding season. These 'fights' are ritualized tests of strength, and as a rule neither animal is injured.

279

Sheep and Goats

Sheep and goats belong to the same family (*Bovidae*) as cattle and antelopes. The two groups are very closely related and differences are slight: sheep have skin glands on the face and feet whereas goats do not, and sheep lack the 'beards' which are typical of goats, especially the males. Rams usually have more tightly curved horns than billy goats.

Both sheep and goats have been extensively domesticated and they are common throughout the world. They originated in Asia and, because sheep had a more northerly distribution than goats, it was sheep rather than goats that migrated across the land bridge between Asia and America (now the Bering Straits) in prehistoric times. There are no true wild goats in the Americas.

Domestication

Sheep and goats were first domesticated by man about 10,000 years ago, before cattle, horses and pigs. In the wild a sheep moults in the spring or early summer, and it was this naturally shed wool that was first spun into a yarn and then woven to yield a fabric. It is difficult to be exact about the date of the earliest weaving, but it probably coincided more or less with successful domestication.

The domestic sheep is descended from one or more species of wild sheep such as the mouflon, *Ovis musimon*. In early times the fleece must have been of poor quality, with a high proportion of coarse rough hair, but gradually over many centuries selective breeding resulted in the fine wool breeds we know today. The main aim of modern breeders is to increase the production of fast-growing lambs on the one hand and to develop the weight and value of the wool clip on the other.

The popularity of sheep as domestic animals derives at least partly from their ability to thrive on almost any sort of pasture, from rough mountain grassland to fertile lowland plains. Like cattle, antelopes and deer, sheep and goats are ruminants (they chew the cud) so they are able to make good use of whatever plant food is available. Another advantage of the sheep is that it can survive in fairly severe weather conditions without needing the attention and shelter required by cattle or pigs. Domestic sheep usually live in flocks under more or less natural conditions and this means that they do not need much individual attention from man. Although some of the newer breeds do require more care if they are to achieve the high wool production of which they are capable, a single shepherd can generally look after a large number of animals.

Flocks of sheep which roam freely over the hills produce lambs only in the spring. With intensive farming, however, sheep are more confined and it has become desirable to have two breeding seasons in the year. It has proved difficult to breed a type of sheep that would lamb in the autumn as well as the spring but there has been some success recently.

There are more than 1,000 million sheep in the world and many different breeds. Altogether there are more than 200 distinct types of sheep, which may be divided into categories according to the characteristics of their tails: long, short,

fat or broad. Most of the improved breeds of the western world are long-tailed breeds. Another way of classifying sheep is into medium, long or fine wool types. Of the medium wool breeds, the Hampshire, Shropshire, Southdown, Suffolk, Oxford and Dorset all originated in England, the Cheviot and black-faced highland are Scottish breeds and the Panama, Columbia and Targhee come from the US. The Corriedale is an important medium wool breed developed in New Zealand.

The long wool breeds include the Cotswold, Lincoln, Leicester and Romney from England. As well as mutton they produce wool of unusually long fibre length suitable for rugs and coarse fabrics. One of the most famous British breeds is the Border Leicester; its long, lustrous wool fibres end in a small curl and make ideal wool for hand knitting.

The original fine wool breed was the Merino from Spain, a breed now found all over the world. Its descendant, the French Rambouillet, which prospers in the western ranges of the US, is another important fine wool breed. The Rambouillet is also a good meat-producer. Like the Rambouillet, the Targhee combines high grade wool with good market lamb

Above: An ancestor of present day sheep from the late Tertiary period. This creature, *Pelorovis olduvaiensis*, was larger than a modern buffalo and its horns spanned about 3.6 m (12 ft). A domestic Merino sheep is shown to the same scale. Sheep and goats originated in the mountainous parts of the Old World and so they have developed in many isolated regions, cut off from each other by valleys and lowlands. This has led to a large number of races, each slightly different from the next.

Below: Sheep were the first animals to be domesticated by man. They are able to thrive on almost any sort of pasture and require little attention: a single shepherd can look after a large number of animals. They would have provided the early herdsmen not only with meat and milk but with excellent skins for clothing. As the art of spinning wool into yarn and then weaving the yarn to produce a fabric developed, the importance of sheep increased even further.

Hans Reinhard/Bruce Coleman

Mansell

Left: An illustration from a medieval manuscript showing textile weaving in the 12th century.

Right: Male Barbary sheep, *Ammotragus lervia*, testing their strength. This 'tug of war' with interlinked horns is common behaviour for these animals. More determined contests take place in the breeding season. Then, the rams will charge each other with their heads lowered so that their foreheads clash together with considerable force. Although these fights between rival males do not normally result in injury, deaths do sometimes occur.

YEAR
male lamb
SECOND YEAR
young ewe
young ram
ewe
female lamb

Left: In a flock of sheep the females tend to herd together to the exclusion of the males. In this illustration a ewe is followed by twin lambs, one male and one female. The next year she is still followed by her daughter of the year before, and both are accompanied by their newborn lambs. The young ram from the first year tags along behind.

Below: Bighorn sheep, *Ovis canadensis*, from the Rocky Mountains. The ewe has much smaller horns than the ram.

production. Another favourite mutton sheep is the Suffolk, a very fertile breed which tends to produce twins or even triplets at lambing.

The various breeds of domestic goat are descended from the wild goat, *Capra hircus*, which originally lived in south-east Europe and south-west Asia, from Greece to Pakistan. The domestic goat is raised extensively in heavily populated farming areas. One or two goats are often kept by farmers for milk in poorer areas where a cow is too expensive or the foraging is poor. In addition to its milk, the wool of the animal is used in manu-facturing fabrics and its skin is made into leather products.

The hair of some species is particularly valuable. The Angora goat, for example, has a coat of long silky locks (called 'mohair') and the Cashmere has an under-coat of downy fleece. The word 'mohair' comes from an Arab term meaning 'chosen as the best'. Cashmere goats thrive only in the high mountainous regions of Tibet, northern India and central Asia, and the soft wool makes a fabric which is both light and extremely warm.

Wild sheep

There are various species of wild sheep living in the world today. Belonging to the genus *Ovis* are the mouflon, *Ovis musimon*, the argali, *Ovis ammon*, the urial, *Ovis vignei*, and the bighorn, *Ovis canadensis*. The first three of these are sometimes regarded simply as differ-ent races (subspecies) of a single species rather than separate species in their own right.

The mouflon is a relatively small sheep, weighing no more than 50 kg (110 lb) and reaching a height of about 80 cm (2 ft 7 in). Originally it lived throughout central and southern Europe but now the only truly wild populations live on the islands of Corsica and Sardinia. Fortu-nately, flocks of mouflons were re-established in various parts of Europe in the nineteenth century and so the species is not in any danger of extinction.

The largest species is the argali from central Asia and the Middle East. It stands as high as 120 cm (3 ft 10 in) at the shoulder and has enormous, highly curved horns. Marco Polo's sheep are an Asian race of the argali and their horns measure 180 cm (5 ft 10 in) or more along the curve. The bighorn is a native of the western mountains of North America. As its name suggests, it has thick heavy horns, but they are relatively short. A subspecies of the bighorn inhabits the wastes of eastern Siberia.

The Barbary sheep, *Ammotragus lervia*, is more like a goat than a sheep in its outward appearance. It is an agile crea-ture which lives in the rocky mountain-ous regions of the North African desert. Barbary sheep have long curved horns but perhaps their most distinctive feature is the mane of long hair on the throat and chest which sometimes reaches al-most to the ground. Like other desert animals such as the oryx, Barbary sheep can do without water for a long time. They derive moisture from the sparse veget-ation which forms their diet.

Two other species, the blue sheep, *Pseudois nayaur*, and the tahr, *Hemi-tragus jemlahicus*, are also intermediate between sheep and goats. Blue sheep are mountain-dwellers which live in the

281

Asian highlands from the Himalayas east into China. The tahr looks much more like a goat than a sheep and there are three different races living in eastern Arabia, southern India and the Himalayas.

Wild goats

Apart from the domestic goat's ancestor, *Capra hircus*, there are three species of wild goat: the ibex, *Capra ibex*, the Spanish ibex, *Capra pyrenaica*, and the markhor, *Capra falconeri*.

Goats feed on grass, weeds, shrubs, leaves and twigs, consuming large quantities of food very rapidly and chewing the cud at leisure. They are hardy animals, surviving well where other animals would starve but, while they can endure both very hot and very cold weather, they do not do well in damp regions. Their voracious appetite has led to goats being used to clear land, but so effective are they that in certain areas of the Middle East they have caused considerable damage and led to soil erosion. This is particularly true along the Mediterranean coast of North Africa and on the island of St Helena.

There are various different subspecies of the ibex living in such regions as the Alps, the Caucasus and parts of Egypt and Saudi Arabia. In the Middle Ages the Alpine subspecies was decimated because of the supposed medicinal properties of the animals' blood, horns, heart muscles and other organs. The result of this uncontrolled slaughter was that by the middle of the nineteenth century the ibex had vanished from all its former haunts except for the Gran Paradiso region of north-west Italy, where it was protected as a game animal for King Victor Emmanuel II.

Fortunately by that time zoologists were taking an interest in the fate of the ibex, and a breeding programme was started just in time to save the subspecies. Today there are about 10,000 Alpine ibexes living in Italy, Switzerland and Austria. The Spanish ibex looks much the same as other ibexes but is considered different enough to constitute a separate species: it leads a precarious existence in several small regions of Spain, and will become extinct unless drastic measures are taken to preserve it.

The markhor is one of the largest species of goat, reaching a height of 100 cm (3 ft 3 in). It has spiral horns and lives in central Asia, north of the Himalayas. The wild goat from which modern
282 domestic goats were derived is now quite

Jacana

S. Bisserot

P. Morris

ZEFA

Above: The markhor, *Capra falconeri*, **is easily recognized by its extraordinary corkscrew-like horns. Although at first sight it does not seem to have much in common with other wild goats, there are similarities in the structure of its skull and horns.**

Left: An Alpine ibex, *Capra ibex*, **in typical surroundings. Ibexes live in small groups composed either of males or of females and their young. Young males up to the age of about four years are tolerated in the female herds, but after that they must join a group of males. Ritualized fights are common among older male ibexes; young or weak animals tend to avoid such encounters.**

Left: The chamois, *Rupicapra rupicapra*, **is a goat-like animal of the European and Asian mountains. The older males are mostly solitary while the females and younger animals live in small herds. The main enemies of mountain dwellers such as chamois and ibexes are eagles, and young animals are especially vulnerable to attack. When alarmed the chamois emits a loud whistling call to alert others of the danger.**

Right: Rocky Mountain goats, *Oreamnos americanus*, **from western Canada. Although these creatures are not very common, they are not in danger of extinction for hunting is now forbidden.**

Frank Lane

rare. A few survive on the island of Crete and there are probably a few thousand still living in Turkey, Iran and southern USSR.

Chamois, gorals and takins

There are a number of horned animals which are sometimes classified with sheep and goats and sometimes with antelopes. The best known of these is the chamois, *Rupicapra rupicapra*, which lives in mountainous areas of Europe and western Asia. Chamois are about the size of goats and they are expert climbers. Like all ruminants they have two hoofed toes on each foot, and these are soft and flexible so that the animal can always get a firm grip on the rocky ground of its mountain homelands. The chamois has a North American relation, the mountain 'goat', *Oreamnos americanus*, which is also an excellent climber. It lives in the Canadian Rocky Mountains, negotiating the steepest inclines with ease: it is said that a mountain goat can jump down a vertical rock wall to reach a narrow ledge as much as eight metres (26 ft) below it.

The goral, *Nemorhaedus goral*, and its relation the serow, *Capricornis sumatraensis*, are rare animals of the highlands of eastern Asia. They are about the size of goats and have short pointed horns. Often there is a mane of long hair around the neck and shoulders. Even less common is the takin, *Budorcas taxicolor*, which looks rather like the musk ox of the Arctic but has shorter hair and smaller horns. An oily skin secretion prevents moisture from penetrating the creature's yellow coat—an adaptation to the damp, misty uplands of Tibet and central China where it lives.

Giraffe
and Okapi

Gawky and ungainly though it may appear, the giraffe has survived where many members of its family have not. It has only a single living relation, the okapi, an inhabitant of the impenetrable equatorial forests of Africa so secretive that it was unknown until early this century. Both animals belong to the family *Giraffidae*, which is part of the great mammalian order *Artiodactyla*. They are cud-chewing, hoofed animals found only in the continent of Africa, although they once lived in eastern Europe and many parts of Asia.

Fossil remains of the giraffe have been found in Greece, southern Russia, Asia Minor, India and China, and it is thought that the ancestors of the modern species entered Africa about one million years ago. In more recent times giraffes were brought to Europe in about 46 BC by Julius Caesar to feature as an attraction in the Roman arenas. The giraffe is by far the tallest mammal, reaching a height of almost six metres (20 ft).

Like other ruminants (animals that chew the cud), giraffes and okapis feed exclusively on plants, which they are able to digest very efficiently. They have large back teeth for grinding up their plant diet, but no teeth in the front of the upper jaw. A giraffe's tongue is prehensile and very long (often 45 cm, 18 in); it is used to draw leaves and twigs into the mouth where they are cut off by sharply twisting them over the lower front teeth (incisors).

Giraffes

The most obvious distinguishing feature of the giraffe is its enormously long neck and limbs, clearly an advantage to an animal which browses on the foliage of trees. This arrangement does, however, present some physiological problems. In particular, a high blood pressure is needed to maintain the flow of blood to the head, and the creature has to have a special system of blood channels to prevent a brain haemorrhage when it lowers its head the six metres (20 ft) or so down to the ground to graze or drink. These channels are controlled by reflex muscles and they automatically 'short circuit' the blood flow to stop any rush of blood to the head.

Surprisingly, the neck contains no more bones than that of most other mammals: the same seven cervical vertebrae (bones of the spine) are present in both man and the giraffe, but in the latter they are enormously long. Similarly, the leg bones are basically the same as in man but again they are very long. The forelegs are longer than the hind legs and the shoulder is deep, so accounting for the downward slope of the giraffe's back. All four limbs end in two hoofed toes, each forefoot being about 30cm (one foot) across.

The giraffe's back legs are its chief defence against predators. Few carnivores will take on anything so large as a giraffe, but lions do occasionally attack them if other game is scarce. A single blow from the hind leg of a giraffe is powerful enough to kill a lion and encounters between the

ZEFA

Left: This short-necked giraffe, *Sivatherium*, became extinct in the Pleistocene epoch. It was a large, sturdy animal and its flattened horns were much larger than those of its modern relatives. Although they now live only in Africa, giraffes originated in Asia and Europe. This creature inhabited southern Asia.

Above: Giraffes feed on the leaves and twigs of trees such as acacia and mimosa. They have long, prehensile tongues to tear the foliage from the branches.

Jacana

Left and above: The giraffe's enormous height is a distinct disadvantage when it comes to drinking. It must either splay its front legs wide apart (left) or bend them in a rather ungainly way (above) to reach the water. Giraffes are very vulnerable to attacks from predators when drinking.

Above: A giraffe gallops away from danger in the Kenyan bush. Because it is such a large animal it cannot keep up this pace for long, but its chief predators, lions, usually give up the chase early if they do not succeed right away. Giraffes pursued for long distances have been known to collapse and die of heart failure.

Above and above right: Male giraffes, using their heads and necks as clubs, fight for the possession of females. Each animal tries to swing its head against the opponent's neck or shoulders. Although these contests are normally fairly harmless, they sometimes result in serious injuries and even death.

Left: The giraffe, *Giraffa camelopardalis*, has keen eyesight, unlike its relation the okapi. Also, because it is so tall it has an excellent field of view and these two factors make it a difficult animal for a lion to stalk successfully. Even by night giraffes are watchful, rarely lying down or sleeping.

Giraffes may have anything between two and five 'horns'. The main horns are situated above the eyes and are crowned with tufts of hair. Any additional horns are simply bony protruberances. The animals shown here have three (above) and five (below) horns.

two animals quite often end in the death of the hunter rather than the hunted. Although adult giraffes do not normally attack lions, they will do so if young animals in the herd are threatened.

Giraffes have at least two short 'horns' located above the eyes. These are bony protuberances covered with hairy skin and structurally they resemble deer's antlers more than the horns of antelopes or cattle. Unlike a deer's antlers, however, which are shed and replaced each year, a giraffe's horn is permanent. Moreover the bony part of the horn develops separately from the skull at first but becomes joined to it as the animal grows older. Some giraffes possess four horns and occasionally, in certain northern races, there is a central swelling between the eyes which is almost as long as the horns. In southern races this swelling is so small as to be hardly noticeable.

The giraffe's pale, buff coloured coat is covered to a greater or lesser extent with reddish brown spots that range from regular geometric designs to irregular, blotchy shapes. Various methods of classifying giraffes into species, subspecies and even sub-subspecies have been devised but none is very satisfactory because the animals vary so much; giraffes with different colours and patterns can sometimes be observed even within a single herd. Nowadays a single species is normally recognized, *Giraffa camelopardalis*, with many different forms. Broadly these fall into two types — the reticulated giraffes with clear geometric markings, and the blotched giraffes with irregular or leaf-shaped markings — but there are many intermediate forms.

In the equatorial regions of Africa, where most reticulated giraffes live, there are sharp contrasts between the bright sunlight and deep shadows, so the distinct light and dark markings of the animals' coat blend in well with its natural background. Blotched giraffes are normally larger than the reticulated variety and they have a wider range extending over most of Africa south of

285

the Sahara. Their markings are more suited to the softer light and less well defined shadows of non-equatorial regions.

The giraffe lives in open country; dry bush regions with scattered acacia and mimosa trees are favourite haunts. It never moves to the forest since its long legs and neck would make movement through ·the dense trees and creepers difficult, and wet forest swamps would be deadly traps for its long legs.

Because trees for forage are often scattered over a wide area, giraffes are nomadic. They travel in herds of 20 to 30 animals, the herds usually being composed of an old bull, females and calves. Younger bulls usually keep a small distance apart from the rest of the herd, but when sufficiently mature they may challenge for the leadership of the herd. Giraffes can trot, run or gallop and when in full flight the legs on each side of the body move together though not quite simultaneously. When galloping they can reach a speed of about 50 kph (30 mph).

Mating occurs at any time of the year, and there is considerable competition between the bulls for the females. The bulls fight each other by swinging their heads against the neck and shoulders of their opponent. Since a giraffe's head weighs something like 45 kg (100 lb) and the neck is about two metres (6 ft 6 in) long the blows are severe and can quite easily cause a broken or dislocated neck. Usually, however, these fights do not end in death, merely the exhaustion of one or both animals.

The young are born about 14 months after mating and they are on their feet within 20 minutes of birth. Normally only a single young is produced at one time but occasionally twins are born. The lifespan of the giraffe may be as much as 30 years in captivity, but is probably considerably less than this in the wild.

As with many other animal species, man is the most dangerous enemy of the giraffe. The natives of Africa and the early European settlers prized the giraffe for its palatable flesh and also for its hide which is as much as 2.5 cm (one inch) thick and was used to make the long reins needed for teams of six or eight horses. As a result of indiscriminate killing the numbers were severely reduced and the giraffe has disappeared from large areas of northern, western and southern Africa. It is still fairly numerous in East Africa where it is a protected species, but populations elsewhere are small.

Okapis

The only living relative of the giraffe is the okapi, *Okapia johnstoni*. It is a rare mammal, native to the dense tropical forests of central equatorial Africa, and it has changed little since, like the giraffe, it migrated to Africa from Europe and Asia in prehistoric times. The okapi rarely emerges from its forest home and has hardly ever been seen in the wild.

When European explorers like Henry Stanley penetrated central Africa at the end of the nineteenth century they found that the pygmies of the region were not surprised at the sight of their horses and claimed that similar animals were to be found in the local forests. At first little attention was paid to these reports but when Sir Harry Johnston, governor of Uganda, obtained a skin and several skulls in 1901 the existence of a new species was confirmed. Zoologists were

286

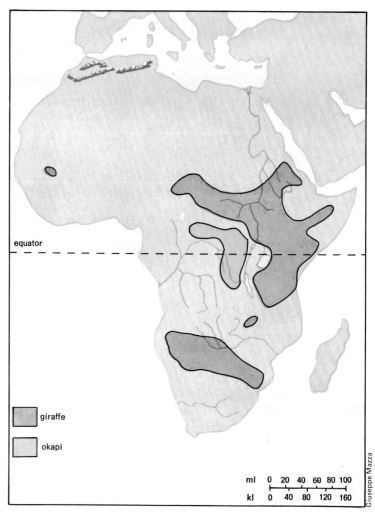

equator

■ giraffe

□ okapi

ml 0 20 40 60 80 100
kl 0 40 80 120 160

Giuseppe Mazza

Above: A map showing the distribution of giraffes and okapis in the wild. Giraffes were once much more wide-ranging than they are today, particularly in western Africa. Even within their present ranges there are large areas where the animals have disappeared. Little is known of the former range of the okapi.

Below: The Masai giraffe with its leaf-shaped body markings is a typical blotched giraffe. Young giraffes are about 2 m (7 ft) tall at birth and they are on their feet within 20 minutes. The young animal suckles for about six months and during this time it never strays far from its mother.

Right: A water hole in Africa attracts all sorts of animals from the surrounding area, both predators and their prey. Because giraffes are so vulnerable when drinking, one of the older members of the herd keeps watch while the remaining animals quench their thirst and feed on leaves.

Giuseppe Mazza

ZEFA

Left: A reticulated giraffe has sharply outlined geometrical markings so that it blends in with its background when seen from a distance.

Below: A white giraffe. Unusual colours and markings do sometimes occur, but albinos, with pure white coats and pink eyes, are rare.

Above: The okapi, *Okapia johnstoni*, which lives in the equatorial forests of central Africa has rarely been seen in the wild, but it is not uncommon in zoos. Although the first okapis to reach Europe were infested with worms and soon died, a healthy, breeding zoo population has now been established.

immediately struck by the resemblance between the new species and the extinct short-necked giraffe, *Helladotherium*, which inhabited Europe and Asia over ten million years ago.

It was surprising that such a large animal could have remained undiscovered for so long, and expeditions were soon mounted to capture an okapi alive. Although several animals were caught in the early 1900s they soon died and it was not until 1928 that one reached a European zoo (Antwerp) and survived there. Today okapis flourish in various zoos throughout the world, and something like half the zoo population has been bred in captivity.

The most obvious points of resemblance between the okapi and its relative the giraffe are the long front legs and the shape of the head. Like the giraffe, the okapi has bony 'horns' above the eyes. These grow independently of the skull but become joined to it as the animal matures. The horns, however, are present only in male animals. An adult okapi stands about 1.8 metres (6 ft) high. Its coat is a rich plum colour over most of the body but the hindquarters and the upper parts of all four limbs are horizontally striped with black and white. The lower parts of the legs, from hock to hoof, are white.

Whereas the giraffe lives in herds, the okapi lives in small family groups of one male and one or two females with their calves: life in the dense tropical forests would be difficult for larger groups of animals. Okapis have rather poor eyesight but they compensate for this by having keen senses of hearing and smell which in fact are much more useful in the jungle where vision is in any case limited. Because okapis are so shy and their habitat so inaccessible it is difficult to estimate their population with any accuracy, and until they have been studied more closely in the wild it will be impossible to say whether or not they are an endangered species. Certainly any attempt to clear their jungle homes for cultivation would threaten their survival.

Natural Science Photos

287

Snakes and Lizards

For about 150 million years reptiles were the dominant form of life on earth. The best known prehistoric reptiles are the often enormous dinosaurs of the Jurassic and Cretaceous periods. The plant-eating *Brontosaurus*, for example, was the largest land animal that ever lived, reaching a length of 18 m (60 ft) and a weight of 20 tonnes. Preying on the many plant-eating species were a variety of carnivorous dinosaurs, the most ferocious being *Tyrannosaurus rex* which walked on its two hind legs, reached a height of about 5 m (17 ft) and had almost 1,000 teeth.

About 65 million years ago, at the end of the Cretaceous period, a profound change both on land and in the sea drastically reduced the number of reptiles, and dinosaurs became extinct. Just what these sudden changes were is not known. Possibly some widespread climatic change affected the plant life on which all dinosaurs ultimately depended for their survival. Today, of the many groups of reptiles which flourished in prehistoric times only four remain: the turtles and tortoises, *Chelonia*, the crocodiles and alligators, *Crocodilia*, the beak-nosed reptiles, *Rhynchocephalia*, of which only one species survives, and the snakes and lizards, *Squamata*.

Snakes

The oldest fossil snakes date from about 65 million years ago. They resembled modern boas and pythons in being stout-bodied and large. Undoubtedly the loss of the limbs, elongation of the body and joined eyelids were originally adaptations to a burrowing lifestyle, though the increase in size probably represents a subsequent adaptation to life above the ground, feeding on the increasing numbers of rodents which developed during the Eocene period. The smaller predecessors of these snakes might not be expected to leave a significant fossil record.

Adapting to a life above ground must have raised enormous problems of locomotion for a legless animal, but it was a problem the snakes overcame well. There are three important methods of movement. The main method is by waves of muscular contraction which produce a side to side undulation from head to tail. In water, their movement is almost identical to that of a fish.

On land, snakes can also move by using ventral (underneath) plates which extend from the throat to the junction of the tail. These overlapping plates cover much of the body and are attached to pairs of ribs by muscles. Since the near edges are free, the muscles can move the plates forwards and backwards and to some extent up and down. Thus, a plate may be lifted, moved forward, lowered and moved backwards. Waves of movement of such plates pass along the body from front to rear, producing a slow crawl which enables snakes to climb steep gradients or squeeze through narrow apertures. For example, the corn snake, *Elaphe guttata*, which can climb vertically up the trunks of trees, uses this method.

288

Anthony Bannister/NHPA

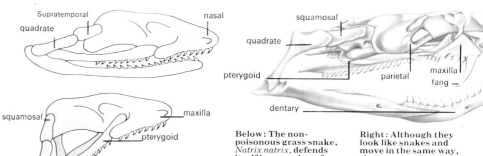

front of lower jaw bones joined only by ligament

Heather Angel

Anthony Bannister/NHPA

Right: South African sand snakes, *Psammophis sibilans*, hatching out. The leathery egg shell is cut open by a special 'egg tooth' which projects forwards from the upper jaw of the young snake.

Below right: The marine iguana, *Amblyrhynchus cristatus*, is one of the unique animals which live on the Galapagos Islands in the eastern Pacific. It is the only lizard which is truly marine, feeding on algae and seaweed. It has special glands in the nose cavities to excrete excess salt.

Below: The bearded lizard, *Amphibolurus barbatus*, from central Australia sunning itself in the open.

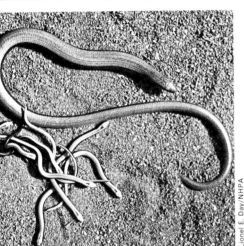

Lionel E. Day/NHPA

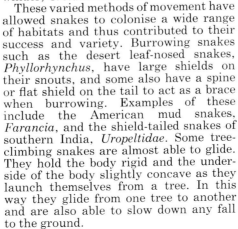

Michael Morcombe/NHPA

Adrian Warren/Ardea

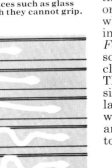

Left: An egg-eating snake, *Dasypeltis*, lives up to its name. The extreme flexibility of the neck and mouth allows the snake to swallow large eggs. The vertebrae which make up the backbone have downward pointing projections to help in swallowing and then breaking the egg. The shell is eventually regurgitated.

Below: A series of diagrams to show how a snake moves through a narrow space such as a burrow. The snake gets a grip by pressing against the sides of the burrow while waves of muscular contraction pass along the body. Snakes can hardly move at all on smooth surfaces such as glass which they cannot grip.

Another method of movement is known as 'side-winding'. This may be used for moving rapidly on very loose soil or in desert conditions. In sidewinding a grip is maintained with a sideways loop. The head is arched forwards so that the front part of the body does not touch the ground. It is then put down in a sideways loop and the back of the body is drawn up. Perhaps the most famous snake to move in this way is the American rattlesnake, or sidewinder, *Crotalus cerastes*.

These varied methods of movement have allowed snakes to colonise a wide range of habitats and thus contributed to their success and variety. Burrowing snakes such as the desert leaf-nosed snakes, *Phyllorhynchus*, have large shields on their snouts, and some also have a spine or flat shield on the tail to act as a brace when burrowing. Examples of these include the American mud snakes, *Farancia*, and the shield-tailed snakes of southern India, *Uropeltidae*. Some tree-climbing snakes are almost able to glide. They hold the body rigid and the underside of the body slightly concave as they launch themselves from a tree. In this way they glide from one tree to another and are also able to slow down any fall to the ground.

Feeding

In their original development from an underground way of life a problem also confronted the snakes in feeding. They were largely carnivorous, but catching prey without limbs posed a considerable problem, as did the chewing or tearing of food with teeth little adapted for the purpose. They developed a number of mechanisms to overcome these handicaps.

Because they have no limbs, snakes do not require a shoulder girdle or pelvis and this made it possible for them to develop a means of swallowing prey larger than their own body diameter. To allow the victim's body to pass through the mouth, a flexible joint was developed in the middle of each lower jaw, and the brain became completely encased in bone to protect it during swallowing. Snakes have well developed ribs which can enlarge to accommodate the swallowed prey.

To swallow, the teeth take a good grip on the prey. The outer rows of upper teeth are alternately moved forwards and outwards and pulled back again into position, in such a way that the curved teeth drag the prey back to the throat. The lower teeth are only used to hold the prey while the upper teeth are freed and refastened but otherwise play no part in the swallowing. As the bulk of the prey enters the throat, the jaws spread out and the neck muscles start to push the prey onwards to the stomach. Once past the head, spine movements help in further swallowing. The process can be slow: it often takes 30 minutes or more to swallow large prey.

Such a slow swallowing process requires the prey to be at least subdued, if not dead. The larger snakes such as boas, 289

Boinae, or pythons, *Pythoninae*, strike at their prey, seizing it in their jaws and then throwing one or more coils around the prey killing it by constriction.

Smaller snakes developed an even more effective way of subduing prey—poison. The evolution of this means of killing prey occurred by modification of some salivary glands into venom glands and the development of fangs. The group with the most specialized fangs include the vipers and the pit vipers, where the fang is situated well forward in the upper jaw. It is not rigid as in other snakes but can be swivelled to lie flat in the mouth when not in use. The venom is forced through an enclosed duct running through the tooth rather than just trickling down a groove in the fang as in some other snakes. This arrangement, like a hypodermic needle, allows the prey to be killed quickly with a minimum amount of venom, thus reducing the risk to the snake.

Among the most venomous snakes in the world are the taipan, *Oxyuranus scutulatus*, of Australia and the banded krait, *Bungarus fasciatus*, from south-east Asia. The latter, however, is virtually harmless for much of the time because it very rarely, if ever, bites during the day, even if severely provoked.

Reproduction

In the breeding season many snakes go through a form of rivalry and courtship. They do not stake out territory, but some species such as vipers indulge in protracted combat in which their heads rear up and each snake tries to push over his rival. The male snake trails a female by picking up the scent left by secretions of her skin. He does this by using not only his nose but also a special organ, called Jacobson's organ, which opens into the mouth and is situated above it. The Jacobson's organ probably acts as a sensor for substances picked up by the snake's tongue as it flicks in and out. Certainly it is common during courtship for the male to rub his chin along the female's back while playing his tongue in and out.

For the act of coitus the two snakes lie extended side by side, and the process frequently lasts for several hours. Eggs are usually deposited in clutches, under stones or in rotting vegetation. Female pythons incubate their eggs in the coils of their bodies. Only a few snakes such as the sea snakes, *Hydrophiinae*, give birth to live young like mammals.

Many snakes hibernate in groups; there are, for example, numerous accounts of rattlesnake dens in the US. How long they live varies greatly from one species to another; large pythons probably live the longest and some have been recorded as living for more than 25 years.

Lizards

The lizards are closely related to the snakes, but there are obvious differences. Snakes have neither limbs nor eardrums, their eyes are covered by a transparent film and a single row of wide scales run along the belly. The 'typical' lizards on the other hand, have four limbs, moveable eyelids, a visible eardrum and many scales

Above and below: A European chameleon, *Chamaeleo chamaeleon*, and a brightly coloured South African species. Chameleons clamber about among the branches of trees, anchoring themselves with their long prehensile tails. They feed mainly on insects which they catch with their long sticky tongues.

Bottom: Diagrams to show how a lizard like a chameleon alters the colour of its skin. Impulses from the spinal cord are transmitted through nerve fibres to melanophore cells which then disperse a black pigment. Thus the colour observed through the outermost layer of the skin (epidermis) darkens.

Above: A giant monitor, *Varanus giganteus*, from Australia. These animals reach a maximum length of about 2.4 m (7 ft). Monitors prey on smaller animals such as birds, rats, snakes and frogs. Like snakes, but unlike other lizards, they can drop the lower part of the jaw when swallowing large prey.

Below: A flying lizard, *Draco volans*, from south-east Asia. These animals have ribs which extend outside the body wall and support a membrane of skin in much the same way as the ribs of an umbrella support its fabric. By spreading this apparatus on each side of its body, the lizard is able to glide from tree to tree in search of insects.

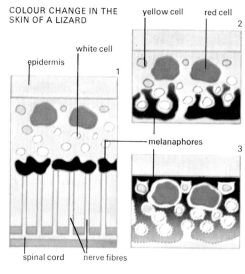

COLOUR CHANGE IN THE SKIN OF A LIZARD

yellow cell
red cell
white cell
epidermis
1
2
melanaphores
3
spinal cord
nerve fibres

Heather Angel

Anthony Bannister/NHPA

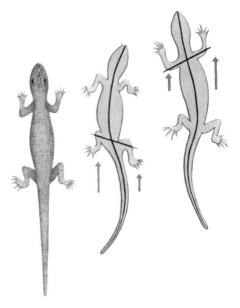

on their undersurface. They differ from
mammals in having legs which stick out
on each side of the body rather than under
it. The belly usually rests on the ground
and the legs push the lizard along, helped
by undulating or wriggling movements.

Lizards found in tropical climates are
often spectacular. The geckos, *Gekkonidae,* are small lizards with flattened
bodies and curious adhesive pads on their
toes which enable them to run easily on
vertical or overhanging surfaces. Most
geckos are partly nocturnal, appearing
in the evenings when they can be seen
stalking insects on walls—they are often
seen lying in wait close to electric lights
where insects collect. There are also some
geckos that live in the desert, and many
of these have enlarged tails which
probably act as a food reserve.

Perhaps the most spectacular, however,
are the huge monitor lizards which look
like incarnations of mythical dragons. Inhabiting a number of Indonesian islands,
the largest of these creatures is appro-
priately named the Komodo dragon,
Varanus komodoensis, and can reach a
length of 3 m (10 ft). Monitor lizards are
predatory; they feed on invertebrates and
smaller vertebrates, including snakes,
and sometimes raid poultry farms killing
chickens and stealing eggs. They are
fierce animals and defend themselves
vigorously with teeth, claws and by using
their powerful tails. Often confused with
the monitor lizards are the iguanas, large
lizards which live in the Americas.

Lizards are sexually mature when they
are two years old and are fully grown at
four or five years. The average lifespan
is about 10 years although some, such as
the slow worm, will live for up to 50 years.

291

Turtles and Crocodiles

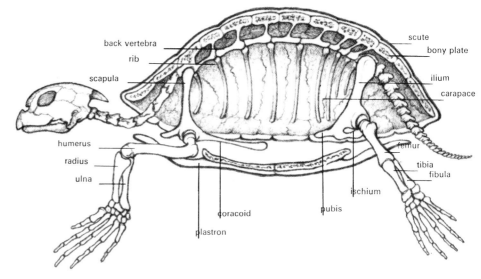

Many reptiles have found the key to survival in the evolution of body armour to protect them from their enemies. Perhaps no other reptiles, however, have armoured themselves so completely as those of the group *Chelonia*. This order includes the typical land tortoises, the amphibious terrapins and marine turtles. It is an ancient order, the members of which have undergone little change since the late Triassic 200 million years ago.

Turtles and tortoises

All turtles and tortoises have shells consisting of two main pieces, the *carapace* above and the *plastron* below. These are usually joined in the middle region of each side, leaving apertures in front and behind for the head, legs and tail. The shell is made up of two materials, an outer layer of horny *scutes*, and an inner layer of bony plates. The skeleton is enclosed in the shell and is partly joined to the carapace. To compensate for the resulting rigidity of the trunk, the neck is long and mobile, and in most species the head can be drawn back until it is almost hidden by the carapace.

The most numerous of the group are the sea turtles and of these the leatherback turtle, *Dermochelys coriacea*, is the largest, reaching a length of over two metres (6.5 ft), a width of about 3.6 m (12 ft) across the front paddles and a weight of over 675 kg (1,500 lb). Like all reptiles they evolved on land, but they have since reverted to an aquatic life. They are a small but fascinating group found in the world's tropical and subtropical seas. To equip them for this life, turtles have evolved special glands around the eyes to dispose of excess salt, their fingers are joined together to form paddles and, compared with those of tortoises, their shells are light and streamlined. The front paddles are considerably longer than the hind ones, allowing turtles to swim well despite their considerable bulk. When swimming, the paddles sweep gracefully up and down with a motion that has been compared to a bird's wings. On land, marine turtles are very clumsy and, like tortoises, have great difficulty in righting themselves when turned on their backs. This is not too much of a disadvantage because they rarely come out of the sea except to lay their eggs.

Turtles often make prodigiously long sea journeys to lay their eggs, returning to the same beaches on remote islands. Whereas there is an obvious advantage to laying their eggs in sparsely populated

Above: The skeleton of a turtle. The shell of a turtle or tortoise is made up of two main pieces, the carapace above and the plastron below. It is composed of two materials, an outer layer of horny scutes and an inner layer of bony plates. The skeleton is enclosed in the shell and is partly joined to the carapace.

Right: A brightly marked terrapin, *Pseudemys dorbicny*. Terrapins live in ponds and rivers, particularly in North and South America. They are often seen basking in the sun on logs or tree stumps. Terrapins are often kept as pets, but these usually die from malnutrition before reaching maturity.

Below, left to right: A female turtle digs a nest hole in the sand before laying her eggs. The young turtles all hatch out together and begin to dig upwards. On reaching the surface they head for the sea.

Above: The extraordinary Mata-mata turtle, *Chelys fimbriatus*, of South America. The turtle's shell is irregular and its head and limbs are covered with folds of skin which

undulate in the currents of water to camouflage it. It lies in wait on a river bottom until a fish touches the skin near the mouth. Instantly the Mata-mata's mouth springs open and the fish is swept in.

Below right: Newly hatched leatherback turtles, *Dermochelys coriacea*, on a beach. Leatherbacks are the largest species of turtle and they have the widest range of any of the world's reptiles.

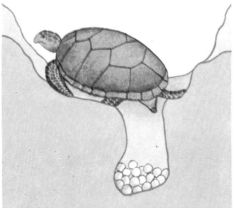

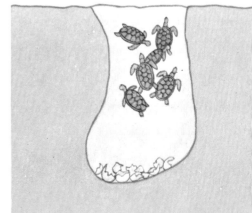

Heather Angel

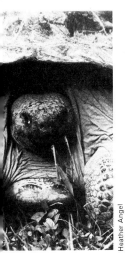

Heather Angel

Above and left: Giant tortoises, *Geochelone elephantopus*, from the island of Isabela in the Galápagos archipelago. These creatures were made famous by Charles Darwin after he had visited the islands in the 1830s. The tortoises spend most of their time in the warm dry lowlands of the islands, but they make regular journeys to the volcanic highlands in search of fresh water. The pool in the picture above lies in the crater of an extinct volcano. A curious feature of some local plants is that they germinate much more effectively if the seeds have first passed through the gut of a giant tortoise. The tortoises feed on all kinds of vegetation.

S. C. Bisserot

Above: An Indian star tortoise, *Testudo elegans*. Star tortoises rest in the middle of the day when the sun is hottest, being most active in the early morning and late afternoon. Curiously, they still rest at noon even when kept in captivity in cool climates.

Left: The alligator snapping turtle, *Macroclemys temminckii*. It lies with its mouth open and part of its tongue is filled with blood to resemble a worm. A fish that tries to take the 'worm' will be caught instantly.

Below: A newly hatched green turtle, *Chelonia mydas*. Its shell is still curved to fit the eggshell and a yolk ball protrudes from its belly. In 24 hours the shell will be straight and the yolk absorbed.

Below right: A map to show the movement of turtles in the Caribbean from the beaches of Costa Rica where many begin life.

Oxford Scientific Films

Frank Lane

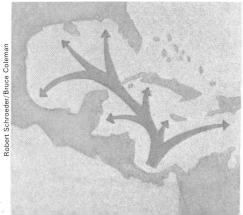

Robert Schroeder/Bruce Coleman

Heather Angel

islands, it seems rather odd that islands so very far away should be chosen. The answer to this problem may lie in the antiquity of the group. Possibly millions of years ago the islands were lying only a short distance from the mainland. According to the theory of continental drift the land masses have moved, over millions of years, so possibly the turtles' nesting island gradually and imperceptibly drifted apart from the mainland. To each successive generation of turtles the distance was no more than on the previous visit but over millions of years inches became many miles.

The nesting patterns of turtles vary, but have many common features. The green turtle, *Chelonia mydas*, comes ashore on an incoming tide, using the waves and her paddles to beach as high as possible. After a few minutes rest she uses her front paddles, advancing both of them at the same time, to drag herself forward. The rear paddles acting in unison with the front ones also assist in pushing the turtle forward. The body is never raised clear of the sand but moves forward a few inches at a time by the pushing and pulling of the paddles. At first the female turtle takes frequent rests of several minutes but as she progresses further up the beach these become shorter. On reaching the softer dry sand, she stops and begins to use her paddles to dig into the sand at a chosen spot. After twenty minutes of digging the action of the rear paddles changes, digging more directly downwards and curving like hands to scoop out the sand.

When finished, the egg chamber is pear-shaped with a narrower neck region and a wider chamber below which will house most of the eggs. This egg chamber is around 40 cm (16 in) deep. The eggs are white and resemble table tennis balls; at first they are discharged singly into the chamber but later in twos, threes, or fours, until up to 500 eggs may lie in the chamber. After laying the eggs the turtle fills in the depression with her paddles, and then, with one strong series of flipper movements, toboggans down to the sea.

After several months the eggs hatch. When emerging from the eggs, the young turtles find themselves underground and it takes them several days to dig their way to the surface. Group effort plays an important part in the emergence of young turtles—the movement of the first to hatch stimulates the others to activity. When they near the surface, the leading turtles will stop moving if the sand is warm because to emerge during the day would leave them open to attack from predators. As the sand cools in the night, activity resumes and the lower turtles again respond to the efforts of those above. In this way most of the young from a particular clutch of eggs will break the surface at more or less the same time.

Late hatchers, without the benefit of the group effort, are doomed.

Once the hatchlings leave the nest they make rapid progress to the sea. However, even during this short space of time they are preyed upon by crabs, particularly the large ghost crab, and birds. This kind of predatory action on land is nothing compared with the hazards which the baby turtles face on entering the water, from attack by carnivorous fish. Those that survive will one day return to lay eggs of their own.

Crocodiles and alligators

In contrast to the generally placid tortoises and turtles are the group of reptiles familiarly known as crocodiles. Those alive today, formidable enough, are not as big as the crocodiles which lived at the time of the dinosaurs. One, called *Phobosuchus*, the 'terror crocodile', was about 14 m (45 ft) long and most probably preyed on the huge aquatic plant-eating dinosaurs. The present day crocodiles can be divided into three groups: the true crocodiles confined to the warmer parts of Africa, Asia and Australia, the alligators and caimans of North and South America and the long-nosed crocodiles called gharials or gavials from India.

There is one small difference between the true crocodile and an alligator: in crocodiles the fourth tooth of the lower jaw on each side fits into a notch in the upper jaw and is visible when the animal's mouth is closed. In alligators it fits into a pit in the upper jaw. The gharials have long slender jaws, very like a beak and set with small teeth.

The largest crocodile now living is the estuarine crocodile, *Crocodylus porosus*,

CAIMAN

ALLIGATOR

Giuseppe Mazza

Above: The eyes of a crocodile are located high on the head so that the animal can see what is going on above the water level while still submerged.

Left: An American alligator, *Alligator mississippiensis*, emerging from the water. With the exception of a single Chinese species, all alligators live in North or South America. As in all reptiles, the limbs project from the sides of the body and are therefore not very good at supporting the body weight on land.

P. A. Milwaukee/Jacana

found in Asia, Southern China and Southern Australia. Although it is mature and can breed when about three metres (ten feet) long, it continues growing throughout its life. The largest one ever recorded was found in Bengal in India and measured 10 m (33 ft) in length and was nearly 4.2 m (14 ft) in girth at the middle of its body. Unfortunately hunting is widespread and consequently very few estuarine crocodiles reach any great age or size: specimens over six metres (20 ft) long are now very rare. The smallest species of crocodile is a South American caiman, *Caiman palperbrosus*, which barely reaches a length of 1.2 m (4 ft).

All crocodiles are adapted for life in water. The tail is flattened from side to side like an oar for efficient swimming and the nostrils are situated in a small dome or bump on top of the snout so that the animal can breathe when almost completely submerged. They can also spend a long period under the water without breathing: up to 5 hours in the case of the alligator. The teeth are conical

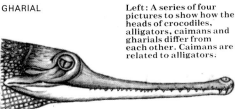

Left: A series of four pictures to show how the heads of crocodiles, alligators, caimans and gharials differ from each other. Caimans are related to alligators.

Jen & Des Bartlett/Bruce Coleman

Above: Most reptiles lay eggs rather than bear live young, and crocodiles are no exception. This picture shows a young crocodile breaking out of its egg.

Left: A long-nosed crocodile or gharial, *Gavialis gangeticus*, from India. These animals are fish eaters and are not dangerous to man. Another type of gharial, the false gharial, *Tomistoma schlegelii*, lives only in the Malay peninsula and Sumatra. It is more closely related to true crocodiles than to its Indian namesake.

Ron Boardman

and pointed, designed for holding prey, not for chewing or cutting it up, so crocodiles have to swallow their food in large lumps. This does not help the digestion processes. Stones are often found in the stomachs of crocodiles, which might assist in digesting the food by crushing and grinding it. This is only a possibility however, since they may just be swallowed by accident.

Like most other reptiles, crocodiles lay eggs. These are laid on land and may be as large as geese eggs. The Nile crocodile, *Crocodylus niloticus*, of Egypt and Northern Africa, buries its eggs in the sand; others, including the estuarine crocodile, make a sort of nest consisting of a heap of water weeds and vegetable debris in which the eggs are buried. This not only helps to keep the eggs hidden, but also maintains them at a constant and fairly high temperature because of the heating effect of the moist, decaying vegetable matter. The mother crocodile guards the nest area until the young hatch out, but does not tend her offspring after they emerge. The nest-building habits of crocodiles are reminiscent of those of birds; indeed, crocodiles are their nearest living relatives.

The emerging crocodiles are miniature adults. They grow rapidly at first, especially if food is plentiful. Alligators, for example, grow about 30 cm (one foot) a year for their first four years of life, achieving sexual maturity after six years when they are around two metres long. Individual alligators and crocodiles are known to have lived for about 45 years, and some may well reach greater ages.

Characteristics of reptiles

All reptiles have a number of features in common. To begin with, like fishes and amphibians, they are all cold blooded, or *doikilothermic*. This means that they have no effective internal mechanism for regulating the body temperature; in conse-

quence it varies widely, depending mainly on the temperature of the environment. When the outside temperature is low, for example at night, a reptile will be very sluggish because the biochemical processes in its body will proceed only slowly.

Reptiles breathe air by means of lungs; they never possess gills like fish or amphibian larvae. The ventricle of the heart is usually only partly divided by a *septum* and, as a result, some mixing of arterial and venous blood occurs. This is an important point of distinction from adult birds and mammals where arterial and venous blood never mix.

The skin of a reptile is comparatively waterproof, being made up of an *epidermis* on the outside and an inner *dermis*. The epidermis forms the scales or scutes (in turtles) which are characteristic of reptiles and distinguish them from amphibians. The scales are composed of dead, horny tissue of which the protein *keratin* forms a large part. They are continually being shed from the surface of the body, either flaking off piecemeal or being sloughed off in one piece as in snakes. This loss is made good by the proliferation of living cells in the epidermis.

A reptile's teeth are shed and replaced throughout its life, instead of there being just one or two sets as in mammals. In some reptiles the replacement of teeth follows an alternating pattern. Between any two functional teeth there is often an empty space. As a new tooth grows in the empty space and begins to function, the teeth on either side of it are shed. This prevents the reptile from losing all its functional teeth at the same time. The teeth are capped with enamel, but its composition is different from that of mammalian tooth enamel.

Reptiles have a well developed sense of sight. The eyes are often brightly coloured, the iris being yellow or red, or sometimes blending in with the camouflage pattern of the rest of the animal. The sense of hearing varies considerably from one reptile group to another. Crocodiles and certain lizards, for example, have fairly keen hearing whereas snakes are almost deaf. Reptiles do not have an external ear and the exposed eardrum is often visible on the surface of the head behind the eyes. Whereas mammals have three bones for conducting sound from the eardrum to the inner ear, reptiles have only one.

Left: The spectacled caiman, *Caiman sclerops*, is common in the northern parts of South America. It rarely grows to more than 2 m (6 ft).

Right: One of the largest crocodiles is the Nile crocodile, *Crocodylus niloticus*. Once common in Africa it is now found only in isolated preserves.

Bavaria

Amphibians

The amphibians were the first group of vertebrate animals to have made a serious attempt at a life on land. Their history is long and complex from a fish-like ancestor to the three groups of modern amphibians, the *Anura* (frogs and toads), the *Urodela* (newts and salamanders) and the *Apoda* (worm-like animals called caecilians).

To trace the origin of the amphibians we must look back over 350 million years to the Devonian period, a time of seasonal drought and wet periods. Prototype amphibians are thought to have arisen from a fish-like ancestor related to the modern coelacanth. These ancient fish had primitive lungs and a skull structure resembling that of later amphibians; they were also probably capable of surviving the periods of drought.

Since the Devonian period many amphibians have evolved and adapted to terrestrial life while others have reverted to a mainly aquatic existence. *Ichthyostega* is the oldest and best known fossil form, resembling a cross between a fish and a salamander. It probably had the five-fingered (pentadactyl) limbs of all higher four-legged animals. *Ichthyostega* belonged to a large group of fossil amphibians called the *Labyrinthodontia*, named from the folded nature of the surface of their teeth. The most successful members of this group were the *Temnospondyli* which grew to a length of up to three metres (ten feet).

Another great branch of fossil forms were the *Lepospondyli*, generally small amphibians with salamander or limbless snake-like forms. Most inhabited the great swamps of the Carboniferous period in areas that now include Europe and North America. There are considerable gaps in our knowledge relating to the evolution of modern forms, but we do know that during the Carboniferous period hundreds of different amphibian forms roamed the swamps and that these

Heather Angel

Above: A tree frog, *Hyla arborea*, resting on the leaf of a *Poinsettia* plant. Clearly visible are the frog's toe pads which enable it to climb trees. Although very obvious in this picture, the frog would normally be well camouflaged by its bright green skin colour against tree foliage. These animals are sometimes found resting in the full glare of the tropical sun. Evaporation of moisture from their body surface helps to keep their bodies at a reasonable temperature.

Right: The eye of a tree frog, *Phyllomedusa trinitatis*. Unlike fish, but like many other land animals, sight is the dominant sense in most amphibians.

Oxford Scientific Films

Right: The mating of common frogs, *Rana temporaria*. The eggs are fertilized by the male (above) as soon as they are laid by the female. A mass of spawn can be seen in the background.

Left: An Argentine horned frog, *Ceratophrys ornata*, is well camouflaged against its background. Unlike most amphibians, these frogs are equipped with biting teeth. Their tadpoles have especially strong jaws and frequently prey on their own kind. The skin of frogs and toads contains poison glands for defence: one of the strongest poisons known comes from a tree frog, *Phyllobates bicolor*. It is used by South American Indians to poison arrowheads.

Jane Burton/Bruce Coleman

H. Rivarola/Bruce Coleman

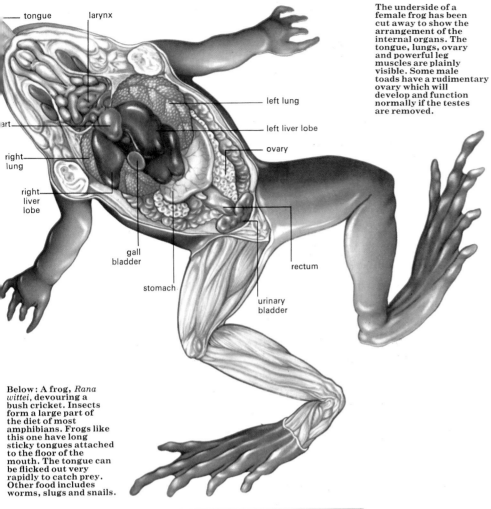

tongue
larynx
left lung
left liver lobe
ovary
~~art~~
right lung
right liver lobe
gall bladder
stomach
rectum
urinary bladder

The underside of a female frog has been cut away to show the arrangement of the internal organs. The tongue, lungs, ovary and powerful leg muscles are plainly visible. Some male toads have a rudimentary ovary which will develop and function normally if the testes are removed.

Below: A frog, *Rana wittei*, devouring a bush cricket. Insects form a large part of the diet of most amphibians. Frogs like this one have long sticky tongues attached to the floor of the mouth. The tongue can be flicked out very rapidly to catch prey. Other food includes worms, slugs and snails.

creatures led easy lives with little competition from other animals and an abundance of fish and insect food.

The change from life in the water to that on land involved relatively few changes in the form and function of amphibians. Apart from caecilians, modern amphibians lost their fish-like scales and developed a soft naked skin that was kept moist to help respiration. This arrangement carried with it the danger of dehydration of the body tissues (water was easily lost by evaporation from the moist skin surface), but provided the amphibians kept to humid regions where the air was already laden with moisture the problem was not a serious one. For effective movement the body was raised off the ground by the development of a sturdy, lightweight skeleton and associated strong muscle systems. The skull lost its stiff connection with the pectoral girdle, giving better mobility. The hind limbs of frogs and toads became well developed for a swimming, and later jumping, habit and in both the anuran (frogs and toads) and urodele (newts and salamanders) groups the pentadactyl limbs became webbed for use as swimming paddles.

Frogs and toads

The anurans are the largest and most widely distributed amphibian group with over 2,500 species. They live in a wide variety of habitats from swamps and marshes to mountain streams and deserts.

Respiration in frogs is effected in three ways. In common with all higher vertebrates, frogs have paired airsacs or lungs. While breathing, the mouth is kept tightly closed and air is sucked in through the nostrils by lowering the floor of the mouth. Air is passed backwards and forwards several times between the lungs and the mouth before finally being exhaled. The skin and the lining of the mouth are also important for respiration. Both areas are richly supplied with blood vessels and are kept moist by secretions of mucous glands.

To help camouflage themselves many amphibians are able to change colour by

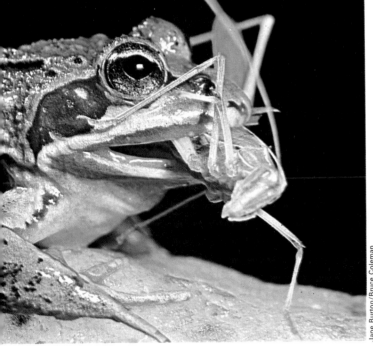

Below: A neotropical toad, *Bufo marinus*, calling to attract a mate. Frogs and toads were the first vertebrates to have a larynx and vocal cords. The inflated vocal sac under the mouth of the toad amplifies the sound and enables it to be heard from a distance of a kilometre or more.

Left: A series of diagrams to show how a frog leaps. The power for the jump comes from the well-muscled back legs which push the frog upwards and forwards. On landing, the back legs are once again drawn up against the body and the impact is taken by the front legs. The frog is then ready for another jump.

expanding and contracting three layers of pigment cells in the skin. The skin is composed of several outer layers which are continuously renewed by moulting. It is often thickened as seen in the warty nature of toads. Apart from mucous glands to keep it moist, the skin contains poison glands used for defence. The poisonous secretion of toads contains substances which have a similar effect to the drug digitalis on the human heart.

The life history of the common frog, *Rana temporaria*, shows the change in body form (complete metamorphosis) common to anurans. Males and females congregate near ponds in early spring and sound is an important factor in bringing the sexes together. Both sexes have vocal cords but only those of the male are fully developed. The typical croaking call is produced by vibration of the vocal cords, a pair of folded membranes in the larynx. Prior to mating the male frog develops a horny 'nuptial pad' on its forelimbs which helps give a secure grip on the female when mating. The male grasps the female during the whole period of egg-laying which may last for several days.

The eggs are almost always fertilized externally by the male immediately after being laid and swell up on contact with water. A jelly-like covering acts as a food supply for the young tadpole and also as a protection against predators. The tadpoles differ greatly in form from their parents, they are completely aquatic and in the early stages are vegetarian. In early summer, young frogs emerge from the pond to feed on small insect prey.

While the common frog gives us an example of the typically amphibian dependence on water for breeding, some species have devised more ingenious methods to ensure the survival of the species. Asian tree frogs, *Rhacophoridae*, lay their eggs in a bubble mass of rainwater on leaves overhanging streams and pools, so that on hatching the young fall directly into the water to continue their development. The male European midwife toad, *Alytes obstetricans*, protects the eggs by carrying them in a string

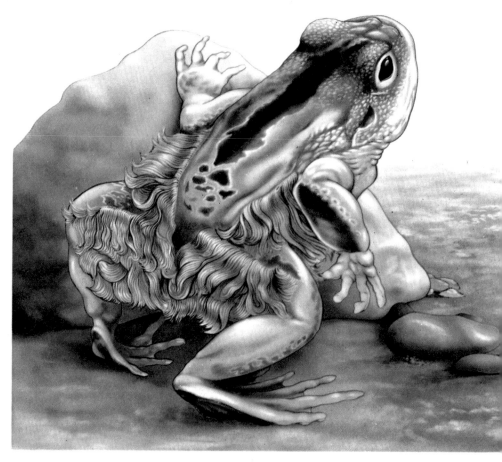

Above: The hairy frog, *Trichobatrachus robustus*. These curious amphibians are found in West Africa and they have small claws on several of their toes. The function of the vascular 'hairs', present only on male frogs, is uncertain. They may be for recognition, camouflage or other purposes.

Above: A pair of mating toads, *Bufo bufo*. Toads mate in much the same way as frogs, but their spawn is in the form of 'ropes' rather than a disorganized mass.

Left: A fire salamander, *Salamandra salamandra*. These amphibians are common in central Europe. They were thought by the ancients to be able to withstand the action of flames. The salamander secretes a milky poison from glands in its smooth skin, and the bright yellow and black markings serve as a warning to potential predators. Fire salamanders give birth to live young.

Right: Pyrenean mountain salamanders, *Euproctes asper*, during courtship.

around his legs until just before hatching when he rushes down to a stream to allow the young tadpoles their freedom. In *Phyllobates* of South America, the tadpoles live on their father's back until they reach an advanced stage of development. The Seychelles frog, *Sooglossus*, goes one step further in parental care, for the tadpoles develop into young frogs while still on the father's back. An extreme short cut in the life history is shown by a few species. For instance in the marsupial frog, *Gasterotheca*. eggs are laid in a brood pouch on the mother's back and the young hatch out in a zipper-like fashion from the pouch. The young of the Surinam toad, *Pipa pipa*, emerge singly from honeycomb depressions on the female's back.

These examples show not only degrees of parental care, but also some independence of water for breeding purposes. Frogs and toads that live in the extremely dry conditions of the Australian desert can imbibe so much water after a rainstorm that Aborigines catch them during the dry season to drink their water store. These desert amphibians often spend the heat of the day in deep burrows and are able to breed almost immediately after a sudden downpour of rain. Since the rainy season is short, the embryos develop very rapidly.

Anurans range in length from a few centimetres to the giant goliath frog, *Gigantorana goliath*, of West Africa which measures up to 40 cm (16 in). Oddities of the group include the Borneo flying frog, *Rhacophorus pardalis*, which can glide from tree to tree and the hairy frog, *Trichobatrachus robustus*, of West Africa.

Newts and salamanders
Most of the 450 species of urodeles live in water or else hidden away in mossy retreats or other humid habitats like the rotting stumps of trees, in caves or under stones. They have long tapering bodies with weak legs, and the adult and larval forms differ little from each other. Urodeles are commonly found in mountainous regions with a temperate, moist climate and have their greatest distribution in the Northern Hemisphere.

The most familiar members are the newts which belong to the large group known as true salamanders. Newts have long, laterally flattened tails and often develop crests in the breeding season. Colour plays an important role in breeding and the gaudy nuptial colours of the males are particularly striking. The pattern of courtship varies with the species, but the secretions of 'hedonic glands' play an important role in initiating sexual response in all cases. These glands are located in the skin, especially in the cloaca and tail region. Among the more common European newts, the male deposits a packet of sperms called the *spermatophore* which is taken up by the female's cloaca. Eggs are commonly laid on the leaves of water plants and from these swimming larvae emerge with well developed feathery gills.

One curious phenomenon observed in many of these amphibians is a tendency for larval features to be retained in the adult. This is called *neoteny*. The giant Asian salamanders, *Andrias*, for example, lose their larval gills, but lack eyelids and retain their larval teeth. Still more modified are the mud puppies, *Necturus*, of North America which keep their larval gills throughout life and have very small lungs. Perhaps the most famous example of neoteny is the axolotl, *Ambystoma mexicanum*, found in Lake Xochimilco and a few other cold water mountain lakes around Mexico city. The axolotl hardly ever changes into the adult form in nature, although of course it does reach sexual maturity. It will, however, metamorphose into a salamander under experimental conditions after treatment with thyroid hormone, extract of pituitary gland (the gland that controls hormone activity in vertebrates) or iodine.

Many urodeles represent the last living species of a previously large and widely distributed group. Some 60,000,000 years ago during the Tertiary period, giant salamanders were found over much of Eurasia. Today there are only three living species confined to China and Japan.

Above: Toads moult regularly throughout the summer months. The process takes about 15 minutes and the old skin is eaten, as seen here. Moulting begins with the secretion of a fluid under the outer layer of dead skin which is to be removed. The toad pulls off the old skin by a series of slow deliberate actions.

Below: An alpine newt, *Triturus alpestris*. Like most other tailed amphibians, these newts prefer a temperate, moist climate. They have a well developed sense of smell which operates under water as well as on land. All amphibians are cold blooded—their body temperatures depend on the surroundings.

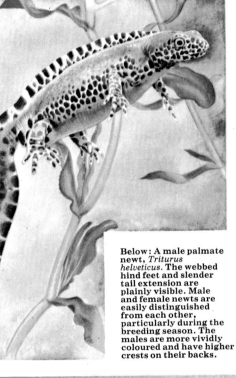

Below: A male palmate newt, *Triturus helveticus*. The webbed hind feet and slender tail extension are plainly visible. Male and female newts are easily distinguished from each other, particularly during the breeding season. The males are more vividly coloured and have higher crests on their backs.

Right: An axolotl, *Ambystoma mexicanum*. In their natural habitats these amphibians remain permanently in the larval state although they mature sexually. The feather-like external gills are typical of salamander larvae. Axolotls can be induced to metamorphose into salamanders by treatment with iodine.

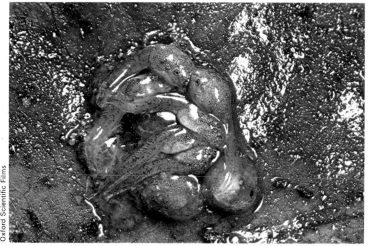

Left: Some frogs have achieved a degree of independence from the water even for breeding. This picture shows young tadpoles of the frog *Phyllobates trinitatis* on a leaf. The tadpoles will eventually be carried on their father's back before being released into a pond or stream.

Below: Five stages in the development of a tadpole. Newly hatched tadpoles have external gills, suckers to help them cling to plants but no eyes. The eyes soon develop and the gills become covered by an operculum. They feed mainly on algae and other plant material. Later the back legs develop and finally the front legs grow out from the gill cavity.

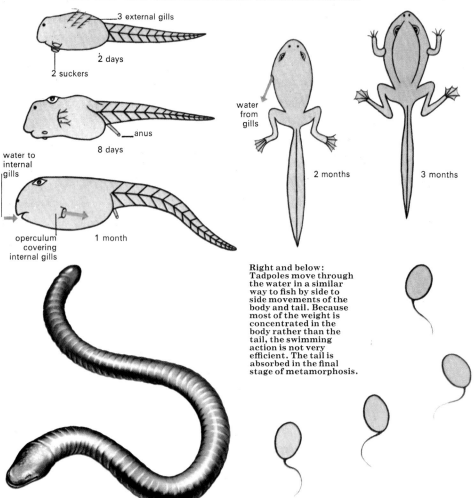

3 external gills

2 days

2 suckers

anus

8 days

water to internal gills

operculum covering internal gills

1 month

water from gills

2 months

3 months

Right and below: Tadpoles move through the water in a similar way to fish by side to side movements of the body and tail. Because most of the weight is concentrated in the body rather than the tail, the swimming action is not very efficient. The tail is absorbed in the final stage of metamorphosis.

Above: A South American caecilian, *Siphonops annulatus*. Caecilians are found in the same sort of habitat as earthworms and are often confused with them. They can, however, be distinguished from earthworms quite easily by their method of locomotion which is much more like that of a snake.

Right: A caecilian from the Seychelles burrows into the soil. Caecilians are blind: instead of eyes they have special sensory tentacles with which they find their way through the earth and locate their prey. They feed mainly on invertebrates, although larger species may eat snakes or small rodents such as mice.

300

These relics grow up to 1.5 m (5 ft) in length and live on the bottom of fast-flowing streams. They are nocturnal and hunt a wide variety of prey from fish and frogs to smaller invertebrate animals.

Another relic group are the cave salamanders, *Hydromantes*. Although they are found above ground they prefer the damp and constant environment of caves. They move slowly, using their prehensile tails for climbing and hunt soft-bodied invertebrates which they catch with their extremely long tongues. The olm, *Proteus anguinus*, is another cave dweller, but this time aquatic. This blind larval urodele with pale unpigmented skin and orange feathery gills, lives in the underground water systems of Yugoslavia.

The largest urodele family is the *Plethodontinae* containing over 60 per cent of known species. These lungless salamanders are mostly found in North America, especially in the Appalachian mountain chain. Such lungless salamanders range from purely aquatic forms like the larger dusky salamanders to the tree-climbing salamander of California.

These creatures demonstrate that an animal can survive on land even without lungs. They breathe through their moist skin and through mucous covered membranes inside the mouth. To survive in this way it is obviously an advantage for the surface area of the body to be as large as possible for a given body weight, so plethodont salamanders are usually long and slender.

The Congo eels or *amphiumas* form another curious group of urodeles. Their common name is singularly inappropriate since they have no connection with eels and are not found in Africa. All amphiumas live in the south-eastern United States. They have long cylindrical bodies equipped with very small weak limbs, often only a few millimetres long.

Caecilians

The apodans are all blind, limbless, burrowing animals and are the least known of the three amphibian groups. They lack both shoulder and pelvic girdles and their long, ringed, worm-like bodies are often scaled. They range in length from several centimetres to the giant *Caecilia thompsoni* which grows to a length of 1.5 m (5 ft).

Caecilians are all confined to tropical and sub-tropical regions of the world, especially Africa and South America. The best known member is the Ceylonese caecilian, *Ichthyophis glutinosus*, a striking blue-black creature with a bright yellow longitudinal stripe. This species shows a curious feature in that parental care is often very well developed. After laying her eggs, the female wraps herself around them until the larvae hatch out. Other caecilians give birth to live young which hatch out from eggs inside the mother. The young larvae feed in the oviduct on 'uterine milk' consisting of oil droplets and sloughed-off cells from the oviduct.

Many amphibians have made a good attempt at a life on land and are not just a precarious remnant of a once more widely distributed group. In habitats like swamps and marshes and mountain streams, they are often quite numerous and have evolved into a variety of forms. However, their survival has often meant evasion rather than total adaption to the more severe conditions of a terrestrial life.

The Big Cats

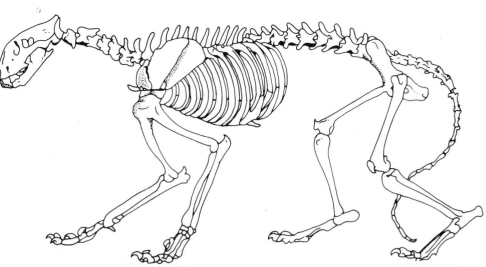

As long as animal life has existed on earth, most animals have eaten plants, leaving the way open for a fiercer minority to become meat-eaters. During the course of evolution a succession of carnivorous animals has appeared, and among the terrestrial mammals the cat family (*Felidae*) of the order *Carnivora* contains in many respects the most highly-developed and efficient carnivores of all.

Like the other members of their order they are descended from the weasel-like miacids that flourished about 50 million years ago, becoming a recognizable group on their own account about 35 million years ago. For most of the time since then there have been two very distinct types of cats, one of which, the sabre-tooths, died out only a few thousand years ago. With their huge fangs—those of the sabre-toothed tiger were up to 20 cm (8 in) long—the sabre tooths are thought to have hunted large plant-eating animals such as rhinoceroses by making slashing attacks.

The other group of cats, the one that survives today, relies instead on stealth. Moving on tip-toe with retracted claws, so that only the soft pads touch the ground, the typical cat approaches its prey silently, before springing, using the powerful muscles of the hind legs and back. The killing weapons are the claws and teeth. Cats have shorter jaws than any other carnivores, and this gives them great biting power. The pointed canine teeth are primarily used in killing, and the large last upper premolars and first lower molars (the *carnassial* teeth) for crushing and slicing the flesh before it is swallowed. Most cats hunt prey smaller than themselves, for there are many more small herbivores than large ones, but the biggest and most impressive cats of all usually hunt prey even larger than themselves.

Above: The skeleton of a tiger, *Panthera tigris.* **It has a strong flexible backbone to enable it to pounce swiftly on its prey, and a long body with most of the weight carried by the front legs so that it can negotiate uneven ground and steep inclines with ease. Although tigers and lions look quite different from each other, their skeletons are almost identical and it takes an expert to tell them apart.**

Right: A tiger cub. Normally a tigress gives birth to between two and four cubs after a gestation period of 105 days. They are born in a secluded den and are at first blind and helpless. Full maturity is not reached until the animals are more than three years old, but they learn to fend for themselves long before this.

Below: A sabre-tooth, *Machairodus lapidens,* which lived in the early Pleistocene epoch, less than 2,000,000 years ago. Sabre-tooths were members of the cat family but did not belong to the same sub-family as modern cats.

301

The big cats make up the genus *Panthera*, and apart from their size resemble each other in various ways. Unlike the smaller cats they have eyes with round pupils, and their larynxes or voice boxes are flexibly joined to the skull.

This may seem to be rather an unimportant anatomical detail, but it has important effects on sound production. Small cats yowl, but big cats roar, small cats can purr almost continuously, but when big cats purr they must pause for breath between each reverberation. Finally, in relation to their size the big cats have even larger heads than the small ones.

The first big cats evolved about a million years ago, as fossils from southern Europe and China prove. It may be that the arrival of this genus was a major cause of extinction of the sabre-tooths, for members of both groups hunted large prey, and may therefore have been in competition with each other. Travelling by land bridges, often temporary, which linked the major land-masses the big cats invaded Africa, the islands of south-east Asia, and (passing through North America) South America.

There were never very many species of big cats, but until man as a hunter com-

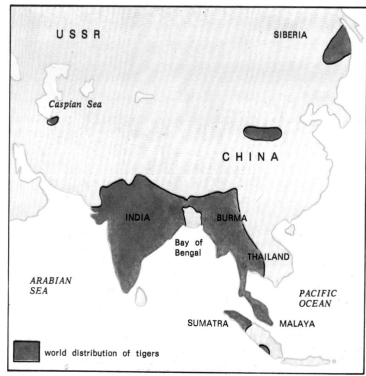

Left: Tigers are much less common than they once were. Not only has their jungle habitat been cleared for cultivation in many places, but the animals themselves have been hunted for their skins and for 'sport'. Sometimes tigers become man-eaters and have to be hunted and destroyed, but this is relatively rare. Man-eaters are usually injured animals which can no longer catch their normal prey; the injury is often a gunshot wound or a porcupine quill lodged in one foot. A single man-eater has been known to kill more than 100 people in the course of its career.

Right: A cheetah, *Acinonyx jubatus*, feeding on the carcass of a Thomson's gazelle.

Below: The cheetah is the fastest of all mammals. It has a highly flexible backbone which allows the powerful back muscles as well as the leg muscles to be used in running. Hoofed animals such as zebras and antelopes have much more rigid backbones than cheetahs and rely on their leg muscles for running.

Left: The most distinctive feature of the tiger is its striped coat which blends in well with the strong shadows of the trees and grass in its jungle homeland. Tigers range from South-East Asia to Siberia, and their prey varies accordingly. Russian tigers hunt roe deer, elk, musk deer and sometimes wolves or bears, whereas in tropical Asia tigers pursue deer of other species, nilgai (large antelopes), wild boar and even young elephants. Throughout their range tigers will take domestic animals when they can.

Right: Unlike most members of the cat family, tigers are not afraid of water and are strong swimmers.

peted with them, in some cases exterminating their prey, every major part of the world except for Australasia and some remote islands, had its own big cat population. For example, there were lions in Europe until only a few thousand years ago. The lion *Panthera leo*, was the biggest cat of Europe, western Asia, and Africa, being replaced by the tiger, *Panthera tigris*, in more eastern regions of Asia. Over much of the Old World these two species coexisted with the leopard, *panthera pardus*, which, being slightly smaller and a better climber, was adapted for hunting different prey and was therefore not in competition with them. In the mountains of central Asia the snow leopard, *Panthera uncia*, was best adapted for the conditions, and the jaguar, *Panthera onca*, was the only

member of the group to find its way to America, where it lived in the warmer and more forested regions.

Human activity has whittled down the original ranges of the big cats. Not only have the lions gone from Europe, but more recently they have also become extinct in what was then Palestine and North Africa. Almost all surviving lions now live in Africa south of the Sahara Desert, but a few still live in the Gir Forest of north-east India.

Not all wild members of the same species are the same colour: the colour of lions' manes is very variable, ranging from black to tawny, and in both leopards and jaguars dark individuals are not uncommon in some parts of the world. These are very dark brown with black spots, and at a quick glance appear to be

plain black. A 'black panther' is simply a dark-haired leopard. Similarly, 'white' tigers, which have dark stripes and blue eyes are merely a paler version of the usual colouring. Like red hair in humans, these variations sometimes appear naturally in the wild.

Lions and tigers are the biggest members of the genus, tigers being slightly bigger than lions and can weigh up to 200 kg (440 lb) or more. Leopards and snow leopards are only a little shorter than the biggest cats, but much of their length consists of a long tail, useful in balancing on overhanging branches, and 45 kg (100 lb) is a good weight for either animal. Jaguars are superficially similar to leopards, and only a little shorter in overall length. However, they have shorter tails and are much more heavily

Above: A jaguar, *Panthera onca*, with its prey—in this case a domestic goat. Jaguars are the only large cats of the Americas, and they hunt deer, peccaries and some of the huge rodents of tropical America such as the sheep-sized capybara. The home range of a single jaguar may extend over 500 sq km (190 sq miles) or more.

Below: The clouded leopard, *Neofelis nebulosa*, hunts such prey as deer and wild pigs in the forests of South-East Asia.

built, weighing about 90 kg (200 lb). Being the only big cats of tropical America, they fill the ecological niches occupied in the Old World by both the lion or tiger and the leopard, and this may be the reason why jaguars are intermediate in size. Ecologically speaking, they are a compromise.

Most cats live and hunt on their own, and the majority of the big cats are no exception. Sometimes more than one individual of species such as the tiger are seen together, but these are almost certainly pairs during their brief courtship, or part of a growing family. There is no certain proof that any of the big cats defend fixed territories against other members of their own species, but it seems probable that they do, for all of them make scent marks using both dung and urine, and also scratch on trees or the ground. This sort of behaviour looks very much like territorial demarcation. Certainly a large carnivore must range over a wide area for it must not deplete the local population of prey animals faster than they can reproduce or it will eventually run out of food. Individual leopards range over an area of roughly 22 sq km (8 sq miles), and tigers range over about 65 sq km (25 sq miles). On scantier evidence the ranges of both jaguars and snow leopards are thought to be even larger.

Lion families

The lions of the grasslands of eastern and southern Africa live in groups known as prides whereas other big cats are solitary animals. This seems to be an adaptation to their environment, for of all the big cats lions are the only ones to live where their prey species occur in large herds. In order to outwit the combined vigilance of the herd, lions co-operate, making combined rushes, or lying in ambush for their prey. Because prey is usually numerous, the territory occupied by a pride is not particularly large—perhaps 33 sq km (13 sq miles). Although lions are the only big cats which are easy to observe in the wild, it is only very recently that detailed studies have been made of their social behaviour by zoologists working on the Serengeti Plain of Tanzania.

A typical pride consists of two or three adult males, perhaps twice as many mature lionesses, and their young. Before they become mature, at between 2 and 3 years old, the adolescent males

303

Giuseppe Mazza

Above: The leopard, *Panthera pardus*, is an expert climber. It hunts antelopes, monkeys (including baboons), hyraxes and large rodents, often wedging the remains of a kill in the fork of a tree to protect it from hyenas, jackals and other scavengers. Leopards live in Africa and southern Asia and, as with other big cats, old or injured animals occasionally become man-eaters.

Right: The snow leopard, *Panthera uncia*, has the longest fur of all cats for it inhabits the cool plateaux and mountain slopes of central Asia. It ranges over a wide area, hunting small deer, mountain goats, ground squirrels and some domestic animals.

Below: A lion, *Panthera leo*, splashes through a shallow pool. This is an African lion, recognizable by its thick mane. A few hundred lions also live in north-east India: they are a different race of the same species and have noticeably shorter manes than their more numerous African cousins.

Above: A lioness with her cub. Lions are the only cats of the genus *Panthera* to live in family groups consisting of males, females and cubs. This is probably an adaptation to life on the open plains where prey animals live in large herds. Tigers, leopards and jaguars are solitary animals of the forest and bush.

Jacana

Above right and right: Within a pride of lions hunting is normally carried out by the females, who kill zebras, wildebeests and other antelopes. Related lionesses form the permanent core of the pride, for the males are ousted every few years by stronger males from outside, thus ensuring an influx of new blood.

and some of the females too are expelled by the adults. The females that are allowed to remain become part of the pride, but the others must live more solitary, less successful, and probably short lives. The young males wander in company, hunting on their own account, and growing powerful. When they are adult two or more of them will move in on another pride, take on the reigning males one at a time and kill or expel them, taking over the pride as their own. They kill the young cubs and, probably as a result of shock, any of the lionesses that are pregnant tend to lose their litters. Later the new males mate with the lionesses and sire their own cubs—in this way their social system is perpetuated and an influx of strong new blood ensured.

This life-style is very different from that of tigers, but nevertheless the two largest species of cats are quite closely related. In zoos hybrids between lions and tigers have been bred. They are called 'ligers' if a lion is the father and 'tygons' if a tiger is the father. Beyond this, the fact that the geographical ranges of the two species do not overlap indicates that they are both filling the same ecological niche—that of the strongest, and fiercest of predators.

Cheetahs

The cheetah, *Acinonyx jubatus*, is in many ways the most distinctive member of the otherwise rather homogeneous cat family. It is taller than a leopard, measuring about 90 cm (3 ft) at the shoulder, and nearly as long but is very lightly built weighing only about 54.5 kg (120 lb). Unlike those of the leopard and jaguar, the cheetah's spots are not grouped into rosettes, but are scattered singly all over the sandy-brown coat. Alone among the cats the adult cheetah is unable to retract its claws.

Other cats hunt by pouncing on the prey from close range, but the cheetah which is able to reach a speed of up to 100 kph (62 mph), catches its prey by sheer speed. However it has no stamina, and can maintain high speeds only over a few hundred yards or metres.

Cheetahs live in grasslands and semi-deserts of southern Asia and Africa. In many parts of their range, especially in Asia, they are now very rare. They hunt small, fleet-footed antelopes such as the Indian blackbuck and Thomson's gazelle of East Africa, and are usually most active early in the morning and in the evening. Either they stalk their prey, using the sparse cover that is available

before launching the attack from some dozens of metres away, or else they move towards the prey first at a walk, then a trot, and then a full-blooded gallop.

Living in herds, the prey species are watchful for such an attack, and usually stay well away from cover that could conceal a cheetah. If a sprinting cheetah succeeds in catching its prey (and often it does not), it bowls the animal over with its paws, and bites into the throat in order to kill.

Clouded leopards

Although smaller than some so-called 'small' cats, the clouded leopard, *Neofelis nebulosa*, is regarded as an intermediate species between the smaller cats and the big cats. Anatomically it possesses features of both major groups of cats in almost equal parts. It purrs like a small cat, and has neither round pupils (typical of big cats) nor vertical slit-like ones (like small cats), but horizontal oval ones. In relation to its size it has longer canine teeth than any other living cat. It lives in the forests of South-East Asia from Nepal to southern China and Sumatra, hunting quite large prey species, including deer and wild pigs—it has even been known to attack man.

305

The Smaller Cats

The cat is by nature a solitary animal and a hunter, relying chiefly on stealth to catch its prey. Its independence of spirit has always held a fascination for man, and cults and superstitions involving cats date back for thousands of years. One of the earliest records of domestic cats dates from 900 BC when worship of the Egyptian goddess Bastet was closely connected with a cat cult. More recently, in the Middle Ages, cats became the symbols of witches and the black arts, and even today many people consider that to cross the path of a black cat brings bad luck (or, according to some people, good luck).

Medium sized and small wild cats inhabit all continents except Australasia. They differ from each other in size, colour, markings, and other details, but all have broadly similar life styles. The domestic cat, *Felis catus*, is almost certainly descended from a now extinct African race of the wild cat, *Felis silvestris*, so it is not surprising that the two species resemble each other quite closely. The wild cat is a little larger than the average domestic cat, it always has a tabby coat and a rounded tip to the tail, and it breeds only once a year. In many ways the wild cat is typical of the smaller members of the family *Felidae*, and various races are found in Europe (including Scotland), Africa and the Middle East, and the steppes and plains of Asia.

Wild cats

The European wild cat inhabits woods and rocky treeless slopes of isolated areas. In northern Britain it lives mainly in the Scottish Highlands although its range is expanding slightly. Nevertheless, it is a shy creature and rarely seen: no good photograph has yet been taken of a British wild cat in its natural habitat. Wild cats are most active in the early dawn, late dusk and at night, and they hunt either on their own or in pairs. They attack their prey by stalking or by lying in ambush, and their most acute senses are sight and hearing, smell being less important. Usually their prey consists of wood mice, short-tailed voles, squirrels, hares and game birds, but occasionally they will attack young roe deer.

The male wild cat defends a hunting territory of about 65 hectares (160 acres) which includes favourite paths, resting places and claw-sharpening trees. The territory is marked out by the cat with its urine and faeces, which are not buried as are those of the domestic cat. Although a female may also occupy the territory for much of the year, she will move away from the male after mating to rear her offspring alone.

Mating takes place in the spring, and during courtship the males yowl rather than roaring as the big cats do. The kittens, usually from two to four in number, are born after a pregnancy of 63 days in a den among rocks or under the roots of a fallen tree. The kittens are playful when they are a month old, but by

the age of three months they are following their mother as she hunts. They are weaned at about four months, and about a month later the family breaks up and they become independent, reaching maturity when they are one year old. The majority of the kittens never reach maturity, but those that do have life-spans comparable to that of the domestic cat.

Closely related to the wild cat are five other species of the Old World. These include the pale, yellow-grey sand cat, *Felis margarita*, of the semi-deserts of North Africa, the Middle East and southern Russia, which has large, widely spaced ears equipped with hairs to keep out sand. The black-footed cat, *Felis nigripes*, is another desert species, from southern Africa. The Chinese desert cat, *Felis bieti*, is a lightly coloured species which inhabits the dry parts of China and Mongolia. Little is known about it— it was discovered only in the form of two skins collected by a scientific expedition in 1889, and further evidence was not forthcoming until a skull was discovered in 1925. This state of affairs is by no means unusual among the cats: very little is known about some species which may nevertheless not be particularly rare in the wild.

The jungle cat, *Felis chaus*, is a slightly larger species weighing up to 9 kg (20 lb) and is widely distributed from Egypt, through much of southern Asia to Thailand. It lives in reed beds, thick bushes and swampy low-lying forests. Pallas's cat, *Felis manul*, is found in Asia from the Caspian Sea to China. It is a yellow-grey colour, and its long coat and short ears adapt it to the cold winters that it has to endure.

Above: A black-footed wild cat, *Felis nigripes*, **from South Africa. Although this animal is even smaller than a domestic cat, it is a fierce predator. It has been known to attack and kill sheep by biting and hanging on to the jugular vein. More usual prey includes rodents, lizards and insects.**

Below: Pumas, *Puma concolor*, **and a bobcat,** *Lynx rufus* **(with pointed ears) at a kill. The prey was probably killed by one of the pumas because bobcats normally restrict their hunting to cottontail rabbits, hares and rodents. Both creatures inhabit North America, the bobcat being the most common wild cat of the US.**

Below: The caracal, *Lynx caracal*, hunts a wide variety of prey on the African savannahs. It can even catch low flying birds by leaping into the air. The pupils of its eyes are normally vertical slits (as they are in most small cats), but when they contract, as seen here, they become round like those of the big cats.

Right: A serval kitten, *Leptailurus serval*, from Uganda. As with most cats, servals are born in carefully selected dens: usually the abandoned homes of wild pigs or porcupines. Unlike caracals, which can do without water for long periods, servals always remain close to water and they are good swimmers.

3

4

Above: The ability to land on all fours is an obvious advantage for an animal like the domestic cat which spends much of its time high above the ground in trees or on roofs. As the cat falls through the air the front part of its body begins to rotate, closely followed by the back part, and by the time it reaches the ground all its feet are pointing downwards. Cats are remarkably resilient animals and can fall from considerable heights without serious injury provided they land feet first. It is not uncommon for cats to survive falls of 12 m (40 ft) or more—about the height of the fourth floor of a building.

Lynxes

The lynxes are easily distinguished from other cats by their tufted ears and short tails. Since cats use both their ears and their tails in signalling their mood to each other, the ear tufts, which emphasize ear movements, can in some respects be regarded as compensation for lack of tail length, but why the lynxes should have short tails in the first place is not at all clear.

The powerfully built northern lynx, *Lynx lynx*, inhabits parts of Europe, temperate Asia and North America where it hunts small deer, rabbits, hares and grouse. Like that of many other wild cats, its range has been reduced by man, and the Spanish race of the species is now in danger of extinction. The slightly smaller bobcat, *Lynx rufus*, is the most common of the North American wild cats. It looks very like the lynx, but whereas the lynx is rarely seen outside regions of coniferous forest, the bobcat is at home in more open country so long as there are some trees or shrubs to provide cover. Bobcats are unpopular with farmers for they prey on domestic animals such as sheep and poultry when they get a chance.

The caracal, *Lynx caracal*, replaces the northern lynx in grasslands of the warmer parts of the Old World, including southern Asia, the Arabian peninsula and parts of Africa. In the bush country of Africa south of the Sahara it is joined by the long-legged serval, *Leptailurus serval*, which has a slightly longer tail and lacks the ear tufts of the lynxes. The caracal has a tawny-brown coat which blends well with dry grasslands, but like most cats of leafy areas, the serval has darker markings to blend in with the shadows.

Zefa

Above: Cats often 'play' with small prey such as mice before killing them. By behaviour of this sort a cat teaches its kittens how to hunt and kill. Once learnt as a kitten, the habit of 'playing' with prey is frequently retained whether or not the cat has offspring to teach. Whereas most cats catch their prey by careful stalking, some, such as the cheetah, rely purely on speed.

Left: Leopard cats, *Prionailurus bengalensis*, are about the size of domestic cats and are found throughout southern Asia, from India to Borneo and China. They live in wooded country where they hunt rodents, hares and birds.

Below: A puma attacks a black bear. The puma is the largest of the North American cats and it preys on most of the mammals which live within its range, from small rodents to the enormous moose. Like many cats it usually kills its prey by biting the nape of the neck: one of its canine teeth penetrates the vertebral column of the prey and death is instantaneous.

Some cats have much more limited geographical ranges. The handsome African golden cat, *Profelis aurata*, usually plain in colour except for darker markings on the head, and about twice the size of a domestic cat, is found only in open forests of mountain slopes of central and western Africa. Its nearest relative, the similar Temminck's golden cat, *Profelis temmincki*, lives in the Himalayan foothills of Asia. The third member of this group is the rare and smaller bay cat, *Profelis badia*, of Borneo. Almost equally rare is the little marbled cat, *Pardofelis marmorata*, which has beautiful blotched markings, and inhabits forests of tropical Asia.

Another group of small cats found only in Asia is typified by the leopard cat, *Prionailurus bengalensis*, which is marked with dark spots and streaks. It lives in hilly areas and secondary forests, and hunts birds and small mammals. The more heavily built fishing cat, *Prionailurus viverrinus*, lives in swampy tropical forests. For many years there was considerable controversy as to whether fishing cats actually catch and eat fish, and only recently has this been resolved. Sometimes the fishing cat hooks fish from streams with its paws, in very much the same way that domestic cats catch goldfish. However the fishing cat is not closely related to the domestic cat, so this provides no answer to the interesting question as to where domestic cats get their

Bruce Coleman

taste for fish. The tiny flat-headed cat, *Prionailurus planiceps*, of Borneo, Sumatra and Malaya also eats some fish.

The discovery of a new species of mammal is a rare event nowadays, but in 1967 a new species of this group—*Prionailurus iriomotensis*—was discovered on Iriomote, a small mountainous island in the China Sea 200 km (124 miles) east of Taiwan. However, the Iriomote cat has a strong resemblance to the leopard cat, and may be only an island race of that species.

American cats
Central and South America have for much of their history been cut off from the other continents, and it is therefore not surprising that their animals tend to be rather distinctive. The American cats of the genus *Leopardus* are alike in having only an incomplete ring of bone round the eye. Best known is the ocelot, *Leopardus pardalis*, which is widely distributed in warm and hot American forests. Weighing about 14 kg (31 lb), it has a handsome blotched coat and for this reason has been hunted by man. The slightly smaller margay, *Leopardus wiedi*, and smaller still oncilla or tiger cat, *Leopardus tigrinus*, are very similar in appearance and occupy much the same range. Since these creatures live in much the same habitats each must be filling an ecological niche of its own. The largest species can take larger prey, while the smallest is able to climb on more slender branches to catch prey which is not available to larger cats.

Not all American cats belong to such neatly rounded groups. The pampas cat, *Lynchailurus colocolo*, is greyish and thinly striped. Once it was widespread in the south American grasslands, but it is now quite rare. The Andean or mountain cat, *Oreailurus jacobita*, is even less well known. It has a very distinctive skull with double-chambered auditory regions, but very few specimens have ever been discovered. The jaguarondi, *Herpailurus yagourarundi*, is even more unusual, for in shape it in some ways resembles a weasel or an otter rather than a cat, and it has a very long, flat skull. Weighing about 7 kg (16 lb), it has a uniform greyish or reddish coat, and is found from Arizona to northern Argentina. It lives in lowland forests and hunts birds and small mammals, including guinea pigs.

If judged by size alone the puma or cougar or mountain lion, *Puma concolor*, would be considered to be one of the big cats, for an average specimen weighs roughly 70 kg (154 lb). However, in most other respects it is more like the smaller cats, having a relatively small head, an almost continuous purr and a yowling voice. However, like the jaguarondi alone among the smaller cats and like all big cats it has round rather than slit-like pupils. Pumas vary greatly in size and in colour although most are tawny with black markings on the face and tail tip. Their range originally extended from Maine to the tip of South America. Each individual usually occupies a territory of about 30 sq km (12 sq miles) although if prey is scarce it will range even more widely. Naturally the prey varies in different parts of America, but pumas hunt elk, mule deer, smaller deer, rabbits, monkeys, giant anteaters, mice, squirrels, coyotes, raccoons, and various birds, including the rhea, the South American equivalent of the ostrich.

Above: The domestic cat communicates its mood by easily recognizable body postures. These range from the cringing submissive posture to the straight-backed threat posture (both seen above). When a cat adopts either of these postures it has already decided its course of action—flight or attack. In another common posture the cat arches its back, holds its tail erect and spits. This is a combination of threat and defence, and indicates that the animal has not decided what to do next.

Left: The face of a cat also reflects its mood. Flattening of the ears is a typical defensive posture.

Below: The ocelot, *Leopardus pardalis*, lives in central and South America. Its beautiful spotted coat blends in well with a leafy background but makes it a target for the fur hunter.

Keystone

Bruce Coleman

Hyena, Mongoose, Civet and Genet

The ancestors of the modern carnivores became extinct nearly 40 million years ago. Known as *miacids*, they were small animals with long, slender bodies, long tails and fox-like heads. They looked more like genets, civets and mongooses (family *Viverridae*) than the familiar carnivores of the cat, dog and bear families. In spite of their outward resemblance to these early carnivores, viverrids are in other respects highly evolved. Their jaws, for example, are like those of cats, having fewer molars and premolars than dogs, bears, raccoons or weasels.

Viverrids are all small carnivores, weighing between 680 g (1.5 lb) and 14 kg (31 lb). They have relatively long bodies and rather short legs, almost always with five toes on each foot, and only partly retractible claws. Some are plantigrade (walking with the sole of the foot touching the ground at each step) while others are digitigrade (moving on their toes). The earliest viverrids known from fossils lived in Europe during the Eocene epoch about 50 million years ago while the miacids were still living. Later they migrated to Asia, then Africa and finally the island of Madagascar. Unlike members of the weasel family, however, they never managed to invade the New World by natural means—although they were eventually introduced by man—and they appear never to have been very successful in cold climates. Whereas weasels have dense, warm fur, that of the viverrids is much less luxuriant and is usually a drab brown, but is sometimes spotted or striped.

The family contains about 80 living species and is much more varied than some other families of carnivores, such as bears or cats. Because of this variety, and because the fossil record is by no means complete, there is considerable disagreement among zoologists as to how it should be subdivided.

Genets and civets

Among this diversity of animals the genets are perhaps most typical of the family. The blotched genet, *Genetta tigrina*, looks like a combination between a fox and a cat—it has the head and body of a fox and the legs, feet and tail of a cat. The black blotched and spotted markings on the body, and the rings on the tail are also reminiscent of some cats. The blotched genet is a solitary, nocturnal animal which preys on small mammals and birds. It lives in southern and eastern Africa and because it is a good climber, hunts in trees as well as on the ground. By day it hides in rocky crevices, hollow trees, thick cover or a burrow taken over from another animal. Various other species of genet are found in different parts of Africa, and one species lives in southern Europe.

The civets are larger and more heavily built than genets and they are found both in Africa and tropical Asia. An example is the African civet, *Civettictis civetta*, a

Bruce Coleman

Above: A pygmy mongoose, *Helogale*, with an egg, one of its favourite foods. These creatures are active during the day, hunting in small groups for insects, lizards, mice and other small animals. They are playful, sociable animals and all the members of a family group help in the rearing of the young.

Below: A mongoose, *Herpestes*, tackles an Indian cobra. The mongoose has been renowned for its snake-fighting abilities for thousands of years, and it is a welcome inhabitant of snake infested regions of India and South-East Asia. Although a mongoose will normally win such a contest, it does not always do so.

Left: Like other members of the mongoose sub-family *Herpestinae*, the suricate, *Suricata suricatta*, can close its ear openings to prevent sand or water from entering.

Right: The banded mongoose, *Mungos mungo*, breaks open hard-shelled food such as a snail's egg by grasping it between the front legs and throwing it backwards or against a rock or downwards on to the ground. The procedure is repeated as often as may be necessary. The pygmy mongoose (above) behaves in very much the same way. These mongooses inhabit dry regions of Africa south of the Sahara, often living in old termite hills or abandoned rabbit holes.

Bruce Coleman

Left: A small-spotted genet, *Genetta genetta*, eating a bird. The species occurs in Spain, southern France and throughout Africa (except the Sahara). Like many animals which prey on birds, these genets are active by night and are good climbers: they can climb trees extremely quickly, and generally descend head first.

Right: An African palm civet, *Nandinia binotata*. Like most palm civets this creature is lightly built, has a long tail and spends much of its time in trees feeding on fruits, seeds and insects. This is the only African species—most palm civets inhabit India and South-East Asia.

Below: In the early morning suricates (sometimes called meerkats) come out of their burrows and stand upright, warming themselves in the sun. They are sociable animals and their burrows consist of a network of tunnels which they excavate with their long claws. Often they share their burrows with squirrels.

nocturnal animal about 1.2 m (4 ft) long from nose to tail which feeds not only on small animals but also on plant material such as juicy stems, tubers and fruits. It lives in bush country south of the Sahara and spends most of its time on the ground, climbing trees only when in danger.

In Ethiopia the African civet is kept in captivity for its musk, a secretion from scent glands beneath the tail. The musk is squeezed from the glands by means of a horn spoon and in a week each animal yields about 4 g (0.14 oz). Musk is very valuable and has been used in the manufacture of expensive perfumes for centuries: King Solomon is said to have obtained musk from East Africa.

The palm civets are usually placed in a sub-family of their own. More lightly built than the true civets, and with very long tails, they spend much of their time in trees. Their fur is either plain or faintly blotched. A typical palm civet is the toddy cat, *Paradoxurus hermaphroditus*, of India, Ceylon, southern China, Malaysia and the East Indies. About one metre (40 in) long, it is active by night and feeds on insects, small vertebrates, fruits and seeds. It gets its common name from its habit of raiding bowls placed beside palm trees to collect the juice or 'toddy'.

The largest living viverrid is the binturong, *Arctictis binturong*, a palm civet from southern Asia and the East Indies, which weighs about 14 kg (31 lb) and has a shaggy grey-brown coat. It is nocturnal and feeds primarily on plants. Like only one other member of the order *Carnivora*—the kinkajou of tropical America which belongs to the raccoon family—it has a prehensile (grasping) tail as an adaptation to climbing.

The otter civet, *Cynogale bennetti*, of southern Asia, Sumatra and Borneo looks much like an otter, and has dense brown fur speckled with grey. As adaptations to aquatic life it has nostrils and ears which can be closed and webbed feet. Its tail, however, is not very strongly muscled, so it is not a particularly fast swimmer; when pursued by larger predators it climbs trees for safety rather than taking to the water. It feeds on slow-moving fish and crustaceans, as well as some small land animals and some plant material.

The viverrids of Madagascar are unusual, and very little is known about them. They consist of the Malagasy civet, *Fossa fossa*, (which is more like a palm civet than a true civet); the falaonoucs, *Eupleres*, which have affinities with the mongooses but have much smaller teeth; 311

Left: Scavengers collect at the site of a kill. A spotted hyena, *Crocuta crocuta*, is surrounded by vultures and in the background are two marabou storks. Although they are often thought of only as scavengers, spotted hyenas are quite capable of killing large antelopes and zebras for themselves. In some parts of Africa lions regularly scavenge off kills made by spotted hyenas.

Right: For their size hyenas (this one is a spotted hyena) have stronger jaws than any other mammal and their teeth are large and well developed. This enables them to feed by scavenging for they can crack the bones of animals which have been killed and partly eaten by other predators such as lions. Spotted hyenas are sometimes called 'laughing hyenas' for when excited they make a sound which is very similar to a human laugh. This strange cry is most often heard at night when the hyenas are feeding. They are mainly nocturnal animals, lying up during the day in burrows or patches of bush.

eight species of mongoose very different from those found elsewhere, and the fossa, *Cryptoprocta ferox*. The fossa is a sleek, reddish-brown animal about 1.3 m (52 in) long—its tail accounts for about half of this length. It is nocturnal, climbs well and hunts lemurs, large birds and even wild pigs. The viverrids of Madagascar differ from those found elsewhere because the island has been separated from the mainland of Africa for many millions of years, and some of them resemble ancestors of the group whose descendants have become extinct elsewhere.

Mongooses
Unlike other viverrids, mongooses live almost entirely on the ground. Having short legs they can move easily through thick cover, and some of them burrow as well. All of them are good swimmers and some species both from Africa, such as the marsh mongoose, *Atilax paludinosus*, and from Asia, such as the crab-eating mongoose, *Herpestes urva*, feed mainly on fresh water fish, frogs and crabs. There are about 50 species in all, inhabiting almost all types of country from sandy plains to thick forests in Africa and southern Asia. One species, the ichneumon, *Herpestes ichneumon*, has a range which includes southern Europe as well as Africa.

Most mongooses are basically carnivorous, but they supplement their diet with plant material. Usually insects and spiders make up the bulk of the food. For example, the suricate or meerkat, *Suricata suricatta*, of southern Africa digs up grubs, and eats locusts and termites as well as lizards, small snakes, birds and bulbous roots.

Mongooses are best known for their ability to kill and eat venomous snakes, and there is no doubt that the fiercer mongoose species can perform this feat, although others appear to avoid snakes and to be afraid of them. One snake-killing species is the Indian grey mongoose, *Herpestes edwardsi*, which is about 40 cm (16 in) long and can tackle an Indian cobra several times its own size.

Above and left: Examples of hyena behaviour. A young hyena greets a visitor to his den by sniffing at the genital region (top), a young hyena greets an unrelated adult female by 'kissing' (centre) and a mother moves her baby from one den to another. The sense of smell is most important in establishing relationships between members of a group of hyenas.

Right: One striped hyena, *Hyaena hyaena*, with teeth bared and ears erect, asserts its superiority over another. To indicate submission the second animal flattens its ears and shrinks away from the aggressor. In this way a social hierarchy is set up.

Giuseppe Mazza

Bruce Coleman

Above: A spotted hyena carrying away the horns of a waterbuck. Hyena packs are dominated by females, and they hunt within carefully defended territories. Males are occasionally seen outside their own territories but females always remain on home ground. Border clashes between neighbouring packs are common.

Above right: The aardwolf, *Proteles cristatus*, is a nocturnal animal of the African savannahs. It feeds mainly on termites and has a long flexible tongue for probing the nests of these insects. Aardwolves are less common than they were because termites are continually being destroyed by man.

The mongoose makes use of its greater speed to dash in and deliver damaging bites, locking jaws with the snake if possible. Being a mammal and therefore warm-blooded the mongoose tires less quickly than the slower-moving, cold-blooded snake which is eventually killed when it becomes exhausted.

Mongooses are not totally immune to the effects of snake venom, and have been known to be killed in combat, but they are certainly less sensitive to it than most other mammals and do not often lose a fight. However, it seems unlikely that snakes form the major part of their diet. In one study of the stomach contents of wild mongooses living in an area where snakes were common, only 11 per cent of the mongooses were found to have eaten snakes recently. The more predatory mongooses hunt singly or in pairs, or at most in small family groups. They rarely kill prey larger than a rat or a chicken.

Because of their ability to kill pests, mongooses have been introduced to various parts of the world. In the 1870s an Indian species, *Herpestes auropunctatus*, was liberated in parts of the West Indies, including Trinidad, Jamaica, St Kitts, Antigua, Barbados and St Vincent. In some places, such as Dominica where the climate was too wet, the introduced stocks died out, but elsewhere they flourished, killing many rats and a few snakes as had been hoped. As their numbers increased, however, the mongooses turned their attention to less harmful wild animals and to domestic chickens, and it was realized that they themselves had become serious pests.

Although a price has been placed on their heads it is now too late for them to be exterminated for they are much too well established. In Trinidad, for example, over 30,000 mongooses a year have been killed for several consecutive years without any apparent effect on their numbers. The same mongoose species was introduced into the Hawaiian Islands in 1883 and with the same dire results. Now that the lesson has been learned it is unlikely that the same mistake will be repeated.

Bruce Coleman

The hyena family

The aardwolf, *Proteles cristatus*, and the three living species of hyena make up a family of their own, the *Hyaenidae*. These carnivores are superficially dog-like, walk on their toes and have backs that slope down towards relatively weak hind-quarters. The hyena's snout is thick and quite long but the jaws contain few teeth which, being much more like those of cats than dogs, reveal the animal's true affinities.

The aardwolf (whose name means 'earth wolf' in Afrikaans) is very different from the hyena in its habits and is usually placed in a separate sub-family. It is about 50 cm (20 in) tall at the shoulder, lightly built and has a pointed muzzle armed with small, widely spaced teeth. Its long fur is sandy-grey with black stripes and it lives in southern Africa from the Cape of Good Hope to the Sudan, preferring dry open plains or bush country.

Spotted hyenas, *Crocuta crocuta*, (sometimes called 'laughing hyenas') are most active at night, lying up during the day in burrows or patches of bush. They are noisy animals and, as dusk approaches, they make loud hooting calls as they roam the African plains in loose packs searching for dead animals or suitable prey such as young antelopes. When excited the spotted hyena utters the characteristic 'laugh' for which it is well known.

The other hyenas are slightly smaller. They are the striped hyena, *Hyaena hyaena*, which lives in northern Africa and southern Asia from Turkey to India, and the now rare brown hyena, *Hyaena brunnea*, of southern Africa. Both species have manes of long hair along the neck and back. Like the spotted hyena, they are mainly nocturnal animals, hiding during the day among rocks. Their diet consists mainly of carrion although they do sometimes attack sheep, goats and small wild animals. The brown hyena sometimes lives on the sea shore where it eats crabs and other such animals. It also scavenges on the bodies of larger dead animals brought in by the tide.

Dogs, Wolves and Foxes

Of all domestic animals, the dog is the most familiar and the most dependent on man. Just how the association began is uncertain, but for many thousands of years both prehistoric man and wolves (from which domestic dogs are descended) hunted the same prey. From time to time wolves must have scavenged on the remains of kills made by man, just as man must have used animals killed by wolves whenever he could, and this probably led to some sort of working relationship between the two. At any event, domestic dogs were a feature of Neolithic farming communities as long ago as 9,000 BC.

Domestic dogs, together with wild dogs, wolves, jackals and foxes are members of a family of carnivores called the *Canidae*. True wild canids are found all over the world with the exception of the Antarctic, some oceanic islands, Australia, New Zealand and Madagascar. The Australian dingo, which is often regarded as a wild dog, is probably descended from domestic dogs introduced by Stone Age man when he entered the continent about 8,000 years ago. As a general rule the 37 or so species in the family live in open areas—grassland and light woodland are favourite haunts—but a few live in tropical forests and others have come to terms with the freezing Arctic wastelands or the searing heat of the desert.

The first canids probably appeared about 40 million years ago in the late Eocene epoch. They may have evolved from unspecialized carnivores which walked on the soles of their feet like bears, lived in burrows and ate a variety of animal and plant food. Their more specialized descendants were successful predators, being long-legged, speedy runners with keen sight, hearing and smell. Gradually the thumb and big toe became smaller and were eventually lost altogether, so they began to run on their toes rather than their soles. This enabled them to run at speed for long distances and so catch their prey by sheer endurance rather than by a short burst of speed like members of the cat family.

The wild canids of today differ little from their ancestors. They are usually light animals with long, thin legs, five toes on each foreleg and four on each hind leg, and non-retractable claws. They have powerful jaws equipped with stabbing canine teeth and modified molars or premolars, called *carnassial* teeth, for shearing meat. Many of them mark out territories with scent glands and have a well developed system of vocal and visual communication. They tend to live in burrows, either self-made or abandoned by other animals. Pairs often mate for life and they breed once a year, the young being born after a gestation period of about 45 days. The puppies or cubs are reared by both parents and in the wild they can expect a lifespan of no more than 14 years.

Wolves, coyotes and domestic dogs

The heaviest and largest canids are the wolves. There are two species: the grey or timber wolf, *Canis lupus*, of Asia and

Right: All modern canids are descended from this creature, *Hesperocyon*, which lived about 30 million years ago.

Below: A wolf, *Canis lupus*, strides across a clearing in a wood. Contrary to popular belief this, the largest member of the family *Canidae*, is a shy creature which avoids contact with man whenever possible. The fear that many humans have of the wolf is largely unfounded: although there are cases of humans being killed by wolves these are relatively rare and the animals were often suffering from rabies. In North America it is difficult to find a single instance of a human having been killed by a wolf.

Frank Lane

Des Bartlett/Bruce Coleman

Left: A coyote, *Canis latrans*, swimming across a pool. Coyotes are found throughout North America and unlike wolves, whose population decreases year by year, are highly adaptable. In some Californian towns they have adopted suburban life, eating domestic pets and boldly strolling down busy streets.

Below: Modern domestic dogs, like these racing Afghan hounds, are descended from the wolf. Selective breeding has led to the great variety of types known today, from the Pekinese to the Irish wolfhound (the largest domestic breed). Greyhound-like dogs were first bred by the Egyptians about 3,000 years ago.

Popperfoto

Left: A dingo pup. Dingos are descended from early domestic dogs which crossed into Australia with the first human inhabitants. They prey mainly on kangaroos and rabbits, but will attack sheep when the opportunity arises. This last habit has, not surprisingly, made them unpopular with farmers.

Right: An adult wolf asserts its superiority over a younger pack member. Wolves, like most other species of the dog family, have characteristic body postures to indicate particular moods.

Below: A black-backed jackal, *Canis mesomelas*, scavenging on the carcass of a zebra. These creatures also eat rodents, insects, lizards and birds.

North America which is almost one metre (three feet) high at the shoulder and weighs up to 79 kg (174 lb), and the red wolf, *Canis rufus*, of Texas, which is smaller and lighter. Once common throughout the northern hemisphere wolves have been persecuted by man wherever they threatened domestic stock, and have been driven to remote areas in Europe and Asia and the wilder parts of North America. In 1974 there were fewer than 200 red wolves and less than 20 Northern Rocky Mountain wolves (a sub-species of the timber wolf) left in North America. The timber wolf is also endangered elsewhere although there are some thriving populations, particularly in Canada and Alaska and in the USSR, where there could be as many as 50,000 wolves.

While wolves have decreased in numbers, their cousin the coyote, *Canis latrans*, has increased its range in North America. It hunts in smaller groups and because it is more cunning and adaptable has been able to cope with the threatening presence of man.

Fossil skulls suggest that domestic dogs were selectively bred from timber wolves. With a well developed social hierarchy they were ideal animals to domesticate—the dependence of inferior dogs on superior ones was simply either transferred to man or, in the case of a team of huskies, used for man's benefit. Like their wild ancestors dingos and pariahs breed only once a year, but most domestic dogs, *Canis familiaris*, come into season and breed twice a year. Selective breeding through the ages has also eliminated many other ancestral characteristics and produced a weaker animal with degenerate jaws and teeth.

Jackals and foxes
Jackals are delicately built, solitary and nocturnal members of the genus *Canis*. The three species are all about 40 cm (16 in) high at the shoulder and weigh about 9 kg (20 lb). The common jackal, *Canis aureus*, lives in open and wooded savannah throughout Africa, Asia and parts of Europe. It is a nocturnal animal and hunts small animals such as rodents, birds and lizards as well as scavenging for food: in Africa it is seen alongside hyenas and vultures at kills. It has also

Left: The fennec, *Fennecus zerda*, is a shy nocturnal animal. Its huge ears give it an acute sense of hearing and its large pupils enable it to make the most of dim light. The large ears, being good radiators of heat, may also play a part in regulating the body temperature.

Right and far right: Although they are not closely related and live in quite different parts of the world, the fennec and the kit fox, *Vulpes velox*, look remarkably alike. This is an example of 'convergent evolution', where two species evolve in much the same way in similar habitats. Both these animals are nocturnal and live in desert areas.

Kit Fox

become the counterpart of the European red fox in its nightly raids on villages in search of food.

The attractive African black-backed jackal, *Canis mesomelas*, is occasionally seen during the day but usually hunts at night. Sometimes it forms packs of up to 30 animals in order to hunt down large prey such as gazelles. Its relative the African side-striped jackal, *Canis adustus*, is a shy, nocturnal animal which scavenges and hunts for small mammals and insects.

Foxes are found in nearly every part of the world and in most environments except dense forest. One species, the eastern grey fox, *Urocyon cinereoargenteus*, of North America will even climb trees. Foxes are smaller than wolves or jackals and they have shorter legs and longer bushy tails; they tend to be nocturnal and solitary. The smallest of all wild canids is the African desert fox or fennec, *Fennecus zerda*, weighing about 1.5 kg (3.3 lb). It escapes the heat of the day in sand burrows and feeds at night on whatever it can find. It has enormous ears and its acute hearing helps it to locate prey in the dark. To equip it for life in the desert the fennec has hairy feet which enable it to run over soft sand, and most of its water requirement is derived from its diet.

The New World counterpart of the fennec, the kit fox, *Vulpes velox*, has similar adaptations. The northern sub-species of the kit fox may be extinct as a result of trapping, poisoning and hunting for fur. Another species of fox which has adapted to a hostile environment is the Arctic fox, *Alopex lagopus*, which can survive temperatures of −50 °C (−58 °F). It is insulated by a coat composed of long guard hairs and a thick underfur, has short ears to conserve heat and hairy feet to give footing in the snow.

This remarkable animal roams the Arctic all year round in search of lemmings and hares or the remains of polar bear kills. As summer approaches the white form exchanges its bushy coat for a sleek brown-grey one. Arctic fox popula-

Right and below: The Arctic fox, *Alopex lagopus*, occurs in two different colour forms. The white variety (right) is more common in those regions with the heaviest snowfall—its coat changes to a grey-brown colour in the summer months when the snow recedes. The rare 'blue' form (below) remains the same colour throughout the year. The Arctic fox is one of the few mammals which can survive north of the Arctic Circle. It feeds on lemmings, eggs, young birds, the remains of polar bear kills and other carrion, and is a common and enterprising scavenger around human settlements. Unlike most of their cousins, Arctic foxes are solitary, nomadic creatures.

Right: A European red fox, *Vulpes vulpes*, devouring a bird. This is probably the most familiar wild canid and is certainly one of the most successful. It can adapt to most habitats and in some countries, such as Britain, it even scavenges for food among domestic refuse.

Fennec

tions rise and fall with the lemming populations. When they are relatively abundant they provide local people with a valuable fur trade: the blue-grey coat of the blue form of Arctic fox was once particularly sought after.

The red fox, *Vulpes vulpes*, found throughout the northern hemisphere, has been farmed for fur for over a century. Highly prized are the wild, silver-coated specimens with their black-tipped guard hairs, and the selectively bred platinum foxes. As well as supplying the fur trade and giving sport to hunters the red fox helps the farmer by keeping down the populations of mice and voles which damage crops. Red foxes are monogamous, they breed in winter and four to ten cubs are born in spring. Both parents are involved in rearing and the cubs leave the den when they are about five months old. In some urban areas the red fox has become a pest as it scavenges among refuse. Like the red fox, the Northern Semien fox, *Simenia simensis*, of Ethiopia has been accused of killing domestic stock and has been exterminated in most of its range. In 1969 with the establishment of the Semien National Mountain Park it was decreed that the fox could only be hunted with the highest authority.

Wild dogs

The remaining group of canids are the wild dogs. By far the most notorious is the mottled African hunting dog, *Lycaon pictus*, which is almost as tall as the wolf but only a third as heavy. Like wolves, hunting dogs are communal animals, living in packs with a well defined 'pecking order' beneath a dominant male and female. They communicate with each other by squeaks and howls, and a variety of facial and postural expressions.

Burrows protect them from the hot sun and strong wind of the savannah, and in the cooler morning and evening they travel long distances in search of prey. The leader selects the prey, often an old or sick animal, and the members of the pack run in relays to maintain the chase, which may last for 5 km (3 miles). If caught the prey is disembowelled and often eaten completely in 15 minutes. The pack returns home and will feed pups communally by disgorging meat. African hunting dogs are now relatively rare as a result of a decline in their natural prey and persecution by man.

Wild dog species are well represented in South America though numbers are declining and some species may be extinct. The sausage-shaped bush dog, *Speothos venaticus*, which inhabits wooded and grassy savannah, is extremely rare and in 1967 was reported to be unknown by native peoples. The similar looking and stocky small-eared dog, *Atelocynus microtis*, of the Amazon basin is also very rare as a result of depletion of its woodland habitat. The pampa fox, *Dusicyon gymnocercus*, has been mercilessly hunted in farming areas where it takes sheep and poultry.

One of the most attractive South American dogs is the maned wolf, *Chrysocyon brachyurus*. It has long yellow-red hair, almost black legs and a white chin and tail tip. Almost as tall as true wolves it has far longer legs which enable it to travel for long distances across the pampas. Nocturnal and very shy it feeds on anything from agoutis (rabbit-sized rodents) to fruit. Another nocturnal South American dog is the crab-eating fox, *Cerdocyon thous*, which despite its name lives mainly on rodents.

The Indian dhole, *Cuon alpinus*, is an Asian species of wild dog. Like other forest-dwelling canids it trails its prey by scent rather than sight and sound. These brave fox-like dogs, now very rare, assemble in packs to hunt down deer, sheep and pigs and occasionally even bears and tigers. They are considerably slower than African hunting dogs, but they have great stamina and can pursue their prey for long periods without a break. Although rare, the dhole can apparently adapt to the most extreme climatic conditions, from the heat of the tropics to the sub-zero temperatures of the Asian mountains.

Another canid species, the raccoon dog, *Nyctereutes procyonoides*, of Asia lives in forested river valleys and near lakes. It is unique among dogs in that it hibernates, though only for short periods at a time. It is also unusual in its feeding habits. Besides eating small rodents, berries and carrion it is very partial to fish and amphibians, pouncing on them in shallow streams and by the side of lakes. The Japanese hunt it for food, using the skins to make clothes and the bones to make medicines.

H. W. Silvester/Bavaria Verlag

P. Castel/Jacana

J. Robert/Jacana

Left: A group of African wild dogs, *Lycaon pictus*. **These creatures live in packs of up to 50 animals and they hunt gazelles and the young of larger antelopes. The leader of the pack normally brings down the prey by biting at one of its hind legs. Wild dogs rarely scavenge off the kills of other animals.**

Above: The long-legged maned wolf, *Chrysocyon brachyurus*, **of South America has an undeserved reputation for attacking young domestic animals and so has been driven from many of its original haunts by man. In fact it feeds almost exclusively on small mammals, birds and some plant material.**

317

Pandas, Raccoons and Badgers

The weasels and their relatives, which together make up the family *Mustelidae*, have the short legs and long muscular bodies which were typical of the remote ancestors of the carnivores. Although this shape is a primitive one it can, with just a little modification, be adapted to the varied life-styles of the small to medium-sized species that make up the family.

The typical weasels hunt through thick cover, sometimes pursuing their prey into burrows beneath the ground. The more heavily built badgers dig their own burrows. Martens chase squirrels through the treetops, catching their prey by a combination of speed and agility. With the addition of webbing between the toes, otters can swim fast enough to catch fish. It is not surprising that members of this family are successful in all parts of the world that they have been able to colonize: they are found in every continent except Australasia.

Mustelids are more closely related to dogs than to the specialized carnivores of the cat family. Like dogs they have relatively long jaws containing rows of molar and premolar teeth—typically three teeth of each type on either side of both the lower and upper jaws. Their eyesight is only fair, but they have keen hearing and an excellent sense of smell. They have five digits on each limb, and the claws are often partially retractable.

Females are usually appreciably smaller than males, and have a fixed breeding season. In some species the ovum, fertilized during mating, does not immediately implant itself on the wall of the uterus and start to grow. Instead it only becomes implanted after a delay of some months, making the gestation period very long—nearly a year in the case of some martens. A few mustelids, such as weasels and polecats, may have two litters in the same year, but most have only a single litter usually consisting of about four young. Sea otters generally have only one young one at a time.

Weasels and badgers

The *Mustelidae* is divided into five subfamilies, the first of which contains the most typical members of the family including the weasels, polecats, minks, ferrets and stoats of the genus *Mustela*, and the longer-tailed, arboreal martens of the genus *Martes*, about 30 species in all. Many members of the group inhabit cool climates of northern Europe, Asia, and America. Being small, long and slender their bodies do not hold heat well, and so the mustelids of northern climates have superbly soft, dense fur. It is no accident that some of the most expensive and sought-after furs used in the fashion trade come from members of this group. Like other mammals of cool climates, many mustelids grow especially thick winter fur and for this reason the early fur-trappers of the Canadian north used to ply their trade in winter.

Left: A stoat, or ermine, *Mustela erminea*, with its prey. Stoats hunt a wide variety of small animals, including insectivores, rodents, rabbits, birds, lizards and insects; only rarely do they eat any plant material. Stoats are territorial animals, marking stones, tree stumps and other prominent features in their home ranges with a strong-smelling secretion from scent glands to warn off their rivals. They move quickly, stopping from time to time to survey their surroundings, sometimes standing up on their hind legs.

Right: A spotted skunk, *Spilogale putorius*, performs a 'handstand' before spraying its scent at an enemy.

Right: The wolverine, *Gulo gulo*, is the largest member of the weasel sub-family. It lives in northern Asia and North America where it feeds mainly on carrion, eggs and insects. It is an efficient predator, especially in the winter months when it can move noiselessly across the snow, but it usually hunts only when carrion is scarce. The wolverine can successfully tackle prey as large and strong as elks and lynxes.

Below: A female polecat, *Mustela putorius*, with her young. The babies are born in early summer after a pregnancy of six weeks and are weaned at one month. By the end of the summer they will be fully grown.

The largest of the weasels is the wolverine or glutton, *Gulo gulo*, of northern pine forests and tundras, which weighs about 18 kg (40 lb). It has long dark brown fur with unique water-repellent qualities. For this reason the fur is used to line the edges of the hoods of Eskimos' parkas. The wolverine normally feeds on lemmings, although it occasionally also kills reindeer. It owes its reputation for gluttony to its habit of using its powerful scent-glands to mark uneaten kills, thus seeming to spoil the meat that it cannot immediately eat. Its smaller relatives feed mainly on rodents and birds: the European polecat, *Mustela putorius*, has a well-deserved reputation for raiding chicken runs. Members of the subfamily are common in Europe, Asia and North America, but also occur in

Below: One of the most familiar mustelids is the Old World badger, *Meles meles*. It is active mainly in the evening and at night when it searches for fruit, roots, insects and other small animals. Badgers live in dens, or *setts*, which consist of numerous chambers and tunnels, with several entrances.

Right: An African clawless otter, *Aonyx capensis*, devouring a fish. This species differs from most other otters in having no claws and only very short webs between the fingers. This makes it considerably more skilful at grasping prey and other objects in its front paws than other species.

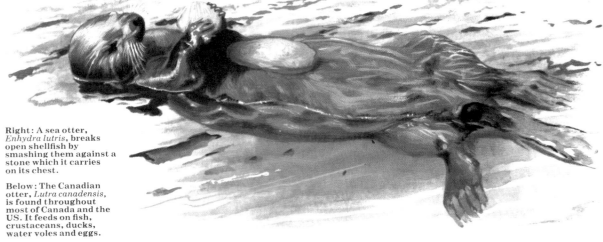

Right: A sea otter, *Enhydra lutris*, breaks open shellfish by smashing them against a stone which it carries on its chest.

Below: The Canadian otter, *Lutra canadensis*, is found throughout most of Canada and the US. It feeds on fish, crustaceans, ducks, water voles and eggs.

South America and in Africa, where one of them, the zorilla, *Ictonyx striatus*, has paralleled the evolution of the skunks in its black and white coat and defense behaviour.

Placed in a sub-family of its own is the ratel or honey badger, *Mellivora capensis*, of Africa and southern Asia. This species is best known for its relationship with the indicator bird, which postures and chatters in order to lead the ratel to wild bees' nests. The ratel, heavily built and strikingly marked in black and grey, rips open the nest with its claws and feeds on the honey, incidentally providing food for the birds. This is a good example of *symbiosis*, a partnership between two species from which both benefit.

The badgers and the slightly smaller ferret badgers of southern Asia make up another sub-family which contains eight species. They are heavily built and usually eat both animal and plant food. For example, the common badger, *Meles meles*, of the woodlands of Europe and temperate Asia, which weighs about 13 kg (29 lb) and spends the day in extensive burrows, feeds on berries, roots, bulbs and acorns as well as invertebrates and mammals of up to the size of a rabbit. In North America it is replaced by a slightly smaller species, *Taxidea taxus*, which prefers open sandy plains.

Skunks and otters

The nine species of skunks are found only in the Americas, and make up the fourth sub-family. They too feed on a wide variety of plant materials as well as invertebrates and rodents. Presumably it

319

is because they are among the least fierce of the carnivores that they have evolved their remarkable defensive system. Like many other mammals, mustelids have special scent-glands, which have primarily evolved as a means of signalling to other members of their own species. Like other glands in the skin, these glands tend to release their odour when the animal is under stress;

The paired scent-glands of the skunk, situated beneath the tail on either side of the anus, have become modified to serve as weapons of defence in situations where the animal feels threatened, and the scent itself has become virtually a poison gas. Armed in this way, and giving warning of their deterrent by means of bold black and white markings, skunks are quite fearless and rarely flee from potential enemies. If they are threatened they emphasize their markings by means of special displays: the spotted skunk, *Spilogale putorius*, of Central and North America performs handstands as a threat. Only if this does not deter the enemy is the secretion of its tail glands discharged, being squirted with considerable accuracy for up to 3.6 m (12 ft). Starting as a liquid, it rapidly becomes a poisonous and foul-smelling vapour. No enemy would willingly face an angry skunk twice.

The fifth mustelid sub-family contains the 18 species of otters. These have very thick fur which, even when the otter is swimming, always retains plenty of trapped air, forming a warm and flexible diving suit. In addition to the webbed feet, the powerful tail, which is horizontally flattened, is also used in swimming. Otters live near lakes and rivers, and sometimes on estuaries and sea coasts, in most parts of the world.

The Eurasian otter, *Lutra lutra*, occurs from Britain to North Africa and Sumatra, and is in many respects typical of the group. It weighs up to about 15 kg (33 lb) and feeds on invertebrates including crayfish, fish, frogs and small aquatic birds. The largest of the otters is the giant otter, *Pteronura brasiliensis*, of South America, which may be up to 2.2 m (7 ft) long and weigh 24 kg (54 lb). The rarest is the sea otter, *Enhydra lutris*, from the north Pacific which has been hunted almost to extinction for its fur. Sea otters live in groups on remote coasts, feeding on sea urchins, molluscs, crabs, fish and sea weed, and often swimming lazily on their backs.

Raccoons

The raccoon family, *Procyonidae*, is found only in the Americas. It contains 16 species, and its members are much more alike than those of the weasel family. Like mustelids and dogs, raccoons have long jaws, usually with four premolar teeth and two molars in each corner of the mouth. They have moderately long legs with five toes on each foot, and are usually plantigrade, the soles of the feet making contact with the ground at each step. The best-known member of the family is the North American raccoon, *Procyon lotor*, which lives in woods and forests, usually not far from water. The favourite food of this species is the fresh water crayfish.

The North American cacomistle, *Bassariscus astutus*, has a shorter nose and larger ears than the raccoon. It lives in woods and on dry, rocky hills, and is an efficient predator, catching small rodents

Des Bartlett/Bruce Coleman

Above: A North American raccoon, *Procyon lotor*, searching for food near the edge of a lake. It will eat almost anything, from leaves and grass to snails, small mammals, fishes, crayfishes and occasionally birds. The habit of searching for food underwater with its fore-paws is retained in captivity: zoo animals place food items into water and then go through the motions of searching for them. This behaviour has led to the popular misconception that the raccoon washes its food.

Right: A ring-tailed coatimundi, *Nasua nasua*, from Brazil. Coatis spend much of their time on the forest floor searching for food, but seek refuge in trees when danger threatens.

Michael Freeman/Bruce Coleman

with great skill. The coatimundis, *Nasua*, have long, pointed noses and live in the forests and bush of Central and South America. They travel in troops, poking their noses into the soil and into crevices in the bark of trees as they search for food. The most arboreal member of the family is the kinkajou, *Potos flavus*, which inhabits tropical forests and has a prehensile tail. It is nocturnal, and feeds primarily on fruit, using its long tongue in order to extract the pulpy flesh. The olingos, *Bassaricyon*, are very similar, but are unable to cling by means of their tails.

Pandas

The precise relationships of the two living species of pandas are still the subject of much argument among zoologists. When

the giant panda, *Ailuropoda melanoleuca*, was first discovered on the remote, bamboo-covered plateaus of China by Père David, a French missionary, it was very understandably described as a black and white bear. Later, after a detailed examination of its anatomical features, it was classified as one of the raccoons. This was not such a startling change as it might appear to be, for the raccoons and the bears have evolved from the same ancestors, and a large raccoon will inevitably look bear-like. Today some zoologists once more believe that the giant panda rightly belongs to the bear family. It is no wonder that many experts, seeking to answer the problem of classification, place the pandas in a family of their own, the *Ailuropodidae*.

The giant panda's closest living

320

Below: The kinkajou, *Potos flavus*, is an expert climber and is the only member of the raccoon family to have a prehensile tail. Feeding mainly on fruit, such as wild fig, guava and mango, it occupies much the same ecological niche as the New World monkeys. It is, however, active at night rather than in the day.

Right: The lesser panda, *Ailurus fulgens*, lives in mountain forests and bamboo thickets from Nepal to western China. It is a nocturnal animal and feeds on bamboo shoots, grasses, fruit and occasionally insects and small mammals. When attacked the lesser panda defends itself efficiently with its long sharp claws.

P. Morris

Right: The giant panda 'Chia Chia' eating bamboo shoots at London Zoo. Giant pandas, *Ailuropoda melanoleuca*, have never been very common because they can thrive only in cool mountainous regions where bamboo is abundant. Today they live in the western part of Szechwan province in western China at altitudes of between 1,500 and 4,000 m (5,000 to 13,000 ft). In spite of their restricted distribution giant pandas are probably not in danger of extinction because the Chinese government conserves them with care.

Left and below: The curious 'playing' behaviour of the giant panda makes it a popular, if rare, zoo animal.

Zoological Society of London

relation is undoubtedly the red panda, *Ailurus fulgens*, which looks much more like a raccoon than a bear. It is long-tailed and arboreal and lives in Asia on forested slopes of the Himalayas. The red panda is mainly active at dawn and dusk, when it feeds on lichens, acorns, and bamboo shoots. It spends much of the day sleeping either in the fork of a tree or in a hollow tree. Weighing only about 5 kg (11 lb) it is much smaller than the giant panda, but has the same pigeon-toed walk.

The giant panda eats a variety of foods, including some small animals, but the bulk of its diet consists of bamboo shoots which are like large, tough, woody grasses. It holds the shoots by means of a long wrist bone that works rather like a thumb. Its teeth are powerful, the molars having flattened crowns designed to crush and chew bamboo. Giant pandas need bulky bodies in order to be able to hold enough of their rather unpromising diet, and they weigh about 135 kg (300 lb). Despite their weight and their short tails, they can climb quite well, if rather clumsily, and climbing is their main defence against predators such as wolves.

It was not until the 1930s that giant pandas first appeared in zoos, and in the early 1970s they became instruments of diplomacy as the Chinese government presented pairs of them to zoos in Japan, the US, France and England. So far giant pandas have never bred in zoos outside their native continent, but the probability that they will soon do so is good. The female panda suckles her one or two young sitting up and holding them in her arms in a manner rather like that of primates.

321

Anteaters, Sloths and Aardvarks

In outward appearance the armadillos, sloths and anteaters of South America, the pangolins of tropical Asia and Africa and the aardvarks of southern Africa hardly resemble each other at all, but they do have one thing in common—jaws which are either toothless or have only very poorly developed teeth. With the notable exception of the sloths, which are herbivorous, they feed almost exclusively on insects.

When the Swedish naturalist Carl von Linné (Linnaeus) prepared his pioneering classification of the animal kingdom, the first to be done on a scientific basis, he grouped all these mammals together in a single order, the *Edentata*. Nowadays, however, the pangolins and aardvarks are placed in different orders, for animals are no longer classified purely by their anatomical features but by their evolutionary relationships which may or may not be reflected in structural details. In the 200 years since von Linné's time fossil evidence has shown that several quite different groups of mammals simplified or lost their teeth during the course of evolution.

The three living groups of animals that now comprise the edentates, namely the anteaters, sloths and armadillos, differ from each other more than the members of any other mammalian order.

Above and right: The heavily armoured glyptodon was a giant armadillo from South America which flourished in the Pliocene epoch about three million years ago. For many millions of years South America was separated from North America and its animal and plant life evolved in isolation. At the end of the Pliocene, however, the two continents were reunited and many species, including carnivores of the cat family, were able to migrate southwards into new ranges. Several South American species perished as a result of this new competition from the north, but the glyptodon was well protected and even managed to increase its range into North America. It was finally hunted to extinction by prehistoric man.

Right: The collared anteater, *Tamandua tetradactyla*, like many insect-eating animals, has an exceptionally long and slender tongue.

Below: A dwarf anteater, *Cyclopes didactylus*, ripping open a nest of insects.

Okapia

Okapia

Their relationship to each other is established by series of fossils dating back for 60 million years. In much of their basic structure the edentates resemble their early ancestors, but externally they have adapted to some highly specialized ways of life. The only visible external feature shared by all edentates is their powerful, curved claws.

All edentates lack front or incisor teeth. In the anteaters all the other teeth have also been lost, while in the sloths and armadillos the remaining teeth have become small and simple in structure. Nevertheless these teeth can be numerous: the giant armadillo has up to 100 tiny, cylindrical, rootless teeth—more than any other land mammal.

Anteaters

Four species of American anteaters make up the family *Myrmecophagidae*, and they all have very long skulls. Like pangolins and aardvarks, they have lost their teeth during the course of time because their insect prey is very much smaller than they are and does not need to be broken up before it is swallowed. Other ways in which the American anteaters are adapted to their diet include their simple stomachs, their long thin tongues, and the superb sense of smell which they use to find the nests of ants and termites. Their eyes and ears are small and not very efficient. All of them have thick, powerfully muscled tails and, except for that of the largest species, these tails are prehensile and useful in climbing trees. Having located the insects' nest, they rip it open with the claws of their forefeet, which also make formidable defensive weapons, and rapidly mop up the exposed insects and grubs with their tongues.

The giant anteater, *Myrmecophaga tridactyla*, is about 1.8 m (6 feet) long from the tip of its long snout to the end of its bushy tail. This is a purely terrestrial species which roams the grasslands and forests of Central and South America, walking on the knuckles of its forefeet and the soles of its hind feet. Its bold black and white markings, superimposed on the predominantly brown body, break up the outline and act as camouflage. The two species of the genus *Tamandua* are smaller, being about 1 m (40 in) long, and inhabit tropical forests, where they spend part of their time on the ground and part of it in trees. The squirrel-sized dwarf anteater, *Cyclopes didactylus*, lives in the same forests, but is exclusively arboreal.

Sloths

The seven species of sloths make up the family *Bradypodidae* and they live only in the forests of tropical America. They are one of the few groups of mammals that do not always have seven joints in the vertebral column of the neck. In sloths the numbers of these vertebrae can vary even from individual to individual of the same species, but Hoffmann's sloth, *Choloepus hoffmanni*, usually has six, the two-toed sloth, *Choloepus didactylus*, usually has seven, and the several species of three-toed sloths of the genus *Bradypus* usually have nine. Each limb bears long, curved claws, and it is with these claws that the sloths hook themselves upside down under the branches as they climb. Sloths can swim far more efficiently than they can walk: their limbs are almost useless on the ground.

A sloth's shaggy hair grows from its

Above: A giant anteater, *Myrmecophaga tridactyla*, investigates a termite hill on the Mato Grosso of Brazil. Giant anteaters consume about 30,000 ants and termites each day. The insects stick to the anteater's tongue, which flicks in and out as many as 150 times a minute, and they are swallowed whole.

Below: Hoffmann's sloth, *Choloepus hoffmanni*. Sloths are extremely hardy animals: they can go for long periods without eating and can survive injuries which would soon prove fatal to other mammals. Their upside-down way of life has led to internal changes, notably in the position of the liver, spleen and pancreas.

Right: This magnified view of a sloth's hair shows the characteristic growth of green algae which covers the surface. These tiny plants give the animal's coat, which is actually brown, a greenish tint and this helps to camouflage the sloth against the foliage of the tropical rain forests.

323

Left: A three-toed sloth, *Bradypus tridactylus*, from northern Colombia. Sloths fall into two distinct genera—those belonging to the genus *Bradypus* have three toes on all four limbs while those belonging to the genus *Choloepus* have three toes on each hind leg but only two on each foreleg.

Below: A young two-toed sloth clings to its mother. Sloths are born after a gestation period of about six months. The mother hangs by her arms from the branch of a tree during the birth and from the beginning the newborn sloth, which is already well developed, is able to cling tightly to her with its claws.

undersurface (which normally points upwards, since sloths live upside-down) towards its back, so that the torrential rain can run off easily. Sloths usually have brownish hair, although male three-toed sloths also have a glossy black stripe bordered by yellow or white across their backs and orange ear-patches. Wild sloths generally carry a population of up to 130 small moths. What the moths feed on has yet to be discovered—perhaps they do not feed at all, for some adult insects do not.

Two-toed sloths feed on a wide variety of juicy stems, leaves and fruits, but three-toed sloths are much more choosy, and for this reason they are impossible to keep in zoos. In the wild the only food that they are known to eat is the fruit of the hog-plum and the leaves of cecropia, a tree related to the mulberry. To deal with this diet each sloth has only 18 or 20 simple cheek teeth which, by comparison with the teeth of other plant-eating mammals, provide a rudimentary and inefficient grinding system. Sloths move slowly, live slowly, and digest their food slowly too. Typically they defaecate only about once a week. Their control of body temperature is erratic, so that a healthy sloth may have a temperature anywhere from 28 to 35 °C (82 to 96 °F). In the equable forest climate, where air temperatures are always warm and vary little, this is not a serious disadvantage.

Armadillos

Armadillos are easily recognized by the thick plates and bands of armoured skin that cover their heads, backs, legs, and tails. Their name means 'little armoured one' in Spanish. There are about 20 species of them, making up the family

Right: A hairy armadillo, *Euphractus villosus*, from Argentina. Like other armadillos this creature feeds on a wide variety of food including insects, plants, carrion and even snakes, In some parts. of South America armadillos are numerous enough to be regarded as pests—they are particularly attracted to newly ploughed fields where they find a plentiful supply of roots and insects. When faced with a predator, an armadillo will roll itself into a tight ball, flatten itself against the ground or rapidly dig a shallow burrow. Whatever the method of defence, the armour proves highly effective—even jaguars have difficulty tackling armadillos.

Left: A Malayan pangolin, *Manis javanica*, from South-East Asia. It is a nocturnal creature, equally at home in trees or on the ground and it feeds on ants and termites. Because the pangolin has no teeth its stomach is specially adapted to crush the insects when they are swallowed. Horny ridges projecting from the inner surface of the stomach act as teeth and some species also swallow sand and small stones which help to grind up the food.

Right: The babies of arboreal pangolins ride on their mother's back for the first few months of their life. The young of exclusively ground-based species, however, travel on foot.

Above: A female giant anteater carrying her offspring. The young animal travels about in this way for a remarkably long time—even when it is almost a year old and nearly the same size as its mother it still rides on her back. Giant anteaters often travel long distances in search of termite hills.

Below: The aardvark, *Orycteropus afer*, is an insect-eating mammal of the African savannahs. It is quite a large creature, reaching a length of about 2 m (6 ft) from nose to tail, and is an expert burrower. When attacked by one of its many enemies (for example a leopard or hyena) it retreats to its burrow.

Dasypodidae. All have short, thick legs armed with strong claws, heavy, rounded bodies, longish, pointed snouts and small, cylindrical cheek teeth. They feed on plant material, insects and other invertebrates, and carrion.

When armadillos breed the fertilized ovum does not immediately become implanted in the wall of the uterus, but remains free and dormant for several months before becoming implanted and starting to grow. At this early stage the single tiny embryo divides several times to form several smaller identical ones. Thus in some species of armadillos identical quadruplets—all the same sex and alike in every other possible way—are the typical litter, and up to 12 identical young can occur. In this respect the armadillos are unique among mammals. The carapace or armour of the young armadillo is at first soft, but hardens rapidly on exposure to air.

Adult armadillos usually live alone or in pairs. All species are energetic and efficient diggers. They vary in size from the little fairy armadillo, *Chlamyphorus truncatus*, which is only 15 cm (6 in) long to the giant armadillo, *Priodontes giganteus*, which is 1.2 m (4 ft) long. The giant armadillo sometimes walks on its two hind legs, but all other members of the family scurry along on all fours. Armadillos live in forests and on grassy plains, mostly in the tropics. The species which occurs the farthest north is the nine-banded armadillo, *Dasypus novemcinctus*, which, during the past century, has gradually moved northwards and eastwards into large areas of the US. Its spread has probably been helped by human action in cutting down forests and killing off natural predators which would otherwise hunt armadillos.

The most obvious difference between the various species of armadillos is in the way in which the armour is used. Individuals of the two South American species that make up the genus *Tolypeutes* can curl up into a ball, the armour on the upper surface of the tail fitting neatly beside that of the back of the head so as to give complete protection. The six-banded armadillo, *Euphractus sexcinctus*, on the other hand, has a more rigid carapace which has little flexibility at the thinner joints between the plates of armour; it flattens itself against the ground if it is caught in the open. The fairy armadillo either dives into a nearby burrow or else hastily digs a shallow one, and then uses its armoured back to seal the entrance.

Pangolins

The pangolins of tropical Africa and Asia bear some resemblance to the American anteaters because they have separately evolved the same adaptations to a diet of ants. They have weak, toothless jaws, very long, sticky tongues, and long curved claws, those on the forelimbs being particularly large. Having armoured backs they also bear some resemblance to the armadillos. The pangolins' armour consists of overlapping brown scales which are formed of hairs fused together and give their owners the appearance of large, animated fir-cones. Between the scales and on their undersurfaces the pangolins have soft, normal fur.

Desite their resemblances to the edentates the pangolins are now placed in an order of their own, the *Pholidota*, which contains but a single family, the *Manidae*. Beyond this, the four African species and three Asian species are all so similar that they are grouped together in a single genus, *Manis*. The smallest species is the African tree pangolin, *Manis tricuspis*, which is about 76 cm (30 in) long, including its long prehensile tail, and the largest is the African giant pangolin, *Manis gigantea*, which is 1.7 m (5.5 ft) long, and is purely terrestrial.

Aardvarks

The aardvark, *Orycteropus afer*, whose name means 'earth pig' in Afrikaans, is another anteater. Having no close relatives it is placed all by itself in the order *Tubulidentata*. Its very few teeth are small and superficially simple, but in fact their structure is quite complex and reveals that the aardvark's distant ancestors were a group of plant-eating mammals which also gave rise to hoofed animals such as horses and deer. The aardvark is a heavily built animal weighing up to 68 kg (150 lb). It has huge ears, which may help it to locate termites within their nest, four tiny hoofs on each forelimb and five on each hind limb. Like other animals which feed on termites it has a long tongue and produces copious sticky saliva.

Aardvarks live on the grasslands of Africa south of the Sahara—anywhere where termites are also to be found. By day they are seldom seen, for they rest in large burrows which slope down to a depth of about 1.5 m (5 ft). They come out to feed at night. If they are surprised in the open aardvarks gallop clumsily away, but they are easily outpaced and when cornered roll on to their backs and defend themselves with their hoofs. On cultivated ground aardvarks' burrows can be a considerable nuisance to farmers, for although aardvarks tend to be solitary and to move about on their own, where termites' nests are common as many as 60 burrows may be crowded together in quite a small area. Little is known of the aardvark's breeding habits, but usually a single baby is born around June.

325

Hares, Rabbits and Pikas

Until early this century rabbits, hares and pikas (small animals which look like guinea pigs) were thought to be rodents. Their continuously growing incisor teeth, which are kept sharp by wear, and their high-crowned, rootless premolars and molars are very similar to those of rodents, and are used in much the same way to gnaw and chew tough vegetable matter. Like the rodents, too, they have no canine teeth, but have instead a long toothless gap called the *diastema* between the incisors and the premolars. However, it is now realized that the resemblances between the rabbits and their allies on the one hand, and the rodents on the other are only superficial.

In fact the two groups are entirely separate, and have been so since the earliest known rabbit-like fossils were formed about 50 million years ago. The rabbits, hares and pikas belong to a separate order called the *Lagomorpha*, which means 'hare-shaped ones' and they can be distinguished from rodents quite easily. Rodents always have two incisor teeth in both the lower and the upper jaws. Lagomorphs also have two incisors in the lower jaws, but they have four in the upper jaws, although in adult animals two of these lie immediately behind the larger front pair and are not obvious. The skulls of lagomorphs are less heavily constructed than those of rodents and this is another distinguishing feature.

It is now thought that the early ancestors of the even-toed hoofed animals (the artiodactyls) were probably also the ancestors of the lagomorphs, although in the absence of fossils which link the two groups there can be no certainty. During their evolution lagomorphs varied little; there have only ever been three families of them, and one of these has been extinct for almost 50 million years. The survivors are the pikas, which form the family *Ochotonidae*, and the rabbits and hares of the family *Leporidae*.

Rabbits and hares

The family *Leporidae* contains about 50 species. These differ from the pikas most obviously in having longer hind legs than front legs, short but clearly visible tails, and long ears. The first fossils which can be attributed to this family come from North America, but rabbits and hares have now successfully colonized most parts of the world except southern South America, Madagascar, and—but for human intervention—Australasia. The story of man's relatively recent introduction of rabbits to New Zealand and especially to Australia illustrates the value of the two features that have contributed most to the lagomorphs' evolutionary success—their ability to thrive on all sorts of different food materials, and their legendary ability to breed rapidly.

The names 'rabbit' and 'hare' were first used for European species, and the distinction was originally made on the basis of reproductive habits. Young hares are born after a slightly longer gestation period—39 days in the case of the European brown hare, *Lepus europaeus—*

Above: In the spring male European brown hares, *Lepus europaeus*, fight among themselves for the possession of females, kicking out with their strong hind limbs and punching with their forepaws. During these contests they seem to throw caution to the wind and their behaviour has given rise to the expression 'mad as a March hare'.

Right: An African savannah hare, *Lepus whytei*, seen at night. Hares are most active in the evening and early morning, resting during the day and in the hours of total darkness. On moonlit nights they are often active right through from sunset to sunrise.

Below: Mountain hares, *Lepus timidus*, from the Arctic have white coats all the year round, even when the snow recedes. Sometimes these animals are called snow hares.

and they are born in the open, fully furred and with their eyes open. Young European rabbits, *Oryctolagus cuniculus*, are born blind, naked, and helpless within the safety of a fur-lined nest in a burrow.

Zoologists tend to define the differences between rabbits and hares in ways which can be applied only when studying dead specimens in museums. For example, hares of the genus *Lepus* have shorter bony roofs to their mouths than do rabbits. When English names have been given to members of the family *Leporidae* from other continents the terms rabbit and hare have sometimes been used indiscriminately. For example, *Caprolagus hispidus*, a rare species from the foothills of the Himalayas in Assam, is sometimes called the bristly rabbit, and sometimes the hispid hare.

The most widely distributed genus of the family *Leporidae* is the typical hare genus, *Lepus*, with 30 species in Europe, Asia, Africa, and North and Central America. Second comes the purely American genus, *Sylvilagus*, with about a dozen species. An example is the eastern cottontail, *Sylvilagus floridanus*, which inhabits woodlands from Canada to Venezuela. Cottontails give birth to naked, blind young, and are referred to as rabbits, but the eastern cottontail does not dig its own burrows. Instead the female takes over a simple, very shallow burrow made by some other animal such as a small rodent and uses it as a nursery for her young. Since the nest cavity is so small the mother is unable to enter it herself, and the babies have to climb up to the lip of the burrow in order to suckle.

Included in the hare genus, *Lepus*, are the American jack rabbits which, despite their English name, are hares by any definition. Two species of hares are found in Britain: the brown hare, which has a range extending to western Asia and north Africa, and the blue or mountain hare, *Lepus timidus*, also found in other cool parts of Europe and Asia. In winter the mountain hare becomes partly or almost wholly white, the extent of the change depending on the location.

Rabbits feed mainly on grass, but also eat other vegetation and, especially when other food is scarce, they gnaw the bark of trees. Where they are common it can be impossible for young trees to survive. Rabbits can live anywhere where there is enough food, and where there is soil in which to dig their burrows. These may be simple, with only one or two entrances, but are more often complex, branched, and with many openings. Adult males are

Above: A European brown hare flees across a field. Hares are larger than rabbits, have powerful hind legs and are speedy runners: they can reach a speed of about 65 kph (40 mph). Although rabbits can run almost as fast, they have no staying power and bolt into their burrows to escape from predators such as foxes.

Above right: Three leverets (young hares) crouch in a small area of flattened grass called a 'form' where their mother visits them only at intervals. Unlike rabbits, hares do not dig burrows so their offspring must be raised in the open.

Right: A pika, *Ochotona princeps*, from Alaska. A remarkable feature of pikas is their habit of making their own hay to overcome the possibility of a food shortage in the winter. In late summer they gather large amounts of grasses and other plants and expose them in the sun to dry. If necessary they move their bundles from one place to another so as to keep them fully exposed to the sun's rays.

to some extent territorial, defending their own part of the warren and grazing area against other males.

Breeding can take place at any time of the year, but is most frequent in the spring and early summer. During courtship the buck sprays the doe with urine and displays the conspicuous white tuft on his tail. The litter consists of between three and nine young, which are weaned when they are one month old. Young females can breed at three months, before they are quite fully grown. Does mate again almost immediately after giving birth, and as the act of mating causes the ova to be released by the ovaries, conception is almost certain. Because of this each doe can produce one litter every month, and so rabbits well deserve their reputation for being prolific breeders. They would, however, be even more prolific were it not for the fact that about 60 per cent of the young conceived die at about the 12th day of pregnancy, and are reabsorbed into the doe's body. Most often complete litters are lost in this way, but sometimes only part of a litter is lost. Despite this strange biological fact, only known to occur in rabbits and hares, the average doe produces ten or more young each year.

Several million years ago the rabbit was widespread in Europe, but during the bitterly cold Ice Age it became extinct over much of this area. By the beginning of historic times it was a species of southern Europe only. Popularly it is supposed to have been brought back to Britain by the Romans, but there is no hard evidence to support this view. There is no written mention of it until the 13th century when it was regarded as quite valuable, which tends to suggest that it had only just been imported. Warrens were deliberately established by man as a useful source of food. By the time myxomatosis was introduced about 40 million British rabbits were used annually by the meat and fur trade, and millions more were gassed in their burrows by farmers for damaging crops.

Pikas

The evolution of pikas has always been centred on Asia, north of the Himalayas where 12 of the 14 species now live. The other two species live in mountainous areas of western North America, which their ancestors must have reached by way of the land-bridge which once existed between Siberia and Alaska. Some of the Asian species live on rocky mountain-

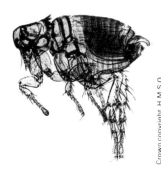

Left: The rabbit flea, *Spilopsyllus cuniculi*, is the chief carrier of the virus disease myxomatosis which decimated the populations of Old World rabbits, *Oryctolagus cuniculus*, in Europe and Australia in the 1950s. The disease was first noticed in 1897 among wild South American rabbits but in those animals infection hardly ever resulted in death. In fact it is now known that myxomatosis is only generally fatal to the Old World rabbit.

Below: Myxomatosis virus was introduced to Australia in 1949 to control the enormous rabbit population. The map shows where it was released and how far it ultimately advanced.

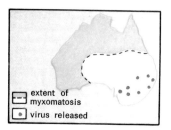

extent of myxomatosis

virus released

Right: Old World rabbits at a water hole on Wardang Island, South Australia before myxomatosis. Rabbits were first successfully liberated in Australia in 1859, and by the time myxomatosis was introduced the population had reached plague proportions. The newcomers caused widespread damage both to crops and to native animal and plant species.

Below: A rabbit suffering from myxomatosis. The swellings around the eyes and ears make the creature blind and deaf before it finally dies.

Below left: The antelope jack rabbit, *Lepus alleni*, inhabits the deserts of north-west Mexico and south-west USA. Like other jack rabbits it has enormous ears, and by operating like radiators these probably help the animal to keep down its body temperature in the searing heat of the desert. At night, when the temperature has dropped, the animal holds its ears close to its body in order to conserve heat.

Below: A large number of domestic breeds have been developed over the years from the Old World rabbit. These huge show animals are angora rabbits, each weighing 4 kg (9 lb) and producing 900 g (2 lb) of fur every year.

sides, but others inhabit forests, grasslands, and semi-deserts. Pikas are between 12 cm (5 in) and 30 cm (12 in) long and have short legs, thick-set bodies, rounded ears, and no visible tails.

Most pikas are grey-brown in colour, the winter coat being slightly greyer than the summer one. Some species are solitary and defend territories while others live in colonies. Those that live on mountains and screes have dens among the rocks, and those of the deserts and plains live in burrows. They are mostly active by day when they often sit sunning themselves.

All pikas are quite closely related to each other and belong to a single genus, *Ochotona*. All of them share with the rabbits and hares a remarkable method of feeding whereby all of the food that they eat is passed through the alimentary canal not once, but twice. During the night they produce droppings which are black, sticky and covered with mucus. These droppings are taken into the mouth direct from the anus and swallowed—a process known as *refection*. During the day small, oval, greenish droppings are produced, and these are left on the surface of the ground. This habit gives the bacteria in the alimentary canal a better chance of splitting up the cellulose, which is the main constituent of the plant diet, into other carbohydrates which can be absorbed and used. The habit of chewing the cud by ruminants such as cattle and sheep serves the same purpose. Refection may also give the lagomorphs a better chance of absorbing valuable vitamins.

Pikas breed in late spring and summer. After a gestation period of about 30 days the female gives birth to two or three young. The babies are at first blind, naked, and helpless, but they grow rapidly. This is essential, for like many rodents, female pikas mate again almost immediately after giving birth, and one litter must be independent before the next arrives. Each female has two or three litters every year. The young are fully grown when they are two months old, and probably live for an average of about two years, although some live longer.

Squirrels, Beavers and Gophers

More than half of all living mammal species belong to the order *Rodentia*, including mice, rats, voles, porcupines and guinea pigs as well as squirrels, beavers and gophers. Rodents are all gnawing animals, equipped with a pair of long, curved incisor teeth in each jaw. These teeth grow continuously throughout the animal's life, but always remain more or less the same length because they are constantly being worn down with use. Only the front surface is covered with hard tooth enamel so the inner side wears down more quickly than the outer, and this ensures that the end of each tooth is always sharp. The rodents are among the few groups of animals to thrive in association with man.

In many of their fundamental characteristics rodents have remained unchanged for many millions of years. One of the earliest genera known from fossils, *Paramys*, which lived about 60 million years ago in the Palaeocene epoch, had the same arrangement of teeth as modern species—large incisors and molars separated by a gap called the *diastema*, and no canine teeth. Like the primates, rodents probably evolved from a group of early insectivores at the end of the Cretaceous period some 70 million years ago.

Classification of the rodents is complicated by the fact that many unrelated species have evolved confusingly similar features simply in response to closely similar environmental conditions. Nowadays the various families, genera and species are sorted out on the basis of the structure of their jaw muscles and other fundamental characteristics, and they are usually distributed between four sub-orders: the squirrel-like rodents or *Sciuromorpha*, the mouse-like rodents or *Myomorpha*, the porcupines or *Hystricomorpha*, and the guinea pigs or *Caviomorpha*. In addition to the familiar grey and red squirrels, the sub-order *Sciuromorpha* includes the woodchuck, the prairie dog, the chipmunk, the flying squirrels, the beaver, the gundi, the pocket gopher and the kangaroo rat.

Tree squirrels

Squirrels are medium-sized rodents belonging to the family *Sciuridae*. They have short rounded ears, long bushy flattened tails and long fingers and toes with sharp, hooked claws for climbing. The characteristic tail is not merely for decoration: it serves to correct the balance of the animal in its flying leaps from tree to tree or as it runs along branches high above the ground. Once the squirrel has launched itself into the air its tail acts as a rudder enabling it to turn left or right or to modify the angle of fall, and in long drops from high branches to the ground it may act as a parachute brake. Squirrels usually gallop along, the fore and hind legs moving together in pairs. Descending the trunk of a tree the squirrel is more cautious,

Left and below: Western pocket gophers, *Thomomys bottae*, build complex burrows with separate chambers to serve as living quarters (1), food store (2) and latrine (3). In addition to the main entrance (4) there is usually a back entrance (5) leading into the burrow from foraging tunnels (6) near the surface.

Left: The jumping hare, *Pedetes cafer*, of southern Africa is a nocturnal, burrowing rodent. It either moves about on all fours or it hops from place to place on its large hind legs like a kangaroo, covering as much as 8 m (26 ft) with a single leap. Jumping hares often live together in colonies.

Above: The scaly-tailed squirrel, *Anomalurus peli*, from West Africa can glide from tree to tree like a flying squirrel. Not being closely related to the true squirrels of the family *Sciuridae*, the various species of scaly-tailed squirrels are classified in a family of their own, the *Anomaluridae*.

running down head first and using its feet alternately.

The red squirrel, *Sciurus vulgaris*, is the only species native to Britain, but it is much less common than it was a century ago. The cause of its decline was the wholesale destruction of its woodland home for agricultural and other purposes. Also, many red squirrels were shot as pests. The introduction of the grey squirrel, *Sciurus carolinensis*, from North America cannot have helped the red squirrel but was not a prime cause of its decline. Squirrels are active in the day, waking at dawn to gather beechnuts, acorns and hazelnuts. They also eat corn, mushrooms, edible toadstools and flowers, and occasionally insects, birds' eggs or even young birds. Squirrels feed sitting up on their haunches with their tail curved up over the back and holding the food in the front paws.

The grey squirrel mates in mid-winter and the young are born about 44 days later in February, March or April. The young are raised in a nest usually constructed in a hollow tree, although if this is not available a nest will be built outside in the branches. The litter numbers from two to six. Young squirrels are blind and hairless at birth, and it takes about five weeks for their eyes to open and fur to develop. Sexual maturity is reached after a year although they are not fully grown until two years old. Their life span is normally about ten years.

Strictly speaking squirrels do not hibernate, but on very cold days they remain asleep in their nests and do not venture out. They moult in early summer and autumn, the latter giving rise to a thick winter coat which provides some protection from the cold. Squirrels are not very sociable animals although they do sometimes gather together for migration. Once on the move nothing stops an army of squirrels. Devouring everything in their path, they may scale mountains and cross rivers or lakes. Many thousands die on the way, victims to predators or simply from starvation, exhaustion or drowning.

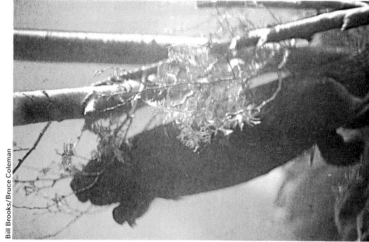

Above: Beavers, *Castor fiber*, construct their dams and island homes or 'lodges' from trees which they fell and float into position. The lodge is carefully built with a ventilation hole in the roof and an underwater entrance, which allows the beavers to forage for food on the lake bottom in winter when ice covers the surface. Beavers mate early in the year and the young, usually two or four, are born about four months later in the security of the lodge. At birth they weigh about 400 g (14 oz) and are covered with soft fur. The young animals live with their parents for about a year, finally leaving them shortly before the next year's litter arrives.

Bill Brooks/Bruce Coleman

Although red and grey squirrels are well-equipped for life in the trees, they are not so comprehensively adapted as the flying squirrels which have great flaps of fur-covered skin extending between the fore and hind limbs. These webs fill with air when the animal jumps from a branch or tree trunk, allowing it to glide for considerable distances. By adjusting the angle of its flight skin and the position of its tail, the flying squirrel can alter its line of flight. The ability to glide in this way is an excellent defence against predators such as martens but less effective against owls and birds of prey which are consequently the chief enemies of flying squirrels in the wild. Flying squirrels are found in North America (genus *Glaucomys*), eastern Europe and northern Asia (genus *Pteromys*), and southern and eastern Asia (genera *Hylopetes* and *Petaurista*). There are also a few species of flying squirrels which inhabit the forests of central and western Africa, but these belong to a different family, the *Anomaluridae*.

Ground squirrels

Among other members of the family *Sciuridae* are the ground squirrels, in-

ZEFA

cluding the marmots, genus *Marmota*, the prairie dogs, genus *Cynomys*, the true ground squirrels, genus *Citellus*, and the chipmunks, genus *Tamias*. The marmots are found in Europe, Asia and North America, and they are sociable animals, often living in large communal burrows.

One of the largest marmots is the Alpine marmot, *Marmota marmota*, which can weigh as much as 8 kg (18 lb) when fully grown. It feeds mainly on roots, herbs and grasses with which it also lines its nest chamber. Unlike tree-dwelling squirrels, most ground squirrels hibernate and the Alpine marmot is no exception. It prepares for hibernation by stocking its nest chamber with hay and by blocking up the entrance to the burrow with earth, stones and grass for a distance of about 1.5 m (5 ft). Hibernation can last for more than six months, and when the animals leave their burrows in the spring they are not surprisingly weak and emaciated. The woodchuck, *Marmota monax*, is a well known North American marmot. Slightly smaller than the Alpine marmot, it behaves in much the same way. Woodchuck burrows are generally to be found in sandy soil, under the roots of trees.

Another common North American ground squirrel is the eastern chipmunk, *Tamias striatus*. It has a striped face and is often seen sitting up on its hind legs on a log or rock. It feeds on plant material such as grass and nuts, and food is often carried in cheek pouches until it can be stored in the animal's underground nest. The eastern chipmunk is a solitary creature, hibernating only in the colder northern parts of its range. There are various other species of chipmunks in the US and a single species, the burunduk, *Eutamias sibiricus*, from northern Asia. Prairie dogs are found only in the midwestern states of North America. They are highly sociable animals and live in small family groups each inhabiting its own burrow system which is vigorously defended against intruders. Often a large number of burrows are grouped together into a prairie dog 'town' which may extend over an area of as much as 60

Left: A Canadian beaver leaves the underwater exit to its lodge. Whereas North American beavers regularly build dams and island lodges, members of the European subspecies more often construct burrows in the banks of lakes.

Below: The red squirrel, *Sciurus vulgaris*, is one of the best known European mammals. After years of decline, caused by the felling of woodland and hastened by the introduction of the grey squirrel from North America, the population of British red squirrels has stablized and is even increasing in some areas. When food is abundant squirrels hide some of it (especially nuts and pine cones) for use in the winter.

Left: A beaver holds a branch in its forepaws as it strips off the bark with its teeth.

Below: Hoary marmots, *Marmota caligata*, from Alaska. There are about 12 different species of marmots and they are distributed throughout Europe, Asia and North America. They are colonial animals which live in borrows or natural crevices in the ground. The more northerly species, such as the hoary marmot, hibernate for many months, waking every six weeks or so to urinate and defecate. Marmots are relatively noisy animals and produce a variety of chattering calls—their alarm calls are often very distinctive and serve to alert other animals.

Above: A series of diagrams to show how a southern flying squirrel, *Glaucomys volans*, glides through the air and lands on a tree. While it is in mid-air the squirrel is conspicuous to predators such as owls and martens, so as soon as it lands it runs to the opposite side of the tree trunk and faces down towards the ground.

Left: An Indian giant squirrel, *Ratufa indica*. These creatures, which belong to the family *Sciuridae*, build large nests of twigs and leaves high above the ground. They feed mainly on nuts and fruit.

Right: A grey squirrel, *Sciurus carolinensis*. These creatures are found in the woodlands of eastern North America and, since their introduction by man at the end of the 19th century, in Britain and South Africa as well. They lack the ear tufts of red squirrels.

hectares (150 acres).

Beavers

The beaver, *Castor fiber*, is the only member of the family *Castoridae*. It is highly specialized for an aquatic life having large, webbed hind feet and a broad, flat, scaly tail. The webbed hind feet are used for propulsion when swimming and the tail serves as a rudder. The smaller forepaws are used for walking when on land and for carrying the loads of mud and rock that it uses in constructing its unique dams and partly submerged 'lodges'. The beaver's fur is very thick and comprises a dense underfur mixed with an abundant growth of longer, coarser hairs.

Beavers are moderately common in North America from Canada to Mexico, but are much rarer in Europe, being confined to Scandinavia, Poland, the Rhone, Danube and Elbe and parts of southern USSR. Their most notable characteristic is the ability to build dams. The dam serves two purposes; firstly it creates a lake in which an island den or lodge can be built safely out of reach of predators, and secondly it brings a new supply of wood within the beaver's reach. It does not take long for the wood near home to become exhausted, and the beaver can only use trees growing close to the water's edge which, once felled, can be manoeuvred by floating.

To build a dam, the beaver first cuts down a tree to get at the branches, since it cannot climb. It takes a mere 10 to 15 minutes to gnaw through a tree trunk 10 cm (4 in) in diameter. Usually, two or more beavers take turns in gnawing splinters of wood from a large tree trunk.

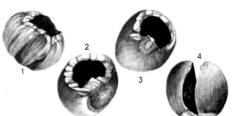
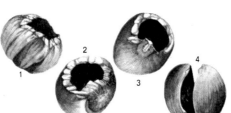

Above: The European souslik, *Citellus citellus*, is the only true ground squirrel to be found in Europe. Smaller than red squirrels, these creatures live together in colonies and are active mainly in the early morning and evening.

Left: A group of prairie dogs, *Cynomys ludovicianus*, on a tree stump. The prairie dog gets its popular name from its alarm call which sounds rather like the bark of a dog.

Below left: Hazel nuts broken open by a squirrel with varying amounts of practice. At first the animal is very inexpert and a ragged shell is left (1). As its technique improves the broken shells become neater (2 and 3) until finally it opens the nut along its natural grain direction and the shell splits cleanly into two parts (4).

Below: An eastern chipmunk, *Tamias striatus*, carries nuts and other food in its cheek pouches. It stores food in its nest for the winter months.

Left: The central European subspecies of the red squirrel exists in two forms: the mountain form (shown here) has a dark grey coat whereas the lowland form has the more normal reddish coat. The colour difference must be at least partly hereditary for the two forms can occur in the same litter.

Once the tree is felled the branches are cut into lengths, floated downstream and anchored in place with the thick ends pointing upstream and then weighed down with mud and rocks. One layer is piled on top of another until a suitable height has been reached. The resulting dam is very strong and has no weak spots to break under the accumulating pressure of water.

Gophers

These burrowing rodents belong to the family *Geomyidae* and they look like rats or mice although they are not closely related to them. The name 'gopher' was given to them by early French settlers in North America: the French word *gouffre* means 'pit', a reference to the complex earthworks constructed by gophers which sometimes undermine whole hillsides. Gophers have strong claws on their forefeet and strong incisors both of which are used for digging. Their lips close behind the incisors to prevent earth from being swallowed as they dig.

All gophers have fur-lined cheek pouches with external openings which they use for carrying food to their tunnels. Food is stored in one of several living chambers in the gopher's tunnel system which it occupies alone. Apart from foraging expeditions, gophers leave their tunnels only for courtship, and as soon as mating is over the two animals separate.

Kangaroo rats and jumping hares

A number of small North American rodents belong to the family *Heteromyidae*, including the kangaroo rats, *Dipodomys*, and pocket mice, *Perognathus*. As their name suggests kangaroo rats have powerful hind legs and move about by jumping. They inhabit dry, semi-desert areas and are active mainly at night when they search for green plants and seeds. Kangaroo rats live in shallow burrows lined with grass, leaves and feathers.

Jumping hares, *Pedetes*, belong to the family *Pedetidae* and are residents of the dry grasslands of eastern and southern Africa. About the same size as common hares, they either move about on all fours like other four-legged animals or they hop from place to place on their large hind legs like small kangaroos. They are nocturnal and feed on grasses and roots. During the day they lie up in their burrows, which are often quite deep and complicated, where they are relatively safe from predators. Difficult to classify, jumping hares probably belong to a separate sub-order, the *Phyomyomorpha*, rather than to the *Sciuromorpha*.

Mice and Rats

For as long as man has lived in settlements and farmed the land he has been only too well aware of the presence of mice and rats. They will eat almost anything destined for human consumption, stored grain being a particular favourite, so they have found it an advantage to live in close association with humans, in roofs and under the floorboards of houses and barns. This close contact with man not only provides them with a ready source of food but also keeps many of their natural predators at bay, for stoats, weasels and foxes are usually reluctant to approach human habitations.

The damage done by mice and rats is not restricted to the human food they actually consume; even larger quantities of food have to be destroyed each year after being fouled by their droppings. Also, by gnawing through walls, wooden beams and even lead pipes in their search for food and nesting material they cause considerable structural damage to buildings. As if all this was not enough, rats or their parasites transmit a number of human diseases, including typhus, bubonic plague and Lassa fever.

Mice and rats belong to the rodent sub-order *Myomorpha* which also includes the voles, hamsters, gerbils, lemmings, dormice and jerboas. There are several thousand species in the sub-order and these are classified in nine families, the most important being the *Muridae* (Old World mice and rats) and the *Cricetidae* (New World mice and rats, hamsters, voles, lemmings and gerbils). All of them have the typical rodent arrangement of teeth—long, curved incisors for gnawing and large molars for grinding up their plant diet, but no canines.

Mice and rats

There are more species in the family *Muridae* than in any other mammal family and they range in size from the tiny African native mice, *Leggada*, with a body length of only 5 cm (2 in) to the cloud rats, *Phloeomys*, from the Philippines which are almost ten times as large. The terms 'mouse' and 'rat' have no well defined zoological meaning, and whether a particular animal is one or the other depends only on its size: murids are called mice if they are smaller than about 15 cm (6 in) and rats if they are larger. When the species is unspecified the word 'mouse' usually means the house mouse, *Mus musculus*, and the word 'rat' means the black rat, *Rattus rattus*.

The black rat and its cousin the brown rat, *Rattus norvegicus*, originated in India and around the Caspian Sea, and in the period following the last Ice Age gradually spread westwards into southern Asia and Europe. In relatively recent times they have colonized every other continent except Antarctica by travelling as unwelcome passengers aboard ships. The brown rat is the larger of the two species, reaching a maximum weight of about 450 g (1 lb). It is a burrowing animal and a good swimmer and is common in warehouses, refuse tips, sewers and around farms. The black rat rarely exceeds a weight of 250 g (9 oz) and is unable to burrow. Its ancestors were probably tree-dwelling creatures and this may be the

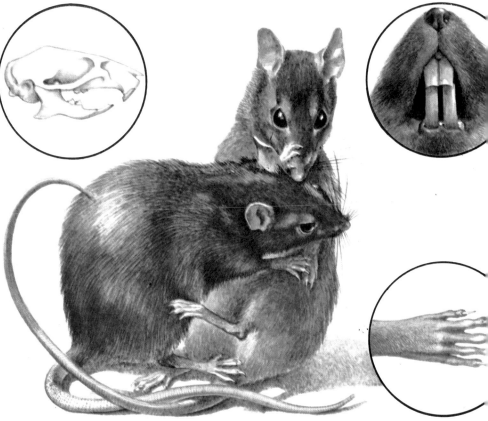

Above: A brown rat, *Rattus norvegicus*, bites a rival in the neck. Only rarely do fights between rats reach this stage when the losing combatant will almost certainly be killed. Usually a brown rat defends its territory simply by pushing intruders away with its flanks or by kicking out with its feet. The insets show the incisors, skull and foot of a rat. A highly efficient jaw mechanism combined with incisors which are kept sharp by wear are important contributing factors to the rat's success throughout the world.

Right: A black rat, *Rattus rattus*. These rats were responsible for spreading bubonic plague in the mid 1300s.

Bruce Coleman

Jane Burton/Bruce Coleman

Above right: A common hamster, *Cricetus cricetus*. Although most common hamsters are predominantly brown with patches of lighter fur along the flanks and dark fur covering the belly, colour variants like this white individual are not uncommon.

Left: The Gambian pouched rat, *Cricetomys gambianus*, is a West African member of the family *Muridae*. These creatures are among the largest of all rats, reaching a body length of 40 cm (16 in) and a weight of 1.5 kg (3.3 lb) in some cases. As their name suggests they have cheek pouches with which they transport food back to their burrows. They are great hoarders and will collect all sorts of completely inedible objects such as small pieces of jewellery.

Right: Three tiny African native mice, *Leggada diminutoides*, feed on rice and fruit in a gourd. These tiny rodents, which are found in most parts of Africa south of the Sahara, are closely related to the mice of the genus *Mus*.

334

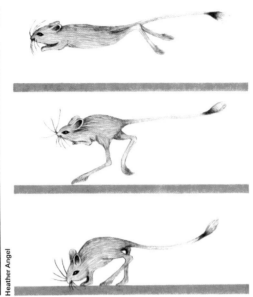

Below: The desert jerboa, *Jaculus jaculus*, from northern Africa and the Middle East can move very rapidly by leaping along on its powerful hind legs like a kangaroo (top). For slower movement it either runs on its hind legs (centre) or walks on all fours (bottom).

reason why black rats are more usually found on the upper floors of buildings.

Both species live in family groups which defend their territories against strange males and against rats of other species. In favourable conditions, both species can reproduce all the year round. The gestation period is about three weeks, a female producing around six litters a year with six offspring on average per litter, and the young are mature when only four months old. With this sort of breeding capacity it is not surprising that the world's rat population is enormous: there are said to be as many rats in the US as humans.

Unlike rats, which soon learn to avoid traps, the house mouse is not an intelligent animal; it has learned surprisingly little from its long association with man and will blunder into almost any trap. Its breeding rate, however, is high and it soon replaces its numbers. It breeds all the year round, a litter of four to six young being born after a gestation of 21 days. The young are born blind and naked but mature quickly; they are capable of breeding when just three months old.

Wood mice and field mice of the genus *Apodemus* are found in Europe and Asia from Spain to Japan. They live in the undergrowth of woods and parkland

Above left: The common house mouse, *Mus musculus*, is probably the most familiar of all rodents. The house mouse originated in central Europe and, like the rat, became world-wide in its distribution as ships travelled the world. It usually seeks shelter and food in human dwellings, and will eat almost anything, including newspaper (as in this picture), soap and even glue. In the summer it may make excursions into the fields but will return to the comfort of a heated house in the autumn.

Right: A long-tailed field mouse, *Apodemus sylvaticus*, having climbed into a jar of jelly cannot escape.

335

Left: The harvest mouse, *Micromys minutus*, is a common member of the family *Muridae*. It spends the summer months among the stems of long grass feeding on seeds, insects and the grass itself. As can be seen in the picture they build roughly spherical nests with one or two entrances. The nest is made of intertwined grass and is supported above ground level by the grass stems.

Below: A common dormouse, *Muscardinus avellanarius*, during its long hibernation. Dormice hibernate on the ground under cover of fallen leaves, curling up into a ball to reduce heat loss. Their body temperature may drop as low as 1°C (34°F).

where they feed on nuts, such as beech-nuts, acorns and hazelnuts, grasses, fruits and berries. They are good climbers and often forage for food among the lower branches of bushes. Some species, such as the long-tailed field mouse, *Apodemus sylvaticus*, will invade houses and outbuildings, especially during cold winter weather. Although they belong to a different family (*Cricetidae*), the white-footed mice, *Peromyscus*, from North America are remarkably like the Old World wood mice both to look at and in their habits. There are many different species and subspecies and they are mostly terrestrial, though a few have adapted to life in trees.

Hamsters and gerbils

Like the New World mice, hamsters belong to the family *Cricetidae*, but they live in Asia rather than America. The best known of these creatures is the golden hamster, *Mesocricetus auratus*, which originally came from a small region in the north of Syria: it was introduced to Europe and the US in the 1930s and quickly became a popular pet. More abundant in the wild is the common hamster, *Cricetus cricetus*, a distinctively marked animal from eastern Europe and central western Asia which is about 30 cm (1 ft) long when fully grown.

Common hamsters live alone or in small family groups in burrows on fields and grasslands. The burrows are often extensive and deep, and they include a large storage chamber for grain which will last the occupants through the winter. Hamsters are active in the evening and early morning, collecting grain and transporting it in their cheek pouches to

their burrows. They hibernate through the winter months, waking every six days or so to feed, defecate and urinate.

Gerbils are small, burrowing rodents common in the desert and semi-desert regions of Asia and Africa. There are several different genera, the most important being *Gerbillus*, *Meriones* and *Tatera*, and hundreds of different species. Gerbils are well adapted to their desert environment, feeding on the sparse vegetation and surviving on the water they get from their food. The life span of the gerbil is from three to four years. The female breeds only in the first two years of her life, but during that time she may have as many as 15 litters of between five and ten offspring each. Many gerbil species, for example the Mongolian jird, *Meriones unguiculatus*, make ideal pets for they are easy to keep and produce little urine (an adaptation to life in the desert where water loss must be minimized). With a few notable exceptions gerbils are gentle animals when kept as pets and, unlike hamsters, will rarely bite or scratch.

Lemmings and voles

Particularly interesting rodents are the brown lemmings. They belong to the genus *Lemmus* of the family *Cricetidae* and live in the colder regions of the northern hemisphere. They are between 12 and 16 cm (5 to 6 in) long with short bobtails and their feet are covered with fur (even underneath) as protection against the cold. The Norway lemming, *Lemmus lemmus*, has a yellowish brown coat with a broad dark stripe on the back whereas the Siberian lemming, *Lemmus sibiricus*, has a brown coat in summer which changes colour to white in the

Stephen Dalton/NHPA

Hans Reinhard/Bruce Coleman

Heather Angel

Above: A European water vole, *Arvicola amphibius*, eating a leaf. Although these creatures are often found along the banks of rivers and are good swimmers, they are not restricted to aquatic environments and in many parts of their range are found far from the nearest water. Water voles are often incorrectly referred to as 'water rats'.

Left: Gerbils are nocturnal desert rodents with well developed hind legs. When alarmed they hop away at great speed with kangaroo-like jumps. Their pale grey-brown colouring provides good camouflage, blending in with the sand and rocks among which they tunnel and build their nests.

Left: Harvest mice climbing on wheat plants. These mice are expert climbers and they are able to use their long tails to help them cling to the stems. When threatened by predators such as kestrels they either 'freeze' flat against a stalk or else drop to the ground where they are better camouflaged.

Below: Many rodents, including this Norway lemming, *Lemmus lemmus* (left) and field vole, *Microtus agrestis*, remain active through the winter. When snow lies on the ground they live underneath it in the air space created by the undergrowth. The blanket of snow protects the rodents from cold winds and predators.

Above: A female fat dormouse, *Glis glis*, with her young. It is the largest species of dormouse, reaching a body length of nearly 20 cm (8 in), and it inhabits most of Europe and western Asia. It was regarded as a delicacy by the Romans and is sometimes referred to as the edible dormouse.

winter. A lemming's nest is relatively simple, being made of dried grass and moss, and it is located above ground, usually hidden in vegetation. Mating takes place in the spring and litters of from four to six young are produced through the summer until September.

Every fourth year or so, instead of producing litters of about five young, lemmings suddenly start giving birth to litters of ten or more. The result is a population explosion which soon leads to the almost total consumption of the vegetation in the area. Lack of food, overcrowding and possibly other factors yet to be determined then trigger off one of the mass migrations for which lemmings are famous. The migration is usually along pathways or tracks and is constant in direction but is not continuous. Odd groups may stop on the way to eat or even produce litters.

Migrating lemmings do not detour even around lakes, rivers or other large obstacles. When they reach a river, however, they do not rush headlong into the water but scurry up and down the bank trying to find a crossing point. If none is found they will reluctantly enter the water and after swimming for 15 to 20 minutes become exhausted and drown unless they can reach the opposite shore. The majority of the migrating lemmings die by drowning, but predators such as Arctic foxes, weasels and wolves also take their toll and eventually the entire horde is destroyed. Only those lemmings that do not migrate remain to perpetuate the species, and for the first year or two after migration reproduction is slow.

Voles are mostly mouse-sized animals with short tails and small ears, and they are among the most common inhabitants of the woods, hedgerows and banks of Europe, Asia and North America. Because they are so vulnerable to predators like the kestrel, voles usually remain hidden in the undergrowth, moving along runways under the tangle of surface vegetation. They feed mainly on grass. During the summer voles build nests of dry grass on the surface of the ground but have their winter sleeping quarters below ground. The best known vole genera are *Microtus* with about 50 species and *Clethrionomys*, the bank voles.

Dormice and jerboas

The dormice and jerboas belong to myomorph families of their own, the *Gliridae* and *Dipodidae* respectively. Dormice are nocturnal animals with pointed heads, large eyes and well developed toes on both front and hind feet for climbing. Dormice live in wooded country, gardens and parkland where they feed mainly on seeds. The smallest species, the common dormouse, *Muscardinus avellanarius*, is found throughout Europe and western Asia.

Jerboas are small jumping rodents found in the arid regions of Asia, Africa and parts of Europe. They stand on their hind feet like a kangaroo and can cover up to 2 m (6 ft) with a single leap, covering the ground faster than a man can run. Jerboas are nocturnal animals, avoiding the heat of the day by remaining in their cool underground dens and sealing the entrances to preserve body moisture. Like the gerbil, the jerboa gets all the water it needs from its food (mainly seeds), and additionally it is able to concentrate its urine, thus further reducing water loss.

Cavies and Porcupines

The Americas are the home of one of the four rodent sub-orders, the *Caviomorpha*. While a few members of the group are to be found in North and Central America and some Caribbean islands, the majority live only in South America. The sub-order is normally divided into five superfamilies and includes the capybara, the cavies (guinea pigs), the agoutis, the coypu, the chinchillas and the American porcupines. They occupy much the same ecological niches as other rodents in other parts of the world and they have the usual rodent arrangement of teeth (large incisors and molars but no canines) which enables them to gnaw through the stems of plants and grind up their tough vegetable diet. The porcupines of Africa and Asia belong to a separate sub-order, *Hystricomorpha*.

Capybaras and cavies

The capybara, *Hydrochoerus hydrochaeris*, of South America belongs to the caviomorph superfamily *Cavioidea*, and it is the largest of all living rodents. Reaching a length of more than 1.3 m (4 ft) when fully grown, it looks rather like a giant guinea pig and lives in the tall grass which borders rivers and lakes. An inoffensive creature, it is an excellent swimmer and is never found far from water which provides it with an escape route from predators. The capybara's fur is coarse and yellowish brown in colour, its limbs are short with four small toes on each front foot and three on each hind foot and it has no visible tail. As an adaptation to its aquatic existence the capybara's toes, which have hoof-like claws, are webbed.

When not feeding on the succulent stems of grasses and aquatic plants, capybaras frequently lie sunning themselves on the river banks. They are interesting not only because they are the largest rodents but also because they are the only rodents that live in herds, even though these are usually small. Most herds consist of about ten animals—a single male and two or three females with their young—but occasionally there may be as many as 50 individuals in a herd.

Capybaras breed once a year and produce litters of four to eight young about four months after mating. Like most rodents young capybaras mature quickly, but they do not reach full size until they are two or three years old. Old age, which would be about ten years for a capybara, is rare because most of them fall prey to animals like cougars, snakes, alligators and eagles. Even man pursues the capybara, for its flesh is good to eat and its hide makes excellent leather.

Belonging to the same superfamily are the guinea pigs or cavies. The most common species, *Cavia aperea*, from which the domestic breeds are derived, is found in all South American countries in both highland and lowland habitats. They are social animals and construct complex and extensive burrow systems which often prove a nuisance near human dwellings. In Bolivia cavies are kept by almost every Indian family as a source of meat and as pets. Most cavies are small, stout, nocturnal animals with short ears, short

Jacana

NHPA

G. Mazza

Left: A spotted paca, *Cuniculus paca*, from the tropical forests of Brazil. The paca feeds by night on a variety of vegetable material, including stalks, roots and fruit, and, being a largish animal (about 60 cm, 2 ft, long) it can cause considerable damage to crops. In many parts of its range the paca is enthusiastically hunted by man not only because it damages crops but also because its meat is rich and good to eat. The mountain paca, *Cuniculus taczanowskii*, from the highlands of Colombia is slightly smaller and much less common.

Right: The skull of a paca looks rather like that of a reptile with its ridged cheek bone.

Above: A female Patagonian cavy, *Dolichotis patagonum*, suckling her young. Like all cavies, Patagonian cavies are born in an advanced state of development: their eyes are open, their bodies are covered with fur and they can move about within minutes of birth.

Left: A domestic guinea pig, *Cavia aperea*. Guinea pigs are descended from the wild cavy which is found in many parts of South America and has smooth brown hair. There are many different breeds of guinea pig, including multi-coloured and long-haired varieties like this one.

Right: Viscachas, *Lagostomus maximus*, are South American rodents which belong to the same family as chinchillas. Colonies of as many as 50 animals live together in large burrows which consist of complex networks of tunnels with many entrances. Excess earth and other unwanted material is carefully piled up into mounds. For reasons unknown, viscachas collect objects like bones and pieces of glass.

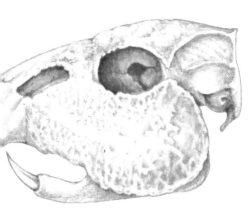

Right: The coypu, *Myocastor coypus*, lives in the temperate regions of South America. Like the beaver of the Northern Hemisphere, it lives along the banks of rivers feeding on reeds and aquatic plants. For shelter it digs a simple burrow in a river bank or constructs a well-hidden nest of reeds, and here it raises its young.

Below: The chinchilla was once a common inhabitant of the Andes Mountains in Peru and Chile, but today it is quite rare. At the beginning of this century about 250,000 furs were being exported each year from Chile alone, so it is hardly surprising that the population went into rapid decline.

legs and no visible tail. They breed twice a year, giving birth to one or two young on each occasion. Unlike most cavies the Patagonian cavy, *Dolichotis patagonum*, and the salt-desert cavy, *Pediolagus salinicola*, have long legs and they look more like hares than cavies. Also, they are active during the day rather than at night.

The pacas and agoutis also belong to the superfamily *Cavioidea*. The spotted paca, *Cuniculus paca*, is found throughout South America north of Argentina and east of the Andes. Like the capybara it is a good swimmer and will take to the water in times of danger. About 80 cm (32 in) long, it has a brown coat marked with horizontal rows of pale spots which provide excellent camouflage in dappled shade. The agoutis are tailless inhabitants of Central and South American forests from Mexico to Paraguay. They look rather like rabbits but stand higher off the ground on long, slender legs ending with hoof-like claws on the toes. Their fur, which is particularly long on the lower back, is sleek and its colour varies from red to brown or black.

Coypus and chinchillas

The best known member of the caviomorph superfamily *Octodontoidea* is the coypu, *Myocastor coypus*. Sometimes called the swamp beaver, it is a native of the southern part of South America and, thanks to man's intervention, it is now also found in North America and Europe. In England the wild population of coypus, centred in East Anglia, originates from escaped animals bred for the fur trade.

The coypu is a large animal, about 1 m (3 ft) long and weighing about 8 kg (18 lb). It lives along the banks of slow-moving rivers where it feeds on aquatic plants and the reeds and grasses which grow at the water's edge. It is a good swimmer and the toes of its hind feet are webbed. Constructing burrows in the river banks, it produces only one litter of about four young each year. The offspring develop quickly and soon leave the burrow with their mother, riding on her back and clinging tightly to her fur when she dives.

The tuco-tucos make up another family of South American rodents. Like the coypus they belong to the superfamily *Octodontoidea* and they look rather like gophers. Their alarm call can be heard over a considerable distance and is most extraordinary: it sounds like a hammer striking metal. Tuco-tucos feed mainly on plant stalks, bulbs and roots.

The superfamily *Chinchilloidea* contains the most economically important of all caviomorphs, the chinchilla. For over a thousand years this animal has been valued for its fur and today large numbers are kept in captivity to supply the fur trade. Merciless hunting in the past drastically reduced the population in the wild, and chinchillas are now rare in their natural home, the Andes mountains. About the size of a young rabbit, the chinchilla has large eyes and ears and a bushy tail. It lives in rocky ground and is equipped with rubbery pads on its toes to help it get a grip on the smooth surfaces of rocks. In the wild chinchillas live in colonies, usually in burrows, breeding twice a year and producing litters of between one and six young. They are sexually mature at about nine months and in captivity can live for seven years or more. The activities of predators considerably reduce their life expectancy in the wild.

Chinchilla fur is a soft bluish grey colour. Of the three main species, *Chinchilla boliviana* has the finest fur and no longer exists in the wild. *Chinchilla cordilberana* has moderately fine fur and *Chinchilla costina* only relatively low grade fur which probably accounts for its continued existence in the highlands of Chile. Strict conservation laws now protect this remaining species.

The only living member of the once large superfamily *Dinomyoidea* is the rare pacarana, *Dinomys branickii*. After the capybara and the beaver it is the largest living rodent and it is found only in the foothills of the Andes. Among its extinct relations were some remarkably large creatures—a species from the tiny West Indian islands of Anguilla and St Martin, for example, was as big as a black bear.

Porcupines

The last of the caviomorph superfamilies, *Erethizontoidea*, contains the American porcupines. These are large, slow-moving rodents with strong, curved claws which enable them to climb trees. They feed on leaves, nuts, fruit and tree bark. All the exposed parts of the body are covered with short protecting spines, called 'quills'. The Canadian porcupine, *Erethizon dorsatum*, which is found in many parts of North America, has a dense hairy coat which largely conceals the quills except when the animal is aroused. Each quill, which is about 10 cm (4 in) long, has a hard outer surface tapering to a needle-sharp point and at the end of the quill, just below the tip, there are about 1,000 tiny barbs which normally lie flat against the quill's surface. As there are about 40 quills to each square centimetre of the porcupine's body surface, including the head, legs, feet and tail, it is well protected.

The Canadian porcupine's tail is a highly effective weapon. With a single lash, directed with great accuracy, it can drive quills deep into the flesh of an adversary. The porcupine's quills are only loosely attached to its body, so they easily become detached. Once in the flesh of an enemy the barbs at the end of a quill come into play and prevent it from being pulled out without ripping the flesh. The barbs not only prevent easy removal but may also cause the quill to work its way inwards so that it may eventually pierce a vital organ and cause death. Animals as large as mountain lions have been killed

L. Lee Rule/Bruce Coleman

Right: Old World porcupines belonging to the genera *Hystrix*, *Thecurus* and *Acanthion* emit a loud chattering sound from a 'rattle' at the end of the tail when they are alarmed. The rattle (shown here) consists of a number of short, cup-shaped quills which clap together like castanets when the creature shakes its tail. This threat noise is usually enough to deter a potential predator.

Below: A brush-tailed porcupine, *Atherurus macrourus*, from South-East Asia. This creature lives in tropical forests and has a distinctive tuft of quills at the end of a long tail.

M. P. L. Fogden/Bruce Coleman

Left: The Canadian porcupine, *Erethizon dorsatum*, has a coat of long, coarse hair which hides its quills. It is a solitary, nocturnal animal which spends the day in the safety of a tree (as seen here) or in holes or crevices on the ground. Although it can successfully defend itself against most predators by lashing out with its quill-covered tail, it has a number of formidable enemies. The Virginian polecat, *Martes pennanti*, and the great horned owl, *Bubo virginianus*, both regularly prey on porcupines.

Right: Old World porcupines like this crested porcupine, *Hystrix cristata*, attack their adversaries, in this case a jackal, by turning round and reversing into them at high speed.

Below: A prehensile-tailed porcupine, *Coendou prehensilis*, from South and Central America. As its name suggests this creature has a long, grasping tail which helps it to climb from tree to tree in its forest home. It will hold on to one branch with its tail and back legs while reaching out with its front legs for a new foothold. There are various other South American porcupine species, including the thin-spined porcupine, *Chaetomys subspinosus*.

Francisco Erize/Bruce Coleman

Below left: All rodents have a pair of long, curved incisors in both the upper and lower jaws. These teeth grow continuously but are normally kept to a reasonable length by constant wear. In the case of this mole rat, however, one of the lower incisors is wrongly positioned and consequently much longer than usual through lack of wear.

Below: The naked mole rat, *Heterocephalus glaber*, must rank as one of the ugliest of all mammals. It spends almost all its time underground, has tiny eyes, no external ears and practically no hair. It feeds mainly on roots and insects.

Jane Burton/Bruce Coleman

Jane Burton/Bruce Coleman

in this way by porcupines.

The porcupines from Africa and southern Asia belong not only to a different superfamily from the American porcupines but also to a different sub-order, the *Hystricomorpha*. The two groups of porcupines seem to have evolved quite independently of each other, and fossil evidence suggests that they first appeared in Europe and South America at about the same time some 40 million years ago in the late Eocene epoch. The reason for the remarkable similarity between these two groups of animals so widely separated geographically is obscure.

The largest of all porcupines is the crested porcupine, *Hystrix cristata*, from western and northern Africa and southern Italy. It is about 60 cm (2 ft) long and has a short tail. Its body is covered with quills and those extending from the top of the head along the centre of the back are longer than the rest, forming a mane or crest. Porcupines produce litters of one or two young once or twice a year. The spines of newborn porcupines are soft and harmless, but become needle-sharp within a few days.

There are 21 species of Old World porcupines distributed throughout Africa and southern Asia. A representative from South-East Asia, the Bornean long-tailed porcupine, *Trichys lipura*, has a long body and only short quills so it looks like a rat as much as a porcupine. The white-tailed porcupine, *Hystrix leucura*, is a common Indian species which is found throughout the Middle East. As well as the Old World porcupines, the sub-order *Hystricomorpha* includes the cane rats, the mole rats and the rock rats from central and southern Africa. These small sturdy rodents are equipped with large incisors and have a typically rodent diet of grass, seeds, roots and sometimes insects.

Seals, Walruses and Sea Cows

Seals, sea lions and walruses are aquatic mammals belonging to the carnivore suborder *Pinnipedia*. This suborder is divided into three families: the true or earless seals, *Phocidae*, the eared seals, *Otariidae*, and the walruses, *Odobenidae*. The pinnipeds evolved from terrestial carnivores but it is not known exactly when the transformation took place. Although fossil remains of seals from each of the three modern families have been discovered (dating from the Miocene epoch some 20 million years ago) they are from animals which already closely resemble their modern relatives. Many zoologists believe that the true seals have a separate ancestry from the eared seals and the walruses: they suggest that true seals evolved from a creature resembling an otter while the other two families had a bear-like ancestor.

Modern pinnipeds are very well adapted for an aquatic existence. Their bodies are streamlined and the digits of both front and hind limbs are fused together to form paddles or flippers for swimming. Although able to spend considerable lengths of time at sea, all seals must come ashore, on to land or ice, in order to breed. A female normally gives birth to a single calf which is suckled on land from one or two pairs of nipples which are hidden from view in pouches on the underside of her body.

True seals

The true seals have no obvious external ears. Their bodies and limbs are covered with a pelt of short, coarse hair which is moulted annually. The hind flippers are directed backwards, beside the tail, and are no use at all when the creature is moving on land. In the water the hind flippers spread out sideways like the tail-flukes of a porpoise and are used to propel the seal forwards while the front flippers are used for steering. True seals are, at best, rather awkward on land, moving forward by a series of wriggling jerks involving muscular contractions of the whole body.

The largest of the true seals are the elephant seals of which there are two species. The southern elephant seal, *Mirounga leonina*, is a huge animal found in Antarctic waters. A large bull may be as much as 7.6 m (25 ft) long and weigh up to three tonnes. The cows are about half this size. Breeding colonies, called 'rookeries', form each year on many Antarctic islands. The cows arrive at the rookeries in September and shortly after this each gives birth to a single calf. The bulls begin arriving in October for the next mating season and each one takes possession of a 'harem' of cows. Rival bulls are constantly fighting over the ownership of the largest harem and the losers of these fights are often severely wounded. During the 19th century, elephant seals were hunted almost to extinction for the sake of their blubber which was processed to yield an oil.

True seals are most numerous in the Antarctic and the crab-eating seal, *Lobodon carcinophagus*, is particularly abundant.

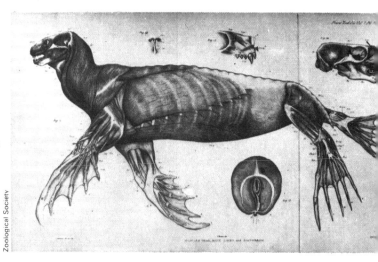

Right: This early anatomical illustration of a sea lion shows how the creature's outer muscles are arranged. Movement through the water is effected by flexing the body as well as moving the flippers.

Below: A herd of walruses, *Odobenus rosmarus*, lying on a rocky shore on the coast of Alaska. These creatures are much less common than they were a century ago having been hunted by man for their skin, meat and blubber. Apart from man, they have few enemies for they can defend themselves very effectively with their huge canine teeth. Polar bears and killer whales occasionally take young walruses, but rarely molest adults.

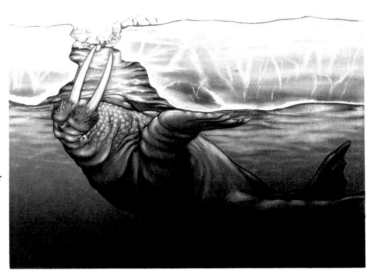

Left: A young walrus supports itself on one of its front flippers. Walruses, like sea lions, have quite well developed front limbs and can move about surprisingly rapidly on dry land.

Right: Walruses spend much of their time feeding beneath the pack ice, and they use their tusks to prevent breathing holes from freezing over. Walruses also use their tusks, which are enlarged upper canine teeth, to help haul themselves out of the water.

Below: The dugong, *Dugong dugon*, is found around the coasts of the Red Sea and the Indian Ocean as far east as northern Australia.

Allan Power/Bruce Coleman

Rex Features

Erik Pabst

Below: Bull elephant seals, *Mirounga angustirostris*, fight for the possession of females on the Pacific coast of Mexico. Elephant seals are so called because the nose of the male is long and pendulous and can be inflated with air to form a proboscis reminiscent of an elephant's trunk.

Right: A sea lion about to eat a fish. The majority of sea lions are found in the southern oceans where fish are plentiful, but a few species live in the Northern Hemisphere. The Californian sea lion, *Zalophus californianus*, for example, inhabits the rocky coastal areas of the US West Coast.

A survey in the early 1970s estimated the total population of these seals at between two and five million animals. It is a slender and fast moving seal with an unusual method of feeding. Whereas the majority of seals feed on a variety of fishes, cephalopods and crustaceans the crab-eating seal feeds only on a type of small, free-swimming shrimp, known as *krill*. When feeding the seal swims into a shoal of krill, takes in a mouthful of the shrimp-filled water and then squeezes the water out between its cheek teeth which are specially shaped to trap the shrimps within the seal's mouth. Weddell's seal, *Leptonychotes weddelli*, is another inhabitant of the Antarctic pack-ice. It is larger than the crab-eating seals and is capable of underwater dives of prodigious depth and duration.

Around the British coastline there are only two resident species of seal, the larger of these being the grey seal, *Halichoerus grypus*. An adult bull may be over 2.7 m (9 ft) long. Grey seals are gregarious and large rookeries exist on various rocky islands and beaches around Britain. Breeding takes place in the autumn, and the pups grow extremely quickly, doubling their size and weight within a week of birth. The pups are born with a shaggy coat of white fur which is moulted when they are weaned at about three weeks. At this early age the pups are deserted by their mothers and must thereafter fend for themselves. The other resident British seal is the common or harbour seal, *Phoca vitulina*, a small seal about 1.7 m (5.5 ft) long. Common seals are monogamous and less gregarious than grey seals. Breeding takes place in midsummer on offshore sandbanks and secluded beaches.

Eared seals

The eared seals are divided into two sub-families—sea lions, *Otariinae*, and fur seals, *Arctocephalinae*—and they differ from true seals in having small but distinct external ears. Their hind flippers, as well as providing the main propulsive force in the water, can also be brought forward sideways to help the animal move about on land. The front flippers are larger and more supple than those of true seals and they can be flapped together underwater to provide some propulsion as well as providing steering power. On land the front flippers support the forward part of the body and are used as true walking legs. Eared seals are a great deal more mobile on land than true seals.

Steller's sea lion, *Eumetopias jubatus*,

James Tallon/NHPA

is one of the largest species of seal, adult males reaching a length of more than 3 m (10 ft) and a weight of one tonne. Each summer many thousands of these sea lions migrate to the Aleutian Islands to breed, the adult bulls arriving first, in early May, to establish territories. Pregnant females are the next to arrive and almost immediately each one gives birth to a single calf. The calves of sea lions are suckled by their mothers for a great deal longer than those of true seals; weaning is rarely completed in less than two or three months.

The Californian sea lion, *Zalophus californianus*, is a smaller, more agile species which inhabits the rocky coastal areas of California. This is the sea lion commonly seen in zoos and circuses around the world. It is a playful and intelligent animal and it appears to have a natural talent for performing tricks which require a fine sense of balance.

In their habits fur seals closely resemble their relatives the sea lions. The Alaska fur seal, *Callorhinus ursinus*, is found in the northern Pacific and breeds only in the fog-bound Pribilov Islands of the Bering Sea. At the height of the summer breeding season as many as two to three million seals congregate at the Pribilov rookeries. There are several other species of fur seal belonging to the genus *Arctocephalus* from the Southern Hemisphere.

The walrus

The walrus, *Odobenus rosmarus*, is the sole representative of the family *Odobenidae*. It has features in common with both true seals and eared seals although it is more closely related to the latter. Like true seals, walruses have no external ears, but they use both front and hind flippers when walking on land like the eared seals. The walrus inhabits the shallow Arctic coastal waters of the Atlantic and Pacific oceans, always living close to land or ice. Adult males reach a length of 3.7 m (12 ft) and weigh up to 1.5 tonnes, while the females are somewhat smaller and slimmer. Walrus skin is enormously thick and wrinkled and adults are almost completely hairless. In both sexes the upper canine teeth are greatly enlarged to form tusks which, in old males, may reach a length of 76 cm (30 in). Walruses feed mainly on shellfish, the tusks being used when feeding to rake the shellfish up off the sea-bed. Once inside the mouth they are crushed between massive cheek-teeth and the soft contents are sucked out and swallowed. Walruses breed during April and May.

The bulls are polygamous and use their tusks as formidable weapons when fighting for possession of the females; old bulls are invariably heavily battle-scarred. Young walruses are not fully weaned until the end of their second year, probably because they are unable to feed properly until their tusks have grown.

Sea cows

Although sea cows are aquatic mammals and superficially resemble seals in many respects, they are quite unrelated and belong to a different order, the *Sirenia*. Indeed, the closest living relatives of sea cows are elephants. The order *Sirenia* is extremely ancient and sea cows were widespread in the oceans of the world as far back as the Eocene epoch some 40 to 50 million years ago. The order is divided into two families: the manatees, *Trichechidae*, and the dugongs, *Dugongidae*.

Sea cows are completely aquatic and they die very quickly if they become stranded on land. They are shy, slow moving creatures and they are entirely herbivorous, feeding on various water plants and sea-weeds. Their bodies are bulky and the tail is flattened horizontally to form a broad paddle, or 'fluke', which is used to propel the animal through the

Left: A leopard seal, *Hydrurga leptonyx*, pursues a penguin off the coast of Antarctica. Penguins form a major part of the diet of the leopard seal, along with fish and the young of other seals. Penguins are notably reluctant to enter the water when leopard seals are patrolling nearby. When a leopard seal catches a penguin it shakes it vigorously and then swallows it complete with feathers and skin. Leopard seals get their name from their spotted markings. They are true seals, belonging to the family *Phocidae*. They are the only pinnipeds to feed on warm-blooded prey. Most seals feed exclusively on fish and invertebrates such as squid.

water. The hind limbs have disappeared completely and the front limbs are small and oar-shaped. The eyes of sea cows are very small and their faces are curiously grotesque because the upper lip is huge and mobile and adorned with a fringe of stiff bristles. The skin of the sea cow is thick and tough and beneath it is a layer of fat or blubber which helps to insulate the animal from the cold.

There are three species of manatee: the Florida manatee, *Trichechus manatus*, which is found in small numbers around the Gulf of Mexico and the Caribbean, the Amazonian manatee, *Trichechus inunguis* from the northeastern coast of South America and in the rivers Amazon and Orinoco, and the West African manatee, *Trichechus senegalensis*, which is very rare and occurs along the tropical west coast of Africa. Manatees vary in length from 1.8 to 4 m (6 to 13 ft) and weigh from 270 to 900 kg (600 to 2000 lb). They are slate grey or black in colour and the huge upper lip is deeply divided in the centre into two prehensile halves which can be moved independently when gathering food into the mouth. The tail fluke is smooth and rounded and the flippers are sufficiently supple to be helpful in collecting food. The flippers are equipped with short nails and the body has a sparse covering of short hairs.

There is one living species of dugong and one species which became extinct within the last 200 years. The dugong, *Dugong dugon*, is found around the coasts of the Indian Ocean. Dugongs are slightly smaller than manatees and are more highly adapted for aquatic life. The upper lip has no cleft in it and the tail fluke has a deep indentation in the centre. The clawless flippers are less supple than those of manatees and are no use in feeding. The body is completely hairless and male dugongs have two short tusks in their upper jaws.

Steller's sea cow, *Hydrodamalis stelleri*, an extinct member of the dugong family, was first discovered in the cold Bering Sea in 1741 by the German naturalist Steller. It was a huge animal which grew to a length of 7.6 m (25 ft). Its skin was curiously rough and bark-like and instead of teeth it had horny plates on the inside of its mouth which it used to chew the seaweed on which it fed. Within 17 years of their discovery, the Steller's sea cows had been completely exterminated by hunters and traders.

Whales

Of all the mammals, both living and extinct, whales are the most perfectly adapted to an aquatic way of life. So perfect is this adaptation that, until comparatively recent times, naturalists mistakenly classified them as fish. Belonging to the order *Cetacea*, they are descended from four-legged, terrestrial mammals, although there is some uncertainty as to precisely which early mammals were their true ancestors. The change from terrestrial to aquatic habitat probably took place in the Palaeocene epoch some 65 million years ago.

Whales have streamlined, fish-shaped bodies and they lack a proper neck as a result of shortening or, in some cases, joining of the neck vertebrae. The body tapers smoothly towards the tail which is expanded out horizontally on both sides to form two flat, pointed tail flukes which provide the whale with propulsive power when they are beaten up and down in the water. Cetaceans show no trace of hind limbs and the front limbs have evolved to become smooth paddle-shaped flippers which are used for balancing and steering. Most whales have a dorsal fin positioned on the midline of the back which varies considerably in size and shape depending on the species.

Like all mammals, whales breathe air. Air is inhaled and exhaled through a special nasal opening known as the blowhole which is situated on the highest point of the head behind the snout.

Museum of Natural History/Leiden

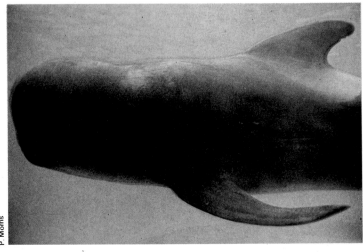

P. Morris

The position of the blowhole allows the whale to breathe when only a small portion of its head and back are above the surface of the water. The blowhole has a characteristic shape for each species, and a few of the larger whales have two blowholes instead of the more usual one. Air is exhaled from the blowhole explosively, producing a blow or spout. The spout consists of mucus and water which forms as the whale's breath condenses in the air. The whale's windpipe is completely separated from its throat or pharynx so that it can open its mouth under water and breath at the same time.

The openings of the female's reproductive organs lie in a narrow slit on the underside of the body in front of the anus. The nipples are hidden in recesses on each side. When suckling, the nipples

Above: A Dutch engraving dating from about 1600 shows a stranded male sperm whale, *Physeter catodon*. The artist was clearly more interested in showing the size of the creature, which is slightly exaggerated, than in anatomical accuracy, for the eye (which is too large) and the flippers are wrongly positioned.

Right and far right: Sections through the skin of a dolphin and skin from a human palm. The dolphin's skin is perfectly smooth to reduce water resistance, and the dark cells (1) show through the outer transparent layer (2). It lacks the ridges (3) and sweat glands (4) which are typical of human skin.

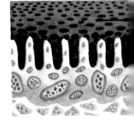

Above: A pilot whale, *Globicephala scammoni*, from the Pacific Ocean. These animals are toothed whales and they live in herds of 100 or more individuals, feeding on fish and marine invertebrates, notably cuttlefish. They belong to the same subfamily as the killer whale and can grow to a length of 8.5 m (28 ft).

Right: The white whale, *Delphinapterus leucas*, is a close relation of the narwhal, and it is found in the oceans of the Northern Hemisphere. Although preferring Arctic waters, white whales are sometimes found along the coasts of northern Europe. The creature's blowhole and broad tail flukes are plainly visible in this picture.

P. Morris

Right: A dolphin drives itself through the water by beating its tail flukes up and down with its powerful body muscles.

346

are protruded and milk is rapidly injected by the female directly into the calf's mouth. Suckling is rapid and takes place while both cow and calf are fully submerged. In the male the testes are internal and the penis lies beneath the abdominal skin in an almost coiled form. Beneath the skin, the whale's body is completely encased in an envelope of thick fat or blubber. For hundreds of years whales have been hunted by man for the sake of this blubber which, once refined, gives rise to a commercially valuable whale oil. Whale flesh is used in the manufacture of pet foods and is eaten by humans in some countries.

The whales are divided into two suborders: the baleen or whalebone whales, *Mysticeti*, which include the right whales, rorquals and humpback whales, and the toothed whales, *Odontoceti*, which include the sperm whales, beaked whales, narwhals, dolphins and porpoises.

Toothed whales

The *Odontoceti* or toothed whales are generally smaller than the whalebone whales and they have only a single blowhole. Toothed whales feed on fish, squid and cuttlefish, and one species, the killer whale, also feeds on sea birds, seals and other whales. The behaviour of toothed whales is better known than that of whalebone whales because many of the smaller species are kept and studied at marine parks and oceanariums around the world. They are gregarious, playful animals and communicate with each other by means of clicks, whistles and quacking sounds.

Many, if not all, of the toothed whales are able to navigate in the dark by echolocation: the whale emits a pulse of ultrasonic clicks and then listens to the echoes of these clicks reflected off nearby objects. The pattern and quality of the returning echoes gives the whale detailed information about its surroundings and enables it to hunt for food in total darkness. As far as is known, whalebone whales cannot navigate by echolocation.

The sperm whale, *Physeter catodon*, is by far the largest of the toothed whales, adult males growing to a length of 18 m (60 ft). The females are considerably smaller. Each tooth is about 20 cm (8 in) long and weighs about 2.7 kg (6 lb). Sperm whales have a characteristic, domed forehead containing a large organ filled with a waxy substance called *spermaceti* which was once highly valued as an industrial lubricant and was also used in the manufacture of candles. The purpose of the spermaceti-producing organ is unknown but it may be involved in echolocation. Sperm whales were extensively hunted for their spermaceti and blubber, and in the days of sailing ships and hand-thrown harpoons the capture of these whales was a dangerous business. Unlike most other whales, sperm whales have been known to attack whaling boats, either ramming them

Below: A series of photographs showing the birth of a dolphin. Whales are born tail first, unlike most large mammals, and because they are born underwater they do not attempt to breathe at once. Only when the mother has nosed her newborn calf to the surface does it fill its lungs with air.

Below right: Bottle-nosed dolphins, *Tursiops truncatus*, are familiar performers at oceanariums throughout the world. They seem to delight in co-operating with their trainers and soon learn to perform the most remarkable tricks. They grow to a length of 3.6 m (12 ft) and come from the North Atlantic.

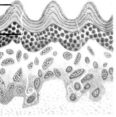

Below: Like all other whales, killer whales, *Orcinus orcas*, mate by swimming alongside each other belly to belly. Killer whales are the only cetaceans which regularly tackle warm-blooded prey such as dolphins, seals and penguins. Packs of 40 or more killer whales have even been known to overcome baleen whales.

Francisco Erize/Bruce Coleman

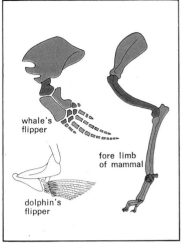

whale's flipper

fore limb of mammal

dolphin's flipper

Left: An Amazon river dolphin, *Inia geoffrensis*, is caught for an aquarium. It has a longer snout and smaller eyes than its salt-water cousins.

Above left: A black and white dolphin, *Cephalorhynchus commersoni*, skims the surface of the southern ocean off the coast of Argentina.

Rex Features

with the snout or splintering them like matchwood between their massive jaws.

The narwhal, *Monodon monoceros*, is a peculiar, small whale inhabiting Arctic waters. Adult narwhals have only two teeth in the upper jaw, and in the male one of these teeth, usually the left one, is enormously enlarged to form a long, straight, spirally twisted horn or tusk which projects to a length of 2 m (6.5 ft) from the whale's snout. Although many suggestions have been made, it is not known how the narwhal uses its tusk.

Dolphins and porpoises

The dolphin family contains many species of small toothed whales. The largest of these is the killer whale, *Orcinus orca*, which grows to a length of 9 m (30 ft), has a striking black and white coloration and a very tall dorsal fin. Killer whales have about 50 sharp, conical teeth and are, as their name suggests, fierce predators. Their reputation as man-eaters, however, is probably undeserved for in captivity they have proved to be surprisingly gentle and co-operative.

The true dolphins are among the fastest of marine animals and are capable of reaching a speed of 25 knots in pursuit of the fish on which they feed. Dolphins usually travel around in large schools, sometimes containing hundreds of animals. They are natural acrobats and in the wild they frequently jump high out of the water when playing. Schools of dolphins often accompany ships at sea, positioning themselves at the front of the ship where they ride the bow-wave like surfers. They seem to enjoy this activity immensely and jostle each other for the best positions for wave riding.

Dolphins are curiously friendly towards humans and there are a few authenticated cases of dolphins attempting to rescue drowning swimmers by swimming underneath them and pushing them towards the surface. They will behave in the same way with injured members of their own species. In captivity, no dolphin, however severely provoked, has ever been known seriously to attack its trainer. In the wild, dolphins attack and kill sharks without hesitation and in the breeding season the males sometimes injure each other in fights, so there is little doubt that they could kill or maim a human if they wished to do so.

Many small toothed whales, dolphins included, have relatively large and complex brains and there seems to be little doubt among scientists that these are highly intelligent animals. Some zoologists who have studied dolphins firmly maintain that they must have a language of their own which is sufficiently complex to allow them to convey complicated instructions to each other. If this is true then dolphins must have an intellectual level comparable to man's and far above that of our nearest living relative, the chimpanzee which is highly intelligent, but has no language of its own.

The common porpoise, *Phocaena phocaena*, is one of the smallest whales, measuring 1.5 to 1.8 m (5 to 6 ft) in length. It is found in the North Atlantic and is one of the most familiar whales to be found along the coasts of Europe. Occasionally porpoises enter the mouths of large rivers, such as the Seine and the Thames, and they may travel upstream for several kilometres.

Whalebone whales

The most characteristic feature of a whalebone or baleen whale is its enormous mouth equipped with rows of whalebone plates which are used to strain food from the water. Each strip of whalebone is made up of thousands of long hairs which have grown together to form a single rigid plate with a fringe of stiff bristles

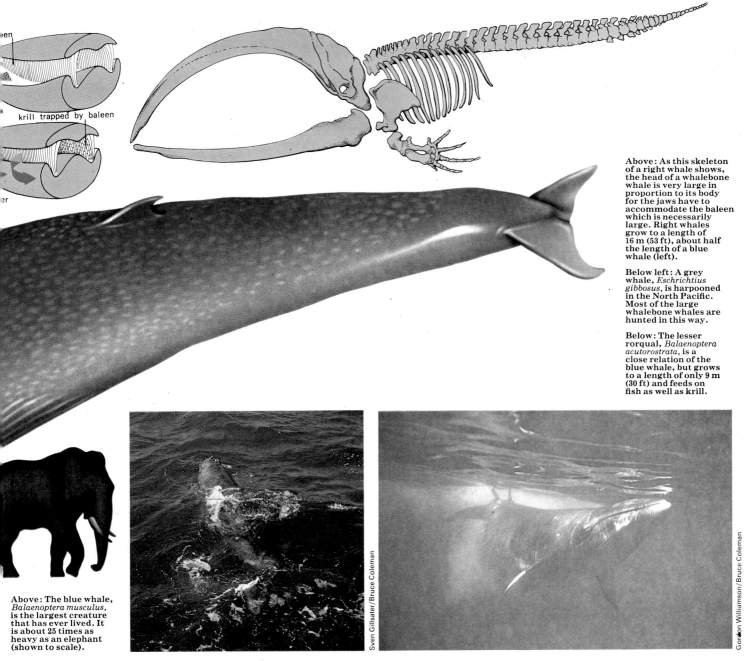

krill trapped by baleen

Above: As this skeleton of a right whale shows, the head of a whalebone whale is very large in proportion to its body for the jaws have to accommodate the baleen which is necessarily large. Right whales grow to a length of 16 m (53 ft), about half the length of a blue whale (left).

Below left: A grey whale, *Eschrichtius gibbosus*, is harpooned in the North Pacific. Most of the large whalebone whales are hunted in this way.

Below: The lesser rorqual, *Balaenoptera acutorostrata*, is a close relation of the blue whale, but grows to a length of only 9 m (30 ft) and feeds on fish as well as krill.

Above: The blue whale, *Balaenoptera musculus*, is the largest creature that has ever lived. It is about 25 times as heavy as an elephant (shown to scale).

Sven Gillsäter/Bruce Coleman

Gordon Williamson/Bruce Coleman

projecting from the end. There may be hundreds of individual plates within the jaws of a single whale. The plates are rooted at their bases to the inside of the upper jaw and can be raised when the animal has its mouth closed to lie along the roof of the mouth. When the whale is feeding the plates are lowered to form a dense barricade, called the *baleen*, at the entrance to the mouth. The whalebone whales are filter-feeders and they use their baleens as gigantic sieves to extract shrimp-like organisms called *krill* from the water. After feeding, a large whale may have as much as ten tonnes of krill in its stomach.

Surprisingly little is known about the behaviour of whalebone whales. Most of them are migratory, spending the winter in tropical and temperate waters and migrating to the poles in summer, those in the Northern Hemisphere wintering in the arctic and those in the Southern Hemisphere in the Antarctic. Though occasionally observed on their own, these whales are sociable animals and are usually seen in pairs or small groups called *pods*. When migrating some species form huge schools of more than a thousand individuals. To communicate with each other, certain species produce an extraordinary 'song' made up of a series of peculiar squeals, grunts and moans. Many species migrate to specific areas in order to breed. Calves are born after a gestation period of about 11 months and are suckled by their mothers for from four to seven months depending on the species. Their rate of growth is astonishing: a whale calf may double its weight within the first week of life.

Right whales are unusual in having no dorsal fin and, unlike other whalebone whales, the right whale has no grooves on the underside of its throat. The mouth is a curious shape with the upper jaw being strongly arched and containing up to 600 plates of whalebone, each with a maximum length of 3.6 m (12 ft). Right whales formed the basis of the earliest whaling industries, indeed they are thought to have got their name simply because early whalers considered them the 'right' whales to hunt. They are unable to swim very fast and were successfully pursued and killed from rowing boats. The Greenland right whale or bowhead whale, *Balaena mysticetus*, is now very rare but still occurs in the Atlantic west of Greenland. It is dark grey in colour and grows to a length of 18 m (60 ft).

Rorqual whales are usually more slender and streamlined than right whales. The mouth is smaller and less grotesque, the back is equipped with a dorsal fin and there are conspicuous grooves on the throat. It is believed that these grooves enable the throat to expand when the whale is feeding so that a greater volume of water can be taken into the mouth. Until the advent of motorized whaling ships and harpoon guns, the rorqual whales were virtually unmolested by man because they are too swift to be pursued by a rowing boat. In this century, however, they have been the subject of a terrible slaughter and many are in danger of becoming extinct.

The blue whale, *Balaenoptera musculus*, is the largest of the rorquals and is also the largest animal which has ever lived. Blue whales sometimes reach a length of 33 m (110 ft) and a weight of 130 tonnes. Once widespread throughout the world, these whales are now exceptionally rare having been hunted almost to extinction by the whaling industry. Many scientists believe that the population of blue whales is now so drastically reduced that it has no hope of recovery and that the species will inevitably disappear in the near future.

Lampreys, Sharks and Rays

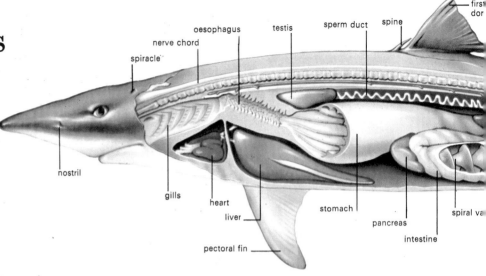

The earliest vertebrates of which we have reasonably detailed knowledge were fresh-water fish, known as *agnathans*, which lived well over 300 million years ago. While not totally dissimilar from modern fish in form, these primitive fish lacked bony jaws. Most were flattened from the back of their bodies to the front, and lived near the river or lake bed. Almost certainly they fed on small organic particles which they found on the ooze and mud.

The living descendants of these fish are known as *cyclostomes*—like their ancestors they are jawless. Their skeletons are made of cartilage, they have long slender bodies and look rather like eels. There are two groups of cyclostomes, the hagfish and the lampreys.

Lampreys and hagfish

Hagfish live only in temperate or cold sea water. By day they bury themselves in the sea bed, emerging to feed at night. They are blind, for their eyes are covered with pigmented skin, but each of them has a single, very efficient nostril which helps them to find the dead or dying fish, as well as invertebrates such as ragworms and shrimps which live on the sea bed—on which they feed. A hagfish also has finger-like feelers around its mouth.

Like their relatives, the lampreys, hag-fish have no scales and instead their skin is protected by a copious secretion of slime. For respiration they have between six and fourteen pairs of gill-slits each, but their relatives the lampreys always have seven pairs. Another important difference between the two groups is that adult lampreys have well-developed eyes. The heart of both hagfish and lampreys is a very simple structure being a mere muscular thickening of a curved part of the main artery.

All lampreys breed in fresh water and the sexes are separate. (Although not all invertebrate animals have separate sexes, it is always the case among vertebrates). Both sexes gather in swift-running water and, using their mouths, make a simple nest by moving the stones. The males then fertilize the eggs while the females spawn, and the eggs are buried in the sand by the movement of the parents' bodies. After about 20 days each egg hatches as a larva, called an *ammocoete*, which lives for about five years before metamorphosing into an adult.

The lamprey larvae are in many ways like their distant relative, the inverte-brate chordate *amphioxus*. They bury themselves and feed by taking water in at the mouth and passing it through the pharynx where mucus traps the small planktonic food particles. Cilia on the wall of the pharynx pass the mucus together with the food to the simple, uncoiled gut for digestion. This is very similar to the feeding of amphioxus, although in the lamprey larvae the water current passes in at the mouth and out of the gills as a result of muscular action—a fish-like procedure—rather than by ciliary action.

Some kinds of lampreys spend their

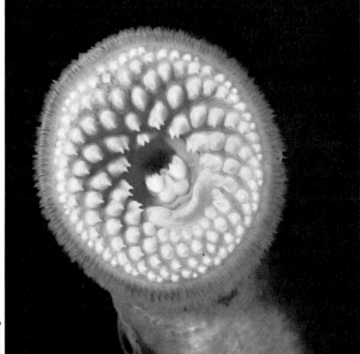

Heather Angel

Below and left: A sea lamprey, *Petromyzon marinus*, clinging to a host fish and a close up of its sucker. Like the earliest vertebrates, lampreys do not have jaws. They are usually parasitic, feeding on the body tissue and blood of a host fish. The sucker is equipped with rows of hooked teeth surrounding the central mouth opening. Within the mouth can be seen a tongue carrying two larger teeth for tearing away the flesh of the host. Around the edge of the sucker is a circular lip. The lamprey's sucker is extremely powerful and it is almost impossible for a fish to dislodge the parasite. In the end the host usually dies from loss of blood or tissue damage.

Right: A nurse shark, *Ginglymostoma cirratum*. These animals are found in the shallow coastal waters of warm seas. Indeed they often lie in such shallow water that their dorsal fins break the surface. They reach a length of about two metres (six feet). As in many sharks the upper lobe of the tail fin is larger than the lower one.

Seaphot

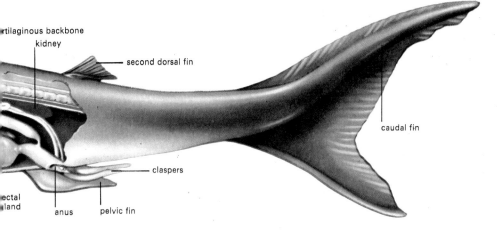

tilaginous backbone
kidney
second dorsal fin
caudal fin
claspers
ectal
land
anus
pelvic fin

adult lives in the sea, migrating into rivers only to breed, while others spend their entire lives in fresh water. Most are parasitic, and have rounded, sucker-like mouths. They cling on to the host fish with their teeth, feeding on its muscle and blood. Anticoagulants in the lamprey's saliva prevent the blood of the host fish from clotting as the parasite feeds. They will attack a variety of fish including mackerel, cod and salmon, and marks left by lampreys have even been found on the skin of whales.

Although they are sometimes caught for human consumption while they are migrating, the chief economic significance of lampreys lies in the damage they can do to commercial fisheries. The best-known case concerns the lampreys which entered the Great Lakes of North America through newly dug canals and, in a very few years, so decimated the population of lake trout and other fish that a formerly valuable fishery became worthless. Despite their primitive features the cyclostomes are evidently still a force to be reckoned with.

Cartilaginous fish

The best known cartilaginous fish are the sharks, dogfish, skates and rays which all belong to one subclass, the *Elasmobranchii*. Despite the fact that they are often grouped together with bony fish, cartilaginous fish form a distinct class on their own, little more resembling bony fish than the bony fish themselves resemble amphibians. Like hagfish and lampreys they have skeletons made up of cartilage rather than hard bone.

Although not as strong as bone, cartilage is lighter and it is strong enough to provide support in the water where buoyancy makes large animals almost or completely weightless. Another characteristic of most of these fish is the *spiracle*, an opening behind the eye leading to the gill system. Drawing at least part of the oxygenated water required for respiration through the spiracle is particularly helpful to a flat-bodied fish like a skate or ray. Their mouth, being on the under surface of the body, would supply sandy or muddy water to the delicate gills if it was used for breathing. Elasmobranchs have separate gill slits opening directly on to the body surface. There are usually five pairs of gill slits but no gill cover, or *operculum*.

The entire body surface including the fins of sharks and the other cartilaginous fish is covered in pointed scales. In structure, these scales are very similar to the teeth of other vertebrates, containing a pulp cavity and nerves. This is not surprising, for the elasmobranchs' teeth are simply specially adapted scales round the mouth. Other vertebrates, including man, are descended from the same ancestors as the elasmobranchs, and it is these teeth which we have inherited. In the case of mammals, the teeth are the only scales that we retain.

Sharks and dogfish

Sharks and dogfish belong to the order *Selachii* and they are perhaps the most typical of the cartilaginous fish. There are some 200 different species all of which are good swimmers with streamlined bodies. But even with their light cartilaginous skeletons they are slightly heavier than the water in which they swim and so have the same problem as aeroplanes;

Above left: A reef shark partly cut away to show the internal body structure. The animal has a skeleton made of cartilage. The backbone encloses a notochord and, above the notochord, is a spinal chord. The brain is protected by a case called the cranium, a feature typical of vertebrate animals. The gill slits are used for respiration, and oxygenated water is supplied through the mouth and through openings in the body wall called spiracles. The intestine is fairly short and shaped in the form of a spiral.

Left: A large wobbegong shark, *Orectolobus maculatus*, is well camouflaged against the sea bed. The animal has a wide, flat head fringed with skin flaps which look like seaweed and break up the body outline.

Below: A tiger shark, *Galeocardo cuvieri*. These animals are found along the coasts of warm seas where they reach a length of about 4.5 m (15 ft). They feed on almost anything, even rubbish from rivers, and they can be a threat to swimmers.

Ben Cropp

Flip Schulke/Black Star

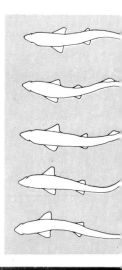

Left: Sharks are among the most successful predators in the sea. Three characteristics contribute much to their success: sharp biting teeth, mobility and an efficient nervous system. The long thin teeth of these sand sharks, *Carchariidae*, are plainly visible.

Right: A series of diagrams to show how a shark moves through the water by sideways movements of the body.

Below: The birth of a shark. The embryo develops in the sea protected by a horny case secreted by a special gland in the mother. The young of some sharks reach an advanced stage of development in the oviduct of the female and are born live.

they must use power to stay up. Their bodies are somewhat flattened at the front, and thick-based immobile pectoral fins project from each side like stubby delta wings. The whole front end of the body thus works like an aeroplane's wing to provide 'lift' as the animal moves through the water.

A few kinds of selachians have evolved mechanisms enabling them to float weightlessly. For example, the huge oily livers of the basking sharks, *Cetorhinus maximus*, act as buoyancy organs, for oil is lighter than water. The sand tiger shark, *Carcharias taurus*, swallows air and uses its own intestines as water wings. Most sharks and dogfish, however, must either keep swimming or sink, and some, like the leopard shark, *Triakis semifasciata*, of the Pacific Ocean, just keep swimming endlessly, day and night, as automatically as we breathe. Others, such as the dogfish, *Scyliorhinus canicula*, which provide us with 'rock salmon', live in shallow seas and spend much of their time lying on the bottom.

For the predatory shark, being unable to hang suspended in the water means that after it has homed in on its prey, it is unable to keep still and take a leisurely bite—it would sink before it could do so. Instead it must keep swimming, biting as it passes. However, this does not seem to be much of a disadvantage since sharks are among the fiercest and most successful predators in the sea.

Not all selachians are hunters. Dogfish, for example, are scavengers and the huge basking sharks, which may be up to 12 m (40 ft) long, swim only sluggishly and feed on plankton which they strain from the water using projections of the gill skeleton known as gill rakers. However, in warm and tropical seas there are a number of fierce predatory sharks. The great white shark, *Carcharodon carcharias*, is greatly feared along the coasts of Australia. A relatively small specimen 4.5 m (15 ft) long can quite easily bite a man in half. The largest great white sharks reach a length of up to 12m (40 ft) and weigh about three tonnes. Among

other species which are dangerous to man are the great blue sharks, *Prionace glauca*, the tiger shark, *Galeocardo cuvieri* and the mako, *Isurus oxyrinchus*.

Sharks usually hunt alone, but they will sometimes attack in packs especially if there is blood in the water. When attacking humans, sharks seem to single out a victim, often a bather, and then completely disregard all others who may be in the vicinity.

Sharks in action

Defensive measures adopted by swimmers in shark-infested seas have varied over the years. At one time it was thought sensible to thrash about in the water, using noise to frighten the sharks away. This is definitely a mistake. During the Second World War the American forces in the Pacific used shark repellent tablets which, by dissolving in the water, were thought to ward off sharks. These tablets had psychological value, helping struggling swimmers to keep their spirits up, but are now known to have had little effect upon the sharks. Presumably where the tablets failed, dissatisfied customers did not return to complain.

Modern research on the sharks' senses reveals that they have very good hearing. They often feed on wounded or unhealthy fish, which swim clumsily, making a noise in the water as they do so. Homing in on the sound, sharks then use their efficient noses to pick up such clues as traces of blood in the water. When they are very close indeed to their prey their inefficient eyes, able to see only in black and white and incapable of seeing detail, guide them for the last few feet.

Above: A great blue shark, *Prionace glauca*. This animal feeds mainly on herring, mackerel and tuna, but will attack almost any other animal including other sharks and man. It is an open sea fish and is therefore only rarely a danger to bathers. Blue sharks sometimes damage fishing nets in an attempt to reach the catch.

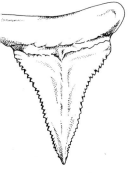

Left and above: A great white shark, *Carcharodon carcharias*, and a drawing of one of its upper teeth. White sharks feed on animals as large as dolphins and sea lions, and they are reputedly the fiercest of all sharks.

Right: Whale sharks, *Rhincodon typus*, are completely harmless to man and, as this picture indicates, they are not at all shy. They are reported to reach lengths of up to 18 m (60 ft) but this one is only 10 m (34 ft) long. Like basking sharks, whale sharks feed on plankton. They are found in the warmer parts of most oceans.

Ben Cropp

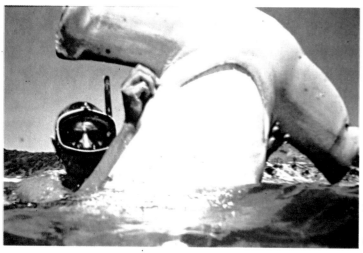

Left: A hammerhead shark, *Sphyrna*. The animal's eyes are carried on the two opposite ends of the hammer-shaped snout. Unlike most sharks, hammerheads do not have spiracles.

Below: A giant manta ray, *Manta birostris*, flaps its way through the water. Mantas can have a 'wingspan' of as much as 7 m (23 ft) and reach a weight of two tonnes. They swim along with their mouths held wide open to catch small fish and crustaceans. Mantas are sometimes seen to leap right out of the water, landing back on the surface with a slap that can be heard from a distance of a mile or more. This behaviour may be an attempt to dislodge parasitic crustaceans.

Transworld

Okapia

Left: A series of diagrams to show how a manta ray swims along by flapping its huge pectoral fins.

Below: A blue-spotted stingray, *Taeniura lymna*. These animals reach a length of about two metres (six feet) and they inhabit the coastal waters of the Indian and Pacific oceans. The whip-like tail carries a sharp spine with a poison gland at its base. It is used by the ray as a defensive weapon and can cause severe injury and prolonged illness in man: the spine often breaks off and remains in the wound. Their flattened bodies and back markings equip rays for life on the ocean floor. They feed mainly on invertebrates such as mussels and snails.

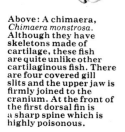

Above: A chimaera, *Chimaera monstrosa*. Although they have skeletons made of cartilage, these fish are quite unlike other cartilaginous fish. There are four covered gill slits and the upper jaw is firmly joined to the cranium. At the front of the first dorsal fin is a sharp spine which is highly poisonous.

Even the fiercest of sharks do not always attack. Their moods are difficult to predict. The fact that attacks by sharks on humans have tended to increase in recent years has much more to do with changes in human behaviour than that of the sharks. Skindiving in warm waters provides sharks with tempting targets. In cooler waters, such as those around Britain's coasts, man-eating sharks are not found.

Skates and rays

Skates and rays belong to the order *Rajiformes*. In structure they are very similar to sharks, but they are even more flattened, with wing-like pectoral fins merging smoothly with the sides of the body. This flattened shape enables the animal to lie on the sea bed without being seen and also helps in swimming. Rays can glide through the water in much the same way that paper darts fly through the air. Some, like the thornback ray, *Raja clavata*, found along the Atlantic coasts of Europe feed on shrimps and other crustaceans, while the huge manta ray *Manta birostris*, flaps its way through the surface waters of the Atlantic feeding on plankton. The sawfish *Pristis pectinatus*, of tropical seas, kills fish for food by flailing its long toothed snout from side to side.

Rays usually avoid predators by remaining concealed on the sea bottom, but they are often well equipped to protect themselves if attacked. Electric rays are capable of delivering a severe electric shock to any potential assailant, and the mechanism is also used to disable prey. The most common of these animals is the eyed electric ray, *Torpedo torpedo*, found in the eastern Atlantic and the Mediterranean. Stingrays have poison spines which can inflict deep wounds and break off to remain in the attacker's body. In man such an injury is extremely painful and can lead to an illness lasting many weeks.

The guitar fish, *Rhinobatos rhinobatos*, looks rather like a combination between a ray and a shark. The front part of the body is flattened like that of a ray, but the tail is fairly thick and carries fins like a shark's tail. The animal is found in the eastern Atlantic and in the Mediterranean living in shallow coastal waters. It feeds on invertebrates which live on the sea bed and can therefore cause considerable damage to oyster beds.

Unlike most bony fishes, sharks, dogfish, rays and skates produce relatively few eggs. These are fertilized inside the mother's body, and in a few cases the eggs are retained inside the mother's body until they emerge as live young. In most species, however, the large yolky eggs are laid in a horny egg-case. When empty these are sometimes washed ashore to be picked up by holiday makers who call them 'mermaids' purses'.

Chimaeras

The chimaeras or ratfishes are also cartilaginous fish, but they are placed in a subclass of their own, the *Bradyodonti*, because they differ from elasmobranchs in a number of ways. In particular, the upper jaw is fixed firmly to the cranium. They have flattened, grinding teeth, feed on small fish and invertebrates, and never attain any great size. Although they are found throughout the world, there are only about 25 living species of chimaeras. Unlike their larger relatives they are weak swimmers.

Allan Power/Bruce Coleman

Rays, like sharks and dogfish, belong to the sub-class *Elasmobranchii*. They have skeletons of cartilage, not hard bone, and their separate gill slits open directly on to the body surface.

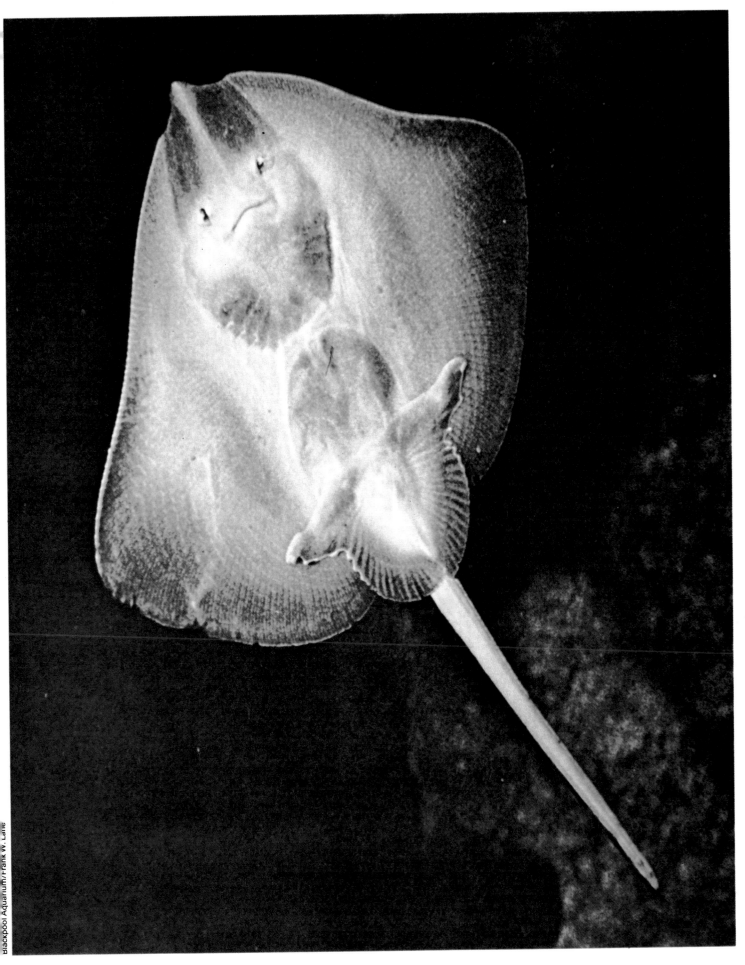

Lungfish and Sturgeons

Almost all the bony fish living today belong to a single group, the superorder *Teleostei*. There are, however, a few bony fish which cannot be classified with the rest and these are interesting because they help us to understand what the bony fish of the past were like. They all branched off from the evolutionary tree before the teleosts developed.

Lungfish and coelacanths

Perhaps the most interesting of all are the lungfish and the coelacanths which belong to the subclass *Sarcopterygii*. The discovery of living coelacanths was one of the most surprising events in the history of zoology because although similar freshwater fish were known to scientists as fossils, in the absence of any other evidence they were believed to have died out over 100 million years ago. The appearance of a dead, but only recently killed, specimen in a South African fish market in 1938 was therefore a total surprise. Little but the skin on this coelacanth was recovered to be examined by zoologists, but it stimulated a great coelacanth hunt after the war. About 100 specimens have now been caught in deep water in the Indian Ocean, and one of these actually lived for some days after capture, so that its appearance and behaviour could be observed while it was alive. Live coelacanths are mostly greyish-blue, but the colour fades rapidly once they are dead.

One of the reasons that coelacanths remained undiscovered for so long is that they only inhabit a small area of the Indian ocean around the Comores Islands north of Madagascar. The first specimen to be caught was almost certainly a stray; it was probably carried to the South African coast by the strong currents in the Mozambique channel. Although relatively new to science, coelacanths have long been known to the natives of the Comores under the name *kombessa*.

Coelacanths, *Latimeria*, are large, deep bodied fishes with three-lobed tails. The largest caught so far weighed 92 kg (180 lb). The paired lungs (or swim-bladders) are small, for coelacanths breathe by means of gills, but the paired pectoral and pelvic fins are remarkable.

They have fleshy, muscular bases inside each of which there is one thick, long bone near the body, and two similar bones a little further out. Although the remainder of the bones in the fins are small, these large bones clearly correspond to those in the limbs of land vertebrates, where one bone in the upper arm or leg is followed by two in the forearm or shin. A coelacanth is therefore the nearest thing there is to a fish with true limbs.

Only a few mature female coelacanths have been caught, and they are remarkable for the size of their eggs. The eggs measure about 9 cm (3.5 in) across and weigh as much as 320 g (11 oz). They are unprotected by shells or cases.

The distantly related lungfish have equally unusual features. For example, although they are undoubtedly vertebrates they never have bony vertebrae, but retain the main girder of vertebrate embryos, the *notochord*, throughout adult life. In this respect they resemble some of the sturgeons. In both cases the absence of vertebrae is a late development; the ancestors of both groups possessed perfectly well developed backbones. Lungfish have fleshy bases to their paired fins, but the fins' skeletons are not limb-like; only in their position on the heavily built, almost newt-like body do they hint at the limbs of land vertebrates.

Lungfish have hollow lungs opening on to the ventral surface of the gullet. Their walls are well supplied with blood vessels so that respiration can take place. There are six species of lungfish—one in Australia, *Neoceratodus*, one in South America, *Lepidosiren*, and four closely related species, *Protopterus*, in tropical Africa. The Australian lungfish live in

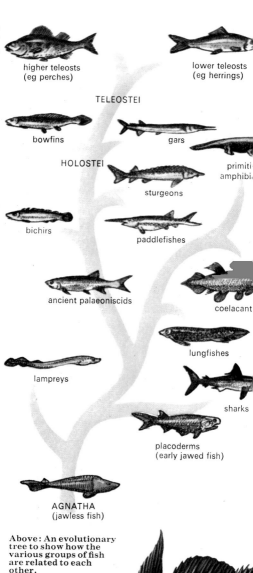

higher teleosts (eg perches)

lower teleosts (eg herrings)

TELEOSTEI

bowfins

gars

HOLOSTEI

primiti amphibi

sturgeons

bichirs

paddlefishes

ancient palaeoniscids

coelacant

lungfishes

lampreys

sharks

placoderms (early jawed fish)

AGNATHA (jawless fish)

Above: An evolutionary tree to show how the various groups of fish are related to each other.

Left: A preserved specimen of a coelacanth, *Latimeria chalumnae*. These fish are found on the sloping sea floor around the Comores Islands in the Indian ocean near Madagascar.

COELACANTH

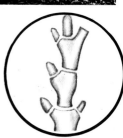

Near right: The bones of a coelacanth's pectoral fin resemble those in the limb of a land vertebrate.

Below: Three or four coelacanths are now caught each year off the Comores. They live at a depth of about 200 m (650 ft) and feed mainly on other vertebrate fish and cuttlefish.

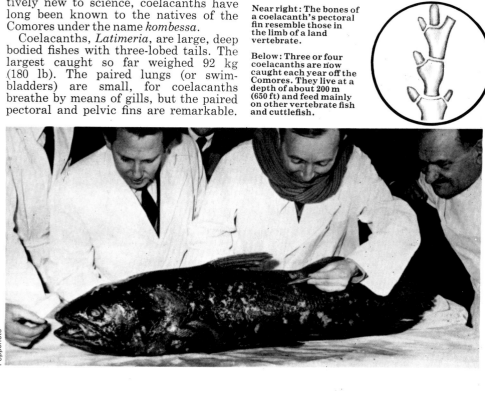

Left: An Australian lungfish, *Neoceratodus forsteri*. Lungfish have lung-like bladders for respiration. Coelacanths differ from other bony fish in having nostrils which are not blind alleys but lead through into the mouth. Their ancestors lay on the evolutionary line which led to the first amphibians.

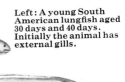

30 days

40 days

Left: A young South American lungfish aged 30 days and 40 days. Initially the animal has external gills.

Left: To survive a drought the African lungfish, *Protopterus*, builds itself a 'cocoon' in the mud. It can survive for several years in this condition because its swim bladder is well equipped with blood vessels and so acts as an efficient lung. The Australian lungfish cannot survive out of water for long.

the Burnett and Saint Mary Rivers of Queensland, which never completely dry up, but are sometimes shallow and choked with decaying vegetation, and therefore short of oxygen. Under these conditions the lungfish's gills are useless and it surfaces to take air into its single lung through its mouth. At other times it has no need to breathe air.

The South American lungfish has paired lungs and only small gills. At all seasons it must breathe at least some air. When the Amazon tributaries in which it lives dry out it survives by burrowing in the mud, and breathing only air. Similarly, the African lungfish build themselves muddy cocoons during the dry season, and are capable of surviving several months without water.

Bichirs and sturgeons

These bony fish belong to the superorder *Chondrostei*. They have fins with fan-like bony rays, and are in fact more closely related to the teleosts than to the lungfishes or coelacanths. The bichirs and the more slender but related reed fish, about 12 species in all, are found only in fresh water in Africa. They have some features reminiscent of the coelacanths and lungfishes. For example, they have paired lungs and can breathe air, and have rather fleshy bases to their paired fins. Their scales are thick, do not overlap and contain *ganoin*, a hard enamel-like substance. Bichirs and reed fish row themselves along with their large pectoral fins in search of insects and small vertebrates. Their dorsal fins are broken up into rows of small flag-like fins.

The sturgeons probably branched off from the main evolutionary line shortly

after the bichirs. There are 20 or so species and in some ways they resemble the sharks. For example, their skeletons are largely made up of cartilage, they have spreading wing-like pectoral fins and tails whose upper lobe is conspicuously larger than the lower. These shark-like features are not the result of a close relationship, but to the separate evolution of similar answers to the same problem. Like the sharks, sturgeon are heavier than water, and have the same need of a light skeleton and of a shape that provides lift as it passes through the water. Much less shark-like are the sturgeons' five gill openings covered by an operculum, large thick scales and toothless jaws.

All sturgeons live in temperate parts of the northern hemisphere. Some species live only in rivers, while others live in the shallow seas, entering rivers only to breed. They feed on invertebrates which they find at the bottom of the water. The largest sturgeon is the Russian beluga, *Huso huso*, which can grow to be nearly 9 m (30 ft) long. They are caught by man for their roes, which are prized as caviar, their meat, and their inefficient swimbladders, from which *isinglass*, a glue, is obtained. The paddlefishes are related to them and have even flatter, more paddle-shaped snouts, used for digging in the mud of river beds. There are only two species, one in the Mississippi and its tributaries, and the other from the Yangtse Kiang in China.

The American paddlefish, *Polyodon spathula*, has a body shaped rather like that of a shark and indeed the first naturalists to observe the animal, in the early 1800's, described it as a shark. For many years large numbers were caught

Frank Lane

Above: An African lungfish, *Protopterus*. The ancestors of coelacanths and lungfishes flourished over 300 million years ago. They had simple swim bladders which were hollow out-growths from the gullet into the body space. These bladders did not do much to improve buoyancy but they could be used as lungs. These early fish also had paired pectoral and pelvic lobe-fins in the same position as the fore and hind limbs of the first four-legged land animals.

Left: A series of diagrams to show how an African lungfish moves along the bottom.

Right: Three genera of lungfish survive today in Africa, South America and Australia.

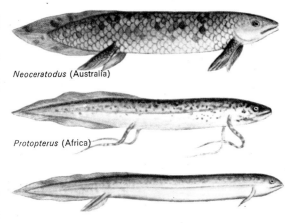

Neoceratodus (Australia)

Protopterus (Africa)

Lepidosiren (S America)

357

each year in the USA for their meat and their roe which was made into caviar. In the 1920's the yearly catch was as much as 1000 tonnes. Nowadays paddlefish are much less common and they have little or no commercial importance.

Bowfins and garpike

The holosteans (of the superorder *Holostei*) are a group of fish closer to the mainstream of teleost evolution. Indeed, the first teleosts evolved from holostean ancestors about 150 million years ago and, as the teleosts became more successful and numerous, they competed with their parent group, almost driving it to extinction. Only two families of holosteans now remain, both living in fresh water in North America. At first glance the living holosteans (there are seven species of garpike and one species of bowfin) look very much like teleosts. However, a closer look at a holostean's tail tells another story. Although superficially symmetrical, with the upper lobe as large as the lower, the tail is really asymmetrical like that of the sturgeons and sharks. The muscular tail end of the body is surrounded by the upper lobe of the tail fin. Like bichirs, the holosteans have thick scales containing ganoin. The scales do not overlap, and those of the garpike are hinged together, so as to provide protection whilst retaining flexibility. So effective is this armour that the harpoons of skindivers usually glance off without harming the fish. Beneath their jaws bowfins have unusual, large bony plates.

Like some of the early teleosts, holosteans have swimbladders which open externally through the throat and mouth. Internally these swim bladders are divided up into compartments, the walls of which have a rich blood supply, and they therefore make reasonably efficient respiratory organs. All living holosteans breathe air to some extent, and bowfins can survive out of water for many hours. A swimbladder cannot, however, be equally efficient when serving both as a lung and a buoyancy chamber. Lungs must gain and lose air, but for buoyancy

P. Morris/Ardea

Above: A bichir, *Polypterus*, from West Africa. These fish live in muddy, poorly aerated water. Their gills are backed up by a swim bladder which can act as a lung. Like lungfish they can survive periods of drought by digging into the mud.

Above right: A reedfish, *Calamoichthys*.

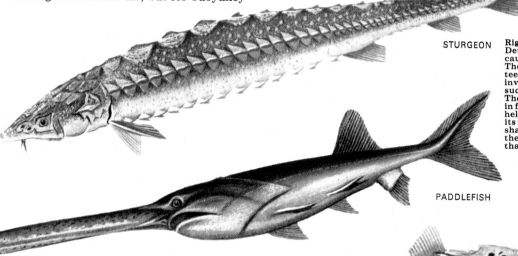

STURGEON

Right and below right: Details of the mouth and caudal fin of a sturgeon. The adult fish has no teeth and feeds on small invertebrates which it sucks up off the bottom. The four sensory barbels in front of the mouth help the animal to locate its food. As in most sharks, the upper lobe of the tail fin is smaller than the lower one.

PADDLEFISH

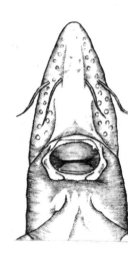

Above: An Atlantic sturgeon, *Acipenser sturio*, an American paddlefish, *Polyodon spathula*, and a shovel nosed sturgeon, *Scaphirhynchus*. The strange looking paddlefish was once common along the Mississippi and in the Great Lakes but its numbers are now dwindling rapidly.

SHOVEL-NOSED STURGEON

a constant volume of air is better. The position in the water of a garpike varies according to the state of its swimbladder. When it has just inhaled air the fish may be just under the surface, with its dorsal fin protruding slightly. A little later it may be hanging weightless in the middle of the water. The loss of only a little more air from either the mouth or the gill opening will then cause it to sink to the bottom.

After spawning, the young of both bowfins and garpike are guarded by the adult males. The young fish cling to water weeds by means of suckers on their foreheads. It seems that these suckers evolved at an early stage because both have similar structures.

Bowfins are found in rivers and lakes of the eastern United States. They grow to be up to one metre (three feet) long. They feed on insects, other invertebrates and smaller fish. Although they can swim quite rapidly in the same way as most other fish, rippling their bodies from side to side and from front to back, for much of the time they move more slowly, rippling only the single long dorsal fin.

Garpike (or gars) are fiercer predators than bowfins. Sometimes they seize other fish with a lazy side-swipe of their long, needle-toothed jaws, but more often they lie in wait to surprise their prey with a short, fast spurt. Their muscular bodies are well adapted for this kind of activity. The dorsal and anal fins are near the tail end of the body so that they can assist the tail fin in providing propulsion. Apart from the garpike's longer fish-eating jaws, its outline is remarkably similar to that of the European pike which, being a teleost, is not at all closely related. The longnose gar, *Lepisosteus osseus*, has the most exaggerated jaws, and lives in the Mississippi and its tributaries. The largest of the group is the giant alligator garpike, *Lepisosteus spatula*, of Mexico, which may grow to be 4 m (12 ft) long. Garpike are found from southern Canada to Panama (although never to the west of the Rocky Mountains) and some species even live for a time in salt water.

Below: A longnose gar, *Lepisosteus osseus*. This North American fish catches its prey by snapping its long thin jaws in much the same way as an alligator. The needle-sharp teeth hold the victim until it is swallowed by the gar. Longnose gars are found in still, shallow water where they can lie in wait for their prey.

Left: A male bowfin stands guard over its offspring protecting them from the attention of predators.

Below: A bowfin, *Amia calva*, from North America. Bowfins and gars have lunglike swim bladders which help in respiration. This is important when oxygen levels are low.

LONG-NOSED GAR

Teleost Fish

There are about 20,000 species of fish within the group known as teleosts. This is almost as many as the total number of species of birds and mammals, but it is not really a surprising number since most living bony fish belong to this group. Indeed, as three-quarters of the earth's surface is covered by water it may seem more surprising that there are not more teleost species. However, because any successful species can have a very wide distribution, limited only by the availability of food and suitable water conditions, the need to evolve separate species has been less critical than for land-based animals.

Swimming

The characteristic features of teleosts include flattened overlapping scales, fins which are strengthened by jointed fan-like rays, and strong but flexible, bony skeletons. The swim-bladder, which first evolved as a lung-like outgrowth from the gullet, tends to be used for buoyancy rather than respiration. In many teleosts it has lost its primitive connection with the gullet and is completely sealed off inside the body.

In these circumstances the only way that gas can enter the swim-bladder is via the bloodstream of the fish—an efficient but rather slow process. However, the amount of gas in the swim-bladder only needs to change slowly to keep a teleost weightless in gradually changing environmental conditions. Supported by the swim-bladder, many kinds of teleosts can effortlessly remain suspended in the water. When swimming, they only have to work to propel themselves. Yet in bottom-living teleosts, buoyancy would be a great handicap so the swim-bladder has degenerated so that as soon as they stop swimming they begin to sink.

In swimming, the typical teleost uses segmented muscles to ripple its body from side to side, the bends passing down the body from head to tail. Even in a fish with no fins this action, pushing backwards and sideways against the water, would cause forward movement. Slender, elongated fish, such as eels, tend to swim in this way. In more typically shaped teleosts, however, additional propulsion is provided by the symmetrical tail. Powered by the muscles making up most of the body's weight, the tail sculls from side to side, working as a propeller.

The beautifully streamlined sailfish *Istiophorus* of tropical seas is reputed to be able to reach speeds of about 96 km/h (60 mph) over short distances. However, cold-blooded animals are incapable of keeping up a sustained effort for very long as the vigorous activity tends to raise their body temperature too much. Not that all fish are totally cold-blooded. Despite the fact that a fish's gill system must also be a highly efficient cooling system, the body temperature of large active fish, such as tuna, is normally several degrees above that of the surrounding water. A bluefin tuna *Thunnus thynnus* has been accurately measured swimming at 69.4km/h (43.4 mph).

The lateral, wriggling movements of a teleost when swimming cause the body to tend to yaw or wobble from side to side. To counteract this there are keel-like

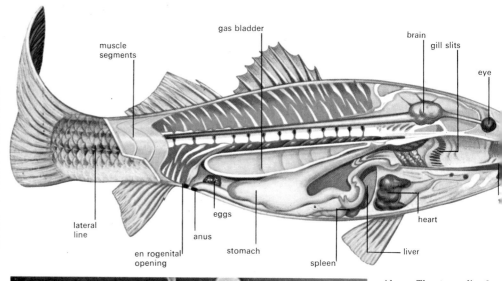

muscle segments — gas bladder — brain — gill slits — eye — lateral line — eggs — anus — en rogenital opening — stomach — spleen — heart — liver

Oxford Scientific Films

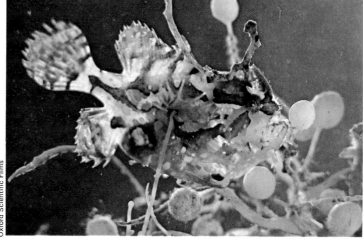

Grossa/Jacana

Above: The streamlined shape of a striped bass, *Roccus saxatilis*, is ideal for manoeuvrability. Its internal organs fit compactly into the muscular body: it has a swim-bladder for adjusting buoyancy at various depths, and a lateral line vibration-sensing system. The brain is less highly-developed than in other vertebrates.

Above: A striking form of disguise. The small Sargassum fish, *Histrio histrio*, has evolved mottled markings and weed-like filaments that enable it to blend in remarkably well with the masses of seaweed floating in the Sargasso Sea. A member of the highly specialized anglerfish group, it also has a dorsal fishing 'lure'.

Below: A pair of sea-horses, *Hippocampus kuda*, looking for shrimps among coral. They are unique among fish, the head being at right angles to the body. The female lays about 100 eggs which are fertilized by the male and incubated within a pouch on his body for about 50 days until the father gives birth.

Right: Tiny clownfish, *Amphiprion percula*, of the Indo-Pacific seas, spend their lives among the tentacles of sea anemones that capture and eat other fish. How they escape the stinging tentacles is unknown, but it is thought that they may acquire a slime which identifies them to the anemone.

Jane Burton/Bruce Coleman

continental shelf

PLANKTON

continental slope

abyss

SOME COMMON TELEOSTS

1 Seahorse
2 Flying fish
3 Common eel
4 Herring
5 Cod
6 Swordfish
7 Blue fish
8 Halibut
9 Haddock
10 Puffer fish
11 Tuna
12 Flounder
13 Anglerfish
14 Bristlemouth
15 Hatchet fish
16 Lantern fish
17 Deepsea stalkeye

dorsal and ventral or anal fins on the body. The body itself often tends to be flattened from side to side, as an efficient swim-bladder means that there is no need to get lift from a horizontally flattened, aerofoil-shaped body.

In many kinds of teleosts this bilateral flattening has become still more highly exaggerated for other reasons. A fish which is little thicker than an envelope looks insubstantial from the side, and is almost invisible head-on. When lying on one side, flat and shadowless, a fish with this shape can be almost invisible, especially when it can change colour to match the sea-bed. In relatively calm water such a fish can also be very manoeuvrable, cornering swiftly with little tendency to 'skid'. However, in more turbulent water extremely flat sides would be a disadvantage. Furthermore, a very flattened body cannot be as muscular and powerful as a more rounded one. Fast swimmers in open waters, like mackerel, for example, have only slight flattening.

The teleosts' narrow-based and mobile paired fins are used for steering and balancing, especially when swimming at slow speeds. The pectoral fins are always located in the shoulder region, just behind the gill opening which in most teleosts is covered by a bony *operculum*. The paired pelvic fins are usually further back on the body, which is not surprising since they share a common origin with the hind limbs of land-living vertebrates. However, unlike most land animals, fish have no need of support at each corner of the body, and during the course of evolution the pelvic fins of many kinds of fish have moved forward, until in many species they are as near to the head as the pectoral fins.

Above right: The plankton floating in the upper sea is a rich food source for many fish. It consists of tiny plants, one drop of water contains about 500, and small animals: shrimp-like copepods, fish eggs and larvae. Plankton eaters swim with their mouths open and the plankton is strained from the water by gill rakers, attached to the gill arch, and the water flows out through the gill slits.

Left: Many deepsea fish can swallow very large prey. To do this the Viper fish *Chauliodus* swings its hinged jaws forward and upward. Adaptations for the dark depths include huge eyes to see better and light-organs for identifying themselves and also seeing prey.

Oxford Scientific Films

361

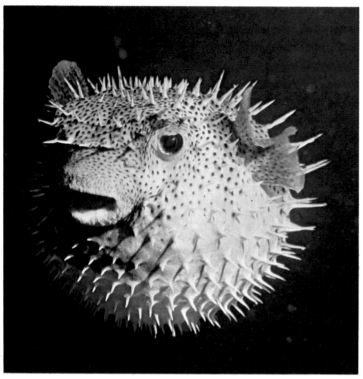

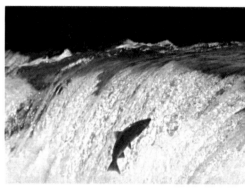

Left: When on the defensive, a porcupine fish, *Diodon hystrix*, inflates its body with water or air, so erecting its spines. Normally the spines, which are modified scales, lie flat against the body.

Right: After spending 3 or 4 years in the sea, the adult salmon 'run' up the rivers to their spawning grounds in swift, shallow streams. The male scoops out a nest, or *redd*, in the gravel using his tail, and the female lays the eggs in the hollow. The male then fertilizes them and covers them with gravel. Time taken to hatch ranges from 5 weeks to 5 months, depending on water temperature. They grow into *parr*, then *smolts* which migrate down to the sea.

Right: Trout eggs and newly hatched larvae, or *alevins*. They have their own food supply in the form of a yolk-sac, which hangs below.

Not all teleosts are conventional swimmers. Some, such as the electric eel of South American rivers, do not ripple the entire body, but merely a long fin which runs along the under-surface of the body. Fish of the wrasse family, which live in rocky coastal waters, only ripple their bodies when they are in a hurry. When swimming more slowly they row themselves along with their large pectoral fins. If the tail is not used as a propeller, it makes a superb rudder, and wrasse steer their way into and out of rocky crevices with great skill.

Fish whose bodies are covered with armoured scales naturally tend to have rather rigid bodies. When swimming they rapidly wave all their fins except the tail fin. Swimming in this way, with the moving dorsal fin as the most obvious means of propulsion, puffer fish look rather like tiny aquatic helicopters. Seahorses necessarily swim in a similar way as they have no tail fin, the tail being adapted as an organ for clinging. They are not streamlined and swim only slowly.

Some teleosts are not confined to swimming. For example, eels sometimes wriggle their way overland as they migrate. Mudskippers walk across the damp mud of coastal mangrove swamps, using their pectoral fins as limbs. Flying fish swim at speed near the surface of the sea until, emerging from the water, they can take off, gliding for some distance with their huge pectoral fins spread out as wings. The little hatchet fish of South America actually flap their wings as they move through the air. They are the only fish capable of powered flight.

Sense organs
In finding their way about teleosts make use of a variety of senses. Most have good eyesight. Their lidless unblinking eyes each have an almost totally separate field of vision on either side of the body. Fish can usually see both detail and colour, although never at very great distance, for even the clearest water is cloudier than air. Because of their good eyesight many teleosts are adapted to

signal to each other when courting or defending their territory. And to enhance their built-in visual signals many teleosts are beautifully coloured.

Teleosts' nostrils are blind alleys, concerned not with breathing, but only with picking up chemical stimuli from the water. They work well, being especially efficient in those species with relatively poor eyesight.

Sound travels well in water and, in spite of their lack of external ears, most fish have very keen hearing; many species use auditory signals when communicating with their own kind. Connected to the same nerves as the ear is the lateral line—a sense organ often visible as a line along the side of a fish's body. This line is extremely sensitive to pressure changes caused by vibrations from another fish or from proximity to some other object. The blind cave characin lives in pitch-black underground lakes, but avoids all obstacles when it is swimming by using its lateral lines. As an alternative, many kinds of teleosts, like catfish, living in rather muddy water have *barbels*—long sensitive feelers on their mouths.

Electric organs
Another means of navigating in murky water is provided by the electric organs of some teleosts, such as the South American eels, and others. It may seem surprising that an animal is able to make electricity but, in fact, all animals are a kind of power station taking in chemical energy in the form of food and, as a result of respiration, liberating some other form of energy such as mechanical energy or heat. The production of electricity is no more amazing than the production of movement by muscles. The two processes are broadly similar and, indeed, electric organs are formed from modified muscles.

Electric fish send pulses of low voltage electricity into the surrounding water. Some of the current is picked up by receptors on the body of the fish. Obstacles in the water change the strength of this current, and the fish is therefore able to detect their presence. When threatened

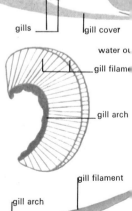

water in

gills — gill cover

Above and right: Respiration in fish is designed to obtain oxygen and remove carbon dioxide, but from water rather than air. The horizontal section of the head shows how water enters the mouth, passes over the gills and leaves from behind the operculum or gill cover. Each gill consists of two flaps fixed to a bony gill arch. The gills contain a network of blood capillaries where the exchange of gases occurs.

Far right: A young pike, *Esox lucius*. Short anal and dorsal fins set far back are typical of predators that lie in wait, then dash out.

water out

gill filament

gill arch

gill filament

gill arch

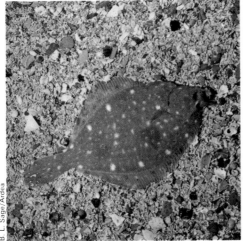

Left: The development of the plaice, *Pleuronectes platessa*. Shown here, at the top of the page, is an egg, shortly before hatching, several larval stages and the bottom-living adult. The early larval stage looks like other fish, but during development the skull starts to twist until eventually it turns right round so that both eyes lie on one side of the fish. Changes also occur in the fins but the mouth and internal organs remain in the usual position. Adults merge well with the sea-bed.

Right: The darker markings on this angelfish, *Euxiphipops*, help to break up its shape and conceal it from predators.

Sargasso Sea

Above, left and above right: The map shows the migration of freshwater eels from Europe and N. America to where they spawn and die in the Sargasso Sea. The eggs hatch into tiny larvae which are leaf-like, transparent and only about 0.5 cm long. These rise to the surface to feed on plankton. They gradually drift across the seas with the currents to the coasts. When the larvae reach the mouths of the streams and rivers they change into elvers (see left), which are small white versions of the adult form (above right). The elvers ascend the rivers where they grow into adults and remain for eight years before returning to the sea.

the electric eel is able to produce a much stronger electric impulse of several hundred volts as a defence mechanism. Exactly how it can do so without electrocuting itself is not clear. To some extent its nervous system is insulated by fatty tissue, and it produces currents which tend to flow across the main nerves instead of along them, which would be more damaging, but this cannot be the entire explanation.

Types of teleosts

Altogether there are 30 living orders of teleosts, containing a vast range of species. For example, the heaviest teleost is the widely distributed ocean sunfish, which can weigh well over a tonne, while the smallest of all fully-grown vertebrates is the dwarf pygmy goby from lakes in the Philippine Islands. Males of this species are smaller than the females and only about 7.6 mm (0.3 inches) long.

The largest single order of teleosts contains the perch and its relatives. Perch are carnivorous, feeding on other fish, as well as aquatic insects, but the order also includes the mackerel, a sea-living scavenger, and the discus fish, a beautiful South American fresh water species, popular with aquarium keepers.

Another order contains the bony flatfish like the soles, plaice and turbots. Most of these lie on their left sides, having both eyes on the right side of the body. However, the flounder, another member of this group, lies on its right side. Cod and their relatives form another order, many species of which are of great importance as human food. About 400 million cod are caught annually by trawlermen and the point has now been reached where cod, together with other species extensively fished, must be harvested more intelligently by man. It is not true that there are more fish in the sea than ever came out of it. This caution applies equally to the herrings and their relatives, members of another order, which tend to live in huge shoals near the surface of the sea or of freshwater lakes. The marine forms are particularly vulnerable to overfishing as

363

Above: The Red piranha, *Rooseveltialla natterei,* **is often kept as an aquarium fish in spite of its reputation. Piranhas are small South American freshwater fish, renowned for their carnivorous habits. They have powerful jaws which are armed with sharp teeth. Their diet is mainly fish or small mammals.**

Right: The exotic Zebra fish, *Pterois radiata,* **a mass of fins and spines. Its unmistakable markings warn would-be attackers to stay clear as the spines contain a poison which is more deadly than cobra venom and very painful. The lion fish, a member of the scorpion fish family, is usually found gliding along fearlessly in tropical seas.**

Below: Also belonging to the scorpion fish family, but even deadlier, is the Stonefish, *Synanceja verrucosa.* **It has 13 dorsal, 3 anal and 2 pelvic spines, all equipped with venom glands. The spines are hollow like hypodermic needles. The stonefish resembles an algae-covered rock—an excellent camouflage.**

not only are mature fish taken but also millions of young, which are fried as whitebait.

The most successful order of freshwater fish includes the carp, goldfish and their relations, the characins of tropical America and Africa. The latter group includes many fish popular in aquariums, such as the colourful little tetras and the carnivorous South American piranha, and the electric eel. Other contrasting orders contain the scavenging catfish, the salmon and trout, the tiny pufferfish, huge ocean sunfish and colourful triggerfish, and the predatory anglerfish. These 'anglers' lurk on the sea bed and use their modified dorsal finray lures to attract other fish towards their huge jaws.

Breeding habits
The breeding habits of teleosts vary as much as their life styles. Some anglerfish of the deep sea provide an extreme example. Presumably to overcome the difficulty the sexes might have in locating each other in the dark, the tiny males have evolved so as to become parasitic on the females, anchored by their mouths with their blood system permanently fused to that of their larger mates. Equally surprising is the species of bass in which all individuals begin their lives as males, but later undergo a natural sex change to become females.

In most teleosts, however, the breeding pattern is more conventional; the females lay numerous small eggs and these are fertilized externally by the males. These small eggs are familiar to us as fish roe. In the ovary or hard roe of a female herring each tiny sphere is an egg. If herring stocks are to remain constant, each parent must be replaced. Although on average only two eggs from each female will reach maturity, this should be enough to maintain stocks. Even so the tiny developing young of many marine species float planktonically, and most are doomed never to reach maturity.

Teleosts such as the salmon and eels make long migrations before breeding. Migration from fresh to salt water or vice versa, however, is not an easy process and is beyond most fishes. Marine fish constantly lose water to their salty environment, and have to 'drink like fish' in order to stay alive, excreting the excess salt imbibed in the process. Freshwater fish tend to gain water from their environment, and need kidneys capable of removing excess water as fast as it arrives. Therefore to swim from fresh to salt water or the reverse calls for a complex and highly adapted physiological make-up.

Once the eggs are laid and fertilized most kinds of teleosts leave them to their fate. In a few cases, however, a degree of parental care has evolved. By increasing their survival chances, fewer eggs need be produced. In the African mouth-breeders the male keeps the eggs in his mouth until they are hatched, and the young return to this refuge when threatened. Among the most remarkable of all fish parents are the South American discus fish. In this species both parents guard the eggs and transfer the newly hatched young with their mouths to suitable surfaces which act as nurseries for the first few days. The young discus then swim to the parents to feed on a special nourishing mucus produced by their skins; feeding continues until they are over a month old.

The tiny puffer fish
(*Diodon holocanthus*) is
armoured by its scales
and static tail fin. When
attacked it reacts as
does the porcupine fish.
(See page 362.)

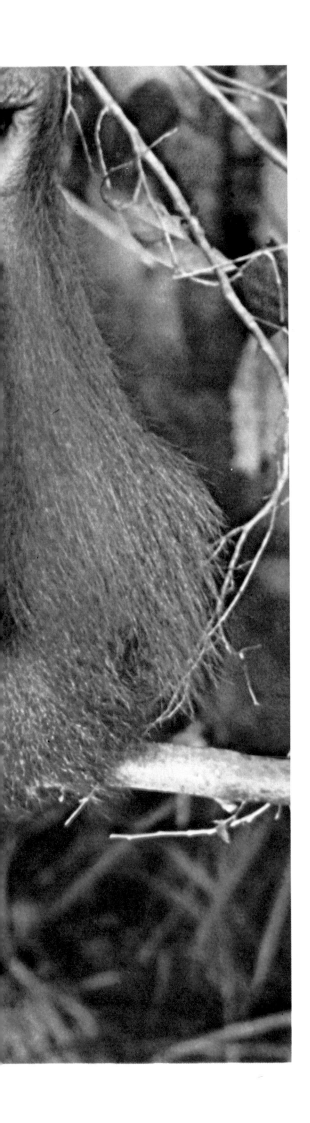

Chapter 4
The Primates

An Orang-utan family. Offspring are
usually born one at a time, after a
gestation period of 8 to 9 months,
average weight at birth being 3.3lbs.

The Lower Primates

In the mid eighteenth century when the great Swedish naturalist Carl von Linné first arranged animals and plants into phyla (the major divisions of the animal and plant kingdoms), orders, families and so on, he recognized that man belonged with a group of animals which he called the *primates*. The most familiar members of this order are the monkeys, the apes and of course man himself, but there are a number of less familiar creatures, including tree shrews, lemurs, lorises and bushbabies, which are also primates. They are often referred to as 'lower primates' and fall into a sub-order of their own, the *Prosimiae*.

The lower primates range in size from that of a mouse to that of a dog. They generally have soft woolly fur, pointed faces and large eyes. Some members of the group, such as the tree shrews, resemble insectivores while others look more like monkeys. These likenesses are not just superficial; tree shrews are still classified with the insectivores (the order which includes hedgehogs, moles and shrews) by some zoologists, and the internal structure of lemurs is remarkably like that of some monkeys. Among other typically primate features possessed by most prosimians are nails on most fingers and toes, the ability to grasp objects by opposing the thumb (or big

G. Cubitt/Bruce Coleman

Left: One of the most common lemurs is the ring-tailed lemur, *Lemur catta*. In the wild it feeds primarily on fig thistles, figs and bananas, these providing most, if not all, of its water requirements. Like all lemurs it is a native of Madagascar. Being easy to keep it is a popular zoo animal.

Above: Black lemurs, *Lemur macaco*, in a forest clearing on the island of Nossi Komba, off the coast of Madagascar. They are very agile animals and can cover 8 m (26 ft) or more with a single leap. These particular animals are males—females have pale brown fur with a ruff of white hair around the head.

Below: Verreaux's sifaka, *Propithecus verreauxi*, is another Madagascan prosimian. Sifakas are most active in the middle of the day when they leap from tree to tree searching for food—mainly fruit, blossoms and leaves. Sometimes they are seen on the ground, walking erect or hopping about like a kangaroo.

N. Myers/Bruce Coleman

N. Myers/Bruce Coleman

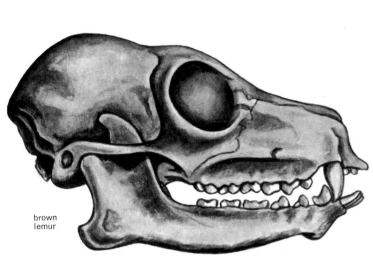

brown lemur

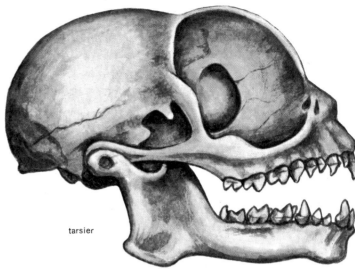

tarsier

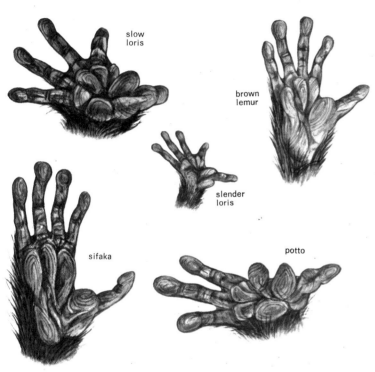

slow loris

brown lemur

slender loris

sifaka

potto

Left: The ability of lower primates to grip objects between thumb and finger is reflected in the structure of their hands. The thumb is positioned apart from the remaining four digits. Slow-moving creatures like the lorises and the potto have very widely splayed hands and reduced second fingers.

Above left: The skull of an adult brown lemur, *Lemur fulvus*. The bony ring around the eye socket, a typically primate feature, is clearly visible.

Above: The skull of an adult tarsier, *Tarsius*. It is relatively deep because it has to accommodate the animal's enormous eyes.

Below: A common tree shrew, *Tupaia glis*, from South-East Asia. Although they are now recognized by most zoologists as primates, tree shrews show clear affinities with some insectivores, especially the elephant shrews. Tree shrews feed on insects, small animals such as mice and frogs, and some fruit.

P. Morris

toe) and a finger (or toe), a bony ring surrounding the eye sockets and, in the brain, a large occipital lobe, the part responsible for vision.

Lemurs

There are three families of lemurs: the true lemurs, *Lemuridae*, the indris or woolly lemurs, *Indridae*, and the aye-ayes, *Daubentonidae*. One of the most curious things about these creatures is their geographical distribution—they are found only on the island of Madagascar where they occupy the same ecological niches as their relatives the monkeys, lorises and bushbabies on the African mainland.

The lemurs are probably descended from a group of early prosimians which travelled south from Europe and Asia to Africa, India and South-East Asia in the early Tertiary period about 65 million years ago. At that time some animals crossed into Madagascar, either by way of a narrow land bridge or, perhaps more likely, on clumps of floating vegetation. Later a second group of early primates migrated southwards but this time they did not cross into Madagascar, reaching only as far as the African coast. This second group of migrants developed into the monkeys and apes we know today,

displacing the mainland-dwellers of the first group (ancestors of the bushbabies and lorises) from much of their original range. The inhabitants of Madagascar, however, were undisturbed by these newcomers and evolved in isolation to become the lemurs.

Most lemurs have bright, distinctively marked coats and long bushy tails, and many species have 'ruffs' of longer hair extending from beneath the chin to the ears. They are quite small animals, none being larger than a cat, and their arms are considerably longer than their legs. Like monkeys, they are expert climbers and spend much of their time in trees searching for fruit, which constitutes the major part of their diet.

One of the more common lemurs is the ring-tailed lemur, *Lemur catta*. Its coat is predominantly grey with white areas on the inside of the legs, and its head has pronounced black and white markings—notably black patches around the eyes. Whereas most lemurs are forest-dwellers, ring-tailed lemurs prefer dry rocky country with relatively few trees, and they can climb steep rock walls with great agility. They are territorial animals, and mark prominent objects within their home range with strong-smelling sec-

retions from glands on the inside of the lower arm, on the upper arm and around the anus. Like many lemurs they enjoy sunbathing with their arms and legs spread out.

Ring-tailed lemurs are quite easy to keep in zoos and breed readily: they are most content when kept in large groups. Gentle lemurs, *Hapalemur*, also adapt well to life in captivity. Like most lemurs they are nocturnal creatures and can be caught without difficulty when asleep during the day. When kept as house pets in Madagascar they soon change their lifestyle and become active in the day rather than at night.

The largest true lemur is the ruffed lemur, *Lemur variegatus*, from northern Madagascar. The colour and marking of its coat varies widely from one individual to another, but most of them have black feet and hands, a black tail and a predominantly black face. The body pattern can vary from evenly coloured brown to strongly marked black and white. The ruffed lemur, like many other species of lemurs, is threatened with extinction: its forest habitat is being destroyed for timber and to make way for cultivation, and during the day the ruffed lemur is an easy target for the hunter. The smallest

Left: One of the rarest Madagascan primates is the aye-aye, *Daubentonia madagascariensis*. Beetle larvae, which live under the bark of trees, form a major part of this creature's diet and it has developed a remarkable technique for catching them. The aye-aye knocks on the bark of a tree until it hears either the characteristic hollow sound of the tunnels or the movement of the larvae themselves. Then it bites through the bark with its incisors and extracts the larvae with its long middle fingers.

Above right: The skull of an aye-aye. The teeth are unusual, being more like those of a rodent than a primate: long, continuously growing incisors, large molars but no canines.

Right: The lesser mouse lemur, *Microcebus murinus*, is the smallest of all the primates. It is known to feed mainly on insects, but because it is nocturnal and lives high in the trees little more has been discovered about its life in the wild. In captivity two or three young are born after a pregnancy of 60 days.

N. Myers/Bruce Coleman

lemur is the dwarf mouse lemur, *Microcebus murinus*, which is only 25 cm (10 in) long from nose to tail. It lives high in the trees where it builds a nest looking rather like a bird's nest.

The woolly lemurs are the sole survivors of a group of large prosimians which once lived in Madagascar. The skull of one extinct swamp-dwelling genus was almost the size of a horse's head. Until man arrived they had virtually no enemies on the island and so they flourished, but today the largest species, the indri, *Indri indri*, is no bigger than a dog. It is nevertheless the largest of all living lower primates.

Apart from its large size and the fact that it is almost tailless, the indri resembles other lemurs. It has large eyes, a pointed snout and well-developed thumbs and big toes. Indris live in trees, either alone or in small groups, and they feed mainly on leaves. They are said to be the loudest of all lemurs, emitting ear-splitting howls to mark their territories.

The sifakas, *Propithecus*, and the woolly indri, *Avahis laniger*, also belong to the family *Indridae*. The sifakas are agile tree-dwelling animals which feed on leaves and fruit. They are capable of leaping considerable distances (up to

370

10 m, 33 ft) from one tree to the next.

The aye-aye, *Daubentonia madagascariensis*, is a curious-looking animal which lives mainly in thickets of bamboo in eastern Madagascar. It is a long-haired creature with a particularly bushy tail, large ears and extremely long slender fingers. The central finger, which alone is used for grooming, is especially long. Aye-ayes eat a variety of foods including eggs, dates, bananas and mangoes, but the bulk of their diet is made up of bamboo pith and beetle larvae.

Many lemur species, such as the indri and the ruffed lemur, were once regarded as sacred animals and so they were safe from hunting. Today, however, as the impact of western civilization becomes felt such beliefs are much less common and the unfortunate animals are increasingly being caught and killed. It is not surprising that the populations of many species are on the decline.

Lorises and bushbabies

Slender lorises, *Loris tardigradus*, inhabit the forests of southern India where they clamber slowly and deliberately from branch to branch in search of leaves, nuts, insects, eggs and lizards. They are tailless, nocturnal animals and have,

Ivan Polunin

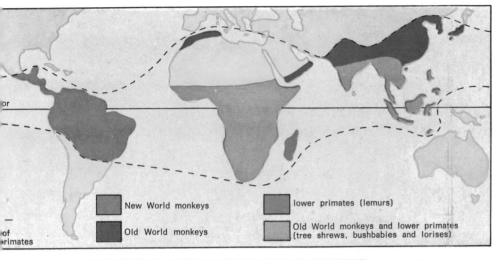

relatively, even larger eyes than the lemurs to enable them to detect their prey in dim light. The slow loris, *Mycticebus pygmaeus*, of South-East Asia is less active than the slender loris, but it is somewhat larger and more sociable.

Belonging to the same family (*Lorisidae*) as the lorises are the angwantibo, *Arctocebus calabarensis*, and the potto, *Perodicticus potto*, of western Africa. Angwantibos live high in the branches of the equatorial rain forest, searching for food by night and sleeping by day. The inaccessibility of their habitat makes them difficult animals to study and little is known of their life in the wild. Like the angwantibo and the lorises, the potto is a slow-moving nocturnal animal with large eyes. When attacked it defends itself by means of spines which grow from two of the spinal vertebrae and project from the back of the neck.

Bushbabies are found in most parts of Africa south of the Sahara. They are small creatures with a body length of no more than 22 cm (9 in) and, unlike their relatives of the family *Lorisidae*, they are agile climbers and can jump accurately from one branch to another. Having exceptionally large eyes, they are active at night and their diet consists of insects, nuts, fruit, snails, tree frogs, eggs, lizards and small mammals. They have good eyesight and an acute sense of hearing which they use to detect their prey. All bushbabies belong to the genus *Galago* and they are often called by this name. The common name 'bushbaby' comes from the resemblance of their cries to the yells of a human baby.

Tarsiers and tree shrews

Tarsiers look rather like small bushbabies and are found only in Borneo, the Philippines and a few neighbouring islands. Like bushbabies they are agile, tree-dwelling animals with an acute sense of hearing and very large eyes; the volume of just one eye is only slightly smaller than that of the animal's brain. Another resemblance to bushbabies is the ability to turn the head through almost 180°. Tarsiers feed mainly on insects and lizards which they hunt by night. There are only three species, all belonging to the genus *Tarsius*.

The tree shrews from India and South-East Asia are nocturnal animals no larger than squirrels and, as their name suggests, they spend most of their time in trees. Occasionally, however, they descend to the forest floor to forage for insects and fallen fruit.

The common tree shrew, *Tupaia glis*, has a coat of brown fur, a long bushy tail and, like the insectivores, a slender, pointed snout. Also, its teeth are more like those of insectivores than lower primates. Prosimian features, however, predominate: each eye socket is surrounded by a continuous bony ring, the visual part of the brain is more developed than the olfactory region, various features of the skull, muscles and reproductive system are unmistakenly prosimian, and it gives birth to no more than two young at a time (insectivores have large litters).

Of all the living primates, the tree shrews are probably most like the early ancestors of the group, and it is likely that the primates sprang from a family of primitive insectivores some 60 million years ago in the Palaeocene epoch.

Above: The distribution of primates is confined to the tropical and semi-tropical regions of the world. Not included on this map are the ape populations of equatorial Africa (chimpanzees and gorillas), South-East Asia (gibbons) and Borneo and Sumatra (orang-utans).

Left: A Philippine tarsier, *Tarsius syrichta*. It is a forest-dweller, most often found close to rivers where it can supplement its normal diet of insects and lizards with fish and crabs. It has unusually long fingers and toes, each bearing a smooth pad which enables the creature to cling to almost any surface. Jumping from a suitable perch, a tarsier can even get a firm grip on a vertical sheet of glass.

Below: A slender loris, *Loris tardigradus*, from India. At night it moves slowly and deliberately among the trees of the tropical forest, searching for insects, birds' eggs, nuts and flowers. Unlike most other prosimians, lorises are tailless.

Jacana

Left: Slow lorises, *Nycticebus coucang*, from Malaysia. Like slender lorises, these creatures are territorial, and they mark out their domains with urine. Scent marking seems to play an important role in the orientation of lorises for they become unsure of their footing in unmarked territory.

Below: The potto, *Perodicticus potto*, is a member of the loris family which inhabits the central West African rain forests. The only other prosimians to come from the African mainland are the bushbabies, *Galago*, and the angwantibo, *Arctocebus calabarensis*, a close relation of the potto.

Frank Lane

NHPA

New World Monkeys

Monkeys are probably the most familiar of all jungle dwellers. They inhabit most of the world's tropical forests, living high in the trees and feeding on fruits, berries, eggs, insects, spiders and occasionally small frogs and lizards. Monkeys are well adapted to arboreal life; their strong, slender limbs, grasping hands and feet, keen eyesight and long, sometimes prehensile tails make them expert climbers and acrobats. Because they can move up and down trees and from one branch to the next with great agility, monkeys can easily escape from most predators.

Monkeys are primates, belonging to the same sub-order as the apes and man himself. Geographically and structurally they fall neatly into two infraorders: *Platyrrhina*, whose members live only in South and Central America, and *Catarrhina*, whose members are natives of Africa and Asia. The New World monkeys differ outwardly from their Old World cousins in a number of ways. In particular, their limbs are usually more slender, their nostrils tend to open to the side rather than to the front, their feet are better at grasping than their hands, and their tails are especially long and often prehensile (Old World monkeys never have prehensile tails).

Throughout the Tertiary period North and South America were separated not by a corridor of land but by a chain of small islands. South America was therefore an island continent like Australia and its fauna developed more or less in isolation until it became joined once again with the north at the end of the Tertiary period, about two million years ago. The ancestors of the New World monkeys probably migrated from North to South America in the Eocene epoch, travelling from island to island on clumps of floating vegetation. Once they had arrived at their destination they flourished and, not surprisingly, developed rather differently from their Old World cousins. In fact the differences are quite minor and the fundamental body plan of all monkeys is very much the same. So either the basic design was already well established by the time the ancestors of the New World monkeys entered South America, or else the New and Old World groups, faced with similar environmental conditions, simply evolved in much the same way.

Capuchins

The capuchins are typical members of a large family of New World monkeys, the *Cebidae*. They inhabit the tropical forests of the Amazon delta and spend almost all of their time high above the ground, descending to the forest floor only occasionally in order to drink. They are sociable animals and live in small family groups within a definite feeding territory. When travelling from one place to another the younger members of the group generally lead the way while the adults bring up the rear. Babies cling on to their mothers' backs or abdomens. Like most monkets, capuchins groom themselves and other members of their family with great care and so they are rarely troubled

MACAQUE (Asia)

CEBUS MONKEY (South America)

Above: Though American monkeys resemble their Old World counterparts in many respects, there are certain differences. For example, the nostrils of the former are usually more widely spaced, as these illustrations show. On the left is a macaque from southern Asia and on the right a cebus monkey from South America. New World monkeys often use their tails as a fifth 'hand' to grasp branches as they leap through the trees. In contrast, the monkeys of Africa and Asia never have prehensile tails.

Right and below: These bald-headed uakaris, *Cacajao*, are residents of the Amazon rain forest. Unlike most other South American monkeys they have only short tails. Uakaris are not common in the wild, but since the late 1960s considerable success has been achieved in keeping and breeding them in zoos.

Frank Lane

Jacana

Right: A female squirrel monkey, *Saimiri sciureus*, leaps through the forest with a baby clinging to her back. Squirrel monkeys are among the most common South American monkeys. They prefer to live at the edges of forests, especially along river banks, where berries, nuts and fruits provide abundant food. They have remarkably large brains, the region responsible for co-ordinating movement and eyesight being particularly well developed.

Below: The night monkey, *Actes trivirgatus*, is easily recognized by its huge eyes which enable it to see clearly in dim light. It is the only nocturnal monkey.

by skin parasites such as fleas or lice.

In some parts of their range capuchins are regarded as pests because they raid plantations of cocoa, oranges and other fruit. They also eat insects and eggs, but fruit makes up the bulk of their diet. The feeding territory of a typical capuchin family is quite small, not more than about 100 m (330 ft) across, but it is carefully marked and defended. Capuchins frequently urinate on their hands and then rub the liquid into their fur—in this way the territory becomes 'marked' with the characteristic scent of the family as they move from tree to tree in search of food.

There are four species of capuchin, the most common being the brown capuchin, *Cebus apella*. In many groups of New World monkeys there is considerable variation in coat colour and markings within a single species, and the capuchins are no exception. Although the coat is usually brownish the face colour and other details vary. Differently marked individuals are usually separated geographically, but often only by a relatively short distance.

Spider monkeys and woolly monkeys also belong to the family *Cebidae* and inhabit the Amazon rain forests. Their most remarkable feature is the long and powerful prehensile tail which serves as a fifth 'hand', being able to cling to branches or stretch for food otherwise out of reach. The spider monkeys, genus *Ateles*, are the most agile of all New World monkeys and can move rapidly through the forest using both arms and tails.

Spider monkeys live in groups of 100 animals or more and are territorial in

Below left: A pale-headed saki, *Pithecia pithecia*. As acrobats, sakis rank with the best of the New World monkeys, and so they spend much of their time high in the forest canopy. When they do descend to the ground they walk upright, holding up their arms for balance. They are relatively small monkeys, measuring no more than about 38 cm (15 in) from the nose to the base of the tail.

Below: Squirrel monkeys are even smaller than pale-headed sakis. They often live in large groups—bands of more than 500 have been seen moving together through the forest. Although common, squirrel monkeys are not easy to keep in captivity.

Left: A spider monkey, *Ateles*, can move rapidly through the forest using both its arms and its tail, covering as much as 10 m (33 ft) with a single leap. Of all New World monkeys, spider monkeys are the most agile. They live high in the forest canopy.

Right: The skeleton of a tamarin, *Saguinus*. To equip the animal for an arboreal life, its bones are slender and light, and long digits on both hands and feet enable it to cling securely to branches high above the ground. Its long tail serves as a balancing organ.

Below right: A brown-headed tamarin, *Saguinus fuscicollis*, from the upper Amazon consumes a mantis.

M. Freeman/Bruce Coleman

their habits. They do not normally stray into adjacent territories and stick to the same trees and paths in their own territories. An intruder into a spider monkey territory is soon surrounded by a crowd of loudly chattering monkeys, and the din soon drives away the stranger. Clearly predators cannot hunt their prey if their presence is being advertised so effectively. Spider monkeys live almost exclusively on nuts and fruit although they do occasionally search for insects in the crevices of tree bark. Most do not have thumbs, so grooming is a relatively difficult operation and is not such a highly developed social habit as in other monkeys.

Of all the creatures of the Amazon jungle, the aptly named howler monkeys, genus *Alouatta*, are by far the noisiest. Their cries, which can be heard for dis-

tances of 3 km (1.8 miles) or more, are used to establish territories. They have long, soft fur and a beard of even longer hair covering the specialized larynx. Although they have prehensile tails and are capable of moving rapidly through the forest, howler monkeys do not normally move very fast as they travel through the trees. In this respect they resemble the woolly monkeys, *Lagothrix*.

One of the strangest New World monkeys is the night monkey, *Aotes trivirgatus*, which is the only nocturnal monkey to be found anywhere in the world. The most striking feature of this creature is its huge eyes which enable it to see clearly in poor light. Also, its nostrils are less widely spaced than those of other New World monkeys and it lacks a prehensile tail. Night monkeys are

quite common in the northern regions of South America. They are most active at dawn and dusk when they search for the same sort of food as other monkeys: fruits, berries, nuts, insects and snails.

Among other members of the family *Cebidae* are the titi monkeys, genus *Callicebus*, the sakis, genus *Pithecia*, the uakaris, genus *Cacajao*, and the squirrel monkeys, genus *Saimiri*. Representatives of all these groups are to be found in Brazil and its northern and western neighbours, and a few species, such as the red-backed squirrel monkey, *Saimiri oerstedi*, live as far north as central America. None of these creatures has a prehensile tail but in most other respects they are typical New World monkeys, living in troops and feeding on fruit and insects high above the forest floor.

374

Below: The pygmy marmoset, *Callithrix pygmaea*, is the smallest of all monkeys, having a body length of 16 cm (6 in) and weighing only about 85 g (3 oz). An expert climber, it inhabits a relatively small region of the Amazon rain forest near the junction of the borders of Brazil, Peru and Colombia.

Above: A young maned tamarin, *Leontideus*, is fed solid food by its mother while it clings to its father's back. A baby maned tamarin is carried solely by its mother for the first week of its life. At the end of this period it transfers to its father, returning to its mother only for short periods in order to suckle.

Right: The colourful cotton-head tamarin, *Oedipomidas oedipus*, lives along the Caribbean coast of Colombia. It is more of a meat eater than most New World monkeys and has well developed canine teeth. It kills its prey, typically a bird or mouse, by biting the unfortunate creature's head.

M. Freeman/Bruce Coleman

Marmosets and tamarins

The other main family of New World monkeys, *Callithricidae*, consists of the marmosets and tamarins, small active inhabitants of the forest canopy. Of all the world's monkeys, the marmosets and tamarins are perhaps best adapted to life in the trees for they are expert climbers and jumpers and they rarely leave the tangle of branches and climbing plants which forms the upper layer of the rain forest. They feed on insects, spiders, lizards and other small animals as well as nuts, fruits and berries. They have long tails and their arms are shorter than their legs. Only the big toe has a flat, wide nail; the remaining toes and the fingers are equipped with claws.

Marmosets and tamarins are attractive animals and were kept as pets by the natives of South America long before the first specimens reached Europe in the seventeenth century. Among the more striking species are the lion marmoset, *Leontocebus rosalia*, with its golden coat and thick mane of hair around the face, the common marmoset, *Callithrix jacchus*, which has a dark coat and long white ear tufts, and the rare emperor tamarin, *Saguinus imperator*, which has a black coat, a brown tail and an outsize 'moustache' of white hair growing from its upper lip. Tamarins can be distinguished from marmosets by their teeth—unlike marmosets their lower canines are longer than the incisors.

Tamarins and marmosets are found mainly in Brazil, but the distribution of a particular species throughout its range tends to be patchy because natural boundaries such as rivers or areas of savannah isolate one community from the next. Not surprisingly, these local populations have developed minor variations on the basic plan, particularly in their markings and coat colour, so there are usually a number of different forms of any given species or subspecies. Quite often these different forms will live quite close to each other, for example on either side of a river.

One of the rarest New World monkeys is the callimico, *Callimico goeldii*, which inhabits forested areas of western Brazil between the rivers Ucayali and Madeira. First discovered at the beginning of this century, it is about 20 cm (8 in) long, has a brown body, black limbs, a black tail and white ear tufts. At first the new monkey was thought to be a hitherto unknown species of marmoset because its external features, such as soft, silky fur and claws rather than nails resembled those of members of the genus *Callithrix*. Later, however, when more specimens became available and when the skull was more closely examined it was realized that the animal also had several features in common with the capuchin-like monkeys of the family *Cebidae*. In particular the callimico has, like capuchins, three molars on each side of the upper and lower jaws rather than just two as in marmosets or tamarins. Nowadays the callimico is regarded as intermediate between the two main families of New World monkeys and is put in a family of its own, the *Callimiconidae*.

The tamarins fall into three distinct genera which are separated from each other geographically. The true tamarins, *Saguinus*, like most other New World monkeys, inhabit the Amazon basin, the bare-faced tamarins, *Oedipomidas*, are found to the north in Colombia, and the maned tamarins, *Leontideus*, are found only in the coastal regions of southern Brazil, close to Rio de Janiero and Sao Paulo.

The negro tamarin, *Saguinus tamarin*, is one of the most familiar New World monkeys because it seems to prefer less densely forested regions than its relatives; it usually inhabits areas of young forest growing on previously cultivated land. The negro tamarin has a hairless face, extremely large ears and, as its name suggests, black fur. It can be seen in most parts of the Amazon delta and is a resident of many suburban areas and some city parks. Typical of the bare-faced tamarins is the cottonhead, *Oedipomidas oedipus*, which has a black face and a brown coat with white underparts.

Old World Monkeys

The monkeys of Africa and Asia belong to the same infraorder, *Catarrhina*, as the great apes and man himself. Although some of them can walk upright on their hind legs for short distances they generally walk on all fours. They have flattened nails on all fingers and toes, and, like all primates except tree shrews, they are able to grasp objects between the thumb and forefinger. Many Old World monkeys have long tails to help them balance when moving through the trees, but these are never prehensile as they are in many African monkeys. Also, the nostrils of Old World monkeys are closer together than they are in their American cousins.

All monkeys and apes are thought to have originated from a family of lower primates, the *Omomyidae*, which inhabited Europe and North America in the early Tertiary period some 60 million years ago. Descendants of these creatures migrated southwards, probably about 50 million years ago in the Eocene epoch, from North America to South America and from Europe to Africa and southern Asia. The two groups thus became geographically separated and evolved along slightly different lines to produce the zoologically distinct New and Old World monkeys we know today.

The African and Asian monkeys are

Mark Boulton/Bruce Coleman

Above: Rhesus monkeys, *Macaca mulatta*, enjoy the protection of a temple at Kathmandu, Nepal. Grooming, as seen here, is an important activity for most monkeys; it not only rids them of parasites but also serves as a constant reminder of social position—high ranking animals receive the most attention.

Below: The pig-tailed macaque, *Macaca nemestrina*, from South-East Asia is one of the largest macaques. The males have longish muzzles and look rather like baboons. This particular animal, from Singapore, has been trained to shin up coconut palms and pick the fruits for its human masters.

divided into two families, the *Cercopithecidae* which includes the macaques, baboons, guenons, drills and mandrills, and the *Colobidae* which includes the colobus monkeys, the proboscis monkey and the langurs. Man has been attracted by monkeys from the earliest times, the obvious resemblances to humans making them particularly fascinating. Two species of baboon were regarded as sacred by the ancient Egyptians and one of them, *Papio anubis*, still bears the name of their god of the dead, Anubis. Monkeys have always been popular research animals. As long ago as the second century AD the Greek physician Galen dissected baboons and other monkeys in the hope that he would learn about human anatomy.

Macaques

Macaques are found in southern and central Asia from India to Japan. They are heavily built monkeys reaching a maximum weight of about 13 kg (29 lb), and their fur is usually a yellowish brown colour. Like many Old World monkeys they have conspicuous pads of hard, hairless skin on the buttocks which develop after puberty and are often reddish in colour.

One of the best known macaques is the Barbary ape, *Macaca sylvana*, which gets its misleading name from the fact that, like the true apes, it has no tail. Living in North Africa and Gibraltar, it is the only macaque to be found outside Asia. Whether it was introduced to Gibraltar by man or whether it has always been a resident there is uncertain, but fossil remains of similar monkeys have been found in various parts of Europe. They live in family troops and are quite bold even in their North African habitat where they frequently raid gardens and fields. This behaviour has, not surprisingly, made them unpopular with the human population and they are killed as pests in some regions.

Another well known macaque is the rhesus monkey, *Macaca mulatta*, from northern India, China, Burma and Thailand. Their true homes are the forests of

Ivan Polunin

The barbary ape (below) is protected in Gibraltar, where a legend dating from French and Spanish attacks of 1779 prophesises that if the apes leave the Rock then the British will lose it.

dominant males
other adult males
juveniles
females
babies

Right: With its arms and legs outstretched and its tail curled upwards behind it, a silvered leaf monkey, *Presbytis cristatus*, prepares to land on a tree in western Malaysia. These monkeys move with great agility when they are disturbed, covering as much as 10 m (33 ft) with a single leap.

both lowland and highland areas, but nowadays they have become adapted to, and even seem to prefer, man-made environments. In some parts of India, where monkeys are protected by religious laws, only about 15 per cent of the total rhesus monkey population lives in the forest, the remaining 85 per cent preferring villages, cities, temples and other human habitations.

Of all monkeys, the rhesus monkey is most commonly seen in zoos. It has played a vital role in medical research for many years, the most important contribution being the identification of the rhesus factor, a blood characteristic which occasionally appears in both rhesus monkeys and man. The unborn offspring of a rhesus negative mother and a rhesus positive father has a high risk of being stillborn because antibodies in the mother's blood tend to destroy the red corpuscles in the blood of the foetus if the latter should prove to be rhesus positive. Nowadays, thanks to research on rhesus monkeys, this dangerous condition can be detected early and the child's life saved by a blood transfusion.

Baboons and mandrills

The baboons, *Papio*, are a group of ground-dwelling monkeys from Africa. They are heavily built animals, reaching a maximum weight of about 50 kg (110 lb), and have well developed teeth, the canines being exceptionally long and pointed. As well as the usual plant diet, baboons eat eggs and small animals. One of the baboon's chief enemies is the leopard, and although the predator usually overcomes its prey in the end, this is by no means always the case. Large male baboons can defend themselves very effectively and will often drive off a marauding leopard; there are even cases of leopards being killed by baboons.

Baboons are active in the day and they spend much of the time in open grasslands close to herds of antelopes and zebra where they feed and groom each other. As well as keeping them free from parasites, grooming is an important social

378

Above: A troop of baboons on the move. The dominant males travel at the centre of the troop with the main group of females and young. Acting as a guard for this central group are the remaining adult males and females. The juveniles travel at the edge of the group but retreat inwards when danger threatens.

Right: When a dominant male baboon encounters rivals he 'yawns' to display his teeth. Because the size and condition of his teeth, particularly the canine teeth, are a good indication of his physical strength, the 'yawning' threat is a clear demonstration of his high social standing in the troop.

W. H. Muller/ZEFA

Left: The mandrill, *Mandrillus sphinx*, is easily recognized by its bizarre face markings. Although it lives in the equatorial rain forests of West Africa, it spends most of its time on the ground searching for roots, fallen fruit, insects and frogs. It uses the same 'yawning' threat display as the baboon (above).

Below: A southern black-and-white colobus monkey, *Colobus polykomos*, from the coast of East Africa. At the beginning of this century colobus monkeys were shot in large numbers for their fur, and they became quite rare in some places. Nowadays their chief enemies are leopards and eagles.

Natural Science Photos

activity and is an indicator of a particular animal's rank: a dominant male will be groomed more frequently than other members of the troop. At night, when predators like hyenas and leopards are active, baboons climb trees for security, and several of the males take it in turn to keep watch throughout the night.

The mandrill, *Mandrillus sphinx*, is another large African monkey. It comes from the rain forests of central West Africa and is easily recognized by its extraordinary face: its long nose is covered by reddish skin and is flanked on either side by patches of pale, often bluish skin which have longitudinal grooves running along them from the eyes to the nostrils. The creature's buttocks are also hairless and brightly coloured. These areas of pigmented skin act as threat

signals to other mandrills for they become markedly more vivid when the animal is excited. They probably also play an important role in attracting mates. Like baboons, mandrills spend the day on the ground, climbing trees at night to sleep. They live in small troops and feed on a variety of plant and animal food. Of similar appearance and habits but less vividly coloured is the drill, *Mandrillus leucophaeus*, also from West Africa.

Guenons

Almost every region of Africa south of the Sahara is inhabited by one or more species of guenon monkey. Although most species are residents of the central African rain forests, some guenons are more at home in open country. Guenons are slender animals with long tails and they have well marked and often brightly coloured coats. One of the most common guenons is the vervet or green monkey, *Cercopithecus aethiops*, which prefers savannah to forest. Having greenish-grey fur, vervet monkeys live in small troops and are quite bold, approaching other animals and even tourists without apparent concern.

Like all monkeys, guenons breed throughout the year, one or, rarely, two

Ivan Polunin

Left: Guenons, genus *Cercopithecus*, can be distinguished from each other by their facial markings. Shown here are (1) the owl-faced guenon, *C.hamlyni*; (2) DeBrazza's monkey, *C.neglectus*; (3) the vervet monkey, *C.aethiops*; (4) the mona monkey, *C.monas*; and (5) the crowned guenon, *C.pogonias*.

There are often differences in colour and marking between the adults and young of the same guenon species. This may serve to prevent young animals from being attacked by the adult males (who tend to be aggressive) by making them easily distinguishable from other members of the family troop.

Below: The odd-looking proboscis monkey, *Nasalis larvatus*, is a native of the island of Borneo. Adult males have huge, bulbous noses which are important secondary sexual characteristics: in the breeding season females select the males with the largest noses. The females have short, turned-up noses.

young being born after a gestation period of about seven months. For the first weeks of its life the baby guenon clings to its mother's abdomen using its tail as well as its arms to help it hold on. This ability to grasp with its tail, so common among American monkeys, is soon lost as the young animal grows. By the time it is two months old the baby guenon is very active and eating its first solid food, and by four months it is fully weaned. It becomes sexually mature at the relatively advanced age of four years.

Colobus monkeys

These are the only leaf monkeys (members of the family *Colobidae*) to inhabit the African continent—they live in the equatorial rain forests south of the Sahara. There are four species of which the southern black-and-white colobus, *Colobus polykomos*, is perhaps the most striking. Its coat is mostly black but there are areas of long white hair on the tail, the flanks and the face. Although it is not a true brachiator (an animal which uses only its arms when moving through the trees) like the gibbons of South-East Asia, the black-and-white colobus is very agile and it does use its arms and hands more than many other monkeys as it moves from branch to branch. This probably explains its lack of thumbs, for these digits appear to hinder brachiation.

Colobus monkeys live high in the forest canopy where they feed on leaves. Unlike that of most other monkeys (except leaf monkeys) the colobus's diet is restricted almost entirely to leaves and shoots; surprisingly it eats very little fruit. To cope with their unpromising diet of leaves, colobus monkeys as well as the other leaf monkeys have compartmented stomachs rather like those of ruminants such as cattle or sheep. In the first two stomach compartments bacteria begin the digestion process by breaking down the cellulose in the leaves into smaller, more manageable carbohydrates. These compounds then pass to the gut proper for normal enzymic digestion.

Langurs and proboscis monkeys

The langurs of the genus *Presbytis* are the most common of the Asian leaf monkeys. They are slender, long-limbed monkeys which inhabit the forests of India, South-East Asia and southern China. Langurs have long tails which no doubt help them to balance as they jump from tree to tree. In fact langurs and the other leaf monkeys are not so restless as most Old World monkeys, but they nevertheless move with great agility when they need to, and can cover 10 m (33 ft) or so with a single jump.

One of the most remarkable leaf monkeys is the proboscis monkey, *Nasalis larvatus*, from Borneo. It is a large, strong monkey immediately recognizable by its long nose. An adult male may reach a length of 76 cm (30 in) from its nose to the base of its tail, and its large, bulbous nose may be 10 cm (4 in) long. Proboscis monkeys spend most of their time in the mangrove forests feeding on buds and leaves. They are reputed to be excellent swimmers. Closely related to the proboscis monkeys are the snub-nosed langurs, *Rhinopithecus*, from China and Tibet and the pig-tailed langur, *Simias concolor*, from Sumatra. These leaf monkeys also have long noses, but not so long as that of the proboscis monkey.

Bruce Coleman

Gibbons and Orang-utans

Of all living animals the true apes are the most closely related to man. As well as having large brains and being highly intelligent, they have the same number of teeth as we do and they lack tails. Nevertheless, in spite of these similarities, the relationship between apes and man must not be overstated: we are not descended from them. We should regard ourselves rather as cousins, for we are both descended from common ancestors who lived in the Miocene epoch, some 25 million years ago. Since that time the true apes and man have evolved along different lines, and it is therefore a mistake to think of apes simply as less perfect versions of ourselves. They are as highly adapted for their way of life as we are for ours.

All of the surviving apes live in or near the tropical forests of the Old World. The gorilla and chimpanzees live only in Africa, and the orang-utan and gibbons in Asia. Of these four groups of apes the gibbons are set rather apart from the others. Not only are they smaller, ranging in height from about 38 to 91 cm (15 to 36 in) when standing erect, but also, like the Old World monkeys, they have on their buttocks leathery patches which are useful when sitting on the tops of branches. The gibbons are therefore usually classified in a family of their own, the family *Hylobatidae*, which means 'tree walkers'.

Gibbons

On the ground gibbons are the only non-human primates which move only on their hind legs. Their arms are so long that in this erect posture their knuckles sometimes touch the ground and are used in rather the same way as crutches. The arms are often held rather awkwardly

Below: The gibbon's lightly-built skeleton reflects its arboreal existence. Its arms are long and its hands act as hooks as it swings from branch to branch.

Above: A lar gibbon, *Hylobates lar*, from Borneo hangs by one arm from the branch of a tree. This species is the most widespread of all gibbons, being found throughout South-East Asia from southern China to Java.

Left: A lar gibbon resting at the top of a tree. Gibbons have dense fur which they keep spotlessly clean and free of parasites by constant grooming. Having such thick coats they can thrive in surprisingly cold climates. Several European zoos keep gibbons in outdoor enclosures or on islands in the middle of lakes for much of the year.

Right: The siamang, *Symphalangus syndactylus*, from Sumatra and the Malay peninsula is the largest and strongest of the gibbons. Siamangs produce a loud and characteristic 'song' at dawn and dusk. The sound is amplified by the creature's throat sac and probably denotes the ownership of territory. Siamangs are considerably less agile than the true gibbons of the genus *Hylobates*.

Norman Tomalin/Bruce Coleman

Bruce Coleman

P. Morris

clear of the ground when the animal runs. However, wild gibbons spend almost all their time in trees, and when they run along branches on two legs, grasping with their opposable big toes, their arms are extended as balancing organs. More often gibbons climb by *brachiation*, swinging on their long arms beneath the horizontal branches. The length of their arms is an adaptation to this mode of progression, and usually they swing hand over hand, although sometimes both arms are used in unison. They are capable of leaping across gaps up to 9 m (30 ft) wide, and can cover 3 m (10 ft) with a single reach of the arms. In gripping the branches the four fingers of each hand are held together and used as grappling hooks. The thumbs are small and are not brought into play. Moving fast and at considerable heights above the ground, it is not surprising that gibbons sometimes miss a hand-hold and fall. Usually they are saved from injury by the lower branches which act as safety nets, but injuries do occur from time to time. Sampling of some wild populations has shown that about one gibbon in three has suffered from a broken limb at some time in its life. Like the other apes, gibbons cannot swim.

The study of the behaviour of wild primates and especially apes is a popular branch of zoological science. The early hope that these studies would throw light on aspects of human behaviour has been fulfilled only in part. It seems that behaviour evolves more rapidly than anatomy, and in their behaviour wild apes differ much more than they do in bodily form. For example, the behaviour of gibbons, first studied in the wild in the 1930s, is in some ways more like that of many birds than that of other mammals. This is not as remarkable as it seems for gibbons, like many birds, live in the trees of dense forests, and have had to overcome much the same problems. Adult gibbons live in monogamous pairs. Each pair defends a territory and, being unable to see the neighbouring pairs, does so primarily by means of vocal signals, uttering loud, ringing and whooping calls. These carry over long distances, and are directly comparable to bird-song. Each pair of gibbons is accompanied by up to four of their young of differing ages, but on reaching maturity at perhaps six years of age the young are driven from the group.

Females give birth to usually only a single young one after a pregnancy of about 200 days. Like other young primates, young gibbons are at first almost completely helpless, able only to suckle and to cling to the mother's breast as she moves through the trees. At night the family sleeps huddled together, sitting erect on branches, with their limbs tucked up against their bodies. Early in the morning there is a burst of noisy territorial defence, and then the group moves round the territory feeding on leaves, buds, fruits and some insects. Some species also eat small birds, which they snatch from the air with remarkable dexterity. When drinking, gibbons usually dip their hands into the water, and then lick the moisture from them. As with other primates, part of the day is spent in social grooming. How long gibbons live in the wild is not certain, but in zoos many individuals have lived for more than 20 years.

Below: The most obvious features of the human skeleton, when compared with that of a gibbon, are the larger skull, longer legs, shorter arms and wider pelvis.

Above: A gibbon can move through the forest very swiftly by swinging hand over hand from one tree to the next. This mode of progression, using the arms rather than the legs, is called *brachiation*, and is typical of the apes.

Left: A large male orang-utan like this one may weigh as much as 150 kg (330 lb). The huge cheek flaps are seen only in males and appear after the animal has reached maturity.

Below: Orang-utans, *Pongo pygmaeus*, live in the forests of Borneo and Sumatra. Although they come from the same part of the world as the gibbons, they are in fact more closely related to the gorillas and chimpanzees of equatorial Africa. Now on the brink of extinction in the wild, orangs were once quite common throughout eastern Asia. Their remains have been found in excavations as far north as Peking. In the last few thousand years orangs have become smaller—early remains show that orangs as large as gorillas once lived on the Asian mainland.

P. Morris

Okapia

Above: The social behaviour of the orangs is quite unlike that of the other great apes. Females and juveniles live in small, widely scattered groups, each keeping to its own home range, while adult males travel, mostly on their own, through a large territory visiting the various groups it contains. Pictured here is a group of young animals in a Sumatran forest. The territorial males father some but not all of the young. Less mature and less assertive males also visit the females when opportunity offers.

Left: A young orang. Like human babies, newborn orangs are almost completely helpless. They are suckled for between three and four years, but are fed some pre-chewed solid food from an early age.

Below: A female orang stands erect and carries her baby in her arms.

In appearance individuals of the typical gibbon genus, *Hylobates*, vary considerably. Even within a single species the thick, shaggy fur of some individuals may be black and that of others brown or silver-grey. The six species are therefore not easy to distinguish. Most often seen in zoos is the lar gibbon, *Hylobates lar*, found throughout South-East Asia, which can be identified by the white fur on the hands and feet and round the face. The hoolock gibbon, *Hylobates hoolock*, of Assam, Burma, and south-western China has prominent white eyebrows and an especially penetrating call. The smallest of the gibbons is *Hylobates klossi*, which is found only on the Mentawai Islands, off the west coast of Sumatra.

Orang-utans

Although it is the only Asian representative of the great ape family, *Pongidae*, the orang-utan, *Pongo pygmaeus*, is more closely related to the gorilla and chimpanzees than it is to the gibbons. Orang-utan means 'old man of the woods' in the Malay language, and in facial appearance orangs are the most like humans of all the apes.

Fossil remains of orangs are widely distributed in southern China and Malay-

sia, but in historic times the species has been found only in Borneo and Sumatra. Even in these islands they are now rare, and the total population numbers only a few thousand. The populations of the two islands are very similar in appearance, both having the same reddish brown, rather sparse hair, but there are differences. Sumatran orangs are on the average slightly larger, while male Bornean orangs have larger cheek flaps. For these and other reasons the two races are regarded as separate sub-species. The present rarity of orangs is chiefly the result of man's destruction of their native forests, both for timber and to make way for plantations. Also, orangs are too often caught as zoo specimens and pets, although this is now illegal. Attempts are now being made to conserve them in the wild: illegally caught young orangs are being rehabilitated for release in the wild, and reputable zoos no longer seek wild-caught specimens, having learned to breed their own orangs. However, economic pressures for forest destruction are strong, and the survival of the orang-utan is by no means certain.

The forests in which orangs live are usually dense, with some very tall trees and little or no undergrowth, and the forest floor is often swampy. Orangs are found in the trees at all heights, and at night they sleep in nests of branches and leaves about 20 m (66 ft) above the ground. The same nest is occupied for only a few nights before a new one is built elsewhere. The ability to make nests appears to be at least partly instinctive. When it rains they cover themselves with large leaves. Orang-utans mainly feed on fruit, especially that of the durian tree, which is their staple diet from August to December, but they also eat some leaves, seeds, bark and birds' eggs.

The gestation period is between eight and nine months, and almost always only one young is born at a time. The average weight at birth is 1.5 kg (3.3 lb) and the young orang clings tightly to its mother with its long arms. It may suckle for several years, but grows up at almost twice the speed that humans do. Orangs can breed when they are about seven years old, and are full-grown at about ten years. More information is needed, but it seems likely that the potential lifespan is comparable to that of chimpanzees and gorillas, about 30 or 40 years.

Although orangs can move with surprising speed when they want to, their movements are normally slow and deliberate. Compared with chimpanzees they appear to be slow and introverted, so it is often believed that they are less intelligent than chimpanzees. There is however, no firm foundation for this view for most of the scientific intelligence testing that has been carried out on apes has been on chimpanzees, whose seeming fondness for showing off makes them cooperative, at least when they are immature. Orang-utans are certainly very intelligent: their brains are about as large as those of chimpanzees, being up to 450 cc (27 cu in) in volume. In captivity orangs show greater mechanical aptitude than chimpanzees do, being able to undo nuts and bolts that would fool a chimpanzee. They use their hands with great dexterity, but because their palms are long, the rather short thumb is less useful than the human thumb for many purposes.

The Sumatran orang-utan (below), lighter coloured than its Bornean relatives, is seriously threatened with extinction. As long ago as 1964 it was estimated that only 100 still existed on Sumatra.

Gorillas and Chimpanzees

gibbon   orang-utan   gorilla   chimpanzee

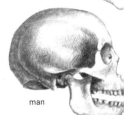

man

Popularly known as the great apes, the chimpanzees and gorillas, together with the orang-utan of South-East Asia, make up the family *Pongidae*. Of all primates these are the most closely related to man, whom they resemble in having no visible external tail, and in their well developed brains. Within the family the chimpanzees and gorillas, which live in Africa, are more closely related to each other than to the orang-utan, having diverged from a common ancestor perhaps seven million years ago.

Both chimpanzees and gorillas have the long arms associated with the arm-swinging method of climbing (*brachiation*) best seen in the gibbons of Asia, but because they are so large and heavy, adult chimpanzees and gorillas rarely brachiate for long. Gorillas spend most of their time on the ground, and chimpanzees spend only about half of their time in trees. One expert, Adriaan Kortlandt, has argued that the immediate ancestors of the chimpanzee were even more terrestrial, living in the African grasslands from which they have since been driven by mankind. This is far from certain. We know only that when chimpanzees were first discovered by Europeans they were living in the African forests.

Gorillas

The gorillas' reputation as savage monsters is entirely without foundation. They are shy vegetarians. During the day the dominant male leads the troop through a home range which has a total area of about 39 sq km (15 sq miles). Home ranges are not defended against other groups of gorillas—if two troops happen to meet, the adults usually ignore each other, although the juveniles may mix together briefly. This cool behaviour is typical of gorillas and reflects their aloof, introverted personalities.

The dominant male is allowed to rest in the most comfortable places, and gets the first choice of the food available without appearing to assert his massive authority. Only rarely, in defence of the troop against the gorilla's only serious enemy, man, or very occasionally when confronting rivals, does he launch into his threat display, hooting, rising on to his hind legs, beating his chest with his hands, and finally charging. Even then he is not very likely to attack; usually the charge is a bluff, and stops short of the intruder. More often at the first hint of danger the troop silently moves off, avoiding confrontation.

Such shy animals are difficult to observe in the wild and so, no doubt, a great deal remains to be discovered about gorillas' behaviour. As far as we know they are purely vegetarian, feeding on leaves, stems, bark, roots and fruit. Some of their favourite foods, for example, are stringy stems with about the consistency of celery. Like most other primates they eat quite a wide variety of foods, but are fussy as to which part of it they accept: before eating they examine their food carefully, pulling it apart, and

Below: A lowland gorilla. Gorillas are vegetarians and they spend much of their time feeding on shoots, leaves and the pith of stalks and branches. Because their food is so low in nutritional value, they have to eat a large quantity each day. Although they are good climbers, they generally remain on the ground.

Bottom: In the wild, gorillas live in groups like this one of about 15 animals. Led by a large silver-backed male, the group consists mainly of adult females with their young, juveniles and one or two other adult males. On reaching maturity most males leave the family group. These are mountain gorillas.

Above and right: The human cranium is larger and more rounded than that of any ape, for it has to accommodate a brain whose volume is about 1,500 cc. The brain sizes of gorillas, chimpanzees and orangutans are about 500, 400 and 450 cc respectively. Man's weaker jaw accounts for many other differences.

Left: A large male gorilla in typical surroundings. Because they feed on bushes and small trees, gorillas prefer to live near the edge of the rain forest where the sunlight can penetrate. Whereas felling trees for timber often provides an ideal habitat for gorillas, wholesale clearing of the forest for cultivation reduces their range.

Below: The male gorilla's threat display can take a number of forms. Usually it begins with a series of hooting sounds and culminates in a chest-beating performance, but a variety of other gestures may intervene. Only very rarely is the threat display followed by a genuine attack.

rejecting any discoloured parts.

Gorillas sleep in nests, but even when tall trees are available these are constructed near the ground. Male gorillas, having nothing to fear from predators, usually make their nests in low bushes or even on the ground. An adult male gorilla standing on its relatively short hind legs may be up to 1.8 m (5.9 ft) tall, and has an arm span of up to 2.75 m (9 ft). Large males may weigh up to 275 kg (605 lb), but this is exceptional. The creature's head is particularly massive because it includes a tall bony ridge on top of the skull to which the powerful jaw muscles are attached. These give the gorilla a very strong bite used primarily to tear through the hard stems of some plants to get at the softer pith inside. Adult male gorillas are larger than the females and can be recognized by the greyish-white fur on their backs.

Females and juveniles climb more often than adult males do. No doubt the gorilla's ancestors were smaller and more arboreal than their modern descendants, for, apart from their size, they are well adapted for climbing, with long, grasping digits, opposable thumbs and big toes, long arms which are potentially useful for brachiation and good binocular vision. The ability to judge distance is essential to an active climber.

Gorillas have a discontinuous distribution in equatorial Africa. The western lowland gorilla inhabits forests of Cam-

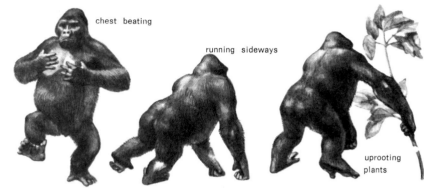

chest beating

running sideways

uprooting plants

Left: Like humans, chimpanzees use a whole range of facial expressions to indicate their emotions. This animal, with its gaping mouth and jutting upper lip, is expressing frustration. Chimpanzees also communicate with other group members by a variety of hoots and grunts, and, to some extent, by touch.

Below: Chimpanzees spend more time in trees than do gorillas. Every evening the adults build nests like the one shown here to provide protection from predators. The nests are made of bent and woven branches covered with a bed of smaller branches and leaves. They may be as much as 30 m above the ground.

Giuseppe Mazza

excitement

elation

Left: Chimpanzees, like the other apes, use their hands more than their feet for climbing about among the trees. As an adaptation for this method of locomotion, they have particularly long arms and relatively short legs. They walk with the soles of the feet flat on the ground and the upper part of the body supported on the knuckles.

Below: A chimpanzee extracts termites from a nest by using a twig stripped of its leaves. When the twig is poked into the nest, angry termites seize it and are drawn out of the nest. Although chimpanzees eat leaves, bark and insects, about 90 per cent of their diet consists of fruit.

eroun, Gabon, and western Zaire. Nearly 1,000 miles to the east, the eastern lowland gorilla inhabits forests from the Lualaba or upper Congo River to the foothills of the mountains beyond. Here on the slopes of the Virunga volcanoes and the mountains bordering Lake Kivu lives the mountain gorilla. These three populations differ slightly from each other in features of the skull and in certain other ways—mountain gorillas, for example, have slightly longer, thicker fur.

However, most zoologists now agree that there is only one species, *Gorilla gorilla*, and that the various forms are only subspecies. Lowland gorillas live in dense forest, preferring areas where fallen trees or rivers break the upper canopy, allowing the sunlight to encourage thick undergrowth, which is a rich source of their food. Mountain gorillas prefer more thinly wooded valleys where ferns and creepers abound. Sometimes they venture above the tree-line in search of bamboo shoots.

The gestation period of the gorilla is about nine months. At birth baby gorillas are even more helpless than those of most other primates. For the first month of life they cannot even cling to their mother, but have to be cradled in her arms. At three months a baby gorilla may start to ride on its mother's back, and at six or seven months it can walk and climb on its own. However, the bond with the mother remains very strong until, three or four years later, she has another youngster. In the rate at which they mature, gorillas resemble chimpanzees. More data is needed, but it seems likely that they have a potential life-span of 40 or more years.

Chimpanzees

There are two main kinds of chimpanzees. The commoner of these, *Pan troglodytes*, is widely distributed in tropical Africa, and several different races or subspecies have been described. However, all chimpanzee populations are rather variable in appearance, and these differences are not very important. The most distinct of all chimpanzees is the pygmy chimpanzee, the only form to be found south of the Congo River. This is regarded by many authorities as a separate species, *Pan paniscus*. The pygmy chimpanzee is less heavily built than the common chimpanzee, which weighs up to 50 kg (110 lb) or more, adult females being almost as large as males.

Chimpanzees are far from being specialized feeders. In mature rain forests they feed mainly on fruit, when it is available, although they also eat leaves and bark. In more open savannah woodland they make up for the smaller supply of vegetable foods by eating insects, and sometimes by hunting and eating other mammals, such as small antelopes. In some parts of West Africa chimpanzees have colonized rubbish dumps outside towns, where they feed on scraps.

Chimpanzees have developed a remarkable technique for obtaining termites, a popular item of diet. Picking a small twig or grass stem they remove all its side branches, and poke it into a termites' nest. Angry termites seize the intruding object with their jaws, and cling to it as the twig is withdrawn. The chimpanzee then pulls the twig through its lips, removing the termites. This action looks highly intelligent, but there is some evidence to suggest that it is purely instinctive. If they are given a slender twig, zoo-bred chimpanzees need little encouragement to poke it into holes, and also draw it through their lips.

One interesting aspect of this behaviour is that in preparing the twigs for use chimpanzees are essentially making tools. They also do this when crushing dry leaves before using them to soak up

fear

sadness

Left: Some common chimpanzee expressions.

Right: A female pygmy chimpanzee with her baby. Like the other apes, chimpanzees reproduce only slowly because the females cannot conceive while they are lactating. Since the female will nurse her young for between two and three years, she can produce only one (occasionally two) offspring every three years or so. The gestation period is between seven and eight months. This particular species, *Pan paniscus*, is found in equatorial Africa, south of the Congo River. The more common species, *Pan troglodytes*, is found throughout central and western Africa, from Senegal to Tanzania.

Above: Chimpanzees in captivity are enthusiastic painters, and their efforts resemble the early works of human children. They seem to have a rudimentary sense of symmetry for their compositions on paper are usually fairly well balanced. They rarely paint only down one side of the paper.

Below: The most significant difference between man and his nearest relatives, the apes, is his much greater mental capacity. The ability to learn and remember things made language possible and paved the way for logical thought. These spectators are watching a chess championship in the USSR.

water for drinking. This means that man is not unique as a toolmaker, and the attempts that were made a few years ago to use toolmaking ability to place man apart from all other animals are not based on fact. The truth is that no absolute distinction can be made between man and all other animals.

Chimpanzees are certainly intelligent. Experiments to determine intelligence have all been carried out with young chimpanzees, for adults are aggressive and uncooperative, and young animals learn more quickly than old ones. Once young chimpanzees have learned that by standing on a box they can reach higher objects—even such an obvious fact has to be learned—they swiftly put their knowledge to good use in obtaining fruit which is otherwise out of reach. Behaviour of this kind enables them to solve problems which could never be solved by instinct alone, and produces flexible behaviour which can be adapted to meet a variety of situations.

In the wild chimpanzees live in large, loosely-knit groups. About 80 animals may occupy an undefended home range of between 20 and 78 sq km (8 to 30 sq miles). They move equally well through the trees or on the ground, where they walk on all fours, touching the ground with the backs of their knuckles. Adult males travel further than the others, acting as scouts for the main party. When they find a tree laden with ripe fruit their drumming and loud hooting calls attract other chimpanzees from up to 3 km (2 miles) away to join in the feast. On these occasions chimpanzees belonging to neighbouring troops mix without hostility. Large males have high status,

and are treated with deference, but within the troop there is no rigid 'pecking order'. When conflicts arise between individuals they are usually solved when one of the individuals concerned moves off to join another troop.

The chimpanzee's essentially peaceable disposition is not even disturbed when the females come into breeding condition, as they do every month or so. At this time females have swellings in the region of the genital organs. They are promiscuous, and may mate with several males in succession. The gestation period is usually between seven and eight months, and at birth the young chimpanzee weighs about 1.9 kg (4.2 lb). For the first two years of life it is completely dependent upon its mother, but as it grows older it is supported by other members of the troop.

By playing with other juveniles it exercises its body, learns about its surroundings and, probably most important of all, becomes socialized and learns how to get on with other members of its species. Until about six years of age the young chimpanzee never goes far from its mother, but it then becomes more independent and, especially if it is a male, may begin to go off with other chimpanzees for increasingly lengthy periods. Chimpanzees are sexually mature at about 8 years, full-grown at about 12 years, and may live for 40 or more years unless they fall victim to a predator. Apart from man the chimpanzee's greatest enemy is the leopard. When threatened by such a predator, chimpanzees arm themselves with missiles and sticks, and confront it aggressively, the combined strength and resourcefulness of the troop being their main defence.

387

Part IV

Plant and Animal Habitats

Moorland and Heath

Since prehistoric times man has felled trees and burned vegetation to clear land for cultivation and grazing. The regions which have been primarily used to support herds of sheep and cattle have become, over the centuries, the uncultivated, treeless moors and heaths we know today.

In everyday speech the words 'moor' and 'heath' are often used to mean the same thing. Ecologists, however, reserve the term *heathland* for areas in which trees or tall shrubs are entirely absent or only very thinly distributed, and the dominant plants are evergreen dwarf shrubs, typically members of the heath family, *Ericaceae*. The looser term *moorland* describes any area with wet, acid soils, usually more than 300 m (1,000 ft) above sea level. Such conditions often lead to the formation of *peat*, a layer of partly decomposed dead plant remains over the surface of the ground. Many areas of moorland support heathland vegetation, while others are *bogs* in which the dominant plant is the moss *Sphagnum*. Grasses, sedges and rushes are also common moorland plants.

Heathlands

The most characteristic lowland heaths are found in Western Europe, from northern Scandinavia to Spain. They flourish in an oceanic climate, with abundant rainfall and lacking extremes of temperature at any time of the year. The soils are typically *podsols*, that is to say well-drained, often sandy soils where rainwater has dissolved the nutrients in the surface layer and deposited them lower down.

Formed from rocks which lack nutrient elements such as calcium, these soils are usually acid. A normally fertile soil develops by the mixing of the surface layer of organic matter with the underlying mineral layer. Under acid conditions, however, few earthworms are present to mix the organic and mineral components of the soil so that the plant litter remains as a separate layer on the soil surface, and decomposes only very slowly.

In Europe, the common heathland shrubs include the common heather or ling, *Calluna vulgaris*, and various species of *Erica* such as bell heather, *Erica cinerea*, and cross-leaved heath, *Erica tetralix*. These genera are not found in North America, but others such as *Vaccinium*—for example cowberry, *Vaccinium vitis-idaea*—are found in heathland plant communities throughout the Northern Hemisphere. Other typical heathland shrubs are bearberry, *Arctostaphylos uva-ursi*, and crowberry, *Empetrum nigrum*.

As their common names imply, the fruits of many of these dwarf shrubs are succulent berries, attractive to animals which disperse the seeds in their droppings. Apart from reproduction by seed, most of the dwarf shrubs also spread by creeping stems, so that one seedling may grow into a mat-like plant covering a wide area. Some of these stems, because they are partly buried, will survive fires, so that burnt areas are re-colonized.

Robin Fletcher

Below right: Two of the most common heathland plants—a lichen of the genus *Cladonia*, and the bearberry, *Arctostaphylos uva-ursi*, recognized by its red-brown leaves.

Below: The growth of a heather plant can be traced through four distinct phases. In the *pioneer phase*, which lasts between three and six years, compact clumps grow from seedlings or from buried stems. This is followed by the *building phase*, in which the plants grow outwards to cover the ground. After about 15 years they enter the *mature phase* during which they reach their greatest height, but growth slackens. After another 15 years or so the plants become *degenerate*.

P. Morris

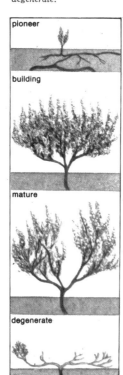

Heather Angel

Left: Desolate, treeless moorland in the north of Scotland. This sort of terrain is inhabited by the red deer, *Cervus elephus*, and is often misleadingly termed 'deer forest'.

Right: The most common herbivores of the heathland are insects like this leaf-hopper nymph, *Fileno spumario*, which lives in a frothy secretion of bubbles. A variety of insects feed on the young shoots and leaves of heather plants, among them thrips, springtails, mites, moth caterpillars and heather beetles. These in turn provide food for animals like shrews, lizards and insectivorous birds such as the meadow pipit.

Below left: Deliberate burning of heather in Scotland. Younger heather plants are more palatable to animals and contain more nutrients, so periodic burning (typically every ten years or so) improves the quality of the grazing for sheep and game birds such as grouse. Normally the heather is burnt in patches and only a proportion of the area is burned each year.

Giuseppe Mazza

Heather Angel

Left: A froghopper, *Cercopis vulnerata*, a typical heathland species. The insect's bold colour and marking probably serve as a warning to potential predators that it would make an unpalatable meal (or make it look like an unpalatable species). Insects form vital links in many heathland food chains. This froghopper, for example, might be eaten by a grouse which could then fall prey to a top carnivore such as a fox, an eagle or a wild cat.

Below: The emperor moth, *Saturnia pavonia*, is another heathland insect. Clearly visible are the 'eye spots' on the wings. These resemble the eyes of a larger animal and so help to deter predators.

Robin Fletcher

Other plant species are found growing among the dominant shrubs. Most conspicuous are the lichens, especially *Cladonia*, some species of which have bright red spore-bearing organs. One species of lichen, *Parmelia physodes*, actually grows on the stems of old heather plants. There are also grasses, such as wavy hair-grass, *Deschampsia flexuosa*, with its conspicuous silvery flower heads. Herbaceous dicotyledonous plants, however, are rare.

Comparable plant communities are found in other parts of the world, for example in some of the 'pine barrens' of the eastern US and Canada, at the extreme southern tip of South America and on some southern Atlantic islands including the Falkland Islands. At extreme northern and southern latitudes, the climate becomes too harsh for shrub species, and heathland gives way to tundra where mosses and lichens predominate. Heathlands are also found on mountains, for example in East Africa, South Africa and in Australia and New Zealand. Tree heaths, such as *Erica arborea*, are found on the East African mountains, but they grow to more than 10 m (30 ft), forming a forest rather than a heathland habitat.

The origin of heathland

The history of vegetation can be investigated by *pollen analysis*. Cores are taken from deep peat deposits or lake sediments, and by laboriously counting the pollen grains of different plant species it is possible to discover the abundance of different types of plants at different times in the past. In some cases, recognizable fragments of plants are found as well as pollen grains, and also layers of ash indicating the burning of the vegetation. The age of different layers in a core can be found by radiocarbon dating. As a rough guide it takes about 1,000 years to form a 1 m (3 ft) depth of peat.

Evidence of the original forest cover of heathland is provided by the appearance in the cores of pollen of trees which once lived in the area. In some places clearance took place in Mesolithic times (around 4000 BC), but the main change from forest to heath began in the Neolithic period (3000 to 2000 BC). Forest clearance resulting in the spread of heathland has continued into modern times.

Once cleared, the forest did not return. Part of the reason may have been the climatic change in Western Europe towards a cooler, wetter climate less favourable for tree growth. Another possibility is that the removal of the trees caused an irreversible deterioration of the soil, resulting in the infertile podsols. However, the main factor—and one which can to some extent be controlled once its effects are properly understood—was grazing. Although tree seedlings are eaten by herbivores such as deer, rabbits and voles, in natural conditions enough survive for forests to regenerate. In contrast, heavy grazing by domestic sheep and cattle can stop any seedlings at all from growing into trees. The absence of trees from large areas of heathland and moorland may therefore be explained by the fact that the main use of these areas in Europe, since early medieval times, has been as grazing for sheep and cattle.

The growth of heather plants generally follows a fixed pattern, ending, after about 30 years, with the plants becoming de-

391

generate. The central branches die, while the outer branches collapse outwards often lying flat on the ground like the spokes of a wheel, There is then an open space at the centre of each plant, in which lichens flourish and where new heather seedlings can germinate to replace the dying plants.

Moorlands

Although many moorland areas can be considered as heathlands, other kinds of vegetation may have originated as a result of overgrazing or excessive burning. Unpalatable plants such as mat-grass, *Nardus stricta*, and bracken, *Pteridium aquilinum*, are common. In other cases, poor drainage and high rainfall create conditions in which heather grows badly, and here the dominant plant is often *Sphagnum*.

Sphagnum bogs are of three types. *Valley bogs* occur where water drains into a valley or depression. This water brings with it nutrients leached from the land around, so a fair variety of plants may be found in such bogs, including the soft rush, *Juncus effusus.* *Raised bogs* develop on top of valley bogs, and have a convex surface, with a thicker layer of peat at the centre than at the edges. The peat is formed of the dead, partly decomposed *Sphagnum*, while the living *Sphagnum* forms a continuous cover over the surface of the bog. *Blanket bog* describes large areas of *Sphagnum* covering flat or gently sloping land. Raised and blanket bogs are both dependent on a continual supply of rainwater, and so the finest examples are found in the west of Ireland, in Connemara and western Mayo, where the rainfall is up to 250 cm (100 in) a year.

The vegetation of wet moorlands is quite varied: in addition to the ever-present *Sphagnum*, there are usually small hummocks colonized by plants of drier habitats. Very often bell heather is found in the drier patches, while cross-leaved heath can grow in the wetter depressions. Among the typical plants of bogs and wet moors are bog asphodel, *Narthecium ossifragum*, with star-like yellow flowers, two sedges called cotton grass, *Eriophorum*, and deer grass, *Scirpus cespitosus*, and the aromatic shrub *Myrica gale*, bog myrtle. The commonest grass is purple moor-grass, *Molinia caerulea*, and there are also the insectivorous plants sundew, *Drosera*, and butterwort, *Pinguicula*. These supplement the inadequate nutrient content of the moorland soils by catching and digesting insects.

Animals of moor and heath

Moorlands and heathlands are not noted for their diversity of animal species, possibly because they are man-made habitats and therefore of recent origin by evolutionary standards. A hectare of typical moorland in Scotland is likely to have only three species of birds: curlew, *Numenius arquata*, red grouse, *Lagopus lagopus scoticus*, and meadow pipit, *Anthus pratensis*. These are all birds which nest on the ground. More species are found where there are trees nearby, and reafforestation causes a great increase in the diversity of birds and other animals.

Frogs and newts are common on wet moors, while the drier lowland heaths provide an ideal habitat for snakes and lizards. Moorland areas with warm, wet

P. Morris

Above: Many moors and heaths owe their existence to the clearing of woodland by man and subsequent grazing by domestic animals. Sheep can thrive on poor pasture and so are suited to such habitats.

Below: The red grouse, *Lagopus lagopus scoticus*, is found only in Britain and Ireland. It is a close relation of the willow grouse found in other parts of northern Europe. Its diet consists chiefly of heather.

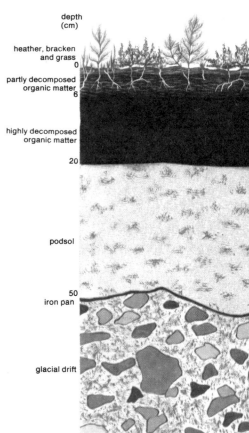

Below: Heathland soils are often *podsols.* Formed from rocks which lack nutrient elements such as calcium, they are usually acid. An acid environment discourages bacteria as well as invertebrates such as earthworms and snails, so decomposition of plant litter is slow and there is little mixing of the soil layers.

depth (cm)

heather, bracken and grass — 0
partly decomposed organic matter — 6
highly decomposed organic matter
— 20
podsol
— 50
iron pan
glacial drift

A. Winspear Cundall/Natural Science Photos

Above: The nightjar, *Caprimulgus europaeus*, is an inhabitant of heath and open woodland. By night it hunts large flying insects, especially beetles and moths, while by day it lies motionless on the ground or in a tree.

Below: A typical moorland blanket bog in Snowdonia, Wales. Visible in the picture are dark green heaths of the family *Ericaceae*, paler green mosses, *Sphagnum*, and the white fruiting heads of cotton grass, *Eriophorum*.

Right: Deerstalking in the Highlands of Scotland. Each year many thousands of red deer are killed, about 15 per cent of the total population in the Highlands. Even so, the deer population is on the increase.

summer weather, such as the west of Scotland, may be infested with biting flies, including midges, *Ceratopogonidae*, and clegs, *Haematopota pluvialis*, a species of the horse-fly family.

The herbivore species have adapted to the extensive areas of moorland to be found in the British Isles. The red grouse, found only in Britain and Ireland, is closely related to the willow grouse found in other parts of northern Europe. Unlike the willow grouse, which has a varied diet of young shoots and willow, birch and bilberry fruits, the red grouse eats mainly heather.

The cock grouse occupy and defend territories, and only those which can obtain territories are able to breed. The rate of increase of the grouse population is therefore limited by the size, and hence the number, of territories. Grouse feed largely on young heather shoots, and after a season of good heather growth the territories may become smaller—down to about 2 hectares (5 acres)—allowing more birds to breed. This is an example of population regulation by the behaviour of an animal, which is interesting because it means that grouse should never become so numerous that they are short of food.

The red deer, *Cervus elaphus*, is found in forests all over Europe, but in Britain it has become a moorland species, smaller and lighter than the original forest deer. Red deer are particularly common in Scottish 'deer forests', which are not forests at all but desolate, treeless moorland. There are about 10,000 sq km (4,000 sq miles) of deer forest in Scotland, although this area is constantly being reduced by the appearance of new forest plantations.

Deserts

Although most of the land surface of the Earth is covered by vegetation there are large areas with only scattered plants or no plants at all. In tropical and subtropical regions, high temperatures all the year round mean that water from rain evaporates rapidly and an annual rainfall of less than 20 cm (8 in) results in a *hot desert*, in which plant and animal life is severely restricted by shortage of water. Similarly barren arid areas, but with cool winters, are found in higher latitudes; the plants and animals of these *cold deserts* have to endure low winter temperatures as well as scarcity of water.

Climate

Taking average figures for a number of years, all deserts are seen to have a low annual rainfall. The pattern of rainfall, however, varies widely from one desert to another. Some deserts, such as the central Sahara, have no rain at all in many years, while others, like the Sonoran desert on the Mexican-US border and the Karroo desert of South Africa, may have two rainy seasons in a year. But however often the rain falls, in most deserts even the low annual rainfall figures recorded (often about 5 mm, 0.2 in, a year) exaggerate the amount of rain likely to fall in any one year. They are the result of averaging, say, one heavy shower over several years. Desert rainfall is unpredictable but in most years it is significantly less than the average.

Above: The starkness of the Namib Desert in southern Africa. Desert habitats can be defined as areas where the overriding ecological consideration is shortage of water.

Below: Deserts are not always hot. Occasionally they can even be cold enough for snow. This is the Mojave Desert, high in the Sierra Nevada of California.

Desert plants

Only specialized plants are able to survive the chronic water shortage of deserts. Different species are adapted in different ways, but perhaps the simplest adaptation is a physiological ability to withstand long periods in which the water content of the plant falls to a very low level. Plants which can do this include lichens as well as flowering plants, such as the creosote bush, *Larrea divaricata*, which grows in the deserts of North and South America. The leaves of a well-watered creosote bush contain about 55 per cent water but this can fall to around 30 per cent during a drought. If the drought is prolonged, the older leaves die while the immature leaves and buds turn brown, losing the ability to photosynthesize but not dying. When rain comes the leaves turn green and the plant starts to grow again.

Other plants, called *succulents*, store water for use in time of drought. The water is stored either in swollen stems, as in the cactus family, *Cactaceae*, and the spurge faily, *Euphorbiaceae*, or in both stems and leaves, as in the stonecrop family, *Crassulaceae*. To eke out what water they can obtain most desert plants have mechanisms for cutting down the amount of water that they lose by transpiration (through the stomata) or by evaporation (through the cuticle).

Water economy is achieved in a number of ways. To reduce transpiration the stomata may be sunk beneath the leaf surface or the leaves may be rolled up with the stomata on the inside. Sunken stomata and rolled-up leaves reduce transpiration because the stomata are then surrounded by a stable layer of air which, because it is in intimate contact with the intercellular spaces within the leaf, is far more humid than the dry desert air. Water loss by evaporation through the cuticle may be cut down by reducing the surface area of the plant relative to its volume (by having small leaves or no leaves at all—in

Camels have adapted thoroughly to desert life. Long eyelashes and muscular nostrils keep out windblown sand, and the camel feeds mainly on plants with a high water content.

From 'Desert Animals' by K. Schmidt-Nielsen, Oxford University Press

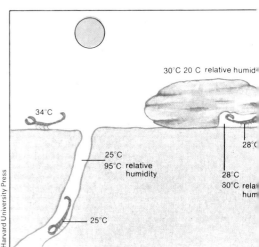

Left: Many desert plants survive dry periods as seeds. There may be 25,000 per square metre (2,500 per square foot) of soil. After rain they germinate, transforming barren areas into colourful meadows. They must, however, flower and reproduce before the soil dries again.

Below: Birds' eggs fail to hatch if left unprotected in the desert sun. They are therefore normally laid in the shelter of bushes, holes, caves or under rocks. The elf owl, *Microthene whitneyi* (shown here) has an ideal solution. It nests in the abandoned holes formed by woodpeckers in the giant saguaro cactus, *Carnegiea gigantea.*

Harvard University Press

which case the stem is used for photosynthesis) or by increasing the thickness of the layer of waxes on the cuticle.

These adaptations of the above-ground parts of the plant are complemented by root systems able to collect such small amounts of rain as do fall. Many desert plants have root systems which extend over large areas. For example, the roots of the bean caper, *Zygophyllum dumosum*, may cover an area of 35 square metres (400 square feet), although the plant itself is no more than 2 m (6 ft) across. It follows that such plants must grow well spaced out from their neighbours, and it is common in desert areas to see shrubs, like the creosote bush, growing several metres apart with more or less bare ground between them.

Instead of rooting outwards, other desert plants send down deep roots, as far as 4 m (12 ft) or deeper, to take advantage of the fact that heavy rain often finds its way, as *surface run-off*, into drainage channels or wadis. Immediately after rain these channels become short-lived rivers, but even after the surface water has disappeared large amounts of water remain deep in the soil. Furthermore, where permanent rivers flow through deserts, there is often underground water for some distance away from the river. Additionally, water flowing down from high plateaus may flow under the desert floor and be reached by deep growing roots. Both river banks and apparently dry drainage channels often support lush vegetation quite different from the barren areas around them.

All the ingenious adaptations of desert plants have but one purpose—they either reduce water loss or increase water up-

396

Photri

Frank Lane

Left: The extraordinary desert gymnosperm, *Welwitschia bainesii*, of the Namib and Kalahari Deserts of southwest Africa. Many Namib plants obtain moisture from sea fogs but *Welwitschia* most often grows in drainage channels and probably obtains most of its water from the soil.

Right: During the hottest weather, some animals like this desert tortoise, *Gopherus agassizi*, aestivate—a process not unlike hibernation but at a higher temperature.

Below: Saharan camels, *Camelus dromedarius*.

Bottom: The gecko, *Palmatogecko rangei*, has webbed feet to prevent it sinking in soft sand.

Above left: The coat of a dog or other hairy animal not only keeps it warm in cold climates but also cool in hot climates. The temperature at the surface of the coat can be very high in comparison with the skin temperature of a man. Although both dog and man gain heat by radiation from the sun and the ground, only man gains significant heat from the air because his skin temperature is lower than that of the air. Loose-fitting clothes will keep him cool in a similar way to the dog's coat.

Left: Invertebrates survive in the desert by hiding in burrows or under stones where the microclimate, both in terms of temperature and relative humidity, is usually far more amenable. This experiment shows how the body temperature of a typical desert dweller, a scorpion, depends on whether it is inside a burrow, under a stone, or directly in the sun.

take, and so allow the plant to continue to transpire when other plants would have to close their stomata because of water shortage. Any plant can reduce its rate of transpiration to zero by closing its stomata, but by doing this it also stops itself from photosynthesizing. This happens because the stomata are not only concerned with transpiration: carbon dioxide required for photosynthesis enters the plant through the stomata as well.

Perhaps the most highly adapted desert plants, mainly members of the stonecrop family, such as *Kalanchoe*, have to some extent mastered even this problem. They have a different kind of photosynthesis which allows them to absorb carbon dioxide at night and to store it as organic chemicals, such as malic acid, which are converted in the daytime to carbohydrates by the normal photosynthetic reactions. These plants can thus close their stomata during the daytime without stopping growth. When their stomata are open at night the lower night temperatures and higher night humidities reduce the rate of water loss.

A final group of desert plants avoid altogether the problem of trying to grow without water. Most of them are annuals and remarkably they germinate only when sufficient rain has fallen for them to grow from germination to seed dispersal before the ground dries again. Others, often members of the lily family such as the desert tulip, *Tulipa amphiophylla*, are able to survive dry periods as underground storage organs, such as bulbs.

Desert animals

The basic problem faced by desert animals is the same as that for desert plants—the

397

Left: Most desert invertebrates are very well adapted to desert conditions. These tenebrionid beetles, *Tenebrionidae*, have very short legs and a flattened body. They burrow into the sand with small alternate sideways movements.

Below: Parental care in a desert arachnid—the scorpion, *Vejovis spinigera*, carrying its young.

Bottom: A carnivorous arachnid, the lady dune spider, *Leucorchestris* (family *Sparassidae*), of the Namib. These animals are nocturnal, hiding in burrows during the day and feeding on insects during the night. Here a cricket has been caught.

Above and right: Only those animals which can travel large distances or can go without water for long periods can rely on drinking from open water to supply their water needs in the desert. Large mammals, like the cape oryx, *Oryx gazella* (above), and the kit fox, *Vulpes velox* (right), will drink when the opportunity permits but rely chiefly on the water in their food. How herbivores, like the oryx, can do this is not well understood, but the problem for carnivores is simpler—meat contains from 60 to 70 per cent water.

need to maintain the water content of their tissues. An animal can obtain water from three sources. The surest of these is *metabolic water*, produced as a by-product of the biochemical reactions of respiration. The amount produced is small, about 0.5 g for each gram of carbohydrate used in respiration, but for some desert animals it is the main source of water. Others rely on eating food containing water: either succulent plants, in the case of herbivores, or other animals, in the case of carnivores. Finally, a few desert animals obtain most of their water by drinking from open water, although this is only useful if they can exist for several days without drinking or if they can travel long distances to water as some birds do.

Set against these three sources of water are the three ways in which an animal loses water. Exposed to the sun, and surrounded by air at temperatures of up to 45 °C (110 °F), mammals and birds need to regulate their body temperature at a roughly constant value, usually in the range 35 to 40 °C (95 to 105 °F). This is chiefly achieved by the evaporation of water—about 600 calories of heat are lost when 1 ml of water evaporates. Water can be lost either by sweating or by panting. In panting the animal takes very rapid breaths to increase the evaporation of water from the membranes of the lungs and from the moist surfaces of the tongue and mouth.

As well as losing water to keep cool, animals also cannot avoid losing water in their faeces and urine. The faeces of a cow, for example, contain about 85 per cent water. This would be an excessive waste of water for a desert animal, and in desert

species much of this water, instead of being excreted, is extracted from the intestinal contents. For instance, a camel without access to water produces faeces with only 45 per cent water. Similarly, desert animals excrete relatively small amounts of urine containing high concentrations of salts and urea. The salt concentration of man's urine is about four times that of the blood plasma; in the camel the urine concentration is eight times that of plasma.

As well as reducing the amount of water lost in excretion, concentrated urine also increases the number of water sources available to the animal. Because the kidneys of desert animals can excrete high concentrations of salt they can drink salt water and eat plants with a high salt content. This is important, because desert soils in dry water channels often contain large amounts of salts, left behind when the water in which they were dissolved evaporated. Birds and desert reptiles go a stage further, and do not excrete urine at all. Instead they excrete *uric acid*, which is almost insoluble and is produced as a semi-solid paste with a very low water content. Nevertheless, this cannot really be considered as a desert adaptation for *all* birds and most reptiles excrete uric acid.

Camels

The camel, *Camelus*, is a very good example of how a large mammal can adapt to desert conditions. The facts about the ability of camels to go without water are remarkable, although often exaggerated in travellers' accounts. There is no doubt, however, that camels can travel across the waterless desert of Saudi Arabia, a distance of about 900 km (550 miles), in 21 days without drinking.

This is done without any special water storage organ—the hump consists mainly of fat—and the ability of camels to survive results from a combination of subtle modifications of normal mammalian physiology. As well as producing dry faeces and concentrated urine, camels also reduce the amount of water which must be lost in body cooling by allowing their body temperatures to increase by up to 6 °C (11 °F) during the day, cooling down at night.

Other animals

Another factor which works in the camel's favour in the desert is its size. Because an animal in a hot environment gains heat energy through its body surface, the amount of water needed for cooling is greater, relative to body weight, in a smaller animal since a smaller animal has a larger surface to volume ratio. To avoid overheating on a typical summer day in the desert a camel needs to evaporate an amount of water equivalent to only 1 per cent of its body weight every hour; for a mouse the equivalent figure is 15 per cent.

Smaller animals are forced to hide from the heat of the daytime sun in order to survive. Most commonly they spend the hot daylight hours in burrows or under stones and come out to feed only at night.

Many nocturnal rodents, for example the kangaroo rats, *Dipodomys*, from the deserts of the southwestern US, survive indefinitely without drinking. Their diet consists solely of dry seeds and other dry plant material. Their nocturnal habit thus allows them to survive on the little water in their food supplemented by the metabolic water produced during respiration.

So long as they can find an adequate supply of prey, carnivores have less of a problem of water supply than herbivores, since meat typically contains 60 to 70 per cent water. Nevertheless, the same basic adaptations for avoiding water loss are found in carnivores as in herbivores. In particular, many of them are active at night—although it is possible, of course, that this simply reflects the nocturnal habits of their prey.

Among nocturnal carnivores which range far into the desert in search of prey are the jackal, *Canis aureus*, the fennec, *Fennecus zerda*, of Africa, and the kit fox, *Vulpes velox*, of Mexico and the southern US.

Invertebrates

Whereas the most striking desert animals are the large mammals, the most numerous, as in most other habitats, are the invertebrates, particularly insects and other arthropods. These animals do not need to maintain their body temperatures within such strict limits as mammals, but they too must conserve water to avoid becoming desiccated. They survive by the same sorts of adaptations as those of smaller vertebrates. In addition, arthropods have an impermeable exoskeleton which reduces water loss to a minimum, and they can also tolerate a large degree of dehydration. By making use of metabolic water and by taking full advantage of the cool, humid *microclimates* found under even small stones or within the rosettes of plants, small invertebrates can live in the hottest and driest deserts virtually uninhabited by larger animals.

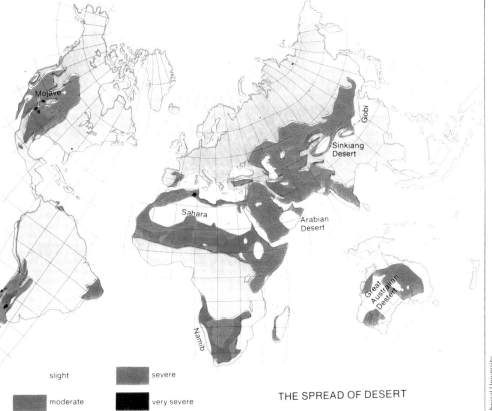

THE SPREAD OF DESERT

his map shows e degree of esertification in the orld. For at least 000 years the total nd area covered by

desert has been increasing, and this has become a particularly serious problem in recent years. The chief reason for

the spread of deserts is over-use of the land by man. If, for example, a tract of land bordering a desert region is used to support too many

grazing animals it will soon be denuded of the grasses which bind the topsoil. This then gets stripped away by wind and water erosion.

slight

moderate

severe

very severe

Mojave

Gobi

Sinkiang Desert

Sahara

Arabian Desert

Namib

Great Australian Desert

The Arctic and Antarctic

Among the most inhospitable areas of the world are the cold polar regions of the Arctic and Antarctic. They are popularly thought to be icebound wastes inhabited by a very few hardy beasts, such as polar bears in the Arctic and penguins in the Antarctic, able to eke out an existence in the intense cold. In fact this is far from the case. The poles themselves are indeed virtually lifeless areas but the polar regions as a whole support an astonishingly large number of plants and animals, especially around the edges of the two regions where the climate is not so extreme.

Differences between the two poles

Both Arctic and Antarctic are cold in relation to tropical and temperate regions but, other than this, differences between them are numerous. Many of these differences spring from the fact that the Arctic is an ocean surrounded by land whereas the Antarctic is a continent surrounded by ocean.

Antarctica has an area of 140 million sq km (5.5 million sq miles), most of which is covered by permanent ice that in places reaches a depth of 3,600 m (12,000 ft)—the average depth being around 1,800 m (6,000 ft). In contrast, the Arctic Ocean is covered by just a few metres of floating ice and has no large ice-covered land areas,

apart from Greenland which has only a tenth as much ice as that of Antarctica. The greater mass of Antarctica makes it many degrees colder than the Arctic which has its climate further modified by the inflow of warm water to the Arctic Basin from the Pacific and Atlantic Oceans. In consequence the cold influence of the Antarctic spreads much further north than the influence of the Arctic does south.

Paradoxically, the Antarctic is a continent but the Antarctic ecosystem derives most of its primary energy from the sea, while the Arctic is a sea whose ecosystem derives most of its energy from the land. This is not surprising, however, when it is realized that both of the polar regions are importers of energy from the milder, more productive areas to the north and south. The Arctic imports from the tundra and forest areas of the American and Eurasian continents, while the Antarctic imports from the highly productive Southern Ocean.

Arctic and Antarctic plants

The *tundra* of the Arctic consists of an area of flat, nearly treeless country which extends from the edge of the northern coniferous forest to the permanent pack ice of the pole. In winter it is covered by snow, but in summer the land thaws to a depth of about half a metre (20 in), although the soil below this remains permanently frozen and is called the *permafrost*. The melting snow reveals a variety of habitats from bare rock to swamp.

The dominant vegetation in the tundra are lichens, particularly reindeer 'moss', *Cladonia*. In addition, algae and moss are common. There are also about 100 species

Suinot/Jacana

Above: The remarkable emperor penguin, *Aptenodytes forsteri*. These birds breed in the late winter— when it may still be continuously dark—so that the chicks will fledge when their food is most abundant.

Left and below left: Some typical Arctic animals.

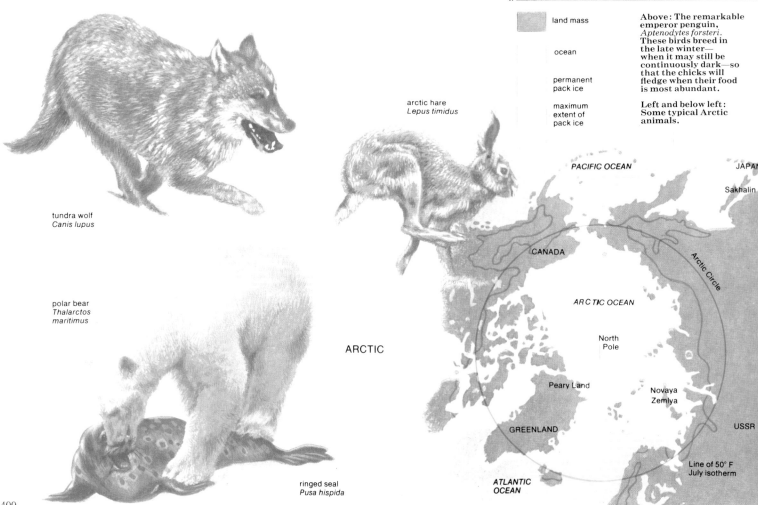

tundra wolf
Canis lupus

polar bear
Thalarctos maritimus

ringed seal
Pusa hispida

arctic hare
Lepus timidus

land mass

ocean

permanent pack ice

maximum extent of pack ice

PACIFIC OCEAN

JAPAN

Sakhalin

CANADA

Arctic Circle

ARCTIC OCEAN

North Pole

ARCTIC

Peary Land

Novaya Zemlya

USSR

GREENLAND

ATLANTIC OCEAN

Line of 50° F July isotherm

of flowering plant, including cranberries and bilberries, *Vaccinium*, the stichwort, *Stellaria crassiflora*, and the dwarf birch, *Betula nana*. Most of the flowering plants grow in a low cushion-like manner which makes them self-sheltering thus reducing the chilling effects of the wind. They are also often dark in colour to better absorb solar radiation.

There are few plants in the Antarctic but the commonest are again the lichens. These plants grow on nearly all rocky faces free of snow. They are often brightly coloured but their most remarkable feature is their ability to tolerate the harshest possible conditions, although they do not grow quickly. Their growth rate is so slow as to be almost undetectable and some colonies are thought to be as much as 4,000 years old.

In more sheltered Antarctic areas, where a minimum of soil has accumulated and a little water is available, mosses develop; and in favourable areas, such as the South Orkney Islands, banks of moss peat several metres deep have been found. In the most favourable habitats just two flowering plants may also occur. These are a grass, *Descampsia antarctica*, and a pink, *Colobanthus quitensis*.

Land animals

Because of the severity of the climate, and because Antarctica has no land connections with more temperate continents over which animal species could migrate, there are very few true land animal species in the Antarctic. They are limited to a species of springtail, *Cryptopygus antarcticus*, several species of mites and a wingless fly, *Belgica antarctica*. In addition the lakes contain a few species of copepod, and a fairy shrimp, *Branchinecto gaini*. Semi-aquatic soil-dwelling protozoa and nematode worms are also fairly common.

In contrast, animal life in the Arctic summer is abundant. Many crane flies, *Tipulidae*, hover flies, *Syrphidae*, and butterflies, *Lepidoptera*, feed on the summer flowers. The butterflies spend the winter as caterpillars, some of which burrow into vegetation and others into rock crevices where they lie dormant until the first warmth of spring. Mosquitoes, *Culicidae*, are also extremely common.

The tundra also supports many land dwelling mammals, though there are none in the Antarctic. The larger mammals include the musk ox, *Ovibos moschatus*, and the caribou (or reindeer), *Rangifer tarandus*. The musk ox is so well protected against the cold that it is able to winter in the Arctic. Caribou migrate to less harsh southern areas for the winter.

On a smaller scale Arctic hares, *Lepus timidus*, lemmings, *Lemmus lemmus*, and voles, *Microtus*, are common. As a regular food source cannot be guaranteed these animals exploit a wide variety of different foods. Lemmings, for example, will eat lichen, fungi, moss and carrion.

Lemmings and voles form the major food source for carnivores such as wolverines, *Gulo gulo*, brown bears, *Ursus arctos*, and Arctic foxes, *Alopex lagopus*. The most aggressive Arctic carnivore, however, the wolf, *Canis lupus*, also preys on herds of caribou and musk ox. Wolves go around in family packs, following the herds on which they feed.

Fred Bruemmer

Below: The Arctic and Antarctic Circles are of little use in defining the limits of the polar ecosystems. The north polar ecosystem is better defined by the 10°C (50°F) *July isotherm* which is a line connecting all those places where the maximum temperature in July is 10°C. It **corresponds closely with the northern limit of trees. The southern polar ecosystem is best defined by the *Antarctic convergence* which is where cold water flowing northwards from Antarctica dips below warmer water flowing southwards from the great oceans.**

Above left: The edge of the tundra. It stretches from the northern limit of trees (shown here) to the pack ice of the pole.

Right: Tundra fruits— the crowberry, *Empetrum nigrum*.

Right and below right: Some typical Antarctic animals.

Fred Bruemmer

Fin Whale
Balaenoptera physalus

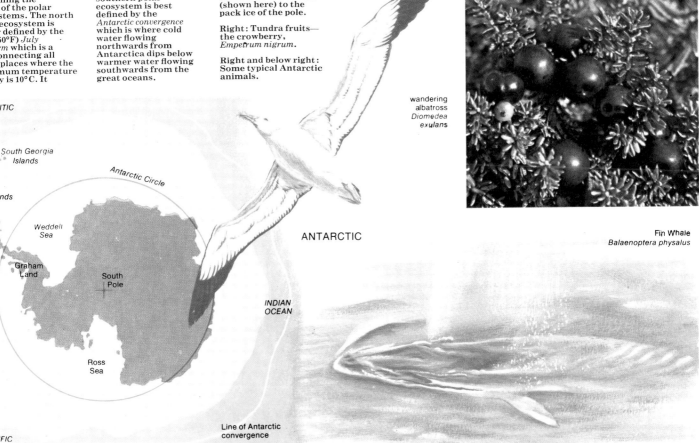

UTH ATLANTIC
OCEAN

South Georgia
Islands

alkland Islands

Antarctic Circle

Weddell
Sea

rica

Graham
Land

South
Pole

Ross
Sea

ANTARCTIC

wandering
albatross
*Diomedea
exulans*

INDIAN
OCEAN

Line of Antarctic
convergence

UTH PACIFIC
OCEAN

Tundra mammals have evolved in several ways to enable them to survive the harshness of the winter. Some adaptations, such as the reduced ears of the Arctic hare and the development of thick winter coats, are anatomical, while others are behavioural. For example, lemmings bury themselves under the snow. Many others, such as caribou and brown bears, migrate south to the coniferous forest during the winter.

Perhaps the most important migratory animals, however, are the birds. Many species (a high proportion of which are water-feeding birds taking advantage of the poorly drained tundra) migrate northwards in the spring to feed and nest. A few birds survive in the tundra throughout the winter. These include two species of ptarmigan, *Lagopus*, the raven, *Corvus corax*, the snowy owl, *Nyctea scandiaca*, and the gyrfalcon, *Falco rusticolus*. The owls feed primarily on lemmings and their population fluctuates in response to that of the lemming. The gyrfalcon feeds on ptarmigan, neatly avoiding competition with the owl.

Sea and shore animals

Unlike terrestrial animals, most sea and shore-dwelling polar animals live in the Antarctic. They are more numerous than those of the Arctic because the Southern Ocean is far more productive than the Arctic Ocean—much of which is permanently covered with ice. The high productivity of the Southern Ocean is due to the constant upwelling of bottom water containing plant nutrients, resulting in a large phytoplankton population. This is especially the case around South Georgia

Right and below: Because of its severe climate and because the Antarctic has no land bridges, connecting it with more temperate continents and over which animals could migrate, there are no large land animals in Antarctica. In the Arctic, however, there are several, including large herbivores like the musk ox, *Ovibos moschatus* (right, shown in defensive formation) and the caribou (reindeer), *Rangifer tarandus* (below). In the Arctic winter the musk ox move to high ground where deep snow cannot accumulate and in the worst storms huddle together in groups to keep warm. Caribou migrate south to warmer areas instead.

Below right: One way of surviving in even the harshest environment is to be parasitic. These are warble fly larvae, *Oestridae*, feeding on the skin of a caribou.

Fred Bruemmer

Fred Bruemmer

S. Bougaeff/Explorer

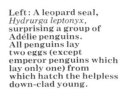

Fred Bruemmer

Left: A leopard seal, *Hydrurga leptonyx*, surprising a group of Adélie penguins. All penguins lay two eggs (except emperor penguins which lay only one) from which hatch the helpless down-clad young.

Below: The largest of the Antarctic petrels, the giant petrel, *Macronectes giganteus*, feeding on a dead penguin. Petrels feed mainly on plankton and krill but most will scavenge when the opportunity arises.

Benoit Tollu/Jacana

Above: An Arctic fox in its white winter coat which provides excellent camouflage against the snow. The summer coat is purple-brown. A rare form, however, much hunted for its beautiful fur, is smoke grey throughout the year.

Left: A white Arctic fox caught by an Eskimo trapper on the edge of the northern forest. There is no native human population in Antarctica but the Arctic has both Eskimos and Lapps. While the Eskimos traditionally hunt and trap animals, the Lapps have semi-domesticated the caribou and follow its herds on migration.

Below: Today, however, Antarctica is not uninhabited—several hundred scientists visit it each year. This experiment is to discover how the long-suffering Adélie penguin keeps warm.

and that area is particularly rich in animal life.

The most important organisms which feed on the phytoplankton are the euphausid crustacea known by the Norwegian name of krill, of which *Euphausia superba* is the most important. These animals are perhaps best known as the food of the great whalebone whales, *Mysticeti*, but the importance of krill does not stop with whales for it is also directly responsible for supporting large populations of fish, penguins, seals and flying birds.

One of the interesting aspects of the polar seas as a habitat is their uniformity. In contrast to the wide variation in temperature experienced over the year by animals on land, those in the sea experience only 2 to 3°C (3 to 5°F) difference between winter and summer. The minimum temperature the sea reaches before freezing is around —1.8°C (29°F), varying with its salt content, while in summer the seas are kept cold by the melting ice. Rises of more than a few degrees above freezing are rare.

Nevertheless, several species of Arctic and Antarctic fish experience winter temperatures below the 'normal' freezing point of their blood. To combat this they employ a number of anti-freeze mechanisms most of which are based on increasing the concentration of salt or protein molecules in the blood which lowers its freezing point. Even so, some species, such as the Antarctic cod, *Notothenia neglecta*, still spend part of the winter in a supercooled state in which they will freeze if they come into contact with ice.

Fish provide food for the best known Antarctic animals, the flightless shore-dwelling penguins. These animals are superbly adapted to dive and 'fly' underwater where they feed on fish and krill. The most numerous species are the chinstrap, *Pygoscelis antarctica*, Adélie, *Pygoscelis adeliae*, and macaroni, *Eudyptes chrysolophus*, which may be found in colonies numbering millions of pairs of birds.

Another well known group of fish-eating carnivores are the seals, *Phocidae* and *Otariidae*. Species of seal live in both the Antarctic and Arctic regions but their close relatives the walruses, *Odobenidae*, are confined to the Arctic. Seals provide food for the best known Arctic animal, the polar bear, *Thalarctos maritimus*. This is one of the few animals which lives permanently on the Arctic pack ice.

Sea-birds are also common in both the Antarctic and Arctic. The Arctic is home for auks, *Alcidae*, puffins, *Fratercula arctica*, and eider ducks, *Somateria;* while in the Antarctic are found the magnificent albatrosses, *Diomedidae*, which feed in the open sea taking squid, fish and crustacea. Recent studies have shown that the various species of albatross are highly specific in the type of food they take, thus avoiding competition.

A few birds are common to both polar regions. For example the Dominican gull, *Larus dominicanus*, is the southern counterpart of the lesser black backed gull, *Larus fuscus*. But the Arctic tern, *Sterna paradisaea*, is probably the most interesting of these species. It spends the northern winter migrating to the Antarctic and back. The Antarctic tern, *Sterna vittala*, however, remains in the Southern Hemisphere throughout the year.

403

Mountains

The plant and animal life of the world's mountains reflects the unusual climatic conditions which prevail in these regions. Because air pressure decreases with height, the air at high altitudes is thin and absorbs little of the sunlight which passes through it. As a consequence, much of the radiant energy of the sun reaches the ground, and so the surface of a mountain can be quite warm while the air temperature is low. However, at night or when the sun is hidden, the surface temperature drops sharply. Night frosts are common in mountainous areas, even in the tropics. The fluctuation of a mountain's surface temperature can be very high over a 24 hour period, but it is usually equalized to a large extent by the wind, and may even be less than on nearby lowland areas.

When an airstream is deflected upwards by a mountain, it becomes cooler and as a result some of its moisture falls as rain. Rainfall therefore tends to increase with altitude on windward slopes, although occasionally low altitude rain belts do form (as on Mount Kilimanjaro and in the Andes) above which the climate is dry. On leeward slopes the descending airmass rewarms, and since it is now dry it has a marked desiccating effect on both vegetation and soil.

Mountain zones

Even when it rises in a tropical rainforest, a mountain, if sufficiently high, can be capped with permanent snow. The nineteenth century scientist and traveller Alexander von Humboldt (1769-1859) noticed that the vegetation changes encountered on a journey from the equator to the poles were similar to those seen on climbing from the tropical base to the icy summit of mountains in Ecuador. At least five vegetation zones could be recognized on these mountains, roughly corresponding to the main lowland climatic types.

The *Arctic zone* occurs above the permanent snow line, above which the snow never melts. In the tropics this occurs at above 4,500 m (15,000 ft), but the snow line is found at progressively lower altitudes as one travels towards the poles, and is also dependent on such factors as the climate and topography of the mountain.

The *alpine zone* lies between the snow line and the tree line, and in many respects corresponds to the tundra. The environment is characteristically cold and moist with melted water, and the growing season is short. However, major differences between the tundra and the alpine zones of mountains at lower latitudes are the lack of a long dark winter and the greater intensity of the sunlight. Also, while the tundra is continuously cold in winter and continuously mild in summer, the daily temperature range is much greater in the alpine zone, particularly if the mountain is in the tropics. Temperatures may reach 30°C (86°F) at midday and fall below freezing at night. Such extreme conditions result in some bizarre adaptations.

At altitudes over about 3,000 m (10,000 ft) in the East African mountains, tree daisies, *Senecio*, reach a height of 5 m (16 ft). These curious plants have cabbage-

Above: Alpine scenery is as impressive as any in the world. This is a view of the Dolomites, a group of mountains lying in the eastern section of the Italian Alps. Plants in this region include the mountain pine, *Pinus mugo*, and the alpine rose, *Rhododendron hirsutum*. One of the most typical animals of the region is the alpine marmot, *Marmota marmota*, a ground squirrel which can weigh as much as 8 kg (18 lb). It feeds mainly on roots, herbs and grasses.

Right: A forest of tree rhododendrons *Rhododendron arboreum*, growing at 2,500 m (8,200 ft) in Nepal. Rhododendrons are members of the heath family, *Ericaceae*, and they thrive in a cool, damp atmosphere.

Below: One of the larger alpine mammals is the ibex, *Capra ibex*, a wild goat. There are various sub-species of the ibex to be found in the Alps, the Caucasus and parts of the Middle East. Once nearly extinct, there are thought to be about 10,000 alpine ibexes living today.

Left: A clubmoss, *Lycopodium*, growing out from a granite rock at an altitude of 3,300 m (11,000 ft). Clubmosses are common in mountain habitats—they are the only living descendants of a group of plants which flourished some 250 million years ago.

Below: The vegetation changes seen on a journey from the equator to the poles are similar to those encountered on climbing a high mountain in the tropics, although the zones are rarely quite as clear cut as suggested in this diagram. Trees may be absent, for example, in a valley which acts as a wind trap, and deep hollows can trap cold air producing conditions colder than would otherwise be expected.

like heads of leaves which open during the day but close at night to insulate the growing point and flowers from as much as 4 °C (7 °F) of frost. A silvery reflective layer of hairs on the backs of the leaves helps to reduce heat losses by radiation. Because the tree daisies only grow at high altitudes they have evolved in isolation, probably from a common lowland ancestor, and mountains such as Mount Elgon, Mount Kenya and Mount Kilimanjaro have their own separate species.

Despite the differences between the climates of the tundra and the tropical alpine zone, the temperate alpine vegetation has many similarities to that of the tundra. Many European alpine plants, such as the purple saxifrage, *Saxifraga oppositifolia*, the golden saxifrage, *Saxifraga aizoides*, the mountain avens, *Dryas octopetala*, the dwarf birches and willows, *Betula nana* and *Salix herbacea*, the mountain sorrel, *Oxyria digyna*, and the alpine grasses *Poa alpina*, *Phleu alpinum* and *Deschampsia alpina*, are also widespread in the Arctic. Some of these species occur in the mountains as far south as the Pyrenees and are also found in North America.

Like the tundra vegetation, temperate alpine plants are typically low, compact, ground-hugging species often forming mats (grasses and sedges) or dense cushions (mosses) which can take advantage of warm patches and hollows exposed to sunlight but protected from the wind. Taller plants would be clipped back by the wind and are generally less well protected from frost. Where there is enough moisture, and especially where the rocks are alkaline, such as limestone, there are abundant wild flowers—for example, mountain speedwell, *Veronica fruticans*, Alpine fleabane, *Erigeron borealis*, campanulas, *Campanula*, primulas, *Primula*, and the mountain azalea *Loiseluria procumbens*.

The *cold temperate zone* forms the lower edge of the alpine zone and the division is marked by the upper tree line, above which conditions become too severe for trees to grow. Below the tree line there is typically a zone, about 50 m (160 ft) wide, of stunted wind-clipped trees and shrubs. Lower still is an uninterrupted belt of coniferous forest. In the American Rocky Mountains this belt is rich in Engelmann spruce, *Picea engelmannii*, and alpine fir *Abies lasiocarpa*, while in the montane coniferous forests of Europe species of fir, *Abies*, predominate. Firs also occur in the Himalayas, Asia Minor, Indochina and Central America. Pines, *Pinus*, are most common in the lower reaches of the coniferous forest zone.

In the Southern Hemisphere the upper forest limit is often formed by evergreen broadleaved trees such as the southern beeches, *Nothofagus*. In New Zealand the black beech, *Nothofagus sclandri*, forms pure forests up to the snow line, and beech forests are also important in the Andes of Argentina.

In the tropics the coniferous forest zone begins in the dry region above the cloud level and *Podocarpus* is probably the most widely distributed genus. Towards the upper forest limit the trees become progressively more branched and stunted, forming a habitat known as *elfin forest*.

The *warm temperate zone* of mountains in the tropics coincides with the cloud belt and an extremely moist habitat

MOUNTAIN ZONATION

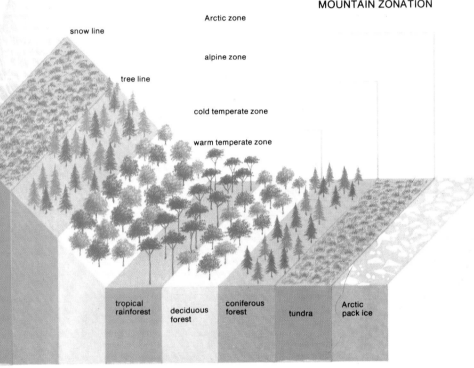

Arctic zone

snow line

alpine zone

tree line

cold temperate zone

warm temperate zone

tropical rainforest | deciduous forest | coniferous forest | tundra | Arctic pack ice

Left: Stemless trumpet gentians, *Gentiana clusii*. About 400 species of gentians are distributed in alpine habitats throughout the Northern Hemisphere and in South America, New Guinea and New Zealand. They are normally pollinated by insects.

Far left: A golden eagle, *Aquila chrysaetos*, with its victim, a jack rabbit, *Lepus alleni*. The golden eagle is found in mountainous regions of North America, Europe and Asia (this picture was taken in Idaho, US). In Europe the golden eagle is one of the few remaining large predators of mountain habitats. Once it competed for prey with mammal carnivores like lynxes, bears and wolves, but man has eliminated these creatures from many of their former ranges. In Europe the golden eagle feeds chiefly on such animals as grouse, hares and marmots as well as the young of larger animals such as ibexes and chamois. In the mountains of the Americas, the puma or mountain lion, *Felis concolor*, is a fairly common predator.

405

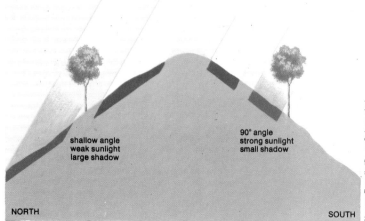

shallow angle
weak sunlight
large shadow

90° angle
strong sunlight
small shadow

NORTH   SOUTH

Norman Tomalin/Bruce Coleman Ltd

known as *cloud forest* develops, usually between 1,000 and 2,500 m (3,300 to 8,200 ft). These forests are luxuriant and rich in epiphytic plants such as Spanish moss, *Tillandsia*, and orchids, mosses and ferns, especially the filmy ferns, *Hymenophyll-aceae*. The canopy is more open than in the lowland tropical rain forest and the floor is carpeted with mosses and *Sela-ginellas*. In higher latitudes, the montane warm temperate zone contains broad-leaved tree species, especially birches, *Betula*, and poplars, *Populus*.

Mountain animals

Many lowland animal species inhabit or visit mountains, but there are a number of species which are especially adapted to the mountain environment. In North America the wolverine, *Gulo gulo*, and

other members of the weasel family, *Mustelidae*, inhabit alpine regions of the Rocky Mountains, and the snow leopard *Panthera uncia*, lives in the mountains of Central Asia and the Himalayas above about 2,500 m, feeding on wild sheep and goats. Otherwise most of the larger alpine mammals are herbivorous.

The bighorn or Rocky Mountain sheep, *Ovis canadensis*, is renowned for its agility in rock climbing and jumping, using soft pads on its feet to absorb shock and to provide grip. Many other species of sheep and goats are mountain inhabitants, including the argali, *Ovis ammon*, a close relative of the bighorn from Central Asia, the markhor, *Capra falconeri*, a mountain goat from the Himalayas, the Rocky Mountain goat, *Oreamnos americanus*, from North America and the chamois,

Rupicapra rupicapra, and ibex, *Capra ibex*, from the mountains of Western Europe. The only member of the ox sub-family which inhabits mountains is the yak, *Bos grunniens*, a long-haired animal of Tibet which has extreme resistance to exposure, living at heights from 4,000 to 6,000 m (13,000 to 20,000 ft).

In the alpine zone of temperate regions insects are extremely seasonal, perhaps only appearing for two months of the year. Insectivorous bird species are therefore rare, and most alpine birds are either ground-living species such as the part-ridges, *Phasianidae*, and grouse, *Tetraonidae*, birds of prey such as the golden eagle, *Aquila chrysaetos*, or car-nivorous scavengers such as the Lammer-geier or bearded vulture, *Gypaetus bar-batus*, which is an inhabitant of high mountains in Europe and flies up to 6,000 m in the Himalayas. Certain mem-bers of the crow family, *Corvidae*, live as scavengers on mountains: the raven, *Corvus corax*, for example is distributed throughout Europe and North America living in rocky areas. The most successful smaller birds of the alpine zone in Eurasia are omnivorous species like the accentors of which the hedgesparrow, *Prunella modularis*, is a common member.

Cold-blooded animals, such as insects, reptiles and amphibia have no tem-perature control mechanisms so their body temperatures are dependent on those of the surroundings and on the amount of solar radiation. They are there-fore active only for short periods of the year in alpine regions, except in the tropics where the daily temperature cycle allows some activity each day. Almost all insect groups are represented in the alpine fauna.

All the reptiles and amphibia of alpine zones, including the European sala-mander, *Salamandra atra*, the European viper or adder, *Viperus berus*, and the common lizard, *Lacerta vivipara*, are ovoviviparous—their eggs develop within the body of the female. This protects the eggs both from predators and from the extremes of cold and heat.

Marion Morrison

Top left: The amount of radiation received by a mountain depends on the angle of its slopes and the direction they face. In the Northern Hemisphere, a given area on a south-facing slope receives sunlight at angles close to 90° and therefore maximum intensity. Shadows are small. On a north-facing slope the angle of the sunlight is shallow so the same area receives less radiation.

Top right: A snow leopard, *Panthera uncia*. These creatures inhabit the central Asian highlands, from the Himalayas north to the Altay, where they feed on wild sheep and goats, large rodents and birds. An adult snow leopard may measure 2 m (6.5 ft) from nose to tail and reach a height of 60 cm (2 ft) at the shoulder.

Left: A herd of llamas in a village high in the Bolivian Andes. The llama was domesticated thousands of years ago from the guanaco, *Lama glama guanicoe*, a South American member of the camel family, *Camelidae*. The llama is used as a pack animal at altitudes up to about 4,000 m (13,000 ft).

The Sea

No man, animal or plant is an island. Each one is part of a community, every member of which is influenced by the others and by the external environment. The study of the inter-relationships between living things and their environment is called *ecology*. It is the study of the biological whole rather than its individual parts.

The place where a particular community of plants and animals lives is called its *habitat*. For example, a habitat may be a forest, a desert, a coral reef, or a freshwater pond. But by far the largest habitat in the world is the open sea—it covers some 70 per cent of the Earth's surface and provides a home for vast numbers of individuals and species.

The Sun as an energy source

Every living community ultimately depends on an external energy source. Energy is needed to build up the organic chemicals which make up the bodies of living things and to allow movement. In the sea, as in most other communities, the external energy source is the Sun. Plants trap this energy in the process of photosynthesis. Animals then feed on these plants and on each other, but at each stage of such a *food-chain* most of the energy is lost as heat. Plants thus make an energy profit which the rest of the community gradually dissipates.

However, the light rays on which the community depends do not penetrate far

Bruce Coleman

Above right: 70% of the Earth's surface is covered by sea—making this the biggest ecological habitat in the world and home to countless living things. The temperature is generally stable—so most members of the sea community do not need to control their body temperatures—and all the materials which plants and animals need for their growth and good health are dissolved in the water around them.

Below: The smallest animals in the sea are *Protozoa* like this radiolarian, *Acanthometron*. Radiolarians have an intricate skeleton of glass-like minerals.

Right: In the shifting oceans, plants are generally unable to grow to any great size and many are very small indeed, falling in the size range 1 μm to 1 mm. Planktonic plants shown: diatoms *Thalassiosira* (1), *Biddulphia* (2) and *Chaetoceros* (3), and dinoflagellates *Noctiluca* (4) and *Ceratium* (5 and 6).

PHYTOPLANKTON

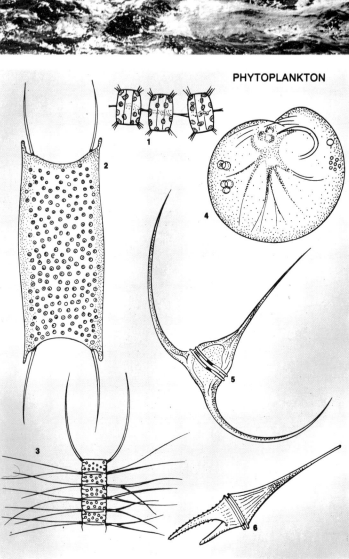

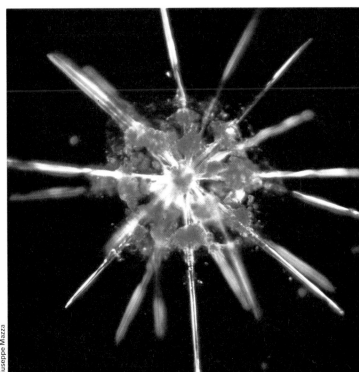

Giuseppe Mazza

407

into the sea because they are absorbed by water. In turbid water, for instance near the coast, they are absorbed even more rapidly than in the clearer waters of the open sea, and the stronger light in the tropics penetrates deeper than the weak light towards the poles: but even in clear tropical seas there is little light below a depth of 100 m (330 ft). In temperate seas in early summer this depth is nearer 30 m (98 ft). Below it plants can do no productive work. Since the average depth of the sea is 3.5 km (2.3 miles) it is evident that plant life will be confined to a very small fraction of the total volume—the rest of the sea being pitch black except for the faint light which some deep sea organisms produce themselves. This productive upper layer, on which all sea life depends, is called the *euphotic zone*.

The different colours which make up white light are not all absorbed by water at the same rate. The longer wavelengths (red light) are absorbed best, then the shorter green waves and finally blue. These differing absorbtion rates have important consequences to the plants which inhabit the euphotic zone. Plants have pigments with which they trap light in the first step of photosynthesis, and different pigments use different parts of the spectrum. Many marine plants have adapted to the marine environment by producing pigments which absorb the shorter wavelengths present at greater depths. In particular many are brown due to a high concentration of the pigment *xanthophyll* which can absorb green light.

Nevertheless, chlorophyll is essential to all plants. It is the only pigment which can actually carry out chemical synthesis. Energy trapped by the other pigments has to be passed on to chlorophyll before it can be used. All marine plants therefore possess chlorophyll but they also have a higher concentration of other pigments than land plants.

Plant types

The plants which live in the euphotic zone and incorporate light energy into the community are generally microscopic and are called the *phytoplankton*. They are mostly tiny *algae* varying in size from 1 μm (a millionth of a metre) to 1 mm. Most of the larger plants of the phytoplankton belong to two groups of algae, the diatoms, *Bacillariophyta* (*Chrysophyta*), and the dinoflagellates, *Pyrrophyta*. In addition there are large numbers of smaller plants, including flagellates, blue-green algae and bacteria, about which little is known.

The range of a particular species depends on light intensity, the availability of nutrients, temperature and the number and type of plant-eating animals (*herbivores*). Of these, temperature is a particularly important factor. Although the temperature range found over the world is not as extreme in the sea as on land, there is still considerable variation. The surface layers in the tropics are at about 30°C (86°F), whereas at the poles near ice they can be as cold as —2°C (28°F). In addition, each great ocean current has its own characteristic temperature which can produce large local fluctuations.

A radical change in the species composing the phytoplankton occurs with these temperature variations, so it appears that temperature is of prime importance in limiting the range of many

Dr. Georg Gerster / John Hillelson Agency

Left: Some species of phytoplankton carry out 'chemical warfare' against other species. Some dinoflagellates in particular produce powerful poisons which, if concentrated because of an 'algal bloom', may result in a 'red tide' as shown here. These can kill large numbers of fish and can severely damage fisheries.

Right: One notable feature of ocean life is the vertical migration which many animals undertake every 24 hours. The reasons for this are not well understood, but it is possible that by feeding near the surface only at night they can successfully avoid predators which hunt chiefly by sight.

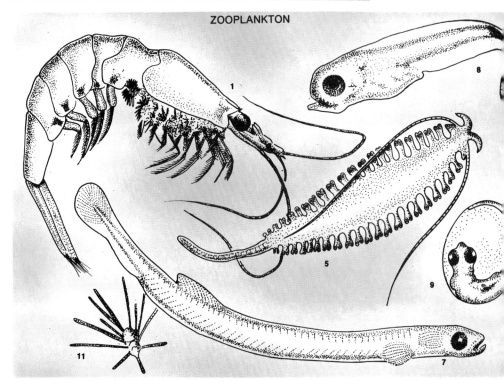

ZOOPLANKTON

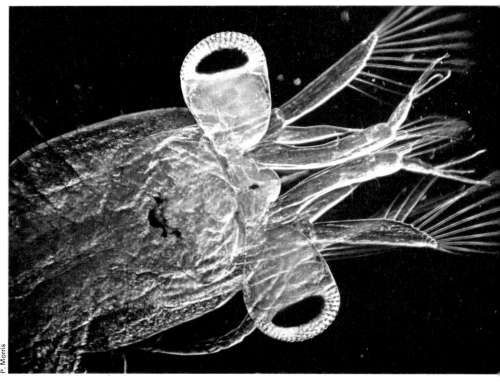

P. Morris

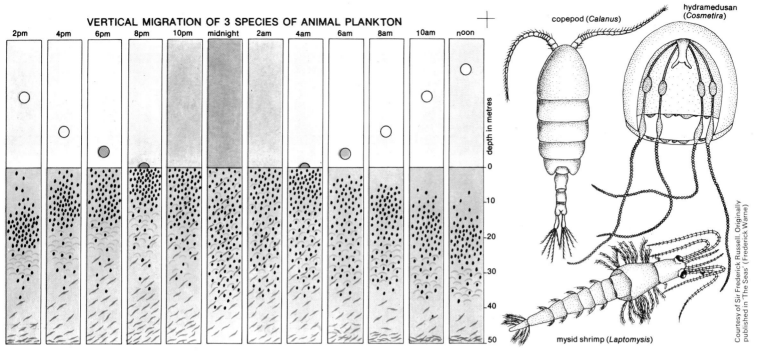

VERTICAL MIGRATION OF 3 SPECIES OF ANIMAL PLANKTON

2pm 4pm 6pm 8pm 10pm midnight 2am 4am 6am 8am 10am noon

depth in metres
0
10
20
30
40
50

copepod (*Calanus*)

hydramedusan (*Cosmetira*)

mysid shrimp (*Laptomysis*)

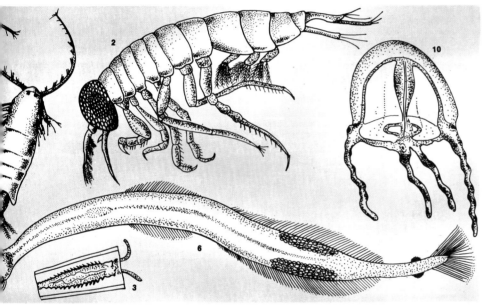

Above: Although whales, the largest animals, live in the sea, most marine animals are smaller than 1 cm (0.4 in) and are called the *zooplankton*. These particular animals are:

1. euphausiid
Meganyctiphanes norvegica
2. amphipod
Parathemisto abyssorum
3. polychaete worm
Lanice conchilega
4. copepod
Labidocera wollastoni
5. polychaete worm
Tomopteris helgolandica
6. arrow worm
Sagitta elegans
7. teleost fish larva
Sprattus sprattus
8. teleost fish larva
Gadus morhua
9. teleost fish egg
Gadus morhua
10. hydromedusan
Sarsia exima
11. sea urchin
Echinocardium cordatum

Left: Many species in the plankton are the immature stages of larger animals. This is the larva (*zoea*) of the hermit crab, *Eupagurus*.

Right: The coral-eating crown of thorns starfish *Acanthaster planci*, which has destroyed much of the Great Barrier Reef off eastern Australia.

species. On the other hand, however, laboratory experiments often indicate that particular species have wider temperature tolerances than their natural range seems to imply. Other factors are therefore involved. Ecologically, the effect of single factors is almost always modified by interactions with other effects. In the seas the effects of temperature interact with other environmental factors, such as salinity, in determining the species present in any area.

Cycles of productivity

The interaction of environmental factors can be clearly seen when seasonal changes in the population of phytoplankton are examined. In temperate latitudes, such as the North Sea, a regular cycle of changes in plankton numbers occurs each year. The numbers are low in winter, start to increase in March and reach a peak towards the end of April. They then fall dramatically and remain low throughout the summer, until there is another rapid increase in the autumn—but the autumn peak is lower than the spring peak. The numbers then gradually return to their low winter level.

The causes of this *cycle of productivity* are now fairly well understood. During the winter the limiting factor for photosynthesis and plant growth is lack of sunlight. In spring, as both the intensity of sunlight and day length increase, this limitation is removed. The algae grow and reproduce rapidly. At the same time, the temperature of the surface water increases. The density of water depends on its temperature—warm water is less dense than cold water—so warming of the surface establishes a layer, about as deep as the euphotic zone, of less dense warm water above the cold body of the ocean. Within this upper layer water mixes freely, but it no longer mixes with the deeper water from which it is separated by the lower boundary of the warm layer, called the *thermocline* or *discontinuity layer*. There is no mixing across the thermocline.

At first, the presence of the thermocline accelerates phytoplankton production because it prevents the algae from being carried beyond the depth at which light penetrates. But it also isolates the surface waters nutritionally from the sea 409

Bruce Coleman

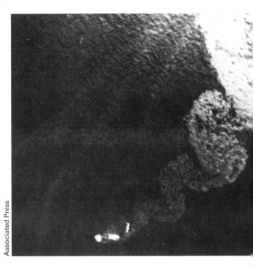
Left and right: Man and the sea. Technological advances, particularly in diving equipment, have allowed man to obtain a greater understanding of the animal and plant life of the sea. (This diver, left, is exploring the beauty of a coral reef). It has also brought the risk of catastrophes big enough to upset the ecological balance even of as large a habitat as the sea. This aerial photograph (right) taken from 1,680 m (5,500 ft) shows part of the huge slick—estimated at 155 million litres (7.6 million gallons) and 161 km (100 miles) long—produced when the Liberian oil tanker *Argo Merchant* foundered off the North American coast during late December 1976.

Douglas Bone

Above and right: Two rare fish. Brilliantly coloured *Pseudochromis fridmani* (right) is found only in the Red Sea, while the Antarctic ice fish, *Chaenocephalus aceratus*, (above) is peculiar because it has no *respiratory pigment* which other animals use to transport oxygen in the blood.

Roger Lubbock

below. Essential nutrients, particularly phosphate and nitrate, are used up by the expanding plankton community and cannot be replaced. Dead organisms and faecal pellets sink through the thermocline, taking their materials with them to the sea bed. There is no way by which these lost nutrients can be reclaimed from the depths where they accumulate.

It was once thought that the resulting nutrient deficiency caused the decline of phytoplankton in early summer. Yet it is now known that numbers begin to fall when nutrients are still adequate, so the beginning of the decline cannot be caused by the lack of nutrients. In fact the decline is probably started by the grazing of herbivores, whose numbers have increased in the wake of the algal bloom. But once the number of algae has begun to fall their further decline continues because of lack of nutrients.

As the summer progresses, these two factors—the level of nutrients and the grazing of herbivores—interact to produce a stable plant population, and the situation remains largely unchanged until the autumn. Then, the cooling of the surface layers begins to reduce the stability of the thermocline and it is eventually destroyed by the gales which come with autumn. The gales thoroughly mix the various water layers and phosphate and nitrate are returned to the surface. This allows growth to be resumed leading to the second peak. Finally, winter sets in. There is less light and plant numbers fall back to their original level.

Throughout the seasons different species of phytoplankton succeed each other within the main cycle of numbers.

Smaller diatoms are prominent in the early spring. Larger species, which take longer to multiply, become dominant later. Dinoflagellates are much more numerous than diatoms during the summer. Diatoms become numerous again in the autumn. The causes of this succession are complex and are not well understood, although there is some evidence that dinoflagellates are more tolerant of a shortage of phosphate than are diatoms.

The same factors which occur in temperate seas also occur in the tropics but in the tropics the thermocline is permanently stable. This explains why tropical seas have a far lower phytoplankton population—there is a chronic shortage of nutrients. The thermocline is normally only broken by an upwelling of bottom water caused by such factors as the trade winds which drive the surface waters away from the west coasts of South America and Africa. In such circumstances the surface waters are replaced from the deeps by water rich in nutrients and a large phytoplankton and dependent fish population can grow up. Such a system is responsible, for instance, for the huge anchovy hauls off Peru.

Animals

The animals of the sea do not themselves need the surface light but can live at all depths. However, herbivores do have to feed in the euphotic zone and they are followed there by their predators. Most marine animals then, like the plants on which they depend, live near the surface. From the surface a steady rain of organic debris falls to support a smaller population of scavengers and their predators in the deeps. Quite large populations, how-

Below: The fate of the Peruvian anchovy fishery is a good example of how the combination of overfishing and adverse environmental factors can reduce a seemingly inexhaustible supply. In 1970, 13 million tonnes were landed, but by 1973 the figure was only two million tonnes. One cause of this dramatic drop in catch was the

intrusion further south than normal of the warm water current, *El Nino*. This upset the mixing of nutritionally rich bottom waters with the surface layers —the basis of this fishery. Restrictions imposed by the Peruvian Government and the retreat of *El Nino* have since prevented further falls in yield.

ZEFA

410

Above and above left:
Some deep sea fishes.
All deep sea animals
are either scavengers
—feeding on organic
matter falling down
from above—or
carnivores feeding on
other members of the
bottom community.
These fish are *Anomalops
catopton* (above left),
Eurypharynx pelecanoides
(top) and *Nemichthys
scolopacus* (above).

Left: Stories of sea
monsters often have
their beginnings in
exaggerated accounts of
real events. This
illustration is of an
occasion in December
1906 when a French
fishing boat landed a
catch of some 1,500
octopuses. The
fishermen saved
themselves by cutting
the trawl rope and
losing the net.

(*cilia*) whereas the massive baleen whales (*Mysticeti*) swim through the water and collect krill on a complicated barricade called the *baleen*. In all cases of filter feeding, however, there is no selection between plant and animal material by the feeder. Filtering involves the selection of food only by size, although a filter with a small mesh size will tend to catch plants, whereas larger meshes, such as are found in whales and herrings, will trap mainly animals.

Finally, besides the filter feeders, there are many carnivores which feed by attacking and gripping individual prey. These range in size from carnivorous protozoans, through arrow worms, *Chaetognatha*, up to sharks, *Selachii*. Large predators, such as sharks and man, represent the last link in the food-chain of the sea.

Food-chains
In a simple food-chain, herbivores eat the plants and carnivores eat the herbivores. Each of the links in the chain is called a *trophic level*. In the seas, however, it is difficult to assign species to a particular trophic level, both because food-chains tend to be long and complex and because the feeding habits of many species change with their age and size.

Nevertheless, whatever the exact composition of a food-chain, most of the energy bound up in the bodies of animals and plants is lost when they are consumed by animals belonging to the next trophic level. As a general rule, only 10% passes up from one trophic level to the next. Thus it takes 1,000 tonnes of plant material to produce just 1 kg (2.2 lb) of great blue shark, *Prionace glauca*.

ever, can live in the deeps—baited cameras on the sea bottom reveal that large crowds of scavengers can assemble remarkably quickly.

A community consists of the *producers* (the plants), the *primary consumers* (the *herbivores*), and various subsequent levels of *higher consumers* (the *carnivores*). In the euphotic zone the primary consumers consist of protozoans (especially tintinnids, *Tintinnidae*, radiolarians, *Radiolaria*, foraminiferans, *Foraminifera*) and copepods, *Copepoda*, of various kinds, which are all less than 2 cm (0.8 in) long. The group *Copepoda* (class *Crustacea*) has been outstandingly successful in the sea. Samples of animal plankton (*zooplankton*) usually consist of between 50 and 80 per cent copepods. In the North Atlantic the commonest species is the

copepod herbivore *Calanus finmarchicus*.

In a slightly larger size range is another very successful group of crustaceans, the euphausiids, *Euphausiidae*. The best known example is the krill, *Euphausia superba*. This animal is about 4 cm (1.6 in) long and forms the staple diet of the great filter feeding whales of the Antarctic—including the largest animal that has ever lived, the blue whale, *Balaenoptera musculus*.

Filter feeding is a very common form of feeding of marine animals. Most of the food in the euphotic zone consists of small organisms, suspended in the water, and these can be most easily removed by filtering. Techniques for achieving this vary from species to species. For example, tintinnid protozoans create water currents towards their bodies by tiny hairs

411

The Seashore

The seashore is home to an enormous variety of living organisms, among them bacteria, seaweeds, barnacles, limpets, oysters and sea anemones as well as visiting sea birds such as gulls and terns. It provides a wide range of habitats, from sand, shingle, boulders and continuous sheets of rock to muddy beaches and salt marsh.

To the organisms colonizing a shore, the particle size of the beach (that is to say whether it is composed of sand, shingle or rocks) is of great importance. Species which thrive among boulders do not necessarily flourish in sand. Particle size is partly determined by whether the shore is exposed or sheltered. Exposed shores pounded by waves are often rocky and steep, while the sand and shell fragments ground off such shores are carried into sheltered coves for beach building.

The tides
Tides, which cover the shore with sea water every 12 hours 20 minutes, make the seashore a relatively hostile environment. Its inhabitants have to be able to withstand the rigours of both aquatic and terrestrial life: at low tide, for example, they risk desiccation in dry weather whereas in rain they need protection against the fresh water which might dangerously dilute their body fluids. At high tide, on the other hand, they are covered by salt water which, although of a much more uniform temperature than the surrounding air, has a much lower oxygen content.

In general, the most hostile part of any seashore is the region near the high tide line, for it is here that organisms are exposed to the air for the longest time. It is a characteristic of all environments that the more hostile they are, the fewer the number of species within them, even though those few may be abundant. This is true of the seashore; there is a reduction in the number of species as one works one's way up from the mid-tide line.

The zones of the seashore
The result of this gradation of shore conditions is that there are a number of distinct zones, each one at a different level up the shore. Each zone has a characteristic set of organisms living in it which are adapted specifically to tolerate conditions at that level.

Below the average low tide line, the *sublittoral fringe*, of a typical rocky shore in Britain is found the seaweed *Laminaria*, the largest of the brown algae, which grows to a length of 4 m (13 ft). In addition there are many red algae, such as *Rhodymenia palmata*. These species are well adapted to thrive when covered by a layer of deep and turbid water which only transmits light of rather short wavelength, and they have a high proportion of pigments capable of absorbing light of of this kind.

In the *eulittoral zone*, the term given to those parts of the shore that are uncovered and covered by the tide every day, is found the seaweed *Fucus serratus*, which gives way to *Fucus vesiculosus* further up the beach, followed by *Fucus spiralis* and finally *Pelvetia canaliculata*. At the upper limits of the eulittoral zone, algae are

Georg Gerster/John Hillelson Agency

unable to survive unassisted and we find the symbiotic partnership known as a lichen, in which an alga and a fungus combine. The black *Verrucaria maura* leads into the *littoral fringe* which is characterised by the silver lichen *Ramalina* and the orange *Xanthora parietina*, both of which extend up the cliff face.

Examination of the animals living on the shore shows a similar zonation. Some, like the limpets, *Patella*, simply follow the algae on which they feed, whereas others are limited by their tolerance of high temperatures, desiccation or lack of oxygen. A good example of an essentially marine creature which has adapted to spend long periods in the open air is the star barnacle, *Chthamalus stellatus*, a suspension feeder. It survives in the open by drawing gaseous oxygen through its *micropyle* (a small aperture). However, allowing oxygen to flow over a moist respiratory surface inevitably entails an undesirable loss of water by evaporation, so the creature has developed an alternative method of respiration. If it loses more than 0.5 per cent of its body weight by evaporation, it closes the micropyle completely and relies on the energy released by *anaerobic* respiration to supply its basic living requirements, so avoiding

any further loss of water.

Living further down the shore is the common barnacle, *Balanus balanoides*. This species is less good at surviving extremes of environment, but it does better than *Chthamalus* when they are matched in a straight competition for space. In the slow process of growth, *Balanus* slowly undercuts *Chthamalus* until the latter is knocked off by the waves. At the bottom of the shore another barnacle, *Balanus perforatus*, is found, which is in turn supplanted by *Balanus crenatus* under overhanging rocks.

One strategy which animals use to populate a particular zone is to lay eggs within the zone where the parents have lived. The eggs are firmly fixed to the rock and have enough food reserves to develop to the stage when the young can

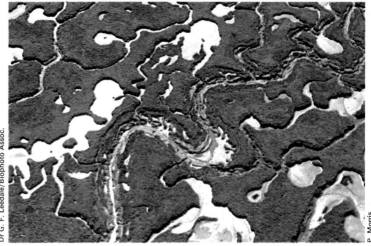

Above: Flowers of the seashore serve the function of binding the sand. They must be able to tolerate a high level of salt and have the ability to conserve valuable fresh water. In order to adapt to their environment, many have reduced leaf size as a protection against evaporation. The flower shown here is the salt-tolerant sea lavender, *Limonium pectinatum*.

Below: An inhabitant of the seashore, and a victim of oil pollution which kills countless birds every year and pollutes increasing numbers of beaches. This oil-covered bird is a Magellanic penguin from Patagonia.

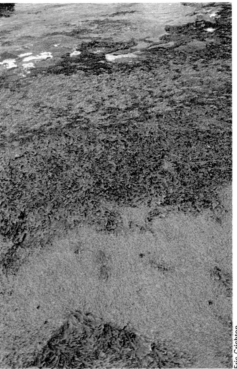

Left: Algae, or seaweeds, are the dominant shore plants, starting at the sublittoral fringe and moving up the shore in zones. Each zone is dominated by the alga best adapted to its conditions. Among the seaweeds on this British shore are *Laminaria, Corallina, Fucus, Pelvetia* and *Enteromorpha*.

Above: Marshes along flat sea coasts are subject to tidal action and because of evaporation the salinity can be even higher than in the open sea. They provide one of the harshest environments for marine animals. The picture shows an aerial view of a salt marsh on the Essex coast of Britain.

maintain their position on the shore. The various species of periwinkle, *Littorina*, do this. In spite of the fact that their eggs cannot drift with the currents, periwinkles are among the most widely dispersed genera of the shore.

In contrast, most shore creatures, especially the immobile ones like barnacles and oysters, have what appears to be a stage specifically adapted for dispersal. In many marine organisms the eggs are released into the planktonic community, where they drift with the vagaries of the ocean current, until the larvae which hatch from the eggs are ready to settle.

The shore community

The organisms found on the seashore make up a community whose members are all affected to a greater or lesser degree by each other's activities. They may be divided into a number of different levels according to their position in the food chain. These are called *trophic levels*: plants (producers) occupy the first trophic level, herbivores (grazers) the second and so on.

At the bottom of the food chain, green plants use the energy of sunlight to photosynthesize new tissue. The food created in this way then passes to the remaining community members by one of two routes: either the plant is eaten by a grazing animal, such as a limpet, or it eventually dies and provides food for saprophytes, such as heterotrophic bacteria. Eventually both pathways lead to carnivores, but not always the same carnivores, at the top of the chain.

On rocky shores, the producers are mainly the various seaweeds which are firmly attached to the rocks by means of *holdfasts*. Various animals graze on these plants, including limpets, chitons and the numerous snail-like molluscs, such as the periwinkle, which are common on most shores. On rocky shores, however, many of the animals are suspension feeders, filtering edible particles out of the water. Barnacles are the most striking of this group. They can take in food particles measuring only 30 μm (millionths of a

exposed rock	encrusting lichen, *Verrucaria*	seaweed *Fucus*
barnacles *Chthalamus* and *Balanus*	seaweed *Pelvetia*	seaweed *Laminaria*

THE EFFECT OF WAVE ACTION

413

Brian Seed/John Hillelson Agency

P. Morris

Erich Lessing—Magnum/John Hillelson Agency

metre) across, so that among other things
they are likely to ingest single-celled
plants, such as diatoms. Diatoms are
really a part of the ocean community, so
suspension feeders in fact import
some material from outside their own
community.

Whatever the origin of the producers,
the secondary consumers are often permanent residents on the seashore. One
example is the dog whelk, *Thais*, which
feeds mainly on barnacles and mussels,
and, nearer low tide, starfish such as the
European starfish, *Asterias rubens*.
Besides these permanent residents of the
rocky shores, there are a number of visitors which can join one of the various
trophic levels for a while and may leave
their faeces or corpses on the shore. They
are, however, more likely to be exporters
than importers of energy. Oyster catchers,
gulls and crows may feed on mussels and
limpets, and also on such secondary consumers as dog whelks and starfish.

On sandy shores, where there is no firm,
stationary surface material, most animals
live below the surface. In the more productive shores, which consist of a mixture of sand and mud, there are probably
three principal groups of producers.
Firstly, the remains of seaweeds and
animals which have been torn from rocky
shores in storms and deposited on sheltered sandy beaches—in this respect the
community of the sandy shore is parasitic
on the rocky shore community. Secondly,
numerous single-celled plants, such as
diatoms and dinoflagellates, lying on or
near the surface of the muddy sand. And
thirdly, various species of *chemotrophic*
bacteria living some distance below the
414 surface of the sand in a black layer al-

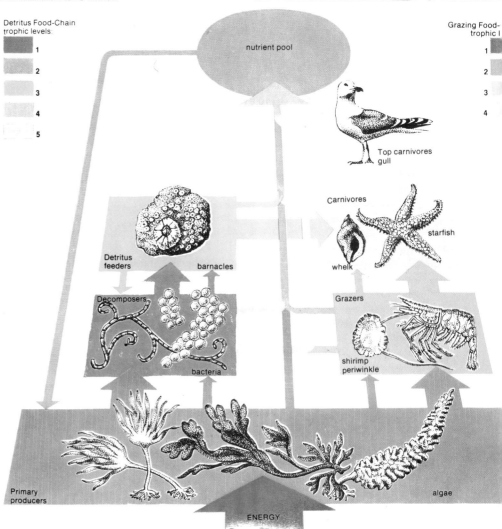

Detritus Food-Chain
trophic levels:
1
2
3
4
5

Grazing Food-
trophic l
1
2
3
4

nutrient pool

Top carnivores
gull

Carnivores

starfish

Detritus
feeders

barnacles

whelk

Decomposers

Grazers

shrimp
periwinkle

bacteria

Primary
producers

algae

ENERGY

Right: Molluscs have various methods for attaching themselves to their habitats, against such threats as pounding waves or predators. Here, the common mussel, *Mytilus*, is putting out sticky 'guy ropes' with its foot.

Below: Acorn barnacles, *Balanus crenatus*, mating. Barnacles are common among shore animals.

Bottom: These white-fronted terns, *Sterna striata*, are among the predators which visit the shore at low tide to feed on the carnivores such as limpets and mussels. They may leave their faeces or corpses on the shore, but chiefly export energy from the ecosystem.

most devoid of oxygen.

Chemotrophic bacteria obtain their energy by oxidizing simple inorganic compounds such as hydrogen sulphide, and so they provide a direct energy input for the whole of the food chain. Nematode worms graze on the bacteria, and these in turn are eaten by animals such as ragworms which are part of the diet of bottom dwelling fish.

Heterotrophic bacteria need complex organic compounds from other living things for food, and are therefore ultimately dependent on green plants for their energy. They are found in huge numbers on the particles of sand near the surface of the beach and are responsible for breaking down much of the flotsam which is deposited on the beach.

Considering the abundance of these surface bacteria, it is not surprising that mud flats are usually packed with animals that feed on the bacteria by swallowing the sand on which they grow. Such animals are called *deposit feeders*. One common British deposit feeder, the spire shell snail, *Hydrobia ulvae*, can reach a population density of as many as 60,000 animals per square metre of muddy beach. Another, the peppery furrow shell, *Scrobicularia plana*, a bivalve mollusc, spends its life burrowing in the sand. It has two siphons extending to the surface, one of which moves over the surface like a vacuum cleaner while the other acts as an exhaust pipe.

The other large group of burrowing molluscs are the *filter feeders*, such as the soft-shelled clam, *Mya arenaria*. Like the deposit feeders they have two siphons, but these are bound together along much of their length, and are not manipulated separately. Particles of food suspended in the water are drawn in through the inhalant siphon and trapped in the mucus overlying the ciliated gills which create the current.

The whole of the shore community then is powered by green plants such as seaweeds and diatoms, chemotrophic bacteria and flotsam brought in by the tide. The material passes to grazers, to heterotrophic bacteria (which are consumed by deposit feeders) or to suspension feeders. These creatures in turn are preyed on by carnivores such as starfish. Ultimately some of these carnivores may themselves fall prey to visiting vertebrates such as fish which come in with the tide or seabirds which feed when the tide is out. When these creatures die their bodies provide food for the humble heterotrophic bacteria and so the cycle repeats itself.

Ponds, Rivers and Streams

It is generally believed that life began in the sea and spread from there to the land. At first glance an obvious first step in this progression appears to be the colonization of freshwater habitats. But the transition from a salt to a freshwater environment is not as easy as it appears. In fact relatively few organisms have managed this step. Rather than land animals and plants evolving from freshwater organisms the reverse is often true.

Chemical factors
The major difference between the stable and cosy environment of the sea and the inhospitable world of freshwater ponds, rivers and streams is the lack of nutrients. Freshwater contains less than one gram per litre of dissolved mineral salts whereas the sea contains about 35 grams per litre. This lack of nutrients effects freshwater organisms in two ways. Plants have difficulty acquiring sufficient salts for growth and animals have difficulty in maintaining their internal salt concentrations above that of the surrounding water.

Chemically, freshwaters can be divided into two types, *acid* or *soft* waters and *calcareous* (calcium-rich) or *hard* waters; though, of course, there are many streams and ponds which fit in between these two categories. In both types of environment the most important organisms in breaking down organic matter—and so releasing the nutrients locked up inside—are bacteria. These simple plants cannot survive in acid conditions and so acid waters have sparse aquatic communities because the breakdown of organic matter cannot take place. (This is why plant material may remain undecayed for centuries in the acid conditions of peat bogs.) In calcareous waters, however, bacteria can break down plant and animal remains,

Above: Fresh water at its most spectacular— 2,800 cubic metres (100,000 cubic ft) flow over Niagara Falls every second during the day. (The flow is reduced at night to produce hydroelectric power.) Turbulence is important in freshwater ecosystems. It causes life-giving oxygen to dissolve into the water.

Right: In stiller waters oxygen is obtained from photosynthesizing plants. This is water crowfoot, *Ranunculus aquatalis.*

Below: In many lakes and streams plant growth is limited by shortage of inorganic nutrients. If these are added, for example from fertilizer leached from surrounding fields (as here), massive algal growth can result.

and so plants can thrive because they have the necessary nutrients for growth.

Consequently, lakes and streams in chalk or limestone areas, rich in calcium, have the largest aquatic communities, both in the numbers of individuals and of species. Acid moorland ponds and streams, on the other hand, contain very few organisms and usually have accumulations of undecomposed organic matter.

Rivers and streams
A community of organisms in which the individuals interact with each other and with their environment is called an *ecosystem*. Most ecosystems are *closed* systems in which nutrients and other materials are constantly recycled between the plants and animals within the system. Streams and rivers, however, are *open* systems. Materials are constantly carried downstream and there is no way in which they can be returned. Hence a community at any place in the stream can only use nutrients once—after that they are lost to the next community further down the stream. In contrast, a lake is a closed system in which nutrients are constantly recycled.

Because they are constantly losing material, stream and river ecosystems

Reeds growing in Wicken Fen, Cambridgeshire. Because its water level is artificially maintained the Fen provides a controlled habitat for birds, insects and plants, particularly willow and alder.

rely on a continual input of organic and other nutrients in order to survive. These materials are largely obtained from animals and plants along the banks. Inorganic nutrients are constantly dissolved from the rocks along the banks and organic nutrients are obtained from both the vegetation and the animals that live on the bankside.

River and stream plants
Very little of the input into a fast flowing stream or river community is produced by aquatic plants within the community itself. This is particularly true of upland streams where plants are few because the swift current makes rooting difficult. Only mosses, particularly *Fontinalis*, and algal films, like *Periphyton*, can survive.

More plants grow in wider streams and rivers where sluggish water flows along some banks and silt and mud are deposited. In such places plants like water milfoil, *Myriophyllum*, and water crowfoot, *Ranunculus*, can take root. Once some plants have rooted they slow the current down further so that more silt and mud is deposited and more plants can grow. In slow-flowing water, too, other, non-rooting plants, such as water hyacinth, *Eichhornia crassipes*, are able to grow. Most importantly the number of *phytoplankton*, minute algae, particularly *diatoms* and *dinoflagellates*, can increase and supply food to the smallest animal herbivores.

River and stream animals
Fast flowing water also presents a problem to stream and river animals. They must prevent themselves being washed downstream, away from their habitat and out to sea. To do this they have evolved three main adaptations. They may be flattened or streamlined to present less resistance to the water, they may have behavioural adaptations, such as *positive rheotaxis* (continuous swimming upstream), or they may have suckers or hooks to attach them firmly to stones. Furthermore, most animals which live in fast flowing turbulent streams are bottom living (*benthic*). Here stones provide shelter and the water current is less because of friction between the water and the stream bottom.

Many benthic animals are young stages (*larvae*) of insects which later emerge from water as winged adults of short lifespan, living only to breed. For example, mayflies, such as *Ecdyonurus* and *Rithrogena*, live for just one day, during which they mate and lay their eggs in flowing water. Immature mayflies (*nymphs*), on the other hand, live for anything from one to three years depending on the species. They are flattened, scarcely 2.5 mm (0.1 in) thick, and have claws which enable them to cling to stones. Other animals which also attach themselves to stones include stonefly nymphs, *Plecoptera*, leeches, *Hirudinea*, flatworms, *Planaria*, and molluscs, such as freshwater limpets, *Ancylastrum*.

Animals which maintain their station in the stream by swimming against the current include the freshwater shrimp, *Gammarus*, commonly found in crevices between stones, and most species of fish. In temperate streams the dominant group of fish are members of the salmon family, *Salmonidae*, particularly brown trout, *Salmo trutta*, in Europe, and brook trout, *Salvelinus fontinalis*, in North America. These fish require cool well-aerated water, typical of upland streams.

Left: The freshwater shrimp, *Gammarus*. This animal prevents itself being swept downstream by a behavioural adaptation, called *positive rheotaxis*, which compels it to swim continuously upstream against the current. Its body is also flattened from side to side so that it presents less resistance to the water. Nevertheless, it cannot withstand a current greater than 45 cm per second (18 in/sec) and is found only where currents are slower among stones and weeds.

Right: Caddis fly larvae of the genus *Phryganea* protect themselves by building cylindrical cases from rectangular pieces of plant material arranged into a spiral.

Below: As a stream gradually widens out into a river there is a profound change in the nature of the ecosystem it provides. In streams less than 2 m (6 ft) wide, 99 per cent of primary food comes, not from plants within the stream, but from the surrounding banks. Leaves, in particular, are constantly being blown into the stream. As the stream widens, however, the influence of the banks slowly decreases and much of the food is produced by plants, particularly planktonic algae, within the river. The range of animals present also varies, determined by the type of food available in the stream or river.

Right: The still water of ponds and lakes allows a stable surface layer to develop on the water. This is the home of many animals. Insect pupae and snails live just below the surface while pond skaters, *Gerris*, (shown here) live on top of it.

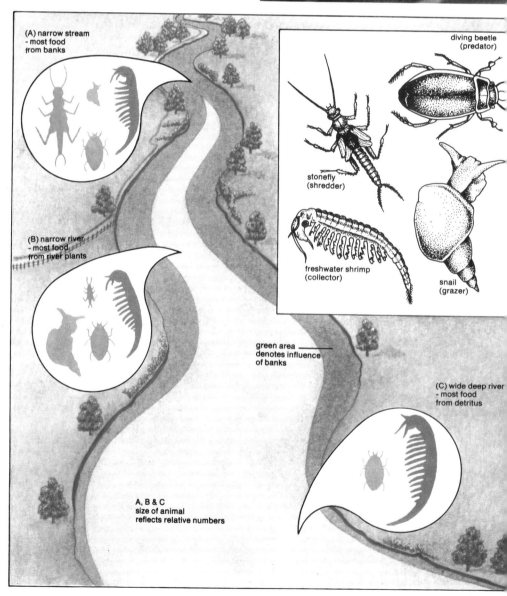

(A) narrow stream - most food from banks

(B) narrow river - most food from river plants

(C) wide deep river - most food from detritus

green area denotes influence of banks

A, B & C size of animal reflects relative numbers

diving beetle (predator)

stonefly (shredder)

freshwater shrimp (collector)

snail (grazer)

Because plants are few, most stream animals feed on decaying organic debris (*detritus*) swept down in the current from vegetation overhanging the bank. Both caddis fly larvae and some mayfly nymphs are *filter feeders*, feeding on detritus. Many stonefly nymphs, however, are *shredders*, eating large bits of decaying organic matter—not for the plant material itself but for the bacteria and fungi growing on it. Shredders break down big pieces of organic matter into small pieces that can be ingested by filter feeders.

Less common are animals that rely on food produced by the stream community itself. Algae provide food for *grazers*, such as limpets and flatworms, while fish feed by maintaining station in the stream and catching drifting animals. Such drift is greatest at dawn and dusk.

Slow-flowing rivers

In wider, more sluggish rivers and streams, the deposit of silt and mud produces a different habitat from that of fast flowing streams so it is not surprising that different animals live there. Few animals, however, actually live in the mud. This is because the mud, particularly if rich in detritus, supports a large population of decomposers, especially bacteria, which use up the available oxygen making it uninhabitable for all but those animals, such as *Tubifex* worms and midge larvae, *Chironomidae*, which can survive where there is little oxygen.

Instead, most animals are found on the mud surface. These include grazers, like the snails *Valvata* and *Bithynia*, detritus feeders, like the water louse, *Asellus*, and predators such as alder fly larvae, *Sialis*.

Right: A trout leaping against the current. Most members of the trout and salmon family, *Salmonidae*, migrate away from their normal habitats to spawn. Some species, especially the Atlantic salmon, *Salmo salar*, migrate many hundreds of kilometres from the sea to spawning grounds in upland streams.

Below: A shoal of tadpoles, *Rana*. Many freshwater animals are the immature stages of land species.

419

P. Morris

Where water weeds have managed to gain a footing an even richer fauna can develop. In such areas dragonfly and damsel fly nymphs, *Odonata*, aquatic spiders, and diving beetles, *Dytiscus*, are common. These are all relatively bulky animals which cannot survive fast water currents because of the resistance of their bodies to the water. They are also all predators, feeding on smaller animals, such as insect larvae and fish fry.

The commonest fish in slow-flowing streams are members of the carp family, *Cyprinidae*, such as roach, *Rutilus*, bream, *Abramis*, and carp, *Cyprinus*. These fish require shallow weeds on which to lay their adhesive eggs and they feed on insects living among the organic debris on the stream bottom and in the mud. Cyprinid's mouths have specialized (*prehensile*) lips which allow them to scoop up mud and silt and sift out the animals contained in it. They are themselves preyed on by large fish predators, such as pike, *Esox*, pike-perch, *Stizostedion*, and perch, *Perca*.

Ponds and lakes

Unlike rivers and streams, ponds and lakes provide most of their own food and are much less reliant on the bank vegetation. In a large lake, 90 per cent of the plant material which supports the community is produced by algae and pondweeds. Algae are fed on by filter feeders, such as the water flea, *Daphnia*, which are in turn eaten by insects or fish. Large pondweeds, however, are rarely eaten directly, and the food they contain usually becomes available only when they die. So the food chain here runs from dead plant to decomposer (bacteria), to insect, to

Above: The grayling, *Thymallus*, a trout-like fish of the family *Salmonidae*. It is found in cold, fast-flowing and well-aerated rivers in North America, Europe and Asia, but is greatly affected by pollution. In North America, in particular, pollution has reduced the numbers of this fine game fish.

Left: An illustration from *The Compleat Angler* by Isaak Walton and Charles Cotton entitled 'Landing the Grayling'. There is no doubt that primitive man obtained food by fishing but the development of the long rod—allowing bait to be cast into deeper water away from the bank—is comparatively recent. Probably the earliest reference to the rod is in the work of the Roman writer Martial, who died in AD 104.

Below: Different species of fish occupy different parts of a large pond or lake depending on their feeding habits. This diagram shows the habitats of some characteristic species of temperate lakes in summer. Most fish, however, move out into deeper water to escape the cold of winter.

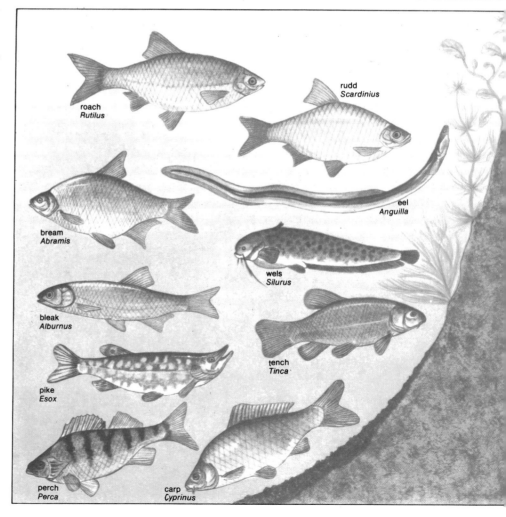

roach
Rutilus

rudd
Scardinius

bream
Abramis

eel
Anguilla

wels
Silurus

bleak
Alburnus

tench
Tinca

pike
Esox

perch
Perca

carp
Cyprinus

420

Brian Seed/John Hillelson Agency

Oxford Scientific Films

Above: The flamingo, *Phoenicopterus*, is a filter feeder—it stirs up muddy water and then sieves out small animals, particularly crustaceans and molluscs, with its bill.

Right: The great crested grebe, *Podiceps cristatus*, on its nest. The feet of this bird are set well back on the body allowing it to obtain greater speeds when diving under water, a tactic it uses to escape from predators.

Left: The rat-like water vole, *Arvicola amphibius*, one of the few mammals in the freshwater habitat.

Stephen Dalton/N.H.P.A.

snail, to worm and finally to fish.

Generally the main algal and water-weed production occurs in the upper layer of a lake where it is warm and light. This layer is called the *epilimnion* and is separated from a colder, heavy and deep layer, called the *hypolimnion*, by a boundary called the *thermocline*. Plants release oxygen as they photosynthesize so that the epilimnion always contains dissolved oxygen. This is not the case in the hypolimnion. Here sinking dead animals and plant remains collect and are fed upon by decomposers. These fungi and bacteria use up the oxygen resulting in low oxygen levels. This lack of oxygen restricts most other organisms to the epilimnion.

The amount of life in a lake is largely determined by the concentration of nutrients, particularly phosphates and nitrates. Lakes containing a low concentration of nutrients are called *oligotrophic* (little food) while those which are nutrient-rich are called *eutrophic* (good food). Oligotrophic lakes occur where the rocks of the surrounding area are hard and little weathering takes place to release the essential salts. Alpine lakes are a good example. Eutrophic lakes occur on soft rocks, such as limestone, which weather easily so releasing minerals into the water. Eutrophic lakes are also associated with a rich vegetation both in the water and on the surrounding banks. The decomposing vegetation releases nutrients into the water.

Algae (*phytoplankton*) and small animals (*zooplankton*) are the dominant groups in open water. The numbers of phytoplankton fluctuate during the year in a similar way to the plankton of the sea. During the winter, the water is thoroughly mixed by winds. Nutrients released by organic decay are brought up to the surface. Then, in the spring, algae rapidly consume this food supply and grow in numbers until an *algal bloom* occurs. This sometimes causes the water to turn green. Algal diatoms, such as *Asterionella*, are typical of these spring blooms.

The numbers of zooplankton are closely related to those of the algae on which they feed. As algae numbers increase in spring the numbers of zooplankton also increase but lag behind those of the algae. When most of the algae die the zooplankton switch to feeding on the bacteria which live on the dead algae. Common in the zooplankton are freshwater crustaceans, such as *Daphnia* and the pear-shaped *Cyclops*. Both of these animals feed on algal remains and on the bacteria associated with them.

Other animals live on the mud which collects at the bottom of lakes. These include midge larvae, water louse, and cased caddis larvae, *Trianodes* and *Phryganea*. But probably the commonest mud dwellers are mosquito larvae, such as *Culex* and *Anopheles*.

In temperate lakes and ponds the commonest fish species are carp, sticklebacks, *Gasterosteus* and *Pungitius*, and tench, *Tinca*. These fish breed and feed in the shallows but move out into the deeper water—over 2 m (6 ft)—in the winter to escape the cold. Ice forms on the surface of water, but because water is at its most dense at 4°C (39°F) the deepest water tends to be at this temperature during the winter. This unusual property of water—most other liquids are at their most dense immediately above their freezing point—is important in the survival of freshwater organisms. Without it lakes, and to a lesser extent rivers, would freeze solidly from the bottom upwards, killing all of the organisms in them except those that produce spores or other protective structures.

An interesting difference between lake and river fish is the size of the offspring (*fry*) they produce. Pond fish lay small eggs which hatch into small fry. In still lakes there is a plentiful supply of plankton for small fry to feed on. In rivers, where plankton is scarce, fish lay larger eggs hatching into larger fry which can cope both with the insect food available and with the water flow.

The number of fish species in a lake depends on the richness of the flora and on geography. Eutrophic lakes may contain from eight to ten fish species in temperate regions or many hundreds in Africa. Oligotrophic lakes, however, may contain only one species.

The number of fish species is also low in small lakes and ponds unable to support many breeding populations. Often the only species present is a large predator, like perch. Predators are able to survive in the absence of other fish to eat by eating their own young. The young perch feed on zooplankton, such as *Daphnia*, and in this way a food chain is formed in which algae are fed on by *Daphnia* which are fed on by young perch which are fed on by adult perch. Cannibalism can thus prevent the extinction of the species when food is short. The adult perch are too large to feed directly on zooplankton themselves and if they did not eat their young they would starve and the species would die out in that particular pond.

Grasslands

One plant family, the grass family, *Graminae*, has attained an economic and ecological importance unsurpassed by any other. Grasses are the dominant feature of a type of ecosystem which now extends over 45 million sq km (18 million square miles). Apart from the sea, only forest ecosystems exceed grasslands in extent; but grasslands far exceed forests in economic importance. The grasses owe their success to structural and physiological characteristics which allow them to withstand, better than other plants, semi-arid climates, poor soils, grazing by animals and burning.

The leaves of grasses are unique. They are produced from a growing point (*meristem*) located not along the stem of the plant, as in most other plants, but at the stem base. Few plants can survive the repeated destruction of their meristems and if they are grazed or cut they die. Because the meristem of a grass, however, is near its base it can be grazed close to the ground and yet grow back new leaves remarkably quickly.

Also important is the volume and aggressiveness of the root systems of grasses. They are large and extensive in proportion to the volume of the shoot— four fifths of living grass is root. Because they have no tap roots this large volume of root can be produced quickly from the base of the stems. They can rapidly absorb most of the available water when it rains in semi-arid areas.

Grasses are also herbaceous plants. With the exception of bamboos, they rarely exceed a metre (3 ft) in height and are often only a few centimetres tall. Because they do not produce permanent woody tissue they can grow up rapidly from seed. They can quickly recolonize land left bare after burning.

Natural grasslands

Grasslands occur wherever low rainfall, poor soil, grazing and burning have prevented the growth of other plant types— particularly trees. They are found in two areas of the world: in temperate regions, where they are called *prairie* or *steppe*, and in tropical regions, where they are called *savanna*. Grasslands reach their maximum extent in continental interiors between humid forests and arid deserts, and they tend to occur on rolling plains or plateaus.

The French gave the name 'prairie' (or meadow) to the North American grasslands while the name 'steppe' is derived from the name of the commonest genera of grass (*Stipa*) in the Eurasian grasslands extending from the Black Sea to eastern Mongolia. In both these temperate grasslands, however, and in contrast to savanna, trees or shrubs of any type are absent or so rare as to be negligible.

The development of the North American prairie is typical of the formation of temperate grasslands. After the last ice age, some 11,000 years ago, the grasses rapidly colonized ground left bare by the retreating glaciers. They have remained dominant ever since as a result of the combined effects of burning and grazing. On the flat plains high winds can develop, fanning and spreading fires which woody plants cannot survive. In addition grazing by

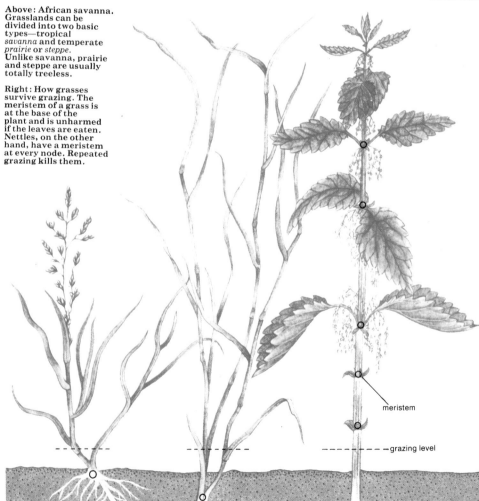

Above: African savanna. Grasslands can be divided into two basic types—tropical *savanna* and temperate *prairie* or *steppe*. Unlike savanna, prairie and steppe are usually totally treeless.

Right: How grasses survive grazing. The meristem of a grass is at the base of the plant and is unharmed if the leaves are eaten. Nettles, on the other hand, have a meristem at every node. Repeated grazing kills them.

meristem

grazing level

Giuseppe Mazza

Left: An illustration dating from 1849 of a prairie fire. Without such fires there would be no prairie. Dry summers and flat open land, on which high winds can develop, are ideal conditions for extensive fires which destroy both woodland and grassland. Grass, however, can recolonize burnt areas far more easily than trees. Where settlers have prevented fires, woodland has gradually spread into the prairie.

Below left: The savanna dung beetle, *Scarabaeus*, collects dung into a ball on which it then lays its eggs.

Bottom left: The largest areas of savanna occur in Africa and South America but it also occurs in large areas of west and north Australia. The typical large herbivore of these grasslands is the kangaroo, *Macropus*. A large kangaroo can cover 9 m (30 ft) with a single leap and can travel at more than 60 kph (40 mph).

Below: Perhaps the most important family of grassland herbivores is the *Bovidae* which includes cattle, bison, buffaloes, giraffe, antelopes, sheep, goats, and the Mongolian yak, *Bos grunniens* (shown here). All of these animals are *ruminants*, containing a part of the stomach, called the *rumen*, in which the otherwise indigestible cellulose part of grass is broken down by bacteria. The food is then regurgitated and digested normally.

bison, *Bison*, pronghorns, *Antilocapra*, and prairie dogs, *Cynomys*, have prevented the spread of woodland.

Tropical savanna is endowed with a greater variety of plants than temperate grasslands. It often includes drought-resistant woody plants, varying from low shrubs to tall trees. Nevertheless, savanna is always open and grass remains the dominant vegetation. It usually occurs where there is a marked seasonal drought but is occasionally found even where the humidity is high enough for forest growth, especially on plateaus.

Plateaus are usually formed when ground is geologically lifted, and the change in environment generally has an adverse effect on the soil. Iron-rich soils, in particular, are oxidized on exposure to the sun and acquire a hard crust, called *laterite*, often with an impervious layer, a *subsoil pan*, just below the surface. Rooting is restricted to the soil above this pan, so only shallow rooting plants, such as grasses, can grow. In addition the soil is usually water-logged in the wet season (water cannot percolate through the subsoil pan) and desiccated in the dry season. Few plants other than drought-resistant grasses and shrubs can survive in conditions like this.

Where deep soils do occur on plateaus, savanna may still be present because of nutrient deficiencies in the soil which prevent the development of woodland. Savannas formed because of soil defects (either nutrient deficiencies or the presence of laterite) are called *edaphic* savannas. Examples include the *cerrado* of South American plateaus, the mountain grasslands of West Africa, the *campo*

limpo of Brazil, and the *pampas* of the Argentine.

A second type of savanna owes its presence more to burning and the activity of man and other animals than to soil type. This is called *derived* or *secondary* savanna and has formed in a similar way to temperate grasslands. Land cleared by fire, caused either by man or by natural causes such as lightning, is rapidly colonized by savanna weeds, such as spear grass, *Imperia cylindrica*. These plants form a tough mat which prevents tree and shrub seedlings from germinating. Additionally, grazing by wild and domestic animals prevents the growth of herbaceous plants other than grasses.

Grassland animals

Open grassland can be a rich habitat but it is also a harsh one with wide fluctuations in temperature and humidity. The shortage of water, in particular, restricts the type of animals that can live there. All water loving animals, such as snails, wood lice and amphibians are rare. But animals which can exist with little water, especially reptiles and insects such as grasshoppers, *Acridiidae* and *Tettigoniidae*, and termites, *Isoptera*, thrive and can be very numerous. These animals obtain all the water they require from their food. Another problem of open grassland is the large difference between daytime and night time temperatures. In the Cameroon savanna, for example, a mid-day heat of 40°C (104°F) in the shade can be followed by a night temperature of 3°C (37°F).

Grasslands also lack shelter from winds and storms, and so grassland animals must provide their own shelter. To do this a great many burrow into the soil. Burrowing is more common among grassland animals than any others. Below a depth of half a metre (20 in), soil temperatures are remarkably static—close to the average annual air temperature for the region. The soil is cooler in summer and warmer in winter than the surface. Burrowing animals are thus able to obtain protection from large daily and annual temperature fluctuations. Furthermore, burrowing also gives a measure of protection from predators. There is little other cover where animals can hide.

Among invertebrate burrowers, ants, termites and earthworms are particularly important. In wetter grasslands earthworms, perhaps more than any other animals, are essential to the health of the grass sward. They help in the circulation of nutrients and decaying organic material, and their tunnels improve the drainage and aeration of the soil.

Larger vertebrate animals, too, burrow for protection. These include reptiles such as tortoises, *Testudo*, and skinks, *Scincidae*. But rodents are the most prolific vertebrate underground dwellers. A good example is the North American prairie dog, *Cynomys*, which forms large colonies, called 'towns', with intricate connecting tunnels.

Insects, such as grasshoppers, are important grassland consumers and can play a crucial role in affecting the quality of grassland vegetation. In areas of New York State, for example, insects were found to consume 94 kg of grass per square metre (19 lb per sq ft) during one summer season. These insects consumed roughly twice as much as cows on the same pasture. Nevertheless the main consumers of

Jacana

Above: The largest land animal, the African elephant, *Loxodonta africana*, is a grassland animal. It is one of the few large wild animals whose numbers are increasing in game reserves—it is often purposely culled.

Right: Grasslands are rarely entirely natural and the most important grazing animals are normally domestic. These are some of the 50 million cattle in the Argentine.

Below: Birds need less water than other animals because they excrete solid *uric acid* rather than urine. They are also able to fly to water. These are red-billed weaver birds, *Quelea*, at a savanna waterhole in Kenya.

Zefa

R.I.M. Campbell/Bruce Coleman Ltd.

Above: Part of the cycle of life and death—vultures feeding on a corpse. Both American vultures, *Cathartidae*, and old world vultures, *Accipitridae*, have few or no feathers on their heads and necks. This allows them to feed on carrion without getting their feathers matted with blood.

Right: A cheetah, *Acinonyx*, surveying the world from a termite hill. Termite hills are very resistant to wind and rain because of secretions produced by the termites which bind the soil together.

Below: A typical savanna food cycle. Plant food eventually passes through the whole community.

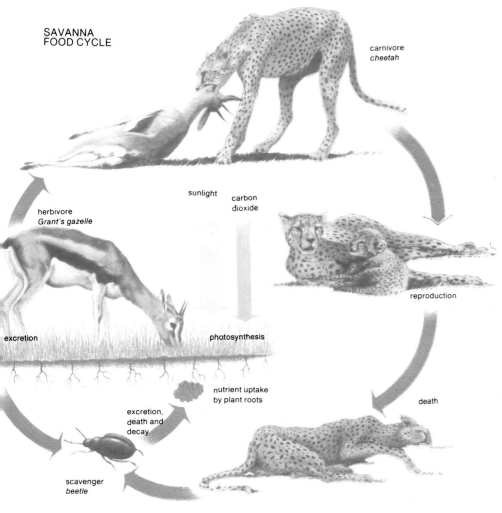

SAVANNA
FOOD CYCLE

carnivore
cheetah

sunlight

carbon
dioxide

herbivore
Grant's gazelle

reproduction

excretion

photosynthesis

nutrient uptake
by plant roots

death

excretion,
death and
decay

scavenger
beetle

grassland (in the absence of interference by man) are normally large mammalian herbivores such as antelopes in Africa and the bison and pronghorn in North America. These herbivores have one noticeable adaptation to grassland life called the *cursorial habit*. Simply, they are adapted for speed of running. In grassland there is no danger of bumping into objects as would occur in forests. Moreover, there is no tall vegetation in which to hide from predators; hence good eyesight, keen sense of smell and, most important of all, speed are required to survive.

Many birds of open country are also adapted for speed of running. The ostrich, *Struthio camelus*, in Africa, the emu, *Dromaius novaehollandiae*, in Australia, and the rhea, *Rhea*, in the pampas of South America have all abandoned flight in favour of running. They have poorly developed wings, long powerful hind legs and feathers which do not lock together as they do in flying birds. They are among the fastest of land animals.

Another interesting protective adaptation is *herding*, exhibited by many grassland animals such as zebra, *Equus*, and gnu, *Connochaetes*. Being in a herd reduces the likelihood of any particular individual being taken by a predator. Additionally, a large group will be able to detect danger and warn each other more easily than individual animals which are widely dispersed. Herding also enables grazing animals to more efficiently exploit the grassland. A large herd covering a large area is able to detect useful food sites that an individual would miss. Once a good grazing area has been found all the attention of the herd can be concentrated on it.

Because large herbivores are so well adapted to protect themselves their predators must be equally well adapted to be able to catch them. In particular, they must be able to run as fast or faster than their prey. Animals which hunt alone, such as the cheetah, *Acinonyx*, can often reach very fast speeds—up to 110 kph (70 mph), though often only for short periods. Other, slower running carnivores, such as the cape hunting dog, *Lycaon*, increase the efficiency of their hunting by attacking in packs which can single out and trap prey from a large herd.

Cultivated grasslands

The biblical statement that 'all flesh is grass' is little short of the truth. The most important of all food plants, the cereals (including wheat, barley and rice), are grasses; and cereal fields therefore technically grasslands. The most productive agricultural areas of the world are often ploughed-up grasslands for this very reason. Those factors which benefit the growth of wild grasses also favour the closely related cereals.

Furthermore, many grasslands which are being used in a more 'natural' way— that is to support grazing animals such as cattle, *Bos*—are also entirely artificial. Without continuous attention from the farmer many of these fields would quickly revert to forest. The distinction between cultivated and natural grassland is certainly not well defined. Very few grasslands exist without some interference from man, even if this only takes the form of occasional burning. Most owe their continued existence, if not their origin, to man and to the domestic grazing animals that he keeps on them.

425

Norman Myers/Bruce Coleman Ltd.

Sassoon/Robert Harding Assoc.

Coniferous Forests

The largest area of forest in the world grows in the cold temperate regions of the Northern Hemisphere. It extends in a band roughly 5,800 km (3,600 miles) long and 1,300 km (800 miles) wide across Europe and Asia to the Far East, between latitudes 55 and 70 degrees north. A smaller, but still considerable, area occurs in North America. Cold coniferous forest merges into treeless tundra to the north and into mixed deciduous woodland and meadowlands to the south. Because none of the southern continents extends sufficiently far south there is no comparable zone in the Southern Hemisphere.

Coniferous forests occur in areas where climatic conditions are too severe for deciduous woodland. Particularly important is the length of the growing season. Unlike most flowering trees, conifers can survive in areas where there are relatively few days in the year when temperatures are high enough for photosynthesis and plant growth.

The largest area of northern temperate or *boreal* forest occurs in central Asia, where it is known as *taiga*. In this region the winter is prolonged, with only three or four months of the year free of frost and January temperatures as low as —30°C (—22°F). Consequently the ground is permanently frozen below a depth of about 30 cm (1 ft) and only the surface thaws in the short summer, when the temperatures may average 10°C (50°F). The permanently frozen ground is called *permafrost*.

Surprisingly, as well as being cold, the taiga is also dry. Winds are dry and, although there is considerable precipitation (usually between 25 and 100 cm (10-40 in) per year), a great deal falls as snow. Especially during the winter months the frozen ground-water is unavailable to plant roots. The environment is said to be *physiologically dry*.

Conifers are well adapted to these adverse conditions. They have tough leathery evergreen needles ready to photosynthesize whenever conditions allow it, and the leaf surfaces are coated with a thick waxy cuticle which reduces water loss by evaporation. The leaves are highly resistant to freezing—even at temperatures well below the freezing point of water—and the narrow leaf shape may help by reducing the rate at which heat is lost by radiation at night. Conifers also have shallow root systems which take water from the thin layer of unfrozen soil. Furthermore, their narrow conical shape not only supports snow but also sheds it quickly when it starts to thaw.

Nevertheless, not all trees in the boreal forest are evergreen or even conifers. In the extreme north two deciduous trees are also common: the coniferous larch, *Larix*, and the most hardy of all flowering trees, the birch, *Betula*. Typically, however, the forest is dominated by evergreen conifers particularly the spruces, *Picea*, with the addition of firs, *Abies*, pines, *Pinus*, and cedars, *Cedrus*, in the southernmost areas All of these trees form a dense canopy which, because there is no autumn leaf fall, produces deep shade throughout the year. For this reason there is no flush of

Above: The largest land habitat in the world is coniferous forest—it stretches in a band roughly 1,300 km (800 miles) wide around the north of the globe. It exists in areas that are too cold for deciduous woodland yet too warm for tundra, where cold-tolerant evergreen conifers can exploit weak sunlight throughout the year.

Right: The cold, waterlogged soils of the boreal forest are strongly acidic and because bacteria dislike acid conditions bacterial decay is negligible. Fungi are the most active decomposers together with small invertebrates likes mites, *Acarina*, and springtails, *Collembola*. This fungus is *Stropharia hornemannii*.

Below: Damp and cold also protect coniferous forests from fire. They are not invulnerable, however, as this photo of burned forest shows.

early spring flowers as there is in deciduous woodland. Few plants, in fact, grow on the coniferous forest floor which instead is often thickly carpeted with fallen needles.

Where there are gaps in the canopy, however, some shrubby plants such as juniper, *Juniperus communis*, and bilberry, *Vaccinium myrtilus*, flourish, along with occasional grasses and herbaceous plants such as the wintergreens, *Pyrola*, wild strawberry, *Fragaria vesca* and cloudberry, *Rubus chamaemorus*. In addition mosses are common on the ground and on the trunks of fallen trees; and vast areas of boggy forest, known as the *muskegs* in Canada and produced because the permafrost prevents drainage of the soil, are covered with carpets of sphagnum moss, *Sphagnum*. Other plants are epiphytes, living on the trees. These are almost entirely lichens, mainly *Usnea*, although some older conifer needles become covered with unicellular algae, *Pleurococcus*, and fungi.

The giant sequoia (*sequoio giganteum*), also called the Wellingtonia, is a species of evergreen found mainly in California and southern Oregon. Specimens have reached 267 feet (91.5m) in height, and 79 feet (24.3m) in girth.

Animals

Animal life in the taiga is greatly influenced by the short summer and severe winter. In the summer months insects are plentiful and mosquitoes and other flies, *Diptera*, briefly achieve very high populations. The conifers also provide habitats for bark boring beetles, *Scolytidae*, sawflies, *Symphyta*, and wood wasps, *Siricidae*, which all have wood-boring larvae which do a great deal of damage to trees in commercial forests.

These and other insects provide food for insectivorous birds, such as flycatchers, *Musicapa*, swallows, *Hirundo rustica*, warblers, *Sylviidae*, and wagtails, *Motacilla*; but since insects are only briefly plentiful, most taiga birds are not insectivorous. Instead most, such as the buntings, *Emberizidae*, finches, *Fringillidae*, and thrushes, *Turdus*, are seed-eaters. Apart from the conifers, taiga plants are commonly fleshy-fruited, probably because wind dispersal of seeds is impossible in the shelter of the forest. Seed and fruit are therefore available for much of the year. Birds are the main agents of seed dispersal.

The crossbills, *Loxia*, are a particularly interesting group of taiga finches. Their beaks have crossed tips and are specially adapted for removing the seeds from conifer cones, their sole source of food. Most taiga birds migrate to more favourable climates in winter. Exceptions are the insectivorous white-throated swift, *Aeronautes sexatilis*, and the poor-will, *Phalaenoptilus nuttallii*, which are among the few bird species known to hibernate.

Many smaller mammals also hibernate in order to survive the winter. During

Fabius Henrion/Jacana

Claude Pissavini/Jacana

hibernation complex physiological changes take place in which the animal becomes temporarily coldblooded. Respiration rates and the requirement for oxygen are reduced to a fraction of their normal level and the carbon dioxide content of the venous blood increases. Hibernation may be *complete*, as in the hedgehog, *Erinaceus europaeus*, and smaller rodents such as voles, *Microtus*, or *partial* as in the brown bear, *Ursus arctos*, and squirrels, *Sciurus*. Partial hibernators wake at intervals during the winter to feed; complete hibernators stay 'asleep'.

Many of the carnivores of coniferous forests are prized as game or hunted for their fur. In the past fur trading often provided the sole means of support for the inhabitants of the taiga who traded the skins for food and other supplies. Valu-

Above: Most coniferous forest birds feed on seeds as little other food, such as insects, is available. This is a male crossbill, *Loxia curvirostra*.

Right: The boreal forest contains the largest of all deer species, the elk or moose, *Alces alces*. The Alaskan moose (shown here) narrowly escaped extinction in the nineteenth century but has since recovered under protection. The European elk is also rare. It was once widespread throughout Europe—an exceptionally large form occured in Ireland—but has now disappeared from all but the northernmost part of its former range.

P. Morris

428

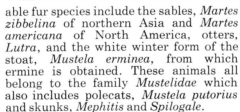

Left: Many forest animals live in the trees. Well known are the squirrels, *Sciurus.*

Above: Monkey-puzzles, *Araucaria,* are conifers native to the Southern Hemisphere. Some grow in the tropical rain forest, but the most heavily exploited *Araucaria* forests are in Brazil and Paraguay.

There, stands of *Araucaria angustifolia* grow within the sub-tropical deciduous forest. This tree, however, is the Chile pine, *Araucaria araucana,* native to Chile and Argentina.

Below: A forest carnivore, the lynx, *Lynx lynx,* washing itself.

Above: The giant parasitic wood wasp, *Urocerus gigas,* boring through tree bark with its ovipositor in order to lay its eggs beneath the bark. The larvae which hatch from the eggs are not themselves immune from parasites however. Another wasp, the ichneumon *Rhyssa,* is able to locate the *Urocerus* larvae beneath the bark. It then lays its eggs on them. When the eggs hatch the developing *Rhyssa* larvae then feed upon the *Urocerus* larvae.

Left: A fox, *Vulpes,* caught in a steel trap set by Eskimo fur trappers in the boreal forest of northwest Canada. Many of the carnivores of the forest are hunted for their fur.

Stephen Dalton/NHPA

Bruce Coleman

Frank Lane

able fur species include the sables, *Martes zibbelina* of northern Asia and *Martes americana* of North America, otters, *Lutra,* and the white winter form of the stoat, *Mustela erminea,* from which ermine is obtained. These animals all belong to the family *Mustelidae* which also includes polecats, *Mustela putorius* and skunks, *Mephitis* and *Spilogale.*

The mustelids are the most important coniferous forest carnivores but the large cats, *Felidae,* are certainly the most spectacular. They include the lynx, *Lynx lynx,* and the fierce European wildcat, *Felis silvestris,* of which there is a subspecies *Felis silvestris grampia* in the conifer forests of Scotland. Finally and surprisingly, because they are now thought of as animals of warmer climates, tigers probably evolved in the coniferous forest of central Asia. The Siberian tiger, *Panthera tigris,* is usually larger in size than the Indian and South-East Asian varieties, and is also paler in colour with less conspicuous stripes and longer hair.

Other coniferous forests

Although the taiga forms the largest area of coniferous forest in the world, conifers are by no means confined to cold temperate climates. They form smaller communities in the entire range of temperate, subtropical and tropical climates both in the northern and southern hemispheres. Indeed some single species grow throughout this range. The white pine, *Pinus strobus,* for example, is found from eastern Canada to the mountains of southern Mexico, although transplanted Mexican plants cannot survive frosts if they are replanted in Canada.

Perhaps the most famous area of tem-perate coniferous forest, because of its enormous output of timber, is found along the west coast of North America in Washington, Oregon and British Columbia. Here long growing seasons, heavy rainfall and good soils encourage the development of dense stands of fast-growing trees. The most important species are Douglas fir, *Pseudotsuga menziesii,* which grows in pure stands or in mixtures with redwood, *Sequoia sempervirens,* pines, western hemlock, *Tsuga heterophylla,* and Sitka spruce, *Picea sitchensis.*

Further south in the coastal regions of northwest California and Oregon, where the climate is warm temperate, there are extensive forests of redwood. Redwoods require a moist environment, and although there is little summer rain in the region there are frequent sea fogs. Moisture from the fog is intercepted by the foliage and provides sufficient water, not only for the trees, but also for communities of the swordfern, *Polystichum munitum,* and redwood sorrel, *Oxalis oregana,* which grow at the base of the trees. When conditions are ideal redwood forests form the heaviest stands of timber in the world and an important timber industry is based on them.

Nevertheless, areas of temperate coniferous forest are greatly outweighed by the mass of deciduous woodland which is the dominant vegetation in most warm and wet areas. The reason there are relatively few conifers in temperate and tropical regions is not that they are unable to survive in hot and wet climates, but that they are unable to survive competition from the more highly evolved flowering trees.

429

Rainforest

The richest and most spectacular vegetation on earth is to be found in the rainforests. Broadleaved yet evergreen trees grow to at least 30 m (100 ft) and an extremely diverse collection of lianas, shrubs, epiphytes and ground flora produce a continuous, many-layered mass of vegetation from the ground to the top of the tree canopy. In it, too, a vast number of animal species have evolved, each filling a particular ecological niche. There are so many rainforest species that they have not all been found and collected, let alone identified and classified.

The climatic conditions which favour the development of rainforest are heavy rainfall—200 to 300 cm (80 to 120 in)—spread evenly throughout the year, and continuous warmth with little seasonal variation in either temperature or day length. Rainforests are therefore almost exclusively tropical, occurring in the Amazon basin of South America, coastal Central America, equatorial West Africa and the Congo basin, and much of tropical South-East Asia including Malaysia, Java, Sumatra, Borneo, New Guinea and the Philippines. Smaller areas occur in Madagascar, Queensland in Australia and the Pacific Islands.

Vegetation layers

Contrary to the popular image of tropical rainforest as a dense, impenetrable jungle, mature rainforest is fairly easy to walk through without resorting to machetes, since vegetation on the forest floor is relatively sparse. It is overhead that rainforest reaches its thickest development. The densest part of all is the *C layer* consisting of trees of heights from 5 to 20 m (16 to 66 ft). Because they are so close together these trees have tapering conical crowns much deeper than they are wide.

C-layer trees are not the dominant trees of the forest, however. Almost half

Heather Angel

Frith/Bruce Coleman Ltd

Left: This picture shows one of the fiercest forest predators, the mantis, *Tenodera*, with its catch, a gecko lizard, *Gekkonidae*.

Below: Epiphytic bromeliads, *Bromeliaceae*, form rosettes in which water collects—so much in some cases that they have been described as 'aerial marshes'. They provide ideal breeding places for tree frogs, *Amphodus* (shown here). Other animals, such as aquatic insects, leeches, *Hirudinea*, spiders, *Arachnida*, centipedes, *Myriapoda*, snails, *Gasteropoda*, and protozoa have also been found in them.

Oxford Scientific Films

430

Oxford Scientific Films

Oxford Scientific Films

Above: The iguana, *Iguana iguana*, is a common large lizard of the rainforests of Central and South America. It is a tree-dweller, eating leaves and fruit (though occasionally it will attack small birds and mammals) and has a camouflaged green skin broken by brown bands. The animal can grow up to 2 m (6 ft) long, including the tail, and its white meat is a delicacy enjoyed by South American Indians.

Left: Ants are probably the most numerous of all rainforest insects. There may be one and a half million in a single column of driver ants, *Eciton*—shown here crossing a living bridge between two tree trunks.

of them are young trees which eventually grow up to form an upper canopy of trees called the *A* and *B layers*. Apart from a few exceptionally tall trees which may grow up to 100 m (330 ft) high, and which are known as *emergents*, the tallest trees in the forest are the A-layer trees. They average about 40 m (130 ft) tall, are widely spaced, and have wide and shallow umbrella-shaped crowns. Beneath them the B-layer trees, reaching heights of 15 to 30 m (50 to 100 ft), form a more continuous canopy—although there are still some gaps—and their crowns are deeper than they are wide. Below these the C-layer trees form an almost continuous canopy.

Lower still the *D layer*, also known as the *shrub layer*, contains saplings, palms, tall herbs such as *Marantaceae*, woody shrubs and bamboos ranging from 2 to about 5 m (6 to 16 ft) in height. Finally, on the forest floor, the *E layer* contains tree seedlings and a few herbaceous flowering plants and clubmosses, *Selaginella*.

Forest plants

As well as containing more layers than temperate deciduous or coniferous woodland, rainforest also contains far more tree species. Temperate woods with more than 20 species per hectare are considered exceptionally rich but in the rainforest there are very often more than 100 species of tree per hectare, not counting many species of shrubs and woody creeper. Nevertheless, vigorous species can become dominant. For example, in Guyana and other areas of the Amazon basin, more than 50 per cent of all trunks more than 5 cm (2 in) in diameter, are wallaba trees, *Dicymbe*.

Despite its great diversity, to the casual observer the first impression of rainforest is often one of monotony. Because there is strong competition for light, trees grow as rapidly as possible to their full height and because of this their trunks are almost always straight, branching only near the top. Although there are many species they all look very much alike. The slender trunks are covered with a thin, smooth bark and even the leaves are surprisingly unvaried, almost all being a glossy dark green and lanceolate (long and narrow) with an undivided margin.

Rainforest trees are often buttressed with triangular sheets of wood, the edges of which may sometimes be as much as 6 m (20 ft) from the trunk, radiating from

431

Left: A South American tree boa, *Corallus caninus*, catching a parakeet. All boas kill their prey by crushing —the snake is sensitive to the minor vibrations produced by the beating heart of its prey and applies just enough pressure to stop the heart beating. *Corallus* can grow to about 1.3 m (4 ft) but the larger *Boa constrictor* may reach lengths of 5.5 m (19 ft).

Above: The Amazon rainforest is the largest natural land habitat which has remained largely untouched by man. Nevertheless, it is steadily being reduced as forest is chopped down and burnt to clear land for crops. It is to be hoped that the construction of the Trans Amazonian Highway (shown here) does not accelerate this process.

Below: African epauletted fruit bats live at the edges of the forest where they hang upside-down in trees during the day. This is *Epomorphorus gambiensis*.

the trunk base. These buttresses can be thin enough to be used as boards and they ring when struck with a stick. Their function is not understood. They may give the trees support, and buttressed trees have been shown to have shallow root systems, but buttressed trees blow down just as often as those without buttresses. Also, if they are for support, it is surprising that they have developed in the rainforest, where strong winds are rare, while they are virtually unknown in temperate forests exposed to severe winds.

The flowers of rainforest trees, like those of most temperate tree species, are usually inconspicuous and greenish or whitish in colour. Unlike temperate trees, however, which always produce flowers on young shoots or on one-year-old growth, the flowers of rainforest trees often grow directly from the trunk or main branches, a phenomenon known as *cauliflory*. Two well-known examples are the cacao, *Theobroma cacao*, a C-layer tree of American origin from which cocoa is obtained, and *Diospyros* (family *Ebenaceae*) from which the hard black wood *ebony* is obtained.

Apart from trees, two other plant groups are particularly characteristic of rainforests. These are the epiphytes and the lianas. Epiphytes, plants which grow attached to, and entirely supported by other plants, occur in all wet forests from the tropics to the tundra, but achieve their greatest diversity in rainforest where they grow on almost every available plant stem, trunk, leaf surface, and even on telegraph lines, if any are present. Rainforest epiphytes include algae, lichens, mosses and liverworts, ferns and flowering herbaceous plants, particularly

bromeliads and orchids. All of these are small plants which have adopted the epiphytic habit to enable them to compete with trees for light.

Some specialized epiphytes send roots down to the ground, become self-supporting, and eventually kill the trees which originally supported them. These are known as *stranglers*, and the best-known are the strangling figs of the genus *Ficus* from Africa, Malaysia and Australia. Some of these become very large trees of the A and B layers.

The most important climbing plants of the rainforest are the lianas, which are woody plants rooted in the forest floor but which use trees for support while they climb to the upper layers of the canopy. Some are of great size, producing crowns comparable with those of the trees they use for support, and compete strongly with trees for space and light.

Rainforest animals

The habitat occupied and part played by any species in a living community is called its *ecological niche*. The difference between two niches may be extremely small, for instance how high up in the air, or at what time of day, two species of bird catch the same insect food; but provided there is some difference there is no direct competition between different species occupying different niches. In a stable community each niche is filled by just one species—the number of species depends on the number of niches.

In a rainforest the diversity of plant species and types produces a bewildering array of habitats and microhabitats each of which provides a niche for an animal species. The result is a vast number of

Left: An Amazonian heron (family *Ardeidae*), *Trigosoma lineatum*.

Above: Most rainforest mammals live in trees and have anatomical adaptations, like well developed hands and feet or a grasping (*prehensile*) tail, for climbing. In the primates these adaptations have taken different forms on different continents. New World monkeys, *Cebidae*, generally have prehensile tails while their counterparts in the Old World, *Cercopithecidae*, have long arms and grasping hands instead. The hands of monkeys also vary. The leaf eating langurs, *Presbytis*, of India and Malaysia have a functional thumb while the leaf-eating *Colobus* monkeys of Africa have a greatly reduced thumb. The monkeys shown here are squirrel monkeys, *Saimiri*, from the rainforests of Central and South America. Easily recognizable by their white faces, they feed on insects and fruit.

species, particularly invertebrates, of which a great many are still unnamed. Despite its high population, the rainforest fauna often appears sparse. There are several reasons for this. First, most of the vertebrates are nocturnal, spending the day in burrows or hidden among vegetation. Second, the main focus of animal activity is not at ground level but in the canopy where there is the greatest abundance of staple foods—leaves, fruits and insects (especially ants and termites). A third reason is that the butterflies and birds of the shaded lower reaches of the forest have dull colours while only those which live higher, like the parrots, *Psittacidae*, toucans, *Ramphastidae*, and the brilliant blue *Morpho* butterflies of South America, have dazzling colours in bold patterns.

The amount of dead organic material in the soil and litter layers is less in the tropical rainforest than in any other land ecosystem. Fallen leaves, trees, fruits and dead animals are rapidly consumed and returned to the nutrient cycle by decomposer organisms. Of these ants and termites are tremendously active and in terms of numbers are probably the most important animal group. Leaf cutting ants, particularly of the genus *Atta*, cut pieces from living and dead leaves and carry them back to the nest where they are processed in fungal gardens to provide a food source for the larvae. Termites are mainly tree-dwelling, although specialist species inhabit dead wood and are the main agents of its decomposition.

Rainforest mammals are mainly arboreal and have anatomical adaptations for climbing, such as well developed hands and feet, and prehensile tails. Probably the most uncompromisingly adapted group are the sloths, *Bradypodidae*, of Brazil. Sloths hang from branches, and have almost lost the capacity to walk on land. They spend most of their lives in sluggish movement or inactivity. Their hair is grooved or scaly and is colonized by algae which gives them a greenish colour of great value as camouflage.

Another characteristic family are the rainforest anteaters, *Myrmecophagidae*. These animals have a specialist diet of ants and termites. Anteaters are confined to the New World but in Africa their niche is occupied by the pangolins or scaly anteaters, *Pholidota*. Like myrmecophagids, pangolins have a prehensile tail and a long, sticky tongue adapted for catching insects.

Man and the forest

Man is by no means a newcomer to the forests. Native peoples have lived in rainforest regions for thousands of years. But modern agricultural man is greatly tempted to replace the forests' immense richness with equally rich crops, and great tracts of forest are felled and burned each year. Although the wood ash acts as a fertilizer, and supports vigorous crops in the first few years, the nutrients are rapidly leached from the soil which is left sterile. Since rainforests are exceedingly complex ecosystems they may take many decades to regenerate, so the current rate of clearance, of the Amazon forest in particular, is of great concern to biologists. Despite its immense size, if future exploitation is not more cautious and better planned its total destruction may become unavoidable.

Hedges, Pasture and Woodland

The dominant vegetation of temperate regions is deciduous woodland. It occurs wherever winters are relatively mild (although frosts may still occur), summers are warm, and rainfall is moderately heavy—75 to 150 cm (30 to 60 in) per year —without a pronounced wet or dry season. Such climates occur between latitudes 30 and 60 degrees north and extend across thousands of square kilo-metres of North America, Europe and Asia. Not all this area is deciduous forest. It is interrupted by the Rocky Mountains in the US—which restrict it to the Eastern states, by a large area of low rainfall and semi-desert in central Asia— which restricts it to the Far East and to Europe, and everywhere by the activity of man, who has continuously cleared woodland for towns and agriculture. In the Southern Hemisphere the continents only just extend far enough south to reach the temperate zone, and deciduous

Above right: Snowdrops, *Galanthus nivalis*, taking advantage of spring sunlight in a deciduous wood. Spring flowers are a feature of deciduous woodland because it is only during the winter and early spring that enough light reaches the forest floor for them to grow. For the rest of the year the floor is shaded by the dense canopy of tree leaves.

Right: Every autumn the forest floor becomes carpeted with fallen leaves. In this way many of the nutrients taken up by the trees during the year are returned to the ecosystem. Invertebrates, fungi and bacteria break down the leaves so returning the nutrients to the soil.

Far right: Just two layers are normally recognized in deciduous woodland—the tree canopy, and the forest floor and leaf litter. The soil can be considered as a third layer, however. Here one underground dweller, a mole, *Talpa*, feasts upon another, an earthworm.

woodland only occurs in New Zealand, Tasmania and the southern tips of Africa and South America.

Plants of deciduous woodland
In its best development, temperate decidu-ous woodland rivals tropical rainforest in height, with trees growing up to 30 or 40 m (100 to 130 ft) tall. But deciduous woodland has quite a different look to it. The trees typically produce a dense, closed canopy of leaves beneath which there is deep shade which inhibits the growth of smaller plants. Life is concen-trated in only two layers: the tree crowns, and the soil surface and leaf litter. Only where the canopy is more open is there a ground layer of herbaceous plants.

The dominant trees are the oak, *Quercus*, beech, *Fagus*, maple, *Acer*, ash,

Fraxinus, and birch, *Betula*. All of these trees produce extensive forests, but only rarely are they found in mixed woodland, growing together. Normally only one or two species grow in any particular area. Which species is domi-nant, and hence the structure of the forest which develops, depends on a wide range of environmental factors. In particular the type of soil is important: acid clay soils, for example, favour oak woodland with few other tree species, while more alkaline clays support a more mixed woodland, richer in tree species and containing shrubs such as privet, *Ligus-trum*, spindle, *Euonymus*, and buckthorn, *Prunus*.

Winter temperatures and levels of sun-shine in temperate regions are sufficiently low that the amount of energy a broad-

leaved tree would consume in winter, if it kept its leaves, is greater than the amount of energy it could obtain by photosynthe-sis. Temperate broadleaved trees, there-fore, save energy by losing their leaves in winter and becoming dormant. (That is, they are *deciduous*.) As a result, the environment of deciduous woodland changes dramatically with the seasons: only in winter and spring can light reach the ground. Herbaceous plants are greatly affected by this seasonal change and many species, such as the wood anemone, *Anemone nemorosa*, bluebell, *Endymion non-scriptus*, and wild strawberry, *Fragaria vesca*, synchronize their leaf production and flowering to take advan-tage of the light of early spring, before the tree buds burst and their leaves shade the ground.

The red deer, *cervus elaphus*, is found in deciduous forests all over Europe. It also has close relatives in Asia, North America and North Africa. In Britain, as forests disappear, it is becoming a moorland species, smaller and lighter than the forest deer.

Other woodland plants have adapted to the deep shade by adopting a *saprophytic* way of life—deriving their nourishment from organic material in the soil, and thereby dispensing with the need for light. The most important saprophytes are the fungi. They are particularly important in the decomposition of leaf litter to release nutrients into the soil.

Woodland animals

Insects and other arthropods, especially mites, *Acarina*, and woodlice, *Isopoda* are also important in the decomposition of forest litter, breaking it down for fungi and bacteria. In turn they are an important food source for birds. A small insectivorous bird may eat up to 20 insects per minute during feeding periods. Insects also disperse fungal spores and pollinate trees. The most important pollinators are honeybees, *Apis*.

Most larger woodland animals are shy species, which live in the woodland for protection. However, the forest habitat has been altered to such an extent by man that many once-common animal species are now absent or rare in areas where man has lived for any length of time. This is particularly true of the larger mammals. For example the wild boar, *Sus scrofa*, and the grey timber wolf, *Canis lupus*, were once widespread throughout Europe but have been extinct in Britain since the 17th century and are uncommon elsewhere.

The disappearance of animals such as these can have far-reaching effects besides the loss of zoologically interesting species. In extreme cases it can lead to the long-term destruction of the forest itself. Smaller mammals, especially rodents such as mice, *Apodemus*, voles, *Microtus*, squirrels, *Sciurus*, and rabbits, *Oryctolagus*, eat the shoots, buds and roots of trees, often killing them. Deer also damage trees by browsing lower branches and by debarking them with their antlers. In an undisturbed forest such damage would be kept in check by predation by carnivores, but where the carnivores have been hunted to extinction the numbers of rodents and other browsing animals may become so large that the forest is prevented from regenerating after it has been damaged.

Cultivated grassland

Where deciduous woodland has been cleared for agriculture, the moist temperate climate' favours the growth of grassland. In most countries of the world livestock is grazed on semi-natural unmanaged grassland known as *rough pasture*, but in Britain and Europe the most productive grasslands are cultivated. They are of two types: *temporary grassland* which is planted, grazed and ploughed all in a few years, and *permanent grassland* in which the turf is left undisturbed for much longer periods. Permanent grassland is also of two types: *pasture*, used for grazing animals, and *meadow*, grown for hay. Grazed pasture generally contains shorter and more palatable grasses, encouraged by the maintenance of a short sward, while hay meadows develop coarser, taller grasses which shade out the smaller plants.

The best pastures are mostly of perennial ryegrass, *Lolium perenne*, but leguminous plants, especially white clover, *Trifolium repens*, and lucerne, *Medicago sativa*, are also widely grown because

they have a high protein content and are able to fix atmospheric nitrogen in their root nodules. Good farmers also recognize the dietary value to their livestock of certain plants which are tasty or are rich in minerals. Among these chicory, *Cichorium intypus*, burnet, *Poterium polygamum*, plantain, *Plantago lanceolata*, and yarrow, *Achillea millefolium*, may be grown, either together with the grasses and legumes or sometimes in separate *herb strips*.

Less well managed grassland is gradually colonized by coarser grasses such as the bents, *Agrostis*, and Yorkshire fog, *Holcus lanatus*. Still poorer meadows provide a home for rushes and sedges and finally scrub. These areas may be poor agriculturally but they are of great interest to the naturalist because they tend to support more plant and animal species than planted pasture.

The typical larger animals of cultivated grassland are those that prefer open spaces to the dense cover of woodland. The skylark, *Alauda arvensis*, common partridge, *Perdix perdix*, and lapwing, *Vanellus vanellus*, are the commonest meadow birds, and they nest on the ground. In addition woodland and hedgerow birds, such as rooks, *Corvus frugilegus*, feed in meadows while kestrels, *Falco tinnunculus*, hunt for small mammals among the grass. Several species of mammals are to be found in meadows though few are truly confined to them. Nevertheless, hares, *Lepus*, and the long-tailed field mouse, *Apodemus sylvaticus*, prefer the open field to hedges or woodland. Other animals like moles, *Talpa*, and rabbits, which prefer cover, create their own by burrowing underground.

Hedges
Hedges form a habitat very similar to that of a woodland edge. A hedge consists of a line of shrubs or trees, often on an earth bank, planted close enough together to provide a barrier to wandering livestock. Often a hedge will follow the line of a drainage ditch in order to avoid breaking up a field more than necessary. Hedges are planted as an alternative to walls and fences, and have the advantage over them in that they are self-repairing. They are grown throughout the world, but reached their most extensive development in Europe, and particularly in Britain, when the Enclosure Acts, passed in the 1790s in the reign of George III, forced farmers to subdivide their fields.

Hedges are man-made and the dominant shrub species are therefore those put there by man. In Europe, hawthorn, *Crataegus monogyna*, is the most commonly planted species because of its rapid growth and because hawthorn hedges are stockproof. Ash, elm and oak are also planted. New hedges, because they are artificial, contain few species. Over the years, however, they are colonized by other hedge plants including trees and

Below far left: Because deciduous woodland occurs in the climatic zone most favourable to man it is the natural habitat which he has most destroyed or severely modified. The larger carnivores, in particular, have been hunted for sport and to protect livestock—though the greatest threat to their survival is the destruction of their habitat. Even in North America, where the forest was virtually untouched until comparatively recently, both the wolf, *Canis lupus*, and the brown bear, *Ursus arctos*, have been eliminated from most of their former ranges. In England one of the few remaining large carnivores, the fox, *Vulpes*, is still ceremoniously hunted.

Below left: Smaller animals are affected by man's activities as well. Forming a ball does not protect hedgehogs from cars, for example—though some (like the one here) have now learnt to run.

Below: A common meadow bird, the skylark, *Alauda arvensis*.

large eddies

h = height of wall

1h 0 0 1h 2h 3h 4h 5h 6h 7h 8h 9h 10h 11h

small eddies

sheltered zone

h = height of hedge

1h 0 0 1h 2h 3h 4h 5h 6h 7h 8h 9h 10h 11h

shrubs such as privet and dog rose, *Rosa canina*, which do not on their own form stockproof hedges.

Besides the hedge shrubs themselves, more than a thousand other plant species have been recorded in hedges. Only about a quarter of these, however, can be regarded as true hedgerow plants. Most are woodland species or are annual weeds, such as nettles, *Urticaceae*, of the type found on disturbed ground and wasteland. The true hedgerow plants are the climbers, like honeysuckle, *Lonicera periclymenum*, hop, *Humulus lupulus*, and old man's beard, *Clematis vitalba*, which must rely on other plants for support.

Hedgerow plants are extremely attractive to insects. Hawthorn, for example, is the food plant of more than 100 species of moths while the flowers of *Umbelliferae*, such as hogweed, *Heracleum sphondylium*, and sweet cicely, *Myrrhis odorata*, attract hordes of hoverflies, *Syrphidae*, longhorn beetles, *Saperda* and *Hylotrupes*, and soldier beetles, *Cantharidae*. Of the 20 butterflies which breed in hedges, the most typical is the brimstone, *Gonepteryx rhamni*, whose caterpillars feed on buckthorn.

Hedges also provide an ideal habitat for amphibia and reptiles—especially if they are planted alongside a ditch—since they possess the ideal combination of warm sunlit spots, cool shade and damp cover. If the ditch contains enough fresh, slow-

Above: A permeable hedge provides far better shelter against the wind than a solid brick wall through which the wind cannot pass. Both force the mass of air up over the barrier, but with a solid wall the creation of a partial vacuum immediately behind the wall causes eddies—whose speed is greater than that of the undisturbed wind in some cases—and a rapid return to ground level of the air stream. The air which filters through a hedge, however, prevents the formation of a vacuum so that the main air stream only slowly returns to ground level. Thin hedges with a permeability of about 40% are the best wind breaks. A thick hedge, or a block of woodland, acts like a solid barrier.

Below: Two hedgerow and pasture animals, a fire bug, *Pyrrhocoris apterus*, and a rabbit, *Oryctolagus*. Rabbits were extremely common in Europe until 1953, when the introduction of the disease *myxomatosis*, which originated in South America, devastated their numbers. The disease is still endemic but the population has now returned close to its old level.

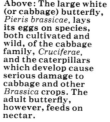

Oxford Scientific Films

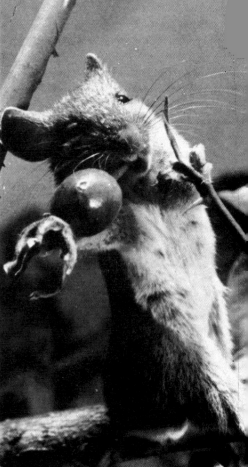

Above: The large white (or cabbage) butterfly, *Pieris brassicae*, lays its eggs on species, both cultivated and wild, of the cabbage family, *Cruciferae*, and the caterpillars which develop cause serious damage to cabbage and other *Brassica* crops. The adult butterfly, however, feeds on nectar.

Right: A long-tailed field mouse, *Apodemus sylvaticus*, eating a rose hip.

running water amphibia lay their eggs there, and their young provide food for snakes and birds.

Most hedgerow birds are woodland species which use hedges as a substitute for woods if the woodland population is high. Some species, however, will not nest in hedges because they offer insufficient cover (nightingale), or because they nest exclusively in mature trees (jackdaws, tits and woodpeckers). Those species which are most typical of hedgerows are the chaffinch, *Fringilla coelebs*, and blackbird, *Turdus merula*, which readily nest in all types of hedge. Robins, *Erithacus rubecula*, wrens, *Troglodytes troglodytes*, and hedgesparrows, *Prunella modularis*, only nest if the hedgebottom is dense enough to give protection from ground predators like stoats and weasels, *Mustela*.

Hedgerow mammals are rarer than birds but several rodent species in particular are common, including the long-tailed field mouse, voles, the brown rat, *Rattus norvegicus*, and shrews, *Sorex*. These smaller mammals are preyed on by stoats and weasels which, together with the brown rat, may also take the eggs and young of birds from their nests.

Deciduous woodlands occur in the climatic zone which is most favourable to man, so it is not surprising that man has greatly affected them, clearing and burning them to make way for agriculture, hunting forest animals for food and sport, and using the timber for fuel and building materials. Only about half of the former area of deciduous woodland now remains. Hedges, too, are now under increasing attack. This is partly because hedges can be a source of insect and fungal pests of crops. For example, a particularly damaging aphid, the black bean aphid, *Aphis fabae*, overwinters on spindle trees before moving on to the bean crop in the spring. Similarly, the fungus which causes the disease *wheat rust*, *Puccinia graminis*, overwinters on barberry leaves, *Berberis vulgaris*. Attempts have been made to eradicate both spindle and barberry from hedges but it is often easier to remove the whole hedge.

Hedges are also criticised for harbouring weeds, often unfairly since most weeds are annuals and the hedge flora is mostly perennial. However good the agricultural reasons for removing hedges, ecologically their loss is regrettable. Hedges contain a reservoir of harmless or beneficial species which can help to replace the populations killed in the fields by ploughing and the use of insecticides.

Below: Railway and roadside verges are often bordered by a hedge and by a strip or bank of flat ground which is equivalent to woodland flanking an uncultivated field margin. They therefore contain species characteristic of hedges, meadows and woodland edges. On roadsides in particular, however, a special set of environmental conditions also applies. Overgrown verges can be a threat to safety on the roads and road authorities, hard pressed for a cheap answer, sometimes remove the vegetation by spraying with herbicides. In the process the perennial plants are destroyed and annual weeds take over. Verges are also subjected to other pollutants from the vehicles themselves, especially lead compounds from the combustion of *tetraethyl lead*, the anti-knock additive in high octane petrol, and common salt, used to de-ice roads in winter. Lead compounds are poisonous to plants, but they may develop tolerance to it in time. Small mammals, however, eating the poisoned plants, concentrate the lead in their body fat and carnivores, such as kestrels, feeding on these animals, concentrate the lead still further. Lethal levels may be reached in this way, the kestrels dying of lead poisoning, although the smaller animals are unharmed.

Above: Where a hedge runs alongside a drainage ditch it provides an ideal habitat for amphibians and reptiles. Here a grass snake, *Natrix natrix*, is swallowing a frog.

Top right: A weasel, *Mustela nivalis*, caught in a spring trap. Weasels can be distinguished from stoats, *Mustela erminea*, by the absence of a black tip on the end of the tail and by their smaller size.

439

Index

442 *Calanus finmarchicus*, 411

443